VICTORIAN MATERIAL CULTURE

VICTORIAN MATERIAL CULTURE

General Editors:
Tatiana Kontou and Victoria Mills

Volume VI

Victorian Arts

Edited by Victoria Mills
and Kate Nichols

Routledge
Taylor & Francis Group
LONDON AND NEW YORK

First published 2023
by Routledge
4 Park Square, Milton Park, Abingdon, Oxon OX14 4RN

and by Routledge
605 Third Avenue, New York, NY 10158

Routledge is an imprint of the Taylor & Francis Group, an informa business

British Library Cataloguing-in-Publication Data
A catalogue record for this book is available from the British Library

Library of Congress Cataloging-in-Publication Data
A catalog record for this book has been requested

ISBN: 978-1-138-22526-8 (set)
eISBN: 978-1-315-40038-9 (set)
ISBN: 978-1-138-22532-9 (volume VI)
eISBN: 978-1-315-40026-6 (volume VI)

DOI: 10.4324/9781315400266

Publisher's Note
References within each chapter are as they appear in the original complete work

CONTENTS

ACKNOWLEDGEMENTS

Particular thanks are due to Jasmine Allen for contributing the stained-glass headnotes and identifying stained-glass sources for this volume. We would also like to acknowledge Lindsay Smith and Luisa Calè for reading and commenting on sections of this volume and Rhiannon Nichols for technical and administrative support. University of Birmingham Library Services provided invaluable assistance with scanning images and supplying documents. Thanks are also due to the Birkbeck Centre for Nineteenth-Century Studies for its ongoing support.

BIBLIOGRAPHY

Primary Sources

[Anon], 'Varieties', *Art-Union*, 3:26 (March 1841), p. 49.

[Anon] 'A Card', *Punch* 8 (1845), p. 238.

[Anon] 'Ancient and Modern Sculpture', *London Review and Weekly Journal of Politics, Literature, Art, and Society*, 4:103 (1862), pp. 567–8.

[Anon] 'Ghosts at South Kensington', *Saturday Review of Politics, Literature, Science and Art*, 47: 1222 (29 March 1879), pp. 391–2.

[Anon] 'Large Bronze Castings', *Illustrated London News*, 16 April 1881, p. 374.

[Anon] 'Stained glass as an accessory to Domestic Architecture', *Chambers's Journal* (1884, June 7), pp. 359–61.

[Anon] 'Stained Glass Windows', *London Journal* (20 March 1858), p. 40.

[Anon] 'The Art-Show at the Great Exhibition', *Dublin University Magazine*, 60:356 (1862), pp. 131–45.

[Anon] 'The Corridor of Statuary Porcelain at Alderman Copeland's, New Bond St', *Art Journal*, 59 (November 1859), pp. 347–8.

[Anon] 'The International Exhibition', *Birmingham Daily Post*, 20 June 1862, p. 2.

[Anon] *Photographic News*, 3 January 1879, pp. 2–3.

[Anon] *The Times*, 22 March 1842, p. 5.

Barnett, E., *The Training of Girls for Work*, (London: Macmillan and Co., 1894).

Barrington, Emilie ("Mrs Russell"), The *life, letters and work of Frederic Leighton*, volume II (London: George Allen, 1906).

Bolas, T., *The Journal of the Society of Arts*, Vol. 28, (30 July 1880), pp. 753–62.

Brewster, D., *The Stereoscope: Its History, Theory, and Construction. With its Application to the Fine and Useful Arts* (London: John Murray, 1856).

Brontë, *Jane Eyre* (London: Smith & Elder, 1847).

Church, A.H., *The Chemistry of Paints and Painting* (London: Seeley and Co., 1890).

Coates, T. F. G., *Lord Roseberry his life and speeches* vol. 2 (London: Hutchinson and Co., 1900).

Duchochois, P., *Photographic Reproduction Processes* (New York: The Scovill and Adams Company, 1891).

Field, G. *Chromatography: or, a treatise on Colours and Pigments, and of their powers in painting, &c.* (London: Charles Tilt, 1835).

Gosse, Edmund, *The Place of Sculpture in Daily Life*, ed. Martina Droth (Chicago: Soberscove Press, 2016).

Hamerton, P. G., *Thoughts About Art* (London: Macmillan and Co., 1873).
Hill, George Birkbeck (ed.) *Letters of Dante Gabriel Rossetti to Willingham Allingham* (London: Fisher and Unwin, 1897).
Holman Hunt, William, 'The Present System of Obtaining Materials in use by Artist Painters, as Compared with that of the Old Masters', *Journal of the Society of Arts* (23 April 1880), pp. 485–99.
Hosmer, H., 'The Process of Sculpture', *Atlantic Monthly* (December 1864), pp. 734–7.
Jameson, Anna, *A Handbook to the Courts of Modern Sculpture* (London: Bradbury and Evans, 1854).
Kennedy, H. A. 'An Art Not Generally Understood', *Contemporary Review* 55 (1889, March), p. 442.
Linton, W. J., *Wood-Engraving: A Manual of Instruction*, (London: George Bell and Sons, 1885).
Macdonald, J. R., (ed.), *Women in the Printing Trades: A Sociological Study* (London: P.S. King & Son, 1904).
Mackail, J. W. *Life of William Morris* (London, New York and Bombay: Longmans, Green & Co., 1899).
Martineau, Harriet, 'The Magic Troughs at Birmingham', *Household Words*, 4:83 (25 October 1851), pp. 113–17.
Maskell, Alfred., *Ivories* (London: Methuen and Co., 1905).
Miller, F., 'George Frampton, A. R. A., Art Worker', *Art Journal* (November 1897).
Mitra, Dinabandhu, *Nil Darpan, or, the Indigo Planting Mirror, a Drama, translated from Bengali by a Native* (Calcutta: C. H. Manuel, 1861).
Mullins, E. R., *A Primer of Sculpture* (London: Cassell and Co., 1890).
Redgrave R., and S. Redgrave, *A Century of Painters of the English School; with Critical Notices of their Works, and an Account of the Progress of Art in England* (London: Smith, Elder and Co., 1866).
Reports by the Juries on the Subjects in the thirty classes into which the exhibition was divided. Presentation Copy (London: William Clowes and Sons, 1852).
Ruskin, J., letter to his father from Padua (October 1845) quoted in *Modern Painters* in E.T Cook and Alexander Wedderburn (eds.) *The Works of John Ruskin* (London: George Allen, 1903).
Ruskin, John, 'On Turner's Recent Works' (1846), in E.T. Cook and Alexander Wedderburn (eds), *The Works of John Ruskin* (London: George Allen, 1903).
Ruskin, John, 'Appendix. Article 1. Notes on the Present State of Engraving in England', *Ariadne Florentina: six lectures on wood and metal engraving: given before the University of Oxford in Michaelmas term, 1872* (Orpington: George Allen, 1890) pp. 256–78.
Salter, T. W., *Field's Chromatography; or, Treatise on Colours and Pigments as used by Artists. An Entirely New and Practical Edition; Revised, Rewritten, and Brought Down to the Present Time* (London: Windsor and Newton, 1869).
Scott, G.G., *Personal and Professional Recollections, by the Late George Gilbert Scott* (London: Sampson, Low, Marston, Searle and Rivington, 1879).
Spielmann, Marion., *British Sculpture and Sculptors of Today* (London: Cassell and Co., 1901).
Stephens, F. G., *William Holman Hunt and his Works: a memoir of the artist's life, with description of his pictures* (London: James Nisbet and Co., 1860).
Street, G. E. 'On Glass Painting', *The Ecclesiologist* 10 (1852), pp. 237–47.

Wedgwood, T and Davy, H., 'An Account of a Method of Copying Paintings upon Glass' (1802) reproduced in Smith, *Colour and Photography*, pp. 101–5.

Weekes, Henry, *Lectures on Art Delivered at the Royal Academy London* (London: Bickers and Son, 1880).

Winsor and Newton's Catalogue of Colours and Materials for Watercolour painting, pencil, chalk, architectural drawing (London: Winsor and Newton, 1882).

Wyatt, M.D, *Fine Art. A Sketch of its History, Theory, Practice, and application to Industry. Being a Course of Lectures Delivered at Cambridge in 1870* (London: Macmillan and Co., 1870).

Zahensndorf, J. W. *The Art of Bookbinding* (London: George Bell and Sons, 1880).

Zerr, G. and R. Rubencamp, trans C. Mayer, *A treatise on colour manufacture: a guide to the preparation, examination, and application of all the pigment colours in practical use* (London, 1908).

Secondary works

Anderson, A. D., and P. H. Smith (eds), *The Matter of Art: Materials, Practices, Cultural Logics, c. 1250–1750* (Manchester: Manchester University Press, 2014).

Anderson, J., 'The First Cleaning Controversy at the National Gallery, 1846–1853', in D. Bomford and M. Leonard (eds), *Issues in the Conservation of Paintings* (Los Angeles: Getty Publications, 2004), pp. 441–453.

Anderson, Jennifer L., *Mahogany: The Costs of Luxury in Early America* (Cambridge MA: Harvard University Press, 2012).

Atkins, G., J. Allen & K., Nichols, (2020). Reframing Stained Glass in Nineteenth-Century Britain: Culture, Aesthetics, Contexts. *19: Interdisciplinary Studies in the Long Nineteenth Century, 2020* (30) https://doi.org/10.16995/ntn.3013

Atterbury, P. (ed.), *The Parian Phenomenon: a survey of Victorian Parian Porcelain Statuary and Busts* (Shepton Beauchamp: Richard Dennis, 1989).

Auerbach, J. A., *The Great Exhibition of 1851: A Nation on Display* (New Haven and London: Yale University Press, 1999).

Bagneris, M. L. 'Miscegenation in Marble: John Bell's Octoroon', *Art Bulletin*, 102:2 (2020), pp. 64–90.

Bailkin, J., 'Indian Yellow: Making and Breaking the Imperial Palette', *Journal of Material Culture*, 10:2 (2005), pp. 197–214.

Banerjee, S., 'Drama, Ecology, and the Ground of Empire: The Play of Indigo', in N. K. Hensley and P. Steer (eds), *Ecological Form: System and Aesthetics in the Age of Empire* (Fordham University Press: New York, 2019), pp. 21–41.

Barker, T. C., R. Dickinson, and D. W. F. Hardie, 'The Origins of the Synthetic Alkali Industry in Britain', *Economica*, 23 (1956), pp. 158–71.

Barnes, M., 'Frederick Scott Archer' in J. Hannavay, (ed.) *Encyclopaedia of Nineteenth Century Photography* (London: Routledge, 2018), pp. 55–57.

Batchen, G., *Burning with Desire: the Conception of Photography* (Cambridge, Mass., London: MIT Press, 1997).

Beach, C., 'John Bell's American Slave in the Context of Production and Patronage,' *Nineteenth-Century Art Worldwide*, 15:2 (2016), http://www.19thc-artworldwide.org/summer16/beach-on-john-bell-american-slave-context-of-production-and-patronage.

Beattie, J., E. Melillo and E. O'Gorman, 'British Empire, 1837–1945', in J. Beattie, E. Melillo and E. O'Gorman (eds), *Eco-Cultural Networks and the British Empire: New Views on Environmental History* (London, 2015), pp. 3–20.

Berger, C. (ed.), *Conceptualism and materiality: matters of art and politics* (Leiden: Brill, 2019).

Bhattacharya, A., 'The Indigo Revolt of Bengal', *Social Scientist*, 5:2 (1977), pp. 13–23.

Bonnell, T. F., *The Most Disreputable Trade: Publishing the Classics of English Poetry 1765–1810* (Oxford: Oxford University Press, 2008).

Brantlinger, P., *Taming Cannibals: Race and the Victorians* (Ithaca N.Y, Cornell University Press, 2011).

Briefel, A., *The Deceivers. Art Forgery and Identity in the nineteenth century* (Ithaca and London: Cornell University Press, 2006).

Briggs, A., *Victorian Things* (London: B. T. Batsford, Ltd., 1988).

Brock, M. G. and Curthoys, M. C., (eds.) *The History of the University of Oxford: Volume VII: Nineteenth-Century Oxford* (Oxford: Oxford University Press, 2000).

Brockway, L. H., *Science and Colonial Expansion: The Role of the British Royal Botanic Gardens,* 2nd edn. (New Haven: Yale UP, 2002).

Brown, B., 'Reification, Reanimation, and the American Uncanny', *Critical Inquiry* 32:2 (2006), pp. 175–207.

Buckland, A., *Raw Materials* (London and New York: Routledge, 2022).

Cameron, J. M., 'Annals of my glass house' (1890) reprinted in B. Newhall (ed.) *Photography essays and images: illustrated readings in the history of photography* (New York: Museum of Modern Art; Boston: New York Graphic Society, 1980).

Carlyle, Leslie, *The Artist's Assistant: Oil Painting Instruction Manuals and Handbooks in Britain, 1800–1900, with Reference to Selected Eighteenth-century Sources* (London: Archetype, 2001).

Chaudri, S. J. McDonagh, B. H. Murray and R. S. Rajan (eds.) *Commodities and Culture in the Colonial World* (London and New York: Routledge, 2018).

Cherry, D., *Painting Women: Victorian Women Artists* (London: Routledge, 1993).

Cheshire, J., 'William Morris and Stained Glass' in Florence S. Boos (ed.) *The Routledge Companion to William Morris* (London: Routledge, 2020), pp. 188–206.

Clarke, Meaghan, 'On Tempera and Temperament: Women, Art, and Feeling at the *Fin de Siècle*', *19: Interdisciplinary Studies in the Long Nineteenth Century*, 23 (2016) http://doi.org/10.16995/ntn.767.

Codell, J., 'Righting the Victorian Artist: The Redgraves' "A Century of Painters of the English School" and the Serialization of Art History', *Oxford Art Journal*, 23:2 (2000), pp. 95–113.

Coole, D. and S. Frost (eds.), 'Introducing the New Materialisms', in *New Materialisms: Ontology, Agency, and Politics* (Duke University Press, Durham and London, 2010), pp. 1–43.

Corbett, D. P., *The World in Paint: Modern Art and Visuality in England, 1848–1914* (Manchester: Manchester University Press, 2004).

Cormier, B. and D. Thom (eds), *A World of Fragile Parts* (London: V&A Publishing, 2016).

Coughlin, M., and E. Gephart, (eds.), *Ecocriticism and the Anthropocene in Nineteenth-Century Art and Visual Culture* (New York: Routledge, 2020).

Curry-Machado, J. 'Global Histories, Imperial Commodities, Local Interactions: An Introduction', in Jonathan Curry-Machado (ed), *Global Histories, Imperial Commodities, Local Interactions: An Introduction* (Basingstoke: Palgrave Macmillan, 2013), pp. 1–14.

Di Bello, P., 'Photographs of Sculpture: *Greek Slave*'s "complex polyphony", 1847–77', *19: Interdisciplinary Studies in the Long Nineteenth Century*, 22 (2016), at http://doi.org/10.16995/ntn.775.

Dominici, Sara., 'Cyclo-Photographers', Visual Modernity, and the Development of Camera Technologies, 1880s–1890s', *History of Photography*, 42:1 (2018), pp. 46–60.

Dootson, K. S., "The Texture of Capitalism: Industrial Oil Colours and the Politics of Paint in the Work of G.F. Watts", *British Art Studies*, 14 (2019), at www.britishartstudies.ac.uk.

Doyle, S., J. Grove and W. Sherman (eds.) *History of Illustration* (New York: Fairchild Books, 2018).

Droth, M., J. Edwards and M. Hatt (eds), *Sculpture Victorious: Art in an Age of Invention, 1837–1901* (New Haven and London: Yale University Press, 2014).

Droth, M., 'The Ethics of Making: Craft and English Sculptural Aesthetics c.1851–1900', *Journal of Design History*, 17:3 (2004), pp. 221–36.

Duncan, D. and A. Smyth, *Book Parts* (Oxford: Oxford University Press, 2019).

Eaton, N., 'Nomadism of Colour: Painting, technology and waste in the chromo-zones of colonial India, c.1765–c.1860', *Journal of Material Culture*, 17:1 (2012), pp. 61–81.

Edwards, J., '*Ex omnia conchis*? Edward Onslow Ford and the problem of Victorian '*animalier*' sculpture', *Word & Image*, 34:1 (2018), pp. 55–63.

Edwards, J., 'The Vegan Viewer in the Circum-Polar World; or, J. H. Wheldon's The Diana and Chase in the Arctic (1857)', in E. Quinn and B. Westwood (eds), *Towards a Vegan Theory: Thinking Veganism in Literature and Culture* (Cham, Switzerland: Palgrave Macmillan, 2018), pp. 79–106.

Edwards, S. The Making of English Photography: Allegories (Pennsylvania: Penn State, 2006).

Evans, C., *Slave Wales: The Welsh and Atlantic Slavery, 1660–1850* (Cardiff: University of Wales Press, 2010).

Fairbairn, L., *Paint & painting: an exhibition and working studio sponsored by Winsor & Newton to celebrate their 150th anniversary* (London: Tate Gallery, 1982).

Feeser, A., M. D. Goggin, and B. F. Tobin (eds), *The Materiality of Color: The Production, Circulation, and Application of Dyes and Pigments, 1400–1800* (Farnham: Ashgate, 2012).

Fielder, I. and Bayard, M. 'Cadmium Yellows, Oranges and Reds', in R. L. Feller (ed.), *Artists' Pigments: A Handbook of Their History and Characteristics*, Volume 1 (London: Archetype, 2012), pp. 65–108

Filipova, M., 'The forefront of English commercial centres: Wolverhampton's exhibitions of 1869 and 1902', in Marta Filipova (ed.), *Cultures of International Exhibitions 1840–1940: Great Exhibitions in the Margins* (Farnham: Ashgate, 2015), pp. 137–159.

Fraser, H., 'Women and the Modelling of Victorian Sculptural Discourse', *Visual Resources*, 33:1–2 (2017), pp. 74–93.

Freedgood, E., *The Ideas in Things: Fugitive Meaning in the Victorian Novel* (London: University of Chicago Press, 2006).

Freedman, W. E., 'Emily Faithfull and the Victoria Press: An Experiment in Sociological Bibliography', *The Library* 29:2 (1974), 138–64.

Fyfe, G., *Art, Power and Modernity: English Art Institutions, 1750–1950* (London and New York: Leicester University Press, 2000).

Gage, J., *Colour and Culture: Practice and Meaning from Antiquity to Abstraction* (London: Thames and Hudson, 1993).

Gentili, R., S. Sgorbati, and C. Baroni, 'Plant Species Patterns and Restoration Perspectives in the Highly Disturbed Environment of the Carrara Marble Quarries (Apuan Alps, Italy)', *Restoration Ecology*, 19 (2011), pp. 32–42.

Gold, S., *The Unfinished Exhibition: Visualizing Myth, Memory, and the Shadow of the Civil War in Centennial America* (New York: Routledge, 2017).

Golden, C. J., (ed.), *Book Illustrated: Text, Image and Culture 1770–1930* (New Castle, DE: Oak Knoll Press, 2000).

Golden, C. J., *Serials to Graphic Novels: The evolution of the Victorian illustrated book* (Gainesville: University Press of Florida, 2017).

Goldman, P. and S. Cooke (eds.) *Reading Victorian Illustration, 1855–1875: spoils of the lumber room* (London and New York: Routledge, 2016).

Goldring, T., 'Recovered or Perfected: The Discourse of Chemistry in the Nineteenth-Century Revival of Stained Glass in Britain and France', *19: Interdisciplinary Studies in the Long Nineteenth Century*, 30 (2020). doi: https://doi.org/10.16995/ntn.2893

Gordon, D.M., 'Precursors To Red Rubber: Violence In The Congo Free State, 1885–1895', *Past and Present*, 236:1 (2017), 133–68.

Graham, F., (ed.), *A memoir of Thomas Bewick: written by himself.* (Newcastle, Frank Graham, 1974).

Grant, A., and A. Patterson, *The Museum and the Factory*: *the V&A, Elkington, and the Electrical Revolution* (London: Lund Humphries, 2018).

Greenhalgh, P., *Fair World. A History of World's Fairs and Expositions. From London to Shanghai 1851–2010* (Winterbourne: Papadakis, 2011).

Guha-Thakurta, T., 'The Production and Reproduction of a Monument: The Many Lives of the Sanchi Stupa', *South Asian Studies* 29:1 (2013), pp. 77–109.

Guha, R., 'Neel-darpan: The image of a peasant revolt in a liberal mirror', *Journal of Peasant Studies*, 2:1 (1974), pp. 1–46.

Hadjiafxendi, K. and P. Zakreski (eds), *Crafting the woman professional in the long nineteenth century: artistry and industry in Britain* (Burlington, VT: Ashgate, 2013).

Hannavay, J., (ed.) *Encyclopaedia of Nineteenth-Century Photography* (London: Routledge, 2018).

Harley, R. D., 'Oil colour containers: Development work by artists and colourmen in the nineteenth century', *Annals of Science*, 27:1 (1971), pp. 1–12.

Hart, I., *Arts and Crafts Objects* (Manchester: Manchester University Press, 2010).

Harvey, J., *Victorian Novelists and their illustrator*s (New York: New York University Press, 1971).

Harvey, M., 'Slavery, Indenture and the Development of British Industrial Capitalism', *History Workshop Journal*, 88 (2019), pp. 66–88.

Haskins, K., *The Art-Journal and Fine Art Publishing in Victorian England, 1850–1880* (London and New York, Routledge, 2017).

Henisch, B. A and H.K Henisch 'Cuthbert Bede and the Photographic Scene in the 1850s', *History of Photography* 28:4 (2004), pp. 348–356.

Herstein, S., 'The Langham Place Circle and Feminist Periodicals of the 1860s', *Victorian Periodicals Review* 26:1, 1993, 24–27.

Hoffenberg, P. H., *An Empire on Display: English, Indian and Australian Exhibitions from the Crystal Palace to the Great War* (Berkeley, University of California Press, 2001).

Hooper, Nancy Langham, 'Unrolled: John Rogers Herbert and the monumental Moses in the National Gallery of Victoria', *Art Journal of the National Gallery of Victoria*, 54 (2016), pp. 71–81.

Hughes, A. and E. Ranfft (eds), *Sculpture and its Reproductions* (London: Reaktion Books, 1997).

Huneault, K., 'Placing Frances Anne Hopkins: a British-born artist in colonial Canada', in D. Cherry and J. Helland (eds), *Local/Global: Women Artists in the Nineteenth Century* (Farnham: Ashgate, 2006), pp. 179–200.

Huzzey, R., *Freedom Burning. Anti-Slavery and Empire in Victorian Britain* (Ithaca: Cornell University Press, 2007).

Igoe, L.T., '"A Gruesome Sight" Randolph Rogers's Nydia in a Marble World', in Coughlin and Gephart (eds.), *Ecocriticism and the Anthropocene in Nineteenth-Century Art and Visual Culture*, pp. 80–92.

Irwin, F., 'Amusement of instruction? Watercolour manuals and the woman amateur', in C,. Campbell Orr (ed.), *Women in the Victorian Art World* (Manchester: Manchester University Press, 1995), pp. 149–166.

Jacob, S., 'Restoration practice in museums and galleries in Britain in the nineteenth century', in Nicola Costaras et al (eds), *A Changing Art: Nineteenth-Century Painting Practice and Conservation* (London: Archetype, 2017), pp. 5–13.

Jacobi, C., *William Holman Hunt: Painter, Painting, Paint* (Manchester: Manchester University Press, 2006).

Jacobson, K. and J., Jacobson, *Carrying Off the Palaces: Ruskin's Lost Daguerreotypes* (London: Bernard Quaritch Ltd., 2015).

Katz, M. R., 'Holman Hunt on Himself: textual evidence in aid of technical analysis', in E. Hermens (ed.) *Looking Through Paintings: the Study of Painting Techniques and Materials in Support of Art Historical Research* (London: Archetype, 1998), pp 415–44.

Kelsey, R., 'Notes from the Field: Materiality', *Art Bulletin*, 95:1 (2013), pp. 21–3.

Kim, J.J. *Painted Men in Britain 1868–1918: Royal Academicians and masculinities* (Farnham: Ashgate, 2012), pp. 17–19.

Kooistra, L., 'Victorian Women Wood Engravers: The Case of Clemence Housman' in A. Easley, C. Gill, B. Rodgers (eds.), *Women, Periodicals and Print Culture in Britain, 1830s–1900s: The Victorian Period* (Edinburgh: Edinburgh University Press, 2019), pp. 277–300.

Kuhn, H. and M. Curran, 'Chrome Yellow and Other Chromate Pigments', in Feller (ed.), *Artists' Pigments*, Volume 1, pp. 187–218.

Kupper T., "Amateur Stained Glass in English Churches, 1830–80", *19: Interdisciplinary Studies in the Long Nineteenth Century* 2020(30). doi: https://doi.org/10.16995/ntn.2895.

Ledger, S., and R. Luckhurst (eds.). *The Fin de* Siècle*: A reader in Cultural History c. 1880–1900* (Oxford: Oxford University Press, 2000).

Leitch, A., 'The life of marble: The experience and meaning of work in the marble quarries of Carrara', *Australian Journal of* Anthropology, 7:3 (1996), pp. 235–257.

Loske, A., 'Mary Philadelphia Merrifield: Color History as Expertise', *Visual Resources*, 33 (2017), pp. 11–26.

Manning, P., 'Wordsworth's 'Illustrated Books and Newspapers' and Media of the City', in L. H. Peer (ed.), *Romanticism and the City*, (Basingstoke: Palgrave, 2011), pp. 223–240.

McClintock, A., *Imperial Leather: Race, Gender and Sexuality in the Colonial Context*, (London: Routledge, 1995).

Menke, R., *Inventions and Technology* (London: Routledge, 2023).

Mintie, K., 'Material Matters: The Transatlantic Trade in Photographic Materials during the Nineteenth Century', Panorama: Journal of the Association of historians of American Art', 6.2 (2020) at https://editions.lib.umn.edu/panorama/article/re-reading-american-photographs/material-matters/

Munro J., (ed.), *Silent partners: artist and mannequin from function to fetish* (New Haven and London: Yale University Press, 2014).

Nelson, C., *The Color of Stone: Sculpting the Black Female Subject in Nineteenth-Century America* (Minneapolis: University of Minnesota Press, 2007).

Nelson, C., 'Vénus Africaine: Race, Beauty and African-ness', in Jan Marsh (ed.), *Black Victorians: Black People in British Art 1800–1900* (Aldershot: Lund Humphries, 2005), pp. 46–56.

Newell, E., and S. Watts, 'The Environmental Impact of Industrialisation in South Wales in the Nineteenth Century: "Copper Smoke" and the Llanelli Copper Company', *Environment and History*, 2:3 (1996), pp. 309–336.

Newman, R., 'Chromium Oxide Greens', in E. Wm. FitzHugh (ed.), *Artists' Pigments, A Handbook of Their History and Characteristics*, Volume 3 (London: Archetype, 2012), pp. 273–94.

Nichols, K., *Greece and Rome at the Crystal Palace. Classical Sculpture and Modern Britain, 1854–1936* (Oxford: Oxford University Press, 2015).

Ormsby, B. A., J. H. Townsend, B. W. Singer and J, R. Dean, 'British Watercolour Cakes from the Eighteenth to the Early Twentieth Century', *Studies in Conservation*, 50:1 (2005), pp. 45–66.

Patrizio, A., *The Ecological Eye. Assembling an Ecocritical Art History* (Manchester: Manchester University Press, 2019).

Patten, R. L., *Charles Dickens and his Publishers* (Oxford: Clarendon Press, 1978; second edition Oxford University Press, 2017).

Patterson, A., and M. Trusted, *The Cast Courts* (London: V&A Publishing, 2018).

Peers, Laura, 'Material Culture, Identity, and the Canadian Fur Trade', in B. Fowkes Tobin and M. Goggin (eds), *Women and Things 1750–1850: Gendered Material Strategies* (Farnham: Ashgate, 2009), pp. 55–73.

Pelizzari, M.A, 'From Stone to Paper: Photographs of Architecture and the Traces of History', in M. A. Pelizzari (ed.), *Traces of India: Photography, Architecture, and the Politics of Representation, 1850–1900* (Montréal: Canadian Centre for Architecture; New Haven: Yale Center for British Art, 2003), pp. 20–57.

Pomeroy, J. '"We Got Upon Our Elephant and Went out After Subjects": capturing the world in watercolour', in Jordana Pomeroy (ed.), *Intrepid Women: Victorian Artists Travel* (Farnham: Ashgate, 2005), pp. 39–50.

Prettejohn, E., *Modern painters, old masters: the art of imitation from the Pre-Raphaelites to the First World War* (New Haven and London: Yale University Press, 2017).

Quinn, E., and B. Westwood (eds), *Towards a Vegan Theory. Thinking Veganism in Literature and Culture* (Cham, Switzerland: Palgrave Macmillan, 2018).

Ray, R., 'The Memsahib's Brush: Anglo-Indian Women and the Art of the Picturesque, 1830–1880' in J. Codell and D. S. Macleod (eds), *Orientalism transposed: the impact of the colonies on British culture* (Aldershot: Ashgate, 1998), pp. 89–116.

Ribeyrol, C., (ed.) *The Colours of the Past in Victorian England* (Oxford: Peter Lang, 2016).

Roberts, J., *Transporting Visions. The Movement of Images in Early America* (Berkeley: University of California Press, 2014).

Roberts, L. 'Nineteenth-Century English Picture Frames I: The Pre-Raphaelites', *International Journal of Museum Management and Curatorship*, 4 (1985), pp. 155–72.

Roberts, L. 'Nineteenth-Century English Picture Frames II: The Victorian High Renaissance', *International Journal of Museum Management and Curatorship*, 5 (1986), pp. 273–93.

Robins, N. A., *Mercury, mining, and empire: the human and ecological cost of colonial silver mining in the Andes* (Bloomington: Indian University Press, 2011).

Rush, S., 'Seeing Red', *19: Interdisciplinary Studies in the Long Nineteenth Century*, 30 (2020). doi: https://doi.org/10.16995/ntn.2897

Shires, L. M., 'On Color Theory, 1835: George Field's *Chromatography*', *BRANCH: Britain, Representation and Nineteenth-Century History*, at www.branchcollective.org

Siegel, J., *Material Inspirations: The Interests of the Art Object in the Nineteenth Century and After* (Oxford: Oxford University Press, 2020).

Silverman, D. L., 'Art Nouveau, Art of Darkness: African Lineages of Belgian Modernism, Part I', *West 86th: A Journal of Decorative Arts, Design History, and Material Culture*, 18:2 (2011), pp. 139–81.

Simon, J. (ed.), 'British bronze sculpture founders and plaster figure makers, 1800–1980', *National Portrait Gallery* (from 2011), https://www.npg.org.uk/research

Sinclair, William, *The Reading Nation in the Romantic Period* (Cambridge: Cambridge University Press, 2004).

Smith, L., *Victorian Photography, Painting and Poetry* (Cambridge: CUP, 1995).

Smith, L. (ed.) *Color and Victorian Photography* (London: Routledge, 2020).

Sprague, A. N., 'The British tempera revival: A return to craftsmanship', *British Art Journal*, 3:3 (Autumn 2002), pp. 66–74.

Stevens, B., 'Wood engraving as ghostwriting: the Dalziel Brothers, losing one's name, and other hazards of the trade', *Textual Practice* 33(4), 645–677.

Suarez, M. F., and H. R. Woudhuysen (eds.), *The Oxford Companion to the Book* (Oxford: Oxford University Press, 2020).

Sunseri, T., 'The Political Ecology of the Copal Trade in the Tanzanian Coastal Hinterland, c. 1820–1905', *Journal of African History*, 48:2 (2007), pp. 201–220.

Taylor, R., *Impressed by Light: British Photographs from Paper Negatives* (Yale University Press: New Haven and London, 2007).

Thomas, J., *Pictorial Victorians: The Inscription of Values in Word and Image* (Athens: Ohio University Press, 2004).

Thomas, S., 'Poetry and Illustration: Amicable Strife' in Charles Mahoney (ed.) *A Companion to Romantic Poetry* (Wiley-Blackwell, 2011), pp. 354–373.

Thompson, A., *blackface* (London: Bloomsbury Academic, 2021).

Tidcombe, M., *Women Bookbinders 1880–1920*. (Newcastle, Delaware: Oak Knoll Press, 1996).

Townsend, J. H., 'The Materials of J. M. W. Turner: Pigments', *Studies in Conservation*, 38:4 (1993), pp. 231–54.

Townsend, J. H., Jacqueline Ridge and Stephen Hackney, *Pre-Raphaelite painting techniques: 1848–56* (London: Tate, 2004).

Townsend, J. H., 'The Materials used by British Oil Painters in the Nineteenth-Century', *Tate Papers*, 2 (2004), at https://www.tate.org.uk/research/publications/tate-papers

Trusted, M., (ed.) *The Making of Sculpture: The Materials and Techniques of European Sculpture* (London: V&A Publications, 2007).

Tucker, J., 'Dangerous Exposures: Visualizing Work and Waste in the Victorian Chemical Trades', *International Labor and Working-Class History*, 95 (2019), pp. 130–165.

von Brevern, J., 'Two or three things photography did to painting' in Nicoletta Leonardi and Simone Natale (eds.) *Photography and Other Media in the Nineteenth Century*, (University Park, Pennsylvania: Pennsylvania State University Press, 2018), pp. 103–115.

Wade, R., *Domenico Brucciani and the Fortmatori of Nineteenth-Century Britain* (New York: Bloomsbury, 2018).

Waterfield, G., *The People's Galleries: Art Museums and Exhibitions in Britain, 1800–1914* (New Haven and London: Yale University Press, 2015).

Wheeler, M., (ed) *Ruskin and Environment: The Storm Cloud of the Nineteenth Century* (Manchester 1995).

Willsdon, C. A. P, *Mural Painting in Britain 1840–1940: Image and Meaning* (Oxford: Oxford University Press, 2000).

Woodcock, S., 'Body colour: The misuse of mummy', *Conservator*, 20:1 (1996), pp. 87–94.

Woodcock, S., 'Leighton and Roberson: An Artist and His Colourman', *Burlington Magazine* 138:1121 (1996), pp. 526–8.

Woodson-Boulton, A., *Transformative Beauty. Art Museums in Industrial Britain* (Stanford: Stanford University Press, 2012).

Yonge, C., *The Clever Woman of the Family* ed. C. A. Simmons (Ormskirk: Broadview Press Ltd., 2001).

Yusoff, K., *A Billion Black Anthropocenes or None* (Minneapolis: University of Minnesota Press, 2018).

INTRODUCTION TO VOLUME VI

Victorian Arts

'There are many difficulties in identifying "works of art" in the "universe of Victorian things"' writes Asa Briggs in his foundational text on Victorian material culture, *Victorian Things* (1987).[1] What, then, constitutes Victorian arts? The term suggests a broad category that might include creative arts (painting, sculpture, photography, musical composition), decorative arts and crafts, and related forms of replication such as prints and plaster casts. Like many of the volumes in the *Victorian Material Culture* series, the scope of *Victorian Arts* is difficult to circumscribe. Necessarily indicative rather than comprehensive, the volume focuses on five categories of Victorian visual art: painting, sculpture, stained glass, book illustration and photography. Rather than engaging in well-rehearsed debates over fine art versus craft, we seek to bring diverse Victorian media into dialogue, through sources which examine the social, cultural and political dimensions of materials and making, and the relationship between different art forms. This introduction offers an overview of key themes that emerge from our selections of primary source material; we explore how questions of class, race, gender, imperialism and the environment were embedded in the production, marketing and consumption of art and its materials in the Victorian period. We draw attention to how the development of new technologies shaped Victorian arts, and we demonstrate how an expanding print and exhibition culture opened up a range of arts to new audiences and, in turn, generated new art forms and modes of engagement with them.

The material culture of Victorian arts was mediated through its varied modes of representation. Sources in this volume include a range of non-fiction prose in the form of exhibition catalogues, artists' and photographers' manuals, and articles on the latest developments in photographic processing and book binding, along with advertisements, novels, poems and reproduced photographs. These different media played an important role in shaping debates on materials and making, as well as providing the means by which a growing audience came to participate in, view and read about Victorian arts.[2] Such debates also discussed the problem of categorisation as the Victorians grappled with a proliferation of new apparatus and materials across all art forms. The classification of photography (was it a science or an art?) was particularly contentious, as the sources

DOI: 10.4324/9781315400266-1

in Part 5 show. Contemporary debates often focus on photography's material components – the camera is viewed as a piece of scientific equipment, but the finished product, the photograph, is viewed as a work of art. The term 'Victorian' is also problematic: suggesting an isolationist British context, it excludes the ways in which the material culture of art was implicated in global systems of trade, manufacturing and intellectual exchange. Indeed, many art objects are collaborative or composite in nature, as indicated by a brief consideration of even the *preparation* of canvases for Frederic Leighton, President of the Royal Academy from 1878 to 1896. As Sally Woodcock has shown, Leighton collaborated extensively with the colourman Roberson, who prepared canvases for him with colour washes of 'mineral grey, blue black, orange cadmium, burnt sienna and golden ochre and the cheaper grades of genuine ultramarine'.[3] We suggest the importance of inquiring beyond the collaboration with Roberson to explore the materials at stake and the range of people and places involved in their manufacture; for example, cadmium was derived from zinc mining (at this point largely sourced from Swansea and Belgium), Sienna and ochre came from clay mined primarily in Tuscany, and genuine ultramarine lapis lazuli was quarried in China, Tibet and Siberia.[4]

There are fruitful dialogues between this volume and *Raw Materials* in this series; both, for example, consider the violent colonial histories of the pigment indigo. In *Victorian Arts*, materials occupy a strange position; they are at times occluded and at times the centre of attention. If, as new materialists argue, 'the power of matter' is fundamental to our understanding of the world, then a focus on the materials of art allows us to better understand the meanings of artworks and their role in global histories of the nineteenth century.[5] By foregrounding the materials that comprise a work of art, for example, we move beyond the politics of representation to question whether *all* Victorian artworks were implicated in colonialism, not just those which feature imperial iconographies.[6] By focusing on the material components of Victorian arts, our sources reveal how they were part of an expanding global network of commodity possession and exchange.[7] Indian yellow, for example, was newly available as a pigment in the production of paint, while gum arabic was imported from North and West Africa for use in photography.

The imbrication of Victorian arts within global trading networks provides another focus for the analysis of materials. As Jennifer Roberts has argued, once we start to pay attention to the mobility of artworks, their material qualities become urgently apparent:

> Although all pictures are in some way material, transit renders their 'thingness' conspicuous in a way that the static equilibrium of traditional modes of display cannot approximate. Everything is heavier when it has to be picked up and moved; pictures hefted through space necessarily become 'ponderous bodies', in the words of the nineteenth-century itinerant painter Rufus Porter.[8]

The intensified movement of artworks in the Victorian period brought in a whole new array of agents who were involved and implicated in the circulation and conservation of these works: those tasked with packing artworks into crates; the dockworkers moving paintings on and off of ships; and curators responsible for carefully unpacking them, as sources in Part 1 in particular explore.

Through its selection of sources, *Victorian Arts* opens up new questions about the labour and forms of colonial exploitation embedded in the material culture of art, the contribution of women to the arts, and the environmental impact of the extraction and transportation of artists' materials.

Expanded publics

Access to and participation in the arts expanded exponentially during the Victorian period. The arts were no longer the exclusive preserve of aristocratic elites and professional artists. Developments in art materials opened up new opportunities for middle-class Victorian women, and a far broader range of 'amateurs' across the class spectrum, to participate in both making and exhibiting painting, sculpture, stained glass, book illustrations and photography.[9]

The whole gamut of 'arts' considered in this volume, from stained glass to sculpture, was displayed (and debated) at international exhibitions in London in 1851 and 1862, which both attracted over 6 million visitors; at a conservative estimate, one in five British people visited the Great Exhibition in 1851.[10] This newfound exhibition culture brought 'fine arts' into dialogue with 'raw materials' and manufacture, and set out to showcase the material resources of the British Empire. The mass culture of viewing art objects at temporary exhibitions extended far beyond London: exhibitions of art and industry took place in towns and cities all over Britain (e.g. the South Staffordshire Exhibition of Arts and Industries, Wolverhampton, 1869, which attracted some 220,000 visitors) and all over the globe.[11] Alongside these exhibitions of art and industry were an ever-growing number of nationwide temporary exhibitions of art forms, spanning watercolours and oil paints to photography. Permanent displays of painting and sculpture were newly accessible to London audiences after the National Gallery was founded in 1824, and by the 1870s, municipal museums and art galleries had been established across Britain.[12] Art forms and materials were transformed by these new exhibitionary cultures. The material preservation of oil paintings, for example, was challenged afresh by damage sustained during transit to exhibitions around Britain and, indeed, around the globe.[13]

A corresponding rich print culture and new genres of writing (such as manuals for the photographer and artist) were directed to these new audiences; these form a number of the sources presented in this volume. The explosion in the popular periodical press allowed an increasing number of readers to come into contact with debates over the materials of Victorian arts. Manuals for 'amateur' artists, like *Ackermann's Manual of Colours*, presented a history of watercolours, closely related to their material properties; exhibition guidebooks (which often dwell on the materials of, for example, sculpture) and reports of exhibitions in periodicals generated a new impetus for these debates over materials and a broader public concern for them. Specialist art periodicals, as well as those aimed at an amateur readership, were established in great numbers in the second half of the nineteenth century. The fast-paced development of photography, for example, led to the establishment of a large range of new journals for the amateur and specialist alike.[14] At the same time, general interest periodicals took a keen interest in this new art form, with satirical journals such as *Punch* often taking a wry look at recent photographic innovation and its possible applications (Part 5). Victorian fiction also shaped the discourse on Victorian arts; included here are examples from novels and poetry, which discuss the materiality of sculpture, book engraving and the idea of photography as a profession for women.

The photographs of the Elkington and Company display at the Philadelphia Centennial Exhibition, reproduced here in Part 2, provide an insight into the productive relationships between materials and the expanded audiences and makers of Victorian arts. The first official World's Fair held in the United States, the Philadelphia Centennial, attracted over 10 million visitors from May to November 1876; the Main Exhibition building, which housed the Elkington stand, was the largest building in the world at the time.[15] The vast array of materials and goods competing for attention at international exhibitions gave rise to a new sort of art object, specifically designed as advertising material for companies like Elkington. One of these objects, an electrotyped plaque titled *Pompeian Lady at Her Toilet*, is visible in this photograph, positioned in the middle of the table at the centre of the image, and is identifiable by its dark rim. Designed by the French sculptor Léonard Morel-Ladeuil, it was electroplated by Elkington and Co. specifically as a showpiece for the Philadelphia Centennial.[16] A diverse array of visitors in Philadelphia might now encounter a shield designed by a French sculptor that was carefully made by a series of highly skilled male and female factory workers in Birmingham, England.[17]

New technologies

Pompeian Lady at Her Toilet is also testimony to the impact of new technological processes on Victorian arts; like the other objects on Elkington's stand at the Philadelphia Exhibition, it was an electrotype, a form of sculptural reproduction patented in Birmingham in the 1830s, which used electrical currents to coat base metal objects with precious metal. Indeed, the rapid growth in new technologies shaped the development of Victorian arts across all of the categories considered in this volume.[18]

Photography, a medium born in the nineteenth century, developed at a rapid pace from the 1840s onwards. With applications across both arts and science, new photographic techniques and materials were invented, patented and marketed at a furious rate.[19] Following the invention of the calotype and daguerreotype processes in the 1830s and 1840s, the 1850s saw the widespread use of the wet collodion process invented by Frederick Scott Archer. Although it involved dangerous chemicals and the need for immediate processing, the great advantage of collodion was its increased sensitivity and faster exposure time. In the late 1870s, the preface of the periodical *Photographic News* reports on a year of momentous change in the development of new photographic techniques, devoting a whole issue to discussing what it describes as 'a history of a revolution'.[20] It draws particular attention to the gradual supersedence of the wet collodion process by dry plates (which enabled quicker processing and is discussed in a range of sources in Part 5), while the development of the 'New Photography', a term referring to the discovery of X-rays by Professor Wilhelm Röntgen, was widely discussed in both trade and general interest periodicals in the mid-1890s. Advertisements from photographic firms including the London Stereographic Company and Marion and Co. attest to the variety of photographic equipment available to the amateur user, from special tents that allowed one to develop one's own photographs in the outdoors to cameras suitable for the new craze of cyclo-photography.

Painting, too, was impacted by new technological developments and influenced by the commercial possibilities of new materials and media. Collapsible metal paint tubes were introduced in 1841, gradually replacing the animal bladders that had been used to supply oil paint. The isolation of new elements (such as chromium, isolated 1797) and encounters with new minerals fed into the development of new colours in the nineteenth century, such as chrome yellows, greens, and reds.[21] Major new firms established in the early nineteenth century, such as Winsor & Newton (1832) and Charles Roberson and Co. (1820), took advantage of a growing market for a wide range of artists' materials. Contemporary debates link these developments to the 'deskilling' of artists, as such 'colourman' businesses would mix paints for both professional and amateur painters.[22]

Nineteenth-century sculpture is characterised by both engagement with new technologies and materials and an intense investment in older craft traditions.[23] The invention of sculpture reduction machines in the 1820s by Benjamin Cheverton and in the 1830s by Achille Collas made it possible for miniature versions of large works to be produced for middle-class audiences, while new replication techniques, such as electrotyping, enabled the widespread and comparatively cheap distribution of these works.[24] New materials such as Parianware – a new, industrially produced ceramic material invented in the 1840s to imitate prestigious white marble from the Greek island of Paros – were also used in the making of miniaturised works, which was vital to the new circulation and transmission of sculpture in the Victorian period. Sculptors also experimented with cast iron produced by the Coalbrookdale Iron Company (famous for building the Ironbridge).[25]

Makers of Victorian stained glass likewise were highly invested in reviving ancient and medieval techniques and processes, but, as Thea Goldring has shown, nineteenth-century chemistry played a significant role in the discourse around this 'revival' and supplied new shades of coloured glass and enamel paint.[26] Further, a number of new glass materials appeared on the market in the Victorian period. Both opalescent glass, or opaline glass, developed in the 1870s in the United

States by John La Farge (1835–1910) and Louis Comfort Tiffany (1848–1933), and Prior's 'Slab' glass developed by English architect E. S. Prior (1852–1932) in 1889 broke away from traditional glassmaking methods. These new glass materials were often of uneven thickness and streaky in colour, lending a jewelled luminosity and sometimes a three-dimensional effect to stained glass. The development of these new glass materials had an enormous influence on the stylistic development of stained glass in the late nineteenth century.

Like stained glass, Victorian book illustration used earlier techniques alongside those newly developed. Printing techniques using woodcuts, which date back to the fifteenth century, were modified in the mid-eighteenth century by Thomas Bewick, who used a steel engraving tool (a burin) to produce a very detailed rendering on hardwoods such as boxwood. The commercial opportunities afforded by the invention of this technique, which enabled the reuse of woodblocks, were quickly taken up by the Victorians, and book illustration burgeoned in the second half of the century though older intaglio techniques, such as mezzotint and lithography, were still widely used.[27] By the end of our period, wood engraving as a reproductive technique for book illustration was gradually being replaced by the cheaper processes offered by photography. Sources in Part 5 reflect on the threat posed by photography to wood engraving and its workforce. Nonetheless, older methods did survive; William Morris used woodcut techniques at the Kelmscott press in the 1890s, and in 1920, the Society of Wood Engravers was established by figures including Gwen Raverat and Eric Gill, artists who were interested in the revival of older techniques.

The art materials of empire

Technological developments enhanced the portability of art materials and enabled amateur and professional painters and photographers to depict (and mediate for audiences 'at home') the peoples and landscapes of the British Empire. But the connections between imperialism and art materials run far deeper than the level of representation or the geographical location of the art maker. Places colonised by Europeans were exploited for commodities and materials used in artistic production, such as pigments and binders (like linseed oil and various plant gums) for making paint, copal (tree resin) for use as a varnish, the India rubber used in bookbinders' rollers and photography, the mahogany used in the production of cameras, and the copper, ivory and silver employed in sculpture.[28] European demand for such commodities and the wealth they generated were fundamental motivators for colonisation from the sixteenth century onwards.[29]

As social historians of commodities have emphasised more generally, and, as Natasha Eaton and Jordanna Bailkin have explored in relation to colonial art materials in particular, these commodities and their violent labour histories were also a crucial locus of subaltern contestation and resistance.[30] This resistance is perhaps epitomised in the career of the pigment indigo; as discussed in Part 1, the hardships that coerced peasant tenant labourers faced on indigo plantations in

Bengal gave rise to the 'Indigo Revolts' of 1859. Dinabandhu Mitra's 1860 play *Nil Darpan, or The Indigo Planting Mirror* was widely performed across Bengal and translated into English in 1861.[31] The extracts from the English translation presented here provide one example of the ways in which imperial commodities became a locus of contestation, and foreground the human cost of commodity production. Many nineteenth-century British sources are not so overt about the violent extraction of colonial commodities upon which art production was based. Yet – for example – advertisements which casually list 'India Rubber' (for book-binding rollers) or 'Indian Yellow' (for painting) among their wares testify to the way in which colonialism underpins the development of materials and making in the second half of the nineteenth century. The very name of the 'Imperial Dry Plate Company', for example, draws on the language of empire to express the expansionist ambitions of a London seller of photographic apparatus.

The materials of art were also implicated in the racial hierarchies used to justify slavery and imperial conquest. This was particularly the case in sculpture, where white-marble-sculpted bodies were closely related to racist hierarchies of beauty, a topic discussed in further detail in the introduction to Part 2. As Bailkin has explored, manuals for painters were also explicit about the importance of keeping distinct the paint colours used to represent different racialised groups.[32] Anxieties over white British women participating in new artistic practices were also expressed through racialised terms and related to particular materials: in an article on photography as a hobby for women, for example, Alfred Harmsworth notes the way in which photographic processing stains white female hands with a black 'Ethiopian tint'.[33] This volume encourages readers to be attentive to the global connections and racialised power dynamics contained in these sources.

Ecology and Victorian art materials

European imperial exploitation was inherently intertwined with environmental degradation.[34] Many art materials sourced from colonial contexts were predicated on invasive changes to colonised environments. This included the introduction and/or intensive cultivation of crops, such as indigo for the eponymous pigment, India rubber used in book binding and photography, or the mahogany used in cameras.[35] Colonial ecosystems were also impacted by the destruction of non-human animal life for artistic materials. As will be explored in Part 2, ivory, for example, was championed in the late 1880s as a material for European sculpture in order to celebrate Belgian colonisation of the Congo and the new organic materials that might be sourced from the local elephant population.[36] Art objects also depended on mining and quarrying, often (but not exclusively) in colonised places, for example, marble, copper and tin used in sculpture, or the silver used in electroplating, photographic plates and silver stain for stained glass.[37]

Environmental issues related to the materials of art were keenly felt in Britain. A number of sources in Part 1, for example, discuss the impact of air pollution from coal burning on the preservation of paintings and their frames.[38] Smog-generating coal was also essential to the industrial foundries that, until the later nineteenth century, were the main sites of production for metal sculpture, both in novel materials, such as cast iron, and in more established media like bronze.[39] The production of sculpture in these industrial settings was no secret. White hot molten metal was particularly well suited to black and white illustrations, and readers of the illustrated press were familiar with dramatic scenes of sculptural production in foundries, as the *Illustrated London News* engraving featured in Part 2 testifies.

As well as being a period of industrialisation and urbanisation, the nineteenth century is also associated with new-found artistic enthusiasm for careful observation and representation of the natural world, enabled partly by new paint transportation and pigment technologies. John Ruskin, the critic most keenly associated with the idea of painters aiming at 'truth to nature', championed the naturalistic effects of the colour 'Chinese White', introduced by Winsor and Newton in 1834.[40] Scholars in nineteenth-century studies have long identified Ruskin as a prescient environmentalist.[41] A focus on materials, however, demonstrates how implicated the arts were in environmental degradation; the Chinese white that Ruskin championed for its ability to capture the natural world was made from zinc oxide, sourced by Winsor and Newton from zinc-smelting plants in Swansea.

Nineteenth-century contemporaries were well aware of the environmental destruction caused by these metalworking industries; the land around works took on 'a volcanic appearance', and the deaths of crops, trees and animals were widely reported.[42] Given the widespread circulation of handbooks (some of which are reprinted in Part 1) detailing the composition of different pigments, many painters would have been aware of the minerals utilised in the making of paint. A consideration of the environmental implications of materials offers new perspectives on some of the most celebrated Victorian evocations of the natural world; J. M. W. Turner, for example, used Chinese white extensively in his oil painting from 1835 to 1840.[43] These paintings were predicated on intensive coal mining, ore smelting, and the contamination of land. What implications might this have for our understandings of these works?[44]

Contemporary scholars are only just beginning to research the relationship between the materials of Victorian art and their impact on the environment; examples include Jennifer Tucker's current work on the relationship between the chemical industry and photography and Jason Edwards' research into the connections between the materials of painting and sculpture and animal bodies.[45] It is our intention to draw attention to the quiet presence of this relationship between art materials and the environment in a wide range of nineteenth-century sources, with the hope that this will support and generate future research.

Labour

An emphasis on the materials of art provides new impetus to consider the range of labour involved in making art, including the work undertaken by those extracting and processing the materials of art, as well as discourse over the ways in which particular materials are seen to promote different types of artistic labour.

While for many in the nineteenth century, art became an amateur leisure activity, the materials of art – and, eventually, the artwork itself – can be seen to embody labour relations. Many of these new nineteenth-century art materials (for example, the chemicals involved in photographic processes) posed a danger to those working with them.[46] These materials are further testimony to the global and imperial reach of 'British' art production and its connections with slavery, indentured labour and violent processes of extraction. And for many nineteenth-century commentators, as a number of sources here demonstrate, the materials of art dictated who was deemed able to create art; marble, for example, was deemed far too physically challenging for women to carve.

Some labour in extracting and processing materials was made widely visible and was valued both financially and aesthetically. The prestige of marble, for example, was partly connected to the expense and intensity of labour involved in quarrying it. Photographs of the Carrara marble quarry in Italy were widely reproduced in this period. Although clearly staged, with the extremely dangerous work of quarrying sanitised, these nonetheless made visible a form of masculine, physical work and related it to the making of sculpture.[47] The image reproduced here in Part 2 hails from the papers of American sculptor Hiram Powers; the act of collecting and preserving this image suggests the significance of drawing connections to this quarry for artists. The dangerous work of copper smelting, however, is never a feature of writing on bronze sculpture.[48] In painting, materials are less self-evidently present than in sculpture, and it is perhaps not surprising that painters seem to have been less engaged with the enslaved and later indentured plantation labour that made access to the pigment indigo possible, as explored here in Part 1. *Ackermann's Manual of Colours*, for example, notes that, 'We pass over, as matters of mere curiosity, and of no importance to the practice of the painter, from what part of the world, or what kingdom of nature his colours come, or how they are produced'.[49] The sources we have selected here attempt to foreground the wide range of human and non-human labour that made possible the materials of art.

Despite pride at the abolition of slavery in much of the British Empire in 1834, many of the materials of Victorian art were either produced by indentured labourers and enslaved people or implicated in these violent practices throughout the period.[50] Copper, for example, was used in bronze sculpture, as well as in the manufacture of paint pigments and glass colours. One prime location for the processing of copper was Swansea (known as 'Copperopolis'). The Swansea mines had been established in the eighteenth century and made the bulk of their wealth from copper used in the slave trade. By the 1820s, copper ore was in shorter supply in Britain, and, from the 1820s to the late 1860s, the ore consumed in Swansea's copper works was shipped from Cuban mines worked by enslaved people of African descent.[51] Copal, a tree resin from Tanzania widely used as varnish for oil paintings, provides another instance. British abolitionists championed the trade in copal as a legitimate alternative to the trade in people, and it seems that copal was unearthed by free men and women; however, before being shipped to Europe, it was cleaned by enslaved people.[52]

As Caitlin Beach has powerfully demonstrated, the complexity of these nineteenth-century relationships between the materials of art and slavery is epitomised in John Bell's *American Slave*, a bronze sculpture of a shackled nude woman of African descent, produced in various sizes and formats in Birmingham by Elkington and Co. from 1853 onwards. Metal objects – be they sculpture or jewellery – produced in the British Midlands were closely associated with items traded for people well into the 1860s, while there was also an uneasy connection between Elkington's mass-manufactured commodities and the commodification of people in slavery. The materiality of Bell's *American Slave* compromised and complicated its ostensibly abolitionist subject matter.[53] Few sources in this book openly discuss slavery or coerced labour, and we encourage readers to consider the significance of these silences and the material entanglements of Victorian arts with enslaved and indentured labour.

The range of materials considered here also acknowledges the role played by a wide range of art workers, many of whom were, however, not regarded or acknowledged as undertaking artistic labour. Consider, for example, the wide range of men and women that Harriet Martineau describes as contributing to the final appearance of Elkington and Co.'s electrotypes, or the men and women who worked in bookbinding factories as discussed in Part 4. The variety of labour was particularly remarked upon in sculpture; as explored in detail in the headnotes for Part 2, contemporaries understood that different materials involved different types of labour. The skilled labour involved in replica making, so crucial in sculpture, was also widely disregarded, conceptualised as mechanical rather than artistic. And as sources in Part 2 demonstrate, in the case of Indian sculptors involved in casting monuments for the South Kensington Museum, this notion of artistic skill was also racialised and related to British imperial claims.

Debates over artistic labour and materials relate to far wider Victorian discourses of gender, class and race. They are also connected to debates over what constituted 'art' and what constituted 'manufacture'. A focus on materials can both draw attention to these debates and demonstrate the wide ranges of people involved in the creation of Victorian arts.

Women and the materials of art

Women played an increasingly significant role in the production, consumption, and marketing of Victorian arts. While many women took up a variety of arts activities, fuelled by the huge growth in manuals and periodical articles aimed at the amateur, for a significant number of women, working in the arts was a bread-and-butter business. Women worked in bookbinding factories, where hand sewing was a physically demanding and low-paid activity, and cheaper female labour was lauded as a way of making the purchase of photographs more accessible to the working classes.

Painters who were female faced specific challenges as a group in the nineteenth century. They had limited opportunities for artistic training, and their presence in the life class was a matter of considerable debate. They were prevented from being members of the Royal Academy (RA); they could still exhibit at the RA, but they received none of the benefits of membership, including reputation-building access to the most prestigious spaces on the walls in the annual exhibition and, pre-eminently, training, status and recognition as professionals. Even the few art societies that did permit women to be members (such as both the Old and New Watercolour Societies) were managed exclusively by men and classified 'lady' members as a distinct category.[54]

However, particularly new media – such as photography – and revived media – like tempera – were embraced by Victorian women with gusto. And, despite expectations, there were a growing number of female sculptors and painters working and exhibiting in Britain. Women were specifically targeted as potential consumers of new technologies of art. Sets of photographic equipment usually consisting of a camera, lens and stand, while largely indistinguishable from other kinds of apparatus, were specifically marketed to 'ladies', and the new less messy methods of paint transportation introduced in the 1840s replaced the use of animal bladders and were considered more appropriate for 'lady artists'.[55]

Developments in both photography and book illustration opened up a range of career possibilities for women. The idea that these arts might provide a way for 'girls' and 'daughters' to support themselves speaks to the growing concern over the spectre of female redundancy caused by a challenging 'marriage market' (explored in Parts 4 and 5). But it is also the case that these arts opened up new vistas for women. Trailblazers such as photographer Julia Margaret Cameron and engraver and illustrator Clemence Housman were an inspiration to women seeking to explore new challenges and commercial opportunities afforded by the development of these media. Our sources discuss such opportunities for middle-class women, from opening their own photographic studios to the importance of having a 'room of one's own' for would-be female wood engravers. Indeed, William James Linton emphasises the high suitability of wood engraving for women in his 1884 manual:

> Let it be said then that wherever in the instructions here given the terms *he* and *him* are used, *she* and *her* may be understood to be equally intended. No artist work can be more suitable for women than our art of wood-engraving, in which already several, Mary Byfield and Eliza Thompson, and others, have distinguished themselves.[56]

The debate about women's participation in the arts often centres on the fitness or aptitude of the female body and is linked to the material specificities of different media. In 1862, for example, the sculptor Harriet Hosmer took out a libel case against those who suggested she was physically incapable of producing the 2-m-high statue of Zenobia that she exhibited in the London International Exhibition.[57] Retouching of photographs was seen as a job suitable for women as it required 'manipulative skill' rather than 'artistic perception', while forms of wood engraving demanded a delicacy of touch suited to female hands.[58] Watercolours and tempera in particular were identified as suitable media for women. Meaghan Clarke describes the development of a network of women including Christiana Herringham, Alice Meynell and Marianne Stokes, who were interested in writing about and experimenting with tempera in the late nineteenth century.[59] Included in Part 1 are essays by Meynell and Mary Merrifield, who produced the first English translation of Cennino Cennini's manual of painting *Il Libro dell'Arte* in 1844, which contains an extensive discussion of the use of tempera. And by working with stained glass women had the opportunity to move beyond the production of small-scale handicrafts for the home (such as embroidery and drawing) to the production of large-scale designs for ecclesiastical settings.[60] Despite the biological essentialism evident in the discourse on women and art, the second half of the nineteenth century saw increased levels of female participation and engagement across all arts.

Through its focus on materials and making, this volume gives a fresh overview of key developments in Victorian arts and enables readers to engage more directly with relevant, yet underresearched primary sources. We hope it will aid the identification of new questions and contribute a new nineteenth-century focus for the growing interdisciplinary field of art history and material culture studies.[61]

Notes

1 Asa Briggs, *Victorian Things* (London: B.T. Batsford Ltd., 1988), p. 45.

2 Jonah Siegel's focus on the '*conceptual* force of matter' and the ways in which the nineteenth century 'thought and wrote and visually represented moments of encounter with the material world' importantly acknowledges the way in which art objects and their material components were discussed, reproduced and remediated within a burgeoning nineteenth-century print culture. See *Material Inspirations: The Interests of the Art Object in the Nineteenth Century and After* (Oxford: Oxford University Press, 2020), also discussed in the introduction to this series.

3 Sally Woodcock, 'Leighton and Roberson: An Artist and His Colourman', *Burlington Magazine* 138:1121 (1996), pp. 526–528, p. 527.

4 Inge Fielder and Michael Bayard, 'Cadmium Yellows, Oranges and Reds', in R. L. Feller (ed.), *Artists' Pigments: A Handbook of Their History and Characteristics*, Volume 1 (London: Archetype, 2012), pp. 65–108; G. Zerr and R. Rubencamp, trans C. Mayer, *A treatise on colour manufacture: a guide to the preparation, examination, and application of all the pigment colours in practical use* (London, 1908), p. 387; Thomas W. Salter, *Field's Chromatography; or, Treatise on Colours and Pigments as used by Artists. An Entirely New and Practical Edition; Revised, Rewritten, and Brought Down to the Present Time* (London: Windsor and Newton, 1869), p. 217.

5 Diana Coole and Samantha Frost (eds.), 'Introducing the New Materialisms', in *New Materialisms: Ontology, Agency, and Politics* (Durham and London: Duke University Press, 2010), pp. 1–43, p. 1.

6 See Bill Brown, 'Reification, Reanimation, and the American Uncanny', *Critical Inquiry* 32:2 (2006), pp. 175–207.

7 For a detailed examination of the relationship between commodity culture and nineteenth-century colonialism, see Supriya Chaudri, Josephine McDonagh, Brian H. Murray and Rajeswari Sunder Rajan (eds.), *Commodities and Culture in the Colonial World* (London and New York: Routledge, 2018).

8 Jennifer L. Roberts, *Transporting Visions. The Movement of Images in Early America* (Berkeley: University of California Press, 2014), p. 8.
9 The distinction between 'amateur' and 'professional' in this period is, however, extremely complex. For further discussion, see Kyriaki Hadjiafxendi and Patricia Zakreski (eds.), *Crafting the woman professional in the long nineteenth century: artistry and industry in Britain* (Burlington, VT: Ashgate, 2013).
10 Jeffrey A. Auerbach, *The Great Exhibition of 1851: A Nation on Display* (New Haven and London: Yale University Press, 1999), p. 1.
11 See Marta Filipova, 'The forefront of English commercial centres: Wolverhampton's exhibitions of 1869 and 1902', in Marta Filipova (ed.), *Cultures of International Exhibitions 1840–1940: Great Exhibitions in the Margins* (Farnham: Ashgate, 2015), pp. 137–159, on p. 144. This figure is particularly remarkable considering that the population of Wolverhampton in 1869 was 68,000. For an overview of international exhibitions, see Paul Greenhalgh, *Fair World. A History of World's Fairs and Expositions. From London to Shanghai 1851–2010* (Winterbourne: Papadakis, 2011). On the British Empire and international exhibitions, see Peter H. Hoffenberg, *An Empire on Display: English, Indian and Australian Exhibitions from the Crystal Palace to the Great War* (Berkeley: University of California Press, 2001).
12 For a comparative history of city art museums established in Birmingham (1867), Manchester (1877) and Liverpool (1883), see Amy Woodson-Boulton, *Transformative Beauty. Art Museums in Industrial Britain* (Stanford: Stanford University Press, 2012). A more general overview is provided by Giles Waterfield, *The People's Galleries: Art Museums and Exhibitions in Britain, 1800–1914* (New Haven and London: Yale University Press, 2015).
13 P. G. Hamerton, *Thoughts about Art* (London: Macmillan and Co., 1873), pp. 368–373; Richard Redgrave and Samuel Redgrave, *A Century of Painters of the English School; with Critical Notices of their Works, and an Account of the Progress of Art in England* (London: Smith, Elder and Co., 1866), Vol. 2, pp. 602–605.
14 These include *The Journal of the Photographic Society* (later *The Photographic Journal*) est. 1853, *British Journal of Photography* est. 1854, *The Photographic News* est. 1858 and *Amateur Photographer* est. 1884.
15 See Susanna Gold, *The Unfinished Exhibition: Visualizing Myth, Memory, and the Shadow of the Civil War in Centennial America* (New York: Routledge, 2017).
16 Alistair Grant and Angus Patterson, *The Museum and the Factory: the V&A, Elkington and the electrical revolution* (London: Lund Humphries in association with V&A Publishing, 2018), pp. 96–99.
17 On the racial and political diversity of this audience, see Gold, *Unfinished Exhibition.*
18 For a broader discussion of the impact of new inventions and technology on Victorian material culture, see Volume 3 in this series, *Invention and Technology,* edited by Richard Menke. On electrotyping, see Grant and Patterson, *The Museum and the Factory.*
19 For an excellent reference text on Victorian photographic techniques, see John Hannavay (ed.), *The Encyclopedia of Nineteenth Century Photography* (New York and London: Routledge, 2008).
20 *The Photographic News: A weekly record of the progress of photography* (vol. xxiii, Christmas 1879).
21 Richard Newman, 'Chromium Oxide Greens', in Elisabeth West FitzHugh (ed.), *Artists' Pigments, A Handbook of Their History and Characteristics*, Volume 3 (London: Archetype, 2012), pp. 273–94; Hermann Kuhn and Mary Curran, 'Chrome Yellow and Other Chromate Pigments', in R. L. Feller (ed.), *Artists' Pigments*, Volume 1, pp. 187–218.
22 William Holman Hunt, 'The Present System of Obtaining Materials in use by Artist Painters, as Compared with that of the Old Masters', *Journal of the Society of Arts*, 23 (April 1889), pp. 485–499.

23 For further exploration, see M. Droth, J. Edwards and M. Hatt (eds.), *Sculpture Victorious: Art in an Age of Invention, 1837–1901* (New Haven and London: Yale University Press, 2014), pp. 18–30.
24 Ibid., p. 67; Susan Beattie, *The New Sculpture* (New Haven and London: Yale University Press, 1983).
25 Droth, Edwards and Hatt (eds.), *Sculpture Victorious*, pp. 259–261.
26 Thea Goldring, 'Recovered or Perfected: The Discourse of Chemistry in the Nineteenth-Century Revival of Stained Glass in Britain and France', *19: Interdisciplinary Studies in the Long Nineteenth Century*, 30 (2020); doi: https://doi.org/10.16995/ntn.2893
27 For a history of engraving techniques, see Susan Doyle, Jaleen Grove and Whitney Sherman (eds.), *History of Illustration* (New York: Fairchild Books, 2018).
28 For example, a detailed overview of the sources for the materials of watercolours in the period is provided by Bronwyn A. Ormsby, Joyce H. Townsend, Brian W. Singer and John R. Dean, 'British Watercolour Cakes from the Eighteenth to the Early Twentieth Century', *Studies in Conservation*, 50:1 (2005), pp. 45–66. Further references and discussions of copal, India rubber, mahogany, copper, ivory and silver are provided later in this introduction.
29 For further discussion, see Jonathan Curry-Machado, 'Global Histories, Imperial Commodities, Local Interactions: An Introduction', in Jonathan Curry-Machado (ed.), *Global Histories, Imperial Commodities, Local Interactions: An Introduction* (Basingstoke: Palgrave Macmillan, 2013), pp. 1–14.
30 Ibid.; see also Adeline Buckland's introduction to the *Raw Materials* volume, which argues for the anticolonial potential of defamiliarising 'raw' materials and attending to their potential: 'Materials constituted as raw have not yet lost the sense that they might still unleash powers in directions unforeseen'. Natasha Eaton, 'Nomadism of Colour: Painting, technology and waste in the chromo-zones of colonial India, c.1765–c.1860', *Journal of Material Culture*, 17:1 (2012), pp. 61–81; Jordanna Bailkin, 'Indian Yellow: Making and Breaking the Imperial Palette', *Journal of Material Culture*, 10:2 (2005), pp. 197–214.
31 For an ecocritical reading of the play and further references, see Sukanya Banerjee, 'Drama, Ecology, and the Ground of Empire: The Play of Indigo', in Nathan K. Hensley and Philip Steer (eds.), *Ecological Form: System and Aesthetics in the Age of Empire* (New York: Fordham University Press, 2019), pp. 21–41.
32 Bailkin, 'Indian Yellow', pp. 198–199.
33 Alfred C. Harmsworth, 'How to take a photograph', *Young Folks Paper* (May 01, 1886), p. 278.
34 On the fundamental interconnection between colonialism and slavery, and human-made global environmental desecration, see Kathryn Yusoff, *A Billion Black Anthropocenes or None* (Minneapolis: University of Minnesota Press, 2018). A useful environmental historical overview and further reading are provided in James Beattie, Edward Melillo and Emily O'Gorman, 'British Empire, 1837–1945', in James Beattie, Edward Melillo and Emily O'Gorman (eds.), *Eco-Cultural Networks and the British Empire: New Views on Environmental History* (London: Bloomsbury, 2015), pp. 3–20.
35 Banerjee, 'Drama, Ecology, and the Ground of Empire'. On the environmental and human cost of mahogany sourced from the Caribbean, see Jennifer L. Anderson, *Mahogany: The Costs of Luxury in Early America* (Cambridge, MA: Harvard University Press, 2012). L.H. Brockway, *Science and Colonial Expansion: The Role of the British Royal Botanic Gardens,* 2nd ed. (New Haven, CT: Yale University Press, 2002), pp. 141–184. For further secondary reading on rubber, see the *Raw Materials* volume in this series.

36 See Alfred Maskell, *Ivories* (London: Methuen, 1905), p. 504.

37 On photography and silver, see Robin Kelsey, 'Notes from the Field: Materiality', *Art Bulletin*, 95:1 (2013), pp. 21–23. A socio-ecological history of the human and environmental costs of silver mining is provided by Nicholas A. Robins, *Mercury, mining, and empire: the human and ecological cost of colonial silver mining in the Andes* (Bloomington, IN: Indiana University Press, 2011). On the ongoing environmental impact of the Carrara marble quarry in Italy, see R. Gentili, S. Sgorbati, and C. Baroni, 'Plant Species Patterns and Restoration Perspectives in the Highly Disturbed Environment of the Carrara Marble Quarries (Apuan Alps, Italy)', *Restoration Ecology*, 19 (2011), pp. 32–42.

38 Hamerton, *Thoughts about Art*, pp. 368–373; Redgrave and Redgrave, *A Century of Painters of the English School*, Vol. 2, p. 599 (see endnote 13 for the full reference). See further Jesse Oak Taylor, *The Sky of our Manufacture: the London fog and British fiction from Dickens to Woolf* (Charlottesville, VA: University of Virginia Press, 2016).

39 An invaluable resource for research into foundries in nineteenth-century Britain is Jacob Simon (ed.), 'British bronze sculpture founders and plaster figure makers, 1800–1980', *National Portrait Gallery* (from 2011), https://www.npg.org.uk/research [accessed 22 June 2021].

40 John Ruskin, 'The Elements of Drawing' in E. T. Cook and A. Wedderburn (eds.), *The Works of John Ruskin*, Vol. 15 (Cambridge: Cambridge University Press, 2010), p. 139. For further information on 'Chinese White', see Hermann Kuhn, 'Zinc White', in R. L. Feller (ed.), *Artists' Pigments*, Vol. 1, pp. 169–186.

41 See, for example, Michael Wheeler (ed.) *Ruskin and Environment: The Storm Cloud of the Nineteenth Century* (Manchester: Manchester University Press, 1995).

42 Edmund Newell and Simon Watts, 'The Environmental Impact of Industrialisation in South Wales in the Nineteenth Century: "Copper Smoke" and the Llanelli Copper Company', *Environment and History*, 2:3 (1996), pp. 309–336 (at p. 311). The Winsor and Newton Archive Database has several references to the sources of zinc for 'Chinese White', referring to zinc smelting in Swansea (URC: 17P038L01) and Belgium (URC: 21P007L12). See 'Winsor & Newton Archive of Nineteenth-Century Artists' Materials' Fitzwilliam Museum Website, https://winsorandnewton.fitzmuseum.cam.ac.uk/database [accessed 21 April 2021].

43 Joyce H. Townsend, 'The Materials of J. M. W. Turner: Pigments', *Studies in Conservation* 38:4 (1993), pp. 231–254 (p. 248).

44 For an overview of the possibilities of an ecocritical art history, with a particular focus on the role of materials, see Andrew Patrizio, *The Ecological Eye. Assembling an Ecocritical Art History* (Manchester: Manchester University Press, 2019).

45 Jennifer Tucker, 'Dangerous Exposures: Visualizing Work and Waste in the Victorian Chemical Trades', *International Labor and Working-Class History*, 95 (2019), pp. 130–165; Jason Edwards, 'The Vegan Viewer in the Circum-Polar World; or, J. H. Wheldon's The Diana and Chase in the Arctic (1857)', in E. Quinn and B. Westwood (eds.), *Towards a Vegan Theory. Thinking Veganism in Literature and Culture* (Cham, Switzerland: Palgrave Macmillan, 2018), pp. 79–106; Jason Edwards, '*Ex omnia conchis*? Edward Onslow Ford and the problem of Victorian '*animalier*' sculpture', *Word & Image*, 34:1 (2018), pp. 55–63. See also the essays in Maura Coughlin and Emily Gephart (eds.), *Ecocriticism and the Anthropocene in Nineteenth-Century Art and Visual Culture* (New York: Routledge, 2020).

46 Tucker, 'Dangerous Exposures'.

47 Leitch's ethnography of the Carrara marble quarries in the 1980s and 1990s provides a fascinating insight into the culture of work and the dangers faced by quarry workers. A. Leitch, 'The life of marble: The experience and meaning of work in the marble quarries

of Carrara', *The Australian Journal of Anthropology* 7:3 (1996), pp. 235–257. On the nineteenth-century context, see Laura Turner Igoe, '"A Gruesome Sight" Randolph Rogers's Nydia in a Marble World', in Coughlin and Gephart (eds.), *Ecocriticism and the Anthropocene in Nineteenth-Century Art and Visual Culture*, pp. 80–92.

48 See Newall and Watts, p. 311.

49 Theodore Henry Fielding, *Ackermann's Manual of Colours, used in the different branches of water-colour painting* (London: R. Ackermann, 1844), p. 39.

50 In the introduction to the *Raw Materials* volume of this series, Adeline Buckland explores the significance of these violent practices for rethinking the very category 'raw material'. On the Victorians and anti-slavery, see Richard Huzzey, *Freedom Burning. Anti-Slavery and Empire in Victorian Britain* (Ithaca: Cornell University Press, 2007). Further interconnections emerge in the manufacture of glass, for example. From the mid-nineteenth century, the synthetic alkali sodium carbonate gradually replaced organic alkalis such as kelp. The demand for a synthetic, mass-produced alkali was primarily driven by the alkali requirements of the UK textile trade, predicated on the exploitation of enslaved men, women and children in the American South. See Sally Rush, 'Seȩing Red', *19: Interdisciplinary Studies in the Long Nineteenth Century*, 30 (2020), doi: https://doi.org/10.16995/ntn.2897 [accessed 15 June 2021]; T. C. Barker, R. Dickinson, and D. W. F. Hardie, 'The Origins of the Synthetic Alkali Industry in Britain', *Economica*, 23 (1956), pp. 158–171. By 1860, 88% of textiles produced in Britain were made with cotton sourced from American slave plantations. See Mark Harvey, 'Slavery, Indenture and the Development of British Industrial Capitalism', *History Workshop Journal*, 88 (2019), pp. 66–88.

51 See further Chris Evans, *Slave Wales: The Welsh and Atlantic Slavery, 1660–1850* (Cardiff: University of Wales Press, 2010), pp. 83–91.

52 T. Sunseri, 'The Political Ecology of the Copal Trade in the Tanzanian Coastal Hinterland, c. 1820–1905', *Journal of African History*, 48:2 (2007), pp. 201–220.

53 Caitlin Beach, 'John Bell's American Slave in the Context of Production and Patronage', *Nineteenth-Century Art Worldwide*, 15:2 (2016), http://www.19thc-artworldwide.org/summer16/beach-on-john-bell-american-slave-context-of-production-and-patronage [accessed June 22, 2021].

54 Deborah Cherry, *Painting Women: Victorian Women Artists* (London: Routledge, 1993).

55 'Varieties', *Art-Union*, 3:26 (March 1841), p. 49.

56 William James Linton, *Wood-Engraving: A Manual of Instruction* (London: George Bell and Sons, 1885), p. 45. Mary Byfield was an engraver and illustrator who produced a number of works for the Chiswick Press. Eliza Thompson is discussed by Patricia Jaffé in *Women Engravers* (London: Virago, 1988), p. 11. See also Lorrainie Kooistra's work on Clemence Housman: 'Victorian Women Wood Engravers: The Case of Clemence Housman', in Alexis Easley, Clare Gill, Beth Rodgers (eds.), *Women, Periodicals and Print Culture in Britain, 1830s–1900s: The Victorian Period* (Edinburgh: Edinburgh University Press, 2019), pp. 277–300.

57 Hilary Fraser, 'Women and the Modelling of Victorian Sculptural Discourse', *Visual Resources*, 33:1–2 (2017), pp. 74–93.

58 Ruth Young, 'Photography as a profession for women', *Atalanta* (April 1, 1898), p. 407.

59 M. Clarke, 'On Tempera and Temperament: Women, Art, and Feeling at the Fin de Siècle', *19: Interdisciplinary Studies in the Long Nineteenth Century*, 23 (2016), http://doi.org/10.16995/ntn.767 [accessed 15 June 2021].

60 T. Kupper, 'Amateur Stained Glass in English Churches, 1830–1880', *19: Interdisciplinary Studies in the Long Nineteenth Century*, 30 (2020), doi: https://doi.org/10.16995/ntn.2895 [accessed 20 June 2021].

61 Recent publications looking to other time periods include Christy Anderson, Anne Dunlop and Pamela H. Smith (eds.), *The Matter of Art: Materials, Practices, Cultural Logics, c. 1250–1750* (Manchester: Manchester University Press, 2014); Christian Berger (ed.), *Conceptualism and materiality: matters of art and politics* (Leiden: Brill, 2019).

PART 1

Paintings

1.1

Artists' materials

DOI: 10.4324/9781315400266-3

1.1 Artists' materials

Paint is perhaps the most obvious of artists' materials, but it is only one among many. Artists' materials also include supports (usually canvas); priming (also often referred to as grounds) applied to the support to prepare it for the application of paint; pigment (which gives colour to paint); vehicles, which bind the pigment to make paint, most commonly linseed in the nineteenth century, as well as poppy seed and in some instances whale oil; brushes and palette knives (and palettes); varnish, applied after painting (egg white as a temporary varnish, usually replaced by either mastic or copal); and picture frames.[1] And these are just the materials that make up the painting, before one considers props, costumes, plaster casts, anatomical models, cadavers (human and animal) or the 'lay figure', a jointed wooden doll, sometimes life-sized, which by the nineteenth century often had a stuffed torso and arms, and was used to model clothing and pose in place of a living model.[2]

Artists' materials underwent numerous changes in the long nineteenth century, and the sources selected here foreground contemporary understandings of these transformations. There is a focus on William Holman Hunt, largely because he was so vociferous on the subject of artists' materials, while Ford Madox Brown's diary provides a more personal insight into an artist's use of a lay figure, and offers a glimpse of the practical ways in which artists discussed their materials. These diary entries demonstrate the physical labour of making art (itself laboured on by Madox Brown in his enumeration of hours worked): the wrestling with lay figures, whose arrangement, according to Madox Brown, seems to have been inordinately time-consuming. The materials of the lay figure had a significant impact on its use, as Brown discovered on leaving his out in the rain. This is not, of course, to suggest that artists in the later nineteenth century, or those outside of the Pre-Raphaelite circle, did not engage with materials.[3] Indeed, as David Peters Corbett and Kirstie Sinclair Dootson have explored, the later nineteenth century was a period of intense scrutiny of the ways in which meaning was created by the physical stuff of paint, with varied political implications.[4]

Collapsible metal paint tubes were introduced in 1841, making painting a much more portable activity. Previously, paint had been supplied in animal bladders, bound at the top; painters would pierce the bladder with a tack and use a stopper of wood or ivory to keep the paint in. They readily burst and were notoriously messy. After the widespread introduction of paint tubes, bladders became obsolete. But as short pieces from *Art-Union* reproduced here suggest, even in 1840 when rival new technologies for paint transportation were being produced (in this case Winsor and Newton's patented – and very expensive – glass syringes), the disappearance of bladders was by no means a foregone conclusion. The *Art-Union* editorial comments favourably on the potential broadening of opportunities that Winsor and Newton's glass tubes might bring to female artists, who had apparently been previously put off by the inconvenience and mess of transporting paint in bladders. A later nineteenth-century Winsor and Newton advert for moist watercolours in collapsible tubes (an innovation of around 1850) shows the range of colours available (including Indian yellow and indigo, discussed in the next section) and their comparative prices. The advertisement's seeming embarrassment in its promotion of these tubes despite them being 'somewhat wasteful' seems particularly noteworthy; as Harley remarked in an article of 1971, the collapsible metal tubes made for artists were also the beginning of disposable packaging for a wide range of commodities.[5]

The suppliers of artists' materials also changed, a topic addressed by numerous sources in the painting section. In the Middle Ages and Renaissance, artists generally manufactured their own paints, passing on recipes through their studios. Victorian artists, like Holman Hunt, became increasingly aware of this practice after the translation into English of Cennino Cennini's *Il Libro dell'Arte* (1437) by Mary Merrifield in 1844. As the status of artists changed, and as more and more people started painting, by the seventeenth century a new business had sprung up: the artist's colourman (although there were also colourwomen, like Elizabeth Emerton who took over her late husband's business in 1741).[6] Colourmen supplied paint and materials, often at first as a sideline (generally they were involved in manufacturing house paints as well). By the nineteenth century, most professional artists also used colourmen rather than making their own paints, and a number of firms emerged, including Reeves, Winsor and Newton, Ackermann's and Robersons. The mid- and later nineteenth-century return to medieval media such as fresco and especially tempera (discussed in detail in the following section) is a key reaction against purchasing ready-made materials.

In the speech reprinted here, Holman Hunt details the alienation of the nineteenth-century painter from their materials, and advocates the formation of a 'society for looking after the material interests of painting'.[7] Holman Hunt draws on mid-century investigations into the history of pigments, including Merrifield's *Original Treatises on the Arts of Painting* (1849) and Eastlake's *Materials for a History of Oil Painting* (1847), and suggests the key *material* role played by new engagements with 'Old Masters' for Victorian artists.[8] He notes the impact that larger political events might have had on the supply of artists' materials, in this case the shift in linseed production for oil paints from the Black Sea to India after the Crimean War. Holman Hunt emphasises the importance of materials for making art; as he understands it, artists are currently in a state of 'helplessness', which is hindering 'our national genius'.[9] Understanding materials had wide-reaching consequences.[10]

Some artists – especially those associated with Pre-Raphaelitism – began experimenting with designing their own one-off picture frames in the 1840s and 1850s. They attempted to move away from mass-produced picture frames and to engage with a Ruskinian 'truth' in materials and textures.[11] From the 1860s onwards, those connected with the Victorian 'classical revival' also commissioned frames to fit their artworks.[12] The importance of frames in contributing to the meaning of artworks is explored in Frederick Stephens' discussion of William Holman Hunt's *Finding of the Saviour in the Temple* (1854–1860), an image that examines the relationship between what Hunt saw as the 'old' (Judaism) and the 'new' (Christianity). Contemporary reviews similarly noted that the painting seemed uncontainable: 'the symbols have overflowed the picture, and expanded themselves all over the frame'.[13] In his 1873 volume of essays *Thoughts on Art*, art critic Philip Hamerton further explored the role of frames in relation to their materials and suggested a range of new technological solutions to the problem of 'the extreme perishableness of frames'.[14] This, Hamerton asserts, was exacerbated in the nineteenth century by industrial pollution, making it nearly impossible to keep the gilt clean, in addition to the damage caused by the regular circulation of paintings at exhibitions, a relatively recent innovation.

Notes

1 An overview is provided by Joyce H. Townsend, 'The Materials used by British Oil Painters in the Nineteenth-Century', *Tate Papers*, 2 (2004), at https://www.tate.org.uk/research/publications/tate-papers [accessed 15 June 2021]. More detailed analysis is provided in Leslie Carlyle, *The Artist's Assistant: Oil Painting Instruction Manuals and Handbooks in Britain, 1800–1900, with Reference to Selected Eighteenth-century Sources* (London: Archetype, 2001). Jason Edwards offers an essential critical reflection on the use of whale oil in Turner's paintings in 'The Vegan Viewer in the Circum-Polar World; Or, J. H. Wheldon's The Diana and Chase in the Arctic (1857)', in E. Quinn and B. Westwood (eds), *Towards a Vegan Theory. Thinking Veganism in Literature and Culture* (Cham, Switzerland: Palgrave Macmillan, 2018), pp. 79–106.

2 Jane Munro (ed.), *Silent partners: artist and mannequin from function to fetish* (New Haven and London: Yale University Press, 2014).

3 A survey of other sources for nineteenth-century artists materials is provided by Townsend, 'Materials Used by British Oil Painters'. Briefly, these comprise: inventories of artists' studios at their deaths (e.g. Turner); archives of artists' colourmen; artists correspondence; surviving materials (such as artists' palettes).

4 David Peters Corbett, *The World in Paint: Modern Art and Visuality in England, 1848–1914* (Manchester: Manchester University Press, 2004), pp. 83–127; Kirsty Sinclair Dootson, "The Texture of Capitalism: Industrial Oil Colours and the Politics of Paint in the Work of G.F. Watts", *British Art Studies*, 14 (2019), at www.britishartstudies.ac.uk [accessed 15 June 2021].

5 R. D. Harley, 'Oil colour containers: Development work by artists and colourmen in the nineteenth century', *Annals of Science*, 27:1 (1971), pp. 1–12.

6 For an overview, see *Paint & painting: an exhibition and working studio sponsored by Winsor & Newton to celebrate their 150th anniversary* (London: Tate Gallery, 1982), pp. 35–44.

7 William Holman Hunt, 'The Present System of Obtaining Materials in use by Artist Painters, as Compared with that of the Old Masters', *Journal of the Society of Arts* (23 April 1880), pp. 485–99, on p. 498.

8 See further Elizabeth Prettejohn, *Modern painters, old masters: the art of imitation from the Pre-Raphaelites to the First World War* (New Haven and London: Yale University Press, 2017).
9 Holman Hunt, 'Present System of Obtaining Materials', p. 498.
10 For more on Holman Hunt and materials, see M. R. Katz, 'Holman Hunt on Himself: textual evidence in aid of technical analysis', in E. Hermens (ed.) *Looking Through Paintings: the Study of Painting Techniques and Materials in Support of Art Historical Research* (London: Archetype, 1998), pp 415–44; Carol Jacobi, *William Holman Hunt: Painter, Painting, Paint* (Manchester: Manchester University Press, 2006).
11 Lynn Roberts, 'Nineteenth-Century English Picture Frames I: The Pre-Raphaelites', *International Journal of Museum Management and Curatorship*, 4 (1985), pp. 155–172.
12 Lynn Roberts, 'Nineteenth-Century English Picture Frames II: The Victorian High Renaissance', *International Journal of Museum Management and Curatorship*, 5 (1986), pp. 273–293.
13 *Manchester Guardian*, 24 April 1860, reproduced in F. G. Stephens, *William Holman Hunt and his Works: a memoir of the artist's life, with description of his pictures* (London: James Nisbet and Co., 1860), p. 115.
14 Philip Gilbert Hamerton, *Thoughts About Art* (London: Macmillan and Co., 1873), p. 369.

1

'VARIETIES'

Art-Union 3:26 (March 1841), p. 49

WINSOR AND NEWTON'S GLASS TUBES. – This is a most valuable invention, and well calculated to supersede every former method of putting up colour for the immediate use of the artist. The advantages of these tubes are important, and not the least so is the perfect cleanliness with which the colour is transferred to the palette. This is effected by means of a small air-tight screw, which acting at one end forces the colour out of a small orifice at the other end, and so perfectly under control, that any quantity can with ease be ejected from a very minute portion to the entire contents of the tube. The colour in these vessels does not thicken and become dry, as is usual in the ordinary bladder packets, but works well and freely to the last, after having been kept any length of time. It is a matter of surprise, that amid the many objections to the old method of putting up colours, nothing has before been devised as an improved substitute. Comparatively few ladies have hitherto practised oil painting, from the inconveniences we have alluded to; but since these are removed by the glass tubes, it may be expected that oil painting will in future become a more general female accomplishment.

BLADDERS OF OIL COLOUR. – Among the many instances of the attention now paid by colourmen to the improvement of the various articles with which artists are supplied by them, we will introduce to notice another ingenious plan now adopted by Messrs. Waring and Dimes. This is a method of preserving for a longer time, and with greater efficacy, the oil colours in bladders. Many have been the expedients hit upon for this purpose, but it is at once manifest that this method has that superiority, which always goes hand in hand with simplicity in all practical matters. The "colour is ejected through the neck of the bladder, and the orifice secured from the air by a cap screwing over it." As the prices of these bladders are very little beyond those prepared in the ordinary way, we certainly can recommend them as most useful auxiliaries, deserving a welcome from artists and amateurs. To the former, indeed, matters of this sort are of less importance, inasmuch as they, by keeping their colours in constant use, preserve them thereby, in great measure, from the unpleasant state into which they generally get when not employed. It is, therefore, in sketching and amateur painting that this method of colour-preserving will be found peculiarly serviceable; as the colours can be kept uninjured for any length of time, and can be easily ejected from the bladder.

DOI: 10.4324/9781315400266-4

2

WINSOR AND NEWTON'S CATALOGUE OF COLOURS AND MATERIALS FOR WATERCOLOUR PAINTING, PENCIL, CHALK, ARCHITECTURAL DRAWING

(London: Winsor and Newton, 1882), p. 20

WINSOR & NEWTON'S MOIST WATER COLOURS

IN COLLAPSIBLE TUBES.

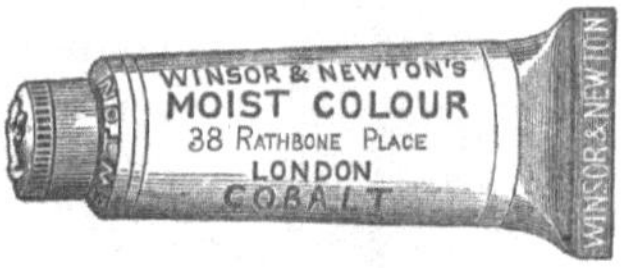

Moist Water Colours in Tubes, though somewhat wasteful, are of assistance as furnishing quickly a quantity of colour, and affording facilities for power of touch and vigor of effect. They should be used within reasonable time, as they do not keep so long, or so well, as the ordinary Moist Colours in porcelain pans.

1*s*. each.

Antwerp Blue	Chrome Yellow	Lamp Black	Raw Sienna
Bistre	Chrome Deep	Light Red	Raw Umber
Blue Black	Chrome Orange	Naples Yellow	Roman Ochre
Brown Ochre	Emerald Green	Neutral Tint	Terre Verte
Brown Pink	Gamboge	New Blue	Vandyke Brown
Burnt Sienna	Indian Red	Olive Green	Venetian Red
Burnt Umber	Indigo	Payne's Grey	Vermilion
Chinese White	Italian Pink	Prussian Blue	Yellow Lake
Cologne Earth	Ivory Black	Prussian Green	Yellow Ochre

1*s*. 6*d*. each.

Brown Madder	Leitch's Blue (or Cyanine Blue)	Purple Lake	Scarlet Vermilion
Crimson Lake		Roman Sepia	Sepia
Mars Yellow	Neutral Orange	Scarlet Lake	Warm Sepia

2*s*. each.

Cobalt Blue	Orange Vermilion	Viridian (or Veronese Green)
Indian Yellow	Violet Carmine	

3*s*. each.

Aureolin	Cadmium Orange	Field's Orange Vermilion	Indian Purple
Burnt Carmine	Carmine	Gallstone	Mars Orange
Cadmium Yellow	French Blue or Ultramarine	Oxide of Chromium	Pink Madder
Cadmium Pale			Rose Madder

5*s*. each.

Purple Madder	Smalt	Ultramarine Ash

DOI: 10.4324/9781315400266-5

3

WILLIAM HOLMAN HUNT, 'THE PRESENT SYSTEM OF OBTAINING MATERIALS IN USE BY ARTIST PAINTERS, AS COMPARED WITH THAT OF THE OLD MASTERS'

Journal of the Society of Arts (23 April 1880), pp. 485, 492–493, 496, 497–498

[p. 485]

The subject about which I feel called upon to address you, I am glad to be able to point out, makes no demand for oratory; although an eloquent lecturer would, doubtless, find means to make the address more attractive. I must premise too that I have no pretension to chemical knowledge. Such science might, at first, be expected in a painter who should address an audience both scientific and artistic; but I have been led to reflect that the chemical investigations necessary for the purposes of art should be left to analysers much more profound than an artist could become. Imperfect knowledge has misguided many experimentalists; it would certainly betray me were I to pretend to teach. One of my main objects is to explain what are our most serious difficulties and wants, and I shall speak, in the hope that a greater interest may be awakened among chemists when they are convinced of our great desire for their help, which they could scarcely yet have been expected fully to realise.

The aim, you will understand, is simply to make a comparison between the system adopted anciently by painters to supply themselves with materials for their work, and that at present in vogue in Europe; to weigh, without prejudice, the good and the bad of this last, and to search for modes of improving the present arrangements which do not prove satisfactory.

[pp. 492–493]

In the necessity of now examining the misfortunes of our system, I feel called upon to avow that I regard the artists' colourmen of London as gentlemen of intelligence, of character, and great enterprise, to which qualities we are

DOI: 10.4324/9781315400266-6

much indebted for the comparatively safe position we enjoy; for, indeed, at the worst, it must be recognised that we might have gone much further astray. It is needful, however, that we should be not only in good hands, but we should give strong proof that we can distinguish between that which is faulty and that which is perfect; and it is the want of discriminating power in the painter which produces all the indifference on the part of the preparer to the permanent character of the materials he supplies. The painter has really not the power to trace the causes of defects. The colour man naturally judges of the character of the materials he vends by the condition they are in while under his own eye. To him, the evils revealing themselves in the work which has passed through his shop do not exist if he never sees them; and, if he hears of them only, as evils untraceable in their cause which have occurred to one of his customers (who may, sometimes, have obtained materials elsewhere), his sense of responsibility is quieted, when he has received the assurance of his men in the workshop that the usual rules, which have hitherto resulted in work of a kind not eliciting complaints, have been strictly adhered to. The workmen, too, in these shops are not permanent, and there is virtually no responsibility for any one preparation. In most cases the complaint is never made, for the evil may be a very serious one, and yet it may not manifest itself before the death of the artist. In one artist-colour establishment, in London alone are colours extracted from their roots; and even there certain colours are purchased from wholesale makers, who are without the feeling of personal pride in the perfection of their products which Mr. Field and the Dutch preparer of vermilion had. The other establishments buy from the wholesale supplier, and thus the user of the colour is so far away from the maker, that there is no real communication between them. So thoroughly is this accepted as proper, that I have been refused both tubes and colours when I have sent for them, the apology being that it did not seem fair to sell direct to the artist. Let us now, by special cases, see how the system works.

Twenty years ago, wanting to have a painting enlarged, I went to a colourman of the best standing, and asked him to explain to me the different systems by which such changes were effected; and he told me that sewing the extra pieces on, as the old masters did, was now found to be quite unnecessary. It caused a great eyesore in the picture, and was no additional source of strength. For many years they had undertaken the enlargement of paintings for Maclise and Landseer, who had been greatly pleased with the manner adopted of relining the central picture on a canvas of the required dimensions, and then fastening down with glue the marginal pieces. I saw specimens of this ingenious treatment of paintings which, in progress, had outgrown their original conception, and nothing could be more satisfactory to the artists' colourman point of view of a few years; but a visit in this day to Maclise' s "Play Scene in Hamlet," and to Landseer's "Field of Waterloo," will at once reveal what a mischievous point of view this is; for the two edges of the adjoining canvas have curled up, and opening lines, every day getting greater, mark the original confines of the composition. This is, in the one case, twenty, in the other thirty years – a time almost out of consideration, by its length, to the tradesman; but it should be a mere tomorrow to the painter, whose work is not worth the doing – to any one but his humbled self – if it will not last for many generations of eyes and minds. The mischief which we have to cure is like a terrible growth requiring the surgeon's knife. We English people are not given to hiding our own weakness; we attribute our vitality to our habit of being the first to speak of our defects; and the rule should certainly not be abandoned in Art matters. I will, therefore, illustrate the weakness of our system by another case. It is now thirty years since that I bought a canvas from the same most respectable house, where before and since I have obtained many excellent canvases. The one I speak of was remarkably sandy in texture; it was so far objectionable in this respect that, after the first two or three days' painting, I should have changed it for another, but I was in the country; and I contented myself by spreading with the palette-knife a filling-up couch of zinc white – then just newly introduced – on the part where my principal work would be. The picture was eventually finished, and for ten years I had no suspicion of its malady. At that time I had my attention drawn to a number of minute particles on the surface of the painting. On experiment, these proved to be microscopic blisters, which, when scraped away, left the white canvas exposed. There must have been 5,000 in the space of two or three square feet. A couple of days' tedious and careful stippling remedied the injury; but, in another ten years, a similar and almost as numerous a crop appeared, with the like need of retouching, which has, in later years, even again occurred. The late John Phillip told me that he had had the same mishap with canvases purchased in Spain, and he had ascertained that the ground had been prepared with sugar of lead as a dryer, and that the mischief would go on until all the particles had come away. I invited my colourman to explain to me the reason of the mischief, telling him the details of my treatment of the canvas while painting. He jumped at the theory that it was the zinc which was in process of disintegration; but this, as I could show him by tracing the greater smoothness of the canvas where I had applied the white, could not be maintained, because the particles had not broken through at all in that part (perhaps, from the greater thickness of the paint, they had escaped through the back). The fact was, I was altogether wasting time to ask this gentlemen any questions about the canvas, which, probably, if prepared on his premises at all – and this, as it happens, is very doubtful – had been trowelled by a workman who never expected to see that canvas or hear of it again one week after he had taken it off the stretching frame. I know of another painting executed on canvas, bought at the same time, and the same shop, which has gone through the same history as mine did; and a third canvas, from the same establishment, had part of its ground peel off like a sheet of paper while the painting was in progress, entirely destroying the artist's labour. I have also had experience of canvas which, if worked at in one intention from the beginning to the end, has proved perfectly equal to the work, but which on any scraping out and corrections has had its ground broken up into facets, on account of the weakness of the cloth; and this has caused obstacles to the happy termination of the work of the most serious kind.

[. . .]

[p. 496]

Let us now examine the state of our oil. I will tell the history of my progressive enlightenment on this important point. An article which appeared about ten years ago in a review explained that, before the Crimean War, our stock of seed for making oil came principally from the ports of the Black Sea. There was then a practice in the trade of a kind somewhat surprising to a stranger. It was to empty into the hold of the vessel one measure of hemp or other common seed to thirty-nine of linseed. This was called legitimate adulteration. The war destroyed this trade, and linseed was subsequently brought from India, where the quality was inferior, and where carelessness in planting and reaping the crops caused the seed to be less unmixed; but, in addition to this inferiority, the trade had thought well to advance its legitimate adulteration to the extent of one measure to every nineteen. After reading this, Dr. Sim told me that he had been unable to find perfect linseed oil in all England, and that he had to procure what he wanted by having the seed carefully sorted out one by one by the fingers. And since then I have had the declaration as to the impossibility of getting pure linseed oil through ordinary channels confirmed by the best chemists.

[. . .]

[pp. 497–498]

In the last fifteen years it may be said that a general conviction has been growing in the minds of painters, that an effort should be made to master the nature of the materials with which the art is conducted. Mr. Barff – who first, I believe, in this room proved his fitness for the post – was appointed by the Royal Academy to deliver lectures on the chemistry of colours. His efforts have, I doubt not, effected much in teaching his hearers the nature of the pigments they use. Together with this manifestation of interest in the material question, artists have made experiments in painting on tempera grounds, and some have strained raw canvas, and laid their own preparations to work upon, which before, I believe, none but two distinguished – but withal, as they were thought, eccentric – artists had done. Mr. Liebreich's lectures at the Royal Institution, and certain articles in the "Portfolio," contributed by various artists, detailing manners of work, and revelations made in the "Athenaeum," are other proofs of the conviction gaining ground that we have still much to learn before we can be in a position of safety. I do not regard anything that is being done as enough going to the root of the difficulty. All is done too much with the determination to keep our clean-handed amateur superiority. But I take these facts as encouragement to think that an appeal to the profession to organise some system by which henceforth the student shall be provided with a knowledge of the servile questions of the craft, may find many others determined to make their life-bought observations a nucleus of knowledge for the benefit of the next generation.

The evidence given amounts, I think, to this, that in this day – 150 years after the commencement of English art – we have no more mastery of our craft, as such, than that with which Hogarth, Gainsborough, and Reynolds commenced their careers. Reynolds's very mistakes testify to his anxiety to establish some certain knowledge of the matter as much as to the blankness of the guidance he had received. The jealousy with which he guarded his secrets from even his pupils was instigated probably by a desire to avow no habits not warranted by success. His enemies had assailed him as one using materials that were perishable. When his weary eyes urged him, finally, to put down his life-kindling brush, the experience that he had gained resulted in no gain to his successors. Hilton, Wilkie, Etty, Turner, and, lastly, Maclise, began their application to the art of painting with no help from their predecessors. The last has left laborious works which, even within 40 or 30 years, or less, are so ruined, from his ignorance of the art of painting, that the uninformed observer would be led to conclude that they had been done by a process – not which had before been tried for 400 years, but which had never before been put to the test. Beside those adduced, which suffered from misdirection by the colourman, "Captain Roche" and "The Marriage of Strongbow" – which I saw only lately – are my justification for thus speaking. What this painter had, in the end, learnt as to what was safe and what unsafe in practice, no one now knows. The lessons of his life's practice all died with him, as had the essence of the experience of previous painters; as will, again, our own dearly-bought knowledge, unless some change be made of radical importance in our system. Will it not be the best proof of our devotion to our art – of our faith in our national genius, and even of the high purpose of the art of the civilised world – if we put ourselves to the task of determining upon some course that shall liberate us from our increasing helplessness. The fear of making a scandal, of hurting the feelings, of exciting the hostility of the many having a vested interest in the present state of the business connected with art, have not been without influence in preventing the evil being laid bare. It is my duty here to insist upon it that there is a sore, and to track the evidence of this, passing by all that betokens independent health; and this determination may easily be construed as signs of prejudice or exaggeration on my part. I do regret this possibility, for I declare again that I have respect for the character of the gentlemen who conduct the businesses which supply us with our materials, and that the intelligence and principle which guide them have saved us from disaster of more serious kind than that I have noted, and have secured good results of great importance, which I have had to pass by. I must not, however, fear to declare that it is high time that the wound should be probed, and that a remedy should be found. In England, we pride ourselves upon being the first to bring out our defects to the light of day. It is, with reason, thought to be a means of ensuring continued vitality. Should we, in art, be the only Englishmen acting on a different rule? The cure that we have to seek is one it is possible to define compactly. It is to establish a means of transmitting the practical wisdom of one generation of painters to another.

4

V. SURTEES (ED.), *DIARY OF FORD MADOX BROWN*

(New Haven and London: Yale University Press, 1981) pp. 4–5, 21, 34, 44, 76

6 September 1847

Have not worked to day – tried to but could not having been out all morning to the costume shop and other places, cam home quite tired, rested and went out again. Got a lay figure from Barbe's[1] at last, bought 10 yards of flannel for draperies, engaged a model for tomorrow, lost myself in Somerstown got into a place where there was no gas thought I should get my throat cut [. . .]

9 September 1847

Got up at seven, breakfasted and then went to Greenvich [sic], came back saw my uncle and Tom ye lauyer [sic], bought some plaid draperies dined and set about aranging [sic] the draperies for Robert Burns[2] in the Lay figure – sweated over it till dark but got it to do at last – Went out till bed time.

28 December 1847

Tried to work did nothing all day but arrange the lay figure for Wiclif [sic] and superintend the making of a gown for Chaucer, I am sadly Idle!![3]

29 December 1847

Got up at half past 8 and to work by half past 9, worked till 11 at arranging the dress of Wicliff [sic]. The Lucy's came in I muddled at a drawing of it till half past 2.

11 March 1848

Got up at half past 7 and to work by 9, altered the hands of John of Gaunt – began painting the Cloak of the lady, interruptions of all kinds [. . .] Arranged the lay figure I had made of the child, took up much time – did nothing more. Walked back to Tudor Lodge with Mrs Lucy. Came back to Studio at 7, Bury[4] did not come, began work at 8 painted the spandril till 12. Lucy called in (5 hours work 2 arranging).[5]

15 March 1848

Got up at quarter past 7, arranged the lay figure for John of Gaunt's jupon. Began painting it at quarter to 10. Left off at half past 3. If I can not better it by Lamp light must rub it out.

DOI: 10.4324/9781315400266-7

17 March 1848

Got up at quarter past 7 to work by quarter to 9. Painted at the Ivy till quarter past 2 and from half 3 till 6 at the Damask back of the chair. Arranged the Lay figure for John of Gaunt. From half past 7 till 10 painted in the ground afresh for the jupon (yellow for the blue and white for the red). Nothing like a good coating of White to get bright sunny colour (9 hours work 2 ½ arranging).

17 July 1848

Went to Paris to see my old fried Casey and buy a lay figure. Did both, enjoyed myself much [. . .] came back to London on the 6th [. . .] The trip in all cost £1.6.6, sheer madness but que voulez vous the thing is done.

16 August 1854

[. . .] The baa lamb picture[6] was painted almost entirely in sunlight which twice gave me a fever while painting. I used to take the lay figure out every morning and bring it in at night or if it rained [. . .] The medium I used was Robersons undrying copal (Flake White)

[. . .]

Twelve days before sending in the Christ picture[7] I had given it up in despair, none of the heads being yet done . . . I afterwards took up the Christ again at the instigation of Millais and painted the heads of Peter, Christ and John (this one the only one laid in) also *all the other figures of* apostles in 10 days and sent it in. This picture was painted in four months the flesh painted on *wet white* at Millais' lying instigation, Roberson's Medium, which I think dangerous like Millais' advice.

Notes

1 Lechertier Barbe, artist's colourman, the Quadrant, Regent St.
2 Burns was one of the figures in the wings of Brown's discarded triptych 'The Seeds and Fruits of English Poetry.' The centre panel of this painting became *Chaucer at the Court of Edward III* (1851, Art Gallery of New South Wales, Sydney).
3 For the painting *The First Translation of the Bible into English* (1847–8; 1859–61, Bradford Museums and Art Galleries).
4 A model.
5 Also for *The First Translation of the Bible into English.*
6 *Pretty Baa Lambs* (1851–9, Birmingham Museums Trust).
7 *Christ Washing Peter's Feet* (1852–6, Tate Britain).

5

WILLIAM HOLMAN HUNT, *THE FINDING OF THE SAVIOUR IN THE TEMPLE* (1854–60)

Birmingham Museum and Art Gallery, Presented by Sir John T. Middlemore Bt., 1896

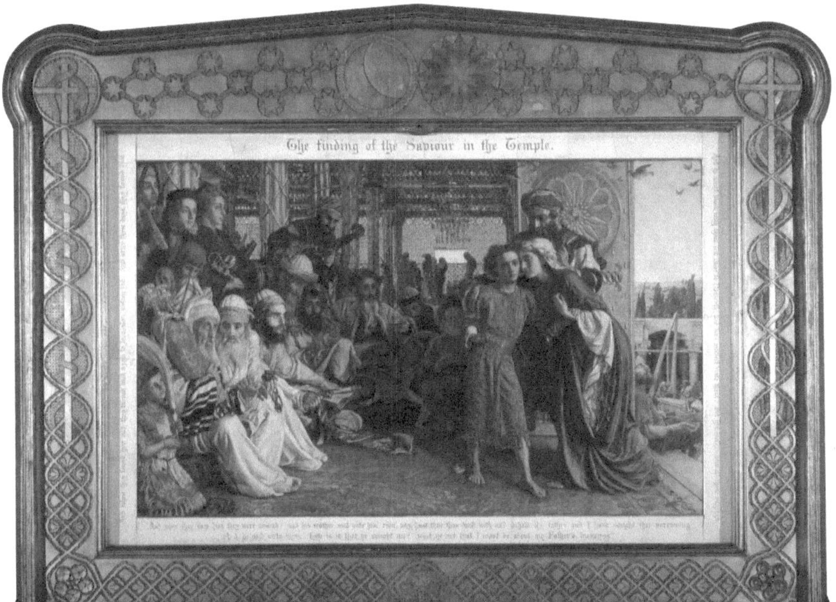

DOI: 10.4324/9781315400266-8

6

F. G. STEPHENS, *WILLIAM HOLMAN HUNT AND HIS WORKS: A MEMOIR OF THE ARTIST'S LIFE, WITH DESCRIPTION OF HIS PICTURES*

(London: James Nisbet and Co., 1860), pp. 78–79

Even the very frame was not without its demands upon the thought of the painter. One side of this, occupied by the cross-staff that sustained the brazen serpent, which twines itself about the head, is typical of the olden Law of Moses, – of the sacrifice and substitution of an animal; on the other a cross of thorns, with a garland of flowers about it, expresses the New Law. The centre is surmounted by the sun at full glory, and the moon eclipsed; the space from this to the corners is filled up with stars. At the foot a diaper of heartscases, the symbols of peace, – and daisies – of humility, devotion, as well as universality.

DOI: 10.4324/9781315400266-9

7

P. G. HAMERTON, 'PICTURE FRAMES'

Thoughts about art (London: Macmillan and Co., 1873), pp. 368–373

THE force of routine, in all matters which concern the working of the common trades, offers such a steady resistance to innovation, that it is almost useless to suggest any reform which would involve the practical abandonment of a trade already learned and in the full tide of an assured prosperity. Picture-frames are made admirably well, and they succeed admirably in the object for which they are intended; that is to say, they show a picture to the best possible advantage. They have two faults; but these faults, instead of diminishing the prosperity of the trade, positively go far to increase it, whilst they injuriously affect only the pocket of the man who buys the picture, or that of the unsuccessful or partially successful artist, who often has pictures left upon his hands.

These two faults are costliness and fragility. A picture-frame of any magnitude is an expensive thing, and, at the same time, one of the very worst investments of money that it is possible to imagine. The ornaments are made in a kind of paste glued upon a wooden frame-work, and then gilt. A very slight shock is sufficient to break them off, for the paste becomes exceedingly brittle with time; and if there is any extra heat – as, for instance, if you hang a picture over a chimney-piece – the mouldings are apt to curl up and detach themselves without the help of any shock whatever. Then the gilding, though extremely pretty when perfectly new and fresh, loses its beauty very rapidly; so that, even in galleries possessed by the very wealthiest owners, the idea of keeping picture-frames always perfectly clean and beautiful has to be abandoned as impracticable. In the country, it is possible to keep them decent a little longer; but even there it is difficult, if the climate produce abundance of troublesome flies: in an English town, however, especially a manufacturing town (such as Manchester or Leeds), the only way of keeping your frames decent without extravagantly frequent regilding, is by covering them with gauze, which, so long as it remains there, spoils both the frame and the picture. Works of fine art are not like things whose use is independent of appearances. For example, you may put a cover on an easy-chair without diminishing its usefulness as a thing to sit comfortably in; but as the only usefulness of a picture-frame is one of appearance, you absolutely arrest the performance of its function in the world

DOI: 10.4324/9781315400266-10

when once you have hidden it. If picture-frames are to have gauze over them, we might as well begin by simply painting them a dull yellow.

The inconveniences to owners of pictures which result from the prevalent system of frame-making are, that an amount of dirt has to be tolerated in frames which would never be tolerated in any other piece of furniture, whilst a constant drain of expense has to be going forward, which, if it could be more wisely administered, might give results of higher and more permanent beauty. Considering, however, that the purchaser of many pictures is of necessity either a rich man who has money to throw away, or an extravagant one, who throws it away without troubling himself about questions of economy, he does not feel the perishableness of frames as a matter seriously affecting him. On the other hand, the successful painter gets rid of his pictures so quickly that a frame has not time to lose its freshness whilst it remains upon his hands; besides which, he can easily stipulate, and often does so, that the frame shall be a separate transaction between the purchaser and the frame-maker. And in any case, if a successful painter has to keep a few old frames in his studio, they serve him to paint other pictures in; and it matters little, when they are used for that purpose, whether an ornament be chipped off here and there, or the general tone of the gilding be somewhat dimmed by ineradicable dust. Those who suffer most from the extreme perishableness of the frames commonly in use are the ordinary crowd of artists, whose pictures are frequently refused at the exhibitions, and are sent from one exhibition to another, till one out of three or four is sold, and the rest come back to their author. The frames of pictures declined at the Academy are *always* damaged; sometimes they come back in a state so extremely unlike their splendour in the month of March, that the comparison which suggests itself the most readily is that of a spruce and brilliant soldier at a review, and the same soldier ragged and dirty after a disastrous battle. All artists complain of this, but the fault lies with the system of frame-making, not with the authorities of the Academy. The pictures are knocked about by agents of artists who go to seek for refused works; and as the ornaments are as fragile as porcelain, a considerable amount of damage is quite inevitable.

A system of frame-making is needed, by which it might be possible to preserve the good appearance of our present frames when they are new, whilst giving greater strength and durability. Some attempts in this direction have been made of late years which may be alluded to. The reader will probably remember the massive frames of carved wood which surrounded Bierstadt's great landscapes when they were exhibited in this country. These were much stronger, no doubt, than the ordinary frames of paste, and were handsome things in themselves. As a cornice for some room, richly furnished in carved wood, they would have been very noble and appropriate; as picture-frames, they had the radical vice of not showing the picture to advantage. In our schemes of reform we must not lose sight of the fact that the function of a picture-frame is purely auxiliary, and that if it fail to be an efficient auxiliary to the work of art it does not signify how beautiful it may be in itself. Many experiments have been tried, but nothing answers so well as gilding. No carved wood helps the appearance of paint as gilding does.

The metallic lustre of gold saves it from injuring the tones of paint which might dangerously resemble it, so that there is never any struggle between them; whilst, on the other hand, there is a pleasant warmth in the colour of gold which silver does not possess. An immensely important collateral advantage is, that gold adds to the *splendour* of a work of art more than any other surrounding. The frames of Bierstadt's pictures, though they were magnificent things, were not splendid things; and a picture-frame ought to be splendid. On the other hand, we have had the pre-Raphaelite experiment in frames – a flat margin, often of solid oak, gilded so as to leave the grain visible. In Mr. Hunt's Temple picture a margin of ivory intervened, which, though useful as adding to the peculiarity of the work (which was an essential part of the pre-calculated effect on the public mind),[1] and useful farther in conveying the idea of sacrifice to the spectator, did not add anything to the artistic effect of the picture, except by separating the painted gilding of the Temple from the rivalry of the real gilding of the frame. The ivory, in short, though more expensive, had only the effect of so much paper of the same tint of white; and it has long been a settled question amongst artists, that oil-paintings are better helped by having gilding close to them than any kind of white or cream-coloured or black margin. The chief defect, however, of the pre-Raphaelite frame was its want of illusory effect, owing to its flatness. The preliminary idea of all picture-frames is the open window, or the bevelled boards that surround the diorama. Although we know that the *trompe-l'œil* is not the object of art, still a certain concession is made to the infantine or instinctive desire to be deceived. The frame, by the recession of its sloping sides, leads us first to the foreground, and then to the successive distances of the picture, preventing the perpendicular lines on each side of the *canvas-stretcher* (or stretching frame) from contradicting the pictorial distances, and so helping to produce the degree of illusion which is right and necessary even in the most elevated art. A flat frame does not sufficiently achieve this (though it achieves it partly), and consequently it misses much of the utility of the typical picture-frame. For the typical picture-frame is not only a margin, but much more. It is to the action or scenery in the picture what the walls and side-scenes of the theatre are to the acting and scenery upon the stage.

The American carved-wood frame and the English pre-Raphaelite frame, though both much more durable than the frames we are usually accustomed to, could not, therefore, be considered as a satisfactory solution of the difficulty. What we want is a kind of frame which shall show a picture as well as the best frames of the ordinary kind, and yet be sufficiently durable to bear dust and coal-smoke, and even a little occasional hard usage in the exhibitions. I have no pretension to be able to suggest any satisfactory solution of this difficulty; indeed, I do not proffer, but ask for a solution. Something, however, may be said as to the direction in which the solution will have to be sought.

The frame *must* be gilded – that is imperative; or, if not gilded, it must look as if it were. It would be interesting to know for what price the ornaments of a frame, or of some of its mouldings, might be done in electrotype, and what gilding of sufficient thickness would cost by the same process. Or, perhaps, the comparatively new compound bronze of aluminium, which is extremely like gold in colour, and can be easily cleaned, would supply the material which we need. Wood-carving, gilded afterwards, is too expensive for ordinary use, besides being brittle, though not so brittle as the common paste. A plain frame of wood, well recessed, and *plated* with bronze of aluminium, might show a picture to advantage, and still be durable and easily cleaned. Projecting ornaments, or the kind of bold carving common in Italian frames, are not at all necessary to the effect of a picture, and are merely a sort of exuberance of Southern taste and invention. We can dispense with these easily enough, but we cannot dispense with the deep recess, nor with the effective contrast between dead and burnished gold. It is clear, that if any ingenious inventor could make for us frames which should be as easily cleaned as silver plate is, and as little liable to injury, we could afford to pay for them at least twice what we pay for the present perishable frames.

The best models, of modern frames, which have come within the writer's experience, are those of M. Bourdon of Paris, who was a painter before he took to the business of frame-making, and who therefore learned what was the utility of a frame as an auxiliary to the effect of a picture. Pictures look better, and more effective, in M. Bourdon's frames than in any others, except those of M. Chercuitte, who is frankly an imitator of Bourdon, and began his present style by simply copying the work of his master. The present writer has employed both these frame-makers, but they have a fancy for putting a wreath or border of laurel on the projecting edge of the frame, which has a pretty effect, but which detaches itself under the influence of damp or of heat, and which has to be removed if the frame is to last long in a trying climate. If we could have such a frame as one of Bourdon's best and most studied productions, in which the exquisite taste of the frame-maker is entirely subordinated to the effect of the picture – like a judicious accompaniment to a musical solo – such a frame as Bourdon's, with the additional virtue of durability, would be all that a painter or collector could desire. Surely, in the present advanced state of the industrial arts, this cannot be altogether unattainable. – 1871.

Note (Hamerton, 1873)

1 This passage has been very widely misunderstood. I intended to convey no unfavourable reflection on Mr. Holman Hunt. Of course all works of art are arranged with a pre-calculated effect on the public mind, as a lady's dress is, or the interior of her drawing-room. This is quite right and innocent; and if an artist concerns himself with a frame at all, it is inevitable that he should think of its effect. Mr. Hunt's frame added to or harmonized with the originality of his picture, so that its eccentricity is to be approved of, but for reasons given above that style of frame is not on the whole the best adapted for helping pictures generally, as works of art. – 1873.

1.2

Colour

DOI: 10.4324/9781315400266-11

1.2 Colour

The materials of colour changed drastically in the nineteenth century. A new range of human-made pigments appeared thanks to new technological developments, while the isolation of new elements, new trade routes established in the eighteenth century and British imperial claims to, for example, India, generated a range of new commercially available pigments.[1] These developments were communicated to both artists and the general public through painting manuals and, as the *Art Journal* article reproduced here demonstrates, in displays at international exhibitions (in this instance, the London 1862 Exhibition). The nineteenth-century literary, philosophical and psychological discussions on the experience of colour have been explored elsewhere; here the focus is more specifically on sources directly exploring the materiality of colour.[2] The sources presented here are quite distinct: an 1862 overview of a commercial pigment display, an instruction manual from the 1830s, a 'scientific' guide to the chemistry of paint from the 1890s, a Bengali play from the 1860s and an 1883 report by Bengali civil servant Trilokya Nath Mukharji. All, however, showcase the diverse range of materials used in creating paint for the palettes of Victorian artists (including plants, animals and even human remains), and the global and often colonial contexts from which these pigments were sourced. The final two sources focus on two controversial pigments sourced from in India: Indian yellow and indigo. The first three sources demonstrate the ways in which these two pigments were promoted and explained to artists. The extracts selected showcase the social and political meanings of pigment: be that the idea of 'national' colour schemes, the gendering, racialising and stigmatising of particular colours, or the ways in which the two pigments under scrutiny here were intertwined with imperial governance, brutal working conditions and subaltern resistance.

Field's *Chromatography* (1835) was a hugely important text for nineteenth-century painters; by 1885 it was in its fifth edition and was widely circulated, used and praised by artists. Field was a colour maker (a manufacturer of pigments), and his book was based on decades of research into the properties of pigments.[3] Handbooks about materials became increasingly important as new, unfamiliar colours appeared on the market, as artists ceased to make up their own paint with the eighteenth-century advent of 'colourmen' (something Holman Hunt laments in the source reprinted in the previous section), and as new artistic groups like the Pre-Raphaelites sought to use materials to create new ways of painting.[4]

The pages extracted here show that even a practical manual is stocked with digressions about the social meanings of colour. Indeed, each section of Field's handbook, divided up by colours and then broken down into individual pigments, is preceded by an overview of the symbolic connections, literary referents and effects of each colour, which Field regarded as essential knowledge for painters (the chapter on 'Of semi-neutral colours – of brown' is reproduced here). In the introduction to the volume, Field sets out the relationships between colour, gender and perception ('the female eye' apparently having a 'judicious and natural . . . taste and feeling' for colour); he extolls the potential for a specifically British school of colouring, and connects 'the human countenance' exclusively with white Europeans.[5] Further, he enumerates the 'beauties of complexion and feature in our females' as a means by which the British might consolidate their apparently superior colour sense.[6] Paint colours were also marshalled to bolster a racist hierarchy of peoples. Field presents the colour brown as 'synonymous with foul or defiled, in a sense opposed to *fair* and pure' (which seems particularly marked considering his widespread use of fair to refer to the complexions of people racialised as white); the quotation describing the 'brown Indian' in the selection of literary renderings of the colour brown only reinforces this interpretation.[7] Artists' materials could be used as a means of describing racial difference or indeed as a means of perceiving the world; Frederick Leighton's 1860s diaries recording his trip to Egypt fixated on the variety of skin colours which he observed in the people around him, describing each in terms of the commercially available paint colours.[8]

I have included descriptions of the range of brown pigments to emphasise the diverse mineral and animal products that contributed to Victorian painting, including bones, ivory, ground-up ancient Egyptian body parts and cuttlefish.[9] In contrast with Field's shorter entries on each pigment, Church's 1890 publication offers a much more detailed breakdown (and a contrasting take on the animal source of Indian yellow; its connection with cow urine was not known definitively in Britain until Mukharji's 1883 report). He provides detailed information about the lifespan and fading of different colours and their chemical compositions. There are no attempts to engage with the cultural connotations of specific colours, and Church adheres to the aim of the book set out in its preface: 'It has been written with the view of explaining to artists . . . the chief chemical and physical characters of the materials with which they deal'.[10] Church was Professor of Chemistry at the Royal Agricultural College in Cirencester, and then from 1879 to 1911 he was the first person to hold this post at the Royal Academy, an indication of the new-found scientific professionalisation of those specialising in artists' materials.

Natasha Eaton suggests that we can think of the artist's palette as a place where the Empire physically came together, before being remixed by the artist on canvas. But she also emphasises the potential of colour for resisting British rule.[11] Indigo – used especially in watercolours – could not help but be connected to the human costs of producing pigment after the Indigo Revolt, which took place across Bengal in 1859. British traders had initially grown indigo on West Indian plantations worked by enslaved African people; the dye was steeped from its beginnings in slavery and violence. After the end of the slave trade in the emancipation acts of 1807 and 1834, the British shifted their cultivation of this dye to Bengal in India.

Planters annexed land from the Bengali peasantry, cultivating indigo instead of crops grown for sustenance and locking peasants (known as ryots) into a system of intensive labour, appalling working conditions and low wages. Even colonial officials compared the conditions of indigo workers to slavery.[12] The Indigo Revolt, a widespread campaign of non-cooperation, began in 1859. Millions of peasants refused to grow indigo; by 1860, they were withholding rent, and some marched on and attacked factories. The subsequent Indigo Commission set up by the British government of India to investigate labour conditions offered a widely cited testimony from one E. W. L. Tower, who claimed that 'not a chest of Indigo reached England without being stained with human blood'.[13] Taking place just a year after the brutal 1858 conclusion of the 1857 Indian Uprising, a major threat to British power in the subcontinent, these events were widely reported in Britain. The first two sources here show the ways in which the material properties of indigo were discussed in colour manuals in the early and later nineteenth century, while dramatist Dinabandhu Mitra's 1860 play *Nil Darpan* focuses on the exploitation and abuse of Indian indigo workers.[14] All are connected to indigo's material properties.

Indian yellow was also subject to considerable controversy.[15] This hugely popular pigment was widely used in creating vibrant flesh tones for persons of colour. In 1883, Sir Joseph Hooker of the Royal Society of Arts commissioned T. N. Mukharji to produce the report on this pigment's origins that is reprinted here. The Government of India reputedly banned the production of Indian yellow in 1908 in response to a number of factors, including the rise of Hindu cow protection movements which threatened British control; Jordanna Bailkin notes, however, that this seems to have been an informal, rather than an official legal ban. Bailkin's incisive exploration of this pigment between nineteenth-century Britain and India suggests the ways in which the ability of British artists to visually represent colonised persons was intricately bound up with the material production of paint, the politics of colonised labour, religion, resistance, and British attempts to govern and control India.

Notes

1 For an overview, see *Paint & painting: an exhibition and working studio sponsored by Winsor & Newton to celebrate their 150th anniversary* (London: Tate Gallery, 1982), pp. 10–23. On the earlier period, see Andrea Feeser, Maureen Daly Goggin, and Beth Fowkes Tobin (eds.), *The Materiality of Color: The Production, Circulation, and Application of Dyes and Pigments, 1400–1800* (Farnham: Ashgate, 2012).

2 See, for example, C. Ribeyrol (ed.), *The Colours of the Past in Victorian England* (Oxford: Peter Lang, 2016). For a more general overview, see John Gage, *Colour and Culture: Practice and Meaning from Antiquity to Abstraction* (London: Thames and Hudson, 1993).

3 See further Linda M. Shires, 'On Color Theory, 1835: George Field's Chromatography', *BRANCH: Britain, Representation and Nineteenth-Century History*, at www.branchcollective.org [accessed 01 March 2019].

4 See Leslie Carlyle, *The Artist's Assistant: Oil Painting Instruction Manuals and Handbooks in Britain, 1800–1900, with Reference to Selected Eighteenth-century Sources* (London: Archetype, 2001); Joyce H. Townsend, Jacqueline Ridge and Stephen Hackney, *Pre-Raphaelite painting techniques: 1848–1856* (London: Tate, 2004).
5 George Field, *Chromatography: or, a treatise on Colours and Pigments, and of their powers in painting, &c.* (London: Charles Tilt, 1835), pp. 12, 19.
6 Ibid., p. 5.
7 Ibid., pp. 155, 159.
8 Leighton's diaries are reprinted in Emilie ("Mrs Russell") Barrington, *The life, letters and work of Frederic Leighton*, volume II (London: George Allen, 1906), pp. 128–187. For further analysis see J. J. Kim, *Painted Men in Britain 1868–1918: Royal Academicians and masculinities* (Farnham: Ashgate, 2012), pp. 17–19.
9 The material contributions of animals to artworks is of increasing interest; this is theorised in Jason Edwards, 'The Vegan Viewer in the Circum-Polar World; or, J. H. Wheldon's The Diana and Chase in the Arctic (1857)', in E. Quinn and B. Westwood (eds.), *Towards a Vegan Theory. Thinking Veganism in Literature and Culture* (Cham, Switzerland: Palgrave Macmillan, 2018), pp. 79–106. On mummy brown, see Sally Woodcock, 'Body colour: The misuse of mummy', *Conservator*, 20:1 (1996), pp. 87–94.
10 A. H. Church, *The Chemistry of Paints and Painting* (London: Seeley and Co., 1890), p. vii.
11 Natasha Eaton, 'Nomadism of Colour: Painting, technology and waste in the chromozones of colonial India, c.1765–c.1860', *Journal of Material Culture*, 17:1 (2012), pp. 61–81.
12 Ibid., p. 69.
13 Cited in S. Bhattacharya, 'The Indigo Revolt of Bengal', *Social Scientist*, 5:2 (1977), pp. 13–23, on p. 13.
14 Ranajit Guha, 'Neel-darpan: The image of a peasant revolt in a liberal mirror', *Journal of Peasant Studies*, 2:1 (1974), pp. 1–46.
15 J. Bailkin, 'Indian Yellow: Making and Breaking the Imperial Palette', *Journal of Material Culture*, 10:2 (2005), pp. 197–214.

8

'NOTABILIA OF THE INTERNATIONAL EXHIBITION: ARTISTS' COLOURS'

Art Journal, 1 July 1862, p. 162

In the Eastern Annexe, not far from the entrance to it from the transept of the main building, placed by the wall on the right hand, is a group of solid, sterling-looking, though altogether unostentatious, mahogany cases, which claim at our hands much more than a passing recognition of their presence. These cases contain Artists' Colours; and they exemplify in a truly splendid manner the high degree of perfection to which skill and enterprise and experience have now brought the *materiel,* that modern Science has provided and placed at the disposal of modern Art. Perhaps in no single class of objects in the entire Exhibition is a grand advance more strikingly demonstrated, than in these collections of artists' colours. They show the results of sustained as well as earnest effort. They have to tell of extended research, and of often-repeated experiment. They declare how thoughtfully the colours of long standing have been subjected to every test that might improve their qualities; while, at the same time, an inquiry after new colours has been carried on with that determined energy, coupled with such masterly intelligence, as rarely fails to result in complete success. And in the present instance the success has been most complete, both in the discovery and preparation of new pigments, and in the improvement of those that have long been in use.

The cases of artists' colours, four in number, are arranged in continuous succession, and they represent respectively the manufacturing firms of Messrs. WINSOR & NEWTON, REEVES, ROWNEY, and NEWMAN – we name them in the order their cases stand. The whole are alike distinguished for the artistic style in which the various pigments are displayed, as for the brilliant and varied colours that are thus exhibited in their most perfect condition. It is to be understood that in these cases the pigments themselves are the objects exhibited, and therefore they appear either in solid masses, or in heaps of powder piled up upon glass *tazzi,* or in bottles of various forms and sizes. The Messrs. Newman have enclosed their specimen colours in small glass spheres, which have a very pleasing and elegant effect. And with their pigments the Messrs. Rowney have very happily associated specimens of the different gums that are used in the Arts.

DOI: 10.4324/9781315400266-12

The case that at once concentrates upon itself the attention of even casual observers is that of Winsor and Newton. It is of large dimensions, and its display of colours is more varied, and also on a much more extended scale, than in the adjoining cases; and in a Great Exhibition it is a matter of no trifling moment that such objects as pigments should be displayed in considerable quantities. This case contains upwards of 250 specimens of pigments, and includes all the rare and costly varieties. Amongst the new colours, introduced by the exhibitors since 1851, are *aureolin* and *cyanoline,* both brilliant transparent yellows, the former rather pale, and the latter having a rich golden tone; both of them are unquestionably permanent; and with these may be associated *viridian* – a perfectly new transparent and permanent green, of the most vivid brilliancy. The same case contains that very rare pigment, platina yellow, and a complete range of orient and other carmines, with specimens of the various cochineal lakes, the madder carmines and lakes, with all the important products of the madder root, the purples, browns, &c.; a perfect series of chromates of lead, of very pure and brilliant tones; as complete a range of pure sulphides of cadmium, in gradations from a pale straw to a deep red orange colour; the varied products of the metal chromium also – transparent and opaque greens, the hydrated brown oxide, citrine brown, and others; the malachite greens, uranium yellow, and the white sulphate of barytes, and all the important pigments that are obtained from the oxides of iron, both pure and in combination with alumina, when they are known as *Mars* colours. We leave to the last of the series the grand display of "Genuine Ultramarine" which is conspicuous in the collection of Winsor and Newton. This noble pigment is here shown in all its varied tints, and under every modification of condition and quality, as it is obtained from the choicest specimens of *lapis lazuli,* from regions that are as far removed from one another as Siberia and South America. The range of tint in these ultramarines, and their perfect purity of tone, command unqualified admiration: they extend from the pale, yet bright, azure of the South American *lapis,* to the full, dark, sparkling blue that is produced in the far north of Siberia, and they comprehend every modification of the deep lustrous colour for which the Arts are indebted to the *lapis* of Persia. It may give some idea of the splendid effect produced by these specimens of pigments, when we add that the ultramarines alone in Winsor and Newton's case weigh upwards of four hundred ounces, and consequently their value may be estimated at about £1,500. As a matter of course, with these new and rare pigments, specimens of all the well-known colours of both foreign and native production are exhibited, and they show that these also have received their own share of careful attention.

In the case of the Messrs. Reeves, the fine smalt blue attracts special attention; and the Messrs. Rowney's case is particularly distinguished for its brilliant pure scarlet, Chinese orange, cœruleum, and Veronese green. In both these collections, as also in the beautiful cabinet of the Messrs. Newmans, all the colours that are exhibited fully vindicate the distinguished reputation of the several exhibitors.

We recommend these cases, and particularly the chromatic museum of Winsor and Newton, to the careful study of artists, and of all who have feeling for that grand element in Art – colour. Here are the agencies which endow great colourists with a power that is absolutely without limit. Iris herself might have been glad to have sought fresh hues from these rich stores of varied pigments; while she would have readily borne her testimony to the excellence of the preparations which qualify human painters to rival her own celestial colouring. Without doubt, these cases of "artists' colours" will be thoroughly appreciated, both here in England, and in every foreign country in which Art has a cherished and an honoured home.

9

GEORGE FIELD, *CHROMATOGRAPHY: OR, A TREATISE ON COLOURS AND PIGMENTS, AND OF THEIR POWERS IN PAINTING, &C.*

(London: Charles Tilt, 1835), pp. ix–xiv, 4–7, 12, 19, 83, 104, 112, 155–159, 161–163

THE progress of the Art of Painting under the happy auspices of this favoured country, the refinement of taste which it has so universally diffused, and the predilection which prevails for its study and practice as a necessary branch of polite education, render acceptable whatever can facilitate the acquisition, or advance the ends, of this useful, elegant, and enlightening accomplishment. Nor are the concerns of this art uninteresting in a still higher view, since whatever refines the taste, enhances the powers and improves the disposition and morals of a people, – and whatever improves the morals, promotes the happiness of man, individual and social. Hence the high moral and political value of this art, to say nothing of its commercial and religious uses, upon which so much stress has been justly laid.

Among the means essential to proficiency in Painting, none is more important than a just knowledge of Colours and Pigments – their qualities, powers, and effects; and there is none to which the press has hitherto afforded fewer helps. There have appeared, it is true, at different times, several works professing this object, and most of our encyclopædias and books of painting treat cursorily on this branch of the art; but not only are these for the most part transcripts of the same obsolete originals, unsuited to the present state of the art, but they are inadequate, irrelevant, and often erroneous or untrue, as every one acquainted with the subject is aware. Hence have arisen several inducements of the author to attempt a guide to the knowledge of colours and pigments generally, and with reference to the Art of Painting in particular.

Most technical readers are fond of recipes and devices communicated as secrets of art, which are accordingly liberally supplied by the caterers to this taste, who compile them in general upon very vague authority; hence the author anticipates some dissatisfaction from those who are in search of royal roads to knowledge, or stratagems and secrets of art: but one principle is worth a hundred processes, – nor was it by prescription, but by the spirit of philosophy, that the Greeks carried the

DOI: 10.4324/9781315400266-13

arts to sublime perfection. Hence it is not a detail of the processes for producing pigments that is here intended, which belongs to another extensive art not to be learnt from brief recipes, and upon which the author has a distinct work in hand;[1] and it is a pursuit accidental and subordinate to painting, in which the pictorial artist can never attain the skill of the chemical colourist without a proportionate sacrifice of his own art, if not, unhappily, of his fortune also, – as was the case with Parmegiano, and has been with others in our own day, who

> Their time in curious search of colours lose,
> Which, when they find, they want the skill to use!
>
> SHEE.

However imperative such sacrifice might have been to the earlier painters, there is no want in the present day of furniture for the palette, – since pigments, and fine ones too, so abound, that nearly as much experience is requisite to a judicious selection of them as was formerly required for their acquisition or production; to which also there is little temptation, since the expence [sic] of the palette, which was immense to the antient masters, is comparatively trifling to our contemporaries. The principal object of the present Treatise is, therefore, by pointing out the true character and powers of colours and pigments, to enable the student to choose and employ judiciously those which are best adapted to his purpose, and thereby to prevent the too frequent disappointment of his hopes and endeavours by a failure at the very foundation of his work. Such failures are often attributed to bad materials; but whatever practices may have formerly prevailed for imposing false and adulterate articles upon the artist, either through ignorance or fraud, it is due to the respectable colourmen of the present day to bear testimony to the laudable anxiety and emulation with which they purvey, regardless of necessary expence, the choicest and most perfect materials for the painter's use; so that the odium of employing bad articles attaches to the artist, if he resort to vicious sources or employ his means improperly. As, however, perfection in all art is a vanishing point, there will be always something to desire in colours, vehicles, and in all the materials of painting; and since the necessity for, and the practice of, the artist in preparing his own materials has ceased, it is the more essential that he should be enabled by precept to select, appreciate, and understand the pigments and colours he employs.

[. . .]

A due selection and employment of colours materially is not alone sufficient, – an adequate knowledge of their reciprocal, sensible, and moral influences in painting, is essential to the production of their full effects on the eye and the mind; and, notwithstanding these effects and influences, belong to the higher aims of the colourist, and are of a theoretical bearing, the subject is so connected with the primary object of the work, that it forms also a feature thereof, in subordination nevertheless to practice; – for colouring, like every other art that has its foundation in nature, refers to a whole, and cannot be rightly comprehended, nor perfectly practised, without some attention to all its parts; – hence also the physical causes, relations, and expression of colours have been briefly investigated therein.

To those who choose to study colours philosophically, or to amuse themselves in the ample field of the colourist, even independently of the art of painting, some details of the author's experience have been appended, interesting for their own sake, and not without reference to the cultivated mind of the painter, who exercises his art with an intelligence beyond mere instinct and imitation. Nor is this department of his work devoted to mere rational amusement or mental satisfaction, but aims at fixing some of the principles of colouring upon the ground of science, – at establishing a metral *standard of colours,* which may be of general practical utility; and contributing toward a new and improved theory of vision, light, and colours.

[. . .]

With respect to the application of colours in painting, recourse must be had to practice under the direction of an able master, several of whom have published valuable works of instruction in the various branches of the art[2] – for of this the student may be assured, that, however useful recipes may be in cookery and pharmacy, the skill of colouring is not to be acquired by any such off-hand processes; and that perfect success therein will require – what no literary work can supply – the constant and united efforts of an able hand, a good eye, and a cultivated judgment – directed in the first instance to the works of good colourists, and perfected by an assiduous application to nature.

But though the records of literature and science cannot alone produce a colourist, nor form the practical painter in other respects, they may become most important auxiliaries, – not merely by recreating his faculties, instructing his hand, and extending the sphere of his art, by endless analogies throughout the field of history and philosophy, and the vast regions of poetic fancy; but also by exciting a just enthusiasm, and stimulating his invention, while they enlarge his judgment and refine his taste; supporting at the same time that connexion with learning which gives dignity to fine art, and raises it above mere manipulation. Indeed there never was a truly great artist who did not unite with his ability somewhat of literary talent, inclination, or acquirement; nor is there a surer mark of a low and groveling genius than a contempt of theory or science, and an over-devotion to the mechanical and practical in art; for the connexion of art with science, theory, and practice, and of these with literature, is most intimate and indissoluble; nor is it likely the artist should paint the worse for being acquainted with the philosophy of his art. We derive hence an excuse for having, even in this lowly performance, attempted to draw philosophy on the one hand, and poetry and harmonics on the other, into intimate connexion with colours and colouring, by a variety of natural analogies and poetical instances.

[. . .]
[pp. 4–7]

So also, according to a correct analogy, colouring may be called the eloquence of painting, – the animating principle which gives life and action to the fine thoughts of the painter [. . .]

In the practice of the individual in Painting, as well as in all the revolutions of pictorial art, in ancient Greece as in modern Italy, colouring has been the last attainment of excellence in every school;[3] thus Zeuxis succeeded and excelled Apelles in colouring, as Titian did Raffael. There is hence just reason to hope the artists of Britain will transcend all preceding schools in the chromatic department of Painting, if even in their progress they should not surpass them in all other departments, and in every mode and application of the art, as they have already done in an original and unrivalled use of water-colours in particular, in the perfection of landscape, in the new and beautiful device of panoramic perspective, and in engraving.

Happily too, a school of colouring has arisen, that confirms this expectation, strengthened also by the suitableness of our climate to perfect vision, – by that mean degree of light which is best adapted to the distinguishing of colours, – by that boundless diversity of hue in nature, relieved by those fine effects of light and shade which are denied to more vertical suns, – and by those beauties of complexion and feature in our females, by which we are perpetually surrounded; – respects in which at least our country is not unfavourable to art. In many obvious references too, this country resembles Venice of old, the greatest of whose antient glories is still her Titian, her Giorgione, and her school of colouring; and England has had her Reynolds, and Wilson, and still has living colourists, of whom we will not offend the modesty, nor distinguish invidiously. It has, however, been urged to the disparagement of the British school, that it excels in colouring; as if it were incompatible with any other excellence, or as if nature, the great prototype of art, ever dispensed with it.

This appeal from the decisions of criticism, in behalf of colouring, is not intended to militate against the necessity the Painter is under, of studying the other branches of his art, nor to assert the redeeming power, or the exclusive excellence, of colouring.[4]

> For 'tis the MIND that makes the body rich;
> And as the sun breaks through the darkest clouds,
> So Honour 'peareth in the meanest habit.
> What! is the jay more precious than the lark
> Because his feathers are more beautiful?
> Or is the adder better than the eel,
> *Because the painted skin contents the eye?*
>
> SHAKSP., TAMING OF THE SHREW.

Colouring alone will not therefore constitute a picture; still colour is the flesh and blood of the art, – and if it be wanting, the finest performances will remain lifeless skeletons, and fail to *please;* and as the proper end of painting is *to please,* and there is a higher and more effectual medium for addressing mind, the most intellectual performances of the painter, and the grandest efforts of his invention, will fall short of their true purpose, if they pass not to the mind by the medium of pleasurable effect through their appropriate sense of sight, of which colour – and colour alone – is the immediate object; and what is Painting altogether but the art of representing visible things by light, shade, and colours? Colouring is therefore the first requisite, the matter and medium of the Painter's art: it is indeed the first quality which engages attention and regard – the best introduction to a picture, and that which continues to give it value so long as it is regarded. In the grosser matters of taste a food or medicine may be both salutary and nutritious, but we nauseate it if it be not also palatable or *well-tasted:* such is Painting without colouring, and so it is with all objects of sense; nor did the first and greatest critic that ever lived assign any higher end than *pleasure* to even Poetry itself.[5]

[. . .]
[p. 12]

For evidence of the natural expression of colours, we need not look beyond the human countenance, that masterpiece of expression, in which are acknowledged – the *redness* indicative of anger and the ardent passions, and the blush of bashfulness and shame betraying a variety of consciousness, – the sallowness or *yellowness* of grief, envy, resentment, and the jealous passions, – the cold, pallid *blueness* of hate, fear, terror, agony, despair, and death; with a thousand other hues and tints accompanied by expressions readily felt, but difficultly described or understood.[6]

If we turn our view from the face of man to that of nature in the sky, we find colour equally efficient in giving character, sentiment, and expression to the landscape, indicating the calm and the storm, and in infinite ways betraying the latent emotions of the spirit of nature.

It is by this influence that the greenness of spring indicates the youth, vigour, and freshness of the season; that the light, bright, warm, *yellow* hues of summer express its powers; that the glowing *redness* of fruits and foliage denote the richness of autumn, –

> Yon hanging woods that, touch'd by autumn, seem
> As they were blossoming hues of fire and gold.
>
> COLERIDGE.

and that *blue,* dark gray, and white tints express the gloom and wintry coldness of nature.

[. . .]
[p. 19]

It may be added, that the female eye seems to be particularly receptive and perceptive of the tender, beautiful, and expressive relations of colours; and we have repeatedly heard it remarked by that graceful painter and colourist, the late lamented President of the Royal Academy, whose subjects were from the high and refined classes of the sex, that in no instance whatever had he occasion to request or desire any change of the colours in which they presented themselves, so judicious and natural was their taste and feeling as to what best suited their peculiarities of character, complexion, and expression.

From the foregoing, it may be concluded that the sentiments effected in the mind by hues, shades, and colours can, next to nature and painting, be nowhere better studied than among the poets; we shall accordingly, as occasion offers, make free use of their productions.

Of Yellow

[. . .]

[p. 83]

XIV. INDIAN YELLOW, brought from India, as its name implies, is a pigment long employed in India under the name *Pwree,* but has not many years been introduced generally into painting in Europe. It is imported in the form of balls, is of a fetid odour, and is produced from the urine of the camel. It has also been ascribed, in like manner, to the buffalo, or Indian cow, after feeding on mangos; but the latter statement is incorrect. However produced, it appears to be a urio-phosphate of lime, of a beautiful pure yellow colour, and light powdery texture; of greater body and depth than gamboge, but inferior in these respects to gall-stone. Indian yellow resists the sun's rays with singular power in water-painting; yet in ordinary light and air, or even in a book or portfolio, the beauty of its colour is not lasting. It is not injured by foul air, but in oil it is exceedingly fugitive, both alone and in tint. Owing probably to its alkaline nature, it has injurious effect upon cochineal lakes and carmine when used with them. As lime does not injure this colour, it may be employed in fresco.

Of Blue

[. . .]

[p. 104]

These analogies and effects of colours are by no means to be disregarded, since they are as various, simply and conjointly, as are colours and their tints; and it is by attention to them that colour conduces to sentiment and expression in painting. Even where the symbolical uses of colours are merely fanciful or conventional, they are not to be totally rejected, since, by association and common consent, they acquire arbitrary signification in the manner of words: it is their natural expression, however, which principally claims our attention. Indeed a just knowledge of the relations of colours, and their effects upon the passions, feelings, and intellect, seems, we repeat, hardly less essential to the poet than to the painter: hence he often employs their ideas and terms with happy effect, and as frequently fails when wanting a proper comprehension, feeling, or taste of their powers: the latter case is however more fatal to the artist than to the poet.

[. . .]

[p. 112]

V. 1. INDIGO, or *Indian Blue,* is a pigment manufactured in the East and West Indies from several plants, but principally from the anil or indigofera. It is of various qualities, and has been long known, and of great use in dyeing. In painting it is not so bright as Prussian blue, but is extremely powerful and transparent; hence it may be substituted for some of the uses of Prussian blue. It is of great body, and glazes and works well both in water and oil. Its relative permanence as a dye has obtained it a false character of extreme durability in painting, a quality in which it is nevertheless very inferior even to Prussian blue.

It is injured by impure air, and in glazing some specimens are firmer than others, but not durable; – in tint with white lead they are all fugitive; when used, however, in considerable body in shadow, it is more permanent, but in all respects inferior to Prussian blue.

Of Brown

[. . .]

[p. 155]

This tendency in the compounds of colours to run into brownness and warmth, is one of the general natural properties of colours, which occasions them to deteriorate or dirt each other in mixture: hence *brown* is synonymous with foul or defiled, in a sense opposed to *fair* and pure; and it is hence also that brown, which is the nearest of the semi-neutrals in relation to light, is to be avoided in mixture with light colours. It is nevertheless an example of the wisdom of the Author of nature that brown is rendered, like green, a prevailing hue, and in particular an earth colour, as a contrast which is harmonized by the blueness and coldness of the *sky,* – both these colours prevailing together, too, in hot climates.

This tendency will account also for the use of brown in harmonizing and toneing, and for the great number of natural and artificial pigments and colours we possess under this denomination: in fact, the failure to produce other colours chemically or by mixture is commonly productive of a brown, which, on the other hand, is the colour of dirt, and defiles all other colours. It was this fertility and abundance of brown that occasioned our great landscape-colourist Wilson, when an acquaintance went exultingly to inform him he had discovered a new brown, to check him, in his characteristic way, with – "*I'm sorry for it: – we have gotten too many of them already*." Yet are fine transparent browns obviously very valuable colours. If red or blue be added to brown predominantly, it falls into the other semi-neutral classes, marrone or gray.

[. . .]
Brown is a sober and sedate colour, grave and solemn, but not dismal, and contributes to the expression of strength, stability, and solidity, – vigour, warmth, and rusticity, – and in minor degree to the serious, the sombre, and the sad; not with the painter only, but also with the rhetorician and poet, with whom, nevertheless, many of the broken colours are yet "airy nothings" and "without a name."

Examples of the applications of brown to the purposes of sentiment abound with the poets. Milton employs this colour in the beginning of his "Monody of Lycidas" thus plaintively:

> Yet once more, *O ye laurels, and once more,*
> *Ye myrtles brown, with ivy never sere,*
> I come to pluck your berries harsh and crude,
> And with forced fingers rude,
> *Shatter your leaves before the mellowing year;*
> For Lycidas is dead – .

And in the following, from an unknown hand, brown is thus beautifully associated with true feeling of the force of colouring:

> Go, mark in meditative mood where Autumn
> Steals o'er his woods with mellowing touch, like Time
> Ripening the tints of some delicious Claude.
> Mark where each elm hangs forth its *golden* bough,
> Like that which Virgil's hero sought;[7] each oak
> Fades picturesquely *brown;* each sycamore
> Mantled with *ruddy* richness. 'Tis a scene
> That o'er us sheds *the mild and musing calm*
> *Of wisdom; breathes, as noblest bards have own'd,*
> *Poetic inspiration; bids us taste*
> *The lonely sweetness of a walk with her*
> *By Milton wooed, "divinest Melancholy."*
> And wouldst thou go, unfeeling, and prefer
> The gorgeous blaze of summer to the charm –
> The dying charm of Autumn's farewell smile?
>
> ANON.

It is apparent that in many instances the colours in which the poet clothes his figures are chosen purely for their expression, as in the following:

> Satyrs and sylvan boys were seen
> Peeping from forth their alleys green;

Brown Exercise rejoiced to hear,
And Sport leap'd up and seized his *beechen* spear.
COLLINS.

– – In *the dun air sublime.*
MILTON.

And see, the fairy valleys fade,
Dun night has veil'd the solemn view!
Yet once again, dear parted shade, –
Meek Nature's child, again adieu!
COLLINS.

Be mine the hut
That from the mountain's side
Views wilds, and swelling floods,
And *hamlets brown,* and dim-discover'd spires,
And hears their simple bell; and marks o'er all
Thy dewy fingers draw
The dusky veil.
IDEM, ODE TO EVENING.

The unsightly plain
Lies *a brown deluge.*
THOMSON.

Byron justly and beautifully contrasts this hue thus:

How throbs the pulse when first we view
The eye that rolls in *glossy blue,*
Or *sparkles black;* or mildly throws
A beam from under hazel brows.

And Goldsmith thus:

Low lies that house where *nut-brown* draughts inspired,
Where *grey-beard* Mirth and smiling Toil retired.

Again, Mrs. Barbauld:

But thou, O nymph! retired and coy,
In what *brown hamlet* dost thou joy
To tell thy tender tale?
The lowliest children of the ground,

Moss-rose and violet, blossom round,
And *lily of the vale.*

ODE TO CONTENT.

And again:

O'er *his fair brow, the fairer for their shade,*
Locks of the *warmest brown* luxuriant play'd.
Blushing he bows – and gentle awe supplies
Each flattering meaning to his downcast eyes;
Sweet, serious, tender, those *blue* eyes impart
A thousand dear sensations to the heart.

MISS SEWARD.

Sir Walter Scott thus contrasts brown with fair: –

Wreathed in its *dark-brown* rings her hair,
Half hid, Matilda's forehead *fair;*
Half hid, and half reveal'd to view,
Her full *dark eyes of hazel hue.*

ROKEBY.

Shakspeare calls brown dissembling, perhaps in the sense of shadowing, as the Italians call burnt umber *falsalo:* –

His very hair is of the *dissembling colour* –
Something *browner* than Judas's.

AS YOU LIKE IT.

And in the following it is accorded with shade, black, &c.: –

To *arched walks of twilight groves,*
And *shadows brown,* that Sylvan loves,
Of pine or *monumental oak.*

MILTON'S LYCIDAS.

Not that our heads are,
Some *brown, some black, some auburn, and some bald,*
But that our wits are *so diversely coloured.*

SHAKSPEARE.

Obscured where highest woods, *impenetrable*
To stars or sun-light, spread their *umbrage* broad,
And *brown as evening.*

MILTON.

Bid this mild summer of my life rebloom;
Bid *every shade embrown* and *cloister gloom.*
MASON.

The *rustic youth, brown with meridian toil,*
Healthful and strong: full as the summer *rose,*
Blown by prevailing suns, *the ruddy maid* – .
THOMSON.

Where beasts with man divided empire claim,
And the *brown Indian marks with murderous aim.*
GOLDSMITH.

Ambitious of the town,
She left her wheel and robes of *country brown.*
IDEM.

The *fields, all iron, cast a gleaming brown.*
MILTON.

[. . .]

[p. 161]

IX. BONE BROWN and *Ivory Brown* are produced by torrefying, or roasting, bone and ivory till by partially charring they become of a brown colour throughout. They may be made to resemble the five first browns above by management in the burning; and, though much esteemed by some artists, are not perfectly eligible pigments, being bad dryers in oil, and their lighter shades not durable either in oil or water when exposed to the action of strong light, or mixed in tint with white lead. The palest of these colours are also the most opaque: the deepest are more durable, and most so when approaching black.

X. ASPHALTUM, called also *Bitumen, Mineral Pitch,* and *Jews' Pitch,* is a resinous substance rendered brown by the action of fire, natural or artificial. The substance employed in painting under this name is black and glossy like pitch, which differs from it only in having been less acted upon by fire, and in thence being softer. Asphaltum is principally used in oil-painting; for which purpose it is first dissolved in oil of turpentine, by which it is fitted for glazing and shading. Its fine brown colour, and perfect transparency, are lures to its free use with many artists, notwithstanding the certain destruction which awaits the work on which it is much employed, owing to its disposition to contract and crack by changes of temperature and the atmosphere; but for which it would be a most beautiful, durable, and eligible pigment. The solution of asphaltum in turpentine, united with drying oil by heat, or the bitumen torrefied and ground in linseed or drying oil, acquires a firmer texture, but becomes less transparent, and dries with difficulty.

A specimen of the native bitumen, brought from Persia by Lieutenant Ford, of which we made trial, had a powerful scent of garlic when rubbed. In the fire it softened without flowing, and burnt with a lambent flame; did not dissolve by heat in oil of turpentine, but ground easily as a pigment in pale drying oil, affording a fine deep transparent brown colour, resembling that of the asphaltum of the shops; and dried firmly nearly as soon as the drying oil alone. Asphaltum may be used as a permanent brown in water, and the native kind is also superior to the artificial for this purpose.

XI. MUMMY, or *Egyptian Brown,* is also a bituminous substance combined with animal remains, brought from the catacombs of Egypt, where liquid bitumen was employed three thousand years ago in embalming, in which office it has combined, by a slow chemical change, during so many ages with substances which give it a more solid and lasting texture than simple asphaltum; but in this respect it varies exceedingly, even in the same subject. Its other properties and uses as a pigment are the same as those of asphaltum, for which it is employed as a valuable substitute, being less liable to crack or move on the canvas. This also may be used, when ground, as a water-colour.

XII. ANTWERP BROWN is a preparation of asphaltum ground in strong drying oil, by which it becomes less liable to crack. See the two last articles. Bituminous coal, jet, and other bituminous substances, afford similar browns.

XIII. BISTRE is a brown pigment extracted by watery solution from the soot of wood-fires, whence it retains a strong pyroligneous scent. It is of a wax-like texture, and of a citrine-brown colour, perfectly durable. It has been much used as a water-colour, particularly by the old masters in tinting drawings and shading sketches, previously to Indian ink coming into general use for such purposes. In oil it dries with the greatest difficulty.

A substance of this kind collects at the back of fire-places in cottages where peat is the constant fuel burnt; which, purified by solution and evaporation, affords a fine bistre. Scotch bistre is of this kind. All kinds of bistre attract moisture from the atmosphere.

XIV. SEPIA, *Seppia, or Animal Æthiops*. This pigment is named after the sepia, or *cuttle-fish,* which is called also the *ink-fish* from its affording a dark liquid which was used as an ink by the ancients. From this liquid our pigment sepia, which is brought principally from the Adriatic, and may be obtained from the fish on our own coasts, is said to be obtained; and it is supposed that it enters into the composition of the *Indian ink* of the Chinese. Sepia is of a powerful dusky brown colour, of a fine texture, works admirably in water, combines cordially with other pigments, and is very permanent.

It is much used as a water-colour, and in making drawings in the manner of bistre and Indian ink; but is not used in oil, in which it dries very reluctantly.

Notes (Field, 1835)

1 Which will complete his original intention, expressed in his "Chromatics," of treating on the *relations,* the *nature,* and the *preparation* of colours, &c.

2 Such are Dagley's Compendium of the Theory and Practice of Painting, in which the elements of the art are treated with classical simplicity and method; – Mr. Harding's

ingenious and admirable Treatise on the Use of the Black Lead Pencil, &c.; Mr. Burnett's elegant performances on Composition, Chiaroscuro, and Colouring; and various others on different departments of the art.

3 And that also of rarest occurrence, if not of greatest difficulty; – hence Du Pile justly remarks, "that for near three hundred years since Painting was revived, we could hardly reckon six Painters that had been good colourists." He might have added – "among thousands who had laboured to become such." – Du Pile's Dialogue, p. 28.

4 As music relates to *sound* simply, and poetry, or *figurative speech,* to signification; and as these when united become *sound significant,* so it is with *colouring* in respect to *Figure, &c.;* the first belongs principally to the harmony of Painting, the latter to its sentiment or poetry, while in the perfect picture they are united.

5 Aristotle's Poetics.

6 Whether these colours of the human countenance are to be variously ascribed to the agency of nerves, blood-vessels, or lymphatics; – whether the *warmth and redness* expressing active feeling be not attributable to *arterial action,* and the *cold hues* of passive suffering to *venous re-action;* – and whether the passions denoted by the *sallow or yellow hue* are not *biliary affections* – are questions we leave to the anatomist.

7 Æn. vi.

10

A. H. CHURCH, *THE CHEMISTRY OF PAINTS AND PAINTING*

(London: Seeley and Co., 1890), pp. 136–138, 192–194, 209

Indian yellow: *Piuri, Purree, Peori – Jaune Indien – Indisch-gelb*

This remarkable pigment is obtained at Monghyr, a town in Bengal, from the urine of cows which have been fed upon mango-leaves. It generally occurs in the bazaars of the Panjáb in the form of large balls, having an offensive urinous odour.

Indian yellow is an impure magnesium salt of euxanthic acid. The essential part of it is a compound containing 4·5 per cent. magnesia, 18·7 per cent. water, and 78·7 per cent. euxanthic anhydride; but this substance is always associated, even in the most carefully purified samples of prepared Indian yellow, with various impurities both mineral and organic. The pure magnesium euxanthate is represented by the formula $C_{19}H_{16}MgO_{11},5H_2O$.

For artistic purposes the crude imported Indian yellow is thoroughly powdered, and then washed with boiling water, until the liquid filtered from it is no longer coloured; a brown impurity, and much of the evil smell, is thus removed. The colour of the washed product is enriched by leaving it in contact for a day or two with a saturated solution of salammoniac, and then repeating the treatment with hot water

Thus purified, this pigment presents a translucent orange-yellow colour of great depth and beauty. Ground in oil, some specimens are practically unchanged, even after long exposure to sunlight, any darkening they show being due either to imperfect purification, or to the change of the associated oil. Such change is reduced to a minimum if poppy oil be substituted for linseed oil, or if the latter be previously treated with manganese borate. On the other hand, I have met with specimens of Indian yellow ground in oil which, after five years' exposure, have lost nearly one-third of their original depth, and have, at the same time, become rather reddish-brown in hue. As a water-colour. Indian yellow retains its hue unimpaired when exposed to diffused daylight; sunlight very slowly bleaches it, the hue it acquires being somewhat brownish. The rate of alteration and of reduction in force caused by sunlight may be approximately represented by these figures:

DOI: 10.4324/9781315400266-14

Original intensity	10
After 2 years	9
After 5 years	7
After 7 years	6
After 10 years	5

As a general rule, Indian yellow suffers no change by admixture with any pigment itself permanent, nor is it affected by sulphur compounds. True Naples yellow, however, most of the chromates, and probably aureolin also, tend to embrown it to some extent.

Indian yellow which has been adulterated with lead chromate (chrome yellow) becomes dark-brown when moistened with ammonium sulphide.

A fine yellow pigment may be prepared from the euxanthic acid, which is the characteristic constituent of Indian yellow, by throwing it down in combination with the two bases – alumina and magnesia. The following directions may be followed: Dissolve 1 part of pure euxanthic acid in just sufficient dilute ammonia. Pour the solution into a liquid prepared by dissolving 45 parts of potash-alum, 15 parts Epsom salts, and 6 parts sal-ammoniac in 250 parts of water. Now cautiously add dilute ammonia to the mixture, stirring all the time, and avoiding any excess of ammonia. The precipitated pigment is to be thoroughly washed, and then pressed, dried, and ground.

Indigo

[. . .]

[pp. 192–4]

Indigo has been used either as a pigment or a dye from very early times in India and in Egypt. It is referred to under the name of *indicum* by Pliny; later on the Byzantine writers called it *azorium Romanum*. 'Indigo bagadel' – that is, indigo of Bagdad – is named as early as 1228 in the Marseilles tariffs; in the early English accounts relating to painting works (1274) it is called 'indebas.' It was first largely imported from India into Europe in the seventeenth century by the Dutch.

A large number of different plants yield true indigo. This pigment was once obtained in considerable quantity from a crucifer, Isatis tinctoria, the dyers' weed or woad, the 'pastel' of the French; but the chief source is now *Indigofera tinctoria,* a leguminous shrub, probably of Indian, or at least Asiatic, origin. The exports of indigo from India in a single year amount to £4,000,000 worth.

Indigo ($C_{16}H_{10}N_2O_2$) does not exist ready-formed in the plants which yield it, but occurs in the form of a colourless compound, or *glucoside,* which, by combining with water, splits up into a sugar and indigo. It is prepared from the freshly-cut plants, or from the dried foliage, by maceration in water and fermentation, followed by boiling (sometimes lime-water is first added); the dark precipitate which forms is thrown on to cloth-strainers, and finally pressed and dried. The mineral impurities which commercial indigo contains are derived partly from the plant itself, partly from the water used in preparing it, and partly from the lime-water above mentioned; moreover, it is sometimes adulterated. Indigo is easily oxidized by a very large number of substances rich in oxygen, yielding a yellow product called isatine; it is converted into a colourless body ($C_{16}H_{12}N_2O_2$) by many reducing agents.

Indeed, several of the processes of purifying indigo depend upon the reduction of the blue colouring substance, or 'indigotin,' into 'white indigo,' and the subsequent precipitation of the blue matter by exposure to the oxygen of the air. Green vitriol is the commonest reducing agent, and is used in association with lime. The purified indigo prepared by this process, though of fair colour, does not, however, work so well as a paint as the best Bengal indigo treated successively with acid, alkali, acid, and alcohol. Indigotin, if quite pure, has a somewhat purplish cast in thick water-colour washes; this hue is observable with this substance whether obtained by sublimation or by Fritzche's process with grape-sugar, caustic soda, and alcohol.

The impurities in commercial indigo constitute from 20 up to 70 or 80 per cent. of its total weight – the average is about 50. They consist mainly of mineral matter, indigo red, indigo brown, and nitrogenous compounds. Much of the mineral matter may be removed by digestion in hydrochloric acid, followed by treatment with boiling water. Sodium hydrate solution dissolves the indigo brown, while strong alcohol takes away the indigo red, which amounts to nearly 4 parts in 100 of the original indigo. After treatment with these three solvents, the residual purified indigo is of an intense and very beautiful hue. Java indigo is generally of very good quality, that from Bengal comes next, and then the indigo from Oudh, Kurpah, and Madras. Japanese indigo is generally poor.

'Mummy'

[. . .]

[p. 209]

'Mummy,' as a pigment, is inferior to prepared, but superior to raw, asphalt, inasmuch as it has been submitted to a considerable degree of heat, and has thereby lost some of its volatile hydrocarbons. Moreover, it is usual to grind up the bones and other parts of the mummy together, so that the resulting powder has more solidity and is less fusible than the asphalt alone would be. A London colourman informs me that one Egyptian mummy furnishes sufficient material to satisfy the demands of his customers for seven years. It is perhaps scarcely necessary to add that some samples of the pigment sold as 'mummy' are spurious. Mummy was certainly used as an oil-paint at least as early as the close of the sixteenth century.

11

DINABANDHU MITRA, INTRODUCTION, AUTHOR'S PREFACE, AND 'PERSONS OF THE DRAMA'

Nil Darpan, or the Indigo Planting Mirror, a Drama. Translated from the Bengali by A Native (Calcutta: C. H. Manuel, 1861), pp. 39–41

Introduction

THE original Bengali of this Drama – the NIL DARPAN, OR INDIGO PLANTING MIRROR – having excited considerable interest, a wish was expressed by various Europeans to see a translation of it. This has been made by a Native; both the original and translation are *bonâ fide* Native productions and depict the Indigo Planting System as viewed by Natives at large.

The Drama is the favourite mode with the Hindus for describing certain states of society, manners, customs. Since the days of Sir W. Jones, by scholars at Paris, St. Petersburgh, and London, the Sanskrit Drama has, in this point of view, been highly appreciated. The Bengali Drama imitates in this respect its Sanskrit parent. The evils of Kulin Brahminism, widow marriage prohibition, quackery, fanaticism, have been depicted by it with great effect.

Nor has the system of Indigo planting escaped notice: hence the origin of this work, the NIL DARPAN, which, though exhibiting no marvellous or very tragic scenes, yet, in simple homely language, gives the "annals of the poor;" pleads the cause of those who are the feeble; it describes a respectable ryot, a peasant proprietor, happy with his family in the enjoyment of his land till the Indigo System compelled him to take advances, to neglect his own land, to cultivate crops which beggared him, reducing him to the condition of a serf and a vagabond; the effect of this on his home, children, and relatives are pointed out in language, plain but true; it shows how arbitrary power debases the lord as well as the peasant; reference is also made to the partiality of various Magistrates in favor of Planters and to the Act of last year penally enforcing Indigo contracts.

DOI: 10.4324/9781315400266-15

The author's Preface

I PRESENT "The Indigo Planting Mirror" to the Indigo Planters' hands; now, let every one of them, having observed his face, erase the freckle of the stain of selfishness from his forehead, and, in its stead, place on it the sandal powder of beneficence, then shall I think my labour successful, good fortune for the helpless class of ryots, and preservation of England's honor. Oh, ye Indigo Planters! Your malevolent conduct has brought a stain upon the English Nation, which was so graced by the ever-memorable names of Sydney, Howard, Hall, and other great men. Is your desire for money so very powerful, that through the instigation of that vain wealth, you are engaged in making holes like rust in the long acquired and pure fame of the British people? Abstain now from that unjust conduct through which you are raising immense sums as your profits; and then the poor people, with their families, will be able to spend their days in ease.

Persons of the drama

GOLUK CHUNDER BASU.
NOBIN MADHAB }
BINDU MADHAB } *Sons of Goluk Chunder.*
SADHU CHURN – *A neighbouring Ryot.*
RAY CHURN – *Sadhu's brother.*
GOPI CHURN DAS – *The Dewan.*
J. J. WOOD }
P. P. ROSE } *Indigo Planters.*
THE AMIN OR LAND MEASURER.
A KHALASI, *a Tent-pitcher.*
TAIDGIR – *Native Superintendent of Indigo Cultivation.*

Magistrate, Amla, Attorney, Deputy Inspector, Pundit, Keeper of the Gaol, Doctor, a Cow-keeper, a Native Doctor, Four Boys, a Latyal or Club-man, and a Herdsman.

Women.

SABITRI – *Wife of Goluk Chunder.*
SOIRINDRI – *Wife of Nobin.*
SARALOTA – *Wife of Bindu Madhab.*
REBOTI – *Wife of Sadhu Churn.*
KHETROMANI – *Daughter of Sadhu.*
ADURI – *Maid-servant in Goluk Chunder's house.*
PODI MOYRANI – *A Sweetmeat Maker.*

Nil Darpan, act 2, scene 3

Enter a ryot, two peadas or bailiffs of the police, and a taidgir of the Indigo factory

Ryot. My elder Babu, preserve my two children; there is no one else to feed them. Last year, I gave eight carts' load of Indigo, and I did not get a single pice for that, and also I am bound, as with cords, for the remainder. Again, they will take me to Andarabad.

Guard. The advance-money of the Indigo and the marking nut of the washer-man, as soon as they come in contact, become mostly joined. You villain come; you must first go to the Dewanji; your elder Babu also shall come to this.

Ryot. Come, I don't fear this. I would rather have my body rot in the Jail than any more prepare the Indigo of that white man. My God! my God! none looks on the poor (*weeps*). My elder Babu, give my children food; they brought me to the field; and I was not able to see them once.

(Exit all, except Nobin Madhab.)

Nobin. What injustice! These two children will die without food in the same way as the new-born young of the hare suffer when the hare is in the hand of the savage hunters.

Enter RAY CHURN.

Ray. Had not my brother caught hold of us, I would have put a stop to her breathing. I would have killed her; then, at the utmost, I had been hanged within six months.[1] That villain!

Nobin. Ray Churn, where art thou going?

Ray. Our mistress ordered me to call Putakur. The stupid Podi told me that the bailiff will bring the summons to-morrow.

(*Exit Ray Churn.*)

Nobin. Oh! oh! oh! That which never took place in this family, has now come to pass. My father is very peaceful, honest, and of a sincere mind; knows not what disputes and enmities are; never goes out of the village; trembles with fear at the name of Court affairs, and even shed tears when he read the letter. If he is to go to Indrabad, he will turn mad; and if, to the jail, he will throw himself into the stream. Ah, such are the misfortunes that are to fall on him, while I, his son, am living! My mother is not so much afraid as my father is; she does not lose hope at once; with a firm mind, she is now invoking God. My deer-eyed is become, as it were, the deer in my volcano;[2] she is become mad with fear and anxiety. Her father died in an Indigo Factory; and her fear, now, is lest the same happens to her husband. How many sides am I to keep quiet? Is it proper to fly off with the whole family; or, is it not right that to do good unto others is the highest virtue? I shall not turn aside hastily. I see, I am not able to do any good to Shamanagara; still, what work is there which is beyond the power of exertion? Let me see what I can do.

Notes (Mitra, 1861)

1 This expression "had been hanged for six months" is only used sarcastically.
2 That is, as the deer feels disquieted when exposed in a volcano, so is my mate troubled by the many anxieties in my mind.

12

T. N. MUKHARJI, 'PIURI, OR INDIAN YELLOW'

Journal of the Society of Arts (23 November 1883), pp. 16–17

The following communication has been received from the India-office: –

Piuri is a yellow dye, used chiefly in painting walls of houses, doors, and railings. It is seldom used for dyeing cloth, owing to its bad smell. It is derived from two sources – (1) of mineral origin, imported from London; (2) of animal origin, manufactured at Monghyr, a town in Bengal. Sir Joseph Hooker has asked for information about the latter.

By inquiries in Calcutta, I found that piuri is made at Monghyr from the urine of cows fed with mango leaves. To substantiate the truth of this statement, I went to Monghyr, and there found that a sect of gwalas (milkmen), residing at a place called Mirzapur in the suburbs of the town, are the only people who manufacture the substance. They feed the cows solely with mango leaves and water, which increases the bile pigment, and imparts to the urine a bright yellow colour. It is said that the cows thus fed die within two years, but the piuri manufacturers assured me that this statement is wrong; and, indeed, I myself saw cows six or seven years old from which piuri has been obtained during the last four years. The cows, however, looked very unhealthy, and the manufacturers of piuri told me that, to keep up the strength of the animal, they now and then allow her grass and other fodder besides the mango leaf, but a mixed food reduces the proportion of the colouring principle in the urine. Owing to the injurious effect which the treatment necessary for the manufacture of piuri has on the cows, the occupation of making piuri is confied [sic] to a very small number of people, who for this reason are looked down upon by their fellow caste-men. I am told that in no other part of the country is the manufacture of piuri carried on. The cows treated with mango leaves are made to pass urine three or four times a day by having the urinary organ slightly rubbed with the hand, and they are so habituated to this process that they have become incapable of passing water of their own accord. The urine is collected during the whole day in small earthen pots, and in the evening put over a fire in an earthen vessel. The heat causes the yellow principle to precipitate, separating it from the watery portion. It is then strained with a small piece of cloth; the sediment is made into a ball, and dried first on charcoal fire and then in

DOI: 10.4324/9781315400266-16

the sun, when it is ready for the market. The merchants (chiefly Marwaries), who advance money to the milkmen for the purpose, purchase the stuff at R. 1 (1s. 8d.) per lb., and export it to Calcutta on the one side and Patna on the other. The price of the imported (mineral) piuri is only 4d. per lb. The animal piuri is of an exceedingly bright colour, and is therefore considered very superior to the mineral piuri. The high price of the animal piuri is probably owing to the deterioration of the live stock consequent on the manufacture of the article, and the cost of procuring mango leaves, which are sold at the rate of Rs. 2 for the produce of a middle-sized tree, say 30 feet high. An average cow passes about three quarts of urine per day, which yields about 2 ozs. of piuri. The animal supply is said to be about 100 to 150 cwts.; but this seems to be an over-estimate, considering the small number of cows employed for this purpose.

I myself saw mango leaves lying before the cows, the collection of urine, and the manufacture of piuri. So the real source of this kind of piuri is now beyond any doubt whatever.

I have sent to Sir Joseph Hooker direct – (1) The mineral piuri brought to Calcutta from London; (2) Monghyr piuri purchased at Calcutta; (3) Monghyr piuri purchased from the manufactures; (4) a bottle of urine from which the piuri is obtained; (5) an earthen pot in which the urine is collected; (6) quantity of mango leaves.

T. N. Mukharji.

27th August, 1883.

1.3

Medium

DOI: 10.4324/9781315400266-17

1.3 Medium

The nineteenth century saw a resurgence and intensification of interest in painting in materials other than oil on canvas. The sources collected here span watercolour, fresco and tempera and have been selected to illustrate some of the social, cultural and aesthetic meanings attributed to the materials of these media in the Victorian period. All three were perceived as important contributions to the formation of a 'national' art school. Further, they offered new opportunities to artists who were women, and as new media they were importantly 'a locus for rethinking gendered aesthetic experience', in a manner distinct from oil painting.[1]

Painting with pigment and water as a vehicle dates back to antiquity, but in the late eighteenth century the watercolour painter emerged as a new category of artist. Solid cakes of colour for watercolour painting were manufactured from the 1780s onwards (and marketed in portable paintboxes), while the development of watercolour as an autonomous medium was bolstered by the foundation of two exhibiting societies known as the 'Old' and the 'New' watercolour societies in London in 1804 and 1832, respectively. By the mid-nineteenth century, watercolour was widely exhibited and increasingly regarded and celebrated as a distinctively British art form. The manufacture of the pigment Chinese white from 1834 onwards makes Victorian watercolour distinct from its predecessors. Rather than building up thin washes of paint and leaving some areas of paper showing through for white contrast, artists started to add in body colour with bright Chinese white. John Ruskin's advice to amateur watercolourists is reprinted here: he champions the ways in which this new material enabled artists to come closer to nature than ever before.

Watercolour paints were relatively stable, lightweight and readily portable. Watercolour painting was typically carried out on a smaller scale than oils; it could be undertaken in a sketchpad or stretched over a board and did not necessarily require an easel. Its material properties (transparency, quick application and rapid drying, enabling new layers to be applied) made it particularly well suited to capturing the fleeting effects of changing weather and light, and the history of watercolour in Britain is closely interwoven with the history of landscape painting (although in the Victorian period a wide range of watercolour 'realist' scenes of daily life also emerged). Watercolour was also perceived and promoted as a particularly *English* undertaking (this too was connected partly to its material suitability for evoking landscape), and guides to watercolour painting – like Ackermann's *Manual of Colours* printed here – were keen to write histories of the medium, emphasising its 'English' genesis. The frontispiece to Ackermann's features Queen Victoria in the company of Prince Albert busily painting with Ackermann's watercolours, with the caption 'Artium Protectores' (Protectors of the Arts), a Royal endorsement for a nationally significant medium. Queen Victoria's presence in the frontispiece to Ackermann's book also underscores another connection between the material properties of watercolour and its social and cultural associations: its connection with women, and especially *amateur* women (at whom many watercolour manuals were specifically aimed). Ackermann's *Manual* is, however, keen to emphasise that the pioneers of watercolour were exclusively male artists.[2]

The portability of watercolour made it particularly keenly utilised by British artists on the move in general, especially artists joining exploration expeditions who were engaged for the purpose of documenting British 'possessions', or who worked in – or were transported to – colonised spaces.[3] These twin aspects of watercolour's material properties are evident in the description of Winsor and Newton's 'moist' watercolours from an 1882 catalogue reproduced here; the limited impact of temperature on these paints allowed their manufacturers to emphasise that 'they are confidently recommended to persons who are going to INDIA (sic) and to all residents in the East'.[4] British women travelling independently – like Marianne North (1830–1890) or Olivia Tonge (1858–1949) – used watercolour to record flora as they moved about the globe to prove their scholarly natural historical credentials. The medium was also employed by British women accompanying their husbands to help work out their new positions in colonial society, to capture and reckon with unfamiliar sights, and to paste into albums and send 'back home', not necessarily with an eye to public exhibition.[5] Others used watercolour to capture new colonial subject matter and to build an artistic career. Frances Anne Hopkins (1838–1919), for example, arrived in Quebec in 1858 with her husband, an employee of the Hudson's Bay Company. Hopkins undertook watercolour sketches on canoe expeditions with her husband, both as studies in their own right (as in her 1870 *Encampment of Voyageurs* reproduced here) and as sketches for larger scale oils, such as her *Canoes in the Fog Lake Superior* (exhibited at the RA in 1869).[6]

Women also made significant contributions to the Victorian fresco and tempera revivals. Both revivals drew on new understandings of fourteenth-century artistic practice, and set out to reform a national style through the employment of alternative materials with connections to celebrated periods in art history. These revivals made extensive use of descriptions of fourteenth-century Italian painting in the Tuscan painter Cennino Cennini's treatise *Il Libro dell'Arte* (1437), the first English translation of which was undertaken by Mary Philadelphia Merrifield and published in 1844. By the 1840s, fresco had become a matter of national interest, and Merrifield was subsequently commissioned by the Royal Commission on the Fine Arts to travel and undertake the research underpinning *The Art of Fresco*, passages from the introduction of which are reprinted here.[7] Fresco is a method of wall painting where pigments resistant to lime are mixed with water and applied to a layer of wet lime plaster; as the plaster dries, the pigments chemically fuse to it, providing a matt and chalky surface. It lends itself to simple, large-scale forms, rather than detail. These characteristics – and especially the idea of patriotic subjects from British history being literally fused to the walls of buildings – made fresco seem particularly appropriate for the new Houses of Parliament. Like Merrifield, the Select Committee formed in 1841 to look into the 'Promotion of the Fine Arts of this country in connexion with the Rebuilding of the Houses of Parliament', saw the simplicity of fresco as a means of improving national artistic and design skills, seeking to use the materials of this medium to establish connections between celebrated figures in art history with present day Britain. The Westminster scheme, however, was ongoing and incomplete, and the reason for its derailing has usually been understood, ironically, to be the medium of fresco, which began to crumble before its painters' eyes. By 1854, the Royal Commission was looking to other media which would be more enduring, and the wall painting technique of water glass was introduced from 1859 onwards.[8]

Tempera is a type of vehicle used to bind together pigments, but it usually refers to the use of egg yolk. Widely used in fourteenth-century Italian painting, it had largely been replaced by oils by the sixteenth century. Tempera dries fast and permanently, requiring careful attention to fine, accurate brushstrokes. This need for careful craft, combined with its medieval heritage, made tempera particularly appealing for a group of British painters in the last quarter of the nineteenth century, some of whom were associated with the Arts and Crafts Movement. These painters sought to return to pre-industrial artisanal modes of artistic production, preparing their own paints rather than purchasing them ready-made.[9] Merrifield's 1844 translation of Cennini provided Victorian readers with extensive descriptions of the use of tempera. This was supplemented in 1899 by a new translation by Christiana Herringham, an early 1870s tempera revivalist. Alice Meynell's 1901 essay on Marianne Stokes identifies tempera as the medium which 'suited her genius' (a highly gendered term usually associated with male artists).[10] Meynell's essay makes connections between materials and ideas of 'primitivism': the material properties of oil painting, she argues, 'separated the art of Europe from simplicity'.[11] She emphasises the importance of materials for the spiritual and emotional resonances of an artwork; these attributes, so often associated with femininity, are not explicitly connected with gender in Meynell's account, instead being set out as the norm, the baseline, for work in this particular medium.[12]

Notes

1 M. Clarke, 'On Tempera and Temperament: Women, Art, and Feeling at the *Fin de Siècle*', *19: Interdisciplinary Studies in the Long Nineteenth Century*, 23 (2016), p. 2, at http://doi.org/10.16995/ntn.767 [accessed 15 June 2021].

2 For more on which see Francina Irwin, 'Amusement of instruction? Watercolour manuals and the woman amateur', in Clarissa Campbell Orr (ed.), *Women in the Victorian Art World* (Manchester: Manchester University Press, 1995), pp. 149–166.

3 For example, John Frederick Lewis in the Middle East; the 'convict artist' Thomas Bock, who was deported to Tasmania; Marianne North, who travelled the globe painting flora.

4 *Winsor and Newton's Catalogue of Colours and Materials for Watercolour paintings, pencil, chalk, architectural drawing &c &c* (London: Winsor and Newton, 1882), p. 11.

5 For an overview, see Jordana Pomeroy, '"We Got Upon Our Elephant and Went out After Subjects": capturing the world in watercolour', in Jordana Pomeroy (ed.), *Intrepid Women: Victorian Artists Travel* (Farnham: Ashgate, 2005), 39–50. For detailed discussion of women and watercolour in India, see Romita Ray, 'The Memsahib's Brush: Anglo-Indian Women and the Art of the Picturesque, 1830–1880' in Julie Codell and D. S. Macleod (eds), *Orientalism transposed: the impact of the colonies on British culture* (Aldershot: Ashgate, 1998), pp. 89–116.

6 For more on the artist and her context see Laura Peers, 'Material Culture, Identity, and the Canadian Fur Trade', in Beth Fowkes Tobin and Maureen Goggin (eds), *Women and Things 1750–1850: Gendered Material Strategies* (Farnham: Ashgate, 2009), pp. 55–73; Kristina Huneault, 'Placing Frances Anne Hopkins: a British-born artist in colonial Canada', in Deborah Cherry and Janice Helland (eds), *Local/Global: Women Artists in the Nineteenth Century* (Farnham: Ashgate, 2006), pp. 179–200.

7 Alexandra Loske, 'Mary Philadelphia Merrifield: Color History as Expertise', *Visual Resources*, 33 (2017), pp. 11–26.

8 Clare A. P. Willsdon, *Mural Painting in Britain 1840–1940: Image and Meaning* (Oxford: Oxford University Press, 2000), pp. 44–6; 59–60.

9 For a useful overview see Abbie N. Sprague, 'The British tempera revival: A return to craftsmanship', *British Art Journal*, 3:3 (Autumn 2002), pp. 66–74.

10 Alice Meynell, 'Mrs Adrian Stokes,' *The Magazine of Art*, March 1901, pp. 241–7, on p. 244.

11 Ibid, p. 243.

12 See further Clarke, 'On Tempera and Temperament'.

13

JOHN RUSKIN, 'THE ELEMENTS OF DRAWING'

The Works of John Ruskin, Vol. 15 (Cambridge: Cambridge University Press, 2010), pp. 157–159

157. Use Chinese white, well ground, to mix with your colours in order to pale them, instead of a quantity of water. You will thus be able to shape your masses more quietly, and play the colours about with more ease; they will not damp your paper so much, and you will be able to go on continually, and lay forms of passing cloud and other fugitive or delicately shaped lights, otherwise unattainable except by time.

158. This mixing of white with the pigments, so as to render them opaque, constitutes body-colour drawing as opposed to transparent-colour drawing, and you will, perhaps, have it often said to you that this body-colour is "illegitimate." It is just as legitimate as oil-painting, being, so far as handling is concerned, the same process, only without its uncleanliness, its unwholesomeness, or its inconvenience; for oil will not dry quickly, nor carry safely, nor give the same effects of atmosphere without tenfold labour. And if you hear it said that the body-colour looks chalky or opaque, and, as is very likely, think so yourself, be yet assured of this, that though certain effects of glow and transparencies of gloom are not to be reached without transparent colour, those glows and glooms are not the noblest aim of art. After many years' study of the various results of fresco and oil painting in Italy, and of bodycolour and transparent colour in England, I am now entirely convinced that the greatest things that are to be done in art must be done in dead colour. The habit of depending on varnish or on lucid tints for transparency, makes the painter comparatively lose sight of the nobler translucence which is obtained by breaking various colours amidst each other: and even when, as by Correggio, exquisite play of hue is joined with exquisite transparency, the delight in the depth almost always leads the painter into mean and false chiaroscuro; it leads him to like dark backgrounds instead of luminous ones,[1] and to enjoy, in general, quality of colour more than grandeur of composition, and confined light rather than open sunshine: so that the really greatest thoughts of the greatest men have always, so far as I remember, been reached in dead colour, and the noblest oil pictures of Tintoret and Veronese are those which are likest frescoes.

DOI: 10.4324/9781315400266-18

159. Besides all this, the fact is, that though sometimes a little chalky and coarse-looking body-colour is, in a sketch, infinitely liker Nature than transparent colour: the bloom and mist of distance are accurately and instantly represented by the film of opaque blue (quite accurately, I think, by nothing else); and for ground, rocks, and buildings, the earthy and solid surface is, of course, always truer than the most finished and carefully wrought work in transparent tints can ever be.

Note (Ruskin, 1857)

1 All the degradation of art which was brought about, after the rise of the Dutch school, by asphaltum, yellow varnish, and brown trees would have been prevented, if only painters had been forced to work in dead colour. Any colour will do for some people, if it is browned and shining; but fallacy in dead colour is detected on the instant. I even believe that whenever a painter begins to wish that he could touch any portion of his work with gum, he is going wrong. It is necessary, however, in this matter, carefully to distinguish between translucency and lustre. Translucency, though, as I have said above, a dangerous temptation, is, in its place, beautiful; but lustre or shininess is always, in painting, a defect. Nay, one of my best painter-friends (the "best" being understood to attach to both divisions of that awkward compound word), tried the other day to persuade me that lustre was an ignobleness in anything; and it was only the fear of treason to ladies' eyes, and to mountain streams, and to morning dew, which kept me from yielding the point to him. One is apt always to generalise too quickly in such matters; but there can be no question that lustre is destructive of loveliness in colour, as it is of intelligibility in form. Whatever may be the pride of a young beauty in the knowledge that her eyes shine (though perhaps even eyes are most beautiful in dimness), she would be sorry if her cheeks did; and which of us would wish to polish a rose?

14

FRONTISPIECE TO THEODORE HENRY FIELDING, *ACKERMANN'S MANUAL OF COLOURS, USED IN THE DIFFERENT BRANCHES OF WATER-COLOUR PAINTING*

(London, 1844), The Bodleian Libraries, University of Oxford

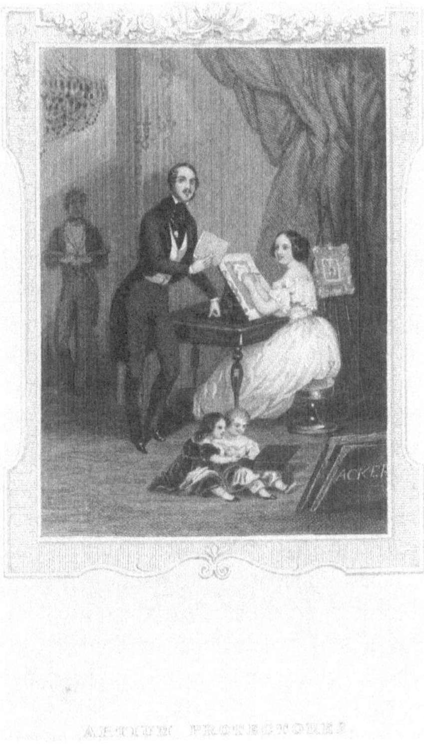

DOI: 10.4324/9781315400266-19

15

THEODORE HENRY FIELDING, 'INTRODUCTION', *ACKERMANN'S MANUAL OF COLOURS, USED IN THE DIFFERENT BRANCHES OF WATER-COLOUR PAINTING*

(London: R. Ackermann, 1844), pp. 3–6

It is an interesting fact, that painting in water-colours, in its present highly improved state, is entirely of English growth. The art may be said to have commenced with Paul Sandby, who was born in Nottingham, 1732, and died in 1809.

The mode of working, adopted by this talented artist, was followed by a numerous class of professors, who advanced the art in a very small degree, by mixing a little blue in the Indian ink, which Mr. Sandby had hitherto used alone; finishing his drawings first with this unpromising pigment, and afterwards staining them with various tints of thin colour. Another improvement was again effected, by working out the foregrounds in brown, but still retaining the blue and Indian ink for skies, clouds, distances, buildings, &c., and then placing the tints of colour over the whole, beginning with a generalizing tint of some warm colour; and so lately has this style of painting in water-colours (if so it can be called) been in vogue, that in a collection of drawings we have seen, there are many done by one of our most eminent artists still living, and in this old fashioned manner. The drawings are, of course, feeble, cold, and with very little colour in them, but, in other respects, they exhibit the great talent which has given this gentleman the very high rank he now holds in his profession. The next innovation was made by Mr. John Couzens, by substituting indigo and Indian red as a mixture for the first washes or shade tint in his drawings; this was called neutral tint, and he produced drawings of great effect, and frequently of romantic grandeur, but it was reserved for Mr. Girtin to break through the trammels of the old school, and at once to rival the richness, force, and depth of oil colours by painting in at once the colours and shadows of objects, with the tints which seemed to him most suitable and convenient.

The next grand desideratum – the power of removing the colours from the paper, in order to fashion the lights on leaves of trees, &c. &c. – was discovered,

DOI: 10.4324/9781315400266-20

we believe, by Mr. Nicholson, and this seemed to give perfection to the art in the hands of its highly talented inventor, and his contemporaries. Lights could now be placed of any form, and in any part of the drawing, resembling the touches of the brush in oil painting, and whoever has attentively regarded the finished water-colour paintings of the present day, will be fully aware of the important step this improvement must have made in the then limited mode of using water-colours. From this time the colour manufacturers may date a constantly increasing demand for every material connected with this branch of the art, occasioned by the extraordinary patronage which it received from the public. It is true, that the miniature and flower-painters were frequently requiring improvements in the manufacture of colours, but their consumption was trifling compared to the increased demand which had all at once arisen, and which has been increasing ever since. The stimulus thus given, has been the means of giving increased facilities to artists by the discovery of new colours, and by producing a greater state of perfection in those already known: – for example – those very beautiful greys made by mixing madder brown, or purple, and cobalt, or madder lake, cobalt, and yellow ochre, a few years back were wholly unknown. The exquisite tints of the rose and carmine madders are also a late discovery, and so essential have they now become, that the practical artist cannot imagine a possibility of being without them – some of the tints from these colours being inimitable. Thus their loss would make a blank on the palette that nothing else could fill. To these things in our department of colour manufacturers, we have paid increasing attention, and we believe that our colours, having received all the attention that the laboratories of modern chemistry can bestow, as well as the utmost skill and care of the colour grinder's art, will be found to possess the many requisites necessary to bear out the splendid attainments of the English school of painting.

16

'WINSOR AND NEWTON'S MOIST WATER COLOURS IN PORCELAIN PANS'

Winsor and Newton's Catalogue of Colours and Materials for Watercolour paintings, pencil, chalk, architectural drawing &c &c (London: Winsor and Newton, 1882), p. 11

WINSOR AND NEWTON'S Moist Water Colours *are prepared after peculiar processes, and by a system of treatment known only to themselves*. Their characteristic qualities of easy solubility and prompt readiness for use are retained unimpaired, for an unlimited time; so that a box of them, which may have been laid aside for two or three years, when required again, will be found *as serviceable as when purchased*. Temperature does not affect these colours; they remain as "Moist" in Tropical climates as in England; accordingly, they are confidently recommended to persons who are going to INDIA, and to all residents in the East. While having the valuable quality of solubility, they possess another and all important one, *of drying perfectly firm on the paper*. Their tints, too, are pure and luminous, and their washes clear and even.

In Sketching from Nature, and when representing transient and evanescent effects, the superiority of the Moist Colours is at once felt and appreciated. Ever ready for instant application, they enable the desired tint to be produced *at once* – a result unattainable by the old tedious method of rubbing dry cakes, which not unfrequently permits the effect, and with it the *thought* of the artist to vanish, before the material can be obtained. It was this quality which, on their first introduction, secured for Winsor and Newton's Moist Colours the eminent popularity that they still enjoy with both professional and amateur artists.

Moist Colours are placed in pans of thin porcelain, and they are afterwards packed in tin-foil for protection. When required for use, and the foil removed, a surface of colour is presented to the artist, which is obtainable in any quantity, simply by the application of a wet brush.

DOI: 10.4324/9781315400266-21

17

FRANCES ANNE HOPKINS, *ENCAMPMENT OF VOYAGEURS* (1870), WATERCOLOUR

Library and Archives Canada/Peter Winkworth Collection of Canadiana at the National Archives of Canada/e000835916

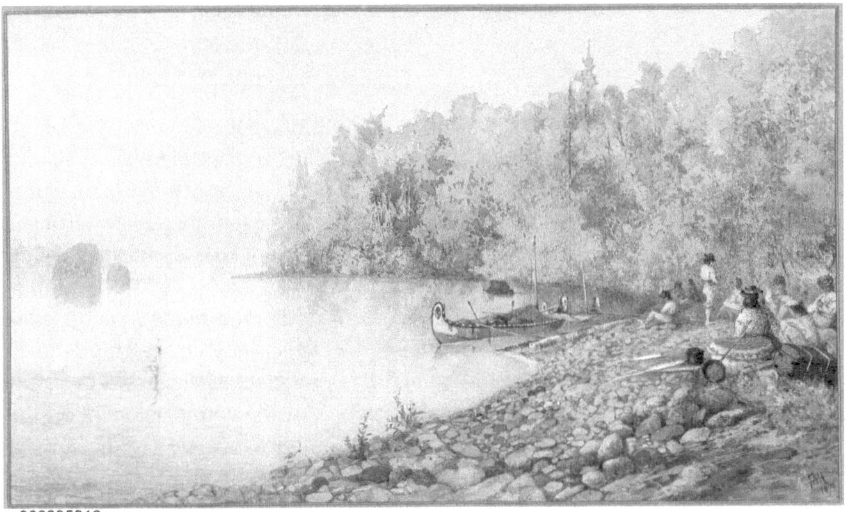

e000835916

DOI: 10.4324/9781315400266-22

18

MARY MERRIFIELD, *THE ART OF FRESCO PAINTING AS PRACTISED BY THE OLD ITALIAN AND SPANISH MASTERS WITH A PRELIMINARY ENQUIRY INTO THE NATURE OF THE COLOURS USED IN FRESCO PAINTING WITH OBSERVATIONS AND NOTES*

(London: Charles Gilpin, 1846), pp. iii–iv, vi–vii

THE revival of the art of *Fresco Painting* in the nineteenth century, will be an epoch in the fine arts, and, will probably, be the means of forming a great school of painting in this country, and lead to the improvement of the sister arts of sculpture and architecture. The moment it was determined to decorate the new Houses of Parliament with fresco paintings, it became important to ascertain the mode adopted by the great masters of the Italian and Spanish schools. To accomplish this desirable object, it became necessary to recur to the old treatises on the subject, especially those written in the Italian and Spanish languages. This inquiry was fortunately undertaken by a gentleman fully competent to the task. The result was presented to the public in the valuable reports of the commissioners on the fine arts. The path of inquiry was well traced out in these reports, and the subject coinciding with my own pursuits and inclinations, I was induced to pursue the inquiry, from the persuasion, that the introduction of the art into this country, would be the means of founding a great English school of painting.

Independent of other considerations, there appear to me to be certain analogies between Italy, during the period the fine arts flourished in that country, and England at the present time, which strengthens this persuasion. The same wealth and splendour of our nobles and merchants, the same commercial prosperity, and, above all, the same spirit of inquiry, which characterised Italy at the period I have mentioned, is applicable to England at the present moment. The advantage is on the side of England.

Almost all the writers of eminence, mention fresco painting, as the highest branch of the art. The most competent judges have expressed opinions, that in

 DOI: 10.4324/9781315400266-23

comprehensiveness of subject, boldness of design, facility of execution, and in durability, it exceeds all other kinds of painting, especially for the decoration of temples, palaces, and great public buildings. It has been practised by men of the highest order of genius. It is only necessary to mention the names of the Carracci, Michael Angelo, Raphael, and Correggio, to shew how highly this branch of the art was formerly appreciated, even if the value set on the cartoons, the rough drafts of paintings in fresco, were not sufficient to establish its superiority. These considerations, added to the favorable reception of my translation of Cennino Cennini, on painting, encouraged me to follow the path of inquiry, traced out in the Reports of the Commissioners.

By long discontinuance, the art had become almost entirely lost. The practice of painting on walls, in the manner described by Vitruvius, that is, partly in *fresco,* and partly in *secco,* appears to have been continued throughout the dark ages, by the Greeks, who instructed the Italians. According to Zanetti, the Greek style was taught by a Greek artist of Constantinople, who, about the year 1200, kept a school for painting, at Venice, to which many foreigners resorted for instruction, and from the same author we learn, that the Greek style was practised until the middle of the fourteenth century.

[. . .]

We must expect that the introduction of the art, will be opposed and condemned by many of those who love the arts, and to whom we are much indebted for their advancement, but who have grown grey in other practice. It were too much to expect otherwise. But the young artist may be assured that fresco painting will succeed, and be most extensively practised in this country. The commencement has been most auspicious. The patronage of government has been offered. The assistance of parliament has been obtained; and with such encouragement and patronage, ability and genius will not be wanting. No opposition can now prevent its success. The die is cast; the path will be trodden. The art has been already revived, and practised with success, on the continent, especially in Germany. It has commenced in this country, and it may be safely predicted, that it will hereafter form the principal part of the decorations of our public edifices. The great, the wise, and the good, with the actions and works, for which they were most celebrated, will be appropriately represented in our public buildings and palaces, if not in our temples. The illustrious dead will be represented as instructive examples to the living, and the art, which it is the object of this treatise to promote, will, by these means, become subservient to the best interests of the country. These are my anticipations. I firmly believe they will be fully realized; and that fresco painting will be extensively and successfully practised in this country, by our own native artists, and will ultimately attain to a perfection, equal to that for which the Italian schools were so justly celebrated.

19

ALICE MEYNELL, 'MRS ADRIAN STOKES'

The Magazine of Art, March 1901, pp. 243–246

Her first conviction of the greatness of colour was gained when she was ready for it, in the galleries of Italy, and in the study of the primitive painters who seem to look not against the light, so as to see the shadows of a luminous world, but with it, so as to see the colours of an illuminated world. Doubtless Mrs. Stokes would hold most important two passages of her life – the conversion to colour, in the first place; and, in the second place, the abandonment of oil-paint as an encumbering material.

[. . .]

The first picture that aimed at both pure decoration and pure spirituality was "Saint Elizabeth spinning for the Poor." But Mrs. Stokes found that she could not attain that aim until she should be free of oil-colour. Something, she thought, had been lost in the practice of art by the association of colour with oil. Too thick, too deliberate, too tolerant of handling and re-handling, too indulgent to the *à peu près* in execution, whilst it works for realism, oil-painting has separated the art of Europe from simplicity. Material controls the painter so far that the very existence of the spirit of realism has come to pass as a consequence of this imitative and yet hindering medium which encourages and hampers at once. This, at any rate, was the conviction of Mrs. Stokes when, being resolved that the grey colours of French painting should not be the final colours of art, she began to search for a ground and material such as the early painters used when art in Europe was born again. She found these in gesso and tempera, and the technique of this painting – the mere material – led to the spirit and the idea. For Mrs. Stokes is evidently not amongst those who stop upon the technique and divide the matter from the form of art, which has never been done in a great school or, indeed, in any school whatever worthy of the name.

The case against oil-painting has been stated in her work on Cennino Cennini by Mrs. Herringham: "It has produced," she says, "many masterpieces, but destroyed monumental painting, not only in developing the taste for petty things, and petty methods, but also in rendering the labour so slow and so arduous that in this method a great undertaking seems impracticable." The same writer says of

DOI: 10.4324/9781315400266-24

tempera: "If the Middle Ages preferred fresco and tempera – that is size-vehicles – monumental painting proves the justice of the preference; and the work of Cennino establishes victoriously that it was not done through ignorance." Mrs. Stokes studied Cennino Cennini in the course of her researches. She found the gesso ground, and the fresh and single medium, that put her in the place of the painters she best loved. For her the recovery of tempera was no less than the restoration of spirituality and decoration – two things long overpowered by the realism, drama, and complexity of oils.

However it may be for other artists, it is certain that Mrs. Stokes found in gesso and tempera the whole convention, and by concomitance the spirit, that suited her genius. She is by nature and grace a primitive painter in tempera, exquisitely sincere in feeling, mistress of a pure method; her handicraft would be rather encumbered than flattered by the facilities allowed by oils to mend and to add. She is direct, in heart and hand, and possesses the composure and the foresight that this simple and severe art of tempera demands. After three years of the practice she is still making experiments. She believes herself to have attained but the first degrees of an art destined to greatness. Great things and large things are to be looked for as a result of this recovery. Fine and vigorous is the hand, single is the vision, and pure is the intellect that have shown the way to an art about to live again. Mrs. Stokes is a painter of keen apprehension in simple things. No man or woman be ginning the world at the time of the re-arising of art in Europe, when Romance began, could have a fresher spirit than hers, a clearer heart, or sincerer sympathies. It needs her noble simplicity to begin the reaction against modern contempt for feeling and thought in art. That contempt itself doubtless had its use as a protest against the sentimentality of the middle of the nineteenth century; but if so, its purpose is more than fulfilled, and the correction is becoming tedious. The century has corrected and bantered itself sufficiently. Let the dead bury their dead. We need no longer to hear hard things said about the anecdote and its literary interest; the suburbs themselves have long been instructed that the anecdote and the literary interest are all wrong, and no one at Clapham would dare to admire a picture because it tells a story. Let the critic, then, consider his work more than done on this point, and let him allow the twentieth century to give back to painting all visible things, emotion that has expression, and histories that make pictorial signs and bear symbols clear to the eye. Mrs. Stokes has never deprived her pictures of these interests, but has used them sweetly in the scheme of direct and frank decoration. Nay, if the beauty of her composition may be made more intelligible by a legend, the legend is added to the decoration of the frame. No one who has seen the picture which shows the mother's vision of her little daughter in Paradise carrying the vessel full of tears, will wish the legend away; but to the greater number of these paintings on gesso of peasant women and children there is nothing to add: they are simple pictures of the wayside figures of the Dutch or German village, in their own nature and aspect. Their round faces, their capped heads, their starched dresses are painted by her with a peculiarly pure brilliance, a daylight radiance of tone that does not seem to owe its clarity and height to any relative depths or darkness. It is – doubtless thanks to gesso and a simple pictorial vision – a positive brightness like that of a white day when we look with the light and meet no shadows. Mrs. Stokes has compassed this brightness with no small art, finding no slight difficulty in keeping the high tone high enough to look brilliant in London. Painted abroad, pictures in tempera as well as in oils seem to sink in the low light. On one detail of her later work – the use of positive gold instead of the representation of the effect of gold according to the convention of painting – there must be opposed opinions. Not so in regard to the delicacy, the bloom, the unhindered colour and unhampered tone, the unclogged expression of the work she has done in her own appropriate medium.

20

MARIANNE STOKES, *CANDLEMAS DAY*, 1901

Tempera on wood, 416 × 340 mm, Tate.
Presented by the Trustees of the Chantrey Bequest, 1977

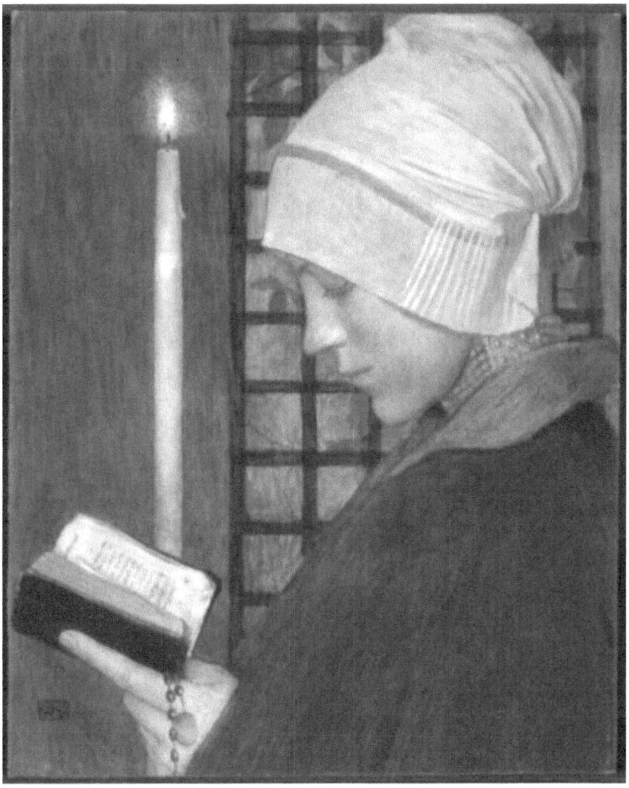

DOI: 10.4324/9781315400266-25

1.4

Conservation

DOI: 10.4324/9781315400266-26

1.4 Conservation

The sources selected here explore various nineteenth-century aspects of the preservation of the physical properties of paintings.

Restoration – and controversies over restoration – were not new in the Victorian period, but they occurred on a new scale and as a matter of public interest. From 1846 to 1853, the National Gallery was embroiled in a controversy over the cleaning and restoration of its old master paintings. As one of the new national museums founded in the nineteenth century (opening in 1824), the controversy at the National Gallery was a matter of public concern, coming under parliamentary scrutiny in a select committee of 1853. This committee interviewed artists, curators, restorers and collectors and produced a nearly 1,000-page report full of conflicting opinions.[1] It created a public platform for discussions about the materials of art, and reveals much about contemporary understandings of the significance of these materials to the making and preservation of artworks. The excerpts printed here are from a collection of essays written in the 1850s by Henry Merritt, a restorer and art critic, in which he virulently defends the role of the restorer. As Merritt sets out, restorers require an intense understanding of materials and their application, artistic techniques, styles and colour preferences. He conceives of restorers as servants, lacking in ego and sacrificing their own artistic expression not just to preserve but to reanimate the art of the past.[2]

Nineteenth-century London changed the material properties of old master paintings exhibited in the National Gallery: the appalling pollution in Trafalgar Square (from steam engines working the fountains, as well as gasworks and factories), combined with the coat of 'gallery varnish' regularly applied to paintings on their arrival, substantially darkened them. It was not, however, only old master paintings that were subject to discussions regarding preservation. The rapid disintegration of some materials and techniques introduced in the eighteenth and early nineteenth centuries was a subject of considerable debate. Contemporaries seem to have believed that there was something particular in the materials used in 'English painting' which led to premature signs of disintegration. Richard and Samuel Redgrave's 1866 history of English painting, for example, devotes an entire chapter to preservation, which is partially reprinted here.[3] Like Hunt's speech in the preceding 'Artists' materials' section, they attribute the problems to a lack of artistic understanding of materials. John Ruskin, well-known for his writings opposing the restoration of buildings in *The Lamp of Memory*, wrote about the rapid deterioration of J. M. W. Turner's paintings in 1846 due to poor technique and materials.[4] In the 1890s, J. A. M. Whistler, keenly concerned with the surfaces of his paintings, wrote and collaborated with his chosen restorer, seeking to combat the effects of time and atmosphere on his work.[5]

In the later nineteenth century, as museums and galleries opened across Britain and around the world – and most especially as colonial museums began explicitly purchasing British art – the long-distance transportation of paintings became an ever more pressing concern. Richard and Samuel Redgrave emphasise the damage done to paintings by changing nineteenth-century display conditions, in particular the circulation of paintings to regional exhibitions. Paintings were usually packed in travelling frames and crates, but works that were not painted on canvas, or that were particularly large, could pose additional problems. When the National Gallery of Victoria in Melbourne commissioned and purchased John Herbert's enormous painting (over 6 m × 3 m) *Moses Delivering the Tablets of the Law* (c. 1858–1877), which was painted on paper and then glued to canvas, Herbert designed his own mode of packing and sent the instructions reprinted here for unpacking the canvas in Melbourne. These painstaking instructions further support Jennifer Roberts' contention that paying attention to the mobility of artworks draws fresh attention to their material properties.[6] On its three-month journey from London to Melbourne, the painting was accompanied by a diverse cargo; the imports noted in Melbourne newspaper *The Age* are reprinted here to give a sense of the ways in which paintings became cargo almost indistinguishable from bundles of steel. This journey fundamentally changed the painting; Nancy Langham Hooper suggests that heat in the ship's hold may have damaged the painting, and it had to be restored before going on display in Melbourne.[7]

Notes

1 This controversy is discussed by J. Anderson, 'The First Cleaning Controversy at the National Gallery, 1846–1853', in David Bomford and Mark Leonard (eds), *Issues in the Conservation of Paintings* (Los Angeles: Getty Publications, 2004), pp. 441–453. See also Jacob Simon, 'Restoration practice in museums and galleries in Britain in the nineteenth century', in Nicola Costaras et al (eds), *A Changing Art: Nineteenth-Century Painting Practice and Conservation* (London: Archetype, 2017), pp. 5–13.

2 On Merritt, the National Gallery controversy, and the relationship between restoration and faking, see A. Briefel, *The Deceivers. Art Forgery and Identity in the nineteenth century* (Ithaca and London: Cornell University Press, 2006).

3 For detailed analysis of this source, see Julie F. Codell, 'Righting the Victorian Artist: The Redgraves' "A Century of Painters of the English School" and the Serialization of Art History', *Oxford Art Journal*, 23:2 (2000), pp. 95–119.

4 John Ruskin, 'On Turner's Recent Works' (1846), in E.T. Cook and Alexander Wedderburn (eds), *The Works of John Ruskin* (London: George Allen, 1903), vol. 3, pp. 249–50.

5 These letters are reprinted – together with a wide range of other relevant sources on the conservation of paintings – in Bomford and Leonard (eds), *Issues in the Conservation of Paintings*, pp. 28–9.

6 Jennifer Roberts, *Transporting Visions. The Movement of Images in Early America* (Berkeley: University of California Press, 2014), p. 8.

7 Nancy Langham Hooper, 'Unrolled: John Rogers Herbert and the monumental Moses in the National Gallery of Victoria', *Art Journal of the National Gallery of Victoria*, 54 (2016) https://www.ngv.vic.gov.au/journal_edition/edition-54/ [accessed 15 June 2021].

21

HENRY MERRITT, *ART CRITICISM AND ROMANCE*

Vol. 1 (London: C. Keegan Paul & Co., 1879), pp. 80, 133–134

[p. 80] In the spring of 1854, on the abatement of the controversy on picture restoration, the author wrote the following protest against the unphilosophical spirit in which the controversy had been conducted.

If the apparent verdict of the public opinion is to be credited, the picture restorers' art is abolished in England. The restorers are in danger of being driven from our public galleries. These unostentatious conservers of the works of genius are described as 'picture rats'; their studies are styled 'shambles'; their careful and patient manipulations 'systematic and wanton destructiveness.' In these controversies the non-restorationists always assume that cleaning pictures means no less than scrubbing out the pictures themselves – repairing small blemishes they regard merely as a pretext for repainting entire works; lining, battening, cradling, and transferring have received no sort of recognition. But will not this judgment suffer reversal when the public shall become practically informed upon it?

[. . .]

[p. 133]

The restorer, like the physician, should have no bias, it is for him to trace with untiring industry, and unerring precision, the many fine distinctions in each particular work he may have to treat. He ought to comprehend, not only the meaning, and spirit of each work, but be able to trace, bit by bit, with microscopic exactness, the means and the method which the artist employed to accomplish it. It is not enough for the restorer to know the results, he must also penetrate their causes – that the effects may not suffer. It would seem that nothing less than a master mind could achieve the successful treatment of a master work, but it comes out in the end, that a restorer of inferior power, profiting by the creations of the artist, may be able to appreciate their excellences though unable to produce them . . . In a word, the restorer has wholly to devote himself to the study of pictures, until he has made himself as familiar with the productions of many pencils as the ambitious painter does with a few select examples.

DOI: 10.4324/9781315400266-27

It is quite possible to conceive an accomplished restorer, fulfilling the high functions of *conserver* to the arts, content in that capacity, and devoting all his energies, with frank good will and hearty self-respect, to the preservation of the works of other – willing to forgo any reputation he might himself achieve as a painter for the general good of art – content to be the servant and the friend of painters, not their rival. He should be favourable to the growth and exchange of congenial sympathies, and he might well become an adviser to them in some minor practical difficulties often experienced by creative genius. The painter not unfrequently works in ignorance of the mechanical department of his art. Through the neglect of what he is too apt to think unworthy of his attention, the rationale of his materials and their uses, he often labours in vain, and grasps at last but that transient reputation which only lives, like the actor's and the musician's in the breath of memory, and by the tongue of report.'

22

RICHARD REDGRAVE AND SAMUEL REDGRAVE, *A CENTURY OF PAINTERS OF THE ENGLISH SCHOOL; WITH CRITICAL NOTICES OF THEIR WORKS, AND AN ACCOUNT OF THE PROGRESS OF ART IN ENGLAND*

(London: Smith, Elder and Co., 1866), Vol. 2, selections from pp. 588–609

It has been said that "pictures have strong constitutions," which, if true, is a wonder, considering the evils they derive from their parent the painter, who indifferently employs in their production bad materials, bad vehicles, and bad execution; clothes them in bad varnishes, and gives them over to the care or carelessness of guardians or keepers, without one word of advice as to their treatment: perhaps even without the knowledge to give it. Passing out of the hands of the painter, what perils beset the after-existence of his works; how indifferently are they sheltered and preserved! Exposed to every variety of light and temperature; to the careless broom of the housemaid, to smoke, and dust, and gas; as premature old age and decay come upon them from all these causes, shrivelling their skins and drying up their juices, quack renovators and conceited restorers are called in, who make it a boast that ignorance of the first principles of art fits them especially for their office, and that from their hands a picture comes forth "better than new." In a work like this, it will not surely be out of place, and most probably will be acceptable, if we point out some of these sources of evil, examine how they arise, show how they may be avoided, and how they may be alleviated, if they cannot be wholly cured.

First, as to bad materials. The painter of the last century took very little thought for the immortality of his own progeny, and from its birth trusted its well-being more to chance than to care. The old painters, as we have already described, would seem always to have prepared their own panels or canvases; that is to say, their preparation was carried on by pupils or apprentices under the painter's eye, and according to recipes handed down from age to age. [. . .]

DOI: 10.4324/9781315400266-28

But when the old art died out in Lely and Kneller, and a British school arose, it deserted the "traditions of the elders," when it repudiated their works; and our great painters began to seek new pigments, new vehicles, and new methods of using them. Up to the time of Kneller, the old practice had prevailed; but when he came to this country, he brought with him a servant whose employment was to prepare all the colours and materials for his work. Northcote tells us this, and adds that Kneller afterwards set him up in business as a colour maker for artists, and that from this man's success – he being the first that kept a colour-shop in London – arose the trade of artists' colourman. Henceforward, the preparation of panels and canvases, and the grounds that cover them, the washing, grinding, and tempering of colours, – the oils and varnishes to use as vehicles, or to protect the surface of the finished work, – passed out of the hand of the painter into that of the colourman, and the former blindly used what the latter had prepared. This is a state of things to be deplored for many reasons; amongst others, that the artist is now too often ignorant of the commonest facts relating to the pigments and vehicles he uses, and so long as they are brilliant in themselves, dry rapidly, and mix well in tints with other pigments, makes little inquiry into their durability or permanency, and uses indifferently those which have received the sanction of the past, with those yet untested, because newly brought into use and notice.

Sir Joshua Beynolds was undesignedly the author of much of this mischief; deeply interested, as we have already seen, in ascertaining the methods of the great masters of colouring, he was continually seeking new and more brilliant pigments, to enable him to rival theirs; new vehicles to give his pigments increased body; using not only the various siccative oils and resinous varnishes, simple and compounded; but the essential oils, wax, and asphaltum, were also pressed into his service, to give brilliancy, impasto, depth, or richness. Of course many of his pictures at the time of their production astonished his brother artists by their surpassing force and beauty of colour, and of course the host of admirers hastened to become imitators, and were prompt to follow his practice. The artists' colourman was called on to supply the demand for orpiment and carmine, for vegetable yellows and pitchy browns; and after a while these fugitive pigments, included with others in his lists, became accepted as of the same value as those sanctioned by use for centuries.

The subject of grounds is of the greatest importance to the future of the picture. Many of our finest works are suffering from want of due care in their preparation. If on canvas, it is essential that the ground, though firm and hard, should have due toughness and flexibility; to which end it should be thin, and have sufficient oil iu its composition, and, whether on canvas or panel, just such an amount of absorbency as will admit of the proper union of the picture with it. If too absorbent, it is troublesome to the painter, and apt to make the picture heavy in the darks, while it prevents, in a degree, the use of the ground as a source of illumination to pigments used over it transparently. If too hard and impervious, the picture is apt to divide from it and blister off. This is often the case with Turner's pictures. "The Regatta at Cowes," and the "Fishing Boats at Yarmouth," in the Sheepshanks' collection, have both a strong tendency to rise from the ground; as have also many other of his works, such as "Pope's Villa at Twickenham," the "Mercury and Herse," "The Beach at Hastings," besides many in the national collection, all which require great care on this account. The fine landscape by Callcott, "Southampton Water," the property of Mr. Gibbs, has suffered largely, and is likely to suffer from this cause; indeed it is a source of evil to many other English paintings of the period. Pictures thus endangered should, if the size permits, be covered with glass in front, and, at any rate, lined behind with painted cloth, to render them impervious to the damp; and they should be kept away from the wall against which they are hung by small blocks of cork at the four corners. [. . .]

But the works of Reynolds and of his followers, and indeed almost all the pictures of the English school up to the end of the first thirty-five years of the present century, have suffered more from the use of improper pigments than from bad grounds; amongst these the worst is bitumen in all its varied forms of asphaltum, mummy, bitumen, &c. These pitchy colours never thoroughly harden; they are readily affected by heat and change of temperature, and as they remain soft beneath the surface, any harder dryer imposed over them, either as a vehicle for the last glazings of the picture, or as a securing varnish, is certain to draw the work together, and to result in deep separation of the parts. Reynolds used this pigment mostly in the darks, for which its luminous richness so well adapts it: indeed its place can hardly be supplied by any known brown; from this cause many of the pictures of our greatest portrait painter have failed terribly in the darks, and every fresh varnishing increases the evil. It is a misfortune to pictures painted with preparations of bitumen, that the evil does not always display itself at once: indeed, under favourable circumstances, they will remain very many years without disruption; but a change in hanging, or in the temperature of the room or gallery, an exposure to the sun's rays, and above all varnishing, will, though heretofore free from harm, crack them in a few weeks.

The works of some of the contemporaries (as Wright of Derby), as well as those of the pupils and followers of Sir Joshua, have suffered from the like cause, and many of the pictures of Northcote, Opie, and Fuseli have, as to their finer qualities, perished from the use of asphaltum.

[. . .]

Such are a few hints at the causes of the decay but too visible in many of our English pictures: and it must be remembered that pictures, so sickly from their birth, require continuous nursing and careful attention to preserve them in any sort of sound condition; yet it too often happens that when once arranged on the walls, either very little further attention is paid to them, or the care and superintendence are of the worst kind. When the pictures were received for the Paris International Exhibition of 1855, and our own of 1862, it was curious to note the condition of such valuable property. Some works had evidently never had any cleansing of their surface since the time they were painted, although they had hung during the whole period of their existence in the heart of this or other smoky towns. The tops of the frames of some and the lower interstices between the canvas and stretcher of others were the harbourage of thick layers of dirt; while the curiosities in the shape of wedges, nails, screws and filth of all kinds that were gathered between the stretcher and the canvas would have served to furnish a little museum. In many respects the loan of works formed a fortunate epoch in their condition; as while deposited in these exhibitions they were most carefully looked after and attended to, and the dust of years removed. Moreover, as to some, the possessors on their return – for once while in their possession – minutely looked them over; and if they laid the evils that had been progressing for so many years to those who had had them temporarily in charge, they were at least awakened to the sense of their decay, and likely to take better measures to preserve them in future.

[. . .]

Almost as much mischief arises from ignorant care as from want of care. The mere dusting of pictures is a work requiring some judgment; it should be done with the softest of feather brushes, and even these are dangerous when the picture has a tendency to scale or blister. Pictures are often carelessly wiped, many persons believing that a silk handkerchief can do no harm; but a glance at any old collection, and even at some of our own public ones, will show how this has been abused: in many pictures, scales have been torn off, the canvases are cracked all round the edges, the corner pieces and the bars of the stretcher marked on the surface, by undue pressure of the hand of the careless operator as he polishes them; at times rubbing even the paint away, but at least rubbing in the dust rather than removing it. [. . .]

Ill-ventilated rooms are another source of mischief to works of art. Hundreds of fine pictures are hung in close rooms lighted with numerous candles or with gas, yet without the slightest means of ventilation. It was shown in the careful report on this subject by Professors Faraday, Hoffman, and Tyndal, that the proceeds from the combustion of coal gas, unless wholly removed from the apartment, are most deleterious to pictures; but that gas unburnt was almost innocuous, and its combustion might be made most useful in promoting an active ventilation sufficient to remove all the resulting evils; and with them, those almost equally deleterious excretions arising in crowded rooms, from condensed breath, and an unchanged atmosphere. While there are those who leave their pictures from year to year untouched and unnoticed, there are others who are continually incrusting them with coats of varnish. Under the dust or dirt of years, the picture may remain intact, and be brought, simply by careful washing, to its first purity and freshness; but those who cover their pictures with numerous coats of varnish, either lock up numerous coats of dirt also, or, if the varnish is continually removed for new applications, remove with it the last tender and most precious finishings of the painter. And here let us again add our warning, at least in respect to British pictures, against the new invention of solving the coats of varnish on a picture, and letting them subside into a new surface. Mastic varnish enters so largely into the vehicle with which such pictures are painted, that under this treatment varnish and pigment may be found floating into one common mass.

It only remains under this head to remark upon a few of the avoidable dangers to which pictures are liable on their occasional removal from place to place. And first as to marking pictures. A practice, but too common, has been to paste paper labels on the back of the canvas or panel indifferently. In the latter case, it is harmless; in the former, the moisture of the paste shrinks the spot of canvas to which it is applied, and the result is a permanent lump on the surface. Again, in passing through the hands of upholsterers or packers, pictures are often numbered or marked with chalk on the back of the canvas – a still more dangerous practice – for in the hurry of so marking them, a little extra pressure cracks the picture, which as it ages, takes that singular form of crack so like a caterpillar with many legs, becoming visible as dirt or varnish gradually fills the lines. On one occasion we saw a large number of works which had been just returned to a London agent from a provincial Exhibition, all so marked on the back of the canvas by the local authorities. Again, blows or pressure from behind should be scrupulously guarded against: the projecting corners of frames, for instance, dragged against the canvas, will result in the crack above described; and a thrust from any bluntly pointed object – from the finger or the shoulder in carrying – will produce the circular crack so often seen in old pictures, and which, from its regular web-like appearance, Turner used to express his belief was occasioned by an insect.

Great care also should be taken not to over-drive the wedges of the stretching frames, more especially when the pictures are liable to any sudden alternations of damp and dryness. Any one who has noted the great shrinkage that takes place on damping the fibres of a stretched string or cord, will be aware that some play must be allowed for these alternations, or the canvas will be torn from the stretcher, and the surface of the picture be broken up into fine hair cracks. These variations of temperature are much guarded against by lining the back of the picture with painted cloth, as already advocated.

Other injuries arise to pictures from careless or improper packing. One of the commonest errors, and certainly one of the most dangerous, is the practice of screwing the picture to the top or bottom of the case; or, when two pictures are in the same case, screwing one to the top, the other to the bottom: this should never be done; they should be slung on battens within the case. Two battens, crossing the back of the picture, should be carefully secured by screws to the most solid part of the back of each frame, the screws being of sufficient length and depth of cut, to allow of the picture hanging beneath the batten without fear of its weight drawing the screws. The ends of these battens, projecting somewhat beyond the frame or frames, should drop, and be carefully secured, into notched racks or ledges, well fastened to the sides of the case; so that the picture should be slung within it, free everywhere but at the end of the battens. Pictures thus packed are partly on springs, and any shock on the outer case is distributed and dispersed without injury. If the case is large and deep enough, a number of pictures may be packed within it in the same manner, merely by placing the racks or notched ledges at proper intervals to keep the pictures well apart.

Before placing the battens across the frames, the wedges should be looked to and slightly tightened, and what is of still more importance, the picture properly nailed into its frame, otherwise the picture may get loose, although the frame remains secure, and rub itself to pieces with the motion in carriage. So carelessly in this respect are pictures sent away by their owners that valuable works are often received at public exhibitions quite disengaged from their fastenings. Another danger to which pictures are exposed in travelling arises from the bad construction of the frames; the flat or inner portion being mostly a separate piece, merely bradded in, or slightly secured by glued wood blocks. Such a construction, although sufficiently strong while the picture hangs on the wall, is most dangerous when it travels horizontally, exposed to the jolting of the railroad; when even if the picture is carefully fastened into the flat, the two break away from the other part of the frame; or when the picture is very heavy – as for instance a lined picture, or a picture on panel – the thin rebate of the flat gives way, and the picture falls through, with the splintered remnants to increase the mischief. The best precaution is, in all such cases, to screw pieces across the back angles of the frame, and to screw the stretcher of the picture to them, which removes the pressure entirely from the flat; but this will not do when the picture is on panel.

Thus a few of the most obvious sources of injury, and of the causes which lead to the premature decay of pictures have been slightly glanced at; it only remains to allude to the doings of those who undertake, qualified or unqualified, to repair their injuries, to renovate their fading glories, and even to restore them to their first freshness and brightness.

Wrong, indeed, would it be to throw discredit on all who practise the restorer's art. Some few there are who are duly qualified; but for our own part we would put up with many blemishes ere we trusted a work we loved out of our own hands. For as in the healing art there are quacks and nostrum-mongers, and shallow or incompetent practitioners; who are always the boldest in their pretensions, and the most boastful of the universality and infallibility of their cures; so it is with the renovators of pictures; and many a one whose qualifications consist only in the reckless impudence with which he dares to use the spirit or the alkali to scour of dirt and art together, places a half-washed portrait in the window, and dubs himself a restorer. Some of these boast that their very ignorance of drawing is one of their best qualifications, since they must of necessity follow the leadings of the painter whose work is under their hands; which is about as logical as it would be to say that we are more fully qualified to decipher a half obliterated inscription by ignorance of the language in which it is written.

[. . .]

There can be no doubt that pictures were, and are, constantly over-toned as well as over-cleaned, and that pictures in our national collections have, in past days, been so treated; but, in view of the terrors of that body of experts the House of Commons, who would venture to bring them back to what the painter thought they ought to be, or he himself would have toned them? To remove such additions would raise up a storm of virtuous indignation that few would be willing to face. This, it is true, is not to be wondered at, in face of the wholesale scrubbings that have taken place abroad, as many even of the works in the Louvre testify; whilst at Dresden, the world-famous Correggios, instead of the delicate, refined, yet luminous glazings which characterize the master's works when in a genuine state, have become solid, dry, and insipid under the hands of the restorer, who has gained fame and reputation at the expense of the poor painter; born, it would seem, only that Palmaroli might be glorified in him. At Rotterdam also the true Dutch spirit of cleanliness has reduced some of the pictures in the public collection to the mere panel.

As individuals, however, will require medical and surgical aid, so occasionally must pictures, whether from accident or premature decay; it may be difficult in an age of quacks to choose a skilled physician, and it is an equally anxious affair to have to make choice of a good restorer. Enough has been said to induce us not to resort to him on slight occasions. On more grave ones, seek out the man of the highest reputation; him, moreover, who promises the least, who has a wholesome dread of doing too much, and the strongest objection to doing anything at all. If the canvas want lining, or the panel parqueting, have it done in the best manner and by the best craftsman; but do not allow the work to be varnished, so that you can see your face in it as in a looking-glass.

23

INSTRUCTIONS FROM JOHN HERBERT FOR UNPACKING AND DISPLAYING THE PAINTING *THE DESCENT OF MOSES*

Letter, 1878, Public Records Office of Victoria, 4363/p/unit 9

The picture was taken from the wall, then placed face downwards on blankets, which covered perfectly the floor to receive it, it was then raised by small blocks at the corners, and in the sides of the frames the tacks which fastened the canvas to the stretcher taken out, and the stretcher lifted from it, the large roller was then brought to one end and that end tacked to cylinder.

Sheets of blotting paper on the surface of picture as it rolls onward, so that rolling onwards the whole surface is at last covered, then sheets of brown paper, and at last bound round with strips of calico.

Now the two great things to be careful of are, first, lifting canvas when unattached from the stretcher, for the weight is immense. There should be no attempt to do this for fear of chinking. – the other thing to guard against is in the unrolling, not the least attempt should be made to separate the blotting paper from the picture, it is almost sure to stick a little, but not the slighted harm need arise from that.

Now when the roll is lifted from the case by the straps of calico, it should be placed again on blankets, unrolled upon them, when the brown paper falls from it as it rolls on, should be gathered quite away; then leaving the picture still to be unrolled, place the stretcher on the ground, of course with all the bevelled edges uppermost. Now as it would be dangerous to put the weight of the roll on any part of the stretcher, the safe way will be to round the spindle of deal so that it will turn while the picture is raised a few inches from the end of the frame thus then three people, one at each edge of the canvas, one in the middle, will bring it downwards, and thus on, while a very careful person, will with a damped sponge, damp the blotting paper, and never to pull at it, every bit will then come off, and he conveniently gets at it to the other end, a dozen tacks then on each side before it is raised a little from the floor, so that it will be impossible that it should in the least bag, or bend while rearing it in order to strain it well on the frame. Being told that there is a damp season in Melbourne, I had for that reason, as well for extra precaution

DOI: 10.4324/9781315400266-29

against sources of injury, the whole of the back prepared to resist damp or decay, if it slackens in damp weather, wedging out will keep it right.

Now for the perfect placing of the picture. – It should be hung not more than four feet from the ground, nor nearer than two feet six inches. It is absolutely painted for a light similar to the one in the Palace of Westminster thus if hung in any other light than this the picture will of course be impaired in its force.

On second thoughts the bottom of the frame should be eighteen inches from the floor, of course if the spectator could see the picture with his eye level with my horizon the whole scene becomes enormously more perfect as it is my point of view.

It should be seen without conflicting objects, that is to say should be alone, spots in the way of pictures up its sides, or under it, would in a word be ruin.

24

ILLUSTRATED INSTRUCTIONS FROM JOHN HERBERT FOR UNPACKING AND DISPLAYING THE PAINTING *THE DESCENT OF MOSES*

Letter, 1878, Public Records Office of Victoria, 4363/p/unit 9

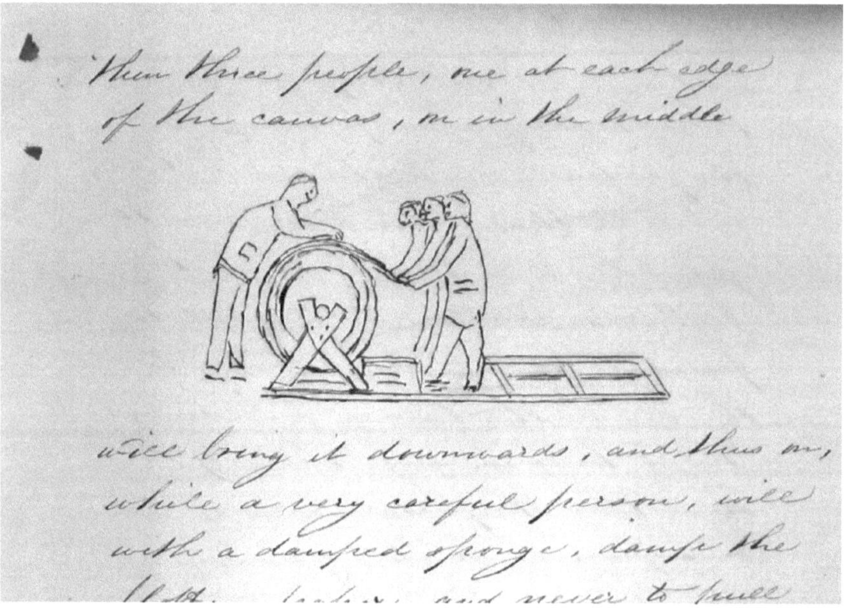

Then three people, one at each edge of the canvas, one in the middle

will bring it downwards, and thus on, while a very careful person, will with a damped sponge, damp the

... and never to pull

DOI: 10.4324/9781315400266-30

25

'SHIPPING. HOBSON'S BAY'

Age, 16 February 1878, p. 4

Key to abbreviations:

Bdl	bundle
Bl	bale
Brl	barrel
Cs	case
Ck	cask
Kg	keg
Pkg	package
Plt	pallette
Tnk	trunk

IMPORTS. – FEBRUARY 15. Hoghton Tower, from London: 55 pkgs marble, 25 csk ink, 25 cs composition; 28 brls tar and pitch, 50 cks mineral water, 8 cs pictures, 6 cks tumblers, 224 girder plates, 5 carboys, 2 qr-cks vinegar, 6 pkgs ship chandlery, 14 cs iron nuts, 20 kgs saltpetre, 19 cs bottles, 139 brls, 301 cs currants, 36 axels [. . .], 40 cs metal, 73 pkgs nails, 15 cs champagne, 85 cs claret, 1870 bdls hoops, 120 axle arms [. . .], 56 bdles tubes, 1800 bxes candles, 125 pkgs herrings, 284 pkgs fish, 200 cs schnapps, 1650 cs geneva, 300 cs bottled beer, 10 cks acetic acid, 40 qr-cks 98 cs wine [. . .], 180 qr-cks 300 cs brandy, 11 tnks 35 pkts hops, 50 cs vestas, 3 tnks fruit, 344 cks 2 tnks 1319 cs and pkgs oilmen's stores, 13s, 43 tanks 20 cks seed, 98 tnks malt, 405 pkgs. drugs, 2808 pkgs oils and paints, 2388 brs 1399 bdls 129 plts iron, 1569 rails, 48 cks fuse, 66 cks shot, 100 bdls wire, 574 pkgs. rails, 963 bxs tin plates, 34 pcs and pkgs machinery, 457 cs galvanised iron, 102 pkgs hard-ware, 49 bls woolpacks, 1579 pkgs softgoods, 105 bales paper, 117 pkgs stationery, 74 pkgs books, 66 pkgs printing materials, 23 pkgs earthenware, 260 pkgs glass, 19 pkgs furniture, 45 cs pianos, music, &c.; 198 pkgs fancy goods, 237 pkgs general merchandise.

DOI: 10.4324/9781315400266-31

PART 2

Sculpture

2.1

Materials and making

DOI: 10.4324/9781315400266-33

2.1 Materials and making

Anna Jameson's 1854 meditation on sculpture as both 'a thought and a thing' brilliantly introduces this section.[1] Here, primary sources explore the relationship between materials and making in sculpture. While of course materials are fundamental to the appearance of all art forms, their physical properties are perhaps most obvious in sculpture. Jameson was writing a primer on sculpture for the new mass audiences of viewers attending the Crystal Palace at Sydenham, and it is striking how prominently this introductory guide features materials, as well as the physical properties of size and setting. Jameson is vague, however, about the actual materials used in sculpture, and traces a continuation between the materials 'in use in ancient times' and the 1850s, primarily marble and to a lesser extent bronze.[2]

Critic Edmund Gosse's review of the Royal Academy in 1890 gives a sense of the dramatic reappearance of bronze at the end of the nineteenth century, which he would go on to label 'The New Sculpture'.[3] By the end of the nineteenth century, a much wider range of materials were being used in sculpture, and often in the same artwork. Fred Miller's 1897 article on George Frampton, reprinted here, offers a prime example. But even a sculpture that appeared to be made of one material alone (e.g. a bronze or marble sculpture) was the product of numerous different materials and processes, as the extracts from sculptor Edwin Roscoe Mullins' *Primer of Sculpture* explain. Mullins emphasises that sculptors need to be continuously thinking about the 'final materials' in which their sculpture will be produced when making initial maquettes in clay or plaster, as the different material properties of each stage dictate the possibilities of the 'final' sculptural form.[4] Marion Spielmann's 1901 tome on *British Sculpture and Sculptors of Today* – aimed more at viewers and patrons of sculpture than at sculptors – likewise emphasises the importance of considering the different properties of materials and their suitability for particular subject matters.

Spielmann considers marble, bronze, plaster and clay, entirely omitting the more industrial material of cast iron, which had been championed in design-reforming circles at mid-century as a particularly national medium: 'Owing to the variety of coal-fields, abundance of the mineral, and improved modes of smelting, England is distinguished above other nations for the exuberance and cheapness of her supply of iron', noted the Great Exhibition Jury reporting on 'Iron and Steel Manufactures' in 1851.[5] The fact that 'iron has been conquered by artistic skill' was proudly remarked upon by the *Birmingham Daily Post* article reviewing regional contributions to the 1862 International Exhibition; yet these industrial associations were precisely why materials like cast iron were so roundly ignored by Spielmann.[6] The 'thing'-iness of sculpture, upon which Jameson had remarked, brought its materials into other debates. What sort of labour was sculpting: artistic or manual? And what were the implications for the status of the sculptor? Different materials involved, apparently, different sorts of labour; Mullins holds that marble carving is more than 'a mere mechanical process . . . it is an art by itself', but the processes of bronze casting were 'not matters of art . . . but rather of science and mechanism'.[7] The *Illustrated London News* account of bronze casting, however, noted the 'great skill' required by founders and provided its non-specialist audience with a detailed account of the drama of bronze casting.[8] The divisions between artistic and manual labour are often understood to have been reconceptualised by the later nineteenth-century Arts and Crafts Movement.[9] Indeed, such an attempt to dissolve these distinctions is evident in Miller's article on George Frampton, which opens by declaring him to be 'an all-round craftsman' who 'prefers to be known as an art worker, and not by the more restricted title of sculptor'.[10] However, the making of sculpture, and its inherent reproducibility, had arguably *always* challenged this division.[11]

Sculptural divisions of labour were also an explicitly gendered discourse. Writing in 1890, Mullins suggested that the 'slighter physique' of women meant that work in marble was more challenging, and he advises that they 'get their marble work done for them'. Importantly, however, he notes that 'in this matter they will not be found to be exceptional; as sculptors frequently, from press of work or disinclination for the hard manual labour, leave this part of the work to their assistants'.[12] This is significant, firstly in its casual acknowledgement of the very existence of female sculptors in marble. Perhaps more importantly, Mullins does not present the use of assistants as something specifically feminine or a source of particular shame. Yet, matters were rather different in 1862, when the American sculptor Harriet Hosmer exhibited her 208-cm-high *Zenobia* at the International Exhibition in London. Hosmer brought a libel suit against two magazines, the *Art Journal* and the *Queen*, which had suggested that the sculpture was not her own work but that of her studio.[13] Hosmer's article in the *Atlantic Monthly* from 1864 is reprinted here in full. It offers a useful overview of the processes of marble carving at mid-century, which Hosmer set out in order to demonstrate that she was not unusual in working with assistants. The photograph of Hosmer standing in the midst of around two dozen Italian workmen operates in a similar manner. The *Atlantic Monthly* article provides Hosmer's view of male and female sculptors' parity, while reinforcing class structures; she is quite clear that the position of 'workmen' in the studio is 'a subordinate one'.[14]

Commentators were not just concerned with the social class associations and fears of 'fine art' appearing like 'manual labour', as the extract from Matthew Digby Wyatt's 1870 Slade Lectures at Cambridge University suggest. Wyatt's overview of the use of different materials in sculpture rapidly descends into Eurocentric cultural stereotypes and connects artistic practices to particular 'races'.[15] The social meanings of materials are explored in much more detail in the following section, but Wyatt's argument that race determines the selection of materials for sculpture makes his a significant text for this introductory section examining Victorian understandings of the relationship between making and materials in sculpture.

Notes

1 Anna Jameson, *A Handbook to the Courts of Modern Sculpture* (London: Bradbury and Evans, 1854), p. 4.
2 Ibid. By 'ancient times' Jameson seems to be referring to ancient Greece and Rome, rather than ancient Egyptian uses of granite in sculpture. For a more recent overview, see M. Trusted (ed.) *The Making of Sculpture: The Materials and Techniques of European Sculpture* (London: V&A Publications, 2007).
3 See Edmund Gosse, *The Place of Sculpture in Daily Life*, ed. Martina Droth (Chicago: Soberscove Press, 2016).
4 Edwin Roscoe Mullins, *A Primer of Sculpture* (London: Cassell and Co., 1890) p. 62.
5 *Reports by the Juries on the Subjects in the thirty classes into which the exhibition was divided. Presentation Copy* (London: William Clowes and Sons, 1852), p. 500.
6 'The International Exhibition', *Birmingham Daily Post,* 20 June 1862, p. 2.
7 Mullins, *Primer of Sculpture*, p. 70; p. 74.
8 'Large Bronze Castings', *Illustrated London News*, 16 April 1881, p. 374.
9 On the limitations of conceptualising this as a coherent 'movement', see Imogen Hart, *Arts and Crafts Objects* (Manchester: Manchester University Press, 2010).
10 Fred Miller, 'George Frampton, A. R. A., Art Worker', *Art Journal* (November 1897), p. 321.
11 See Martina Droth, 'The Ethics of Making: Craft and English Sculptural Aesthetics c.1851–1900', *Journal of Design History*, 17:3 (2004), pp. 221–235. On Victorian engagements with the ambiguous status of sculptors in classical antiquity, see Kate Nichols, *Greece and Rome at the Crystal Palace. Classical Sculpture and Modern Britain, 1854–1936* (Oxford: Oxford University Press, 2015), pp. 136–8.
12 Mullins, *Primer of Sculpture*, p. 70.
13 Similar charges were also levelled against the sculptor Richard Belt in 1882, but in Hosmer's case, this was an explicitly gendered accusation. See Hilary Fraser, 'Women and the Modelling of Victorian Sculptural Discourse', *Visual Resources*, 33:1–2 (2017), pp. 74–93.
14 Harriet Hosmer, 'The Process of Sculpture', *Atlantic Monthly* (December 1864), p. 735.
15 M. D. Wyatt, *Fine Art. A Sketch of its History, Theory, Practice, and application to Industry. Being a Course of Lectures Delivered at Cambridge in 1870* (London: Macmillan and Co., 1870), p. 180.

26

ANNA JAMESON, *A HANDBOOK TO THE COURTS OF MODERN SCULPTURE*

(London: Bradbury and Evans, 1854), pp. 3–5

THE following Catalogue of the works of art assembled in the Courts of Modern Sculpture, being intended for the public at large, has been made as clear and as comprehensive as was possible within the prescribed limits of space and time. If I venture to introduce it by a few prefatory observations, it is not for the purpose of dictating to those who assume in art the right of private judgment and of deciding to their own contentment what they like, and what they do *not,* – but in the first place, to explain the sense in which I have used certain terms, which otherwise might be misunderstood, and secondly with a hope of leading the mind of the observer to certain considerations which may be suggestive of added pleasure, and a more refined and discriminating judgment; for unless we know what to require, we cannot do justice to the artist who has sought in his own way to meet our requirements.

We will begin by a definition.

The word SCULPTURE (from *sculpo,* to carve,) signifies whatever is cut or carved into shape. We apply the word technically to all the productions of the plastic or formative arts: that is to say to all imitations of natural forms fashioned out of any solid material, whether they be modelled in clay or wax, cast in metal or gypsum, carved in wood or ivory, hewn in stone or marble. And we distinguish the productions of sculpture considered as one of the fine arts under two divisions: in the first we comprise all insulated and complete figures single or grouped. These we call in a general way STATUES; they may be *standing,* or *seated,* or *recumbent.* In the second division, we place all figures which are partly raised on a flat plane, which we style in a general way BAS-RELIEFS. But when we would describe accurately we distinguish between – I. BASSO-RELIEVO, *Bas-relief,* or low-relief, where the figures are slightly projected (as in No. 20). – II. MEZZO-RELIEVO, half-relief, where half the figure appears as if sunk in the block, and half above it (as in No. 226). – III. ALTO-RELIEVO, *plein-relief,* high-relief, where the figure is almost detached from the plane behind – standing out from it, though still not wholly detached from it (as in No. 172). In the mediæval sculpture, and the modern imitations of it, we find a mixed style, in which all the three degrees of relief are used – the figures in

DOI: 10.4324/9781315400266-34

the background being in very flat relief, those in the middle ground in half-relief, and those immediately in front in high-relief (as in No. 109).

Now it must be evident to those who use their reason in the observation of works of art that Sculpture, dealing with forms in solid material, must be very different from Painting, which describes with lines and colours on a flat surface; that the aims of each art are distinct; that each has its capabilities, its limits, and its laws, and that these being founded on natural laws cannot be infringed with impunity. Coleridge defined painting as "a somewhat between a thought and a thing." Sculpture is a *thought* and a *thing*. Painting is not what it seems; sculpture is a reality: painting produces its effects to the eye by differences and varieties of colour, by gradations of distance, by multiplied figures. Where sculpture pretends to such manifestations (as in some of the mediæval and modern bas-reliefs) it is apt to wander beyond the legitimate bounds which truth and taste have assigned to it; and that which constitutes its essential excellence and real character is diminished in proportion as it assumes the powers, and proposes to itself the aims of painting, an art which works with different means, and has a far wider range of imitation and representation than that commanded by the art of sculpture.

I have begun by this definition of what sculpture is, and what it is not, and have dwelt a little upon the distinction, because the first principle with which the observer must start, is this: – never to confound the laws and the objects of two arts so perfectly distinct as sculpture and painting, but to consider well the kind of pleasure and the kind of representation which he shall require from each.

One of the first considerations of sculpture is the MATERIAL. In modern times we use the same materials which were in use in ancient times; nor does it appear that we have improved on those mechanical processes which ensured completeness, beauty, and excellence of workmanship, though we have some scientific and mechanical inventions which have facilitated imitation and cheapened material; and with regard to material, we should observe that the management and capabilities of different substances are considerations of great importance; that figures which look well in one material, do not look well in another; that metal requires a different treatment from marble, and is fitted for purposes where marble would be misplaced.

All the specimens of sculpture here (both ancient and modern), are casts made in gypsum (plaster of Paris), and the hard, opaque plaster is so different in effect from the delicate semi-transparent marble, which under the master-hand seems actually to soften into life, that, in judging of some admired works, this difference must be taken into consideration.

SIZE is another of the external conditions of sculpture, which must be well considered. Many subjects which are extremely graceful and ornamental, of small size, become repulsive when enlarged. When a figure is rather above nature, we style it *heroic;* when much above the natural height, it is *colossal*. If a statue be half the size of life, or less, it is called a statuette. Some of the antique colossal statues may be diminished into statuettes, retaining their grace, and even their sublimity; but a subject originally conceived of a small size can seldom be enlarged to colossal dimensions.

The LOCALITY for which a statue is intended is also of great importance; whether for a church, a temple, a hall, a gallery, a room, a garden; whether for a high or a low situation. A statue which is to be placed in the open air, or to enter into an architectural composition, or to form part of a sacred monument, or an historical memorial, requires a different treatment from one which is to decorate a room in a palace. The Milo of Puget (No. 117) was placed in a bocage at Versailles; the Nymph (No. 168) in a public garden; the Angel (No. 67) in a church: all are calculated for height or distance. A central situation in a large space requires that the figure and attitude should display beauties in every point of view.

27

EDMUND GOSSE, 'SCULPTURE AT THE ROYAL ACADEMY'

Saturday review of politics, literature, science and art, 69:1809 (28 June 1890), p. 794

IN spite of the fact that Mr. Alfred Gilbert is not represented at all this year at the Royal Academy, and that Mr. Thornycroft sends no very important contribution, the interest of the sculpture is well sustained. The general average of merit has, perhaps, never been so high, and on every side we see work which would have been a portent fifteen years ago. The most superficial visitor must observe a change of colour in the sculpture-rooms. The uniform white of the old rows of marble is being transformed into black, green, and golden yellow, the hues of the patina of bronze. The new school have discovered the value and the charm of metal, in which their finest touch can be reproduced without modification, and if this movement proceeds much further, we may even have to recall the sculptors to the preciousness of the marble surface. At present about half the exhibition is white, and half is either bronze or plaster bronzed. Everywhere the young men are coming forward with admirably executed work. The honours of the year belong to Mr. Onslow Ford, and to three outsiders – Mr. Bates, Mr. Frampton, and Mr. Goscombe John – young sculptors who have lately served their novitiate.

DOI: 10.4324/9781315400266-35

28

FRED MILLER, 'GEORGE FRAMPTON, A. R. A., ART WORKER'

Art Journal (November 1897), pp. 321, 323–324

GEORGE FRAMPTON is an all-round craftsman, and prefers to be known as an art worker, and not by the more restricted title of sculptor, though it was his originality and skill in this direction which gained him the Associateship of the Royal Academy in 1894.

[...]

I was glad to find that Mr. Frampton does not believe in a high degree of specialisation, the devoting of all one's energies to the production of one class of work. Though he as a student devoted much time to conquering the difficulties of figure modelling. Mr. Frampton does not believe that figure-modelling is the essence of the whole art of sculpture. "I pay as much attention to a leaf as to a figure, for one is just of as much importance as the other in the whole effect, and you can put as much love and thought into the way you use an ivy leaf as a figure." We find Mr. Frampton, therefore, modelling the decoration of a frieze by a clever treatment of the herb "Honesty" in low relief, designing and carrying out a silver casket for the Skinners' Company, as shown in No. 1, in the lid of which is placed one of his enamels, No. 5, working in silver, bronze, marble, and wood, and combining all three in the figure of Dame Alice Owen in this year's Academy in a most original and charming way.

A master of many methods, Mr. Frampton is truly an art worker, and he esteems it an honour to belong to the Art Workers' Guild and the Arts and Crafts Society. This pigeon-holing of people, which compels them to devote all their energies to one small section of work, is one of the outcomes of the factory system. There is no warranty for it if we look to the past, for then we had men who could paint, design, model, etch, and do anything demanded of them, and these many interests tended to keep them perennially young, for the energies and mind grow weary if they are working within too restricted a range. Is not a change of work rest? The artist who has mastered the technique of one craft can quickly become proficient in another, though he may prefer to give his first energies to the one in which he finds he can give his ego freest play. No two crafts appear, at a superficial glance, more dissimilar than painting and sculpture, and yet they are both the expression of the same set of faculties, and may be the work of the same pair of hands.

DOI: 10.4324/9781315400266-36

29

EDWIN ROSCOE MULLINS, *A PRIMER OF SCULPTURE*

(London: Cassell and Co., 1890), pp. 62–64, 70–72, 74–75

Final material

The final material, for which you intend your work, should be before your mind when modelling the clay or wax model, as the treatment required should vary according to the material you have in view. And although it is better in the first sketch not to be hampered by any other thought than how best to treat the subject in hand, yet in the full-sized model it is a necessary condition to take into account whether bronze, marble or terra-cotta is to be the material in which the work will finally appear.

Should the model be intended for marble or stone, the work must be kept tolerably compact, and the effect should be dependent upon the arrangement of the masses rather than upon a varied outline: whilst if intended to be reproduced in metal the reverse is true. Here a varied outline is to be desired, and the work may be kept as light in character as possible, and every part may be as detached as good composition will allow: a thing impossible in a more brittle material. Nor are any fictitious supports necessary to keep the figure upon its legs when in bronze, or to uphold the weight of the body; the metal is strong enough to stand alone, and arms and even fingers can be detached. Again, the hair need not be closely matted to the head, nor both feet planted firmly on the ground; indeed, a greater freedom of composition is possible in every part. But in marble, unless fictitious supports are added, the figure must be kept together for strength, and the parts connected, especially at the base, by the introduction of drapery or other means. This fact applies even more to stone, which is still less strong, as the grain is not so close as in marble.

It is in the beautiful adaptation of means to a certain end that the excellence of a work of art consists. If marble is treated as only bronze can legitimately be, the result is but a *tour-de-force*, and therefore by no means happy.

The different materials have important bearings upon the character of the modelling in other particulars as well. Usually the lines can be kept sharper and more undercut for bronze than for marble; unless the design is for relief work in metal that has to be reproduced over and over again, and in more than one casting. In

DOI: 10.4324/9781315400266-37

this case there should be no undercuts at all, but every part should "pull" straight out of the mould. If one refers to Alfred Stevens' iron work for chimney-pieces, which were brought out some time ago by the Coalbrook Dale Company, it will be seen what I mean; there no undercuts at all are allowed, although the work is in high relief: and yet the effect is so beautifully rendered that the want of it is not felt. But working without undercuts is quite a separate branch of the art and includes modelling medals, although in the latter case the work is easier because it is generally in low relief. Undercuts, of course, are ordinarily used to give stronger shadows, and thus greater distinction.

[. . .]
[pp. 70–2]

Carving

Marble or stone work necessitates that another branch of the art should be learnt, viz., carving. In this field I think women, from their slighter physique, are placed rather at a disadvantage, because the practice requires a firm grip of the tool, and strength of arm and wrist, to ensure good execution. Therefore as a rule I should advise them to get their marble work done for them; in this matter they will not be found to be exceptional; as sculptors frequently, from press of work or disinclination for the hard manual labour, leave this part of the work to their assistants, even to finishing it throughout.

Yet it is a great mistake to assume that carving is a mere mechanical process, and that therefore a carefully trained workman alone can do it; it is an art by itself; and the mere treatment of the surface – the interpretation into marble of that which looked well in clay – may make all the difference to the enjoyment or not of the work.

In choosing a block of marble and stone – and there are several agents in London where such can be obtained, three of whom are Messrs. S. Trickett and Sons, Victoria Stone Wharf, Millwall; Messrs. Goody, Cripps, and Sons, Graham Street, City Road; Messrs. Fabricotti, Buckingham Palace Road, Pimlico – it will be advisable to procure the services of some one who has had experience: for although there is considerable chance as to whether a block turns out well or ill, yet much can be ascertained from the exterior by a practised eye. A man who had long practice told me he always selected a wet day to choose marble, and a dry one for lime- or sand-stone, as the defects of each were under those conditions more easily seen.

The block is first roughed out into shape by a skilled mason, or "pointer," as he is called from the nature of the work, which is called "pointing:" this is purely mechanical, and effected by careful measurements, arrived at with special instruments. Carving requires a great number of tools, which can be procured at Messrs. Buck's, in Tottenham Court Road, or at other large tool shops; and they should be of all sizes and shapes: sharps or chisels, claw or tooth tools, round-nosed (with edges taken off) tools, and prising tools, that is, those for working with the hands alone, to clean out any hollow line. They should vary in size from half an inch to one-sixteenth, or larger than that for stone work: but half an inch will be found to be as wide as will allow of a clean sharp cut on the marble. Iron hammers too are needed, the weight according to requirement, three pounds being as heavy as is usually wanted, and a lighter one for finer work of two or one and a half pounds. Lead hammers are also much used; for stone, wooden mallets are the most serviceable, with mallet-headed instead of cup-headed tools, such as are used for marble.

[. . .]
[pp. 74–5]

Bronze

I do not intend to dwell upon this branch, as the means by which casting is effected are not matters of art, as was stated before, but rather of science and mechanism. The only part in which art is called into play is in retouching the wax model, should the work be cast in the lost-wax process, called *à cire perdue*. This retouching of the wax is very similar to retouching a squeeze for terra-cotta, only the wax used in' this process is usually so hard and unyielding that the task is by no means easy, and the less one has to touch it, beyond removing the necessary seams, the better; but the wax model should always go through the sculptor's hands before being cast.

With the ordinary sand-mould process of casting – the process by which all large work, or the bulk of large work, is done – there is no model to be considered, after once the plaster cast has been made from the clay. This process is, I think, perfectly adapted for out-door statues; there can be no comparison, however, between the *cire perdue* process and the other for small and fine work, or that which is to be seen near the eye. Anything that can be modelled, can be rendered into bronze by the wax process, and all undercuts truly carried out. This process is the old Italian method that we read of in Benvenuto Cellini's Life: it has recently been introduced into England; and now some large firms, as well as enterprising sculptors, are adopting it for busts and smaller work. The colour that charms us so much, and which is an important matter in bronze, is, if on an old bronze, the result of oxidation and the combination of carbonic acid; but if seen on new metal it is caused by washing the surface with acids.

30

MARION SPIELMANN, *BRITISH SCULPTURE AND SCULPTORS OF TODAY*

(London: Cassell and Co., 1901), pp. 5–6

The materials for sculpture

IF the public were better informed as to the materials proper for sculpture they would be less likely to go astray in their encouragement of the art. If they understood that the material should fit the subject they would appreciate the folly of prostituting marble to purposes and subjects which are merely frivolous and amusing. M. Van der Straeten appreciates this fitness of things by executing his charming little *fantaisies* not in marble or dark bronze, but in terra-cotta or in some cheerful coloured metal; and, moreover, he keeps them small. A big sculptural joke or mountebank feat is an impertinence.

MARBLE has, above all things, dignity, and it flatters form, while resenting the elaboration and embroidery of ornament and the like. In a quaint passage in which Ruskin insists on the appropriateness of marble to the rendering of the nude figure, he points out, apart from the somewhat transparent surface (not being opaque and dull like chalk) that the evenness of its white tint is good for flesh, otherwise were the marble spotted, a figure of Venus executed in it, were it never so beautiful, would give us the impression of "a speckled frog." Similarly, a streaked marble Adonis would suggest a zebra. The stately material is for stately, earnest, and poetic subjects.

BRONZE is utterly unlike marble in its peculiar appropriateness, for its shadows are almost black, and its texture in the nature of clay. As bronze is run into the mould in a molten condition, the texture is of necessity entirely different from that of marble, with its brittle quality and its surface susceptible only to the chisel. It follows, therefore, that the handling of the two must be dissimilar; while, on the other hand, if we find in a given work, whether bronze or marble, the treatment natural to the particular material of the other, we know that the artist has offended against the laws of his art and has ignored the virtues of his material, and has forced it to do work for which it is not best fitted. Bronze, which may present the characteristics of clay or wax frozen hard, as it were, may be more playfully handled than marble. It allows a closer rendering of texture and infinite modulation of

DOI: 10.4324/9781315400266-38

colour in its patina; and the elaboration of folds in draperies appears less foreign to the more complaisant material. For that very reason, bronze requires the greater exercise of restraint, for without it good taste will easily be overstepped.

PLASTER, in spite of the dull nature of its whiteness, is not wholly unlike marble in effect. But its surface is relatively unsympathetic. It is generally felt, however, that there is no finality about plaster as there is about other materials, even such as terra-cotta or wax. It is a sort of temporary purgatory to be transmuted to a paradise of marble.

CLAY is the most natural, the most necessary, of all the materials to the modeller's hand – and the most treacherous. For its very virtues may seduce away the artist from the marble to which he ultimately looks, and may lead him to be false to his work and to himself. The proof is simple. Marble, a brittle substance, must be chipped away with mallet and chisel, and carved, as Michael Angelo chipped and carved it. Clay must be built up, modelled, and smeared, or "dragged together," and so receive its "skin." The characteristics of each class or work are different; the very planes are, or ought to be, different. How can clay, modelled with the tool and smeared with the fingers, be properly translatable into chipped marble with the aid of a pointing-machine? The skilled sculptor can, and does, make allowance for the change, certainly; but, as a principle, it is illogical to prepare in one material for work to be executed in another entirely foreign to it in character. In other words, the Plastic art, after centuries of fair companionship, has come to dominate and almost to crush out of existence the purely Glyptic art; and our marble works are to that extent a translation out of another language.

Such are the sculptor's materials, the characteristics of which, as they are successively used in the building up of a statue, Canova so admirably summed up: Clay is the Life; Plaster the Death; Marble and Bronze the Resurrection.

31

'THE INTERNATIONAL EXHIBITION'

Birmingham Daily Post, 20 June 1862, p. 2

No. 9. District Contributions. The Iron Castings of the Coalbrookdale Company

Iron has been conquered by artistic skill, and compelled to do homage to decorative power: the most stubborn portion of the mineral kingdom has been annexed to the realms of taste. How true this is will at once be seen and understood, as the visitor who wanders through the International Exhibition finds himself in the Court which contains the exhibition of the Coalbrookdale Company. At an early period, long ere the general attention of manufacturers or others was awakened to the importance of the association of Fine with Manufacturing Art, the "Dale" Company were energetically at work, giving evidence thereof from time to time by the production of castings in iron which all but rivalled the Berlin ironwork, at one time so much admired. In the Free Trade Bazaar, held in Covent Garden in 1845, the contributions of the "Dale" attracted very general attention, and there were not a few visitors who could scarcely comprehend that the sharp, delicately beautiful, minute and elaborately made out ornamentation which decorated the objects then shown could be produced, from iron by the ordinary process of casting. In the Manchester Exhibition of 1847, we again find the company exhibiting, and in each succeeding display making bolder and more ambitious efforts until in 1851, when the entrance gates in cast iron, erected in the transept of "Paxton's Palace," in connection with the "Boy and Swan Fountain," the rustic dome, &c., in cast iron; the statues modelled by John Bell (the "Eagle Slayer,"' and the "Andromeda," with its elaborate pedestal, the two latter cast in bronze), put an end to any doubt as to the position the Coalbrookdale Company should occupy. Since then it has been admitted that amongst those who produce objects in cast iron, in which utility and beauty go hand in hand, this house holds a place second to none.

DOI: 10.4324/9781315400266-39

32

'LARGE BRONZE CASTINGS'

Illustrated London News, 16 April 1881, p. 374

The pair of colossal Sphinxes, to adorn the pedestal of the Egyptian Obelisk called "Cleopatra's Needle," on the Victoria Thames Embankment, are cast at the foundry of Messrs. H. Young and Co., Eccleston-street, Pimlico. Our Illustration shows the operation of melting the metal at that establishment, where also the colossal equestrian statue of the Prince of Wales, modelled by Mr. Boehm, which Sir Albert Sassoon presented to the city of Bombay, was cast a few years ago. The mixture of metal used at Messrs. H. Young and Co.'s foundry is eleven parts of copper to one of tin; which alloy is similar to that proved to have been used by the ancients. It is a remarkable fact that the density of this alloy becomes greater than the mean density of its constituents; and, by experiments made at Woolwich Arsenal, its tenacity has been found equal to 30,700 lb. per square inch. It is less liable to corrosion than other metals. Great skill is required in the production of the mould. The artist's model being laid on a strong iron frame, the founder begins to mallet the prepared sand over half its surface, in suitable segments, keeping in view the easy extrication of each separate piece at its relative angle. When this tedious operation is accomplished, another iron frame, or mould-box, with cross-stays, or diaphragm plates, is fitted to the model covered with the aforesaid sand segments, which are dusted with a fine material, such as farina, reduced to an impalpable powder, to create a separation or parting, as required by the moulder. This box is fitted in, and rammed tightly with sand by iron rammers; then, by means of the overhead traveller crane, the boxes, with the model inclosed, are turned over. The moulder forms his centre joint and proceeds to make the segment sand pieces, which he covers with the iron frame, precisely in the same manner as he did before, making only, in addition, the "runners" or perforations, down which the metal must pass. When this is accomplished, the mould box is divided, and the sand segments are removed from off the model, and are fitted in their respective positions, in what may be called the top box. A false mould is needed to fit over the exposed half of the plaster model, so that it may be secured in its position whilst being turned over the second time, when the bottom box is lifted off, and all the sand segments are removed and fixed in their impress, as before described. The model is now done with; but we have only yet obtained an impress of the external surface of the sculpture; and it is necessary to form an inner mould,

DOI: 10.4324/9781315400266-40

or "core," for the purpose of lightening the work, allowing a space of half an inch everywhere between the outer and inner mould or core. The formation of this core needs great care. An iron skeleton is formed to take the rough shape of the statue, anatomically constructed, for easy subdivision. The external or outer surface is covered with tissue paper, and upon it a layer of plastic sand is put, representing the required thickness of metal. The skeleton frame is now fitted in position, and the centre of it is filled in with a porous material, while the external part of the core is of a consistency which, when dried, will become perfectly hard and strong. This core, when prepared in the lower half of the mould, is built up to the form of the upper half, the pieces of which are removed as the core is advanced. The top box is now fitted on to ensure accuracy of the mould and core together; then again they are separated for the last time; the pieces are removed, channels are cut between the segments in connection with the perforations down which the metal must run; and then it is finally fixed in the top box. The core is extracted in its divisions, the thickness is pared off, the lower half of the mould is finished as the upper part; and the whole work is removed into a gigantic oven, in which it remains for six or eight weeks until all vapour is expelled. Then it is put together, provisions being made for easy escape of gases; it is lowered into the foundry floor, bolted together, and solidly embedded to prevent explosion or upheaving. A dam or receiver is placed on the top of the mould, for holding the metal by valves, until it is at proper temperature for induction, when it is suddenly released by means of a lever, and the founder's anxious task of months is brought to a close.

33

'MELTING THE METAL FOR THE BRONZE SPHINX TO BE PLACED ON THE THAMES EMBANKMENT'

Illustrated London News, 16 April 1881, p. 373

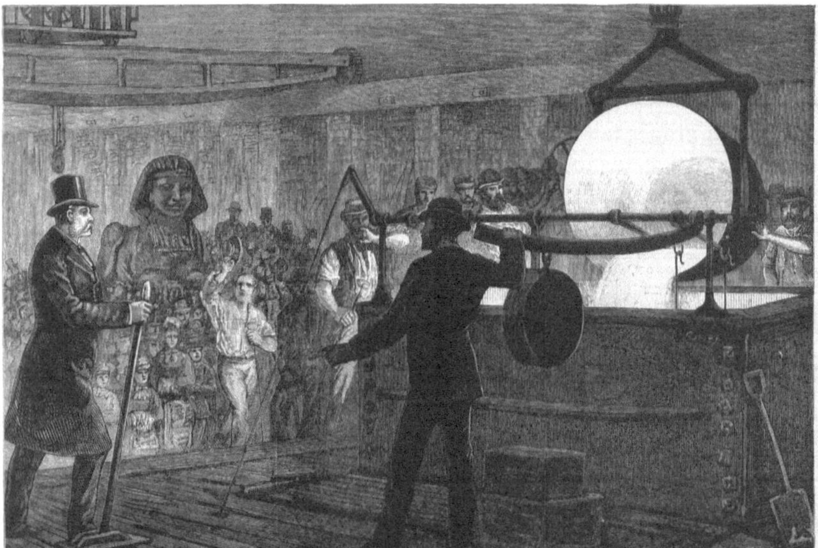

MELTING THE METAL FOR THE BRONZE SPHINX TO BE PLACED ON THE THAMES EMBANKMENT.—SEE NEXT PAGE.

DOI: 10.4324/9781315400266-41

34

HARRIET HOSMER, 'THE PROCESS OF SCULPTURE'

Atlantic Monthly (December 1864), pp. 734–737

I HAVE heard so much, lately, about artists who do not do their own work, that I feel disposed to raise the veil upon the mysteries of the studio, and enable those who are interested in the subject to form a just conception of the amount of assistance to which a sculptor is fairly entitled, as well as to correct the false, but very general impression, that the artist, beginning with the crude block, and guided by his imagination only, hews out his statue with his own hands.

So far from this being the case, the first labor of the sculptor is upon a small clay model, in which he carefully studies the composition of his statue, the proportions, and the general arrangement of the drapery, without regard to very careful finish of parts. This being accomplished, and the small model cast in plaster, he employs some one to enlarge his work to any size which he may require; and this is done by scale, and with almost as much precision as the full-size and perfectly finished model is afterwards copied in marble.

The first step in this process is to form a skeleton of iron, the size and strength of the iron rods corresponding to the size of the figure to be modelled; and here, not only strong hands and arms are requisite, but the blacksmith with his forge, many of the irons requiring to be heated and bent upon the anvil to the desired angle. This solid framework being prepared, and the various irons of which it is composed firmly wired and welded together, the next thing is to hang thereon a series of crosses, often several hundred in number, formed by two bits of wood, two or three inches in length, fastened together by wire, one end of which is attached to the framework. All this is necessary for the support of the clay, which would otherwise fall by its own weight. (I speak here of Roman clay, – the clay obtained in many parts of England and America being more properly potter's clay, and consequently more tenacious.) The clay is then pressed firmly around and upon the irons and crosses with strong hands and a wooden mallet, until, from a clumsy and shapeless mass, it acquires some resemblance to the human form. When the clay is properly prepared, and the work advanced as far as the artist desires, his own work is resumed, and he then laboriously studies every part, corrects his ideal by comparison with living models, copies his drapery from actual drapery arranged upon the lay-figure, and gives to his statue the last refinement of beauty.

DOI: 10.4324/9781315400266-42

It will thus be seen that there is an intermediate stage, even in the clay, when the work passes completely out of the sculptor's hands and is carried forward by his assistant, – the work on which the latter is employed, however, obviously requiring not the least exercise of creative power, which is essentially the attribute of the artist. To perform the part assigned him, it is not necessary that the assistant should be a man of imagination or refined taste, – it is sufficient that he have simply the skill, with the aid of accurate measurements, to construct the framework of iron and to copy the small model before him. But in *originating* that small model, when the artist had nothing to work from but the image existing in his own brain, imagination, refined feeling, and a sense of grace were essential, and were called into constant exercise. So, again, when the clay model returns into the sculptor's hands, and the work approaches completion, often after the labor of many months, it is he alone who infuses into the clay that refinement and individuality of beauty which constitute his "style," and which are the test of the greater or less degree of refinement of his mind, as the force and originality of the conception are the test of his intellectual power.

The clay model having at last been rendered as perfect as possible, the sculptor's work upon the statue is virtually ended; for it is then cast in plaster and given into the hands of the marble-workers, by whom, almost entirely, it is completed, the sculptor merely directing and correcting the work as it proceeds. This disclosure, I am aware, will shock the many, who often ingeniously discover traces of the sculptor's hand where they do not exist. It is true, that, in some cases, the finishing touches are introduced by the artist himself; but I suspect that few who have accomplished and competent workmen give much of their time to the mallet or the chisel, preferring to occupy themselves with some new creation, or considering that these implements may be more advantageously wielded by those who devote themselves exclusively to their use. It is also true, that, although the process of transferring the statue from plaster to marble is reduced to a science so perfect that to err is almost impossible, yet much depends upon the workmen to whom this operation is intrusted. Still, their position in the studio is a subordinate one. They translate the original thought of the sculptor, written in clay, into the language of marble. The translator may do his work well or ill, – he may appreciate and preserve the delicacy of sentiment and grace which were stamped upon the clay, or he may render the artist's meaning coarsely and unintelligibly. Then it is that the sculptor himself must reproduce his ideal in the marble, and breathe into it that vitality which, many contend, only the artist can inspire. But, whether skilful or not, the relation of these workmen to the artist is precisely the same as that of the mere linguist to the author who, in another tongue, has given to the world some striking fancy or original thought.

But the question when the clay *is* "properly prepared" forms the debatable ground, and has already furnished a convenient basis for the charge that it is never "properly prepared" for women-artists until it is ready for the caster. I affirm, from personal knowledge, that this charge is utterly without foundation, – and as it would be affectation in me to ignore what has been so freely circulating upon this subject in print, I take this opportunity of stating that I have never yet allowed a statue to leave my studio, upon the clay model of which I had not worked during a period of from four to eight months, – and further, that I should choose to refer all those desirous of ascertaining the truth to Mr. Nucci, who "prepares" my clay for me, rather than to my brother-sculptor, in the *Via Margutta,* who originated the report that I was an impostor. So far, however, as my designs are concerned, I believe even he has not, as yet, found occasion to accuse me of drawing upon other brains than my own.

We women-artists have no objection to its being known that we employ assistants; we merely object to its being supposed that it is a system peculiar to *ourselves*. When Thorwaldsen was called upon to execute his twelve statues of the Apostles, he designed and furnished the small models, and gave them into the hands of his pupils and assistants, by whom, almost exclusively, they were copied in their present colossal dimensions. The great master rarely put his own hand to the clay; yet we never hear them spoken of except as "Thorwaldsen's statues." When Vogelberg accepted the commission to model his colossal equestrian statue of Gustavus Adolphus, physical infirmity prevented the artist from even mounting the scaffolding; but he made the small model, and directed the several workmen employed upon the full-size statue in clay, and we never heard it intimated that Vogelberg was not the sculptor of that great work. Even Crawford, than whom none ever possessed a more rapid or facile hand, could never have accomplished half the immense amount of work which pressed upon him in his later years, had he not had more than one pair of hands to aid him in giving outward form to the images in his fertile brain. Nay, not to refer solely to artists who are no longer among us, I could name many studios, both in Rome and England, belonging to our brothers in Art, in which the assistant-modeller forms as necessary a part of studio – "property" as the living model or the marble-workers, – and many more, on a smaller scale, in which he lends a helping hand whenever required. If there are a few instances in which the sculptor himself conducts his clay model through every stage, it is usually because pecuniary considerations prevent his employing a professional modeller.

I do not wish it to be supposed that Thorwaldsen's general practice was such as I have described in the particular case referred to: probably no artist ever studied or worked more carefully upon the clay model than he. What I have stated was only with the view of showing to what extent he felt himself justified in employing assistance. I am quite persuaded, however, that, had Thorwaldsen and Vogelberg been women, and employed one-half the amount of assistance they did in the cases mentioned, we should long since have heard the great merit of their works attributed to the skill of their workmen.

Nor should we forget – to draw for examples upon a kindred art – how largely the painters of the fifteenth and sixteenth centuries relied upon the mechanical skill of their pupils to assist them in producing the great works which bear their names. All the painters of note of that time, like many of the present day, had their pupils, to whom was intrusted much of the laborious portion of their work, the master furnishing the design and superintending its execution. Raphael, for instance, could never have left one half the treasures of Art which adorn the Vatican and enrich other galleries, had he depended solely upon the rapidity of his own hand; and of the many frescos which exist in the Farnese Palace, and are called "Raphael's frescos," there are but two in which are to be traced the master's hand, – the Galatea, and one of the compartments in the series representing the story of Cupid and Psyche.

It will thus be seen how large a portion of the manual labor which is supposed to devolve entirely upon the artist is, and has always been, really performed by other hands than his own. I do not state this fact in a whisper, as if it were a great disclosure which involved the honor of the artist; it is no secret, and there is no reason why it should be so. The disclosure, it is true, will be received by all who regard sculpture as simply a mechanical art with a feeling of disappointment. They will brand the artist who cannot lay claim to the entire manipulation of his statue, whether in clay or marble, as an impostor, – nor will they resign the idea that the truly conscientious sculptor will carve every ornament upon his sandals and polish every button upon his drapery. But those who look upon sculpture as an intellectual art, requiring the exercise of taste, imagination, and delicate feeling, will never identify the artist who conceives, composes, and completes the design with the workman who simply relieves him from great physical labor, however delicate some portion of that labor may be. It should be a recognized fact, that the sculptor is as fairly entitled to avail himself of mechanical aid in the execution of his work as the architect to call into requisition the services of the stone-mason in the erection of his edifice, or the poet to employ the printer to give his thoughts to the world. Probably the sturdy mason never thinks much about proportion, nor the type-setter much about harmony; but the master-minds which inspire the strong arm and cunning finger with motion think about and study both. It is high time that some distinction should be made between the labor of the hand and the labor of the brain. It is high time, in short, that the public should understand in what the sculptor's work properly consists, and thus render less pernicious the representations of those who, either from thoughtlessness or malice, dwelling upon the fact that assistance has been employed in certain cases, without defining the limits of that assistance, imply the guilt of imposture in the artists, and deprive them, and more particularly women-artists, of the credit to which, by talent or conscientious labor, they are justly entitled.

HARRIET HOSMER.

35

HARRIET HOSMER AND HER ASSISTANTS, C. 1861

Harriet Goodhue Hosmer Papers, Folder: HGH, [c. 1860], Schlesinger Library, Radcliffe Institute, Harvard University

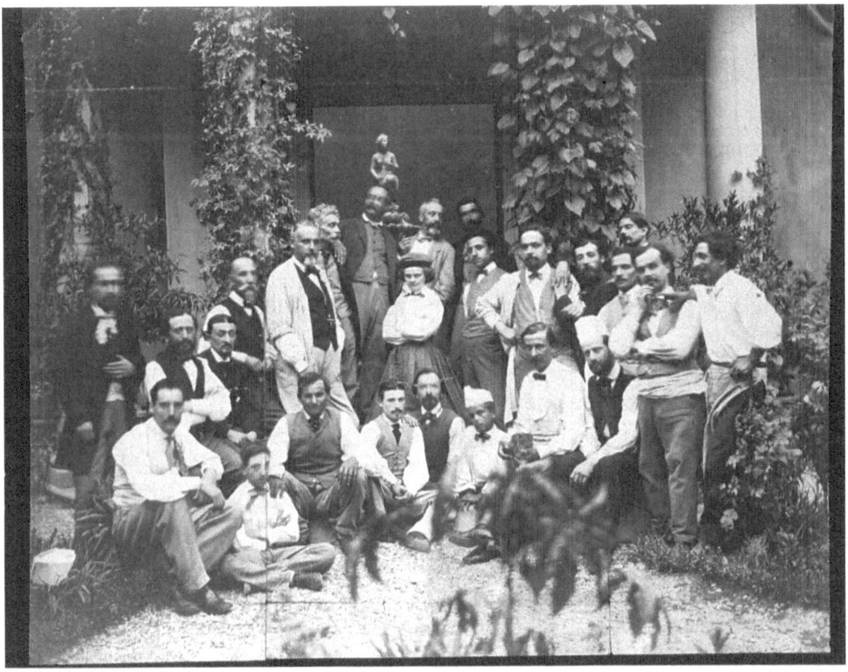

DOI: 10.4324/9781315400266-43

36

M. D. WYATT, *FINE ART. A SKETCH OF ITS HISTORY, THEORY, PRACTICE, AND APPLICATION TO INDUSTRY. BEING A COURSE OF LECTURES DELIVERED AT CAMBRIDGE IN 1870*

(London: Macmillan and Co., 1870), pp. 180–182

There occur to me only four operations by means of which sculpture has ever been executed; and these will be found to coincide with and owe their origin to the properties of the various materials it is their duty to fashion. These four operations are cutting, modelling, fusing and beating.

The operations of cutting convert granite, marble, stone, wood, and some few other materials, such as ivory, precious stones &c., from shapeless forms into any which the sculptor may desire to embody.

The operation of modelling enables him to create the same forms out of any soft matter, and his ingenuity must then be brought to bear to convert that soft material into an approximation to hardness.

The third operation, that of fusing, could come into existence only with man's acquaintance with and mastery over the extraction of metals from their ores; taking advantage of the property of that section of the mineral kingdom to approach fluidity by the action of heat, and to revert to solidity on losing caloric.

The last operation, that of beating, could come only at that subsequent stage of man's technical education, when he would have acquired a knowledge of the relative ductility of metals under various conditions of their textures.

By the first of these operations, as I have said, the sculptor is enabled to convert hard and shapeless materials into the realization of his fancies. With the operation of cutting must of course be united that of abrading, or rubbing down, which is in fact only another form of cutting, – a slow and laborious operation particularly delighted in by those races which multiplied with a rapidity consistent with the teeming productiveness of the soil which gave them birth. Thus, this form of cutting has always been affected in the thickly-populated districts and on the highly productive soils of China, India and Egypt.

DOI: 10.4324/9781315400266-44

Where population has been thinner, and more labour has been requisite to obtain the means of subsistence, men have learnt to be more economical of human labour: and under such conditions they have generally adopted those more speedy processes in art whereby economy of labour may be attained.

To those people to whom labour was a matter of indifference, intricacy and elaboration, amounting often to over elaboration, was a natural source of delight; and hence the highly ornamental character of Oriental Art, especially in the form of sculpture, from its very dawn.

As men rose in the scale of thinking beings their respect for human labour increased, and their desire to avoid its waste led them to eliminate from the scheme and practice of their arts all labour not indispensable to a satisfactory æsthetic result. Hence, no doubt, much of that obvious delight in simplicity which, while it facilitated the execution of Grecian sculpture, preserved its intellectual character, and substituted the beautiful for the difficult as a standard of excellence in art.

I cannot but think that a return on the part of the sculptor of the present day to a correspondent estimation of the dignity of labour, which demands that it should never be spent in vain, would purify many of the manifestations of his art, and only increase, in us and in him, a due appreciation of the really permanent sources of attraction in sculpture.

When the labour of the sculptor was limited to evolving, out of a shapeless form, the image which existed only in his fancy, he was liable in a high degree to misadventure in the operation of cutting. If a stroke too much removed a portion of material which it was essential to preserve for the representation of some important feature of his design, the moment that piece of material was cut away all the previous labour of the sculptor was necessarily sacrificed. It behoved him then in practice, in order to avoid any such great risk, to make for himself a model, in some material which could be easily altered, of what he desired to carve in a permanent form, before commencing the otherwise hazardous operation of cutting. This it was which no doubt led to the application of our second class of operations to the sculptor's art.

In all the history of civilization, and in every race which has ever appeared upon the face of the earth, we find amongst the earliest of the technical arts acquired that which the Greeks distinguished as ceramic; or in other words the softening of certain substances by moisture, and then their hardening by the evaporation of that fluid through the application of heat.

In those intensely hot countries which formed the nursery of mankind, the sun alone would teach this lesson, and the sun-dried bricks of the earliest of the building races attested their acquaintance with that principle which, in the analysis of the technical arts, has been denominated plasticity. The formation of a mould, and the pressing of soft substances into that mould, and their subsequent restoration to hardness under the action of fire, are all successive stages of this ceramic system.

The substitution for fire of that chemical action by which certain materials having lime for their basis acquire in the highest degree the property of changing from plastic to comparatively hard textures, although an early, was probably a subsequent operation.

All of these arts were unquestionably known to the ancient Egyptians, and formed the fundamental basis upon which their practice of sculpture rested.

The progress of antiquarian and anthropological study has recognized the succession of these operations by generic divisions of the successive races of mankind into those which existed in the Stone Age, the Pottery Age, the Bronze, and the Iron Age; [. . .]

2.2

Social meanings

DOI: 10.4324/9781315400266-45

2.2 Social meanings

This section explores both the range of materials used in Victorian sculpture and the social meanings accorded to those materials. Several sources are concerned with the issue of colour in sculpture, a matter of considerable debate throughout the period.

As a raw material, marble was expensive, labour intensive and connoted a certain exclusivity. Widely circulated images such as that of the Carrara marble quarry, the source of the most prestigious marble for neoclassical sculptors, were testimony to its expense and demonstrated the dramatic methods of its extraction from the earth. A 1950s account of the havoc caused in the 1880s by the transport across London of a block of Carrara marble for a sculpture of Queen Victoria demonstrates the phenomenal labour and cost of moving materials *after* their extraction: 'Traffic was blocked, omnibus routes had to be diverted, drivers and pedestrians alike became enraged, cries, lashing of horses and Cockney sarcasm all added to the commotion'.[1]

The early and mid-nineteenth-century taste for white marble sought to reclaim the materials, refer to the physical appearance, and take on the cultural cachet of classical sculpture. The whiteness of marble took on various connotations in the nineteenth century. This is clearly articulated in the passages reprinted here from Nathaniel Hawthorne's 1860 novel *The Marble Faun*, which is set amongst the American and English 'colony' of artists seeking classical precedents in mid-century Rome. It presents sculpting in marble as a masculine, religious, morally upright and, significantly, immortal and permanent legacy; Hawthorne entirely ignores the female artists such as Harriet Hosmer and her circle, from whom he had learnt so much during his late 1850s period in Rome. The 'purity' of white marble has evident moral overtones in this text. Hawthorne expresses horror at the use of colour in one sculpture produced by an 'English artist', referring to (Welsh) sculptor John Gibson's *Tinted Venus*, c. 1851–1856. Tinting sculpture 'robbed the marble of its chastity . . . it became a sin and a shame to look at his nude goddesses'.[2] Colour made sculpture dangerously real, not ideal.

Gibson's *Tinted Venus* was displayed at the 1862 International Exhibition in London, and later that year at the Crystal Palace at Sydenham, in a purpose-built, multicoloured pavillion designed by the architect (and avid apologist for the use of colour in sculpture) Owen Jones. The review of Gibson's sculpture in the *Art Journal*, reprinted here, offers further reflection on the perceived immorality of colouring marble, demonstrating the strong association between white marble and moral propriety. For this critic, Gibson's experiment with materials called into question the very purpose of sculpture.[3] An 1861 review in the *Critic*, however, demonstrates that, before the London debut of the *Tinted Venus*, a large number of 'polychrome' and indeed 'polylith' (multiple stone) sculptures had been exhibited in London to great acclaim, and their innovative use of multiple materials was particularly praised. These were the works of French sculptor Charles Cordier, referred to here as an 'ethnographic' sculptor, whose sculpture depicted people from Greece, Italy, North Africa and China using various coloured marbles, often quarried at these diverse geographic locations. The North African works had been commissioned by the French government to 'document' the peoples colonised by the French. All Cordier's works are idealised. But their status as fine art objects was troubled both by their unusual (at mid-century) mix of materials, and by the peoples they represented. Racist hierarchies of beauty, as Charmaine Nelson has documented, made non-European peoples unsuitable artistic subjects for many Victorians, and these attitudes are readily apparent in the *Critic*'s discussion of the relationship between the ethnicities of Cordier's subjects and the materials chosen to represent them.[4]

The nineteenth-century obsession with the 'purity' of white marble also had racial connotations, as Nelson has explored. This became particularly apparent in marble sculpture depicting people of colour, as indicated by the critical responses reprinted here to two sculptures in white marble depicting women with facial features and body types widely identified at the time as signifying people of African descent. The display of American sculptor William Wetmore Story's *Cleopatra* and *Libyan Sibyl* at the 1862 International Exhibition in London generated concern about employing 'classical sculpture' (i.e. the use of marble materials) to represent people of colour.[5] The *London Review* praises the originality of the pieces, while *Dublin University Magazine* condemns the Sibyl as 'vulgar' and notes that, in his depiction of Cleopatra, 'Mr Wetmore Story has wantonly strayed aside from a field of beauty'.[6] Both articles are underpinned by an assumption that white Europeans are the only aesthetically suitable subjects for white marble statuary.[7]

In the later nineteenth century, colour in sculpture re-emerged, not so much in terms of tinting marble but in the use of numerous different materials, sometimes polylithy or multimedia (marble, bronze, ivory, precious stones). Making use of ivory, bronze, opals and glass, George Frampton's *Lamia* (1899–1900), reproduced here, is one famous multimedia example, which was explored in detail in Maskell's *Ivories*. Many deemed a multimedia approach to be more appropriate to sculpture as a medium than the excessively imitative tinting employed by Gibson, because it did not attempt realism. Royal Academy Professor of Sculpture Henry Weekes' lectures once again raise – and attempt to police the boundaries of – the relationship between sculpture and 'art manufacture'. Colour and new coloured materials for sculpture are, according to Weekes, fitting for the 'lower' activity of 'art manufacture'.[8] Weekes presents the Royal Academy as the guardian of 'the topmost walk of Sculpture', duty bound not to 'advocate what tends to bring it down to the subordinate one', that is, the use of colour.[9] He advises a cautious use of colour and coloured materials – but these materials are presented as dangerous temptations – both for the moral integrity of the sculptor and their art.

Metalwork in sculpture brought about further social concerns, as the passage from Spielmann's 1901 *British Sculptors* indicates. Spielmann interweaves the lower class industrial worker associated with this metalwork ('at the best it suggests rather the man with the anvil, shears, and pincers, than the man with the clay and the chisel') with the vulgar lack of restraint associated with mass audiences, which he believed typified the uses of metalworked items ('The people have a predisposition towards flummery').[10] Maskell's *Ivories* seems similarly concerned at the apparent social debasement of ivory in nineteenth-century culture, 'relegated to the position of an industry', and notes that skills in ivory carving were associated primarily with Japanese, Indian and Chinese sculpture rather than European.[11]

Other aspects of the ethics of materials might seem much more pressing to the twenty-first-century reader. Maskell's cheerful outline of the rebirth of ivory sculpture in Europe as a 'happy idea' emerging out of the Belgian acquisition of the Congo in 1885 points to sculpture's connections with colonial violence (other sources in this section highlight the ways in which sculpture shored up and contributed to the formation of the racist discourses which underpinned such violence).[12] Further, ivory is perhaps the sculptural material most obviously predicated on the destruction of animal life, with complex repercussions for ecosystems. As Jason Edwards has recently argued, however, *all* sculptural production depends on some sort of exploitation of animals.[13] Perhaps we might rethink the image of the marble quarry with which this section opens as one of not just human labour, but also non-human animal exploitation, taking into account the roles played by the millions of compressed molluscs and crustaceans from which marble is composed.

Notes

1 A. M. W. Stirling, *Victorian Sidelights. From the Papers of the Late Mrs Adams-Acton* (London: Ernest Benn, 1954), p. 260.
2 Nathaniel Hawthorne, *The Marble Faun* (1860), ed. Susan Manning (Oxford: Oxford University Press, 2002), p. 104.
3 See M. Droth, J. Edwards and M. Hatt (eds), *Sculpture Victorious: Art in an Age of Invention, 1837–1901* (New Haven and London: Yale University Press, 2014), *Sculpture Victorious*, pp. 184–8.
4 See Charmaine Nelson, 'Vénus Africaine: Race, Beauty and African-ness', in Jan Marsh (ed.), *Black Victorians: Black People in British Art 1800–1900* (Aldershot: Lund Humphries, 2005), pp. 46–56.
5 Cleopatra's ethnic identity was a subject of considerable contemporary interest. For example, the *Dublin University Magazine* refers to a 'Mr Hawthorne' having neglected to emphasise the Greek heritage of Cleopatra; 'The Art-Show at the Great Exhibition', *Dublin University Magazine*, 60:356 (1862), p. 142. This is a sneer at chapter 14 of

The Marble Faun, where Hawthorne praises a sculpture of Cleopatra with more stereotypically African features. See Hawthorne, *Marble Faun* (2002), pp. 98–99.

6 'Ancient and Modern Sculpture', *London Review and Weekly Journal of Politics, Literature, Art, and Society*, 4:103 (1862), p. 567; 'The Art-Show at the Great Exhibition', *Dublin University Magazine*, 60:356 (1862), p. 142.

7 See Charmaine Nelson, *The Color of Stone: Sculpting the Black Female Subject in Nineteenth-Century America* (2007, Minneapolis), pp. 143–178. The complexity of materials in relation to race is further explored in Mia L. Bagneris, 'Miscegenation in Marble: John Bell's Octoroon', *Art Bulletin*, 102:2 (2020), pp. 64–90.

8 Henry Weekes, *Lectures on Art Delivered at the Royal Academy London* (London: Bickers and Son, 1880), p. 171.

9 Ibid, p. 171.

10 Marion Spielmann, *British Sculpture and Sculptors of Today* (London: Cassell and Co., 1901), p. 11.

11 Alfred Maskell, *Ivories* (London: Methuen and Co., 1905), p. 498.

12 Ibid, p. 504. See further Debora L. Silverman, 'Art Nouveau, Art of Darkness: African Lineages of Belgian Modernism, Part I', *West 86th: A Journal of Decorative Arts, Design History, and Material Culture*, 18:2 (2011), pp. 139–181.

13 Jason Edwards, '*Ex omnia conchis*? Edward Onslow Ford and the problem of Victorian '*animalier*' sculpture', *Word & Image*, 34:1 (2018), pp. 55–63.

37

ALINARI BROTHERS, PHOTOGRAPH OF MARBLE QUARRY AT CARRARA, ITALY, C. 1860S

Hiram Powers papers, 1819–1953, Box 11, Folder 9, Archives of American Art, Smithsonian Institution

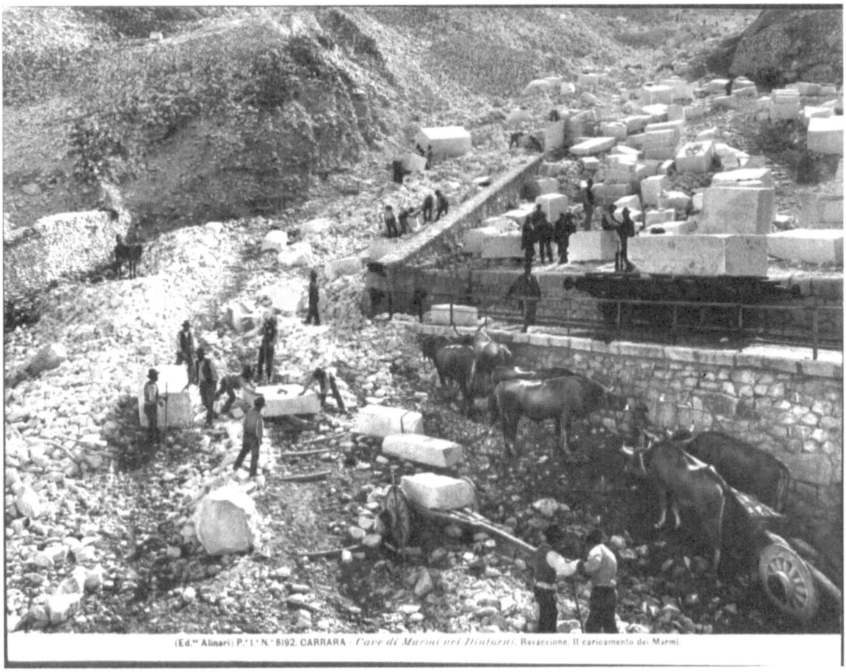

DOI: 10.4324/9781315400266-46

38

NATHANIEL HAWTHORNE, *THE MARBLE FAUN* (1860)

(Oxford: Oxford University Press, 2002), selections from Chapter 15, 'An Aesthetic Company', pp. 104–106

It may be allowable to say, however, that American art is much better represented at Rome in the pictorial than in the sculpturesque department. Yet the men of marble appear to have more weight with the public than the men of canvas; perhaps on account of the greater density and solid substance of the material in which they work, and the sort of physical advantage which their labors thus acquire over the illusive unreality of color. To be a sculptor seems a distinction in itself; whereas a painter is nothing, unless individually eminent.

One sculptor there was, an Englishman, endowed with a beautiful fancy, and possessing at his fingers' ends the capability of doing beautiful things. He was a quiet, simple, elderly personage, with eyes brown and bright, under a slightly impending brow, and a Grecian profile, such as he might have cut with his own chisel. He had spent his life, for forty years, in making Venuses, Cupids, Bacchuses, and a vast deal of other marble progeny of dreamwork, or rather frostwork: it was all a vapory exhalation out of the Grecian mythology, crystallizing on the dull window-panes of to-day. Gifted with a more delicate power than any other man alive, he had foregone to be a Christian reality, and perverted himself into a Pagan idealist, whose business or efficacy, in our present world, it would be exceedingly difficult to define. And, loving and reverencing the pure material in which he wrought, as surely this admirable sculptor did, he had nevertheless robbed the marble of its chastity, by giving it an artificial warmth of hue. Thus it became a sin and shame to look at his nude goddesses. They had revealed themselves to his imagination, no doubt, with all their deity about them; but, bedaubed with buff color, they stood forth to the eyes of the profane in the guise of naked women. But, whatever criticism may be ventured on his style, it was good to meet a man so modest and yet imbued with such thorough and simple conviction of his own right principles and practice, and so quietly satisfied that his kind of antique achievement was all that sculpture could effect for modern life.

This eminent person's weight and authority among his artistic brethren were very evident; for beginning unobtrusively to utter himself on a topic of art, he

DOI: 10.4324/9781315400266-47

was soon the centre of a little crowd of younger sculptors. They drank in his wisdom, as if it would serve all the purposes of original inspiration; he, meanwhile, discoursing with gentle calmness, as if there could possibly be no other side, and often ratifying, as it were, his own conclusions by a mildly emphatic "Yes."

The veteran Sculptor's unsought audience was composed mostly of our own countrymen. It is fair to say, that they were a body of very dexterous and capable artists, each of whom had probably given the delighted public a nude statue, or had won credit for even higher skill by the nice carving of buttonholes, shoe-ties, coat-seams, shirt-bosoms, and other such graceful peculiarities of modern costume. Smart, practical men they doubtless were, and some of them far more than this, but still not precisely what an uninitiated person looks for in a sculptor. A sculptor, indeed, to meet the demands which our preconceptions make upon him, should be even more indispensably a poet than those who deal in measured verse and rhyme. His material, or instrument, which serves him in the stead of shifting and transitory language, is a pure, white, undecaying substance. It insures immortality to whatever is wrought in it, and therefore makes it a religious obligation to commit no idea to its mighty guardianship, save such as may repay the marble for its faithful care, its incorruptible fidelity, by warming it with an ethereal life. Under this aspect, marble assumes a sacred character; and no man should dare to touch it unless he feels within himself a certain consecration and a priesthood, the only evidence of which, for the public eye, will be the high treatment of heroic subjects, or the delicate evolution of spiritual, through material beauty.

No ideas such as the foregoing – no misgivings suggested by them probably, troubled the self-complacency of most of these clever sculptors. Marble, in their view, had no such sanctity as we impute to it. It was merely a sort of white limestone from Carrara, cut into convenient blocks, and worth, in that state, about two or three dollars per pound; and it was susceptible of being wrought into certain shapes (by their own mechanical ingenuity, or that of artisans in their employment) which would enable them to sell it again at a much higher figure. Such men, on the strength of some small knack in handling clay, which might have been fitly employed in making wax-work, are bold to call themselves sculptors. How terrible should be the thought that the nude woman whom the modern artist patches together, bit by bit, from a dozen heterogeneous models, meaning nothing by her, shall last as long as the Venus of the Capitol! – that his group of – no matter what, since it has no moral or intellectual existence will not physically crumble any sooner than the immortal agony of the Laocoon!

39

'NOTABILIA OF THE INTERNATIONAL EXHIBITION: TINTED SCULPTURE'

Art Journal, 1 July 1862, pp. 161–162

Few Art-questions have been more repeatedly discussed, and with a greater diversity of opinion, than the propriety of painting marble statues. Precedents have been sought with more or less success in the finest examples of early Greek sculpture, whence it has been attempted to adduce unquestionable authority for its adoption, Few and unimportant have been the experiments hitherto placed before the public eye in England until the present Exhibition, and in this the results are exclusively from the studio of Gibson, our distinguished countryman. With every consideration for works which have emanated from so gifted a master of his art, and an inclination to accept any exponent of its capabilities which his judgment and taste might approve, we confess our dislike for these coloured statues; tinting, as thus illustrated, is, to our thinking, most unsatisfactory. It has either been carried too far, or not far enough; it is neither flesh nor marble. We consider the adjunct of colour, thus applied, as a departure from the original high purpose of sculpture, which never aimed at more than an abstract type of the subject represented in form and expression; its end being to idealise rather than to realise. This attempt at "too palpable flesh" not only destroys the very essence of the sculptor's art, but violates the delicacy that attaches to the pure material, on which representations are sanctioned that in a coloured medium would be objectionable. As a mere attempt at identity, it fails to do what is done effectually in wax; and, from the quality of the marble, especially observable in the Venus, the veins, as shown through the coloured surface, are particularly unsightly, not to say repulsive. These examples will doubtless settle this vexed question conclusively; few will be bold enough to hope for a success where Gibson has failed. The experiment is for warning rather than for imitation.

DOI: 10.4324/9781315400266-48

40

'ART AND ARTISTS: MR CORDIER'S ETHNOGRAPHICAL SCULPTURE'

Critic, 9 February 1861, p. 190

THOSE WHO, FROM THE TITLE OF THIS EXHIBITION (ignorant of M. Cordier's reputation as a sculptor in his own country), anticipate a kind of Madame Tussaud gathering of painted Red Indians and grinning New Zealanders, will be agreeably surprised by the purely artistic character of the collection. From the ethnological point of view its claims are strikingly incomplete. Of the various races which people the earth, we have the representative forms of only a very few, and those already among the most familiar. Greece, Italy, North Africa, and China, are the favoured nations. What it lacks in value on the scientific side is more than counterbalanced on the æsthetic, by the sculptor's taste and technical attainments, and by the interest attaching to his daring yet judicious experiments in polychromy and mixed materials. To this add a sufficiently unusual variety of types in the subjects chosen, to render the exhibition a novel, picturesque, and singularly interesting one. This picturesque aspect of the exhibition, by the way, would have been greatly augmented by a few specimens of the nobler Asiatic races. Of the various races which cover Hindostan, abounding in contrasted and varying characteristics of form, all eminently suitable to the sculptor, we have not a single example. The idea of such ethnographic study on the part of a sculptor – whose art above all others is fitted adequately to interpret the facts presented by the study – is a good one, and might be worked by competent hands almost to the re-awakening of popular interest in this now languidly-tolerated art: and, if the nobler types were selected, quite consistently with the development of those attributes of beauty and sentiment, robbed of which sculpture ceases to be an art. The factitious, worn-out Greek ideal – which yet is *not* Greek – of our modern sculptors: is not every mortal tired of it? M. Cordier himself cannot emancipate his hands – above all, his eyes – from the venerable fallacy, and under its tyrannous influence often works out (with his hands tied) the lamest, most impotent results.

Perhaps the most remarkable thing in the collection for spirit of conception, vigorous execution, and successfully daring employment of mixed materials, is the bust of an "Arab of El-Aghoual" (No. 1), the head of bronze, the draperies of Algerine onyx. That dark, imposing, treacherous head, lit up by the white burnouse or headdress, and relieved by the broad rich colours of the draped

DOI: 10.4324/9781315400266-49

shoulders, haunts you so long as you are in the room. It is as telling a bit of colour and effect as the bold, prominent, sharply-cut outlines of the face are superb in form. We have small variations of the same, without the bernouse, and in marble and bronze, not nearly so effective. Another very interesting, and on the whole successful, experiment is the bust of a "Moorish Woman singing" (No. 3), in polychrome. Colour is here carried very far, and is wanting here and there, especially in the eyebrows, in delicacy. Though the pose of the head thrown back be somewhat forced, it is not unpleasing. The general *esprit* and verve of that strikingly characteristic and animated face are very remarkable. Noticeable, too, is the help which the colour affords to the *distant* effect of the sculpture. From the other side of the room we see the lines of that piquant face – do not, as in cold marble, merely guess them. There is a small repetition of this head, more delicately tinged with colour, which would be preferred by many; also a small bronze repetition.

A grand type of beauty is that of the noble broad-browed "Greek Woman of Missolonghi" (20), a large bust in Parian: gracious as well as noble. The companion bust, "Roman Woman of Trastevere" (19), is still grander, with her bold, marked features, her broad shoulders, and queenly neck. Worthy to be the mother of heroes, one ejaculates as one gazes; but, alas, no! heroes are *not* now born in those regions of the world. The bust (tinged with colour) of a fair "Neapolitan of the Abruzzi" (21), is a charming head, abounding in soft yet noble outline. How come such heads to be still found in the Abruzzi? There is earnest reading of nature in the bust of a "Young Woman of Paros" (41), with her tender beauty of feature. As to the "Italian Girl" (39), so vague a definition in an ethographic gallery naturally provokes dissatisfaction. In regard to some other so-called "typical" heads a horrible misgiving sometimes seizes one that our sculptor may occasionally be a little lax, and use the same model more than once, with new titles, just as his fellows do. As for the modern Greek men, "Kadji Petros" (31), a bronze medallion, and the rest, they are all disagreeable lying humbugs, and suffice to explain why women of Missolonghi are not nowadays mothers of heroes.

Returning from the familiar pure beauty of Greece and Italy to the *picturesque* subjects, the bust "in bronze, silver, gold, and enamel" of a "Black Moorish Woman" (7) is a very happy example of M. Cordier's art in that direction; though we cannot endorse the inflated language of the catalogue about "Italian languor intensified by Oriental ardour." Such mixture of materials is happily invoked for the representation of these sun-burned denizens of Africa. As again, in the "Negro of the Soudan" (8), a bust in bronze and Algerian onyx; an endurable negro for once, vigorous in character. As for the thick-lipped, low-nosed, low-browed, "Nubian Negro" (9), admirably cast in bronze, the sight of him makes us the very reverse of philanthropic. Our unamiable feeling is only enhanced by the intolerable balderdash and claptrap, calculated for the meridian of Exeter Hall, we find in the catalogue about "manly demeanour;" "sentiment of human dignity and hatred of slavery deeply printed in his noble face;" "reflection of an ardent soul." If ever there were a black scoundrel, that is one. If No. 10, "Negro Woman of the African Coast," be "deservedly surnamed the African Venus," we would rather see no more African Venuses. There *is* something Dantesquely grand, on the other hand, in the hideousness of the "Mulatto Woman" (11), or "Priestess at the Feast of Venus." The round moon face and small features of a Mongol beauty is happily rendered in the bust of a "Chinese Woman" (15), of metal gilt, though the gilding be too overdone; as again in the "Chinaman" (18). The mimetic shrewdness and cunning of that Mongolian face almost sink beneath the human translated into burnished metal. We get back to nobler types in the "Algerine Child" (34), a full-length statue of mixed bronze and coloured marble, and gilt detail. It is felicitous in character, and one of the most picturesque features of the exhibition. "Child of a Highland Kabyle" (5) is of a still purer race.

A bas-relief – which is almost an alto-relief – of "The Nine Muses" (47), studied from various types of "Young Women of Missolonghi," or rather, perhaps, from one or two types in various pose, is an almost infantine failure as a work of art; though one or two of the heads are of great beauty, and have the interest of a naïf reality rare in modern sculpture. When our sculptor utterly forsakes earnest reality for the ambitious ideal, as in his busts of "Diana" (20), "Spring" (29), "Bacchante" (35), &c., the result is as correct and vapid as the work of many another modern sculptor. These things serve as foils to the earnest attempts to interpret the living work of God with which they are interspersed. The statue of "Andromeda" (49) falls below mediocrity in its inanity; and the graceless right-angle of her extended right arm – leaning on something or other – offends against even Academic, as well as higher rules. The ambitious statue, entitled a "Roman Venus" (18), which occupies the post of honour in the room, is a big, hulking, "unmentionable female," attitudinising with an awkward violence and impropriety of demeanour which are only equalled by her utter unattractiveness.

There are some pretty minor statuettes and busts in bronze scattered about the room – of Moor, Turk, and Jew – which call for no special notice.

41

'ANCIENT AND MODERN SCULPTURE'

London Review and Weekly Journal of Politics, Literature, Art, and Society, 4:103 (1862), p. 567

Two most remarkable works by Story, an American artist, afford instances of the very opposite feeling to that of the statues we have been discussing. The subjects, the Libyan Sibyl and Cleopatra, are classical, but the treatment shows a freshness that makes the statues not only original, but, of their kind, more original than anything produced during the last three hundred years. The Cleopatra is fine in the thoughtful expression of the face, the largeness of the type, and the dignity of the position. The last would perhaps have been more pleasing had it been more regular. The Egyptian type of the features is a mistake: Cleopatra was of a Greek family, and her face, as seen on her coins, is sharp and refined, rather what is commonly thought Roman than Greek in its general character. Her headdress, again, is incorrect, for it follows the conventional representation of hair in the ancient Egyptian sculpture. Yet these are trifles, for they do not seriously detract from the great merit of the statue. The Libyan Sibyl deserves still higher praise. The figure is broad in treatment, and the attitude is grand; the expression of the face is thoughtful and noble; and the African features are appropriate. In these two statues, though the subjects are classical, the sculptor has completely freed himself from any conventional shackles. In both the comparative narrowness of the face, the unusual attitude, and the realism of both face and attitude, are startlingly contrary to received opinions. Since Michael Angelo there has been no such powerful realism. That a new sculptor should dare to choose a type not in the face of any high degree of beauty, and depend for his fame upon a truthful and dignified representation of nature, is an innovation in contemporary art that calls for the highest admiration. It is only by works like these that classical subjects can be made interesting by modern artists, but the different treatment from that of the antique, and the essential fitness of that treatment for portrait art, whether historical or contemporary, make it unjust to place these works in the class of modern classical sculpture.

 DOI: 10.4324/9781315400266-50

42

'THE ART-SHOW AT THE GREAT EXHIBITION'

Dublin University Magazine, 60:356 (1862), pp. 141–142

Story's Sybil, leaning forward from her seat, and gazing wistfully into space, has all the air of a mighty seeress, blended with the limbs and body of a vulgar Nubian. Her arms are big and brawny, as those of any fish-wife, and the fat lies in folds below her breast. A little, but only a little, more refined edition of the same work is "Cleopatra Seated;" a figure queenly in attitude, as she rests her chin on one arm, and powerful in the expression of her firmly compressed lips; but no more like to the true Cleopatra, than to Queen Victoria, whether in type of countenance or grace of form. As in all such attempts at realistic faithfulness in matters of the past, great violence has here been done to the truth of history. If Mr. Hawthorne, in puffing off his friend's and countryman's genius without the slightest pertinence to the plot of his own book, chose to forget, many others will not fail to remember, that Cleopatra came of an old Greek line, and that even if any Egyptian blood coursed through her veins, there is no shadow of warrant for moulding her features after the Nubian type. In bodily shape, the true children of Egypt had nothing whatever in common with the Negro races. Their lips and noses were as fine, their hair as far removed from wool, as that of the blackest Hindoo in Lower Bengal. In giving his Cleopatra the Nubian lip and the ungraceful figure, Mr. Story has wantonly strayed aside from a field of beauty which, often travelled over, still remains but partially explored. Did he wish to make Mark Anthony's Circe less of a Ptolemy, and more of a Pharaoh, he should have given her a countenance not unlike that of the "Girl reading," both in point of feature and facial angle! But whatever he aimed at, some show of her traditional beauty ought, at least, to have been preserved. The statue, as a statue, has no small merits of its own; but for truth's sake, let it be called by some other name than that of her whose waning loveliness held Cæsar himself in passing thraldom.

DOI: 10.4324/9781315400266-51

43

HENRY WEEKES, *LECTURES ON ART DELIVERED AT THE ROYAL ACADEMY LONDON*

(London: Bickers and Son, 1880), pp. 171–172

Colour in Sculpture is rather advancing than otherwise. You have heard enough of me on this question, but I believe it will not be wholly without service to you. Many temptations are now being set before you to lead you from the simple feeling of old times, when plaster, terra-cotta, marble, and bronze were looked upon as the only materials necessary for Sculpture, and no others were even sought or desired; and the consequence was that sculptors vied with each other in producing Form only of the most beautiful kind: they were steadily devoted to that one purpose, and nothing tended to divert their thoughts from it. Now the public taste seems oscillating between Form and Colour in Sculpture: more attention is given to the introduction of the latter, and to the discovery of new materials to work upon than formerly. It would not do for me to say that this is a sign of decay in the Art, for I have given evidence to you in this lecture of Colour having existed in the best days of the old Greeks, but I would warn you against lending yourself too much to its temptation: it has before now accompanied decay, and most certainly distracts attention from higher points. Kensington Museum is a condensation of beautiful Colour, almost as beautiful as the airy bubbles which Professor Tyndal exhibited to you lately in his interesting lecture on Light. Nothing can be more instructive than it is in Art manufacture, for there indeed, Colour becomes of equal, if not superior importance to Form. The examples in the collection of the pure style of Sculpture are, in fact, few, scarcely worth noticing. The directors place comparatively no value upon them, and yet, as we know, they do not confine themselves to the lower grades in their teaching. Their defence, however, for the adoption of Colour is a good one when they assert that their schools were established for Art manufactures.

The Royal Academy teaches, or ought to teach, only the topmost walk of Sculpture, and therefore cannot advocate what tends to bring it down to the subordinate one. You will have learnt, I think, from what I have told you that I am not an advocate for the application of Colour to your Art, nor am I wholly antagonistic to it I would have you use it, if at all, with caution – with the

 DOI: 10.4324/9781315400266-52

utmost reserve, as a thing which you may resort to only on particular occasions and under special circumstances: I would have you look upon it as a sort of temptation to which you are liable, but which you may partake of with moderation, without injury to yourself or degradation to your Art. I am, in short, a timid reformer.

44

GEORGE FRAMPTON, R.A., *LAMIA*, 1899–1900

Ivory, bronze, opals, glass, 61 × 55.3 cm,

photographer: Paul Highnam

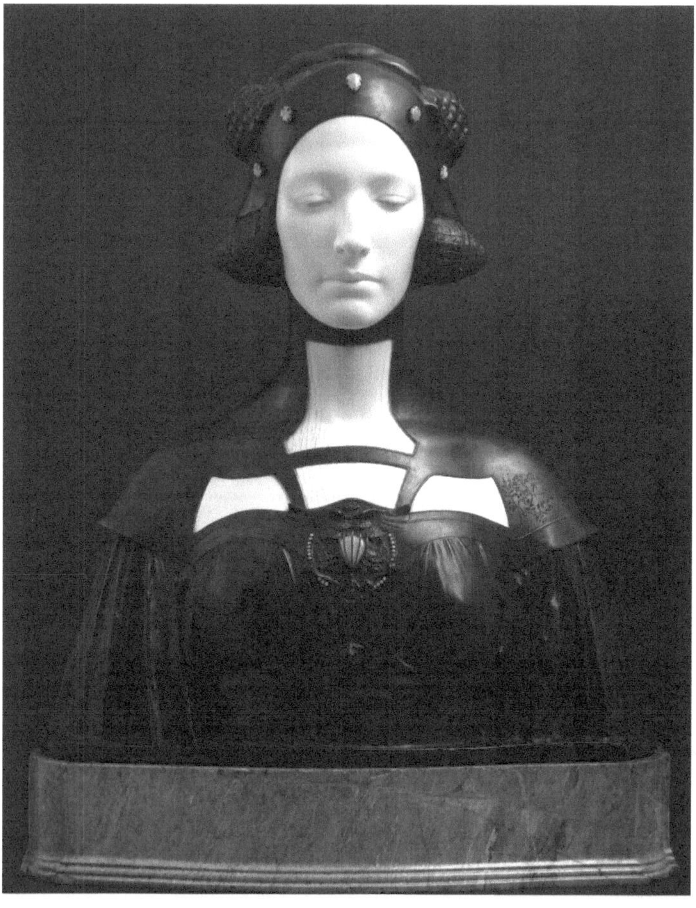

 DOI: 10.4324/9781315400266-53

45

MARION SPIELMANN, *BRITISH SCULPTURE AND SCULPTORS OF TODAY*

(London: Cassell and Co., 1901), pp. 11–12

Sculpture and metal

THERE is, of course, no doubt that the modern movement, like all other movements, has given rise to a good deal of affectation, which, flashy in effect, and attractive to the lovers of the New for New's sake, makes but a poor show against the lofty dignity and true learning of more classic work. Those modellers who have acquired great cleverness of a superficial kind cannot impose upon those who understand and appreciate the high qualities displayed by Mr. Thornycroft, Mr. Gilbert, and their peers; yet in Sculpture, as in Painting, it is dexterity that dazzles the crowd and is apt to lead public taste astray. The people have a predisposition towards flummery.

As has been hinted, it must not be thought that the revival of metal-work, cut, beaten, and twisted, in itself helps sculpture forward very much. Popular as it is, it really seems to divert the attention from Form to Design, and from light and shade, with planes, to ingenuity with pleasing lines – a very beautiful and elevated art, but not sculpture. As an adjunct, it is extremely valuable; and its delightful playfulness is irresistible in the hands of a fine artist, who does not mistake mere wriggles and doublings for harmonious line; but at the best it suggests rather the man with the anvil, shears, and pincers, than the man with the clay and the chisel. No doubt, in the Parthenon frieze and the Ægina pediment horse-trappings and the like were additions in real metal; but as time went on these accessories were rendered like the rest of the work, in marble, as may be seen in the Pergamon frieze.

Nevertheless, in the hands of a man of taste, capable of restraining any tendency towards ostentation and redundancy, the introduction of this offshoot of the goldsmith's art, and the ironsmith's, cannot fail to be very attractive. At any rate, it may give rise to a new school of artistic craftsmen, a community to be welcomed for the educational value of their refinement, but not less for the economic importance of their work. Especially would this be so in the case of cast metal. The point is well appreciated in Paris, where a dozen years ago there were two firms of fine-art bronze-founders employing over five hundred hands, whose work was

DOI: 10.4324/9781315400266-54

very highly paid; while there were innumerable smaller establishments, and more were to be found in other cities of France. Since that time the "new art" movement has there given an impetus to the art-trade such as should startle Birmingham into unaccustomed envy. In England such an industry is practically unknown, and it may be doubted if in the whole kingdom a hundred hands are employed in this production of bronze statuary, as distinguished from the ordinary metal figures and ornaments of commerce. Obviously, there is here an opening for a very beautiful and a very lucrative industry if only the public will understand its charm, and encourage the effort now being made to bring before the world good work by our best sculptors and designers.

For this reason I have included in this volume some reference to metal-workers whose names are not commonly linked with those of the sculptors, except in so far as they may perchance be commissioned to provide ornament for the greater work. At the same time it should be remarked that the beaten and twisted metal-work revived in England mainly by Mr. Alfred Gilbert is not exactly the sort at present understood and cultivated in France, where sculpture is regarded with somewhat more sedate and classic eyes – when, indeed, that sculpture is not avowedly frivolous. Its popularity is less a matter of taste than of fashion; and it is recognised that fashion, even in art, imposes some respect. During a discussion on the advisableness of clearing out from Westminster Abbey the more pretentious and debased statuary that encumbers it, I was startled to hear a distinguished sculptor energetically resist the proposal, quaintly protesting – "Past generations thought it very good; future generations may do the same, and may condemn our finest works of to-day, on which we set some store, as utter rubbish, bad in conception, and false in sentiment!"

46

ALFRED MASKELL, *IVORIES*

(London: Methuen and Co., 1905), pp. 498–499, 504, 515–517, 521–522

The nineteenth century and the present day

IT will come as a surprise, perhaps, to many people to hear that in this present twentieth century sculpture in ivory can be considered worthy of any consideration, or, to put it otherwise, that it is practised by artists of distinction. They will be aware of the neglect into which the art had long fallen, and although the use of ivory for such prosaic things as billiard-balls, paper-knives, the backs of brushes, and other objects of utility which we are accustomed to see in shop-windows is well known, it would appear to be almost entirely forgotten as a material for serious sculpture. It is true that Dieppe is still famous as a centre of ivory carving, that crucifixes and figures, fansticks and nick-nacks from thence are abundant enough, that Chinese and Indian productions fill a void of a certain kind, and that modern Japanese figures of a better type than the latter command comparatively high prices. But it is also true that, for one cause or another, ivory carving has been neglected – it would not be right to say despised – for many years by great sculptors in marble and bronze. It was relegated to the position of an industry, and during the three centuries or more which have gone by since, as has been shown, ivory sculptors occupied a position inferior to none amongst those who practised what have been called the minor arts – a misnomer, for they are often lesser only in point of size – during all this lapse of time the immense output of the beautiful material was restricted in its use either to objects of utility upon which it was not thought worth while to lavish decoration of any kind, or – so far as public taste is concerned – was only good enough for the manufacture of that which we know by the terms "*articles de Paris*" or "*de Dieppe*": bazaar or chimney ornaments with pretensions to nothing beyond prettiness.

[. . .]

The acquisition of the Congo State by the King of the Belgians, and the large amount of ivory imported into the Antwerp market, inspired the king, on the recommendation of M. van Eetevelde, Secretary of State for the Congo, with the happy idea of the encouragement of a long-neglected art. For this purpose tusks of the finest description were placed at the disposition of the leading sculptors, and the desire of the king was well known that efforts should be made to revive

DOI: 10.4324/9781315400266-55

the use of ivory for sculpture, both alone and in conjunction with other materials, and also for furniture, for caskets, and other decorative objects. The response was immediate and gratifying, and the first results were exhibited at the International Exhibition at Antwerp and at the succeeding one at Brussels in 1887. From these a selection was made and is now permanently installed at the exhibition of the Congo State in the Belgian capital.

[. . .]

We come now to England, and if it cannot be said that we can produce an extended list of workers in ivory, on the other hand it will be admitted that those whose work remains to be noticed are in the first rank amongst our sculptors. No pretension is here made to compile a complete list.

The pages of the catalogues of the exhibitions of the Royal Academy during the last ten years or so of the nineteenth century – it would be hardly necessary to go farther back – will show, from time to time, solitary instances of art in ivory. We shall find in 1896 the work of the Belgian sculptor Van Beurden, and again in the two following years, when there was also a "Despair of Cleopatra," by Richard Garbe. In 1899 we have the group by Harry Bates, in 1900 Frampton's "Lamia," in 1901 the frieze by Lynn Jenkins, and "Andromeda," by Clovis Delacour. In 1893 Gérôme, who was an honorary Royal Academician, had exhibited his life-size "Bellona" in ivory and bronze. Now and again there are minor ornamental works, such as a lady's belt in ivory and silver, and some medallions by Garbe, or, in 1897, a mirror frame by the Countess Fédora Gleichen. And we may suppose that other things would have gone direct from the artist's studio into the hands of the purchaser. In any case, it must be admitted that the list is not a lengthy one. But if not extensive, it makes up, as has been said, in quality.

In noticing English ivory sculpture we shall be again struck by the predilection for using it in conjunction with other materials. Again, also, we shall find amongst the artists the diversity of talent that distinguishes them not only as clever statuary sculptors, but skilled as painters and enamellers, in gold and silver smiths' work, or in the execution of bas-reliefs, plaques, and medals. It is hardly surprising that the decorative character of the mingling of materials should appeal to this versatility of genius. It is a difficult method to handle, but we know that in the use of metal or in adding colour or jewellery such an artist as Frampton, for example, will not offend by vulgarity. He does not appeal to purely sensuous feelings. There is no question of trickery or attempt to deceive, nor will the effect be tawdry or claptrap. And, then, how charmingly applicable is such a system – more than marble or bronze – to small sculpture! In the leaning towards modernity could anything be more suggestive than the introduction of portrait figures of everyday life or the poetic ideals such as the labourers and miners of Constantin Meunier? We cannot help thinking of the Tanagra figurines, but can there be any reason why the contrasts and tonalities of the flesh and draperies should not be harmoniously translated by the mingling of ivory with wood and metals? It is another question from that of colouring, and while it must be admitted that both are of too extensive a nature to be strictly within the scope of the present work, the allusion to them will be pardoned.

The work of George Frampton requires but little introduction. He is an all-round craftsman who astonishes us by the variety and fertility of his invention. He appears to be completely unshackled by the traditions of the past and the usages imposed by convention. It has been said that he has been influenced by the study of Donatello. That may be, but in the main it must be seen that he goes to nature. There is, after all, an emancipation from tradition and precedents which is in itself logical and by no means a renunciation. Throughout all his work we find the note of simplicity and exact knowledge, the intuition which knows when to be lavish and where to stop. In the mingling of materials Frampton has already given us numerous examples in his other work. We need only recall his St. George in bronze, agate, and mother-of-pearl, his panels, or his figure of Dame Alice Owen in bronze and marble.

The bust of "Lamia," now in the possession of Mr. William Vivian, which is here illustrated, is an example of modern ivory carving which it is pleasing to be able to give. The face, with its studied serenity – cryptic, snake-like – is carved in life-size from a fine block of beautifully grained ivory. The quaint head-dress and arrangement of the hair in nets projecting on either side of the face, in the style which was fashionable in the reign of Richard II., the dress and covering of the shoulders and neck are of bronze, through openings in which ivory is again used for the flesh. The head-dress is jewelled, and so also is the elegant breast ornament, with opals, and the patina of the bronze should be noticed.

For the same reasons of variety in his work one is not surprised to find that Alfred Gilbert has applied himself to ivory carving. He also is a goldsmith, notably in the case of the fine epergne which he made for the late Queen. Neither, indeed, has he disdained lesser work, such as the designing and executing of necklaces and other objects of jewellery. He seems to revel in richness of decoration.

[. . .]

It may be questioned if even the Belgian sculptors worked solely for love of the material – much as they esteemed it – and not, rather, simply because the government of the Congo had placed in their hands, with a definite object, the superb tusks which came from that colonial possession. The result was to produce a certain movement in the desired direction and to show that a school of ivory sculpture could easily be formed, but that support was necessary for a prolonged existence. It was bounty-fed in fact, and through the apathy or want of tangible recognition on the part of those whose protection is essential in all the arts it was almost strangled at its birth. The public admired, the success was undeniable; but it was a *succès d'estime*. More than this is required. Undoubtedly from time to time the sculptor will use ivory as his medium. It is a delightful material to work, attractive, delicate, and graceful in results; grateful in every way to the artist. It bears to monumental sculpture something of the relation that miniature painting bears to the art of painting on a large scale. No new or special knowledge is required. Any sculptor can work it. What is essential is the creation of the model, to be afterwards reproduced in ivory. But still more essential are patronage and a market, and these at a figure worthy of a great artist. All this must be conceded.

It cannot be denied that ivory sculpture since its most glorious days fell into bad hands and got a bad name. It is from the productions of the workshop that it has been judged. To the public, nowadays, carving in ivory suggests China or India; nothing more. People will pay for industrial art what it is worth, but it is not at such a price that a sculptor of reputation can work. Nor should it be forgotten that from the point of view of the qualities of the material it costs as much to execute a statuette in ivory, a foot or so in height, as to produce a life-size statue in marble.

2.3

Replication

DOI: 10.4324/9781315400266-56

2.3 Replication

The making of all sculpture is dependent on reproduction, whether casting a bronze from a clay, wax or plaster model or carving stone from a clay prototype. All sculpture can be made in multiples, and often has been, rendering nonsensical the notion of an unique original sculpture.[1] In the nineteenth century, new methods, technologies and materials emerged for reproducing sculpture at various scales, while plaster casting, dating back to classical antiquity, was put to new purposes and its methods updated for new contexts. Some sculptures – perhaps most famously Hiram Powers's 1847 *Greek Slave* – became multimedia, appearing in full size in marble, in reduced size in Parian, and in two dimensions in photographs and engravings.[2] Sources in this section highlight the new 1840s materials and methods of electrotyping, reducing sculpture, Parianware and stereograph photography, alongside the revived ancient practice of plaster casting. They explore the Victorian materials of replicated sculpture and their social, cultural and political meanings.

The newfound importance of replicas is perhaps best illustrated by the 1867 'Convention for Promoting Universally Reproductions of Works of Art for the Benefit of Museums of all Countries'. This was drawn up by the founding director of the South Kensington Museum (now the Victoria and Albert Museum or V&A), Henry Cole, and signed by 15 European princes. It inaugurated a new, formalised means of sharing art treasures across borders – although, as the photograph of men making moulds for South Kensington in Delhi suggests, copying took place far beyond Europe, and not always in such a reciprocal manner.[3] Replicas (especially casts and electrotypes) were used to train artists and designers in nascent art and design schools across Britian and the British Empire. They were employed to educate and entertain new mass audiences at newly founded museums and leisure resorts. The *Saturday Review* article discussing the South Kensington Museum's Cast Courts, which opened in 1873, offers a rather sneering account of the new viewers of sculpture that these replicas encourage; these new viewers appear to be as inauthentic as the plaster materials they survey.[4] The public accessibility of these reproductions in new materials formed one of the principal arguments in their favour, however, as the *Saturday Review* itself rather grudgingly concludes. Similar remarks can be found in the *Art Journal*'s 1859 discussion of Parian, and an 1890 *Saturday Review* piece on 'Small Bronzes' emphasises these reduced size versions as a means of disseminating more broadly the innovations of the so called 'New Sculpture', which prioritised the material of bronze. Further, David Brewster's 1856 exposition of the significance of binocular photography for replicating sculpture stresses the potential of this new medium and its compact, portable material properties: 'from such binocular pictures, executed on one side of the globe, an artist, on the other side, may complete an admirable statue'.[5] All three discussions of Parian, small bronzes, and stereophotography suggest the ways in which replicas might be preferable to the 'original'.

Replicas were both commercial objects and expressions of cultivated taste for the middle-class home. This topic is explored in the *Art Journal*'s article on Parian, which suggests the 'peculiar fitness of these beautiful works' as Christmas presents, and captured in the photograph of the exhibition stand for Elkington and Co. at the 1876 Philadelphia Centennial Exhibition.[6] All were made by skilled workers, but the skill of these workers has often been overlooked. The fact that Parian and electrotypes were made in factories, rather than studios, marked these workers out in particular, whereas the predominently Italian migrants making plaster casts in nineteenth-century London seem to have been either criminalised or ignored altogether.[7] The skill of plaster cast making was tacitly acknowledged in colonial contexts, as Indian men in Delhi making casts for the South Kensington Museum were seen to be lacking the skills to create plaster piece moulds (despite the fact that the men in question were themselves experienced soapstone carvers). Instead, they were put to work making 'mechanical' gelatine moulds, a process developed specifically for this context (and one deemed appropriate for the intricate nature of Indian sculpture), as set out in the extracts here from the account of this undertaking by Henry Hardy Cole (Henry Cole's son). The photograph reproduced shows these men at work.[8] Back in Britain, the social theorist Harriet Martineau's account of a visit to the Elkington factory in Birmingham is unusual in its emphasis on the artistic skill of its 'productions which require artistic heads and hands at almost every stage'.[9] This destabilises the dichotomy set up by sculptors in the preceding 'Materials and making' section, who saw artistic labour only in the conceptualisation of a sculpture and were happy to delegate 'manual' work to 'carvers'. New materials brought with them new sets of art workers – wax modellers, metal hammerers, detail-focused silver workers, solderers and chasers. But as Martineau disparagingly sets out, women were not permitted to engage in the more creative aspects of work in Elkington's factory. At the same time, these new materials drew art closer together with manufacture and industry, with reproductions of Greek sculpture and knives and forks made as part of the same undertaking. The *Art Journal* likewise comments favourably on this union of art and manufacture in its deliberations over the new ceramic medium of Parianware.[10]

Despite the fact that plaster casts were embraced anew in the nineteenth century for didactic and leisure purposes on a whole new scale, the limitations of plaster as a material for replicating sculpture emerge in a number of sources. At South Kensington, casts are described as 'ghastly unrealities, visible but intangible, bearing the semblance but not the substance of old and valued friends'.[11] Casts are regularly described in such a contradictory manner: they are acceptable stand-ins for the *form* of sculpture, often discussed with no acknowledgement of their replica status, as in Anna Jameson's introduction to the cast courts of modern sculpture at the Crystal Palace, which opened the sculpture section in this volume. But they cannot replicate the surface properties of marble. The cheapness and inauthenticity of plaster for some critics seem to be connected too to a perceived vulgar and inauthentic audience, which was attracted to new displays like the

South Kensington cast courts and the Crystal Palace at Sydenham before it. Parianware was presented in an altogether different light: unlike the 'ignoble' plaster cast, the *Art Journal* praised its 'delicate and refined' surface, 'eminently sculpturesque in its aspect and tone of colour'.[12] Parian was exclusive (but affordable), its elite status shored up by its name, which is a reference to prestigious white marble from the Greek island of Paros used in the most celebrated sculptures of ancient Greece, the social connotations of which were explored in section 2.2.

Notes

1 For further exploration, see A. Hughes and E. Ranfft (eds), *Sculpture and its Reproductions* (London: Reaktion Books, 1997).
2 M. Droth, J. Edwards and M. Hatt (eds), *Sculpture Victorious: Art in an Age of Invention, 1837–1901* (New Haven and London: Yale University Press, 2014), pp. 244–51; pp. 308–27.
3 See B. Cormier and D. Thom (eds), *A World of Fragile Parts* (London: V&A Publishing, 2016).
4 I have explored plaster and inauthenticity in greater depth in K. Nichols, *Greece and Rome at the Crystal Palace: Classical Sculpture and Modern Britain, 1854–1936* (Oxford: Oxford University Press, 2015. On the V&A cast courts, see A. Patterson and M. Trusted, *The Cast Courts* (London: V&A Publishing, 2018).
5 D. Brewster, *The Stereoscope: Its History, Theory, and Construction. With its Application to the Fine and Useful Arts* (London: John Murray, 1856), p. 185. On sculpture, reproduction and photography, see P. Di Bello, 'Photographs of Sculpture: *Greek Slave*'s "complex polyphony", 1847–77', *19: Interdisciplinary Studies in the Long Nineteenth Century*, 22 (2016), at http://doi.org/10.16995/ntn.775.
6 'The Corridor of Statuary Porcelain at Alderman Copeland's, New Bond St', *Art Journal*, 59 (November 1859), pp. 347–8, on p. 348. On Elkington at the Philadelphia Centennial, see A. Grant and A. Patterson, *The Museum and the Factory: the V&A, Elkington, and the Electrical Revolution* (London: Lund Humphries, 2018) pp. 96–9.
7 See R. Wade, *Domenico Brucciani and the Fortmatori of Nineteenth-Century Britain* (New York: Bloomsbury, 2018), pp. 1–19.
8 On the photograph, see M. A. Pelizzari, 'From Stone to Paper: Photographs of Architecture and the Traces of History', in M. A. Pelizzari (ed.), *Traces of India: Photography, Architecture, and the Politics of Representation, 1850–1900* (Montréal: Canadian Centre for Architecture; New Haven: Yale Center for British Art, 2003), pp. 20–57. For discussion of another famous plaster cast made for the V&A in India, see Tapati Guha-Thakurta, 'The Production and Reproduction of a Monument: The Many Lives of the Sanchi Stupa', *South Asian Studies* 29:1 (2013), pp. 77–109.
9 Harriet Martineau, 'The Magic Troughs at Birmingham', *Household Words*, 4:83 (25 October 1851), pp. 113–17, on p. 114.
10 A general introduction to Parianware is provided by P. Atterbury (ed.), *The Parian Phenomenon: a survey of Victorian Parian Porcelain Statuary and Busts* (Shepton Beauchamp: Richard Dennis, 1989).
11 'Ghosts at South Kensington', *Saturday Review of Politics, Literature, Science and Art*, 47: 1222 (29 March 1879), pp. 391–2, on p. 391.
12 'The Corridor of Statuary Porcelain', p. 347.

47

HARRIET MARTINEAU, 'THE MAGIC TROUGHS AT BIRMINGHAM'

Household Words, 4:83 (25 October 1851), pp. 113–117

ON the 7th of next May, it will be twenty years since the largest meeting ever held in our island was assembled at Newhall Hill, Birmingham. At the bottom of the hill were the hustings, whence it was declared that the Reform Bill should become the law of the land; and from every part of the slope, from tens of thousands of voices, came the solemn chant of the Union Hymn, and the words of the oath, singly spoken, by every man present, to devote himself and his children to the great cause. There is no room now for such a meeting on Newhall Hill. Within these twenty years, buildings have sprung up, over nearly the whole surface; and the roaring of the furnace and the din of the hammer are heard where the hymn and the solemn oath resounded in a less peaceful time.

Among those buildings, at the bottom of the hill, are the large premises of Messrs. Elkington, Mason, and Co. – the firm celebrated for their electro-gilding and plating. They have actually enclosed the canal within their premises – built over it – and their workshops are still extending. There may be seen nearly four hundred men and boys employed, diligently and constantly, upon work of so high an order, that the wonder is how, in the imperfect state of our popular education, so many can be found to manage such processes. As for the diligence – arts of so high an order as these cannot be served by halves. Here must be no Monday laziness after Sunday's rest; no caprice as to going to work or staying away. Like time and tide – like brewing and dyeing – the work at Messrs. Elkington's cannot wait for men's humours. Any one who engages himself here must go through with what he undertakes. He is told, on being engaged, "We find you six days' work, and you are to find six days' labour." And the wages given are such as to justify this compact being made stringent. They rise from twenty-five shillings to three pounds a week, according to the nature and quality of the work.

Any one who has seen the contributions to the Exhibition from this house, will understand that a special education is required for almost every department of this manufacture. The fruit-baskets, twined with the convolvulus and the vine, are graceful enough; but the inkstands, with their groups – Rebecca at the Well; the Milkmaid and her Goats; and the race-cups and the statuettes – are productions

DOI: 10.4324/9781315400266-57

which require artistic heads and hands at almost every stage. And, as yet, this order of art is new in England, and so is the process of manufacture. Formerly, we bought our plated candlesticks, and table-forks, and mustard-pots, and ink-stands from Sheffield. There was a small choice of patterns; very rarely anything new – seldom anything remarkably beautiful. The few who could spend money largely – princes and peers, and half-a-dozen wealthy commoners – might go to Rundell and Bridge, and indulge their taste for works of art in gold and silver; but in plated goods there was little beauty, little variety, and very poor wear. Preparation was making, half a century ago, for the day which has arrived. Mr. Rundell was bringing over works of art – seizing every interval of continental truce to import pictures, statues, and gems, and paying Flaxman six hundred and twenty pounds for his model and drawing of the Shield of Achilles – of which four casts only were made – for two royal princes and two peers: but meantime, the middle classes were served with patterns almost as hackneyed as the willow pattern in our dinner-plates. Preparation was making, unawares, for the other grand improvement, by Mr. Spencer, of Liverpool, and Mr. Smea, of the Bank of England, having applied the process of electro-plating to taking copies of embossed surfaces. Where the discovery originated, is not yet settled. Russia claims it. Italy claims it. But while it was used only for taking copies of gems and coins, we of the middle classes, who cannot afford to buy silver plate, were annoyed by seeing the copper peeping through the edges and prominences of our plated candlesticks, forks, and sugar-basins; and, too often, a bend or a dent here and there, showing that there was as little wear in the metal and its solder in one way, as in its silver covering in another.

Mr. Elkington was one of those who first saw how the process of electro-plating might be extended to the supply of our needs. He saw that by the agency of electricity, the gold or silver plating might become one substance with the material on which it is deposited, instead of being a mere covering, liable to be rubbed off by use. He saw that a whiter and harder metal than copper might be used as a base, and employed German silver for the purpose. He saw that the most various and elaborate designs and ornaments could be produced by this method, in place of the few old forms; and that it would be an inestimable advantage to do the plating last, after all the repairs and finishings, instead of the clumsy old method of smoothing, and finishing and burnishing, after the frail coating of silver had been laid on. Seeing all this, he took out a patent for his process in 1840. About thirty other manufacturers in England are licensed by him to use his process; and there are not more than two houses now which maintain the old Sheffield method of laying silver on copper, and using the old soft tin solder. That any such houses remain, may be very well, because they turn out their work cheap, and keep down the price of the superior article. By the time they also have recourse to the new method, the patent will have expired, and competition will keep prices reasonable. The process has also spread widely over the Continent; so that society may consider that it has the discovery safe for general use. What remains to be wished is, that our Schools of Design should be extended and improved; and that a Museum of practical work, in various departments of manufacture, should be attached to them. We have not enough of fresh and beautiful designs actually offered; but, few as they are, they are more than can be used, from the designers' want of knowledge of the practical business of the manufacture. While we are complaining of the dearth of employment for educated women, here is one, remarkably suited to the female faculties, much needed, and therefore very profitable; but from which young women are at present almost excluded, for want of the practical part of the study. One, here and there, may design a pattern, unexceptionable in taste, and in every sort of fitness but one: but if it cannot be wrought, her labour and her hopes are lost.

Let us send a glance over what we saw at Messrs. Elkington and Mason's the other day, where a friend, connected with the establishment, showed us whatever we wished to see. From the show-room – the Art-chamber – which we shall not describe, because every one may go there, we were conducted to the room where the modellers were at work. There, on a shelf, stood some tall volumes – books on Art, and choice engravings. Engravings, and patterns of beautiful forms were hung up; and at their respective tables sat several artists, modelling in wax. One should come here to understand what pains are spent on the common articles which we use every day. Here is one side of a stand for castors. This one side consists of three pieces; the straight centre, and the two oblique sides, on which the pattern must be reversed, every hair's-breadth of each of which must be modelled with the nicest care, – a smooth stroke here, a gentle touch there. And then there is the stem, with the handle at the top, and two sides again. These common articles surprise one more by the detail than the more luxurious productions – the nautilus shell, for instance, in pink wax, which is the pattern of a flower-stand; or the group of palm-tree and oak, overshadowing the sick Hindoo, and the soldier-surgeon stooping over him, lancet in hand; – the piece of testimonial plate presented to the surgeon of a regiment.

It seems as if as much precision and care were necessary in the coarse interior parts of the work as in the outside finish: for instance, in raising the foundation of a sugar-basin, which must have no join in its circumference, because it is to be gilt inside. It is one of the nicest arts in cookery to make a raised pie a true circle or oval; and, in the hairdresser's business, to make one side of a wig match the other. In forming the foundation of a sugar-basin, the flat sheet of metal has to be raised in a bulge first, and then contracted; and then it must bulge again: and this form must be truly given by turning the metal with one hand, on the vibrating steel bar, which serves for the anvil, while the other hand uses the hammer, with equal and steady strokes. A similar process is used for raising an embossed pattern on the metal, when the form renders casting out of the question. Under the process of *snarling,* as this is called, it is curious to see the bumps rising under the hammer – bumps caused by the round head of the steel bar beneath, and destined to group themselves into clusters of leaves or fruit as the work advances. When a hard mixed metal is used for these foundations, and the copper scales at the surface, the work must go into *pickle* before it can be further dealt with. In a yard, therefore, stand little vats of this pickle, in which sulphuric or nitric acid predominates, causing the copper to scale away.

But the foundations must be annealed before hammering, that the pores of the metal may be opened. In the annealing room is a furnace, such as was formerly blown by bellows, like that of a blacksmith's forge. Now the engine saves that labour. A cock is turned, and there is an instant commotion among the lazy embers. Blue, yellow, red, and white flames dance and leap, and want something to devour. A sugar basin or teapot is held over them on a metal slice; and, in a few seconds, the black metal becomes a deep red; and then, in a few more seconds, scarlet, pink, white; and then it is laid down on the ground, to grow black again at its leisure.

Meantime, the ornamental rims, and little panels, and all the decorations which are to be afterwards attached to the article, are in preparation elsewhere. A man stands at a pair of shears fastened to his counter, and cuts out pieces of German silver, as marked roughly from a pattern. These are the little plates which are to receive the embossed patterns, now in course of being struck off from steel dies in another room, or the slips which are to become rims themselves. In that other room are three or four men, who seem to be seized with a frantic convulsion, at intervals of a minute or so. They are the stampers. Having fixed the concave part of the die under the stamper, and attached the punch to the stamper, they lay on a slip of German silver, throw themselves by one foot and hand into a sling of rope, raising the stamper by their weight, and then let it fall, punching the slip of metal, which then gives place to another. There are no less than thirty tons of steel dies on the premises, each die being a costly and precious article of property. They are the most expensive part of the apparatus; as the castings are the most expensive process of the manufacture, from the time and minute pains required. Of the castings, nothing need be said here, as the process is the same as in every iron-foundry, – the work being only on a smaller scale, and more delicately finished. The sand, employed in the castings, is from the neighbouring Cemetery. As fast as the red sandstone is hewn away there, to make room for new chambers of the dead, and fresh nooks for flowering shrubs and green graves, the rubbish is bought by the manufacturers for their castings, to an amount which materially supports the funds of the Cemetery.

The chasing of the cast articles is one of the most astonishing processes to an observer. It seems as if every man so employed must be an artist. One sits with a salver before him. With the left hand, he turns it this way and that, while with the graving tool which he holds in his right, he runs graceful patterns, without hesitation and without fault. Parallel curves, and curves that meet, are marked off with a roundness and steadiness that no mechanism could surpass. The folded leaf, the pendulous flower, the wandering tendril, grow under his touch; and no one of them wanders out of its place. Near him sits another artist, at work upon a statuette, fixed in the position he wants by being stuck in pitch. A row of little chasing tools is arranged at his side, each pointed with a different pattern. Here he, by gentle taps of the hammer on the tool in hand, makes a rim round the head or arm: there, by using another tool, he produces a diced pattern, where shadow is to be represented. Then, the folds of the drapery are more finely streaked, and a finish is given to the bands of hair. Close by is another man, so intent on his work, that he twists a wire round his head to keep his hair from falling over his eyes. He is engaged on a vase filled with pitch, to preserve the smallest indentations of the pattern from injury, while he hammers away, daintily, at the minutest finishings of the bark of a tree, or the fleece of a sheep.

Next, we see how the stamped rims, or other loose parts, are soldered on to the main body of the work. It is not now as in the old days, when the spout of a teapot was liable to come off, or the top of the nozzle of a candlestick to part company with the cylinder. Those were the days when the soft tin solder was used: and the soft solder was used because the work had to be carried to the fire; whereas now, the fire is brought to the work. On stands in the middle of the room are huge iron pans, like saucers, containing cinders. At each of these pans or saucers stands a man, with pincers in one hand, wherewith he applies the solder, and turns over the article to be soldered; and, in the other hand, a flexible tube, by which he administers air and oxygen gas to the fire among the cinders. This tube consists of two compartments, one of which conveys air, and the other gas; and it is in the power of the holder to increase the flame to any intensity, and apply it in any direction, to this side or that, above, below, and around the most delicate ornament that has to be united with any other piece. The white powder that is thrown on, where the solder has been applied, is borax, which fuses the solder. One sees the metal bubbling and running like a liquid; and when it has diffused itself, and shown by a white streak that it is done enough, and then become cool, the join is evidently as lasting as any other part of the work. Nothing comes to pieces that is soldered under this blowpipe.

There is, of course, some roughness at these joins. Formerly, under the old method of plating, the silver had to be laid on before such blemishes were removed. A finishing process was gone through after the plating. The advantage of electro-plating, in this respect, is great. The gilding and silvering are done the last thing. Now, therefore, the goods are carried from the soldering to receive such touches from the file, and smoothing apparatus, as may make all sharp, and polished, and fit for the final process. When the file has removed all roughness at the joins, the whole surface of the article is smoothed and polished, under the hands of sooty workmen in paper caps, who apply the surface to swift revolving cylinders, which administer a polishing with oil and sand. After being cleansed in vats containing a ley of caustic potash, the goods are ready for the final process. The fumes from a little congregation of vats, direct the observer to the place where this cleansing goes on; and he finds them suspended in the liquor, where they part with the oil, and every other kind of soil that they may have brought from the workman's hands.

The visitor may next find himself introduced to what looks like a dinner-party of nearly fifty people. A second glance, however, shows him that the guests are all women, and that their dress, however neat, is not precisely suitable to the decorations of the table. The long table is set out, from end to end, with epergnes, candelabra, fruit baskets, cruet frames, bottle stands, and silver dishes; and between forty and fifty women are employed in burnishing and finishing, giving the last polish with the hand, and clearing out the last speck of dust or dimness which may lurk in any crease or corner.

As for the gilding and silvering chambers, they are like seats of magic. One might look on for a year, and have no idea of the process, but that it must be done by magic. There is a machine, containing a great wheel, and large bands of a horse-shoe shape, which we are told are magnets. From this machine, loose wires extend to the troughs, and dangle over the sides. In the troughs are plates of silver, standing in a brownish liquor; and in this liquor hang the articles to be silvered, suspended by copper wires from thicker copper wires laid across the top of the troughs. There hang the teapots, and spoons, and trays; and nothing ensues till the magician, in the shape of a man in a dark-blue blouse, takes hold of one of the dangling wires, and unites it with the wires on which the goods are hung. Then, in an instant, they become overspread with silver. The coating is a mere film at first, and it requires some hours (from five to ten, according to the quality of the article) to obtain a sufficient silvering. The brownish liquor in the troughs is a solution of oxide of silver in cyanide of potassium. At the magnetic touch of the loose wire from the machine, the silver is deposited upon the surface of the article communicated with; and not only laid upon it, but intimately united with it. Gilding is done more rapidly than silvering; and the gilding process is therefore that which is usually exhibited to strangers. In this case, a man holds a bent copper wire, from which is suspended the bunch of spoons, plate, scissors, watch-keys, or vinaigrettes to be gilt; he holds, at the same time, the loose wire in connexion with the other, and washes his charge for a few seconds to and fro, and, lo! it comes out golden. Having heard something of a cobweb having been gilded at this trough, in the service of Prince Albert, we made inquiry, and found that it was really so – that a cobweb had been gilt – but it was by accident. A rosebud was gilded in the Prince's presence, and when it came out of the trough, it was found to have been crossed by a delicate thread of cobweb.

We asked, what could be done in the case of articles *parcel-gilt?* where, for instance, bunches of silver flowers or fruit appear on a gold ground, or a gold net-work covers a silver ground, – and we found that the matter was very simple. The parts which are not to be gilt are varnished over, and the varnish is easily removed afterwards. The minutest atoms of the gold and silver are saved, by the goods being dipped in four or five troughs in succession, till every loose particle is washed off. The superintendence of these troughs is a situation of great trust. The value of a pint of the solution may be about fifteen shillings, and, of course, it would not be difficult to carry off small quantities of it. The whole work of the establishment, however, requires a somewhat superior order of men – men who might be supposed superior to the temptation of theft.

But here, alas! comes in the regret which cannot but be felt by the observer of the working-classes in Birmingham – regret for their extreme and unaccountable improvidence. Without doubting that there may be exceptions, we are obliged to see that, as a general rule, the best wages, and the most constant work, are no security against poverty and dependence. It is too common a thing to find that a man who has, for years together, earned from thirty shillings to sixty shillings a-week (twice or three times the income of a multitude of clergymen, retired military and naval officers, poor gentlemen, and widow ladies), has not a shilling beforehand when he falls sick, and must be sustained by a subscription – by private charity – as the only alternative from public relief. It is too common a case that women, employed in the manufactures of the town, buy expensive shawls or gowns, paying for them by weekly instalments (extending over years for a single shawl), and pawning them every Monday morning, to redeem them on Saturday night for the Sunday's wear. It is too common to hear employers speak coolly, if not with satisfaction, of this state of things, because it keeps the workmen dependent and humble, and lessens the danger of those strifes about wages, which are the plague of the manufacturer's life. "Well; never mind!" says the employer, significantly. "Let things be. It may be all very well."

To us, however, it seems not well that men, with incomes exceeding one hundred pounds a-year should fail to secure their own independence; should fail to educate their children; should fail to provide a soft pillow for a time of sickness; while indulging in pleasure and luxury during their best days. To us, it seems not well that, just at present, when the necessaries of life are one-third cheaper than they were when the men were receiving the same wages as now, no attempt at saving should be made by so many as, in Birmingham, exhibit their improvidence to all the world. Here and there, however, something better is seen. In the manufactory we have been describing, every workman above twenty-one years of age, is a member of a relief-club, paying three-pence a-week to secure support under sickness or accident. Many of the people on the premises, also, are members of the Freehold Land Association, and are acquiring property in that excellent manner. One pleasant change in their mode of life appears in their love of reading. At the tea hour, those who do not go home, and who used to gossip over a pot of beer, have turned readers; and under their counters several popular periodicals may be seen stowed away. We must hope that the improvement will proceed, and that, while dismissing from under their hands, to the houses of the great, the articles of luxury and beauty which Birmingham supplies, the men of Birmingham will aspire to have their own humble homes furnished with every needful comfort, and brightened by that intellectual enlightenment, and that peace of mind about their families and their future, without which neither luxuries nor comforts can yield any true and lasting pleasure.

48

CENTENNIAL PHOTOGRAPHIC COMPANY, ELKINGTON & CO.'S EXHIBIT, MAIN BUILDING, PHILADELPHIA CENTENNIAL EXHIBITION, 1876, SILVER ALBUMEN PRINT; 33 × 41 CM

Image Courtesy of the Free Library of Philadelphia, Print and Picture Collection

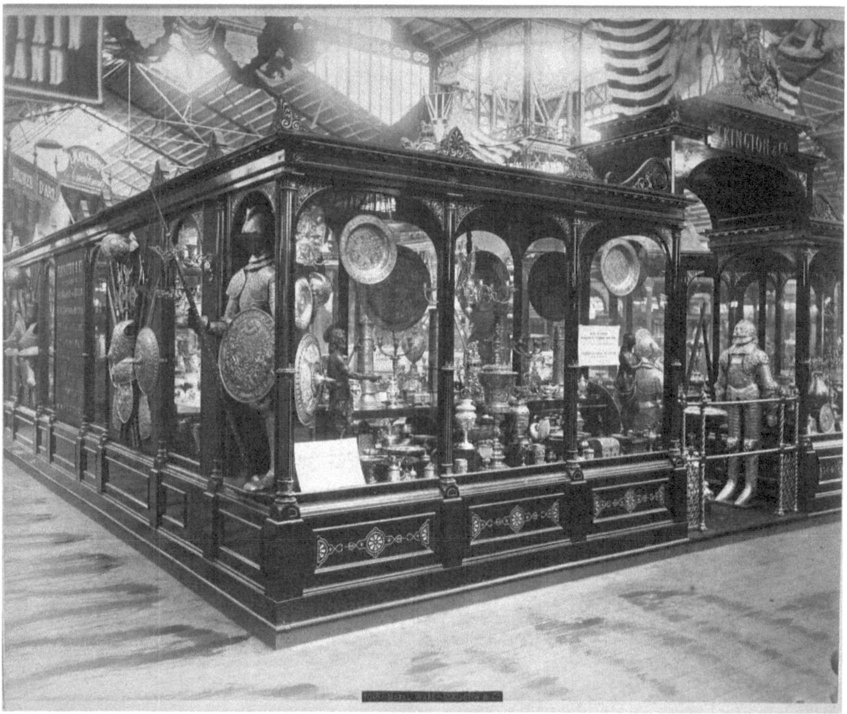

DOI: 10.4324/9781315400266-58

49

CENTENNIAL PHOTOGRAPHIC COMPANY, INTERIOR VIEW OF ELKINGTON & CO.'S EXHIBIT, MAIN BUILDING, PHILADELPHIA CENTENNIAL EXHIBITION, 1876, SILVER ALBUMEN PRINT; 21 × 26 CM

Image Courtesy of the Free Library of Philadelphia, Print and Picture Collection

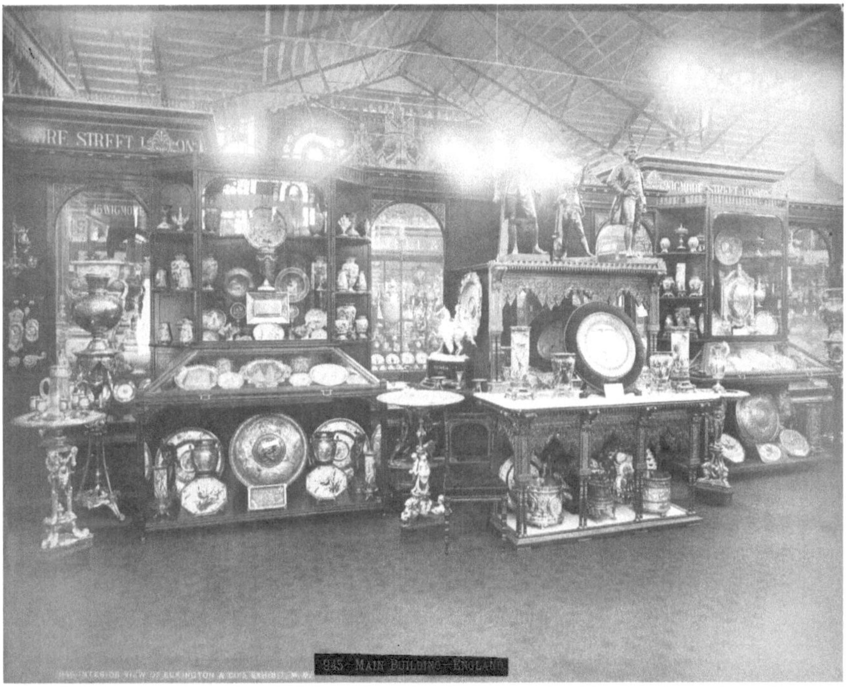

50

DAVID BREWSTER, 'APPLICATION OF THE STEREOSCOPE TO SCULPTURE, ARCHITECTURE AND ENGINEERING'

The Stereoscope; its History, Theory, and Construction, with its Application to the Fine and Useful Arts and to Education (London: John Murray, 1856), pp. 183–185

To the arts of sculpture and architecture, the processes of binocular photography and stereoscopic combination are particularly applicable. The landscape painter has every day within his reach examples of the picturesque, the wild and the sublime in nature. In the fields which surround him, in the river, or even in the "brook that bubbles by," on the shore, on the heath, or on the mountain side, he has the choice of materials for every department of his art. The sculptor has no such advantage. Swathed in impenetrable drapery the human figure mocks his eager eye, and it is only by stolen glances, or during angel visits, few and far between, that he can see those divine forms which it is his business to portray. He must therefore quit his home and seek for the models of ancient and modern art. In the British Museum, in the Louvre, in the Vatican, and in the repositories of art in Berlin, Munich, and other European cities, he must spend months and years in the study of his profession. He must copy, day after day, those master triumphs of genius which the taste of ages has consecrated, and gather from their study the true principles of his art. Transferred to his own studio, these copies will be his instructor and his guide. They will exhibit to him forms more than human, though human still, embodying all that is true and beautiful in what might be man. The value of these copies, however, depends on the skill and care with which they have been taken; but no labour however great, and no power of drawing however masterly, can give even an approximate idea either of the outline or round of solid figures, whether single or in groups. Light and shade can alone evolve those muscular prominences, or those soft and sphere-like relievos which give such power and beauty to forms, male and female; but how can an artist catch and fix those lights and shades which give relief to the parts which they illuminate or obscure?

 DOI: 10.4324/9781315400266-60

The light of the sun, even in a cloudless sky, is ever varying in intensity, and the breadth and direction of the shadows which he casts are varying from hour to hour. In a cloudy day, the motion of the clouds, and the varying reflexions within his apartment, subject the lights and shadows to constant change. The portions of the drawing executed in the morning will not harmonize with what is drawn at noon, or during the decline of day. We consider it, therefore, impossible to execute a drawing of a statue, or of a group of statues, from which the artist can have anything like an accurate idea of the forms which compose them.

From all these difliculties the sculptor has been relieved by the invention of the photographic process. He may thus take copies of statues in a few minutes, and take them in all their aspects, and as seen at various distances, and in this manner he will obtain drawings with the shadows as they existed at a particular instant, so that the lights and shades, upon every individual part of the statue, will be correctly related to each other. But valuable as these drawings are, compared with those executed by the pencil, their value becomes tenfold greater when they are taken with the binocular camera, and with small lenses, as already described. When combined in the stereoscope, he may reproduce the statue in relief, in all its aspects, and of different sizes, and derive from its study the same advantages which the statue itself would have furnished. In one respect the creations of the stereoscope surpass the original. While the artist is surveying and drawing instruction from the marble prototype, its lights and shadows, and consequently the delicate forms, convex and concave, by which they are produced, are constantly changing, whereas, in the stereoscopic statue, everything is fixed and invariable. In taking busts and statues from the living subject, the sculptor will derive great advantage from the stereoscope. Double pictures of the whole, or of any portion of the subject, may be taken and raised into relief, and from such binocular pictures, executed on one side of the globe, an artist, on the other side, may complete an admirable statue. The dying and the dead may thus be modelled without the rude contact of a mask, and those noble forms perpetuated which affection or gratitude has endeared.

51

C. BIERSTADT, PUBLISHER, *1043 UNA AND THE LION*

Date unknown (1882–1903), stereograph card;
17.5 × 8.5 cm, Author's Collection

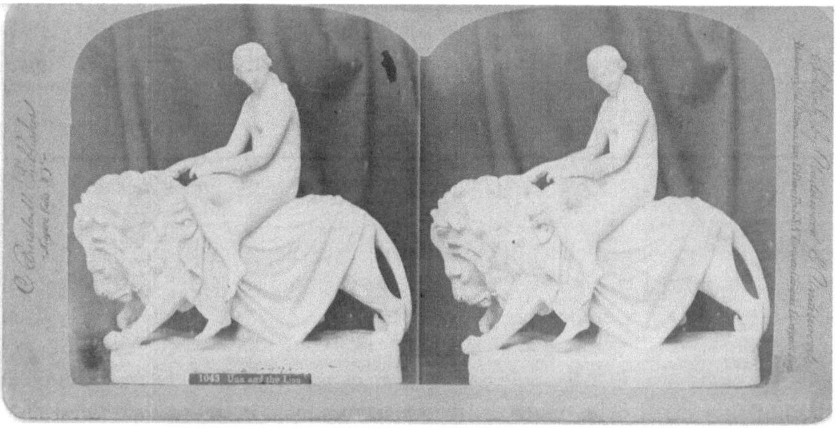

 DOI: 10.4324/9781315400266-61

52

'THE CORRIDOR OF STATUARY-PORCELAIN AT ALDERMAN COPELAND'S, NEW BOND ST'

Art Journal, 1 November 1859, pp. 347–348

THE pure and enduring marble which so deservedly was held in high esteem by the great sculptors of antiquity, has given its name to one of the most beautiful, and also of the most useful, substances employed by modern artists for rendering sculpture a popular art. The life-size marble or bronze is a work of an exclusive order. Its costliness renders it accessible only by the few, while its proportions forbid that it should find a consistent home under any roofs except such as are of a national, or palatine, or a patrician character; it is, accordingly, in the reproduction of great works, on a reduced scale, that sculpture can alone discover the elements of popularity. Small groups and figures, obtainable at a moderate cost, are the statues of the people. *They* are to the originals what fine engravings are to pictures of the highest rank; indeed, they even surpass the utmost powers of the *burin* in their faculty of graphic and impressive translation. The statuette model reproduces the statue, through the agency of another expression of the same art; whereas the engraving is a work of an art altogether distinct from the picture, although the two arts are in close and most felicitous alliance.

Until a recent period the great difficulty has been to reproduce works of sculpture in an artistic material. Skilful manipulators have long been able to reduce the scale of statues, and to produce small models, which, in form and expression, were faithful transcripts of the originals. But, when the reduced model was perfected, there existed no means for executing the desired statuettes under conditions that would impress upon every one of them the unquestionable character of works of Art. A plaster cast might be most valuable as a model, but it never could rise to be anything less ignoble than a plaster cast. A statuette in a fine Porcelain is a different thing altogether; it is a true and a beautiful work of Art in itself. It may be that the sculptor, in the first instance, executed the design which we see before us in the Statuary-Porcelain, for the express purpose of its being produced and repeated in this material; or the porcelain work may have been modelled from some sculpture in marble or bronze. In either case, every Statuary-Porcelain – or, as this material is sometimes called, "Parian" – work, is equally a work of Art: and its value as such is greatly enhanced through the circumstance that it admits of

DOI: 10.4324/9781315400266-62

an unlimited repetition. It is like a painter's etching, in its faculty of being always original, and in its direct transmission of the thought, and feeling, and intention of the sculptor.

There is something also that is peculiarly agreeable in works of sculpture when they are on a small scale. Instead of a large group or statue being degraded by appearing of statuette size, in the great majority of instances the reduced scale imparts a peculiar charm to the composition. This most important quality in statuettes, however, implies that they should be executed in a delicate and refined material. Statuary-Porcelain is exactly such a material. Delicate and refined in the highest degree, it is eminently sculpturesque in its aspect and tone of colour, and, at the same time, it excites no suspicions of fragility or evanescence. Statuettes executed in the Statuary-Porcelain or Porcelain, accordingly, are always regarded with favour and admiration; and all that is needed for them to take a foremost position amongst the Art-productions of the present time is, for their numbers to be considerably increased, and the repetitions of each example to be multiplied to a great amount.

It must also be very distinctly understood, as one of the peculiar excellences of Statuary-Porcelain, that it admits of being applied to the most varied purposes of Art-manufacture no less successfully than to the production of works in the highest departments of the art of sculpture. Parian statuettes may be, and they have already been, very happily introduced into the composition of numerous objects that are made in porcelain; and, in many instances, the material is itself applicable to purposes of practical utility. In dessert-services the Statuary-Porcelain and the ordinary porcelain have been found to work together in delightful harmony. This is one example of the manner in which the highest expressions of Art may be made to bear directly upon the useful applications of manufacture. It is impossible to estimate too highly the importance of such a union of Art with manufacture, since it is thus, and thus alone, that, through the consistent influence and the confederate action of pure Art, all manufactures gradually attain to their most exalted character. The Parian, from its high qualities as a material, empowers the sculptor to extend his range of action far beyond the utmost powers of the chisel: and it also shows him by what means his loftiest ideas may diffuse a vital impulse through the distant and diversified ramifications of Art-manufacture.

By all the most eminent ceramic manufacturers of the present era, Parian is in use for the production of statuettes and other objects, that may be classified under the common title of Statuary Porcelain. And it is not in many instances that the works thus produced prove to be unworthy of the beautiful material. Whatever the degree of success that may have attended the efforts of other establishments, Alderman Copeland has devoted so much attention to his Statuary-Porcelain, and he has produced these works in such numbers, variety, and beauty, that he may justly claim to be considered to stand at the head of this department of Art-manufacture. In his spacious and handsome group of ware-rooms, in New Bond Street, a Corridor is devoted by Alderman Copeland almost exclusively to the display of this class of his productions. Here and there the visitor may encounter some gem in porcelain-enamel, or the Parian works may appear before him in that union with porcelain, of which we have spoken, or perhaps he may pause to examine a piece of pure modern porcelain, such as might stand unrebuked beside the *chefs d'œuvre* of Sèvres.

The corridor, however, is in reality a gallery of Porcelain sculpture; and it is in that capacity that we now introduce our readers to it, in order that they may become familiar with by far the most extensive collection of works of this class, that can be seen together in any one place in London. It will be remembered, that the entire collection is the production of Alderman Copeland's ceramic establishment: and it must also be understood that many other works are either in the course of actual preparation, or their future appearance is in contemplation.

The groups, statuettes, busts, and other compositions are arranged in two long lines on either side of the corridor, some of the more important specimens being brought together to form groups. In the adjoining saloons, other specimens may also be seen, particularly those which have been designed to constitute parts of services, for the most part executed in porcelain. Of the busts which have been executed in Porcelain by Alderman Copeland, several are of the full life-size of the original marbles. Busts of her Majesty the Queen and of the Prince Consort are amongst the most successful; but the work that is still more admirable is the Parian reproduction of the well-known Greco-Roman bust in the British Museum, known as Clytie, with the hair brought down so low on the forehead, and the figure represented as if rising from a bud of the lotus. The busts of Juno and Ariadne, of full size, are of great excellence; and those of Ophelia and Miranda, by Calder Marshall, executed for the Crystal Palace Art-Union, are also very beautiful; and the reduced models of them are more beautiful still. Amongst the busts of this smaller size, is a charming one of Jenny Lind. A group of busts of Indian heroes, with Havelock at their head, will require no special notice to secure for them due regard. Other busts of Wellington and Nelson range consistently with them, and various others extend the series still further. The portrait-statuettes are not so numerous as the busts, but they are equally excellent with them: they include an admirable figure of the great Duke. The ideal statuettes and groups, as would be expected, comprehend the larger portion of these interesting works. They may be divided into three classes: of these the first class consists of fac-simile reproductions of well-known statues and groups on a greatly reduced scale; the second comprises a variety of original figure subjects, modelled expressly for the Statuary-Porcelain; and in the third class may be included miscellaneous subjects, such as groups or figures of animals, vases, jars, jugs, and other similar objects. Every class is well represented. Many are the familiar forms that we have known before of larger proportions, as "Sabrina," "Sunshine," and "the Greek Slave." Others we have learned to know better in their statuette form, than we knew them previously; and not a few come and form their first acquaintance with us, in their capacity of statuettes in Parian. Our readers will find every variety of subject here, from "Venus at the Bath" to "Paul and Virginia," and from "the Wounded Soldier" to "the Boy with a Shell." There are most spirited dogs also, and some noble horses.

The groups that have been incorporated with porcelain, for the most part consist of figures placed around a porcelain shaft, which supports a flat dish or tazza. These works are altogether successful, and both Statuary and ordinary Porcelain accomplish their proper duties, in a manner which attests the judicious discrimination, as well as the true artist feeling of the artists employed in their production. [. . .]

The art of producing sculpture in Porcelain is of comparatively recent introduction into England, and it differs essentially from the old "Bisque," over which time-honoured body it possesses great and manifest advantages. It is foreign to our purpose to enter upon any discussion concerning the priority of the invention of the Statuary-Porcelain, or Parian sculpture. We are well aware that this is a matter that is still in dispute; and, perhaps, like so many other important and valuable inventions, in dispute it may be destined to remain. The introduction of Parian at Alderman Copeland's establishment took place in 1842, at which period Mr. T. Battam was director; and it may interest our readers to be informed of an incident that took place, some twelve years ago, when the Parian was undergoing the ordeal of its experimental trial. We were at that time entering upon the duty, which we have since continued to discharge, of seeking to associate high Art with useful manufactures. With that view we made a tour into the manufacturing districts, when we visited the works of Mr. Alderman Copeland, – then "Copeland and Garrett," – at Stoke-upon-Trent. We there witnessed the first efforts to secure popularity for the new art of Porcelain sculpture. A "new art" it undoubtedly was; but it had not then assumed the character of being a promising one. Two statuettes had been produced in it – one a graceful female bust, and the other "the Shepherd-Boy," after Wyatt; but they had not "sold." The public did not show any sign of being prepared to acknowledge the real worthiness of the novelty; and it is by no means improbable that the process would have proceeded no farther, had it not been our good fortune to urge upon Mr. Garrett (in whose department the matter was placed) the wisdom of perseverance, under the conviction that what in itself was so evidently excellent, must eventually attain to success. A meeting was, in consequence, arranged by us between several sculptors, of whom Mr. Gibson was one, and Mr. T. Battam, the artist of the works. The two honorary secretaries of the Art-Union of London were also present. After a careful examination of the new material, an opinion was pronounced decidedly in its favour, Mr. Gibson declaring it to be "the material next best to marble that he had ever seen," and his brothers in Art agreeing with him. Mr. Gibson, at the same time, expressed a hope that some work of his might be suitable for Mr. Battam to produce in the Statuary-Porcelain. A commission from the Art-Union of London followed; and thus the new art of Parian sculpture was rescued from a peril, that might have proved fatal in the first infancy of its career. The material itself is a species of porcelain body, in which soft felspar is used instead of the more siliceous Cornwall stone. The peculiar tint, that contributes so highly to the beauty of the Parian, is due to the presence of the oxide of iron in small quantities in the clay. A silicate of peroxide of iron is produced through the action of this oxide upon the silica of the clay, which is of a pale buff colour; and thus the colour of the mass is obtained. Full particulars of the processes of producing sculptures and other objects in Statuary-Porcelain have been described in detail in our pages, by Professor Hunt, of the Jermyn Street Museum.

We have invited especial attention to this subject at the present time, in consequence of the peculiar fitness of these beautiful works for those presents which so constantly pass from one friend to another at the coming Christmas season. As the best possible commentary upon our notice of Alderman Copeland's "Sculpture Corridor," we commend to our readers the "Corridor" itself. That they will find our admiration for its contents to be well-founded, we are confidently assured; and we are also disposed to believe that they will accept our proposition, to accord to these beautiful works an honourable position amongst the Art-collections of the metropolis.

53

'GHOSTS AT SOUTH KENSINGTON'

Saturday Review of Politics, Literature, Science and Art, 29 March 1879, pp. 391–392

ALMOST more depressing than to perambulate the Inferno between Virgil and Dante would be the occupation of wandering through large and silent halls haunted by the pale forms of those whom we have known and loved – ghastly unrealities, visible but intangible, bearing the semblance but not the substance of old and valued friends. Nor would our spirits rise if, as we hurried away from one apparition, another immediately presented itself; if the figures were sometimes a ghostly white, and sometimes wore the colour of the familiar forms themselves, though not of their substance. The pale and lifeless image of an old Italian friend might make us shrink in horror, and on turning we might be confronted by the shade of one whom we knew familiarly in Spain some thirty years ago, while old acquaintances made in India and Central Asia might appear, standing motionless and ghastly. The sight of a few men, women, and children sauntering sleepily through these halls, or lounging on benches, apparently unconscious of the presence of the dread forms which haunted the building, though somewhat reassuring, would scarcely cheer the visitor, especially if these human beings seemed affected by the depression of the scene, although they looked not at the grim apparitions. The gloom of such a place would be increased by the sudden chiming of a deep-toned clock, which, on being examined, proved to be but the vain resemblance of a clock which once stood in an old cathedral tower far away in Eastern Germany; nor would the scene be rendered less sombre by the presence of many monuments to the dead. It may easily be imagined that such surroundings as those which we have been describing would be the reverse of hilarious; and yet the British nation has provided for itself a place of entertainment of very much this nature.

The lover of statuary and architecture who has travelled much in Europe may experience some such sensations as those above described by paying a visit to the South Kensington Museum, for, as he wanders through its halls and corridors, he will be confronted by the apparitions – in plaster of Paris – of many of his old friends. We are far from undervaluing that wonderful exhibition, being fully alive to the merits of many of the works of art which it contains, and being ready to admit the usefulness of plaster casts. The latter are invaluable to students of drawing, and serve as useful works of reference to artists and amateurs; they afford opportunities of completing their studies to travellers who have only had time

 DOI: 10.4324/9781315400266-63

to inspect the objects which they represent in a hurried manner, and they help to refresh the memories of the most learned. To the untravelled they are naturally instructive; but it is obvious that they can convey but a very imperfect idea of their originals to those whose artistic travels have been limited to London museums. A work of art which, while to a certain extent complete in itself, forms but a small part of a magnificent whole, loses much of its virtue when taken from its proper place and exhibited alone; much more, therefore, does the plaster representation of a part of a great work, when shown alone, fail to give much idea of the beauties of the original as it stands in its proper position. When a fine work of art is seen in its own place many questions of interest at once occur to the mind of the traveller – such as how it came there, what it is made of, and when it was made; but we do not trouble our heads much about an object which is plainly labelled as made of plaster, and having cost thirty shillings. Then again, in a museum it is next to impossible to avoid crowding things too much together to allow any opportunity for their beauties being fairly appreciated. Let us suppose the case of a cast of some bronze doors. Instead of approaching them from an open piazza, admiring their breadth of treatment in the distance, their general richness at a nearer view, and their marvellous detail on a close inspection, we have to thread our way through a labyrinth of huge casts and stands, and then look at them in an awkward position. We thus can only enjoy a small portion of their beauties. Then the doors themselves, instead of closing the portals of some cathedral or baptistry, lie flat against a wall, and convey no meaning. In a line with them are other plaster doors; this is the door department, and they stand in a row like crows upon a rail. We have more room to look at the cast of the gallery in Santa Maria Novella at Florence. This cast is at the end of an upstairs corridor, and can be seen to advantage from below. The colour of the plaster too is not very strikingly dissimilar from that of the marble of the original, and as we look up we try to fancy that we hear the choir singing High Mass, and see the monks in their white habits. Suddenly the illusion is dispelled. A policeman appears at one corner of the gallery and a nurse with a baby at the other, and we speedily realize the fact that, after all, we are at South Kensington and not at Florence. Models of the splendid pulpits of the cathedral and baptistry at Pisa are placed opposite each other, as if it were intended that rival orators should thoroughly "ventilate" some theological question from their heights. Michael Angelo's David towers above, ready to drop a stone upon the head of the worsted disputant. Shakspeare and Cupid, side by side, help to form the audience, and several human beings are already asleep upon some benches beneath the pulpits, thus helping to give reality to the scene. The shrine of Saint Sebaldus, coloured and gilded in imitation of its original at Nuremberg, is overshadowed by the tomb of a Mogul; and German, Hindoo, and Italian monuments hob-nob in the most friendly manner. It is sweet to recall memories of our childhood, and these models remind us of the days when temples and pagodas used to be represented on the dinner-table in barley sugar. We do not, however, remember any effort of the cook or confectioner – not even a wedding cake – which equalled in originality the arrangement of the cast exhibited at

South Kensington of the splendid Puerta de la Gloria belonging to the cathedral of Santiago. Frederick the Great is complacently riding on his charger through one archway, and Mercury is bounding with a hop, skip, and a jump through the other. These immense doorways are quite dwarfed by the cast of Trajan's Column, which rises immediately in front of them. This column has been broken in two to suit the exigencies of limited space, and the result is about as graceful as would be that of a broken statue of a man, one half consisting of his legs standing upright, and the other of his upper half resting on a cross section of his middle, his thighs and head being level with each other. The Science and Art Department might with as much reason urge that this arrangement would give a correct idea of the man as that their divided cast of Trajan's Column could give a correct idea of its original. Even a bronze-coloured lion, which stands between the two broken halves, looks astonished at this piece of eccentricity; but, in order to palliate any defects in the arrangement of the Column, the thoughtful authorities have furnished a sketch of Trajan's Column as it looked at home, which, with a book telling everything that an ordinary visitor is likely to want to know on the subject, is placed on a desk at the foot of the great cast. When last at the Museum, we noticed two plaster horses in a Biga, galloping eagerly, in the direction indicated by a placard which was placed immediately in front of them. On this placard a finger pointed to the mystic words "To the Refreshment Room." If a visitor liked to follow the proposed course of these horses, and established himself at a table in the grill-room about luncheon-time, he might hear the students recounting their impressions of their studies and the lectures which they had heard during the morning; and he might form his own conclusions as to the edification likely to result from an atmosphere of plaster of Paris, sham antiquities, and museum lectures.

We doubt if the devotion (whether artistic or otherwise) aroused by a gilded plaster model of a magnificent gold reliquary could be very wholesome. There is a fine example of such a model at Kensington. We wonder that coloured casts of the relics which it contained are not placed in an adjoining case. Surely this would be the very acme of modelling – or apedom. Many yards of superficial wall-surface are covered by a ghastly and gigantic diagram, showing the relative proportions of some of the most remarkable buildings of various countries and dates on a scale of about one-sixteenth of their actual heights. The dome of St. Peter's is relieved against the great pyramid of Cheops, above which again peeps the top of the spire of Strasburg Cathedral. Beneath rise the slender proportions of the Albert Hall, which are partly concealed by the Temple of the Giants and the Parthenon of Athens. After gazing at this extraordinary diagram, one is almost disposed to make a vow upon the nearest plaster altar never to look at a cathedral again and to forswear architecture for the future. Surely the erection of the Tower of Babel was not such a sin as a work like this. The large hall in which it hangs is a kind of architectural dissecting-room. Here are parts of some rood-screen, there some choir-stalls, and there again a piece of a cathedral façade. The place is full of pieces and sections, as if the principal buildings in the world had been operated upon by some giant's scalpel. A skinned human arm lying upon a surgeon's table, although interesting in its way, does not give us any very direct enjoyment, neither do casts of bits and scraps of the great works of architects and sculptors. On returning to England from a long tour on the Continent, where we have given special study to architecture, statuary, and woodwork, after suffering Roman fever and the loss of much of our luggage, after being wearied, robbed, and bug-bitten, it is disheartening to find that the model working-man can come from the City by the Underground Railway and see in one morning exact models of many of the works of art which we saw at the cost of so much labour, time, and money. When we look with ungracious eyes at the unsophisticated arrival by the Underground comfortably glancing over in a few hours exact imitations of objects which it took us many months to see, we are reminded of the late Major Whyte-Melville's story of a hard rider who complained at the end of a severe run with the hounds that, after spoiling his hat, tearing his coat, laming his horse, having two falls, and riding first from end to end, he found that a fellow on a coffee-coloured pony arrived at the finish before him after all. The underground tourist is not to be beaten by the Continental traveller, even in the matter of photographs. As he leaves the Museum, he can buy "cartes" or "cabinets" of the various objects of interest which he has been inspecting. He may fill his pockets with photographs "taken direct from the plaster cast," and carry away armfuls of "descriptive catalogues." He may even increase his spoils at the depôt of the Arundel Society within the building, and pocket a small copy of the diagram showing the comparative altitudes of the principal buildings in the world. He has one great advantage over the Continental traveller, which consists in his freedom from the nuisance of cicerones, and he can wander where he will in the Museum, without being disarmed of his umbrella. He may breakfast, lunch, and dine in a mediæval chamber, at a reasonable rate, hear a lecture, wash his hands, and spend an hour or two in an excellent library, "within the precincts of the building." It may be true that at the South Kensington Museum we see little but the ghosts of the statuary and architecture which we admire abroad, but where, let us ask, out of England, can we find a South Kensington Museum?

54

CHARLES SHEPHERD, *VIEW OF MOLDERS WORKING IN THE COURTYARD OF THE QUWWAT AL-ISLAM [MIGHT OF ISLAM] MOSQUE WITH THE COLONNADE IN THE BACKGROUND, QUWWAT AL-ISLAM MOSQUE COMPLEX, DELHI, INDIA*

Published 1872. Image used according to the V&A's terms and conditions

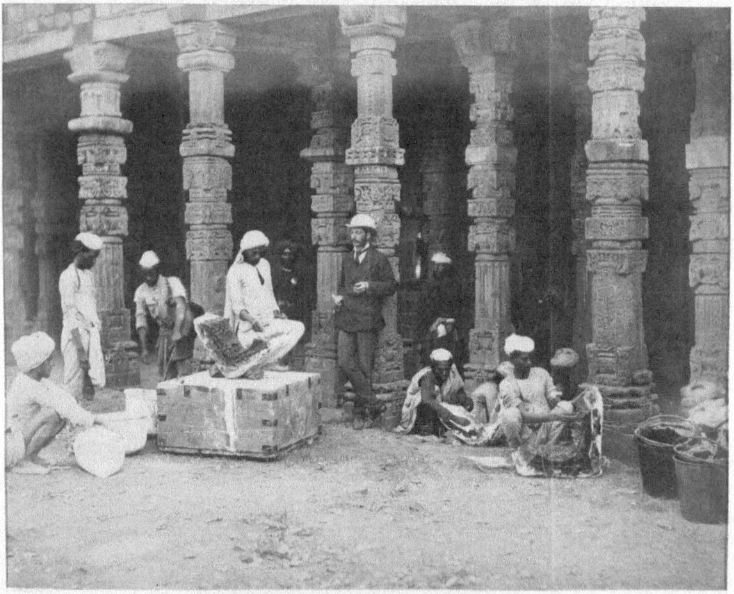

DOI: 10.4324/9781315400266-64

55

H. H. COLE, *THE ARCHITECTURE OF ANCIENT DELHI. ESPECIALLY THE BUILDINGS AROUND THE KUTB MINAR*

(London: Arundel Society, 1872), pp. 5–7

Piece moulding, whether in clay, plaster or any other material, involves considerable skill and time; hence, its unsuitability to reproducing large objects covered with much carving, or sculptures which from palpable reasons must be carried out expeditiously. In every class of "piece moulding" the method of covering the carved surface with a number of inelastic moulds capable of being individually removed with ease is theoretically the same. The perfection of the plaster piece moulding depends on the skill of the moulder in the disposition of the moulds, so as to have the fewest possible joints when the piece moulds fitted together completely cover the carving. Such a process is evidently not suitable, in respect of rapidity, to Indian sculptures, which are mostly of a very elaborate character – partaking largely of what is technically termed an "undercut" quality – and native moulders cannot be trusted to execute any such work alone, as it requires unbroken supervision on the part of some qualified person. A demand was thus created for a process which would be not only more easy and quick, but to a great extent would obviate the necessity of manipulating the casts when they issue from the mould. A process of moulding with gelatine was adopted, and it meets the requirements above stated to a very considerable extent. It is applicable in the reproduction of big objects by reason of the large area which a single mould can cover. As the gelatine is elastic, a great extent of "under-cut" in the carving may be embraced in one mould, thus rendering unnecessary the making of a number of joints. In withdrawing the elastic mould from the object under treatment, the gelatine stretches itself in order to become released from the "undercut," but it regains its shape almost immediately without destroying any of the extreme accuracy with which the gelatine is able to repeat every mark and grain on the surface reproduced. This gelatine process is more mechanical in its nature than piece moulding, therefore it is easily acquired by natives, who, with ordinary care and under supervision, execute it rapidly and well.

[. . .]

DOI: 10.4324/9781315400266-65

The photograph on the opposite page, of the group represents the casting operations at the Kutb in progress. The three moulds under manipulation show the position of the gelatine mould inside the clay wall. That upon the box in the centre of the picture has been cleaned, and is ready for casting from. The other two are being brushed out preparatory to casting. On the left is the plaster of Paris in a bag – the pans in which it is mixed with the water are near to it, and water is being poured out, by the "Bhisti" or water bearer, into one of them. On the right are the copper pails in which the gelatine is boiled.

The casts made at the Kutb weighed about six tons when packed; an equal number of facsimiles were produced under the superintendence of Corporal Jackson, at Fâthpúr-Sikri, near Agra, and the whole collection was sent back to England, overland, and reached London about the end of May, 1871. They then underwent such repairs as had been rendered needful by the casualties of a long voyage, and from them have been reproduced two sets of casts, one for London and one for Edinburgh.

56

'SMALL BRONZES'

Saturday Review of Politics, Literature, Science and Art, 31 May 1890, p. 672

WE have frequently in these columns urged upon the artists who lead our interesting revival of English sculpture to adopt the practice of the French, and to publish their works in a form which might give them circulation among amateurs. It is very well for Mr. Gilbert or for Mr. Thornycroft to exhibit at the Royal Academy a statue of heroic size. We admire, we congratulate British art on a work of great beauty, but we do not buy. Occasionally such a figure may be added to the national collection or to the palace of a connoisseur of exceptional wealth. But it is not merely that the cost of a full-sized imaginative statue is prohibitory; the ordinary householder would have no place to put such an object even if some one should make him a present of it. The gift of a marble statue seven feet high, suddenly delivered at the door by a van, would beat the record of white elephants. In France, where sculpture lives and thrives, there is, of course, the same difficulty; but there the artist really subsists by the publication of reductions, principally in bronze, of large figures or groups which have attracted critical attention at the Salon. English sculptors, it would appear, are not a very enterprising body. Although the revival of our sculpture – one of the most interesting developments of modern art – has now a history of at least ten years, scarcely anything has yet been done by them to bring their work within the range of the pocket and the house of the ordinary buyer of pretty objects.

We are, therefore, very happy to call attention to two simultaneous experiments in this direction which have just been made, each of which deserves, and we hope will meet with, the approbation of the public. Mr. Collie, who published a bronze reduction of Mr. Thornycroft's "Gordon" last year, has been so much encouraged by the success of that solitary effort that he has just opened at his gallery, 39B Old Bond Street, a little collection of small modern bronzes, which he is publishing, as though they were etchings, in a strictly limited and numbered issue. Mr. Onslow Ford's elegant and spirited work specially lends itself to reproduction in miniature. No specimen in Mr. Collie's gallery is more delightful than the "Peace," a little nude female figure, in a caressing and conciliating attitude, waving a palm branch. When this work was originally exhibited at the Royal Academy, in full size, we took exception to one or two points, in which it seemed to us that Mr. Ford had lost beauty by adhering too strictly to the peculiarities of the model before him.

DOI: 10.4324/9781315400266-66

But these are not obvious in the small bronze; they melt into the general impression of grace and fidelity to nature which this charming statuette produces. Other works of Mr. Onslow Ford's at this gallery are a reduction of his "Folly," and a very refined bust of a girl, with a pensive look, somewhat in that Tuscan manner which we commonly identify with Donatello. But, for the particular purpose Mr. Collie has in view, namely, the purchase of these little bronzes for drawing-rooms, it is the "Peace," with its exiguous proportions, its extreme delicacy and finish, and its exquisite thin golden patina, that we hold to be especially successful.

In the same gallery is a small bronze of Sir Frederick Leighton's statue, "The Sluggard." This is a very rough sketch in plaster, transferred to the metal without alteration. There is a great charm about a master's work in this condition, and a freshness of handling which is often lost in subsequent finish. Artists will certainly enjoy this study, and will wish to possess it. But we find it difficult to commend the publication in bronze of a sketch in this rude condition. By the side of the delicate finish of Mr. Ford's statuettes, it is not to be denied that Sir Frederick Leighton's seems a little out of place. The eye inevitably rests on the foot of the figure, which is a mere flattened lump, full of meaning in the clay, of course, but annoying in the bronze. There is here a positive discord, in our idea, between the transitory nature of the work itself and the extreme durability of the metal in which it is imprisoned.

At the same time that Mr. Collie offers these interesting bronzes to subscribers, Mr. Hamo Thornycroft, turning his own publisher, like Mr. Whistler, issues a circular announcing the publication of a limited number of bronze reductions of two of his best-known statues – of "The Mower," which was in the Royal Academy of 1884, and of "Teucer," the original bronze of which now forms part of the national collection. Specimens of these statuettes are now on view at his studio, Moreton House, Melbury Road, Kensington. Each is twenty-two inches high. The sculptor has tried various kinds of patina. One or two of these seem to us a little too thick. We fancy that it destroys something of the extreme delicacy of the modelling, in the same way, though not of course to the same extent, as a coat of paint does on a plaster cast. This is not, however, a fault into which Mr. Thornycroft has fallen in more than one, or perhaps two, cases. Some of his bronzes have an exquisite patina of dark green, as beautiful, in its way, as the golden-brown of Mr. Ford's "Peace." The point which we are anxious to emphasize, however, in the one exhibition as in the other, is that here at last is an opportunity for amateurs to secure, for their private collections, works of the highest individual merit, of an issue more limited than that of most etchings, of convenient size, and of very reasonable price. The admiration so generally expressed now for the best modern English sculpture must be tame indeed if it does not lead to the practical encouragement of the art when the latter takes forms so attractive and so manageable as these. There ought to be no difficulty in filling up both subscription lists without delay.

Part 3

STAINED GLASS

3.1

Materials and techniques

DOI: 10.4324/9781315400266-68

3.1 Materials and techniques

The art of stained glass underwent a significant revival in the Victorian era, following almost three centuries of decline.[1] In the 1840s, the production of stained-glass windows was an occupation for a few specialists, as well as jobbing glaziers and plumbers, but by the 1890s the design and making of stained-glass windows was a large industry and a growing profession for artists. Initially, the growth in popularity of this art form was due to antiquarian interest in ancient stained glass. Medieval stained-glass windows were particularly highly prized and provided the ideal model for modern artists. Yet, modern materials were inferior to their medieval counterparts; glassmakers struggled to produce coloured glass to match the tone and quality of the medieval glass. The ground-breaking scientific and archaeological investigations into the composition of medieval stained-glass windows instigated by the likes of barrister and stained-glass historian Charles Winston (1814–1864), with help from Dr Medlock of the Royal College of Chemistry, helped to inform glassmakers on the manufacture of coloured sheet glass, enabling 'antique' coloured glass to be made using medieval recipes and processes.

Winston's 1847 publication *An Inquiry into the Difference of Style Observable in Ancient Glass Paintings* was one of the first treatises on stained glass published in the Victorian period. Winston investigated the style, technique and materials of ancient glass, including the productions of the sixteenth century (which he championed). Winston described in some detail how glass was coloured, and the extract included here introduces the reader to the three main styles of glass painting, each of which used a different technique or combination of techniques: mosaic, enamel and mosaic-enamel methods. The mosaic technique, which involved constructing a window from pieces of coloured glass onto which vitreous pigment was applied, was championed by the Gothic revivalists because it was a continuation of the medieval mode of making stained glass. Popular from the seventeenth century onwards, the enamel technique, in which vitreous enamel colours were painted onto clear glass, was technically very accomplished by the mid-nineteenth century, but it soon fell out of favour due to the growing popularity of stained glass using the 'mosaic' techniques of the Middle Ages. In reality, many Victorian stained-glass artists used a combination of the mosaic and enamel techniques in their windows, which were constructed using a wide variety of coloured and textured sheet glass.

By the end of the nineteenth century, mouth-blown sheet glass could be purchased in a range of colours; the palette of glass materials available to the Victorian stained-glass artist far exceeded those available in the medieval period. A number of new glass materials also appeared on the market as a result of experimentation with the colouring and forming of molten glass and in response to changing tastes. Both opalescent glass, or opaline glass, developed in the 1870s in the United States by John La Farge (1835–1910) and Louis Comfort Tiffany (1848–1933), and Prior's 'Slab' glass, developed by English architect E. S. Prior (1852–1932) in 1889, broke away from traditional glassmaking methods. These new glass materials were often of uneven thickness and streaky in colour, lending a jewelled luminosity and sometimes a three-dimensional effect to stained glass. The development of these new glass materials had an enormous influence on the stylistic development of stained glass in the late nineteenth century. Artists utilised the coloured streaks, swirls and patterns of the glass material in their designs, to an extent diminishing the role of painting on the glass surface in favour of celebrating the glass material. The second source in this section was published in the British monthly journal *Magazine of Art*. It explores the effects of these new materials, their artistic possibilities and their visual impact, all of which were very appealing to the modern artist.

Note

The stained glass headnotes in this volume are written by Jasmine Allen.

1 On the revolution in the design and production of stained glass in the 19th century see Atkins, G., Allen, J., & Nichols, K, Reframing Stained Glass in Nineteenth-Century Britain: Culture, Aesthetics, Contexts, special issue, *19: Interdisciplinary Studies in the Long Nineteenth Century, 2020* (30) https://doi.org/10.16995/ntn.3013.

57

C. WINSTON, *AN INQUIRY INTO THE DIFFERENCE OF STYLE OBSERVABLE IN ANCIENT GLASS PAINTINGS, ESPECIALLY IN ENGLAND; WITH HINTS ON GLASS PAINTING*

Vol. I (Oxford: John Henry Parker, 1847), pp. 2–7

The glass used in glass paintings is, in its original manufactured state, either *white,* or *coloured.* The ingredients of White glass,[1] of which silex and alkali are the most important, are incorporated by fusion in the melting-pot of the glass-house, having been in general previously *fritted;* i. e. roasted with a strong fire, in order to facilitate their union. When the vitrification in the melting-pot is complete, the glass is formed into sheets.[2] These are afterwards *annealed,* i. e. suffered to cool very gradually, a process which renders them less brittle; and they are then ready for use.

Coloured glass is of two kinds: –

One kind is coloured throughout its entire substance,[3] and is called *pot-metal glass:* the other is coloured only on one side of the sheet, and is termed *covered,* or *coated glass;* i.e. white glass covered with a coat of pot-metal colour.[4]

Red, or *ruby* glass, is almost invariably *coated glass*;[5] other kinds of coloured glass are generally *pot-metal glass;* but they are not unfrequently manufactured as *coated glass.*

Coloured glass is formed by adding a certain quantity of colouring matter to the materials of white glass,[6] and incorporating these ingredients by fusion in the melting-pot of the glass-house. It is manufactured into sheets[7] in the same way as white glass, and is of the same transparency.

The Glass Painter possesses the power of colouring white glass, and even of varying the tints of coloured glass, by the use of *stains,* and *enamel colours.*

All shades of yellow, to a full orange red, may be imparted to white glass by staining it:[8] other colours are produced by means of enamels.

A stain penetrates the glass to some little depth, and is properly as transparent as white glass itself.

An enamel colour[9] only adheres to the surface of the glass, without penetrating it, and is always more or less opaque.

DOI: 10.4324/9781315400266-69

There are three distinct systems of glass painting, which for convenience sake may be termed the *Mosaic method;* the *Enamel method;* and the *Mosaic enamel method.*

Of these the most simple is the Mosaic method. Under this system, glass paintings are composed of white glass, – if they are meant to be white, or only coloured with yellow, brown, and black, – or else they are composed of different pieces of white and coloured glass, arranged like a mosaic, in case they are intended to display a greater variety of colours. The pieces of white glass are cut to correspond with such parts of the design as are white, or white and yellow; and the coloured pieces with those parts of the design which are otherwise coloured.

The glass painter in the Mosaic style uses but two pigments; – a stain which produces a yellow tint, and a brown enamel, called *enamel brown.* The main outlines of the design are formed, when the painting is finished, by the *leads* which surround and connect the various pieces of glass together: and the subordinate outlines and all the shadows, as well as all the brown and black parts,[10] are executed by means of the enamel brown; with *which colour alone* a work done according to the Mosaic system, can be said to be *painted.* The yellow stain is merely used as a colour.

It therefore appears, that under the Mosaic method each colour of the design, except yellow, brown, and black, must be represented by a separate piece of glass. A limited number of colours may however be exhibited on the same piece of glass, by the following processes. Part of a piece of blue glass may be changed to green, by means of the yellow stain. The coloured surface of coated glass may be destroyed by attrition, or the application of fluoric acid;[11] and the white glass beneath it exposed to view. This may of course be wholly or in part stained yellow, like any other white glass. Two shades of yellow may also be produced on the same piece of glass, by staining some parts twice over. But, unless he adopt one or other of the above-mentioned processes, the glass painter under the Mosaic system cannot have more than one colour on the same piece of glass. A variety of *tint,* or *depth,* may often be observed in the same piece of coloured glass, arising from some accident in its manufacture.[12] Of this a skilful glass painter will always avail himself to correct as much as possible the stiffness of colouring necessarily belonging to this system of glass painting.

Under the Enamel method, which is the most difficult of accomplishment, coloured glass is not used under any circumstances, the picture being painted on white glass, with enamel colours and stains.

The Mosaic enamel method consists in a combination of the two former processes; white and coloured glass, as well as every variety of enamel colour and stain, being employed in it.

The practical course of proceeding under each of these three methods is nearly alike.

A cartoon of the design is made, upon which are also marked the shapes and sizes of the various pieces of glass. The glass is cut to these forms, and is afterwards painted, and *burnt,* i. e. heated to redness in a furnace or *kiln,* which fixes the enamel colours, and causes the stains to operate. The number of burnings to which the glass is subjected varies according to circumstances. It is in general sufficient to burn glass painted with only one enamel colour, once or twice; the self-same operation sufficing also to give effect to the stain, if any is used. Where several enamel colours are employed, it is necessary to burn the glass more frequently; each colour, in general, requiring to be fixed by a separate burning.

It only then remains to *lead the glass together,* and to put it up in its place.[13]

The Mosaic system of glass painting, as now practised, may, I think, be considered a *revival* of the system which prevailed throughout the middle ages, and until the middle of the sixteenth century.[14] The glass employed during this period is similar to the modern in its general character, but materially differs from it both in *texture* and *colour*. These differences are the more perceptible in proportion to the antiquity of the glass. It seems to have been always painted, burnt, and leaded together, nearly as at present.[15]

The Mosaic system of glass painting is admirably adapted to the nature of the material. It is however unsuited for *mere* picturesque effect, owing to the nature of its colouring, which being produced by broad pieces of glass, whose tints can scarcely be varied either in the lights or shadows, (the latter being represented by means of the enamel brown,) imparts to works executed in this style the flat and hard, though brilliant character of an ancient oil painting.[16]

The revival of art in the sixteenth century, and the extraordinary efforts then achieved in oil painting, by which the hard and dry illumination of the middle ages was transformed into a beautiful picture, glowing with the varied tints of nature, and expressing to the eye, by a nice gradation of colouring, the relative position of near and distant objects, seem to have excited the ambition of the glass painters. Not content with carrying Mosaic glass painting to the highest pitch of perfection it has hitherto attained, and with borrowing the excellent drawing and composition of the oil and fresco painters, they strove to render their own art more completely an imitation of nature, and to produce in a *transparent* material the atmospheric and picturesque effects so successfully exhibited by the *reflective surfaces* of oil and fresco paintings. The facility of applying colour to glass with the brush, at the pleasure of the artist, afforded by the discovery of the various enamel colours, about the middle of the sixteenth century,[17] soon led to their extensive employment. It was not however until the eighteenth century that they entirely superseded the use of coloured glasses in large works.[18]

The introduction of enamels, though it certainly occasioned a great extension of the scale of colour in glass painting, was not without its disadvantages. The paintings lost in *transparency* what they gained in variety of tint; and in proportion as their picturesque qualities were increased by the substitution of enamel colouring for coloured glass, their *depth* of colour sensibly diminished.

Notes

1 See note *a* at the end of this Introduction.
2 See note *b* at the end of this Introduction.
3 See note *c* at the end of this Introduction.

4 See note *d* at the end of this Introduction.

5 The reason to be assigned for the peculiar manufacture of Ruby glass is, that its colouring matter is so intense, that it would appear opaque, if formed into a sheet by itself of the usual thickness of an ordinary piece of glass. The colouring matter therefore requires a *backing* of white glass, to render the sheet thick and strong enough to resist the weather.

6 The compositions of various coloured glasses are described at large in Fromberg's Handbuch der Glasmalerei. Quedlinburg and Leipzig, 1844; (a translation of which, by my friend Henry James Clarke, Esq., is printed in Weale's Quarterly Papers,) and in p. 268 of Dr. Lardner's work, mentioned in note *a* at the end of this Introduction.

7 It is usually made into cylinders, which are opened out into sheets.

8 See note *e* at the end of this Introduction.

9 See note *f* at the end of this Introduction.

10 See note *g* at the end of this Introduction.

11 This is the only acid known to *rapidly* corrode glass.

12 This appearance generally arises from an inequality in the thickness of the sheet in pot-metal glass, and of the colouring matter in coated glass.

13 See note *h* at the end of this Introduction.

14 See note *i* at the end of this Introduction.

15 See note *k* at the end of this Introduction.

16 It was, I believe, the ancient practice in oil painting, to paint for instance a red drapery, at first entirely red, and afterwards to represent its folds, by relieving the light parts with white paint, and occasionally deepening the darkest shadows with brown, or some other dark colour.

17 Did not experience teach us how much we are indebted to chance for our boasted discoveries, it would seem unaccountable that the art of enamelling, itself of such high antiquity, should have been confined to opaque substances, until the middle of the sixteenth century. An interesting account of the process of enamelling earthenware is given in Theophilus's treatise, book ii. chap. 16, [post Appendix A.] It does not appear to differ materially from the process now in use. See Dr. Lardner's Porcelain and Glass Manufacture, chap. 6.

The art of enamelling was practised by the ancient Egyptians upwards of 2000 years before Theophilus wrote. See Sir Gardiner Wilkinson's Manners and Customs of the ancient Egyptians.

18 Pot-metal glass occurs in a drapery in the glass painting at the end of the library of Trinity College, Cambridge, which was executed by Peckitt, from a design of Cipriani, at the end of the last century. But both the west window of New College, Oxford, executed by Jervais in 1800, after a design by Sir Joshua Reynolds, and the windows of Arundel Castle, are entirely coloured with enamels and stains.

58

'OPALINE GLASS'

The Magazine of Art (January 1897), pp. 334–336

ALTHOUGH this beautiful coloured glass, which was discovered some twenty years ago, has as yet received scarcely any practical recognition in this country, its great merits and unbounded possibilities are well known to artists and to all who have seen in the United States and at the Paris Exhibition, in 1889, examples of the work of John La Farge. The erection of a church window in this material at Wickhambreaux seems to be an opportunity for describing what to many persons is little understood – namely, the manner in which opaline glass is made and how a window in this material is constructed.

The history of stained glass dates back to the early days of Christianity, when Pope Leo III, adorned the Lateran church in the tenth century with coloured windows. Theophilus, in the same century, describes minutely in the second book of his "Divprsarum Artium Schedula" the process of manufacturing stained glass, and the information which he gives is most interesting, as it not only throws light on the art of glass-painting during his time, but throughout many subsequent centuries, when the process remained practically the same.

Undoubtedly the finest specimens of English stained glass are those of the twelfth and thirteenth centuries; of these, however, only few are left, for the great war of the Reformation passing over the country turned the peaceful workman into a fanatic savage whose reckless hand destroyed by thousands the many beautiful monuments which were the glories of the early Middle Ages. In the seventeenth century the glazier's art began to decline, and subsequently in the eighteenth century became practically extinct, stained glass being superseded by the use of enamel and paint. It is not until the end of the nineteenth century that we find a revival of the art, and in the present day many beautiful windows have been designed by such men as Sir Edward Burne-Jones, Ford Madox Brown, Mr. Henry Holiday, and others, not to speak of the many imitations of old windows which are constantly being erected in the churches to fill in the traceries robbed of their beautiful adornments during the time of the Reformation. Not only in England, but in many other European countries, the art of glass-painting has been revived; but we owe to an American artist, Mr. John La Farge, the invention of the new material, which, it may well be said, rivals even the best glass of the thirteenth century.

DOI: 10.4324/9781315400266-70

In 1873 Mr. La Farge accidentally discovered that the white substance of certain imitation chinaware, when insufficiently mixed with the clay and colouring matter, produced a curious opalescent quality, semi-transparent and of great beauty. He subsequently concluded that by perfecting and developing this translucency and opalescence he would ultimately produce a glass more harmonious and varied in colour than anything hitherto known. That his surmise was correct has been abundantly proved by the success of his work, and he is now at the head of an industry which is yearly increasing. The manufacture of this glass differs greatly from the way in which ordinary pot-metal is prepared. Besides having the addition of opal (white), it is often made in sheets containing two or more colours imperfectly mixed. To obtain the desired effect, the different coloured glasses, when in a molten state, are ladled from each pot on to an iron slab, where they intermingle under the pressure of a heavy roller. The sheets vary in thickness, the edges being usually thick and more or less opaque, the centre very thin and transparent.

Advantage is derived from this peculiarity, as through it gradation of tone is given to each sheet. It would be impossible to describe the infinite number of colours and tones of which this glass is capable. The mere fact that two pots of glass are never quite alike shows that the variety is endless.

Much abuse has crept into the making of the glass owing to the lack of discrimination and taste on the part of the manufacturers; artists cannot possibly attend to the making up of the pots, and have to accept what is turned out of the factories, relying upon their own judgment in selection of pieces. Another kind of glass, called Drapery glass, has been brought into the market by one of the leading firms. It derives its name from the fact that it is actually crinkled into shapes like drapery folds, for which reason it is now much used, since it saves a great amount of leading in the delineation of drapery, and so lessens the expense.

The construction of an opalescent window differs somewhat from that of one in ordinary glass, so that it may perhaps be interesting to follow the process.

Having chosen a subject and made a small coloured sketch indicating the composition, colour-scheme, and tone, the artist prepares the cartoon or full-size drawing from which the window is constructed. In designing the cartoon particular attention must be paid to the lead-lines, as all lines in the composition will appear in the window as such, no painting or drawing being done upon the glass except where faces, hands, or feet are introduced.

The cartoon is therefore practically a skeleton design of the lead-lines, and these must be so disposed as to represent the whole composition and define each figure in the window. From the cartoon three tracings are made, two on paper and one on glass; this latter is the so-called glass frame, which is set up against the light to receive the coloured pieces of glass cut from templates, which in their turn are made from the tracings. The selection of glass now commences. Usually some important figure in the design is first glazed, and forms the starting-point from which little by little the work grows, until the whole glass frame is covered with irregular shaped pieces of various sizes fixed on the frame with wax. The necessity of the colour sketch is obvious, as it facilitates the selection of pieces.

The window is now taken down and leaded together over one of the paper drawings. As it is impossible to obtain the desired harmony of colour and depth of tone in one thickness, the window is once more placed against the light and plated – that is, backed by or covered with other thicknesses of glass. This plating largely contributes to the beauty of opalescent windows.

With regard to the semi-opacity of the glass, it may be said that the beauty of colour is enhanced thereby, since the opal, which gives it its opacity, may be said to resemble a film of mother-of-pearl, suggesting complementary colours; it also gives it a certain solidity which makes ordinary modern stained glass seem thin beside it.

Opaline glass is, perhaps, the most perfect colour material ever invented, and in the hands of a sound artist it becomes as precious jewels, beautified by the setting. It therefore lies with those who can and will personally undertake the construction of windows to show the public its possibilities, and it may safely be asserted that if the use of opaline glass be adopted by our brotherhood of artists we may look forward to seeing our cathedrals, our churches, and other buildings become shrines of beautiful and resplendent windows.

3.2

Architectural contexts

DOI: 10.4324/9781315400266-71

3.2 Architectural contexts

The extent to which modern stained-glass windows integrated or harmonised with their architectural framework was a topic of much debate in the nineteenth century, whether the building was ancient or modern, religious or secular. Antiquarian, archaeological and ecclesiological groups such as The Society for Promoting the Study of Gothic Architecture (later the Oxford Architectural Society) and the Cambridge Camden Society (later the Ecclesiological Society) were influential in encouraging the use of the Gothic revival style in church architecture, publishing model designs and critiques and offering advice to church builders.

Gothic revival architect George Edmund Street (1824–1881) became a member of the Cambridge Camden Society in 1845 and regularly contributed to the society's journal *The Ecclesiologist,* which published a number of opinion pieces and critical reviews of contemporary stained glass. His paper 'On Glass Painting' (1852) was influenced by the writings and principles of other Gothic revival architects, including Augustus Welby Northmore Pugin (1812–1852). In it, he lays out his own principles and rules regarding the design of stained glass for ecclesiastical settings and its proper role as 'a vehicle for architectural decoration', as well as its limitations as a high art form.[1] Street believed that architects should have control over every part of an architectural project, including its decoration and furnishings, and he challenged the role of the independent stained-glass 'artist', stating that stained glass

> ought to be *simply* an architectural decoration, schemed out by the architect, forming part of his entire plan, harmonizing with the architecture, and capable of being executed to a great extent by workmen whose powers are little above being merely mechanical.[2]

Street not only supervised the design, execution and insertion of stained-glass windows into his buildings but was often involved in the design process too. Extracts from the article highlight his determined views and the crucial relationship between stained glass and its architectural environment: firstly, that glass is an embellishment of architectural form and therefore subordinate to its architectural surroundings, that is, it 'should never interfere with or oppose the design of the stonework'; and secondly, that glass should integrate with its architectural surroundings.[3]

Much of the debate around stained glass as an architectural decoration focused on ecclesiastical contexts. Yet, from the 1860s and 1870s, stained glass was increasingly incorporated into new secular buildings, including town halls, schools, banks and private homes. 'Stained glass as an accessory to Domestic Architecture', published in the Edinburgh journal *Chambers's Journal of Popular Literature, Science, and Art* and distributed widely, draws attention to the possibilities of stained-glass decoration within such buildings.[4] Written by an anonymous stained-glass designer and published in the 1880s when home decoration was a popular middle-class preoccupation, it especially reveals the growing public appeal of stained glass within domestic interiors – through light, ornament and chromatic harmony. In the latter part of the nineteenth century, stained-glass windows became more affordable, and the secular market was an increasingly important outlet for stained glass, providing additional work for stained-glass studios. Whether placed in the 'lordliest mansion' or 'more humble dwelling', stained-glass windows provided necessary illumination whilst enhancing the beauty of an interior.[5] The author makes the case for the use of stained glass in civic and commercial settings, where windows were used to extol the virtues of public figures and encourage civic pride. Within institutional establishments such as schools, the author recommends cheaper leaded windows using geometric, tinted or patterned glass (known as 'cathedral glass') to relieve the monotony of an interior, prevent external distractions and block out unsavoury views.

The introduction, or reintroduction, of stained-glass windows to old buildings during architectural restoration projects was also common in the nineteenth century. William Morris (1834–1896), designer, socialist activist and founder of the Society for the Protection of Ancient Buildings (SPAB), questioned this practice. He drew attention to the fact that the installation of modern stained-glass windows in ancient buildings caused material and aesthetic damage to old glass and stonework. Although stained glass was a specialty of Morris' successful decorative arts company, Morris & Co. (known as Morris, Marshall, Faulkner & Co. from its foundation in 1861 until 1875), he famously declined to provide estimates for stained-glass windows destined for 'monuments of Ancient Art' on conscientious grounds, with only a handful of exceptions. As Morris' friend and biographer John Mackail (1859–1945) acknowledges, this resolution was undeniably bad for business.[6] Yet, Morris advocated for a preservation-led approach to the protection of ancient buildings and objected to contemporary approaches to 'restoration', which often resulted in irrevocable changes to the architectural structure and decoration.

Notes

The stained glass headnotes in this volume are written by Jasmine Allen.

1 Street, G. E. 'On Glass Painting', *The Ecclesiologist* 10 (1852), 237–47 (p. 241). [selected extracts from a Paper read at 13th Anniversary of the Ecclesiological Society, 9 June 1852].

2 Street, 1852: 241.

3 Street, 1852: 239.

4 Anon., 'Stained glass as an accessory to Domestic Architecture', *Chamber's Journal* (1884, June 7), pp. 359–361.

5 *Chamber's Journal*, 7 June 1884: p. 360.

6 Mackail, J. W. *Life of William Morris* (London, New York and Bombay: Longmans, Green & Co., 1899) vol. 2, pp. 37–40.

59

G. E. STREET, 'ON GLASS PAINTING'

The Ecclesiologist, 10 (1852), pp. 237–247 [selected extracts from a Paper read at 13th Anniversary of the Ecclesiological Society, 9 June 1852]

I HAVE been asked to read before the Society to-day some remarks in further explanation of views stated by me in a very short form in a paper lately read before the Oxford Architectural Society, as to the amount of art which is to be required at the hands of our glass painters, and as to the limits which exist to any attempt at what can properly be called high art in stained glass.

I am quite prepared to be at once met with the common exclamation, that we are bound to attempt to have the best of everything which we devote to the service of GOD, and that therefore the best paintings or the best cartoons drawn by the first artists of the day must be best for use in executing paintings in glass for the church's use. And it is this common and plausible assertion which I wish to meet, and the mistaken assumption on which it proceeds which I hope to make clear to you.

Now it is very true that no modern glass has yet been executed, which either in design, or in the arrangement of tinctures, or in the tinctures themselves is likely a hundred years hence to stand the test of impartial criticism.

The defects in the colours I shall not consider at present, though much remains to be done for their improvement and variety, before even good designs can compete with ancient examples.

The designs of glass and the arrangement of colour, are the two points on which it is most necessary to enlarge, and which most admit in general of improvement. In the first, I include the consideration of the theory of draughtsmanship on glass, and in the second, those arrangements of colour which either give life and brilliancy to the particular window or else add by some general arrangements, e. g. of lines of colour, to the architectural effect of a building.

But I may at once say, that if I appear severe on modern glass, I do not at all wish to depreciate what our stained glass manufacturers have done in the last few years. I consider that if they have failed, it has been mainly because they have been the victims, – 1st, Of the obstinacy of their employers in requiring to have what is not good, and to get as much as possible for their money, and of

DOI: 10.4324/9781315400266-72

the consequent necessity for cheapness of production. 2ndly, The manufacture of immense quantities by one man, making the whole business too much of a trade to allow of the developement of feeling. 3rdly, The practice of allowing glass to be executed without much knowledge of the circumstances which are to affect it, and the fact that it now seldom enters into the province of an architect to regulate in any degree the design of the glass, or to scheme out the general arrangement of colours, subjects, or designs for an entire building.

The history of design in glass is curious; its principle varied considerably in the three great periods of Christian art, and a very short statement of its successive varieties will be useful for my purpose.

In First-Pointed, it was mosaic in its idea, and rather non-transparent than transparent; still the drawing and treatment of the material were generally very true to its requirements.

In Middle-Pointed, the idea was also really semi-mosaic, the glass transparent, whilst the superiority of the draughtsmanship, and the conventional imitation of and use of natural forms, gave it a great advantage over its predecessor.

In Third-Pointed, in its full developement, the design was what we should call artistic, attempting to represent nature as perfectly as on canvass, and consequently the attempt at deep shadows made the glass necessarily often non-transparent, and designs in perspective were continually and unsuccessfully made.

Of these three, I believe the Middle-Pointed to have been the most true in its developement in all ways. For there are certain necessities in the construction of glass paintings which it may be well to recapitulate before proceeding further, and it more than either of the others fulfilled these necessities.

1st. Each piece of glass must be lined round with a black line of lead, unnatural and stiff in its effect.

2nd. The pieces so tied together, must be each of one colour, two colours not being admissible on one piece.

3rd. The object of a window being to let in light, that glass is the worst which again artificially shuts out light. It must therefore if good be very transparent.

4th. The effect of a window must be so decided as to be intelligible from a great distance.

5th. The absence of shading and of perspective are certainly necessities; the first, because it darkens and makes dismal what should be clear and brilliant; and the second, because it can never be so managed as to look correct, or to harmonize with the straight lines of the architecture or the stiff lines of saddle bars, &c. which confine it on every side; and lastly, it is absolutely necessary, that the design of the glass should never interfere with or oppose the design of the stonework, but that it should be treated in all cases as subordinate to it.

Now all these things are of necessity in stained glass, and therefore none can be good without them.

First-Pointed regarded most of them, but as it was purely and entirely conventional in all respects it was inferior to

Middle-Pointed, which in its perfection obeyed all, and taking nature as a guide, but conventionalising her forms, really, as I hope to prove, worked on the most truthful and best of all rules.

Whereas Third-Pointed, pretending to take nature as a guide, and doing so without conventionalising her, and not regarding or obeying those rules of which the necessities of the material require the strict observance, and further attempting to disregard and over-ride all architectural arrangements and restrictions, failed most egregiously.

And having thus stated which of our old styles is in my opinion the most perfect, I proceed to examine more at length the theory of conventional forms which I consider of very great importance in estimating the real necessities and capabilities of art in glass.

I believe then, that unless you can have absolutely perfect representations of natural forms, it is far better to have those forms in a conventional guise. And as perfect representations can only be expected from great artists working on a proper medium, it seems absurd to expect them from very inferior hands (as they must always be) working on a medium which, let the representation be never so exact, would yet never allow it to look really like nature. A wreath of real flowers is worth five hundred artificial imitations; but I doubt much whether such a wreath gives more pleasing feelings, or produces a more perfect effect than does some rich and brilliant diaper of flattened and conventional flowers spreading in endless profusion through window after window of some long aisle. And further, let me observe, that conventional representations of natural forms are usually the absolute forms which nature has produced, taken from the most perfect examples – the best maple leaves or the best lily that can be found. Not twisted about in the wild luxuriance of active life, but still represented in their individual shape and with their fibres and their petals just as they really are. These forms, so obtained, are genuine ornamental forms; they do not require an artist to paint each leaf, but a patient humble workman may do them even more effectively than the most brilliant of painters. And thus these forms are best suited to a manufacture which does not allow of the general employment of great artists. A single practical instance is of more force than a host of theories; and so let me ask any one here who has looked much at modern glass, whether he has ever seen any of that most detestable of all hateful things – shaded foliage in glass? If any one here has noticed it, then he must have noticed the dismal, the heavy, and the unreal effect which always distinguishes it. The slightest amount of knowledge or discernment will suffice for the perception at once of the difference between it and foliage painted in the ancient and proper way, stiff and precise in its form, and transparent in its texture, not attempting unsuccessfully to imitate nature, but happily and successfully reminding us of her, as it were, by a beautiful symbol.

In further developement of the value of conventionalism, let me ask whether e.g. any representation in oak or brass of a real eagle for a book desk ever approached in real grandeur and fitness those quaint and magnificent birds with outstretched wings, stiff feathers, and upturned heads which we call eagles, which symbolize those birds, but which are really best when least like them. Or again, is not the stiff conventional mediæval angel infinitely more solemn and more beautiful than the wretched attempts at natural representations of heavenly beings which for three hundred years have been the fashion?

But I have no time to go into the whole question, and am only able therefore to state in a very general way the exceeding importance of this principle, and its value in all the decorative accessories of good architecture, and I have been particular in stating my opinion, because I perceive that in most modern glass, whilst its importance is recognized in the treatment of representations of foliage and the like, yet in the treatment of figures and subjects it is quite forgotten or ignored.

In these, the existence of a new principle is, I suppose, perceived, but with what reason I am unable to see. The same arguments which make me feel certain that shaded foliage is not effective, prove equally strongly that shaded figures are objectionable. And I am convinced that a careful examination of old glass would at once prove that in old examples, where all other elements of truthfulness in construction and design are found, this last, the most important of all, will not be found wanting. I should therefore, lay down as one of the most important canons, that no shading can be good in glass which is not transparent, and that that glass is best which trusts most to outlines and lines, and least to shading. I have had many opportunities of examining new shaded and old unshaded glass side by side, and I have invariably felt that this was the one point in which more than any other the new failed. It is, moreover, as it seems to me, the one great point at which the line must be drawn, in allowing artists, or men who pretend to be artists, to work. For it involves many other points. For if a figure or group of figures are transparent, and without shading, it follows that they are so far not natural and not exact representations of nature; and this point once allowed, there is a certain degree of conventional licence in attitude, in disposition of drapery, and in arrangement of colour, which may well also be allowed, and which being obviously without any pretence to represent nature exactly, ceases to offend in the degree that those representations of nature do, which it is utterly impossible, owing to their material, to make *exact* in their imitation.

And if this licence is not only allowable, but absolutely necessary in stained glass, then we at once get over one of the greatest difficulties in the treatment of the material, the existence, namely, of the black lines of the lead, and the stiffness, formality, and unnatural effect which they involve. For there is no doubt that the lines should be boldly shown wherever necessary for the construction, and consequently it is satisfactory to think that they need in no way interfere with the true principles of design.

The absence of shading which I have mentioned as one of the points most to be remembered in designing for glass, involves not only the loss of ordinary pictorial effect or chiaroscuro, but also the absence of perspective; and this on grounds additional to those which I have already noted of the incompatibility of perspective with the straight lines of the constructional parts of the window. A coloured subject in perspective, must have not only linear, but just as much aerial perspective. It will never do that the tints of the distant parts should be as forcible as those of the foreground, or that figures in the distance should have robes as bright and sparkling as those of the figures which are close at hand. This seems to be so obvious that it ought at once to expose the absurdity of all attempts to copy in glass cartoons intended for oil or fresco. So for instance, in the Munich glass at Cologne, or in the Church of S. Maria Hilf at Munich, I think every one's feeling must be – much as he may admire the magnificence of the offering or the boldness of the attempt – that it would have been much more delightful to see such subjects represented on the walls, than essayed in windows, where they disobey all the necessities of construction, are deficient in their effect, and disagree in toto with all the architecture, the beauty of which they ought to have heightened and brought out.

So then I think I have shown that high art in the ordinary sense, cannot co-exist with the proper use of the materials at our disposal, that is to say, that the kind of art which is successful on canvas will probably be just the reverse in glass, and that elaborate representations of actual life and of nature, are quite wrong in principle and must always be unsatisfactory in their effect.

There is one other consideration which bears very forcibly on this question; and this is the fact that glass is properly a vehicle for architectural decoration, and not primarily for the introduction of religious pictures into churches. There can, I hope, be no doubt in this room that if we wish satisfactorily to develope a school of Christian artists by giving them work in our churches, it must be done rather by giving them our walls than our windows to work upon: we must ask them to work in fresco or to paint in oil, and take care only that the windows and their glazing let in so much light as may enable us to see all the beauties which their brushes have figured on the walls.

Stained glass ought to be *simply* an architectural decoration, schemed out by the architect, forming part of his entire plan, harmonizing with the architecture, and capable of being executed to a great extent by workmen whose powers are little above being merely mechanical. Very much of the old glass I believe to have been executed on this principle, as for instance, that system which prevailed so extensively in the 14th century of arranging the subjects or figures with a band of rich colour about the middle of a long succession of windows, so as to produce a decided horizontal line of rich colour throughout the building, harmonizing with and assisting the lines of the architecture, as may be seen at Merton College Chapel, or in the nave of York, or in the choir of Cologne, in which last instance no doubt it contributes much to give strength of effect to the clerestory windows which would have otherwise looked weak and wiry and attenuated.

Again the filling in of such windows as those five sisters, as they are called, in the transept of York – to give one example out of hundreds of the same nature – is an instance of the attempt to make the glass simply an architectural ornament; and need I say how successfully this was achieved? May I not appeal to the universal admiration which such glass excites for a confirmation of my views?

I have not space now to say more on this *most* important point, but I am well assured that it *is* of immense importance, and that so long as we are content to treat glass painting, as if it were independent of architecture, so long we may expect to meet with disheartening results.

I should like now to say a few words on the extent to which paintings in oil or fresco may be taken as models by glass painters; because it is very much the fashion to require them to do this, and unfortunately the fashion generally requires the reproduction of the works of an unsatisfactory school, that of the modern Germans.

What I have already said may have been sufficient to show how completely it is a mistake to make a modern lithograph the foundation of a stained window, and yet this is done and admired. All I wish to say now is that if it is done at all, the works of those painters ought to be selected as the best models, which show the least attempt at Chiaroscuro, and the greatest simplicity and decision in the attitudes and details of dresses and figures. Such pictures as those of Memling, Van Meckenen, Roger of Bruges, Van Eyck, William of Cologne, and the like, contain, no doubt, a mine of information which might, with discretion, be turned to much account. But to attempt to turn the paintings of men like Hess or Overbeck or Steinle into glass, is another and a very different thing, and can never be successful; for their works are always deficient in that sternness and decision of purpose which marked the early German school, and which ought to mark any school of painters on glass.

But even more information and more useful knowledge is to be obtained from the illuminated manuscripts of the middle ages than from early paintings. Not only as to the proper mode of treating the various subjects required in the ancient traditional manner, (and this is very important,) but also as to arrangements of colours and the like; for as a large number of the subjects are represented on a gold ground, without attempt at either perspective or shading, they come very near to the requirements of glass.

There is again in modern glass one most glaring fault, which is visible in the works of almost every one, that, viz., of continuing one subject through a number of lights of a window. There can be no excuse for this violation of an absolute law; and if it is right to have such large subjects, then it is high time that architects should be requested to omit the monials from their windows. At any rate, monials and such subjects cannot properly co-exist. But this fault is brought to the very acme of absurdity when a succession of niches and canopies, five or seven in one window, contain only *one* subject, and is even worse when, as is often the case, each of these canopies and each pedestal has its own very peculiar point of sight, and equally peculiar vanishing points, none agreeing with each other, or with the subject which is pleasantly supposed to be visible through openings in their backs.[1]

It is distressing to have to notice such faults, but it is quite necessary, for they are not only done, but persisted in and argued for, because there is ancient precedent for such mistakes. It is high time that in glass, as in other things, men should begin to think a little for themselves, if no further, at any rate so far as to discover which is the *good* ancient precedent. *All* that is old is not good; it is all venerable, all to be preserved where it exists, but not all to be copied because it exists, and yet one hears men argue as if our forefathers never in a single instance made a mistake.

I, for one, with a much deeper admiration than most men for what I believe to be their good works, do not hesitate to confess that many of their works I do not consider good, and should be very sorry to be bound to imitate.

If time will allow, I should be glad now to call your attention to some examples of fine old glass, which I think may furnish some useful hints to us as to principles of design.

The proper use of white glass is one of the most important of all points to be observed. I remember an admirably striking example of the effect it may produce in the cathedral at Chartres, where all the subjects are arranged in regular geometrical forms, – circles, quatre-foils, &c., – each form marked out and defined by lines of white glass. When I was there I was fortunate in finding the cathedral open until very late in the evening, and I availed myself gladly of the opportunity thus afforded for the study of the wonderful and changing effect of the glass, and I found that as the light gradually faded away, an effect was produced which showed strikingly the advantage of the white line, for whilst the rest of the glass became very dark and black in its effect, the white lines stood out brilliantly, and the windows appeared full of regular and beautiful patterns.

The advantage of the white edge to all glass next stone is now generally perceived, but we have not yet attained to sufficient boldness in its use in other parts.

There can be no doubt that its use is founded on a correct principle, and that the contrast which it allows is in the highest degree beneficial in its effect to the rich colours among which it occurs, and it is a great rule that it should be treated as metal in heraldry: either white on colour, or colour on white. White, from its brilliancy and sparkling character, answers to the gold of heraldry, of illuminations, and of mediæval paintings. And in the best glass, it is always observable that the white glass increases in amount towards the head of the window, and the tracery is frequently almost entirely white, with a little yellow stain. Now in modern glass the head of the window is frequently, if not generally, full of colour, and when so, seldom looks well, but always heavy, and always has a tendency to confuse and darken the stonework far too much.

At Ratisbon Cathedral, (perhaps one of the grandest churches and one of the noblest collections of glass in the world,) it is very noticeable that in the apse the colour of the windows, which rise in the same wall one over another in three heights, answering to aisle, triforium, and clerestory, gradually gets lighter as it ascends. Throughout, however, the white is very decided.

In the same cathedral also the Munich glass may well be compared with that of the 14th century, and it is very remarkable how sombre and heavy its effect is. This is attributable, I believe, principally to the elaborate shading, of which it is the victim. Bits of white here and there look brilliant, but the whole looks very dismal.

Sometimes, however, when there is a great quantity of this yellow or white glass shaded, if the shading, from its small surface in any one point, has rather the effect only of lines, the effect is very brilliant. I may instance the celebrated Volkamer window at Nuremberg, and some of the windows in Ulm Cathedral, which however vary much in their merit. In these, however, the *lines* are always very clear and decided, (and this is a very great point,) and the canopies, though they have colour behind them, have it in small quantities. I may observe, too, that the best of the Ulm windows are, owing to the proper use of white, marvellously distinct and intelligible at a great distance.

In England we have magnificent examples of the value of white; among other examples, in

The clerestory of the choir at Winchester, which are some of the finest figure and canopy windows in England, where all the canopies and their supports are white and the figures have all white cloaks, with yellow patterns, the yellow very pale and delicate; and again in the west window of S. George's Chapel, Windsor, and the east window of Gloucester, both examples of late glass, but still very fine and good in principle. At Gloucester the figures and canopies are white and the ground coloured, hair yellow, and edging to robes the same; and again at Wells, a storehouse of the best glass, in the tracery of the choir aisle windows the foliage (which is all in imitation of natural leaves) is only stiffened and conventionalized, the whole is *very white,* the stalks, berries, and acorns only, being yellow, and the most formal patterns and leaves, I may remark, look by far the best. There is a coloured ground, it is true, but the colour is in very minute pieces.

At Rouen a white stem is used next to geometrical lines of lead to increase their definite character, from which the foliage springs.

And finally, it would be ungenerous in the extreme if in speaking on such a subject one were to omit mention of the thorough appreciation shown by Mr. Pugin for the true principles of art in this as in other matters in the glass which he has of late been designing. I believe the brilliant effect of much of Mr. Hardman's manufacture is owing to the proper use of white.

One word more, and I have finished on this point. I doubt whether we have as yet missed any colour so entirely as we have white, if I may call it a colour. There is a certain kind of thickness – obvious and yet transparent thickness that one sees in old glass, but which I have never seen re-produced; and I trust that those glass stainers who feel the importance of using it, will endeavour if possible to improve upon the texture of that which they now generally use.

On subject and canopy windows I have already spoken in condemnation, and may here say that as there is "authority" for subjects without canopies, as e.g. at Ulm, and often in the latest glass, so there is no reason why those who wish entirely to go by authority need insist upon having them. The very beautiful Jesse windows, of which there are magnificent examples at Wells and at Ulm, are excellent substitutes for the subject and canopy, and I do not think that the idea need be restricted to this particular subject.

The grounding of subjects was another point on which much attention was always bestowed, and of course one great element of success in its effect is always that it should contrast decidedly with the figure or subject.

At Freyburg, at Strasburg, and at Ratisbon, the system is very beautiful where subjects in medallions are introduced; a richly diapered and very broad bordered carpet appears to be suspended behind the medallions, whose grounds are much simpler and more transparent, and therefore, well contrasted; and in these examples – and they are almost the best series of 14th century paintings with which I am acquainted, (and all apparently from the same school) – white is very judiciously used to define all patterns.

In England, I think, subjects with canopies and flowered back grounds were more common than abroad, and one always remembers them gratefully by the lovely representations of ferns and other delicate plants which one sees covering the surface of the glass.

There is one other point on which I may touch before I conclude, which is rather a matter for the architect to remember than for the glass painter. The position, in the thickness of the wall, namely, which the glass is to occupy when finished. For this is often very important.

I well remember a very noble new church in which the glass in the clerestory was scarcely visible owing to its being advanced too much toward the external face. Whereas in some of the great foreign clerestories the glass is within a few inches only of the *internal* face, so that the whole is seen from below.

Again in the tracery of many old east windows it will be found that the glass is nearer the *external* face than it is in the lower lights of the window, and the reason is obvious, as it tends to make the exterior tracery more delicate and in better proportion, whilst from the interior the glass is well seen. This is done at Merton College Chapel and at North Moreton and elsewhere.[2]

There are other points on which I should have liked to speak had time allowed, and the most important of these perhaps is the arrangement of subjects in subject windows. In old windows there is generally a vast amount of thought and knowledge displayed in this matter, whereas in modern we very often see great incongruity, if not ignorance displayed in the relative positions allotted to them. But on this subject a treatise might be written, and any one who would draw out and publish regular schemes of subjects as arranged in old windows at home and abroad would do very great service.

One kind of window – the rose – presents apparently great difficulties, and is seldom treated well. At Nôtre Dame, Paris, the south transept rose is successfully managed, all the subjects being in medallions, and all the figures therefore on their feet, instead of tumbling about in all directions as is so frequently and so absurdly the fashion.

And now I must conclude. I leave unsaid much more which might I believe well be said in support of the principles and the rules which I have desired to lay down. I regret, indeed, that I have not been able to work out more clearly and properly the results which we attain if we argue in this matter upon the laws of truthfulness. I am satisfied that in glass as well as in every other detail of Architecture, we are just in the position in which a recurrence for a time to first principles is useful and even necessary. Indeed we want a little pre-Raphaelitism in this as in many other things; above all, we want and shall, I hope, soon have, men who see the necessity of working upon right principles and who will be courageous enough to refuse to work on any others. They might rest assured, that we should have more confidence in them than in men who will do anything in the way of business, and defend it on that score. And then we want much that architects should study the art so far at any rate as to have a general idea, when they design a building, what its ornamentation is to be; not only what the shapes of its openings are to be, but much more, even, what the fittings of these openings are to be. Two more wants there are; first, a greater knowledge of Christian Iconography; and secondly, such a payment for their work as will enable glass painters to think long and carefully on every work that they undertake. All these wants we may I trust in time see supplied, and then I think we shall be in a fair way to equal the noble works of our forefathers.

Notes

1 The new windows in the nave of Cologne Cathedral have each a single subject filling the whole of the four lights. Some of these subjects require central figures, but the central monial prevents this, and the whole subject consequently has a kind of lop-sided effect, and, which is still worse, the limbs and the dresses of single figures passing from one light into another are dissected in all directions by the monials in the most ludicrous manner.

2 One of the most interesting of the many very fine churches with which I am acquainted in France, is that of S. Urbain at Troyes, and the arrangement of the glass in it is quite worth notice here. The choir is apsidal, and its north and south aisles are so also, and do not continue round it. The latter have two-light square-headed windows – one in each bay – the tracery of which is quite on the external face of the wall, and on the inside is partly concealed by beautiful open tracery filling in the spaces between the groining, and set flush with the internal face of the wall. In the choir apse the same idea is continued, but the monials of the detached tracery of the lower tier of windows are continued up as monials for the clerestory. In the lower range, therefore, the glazing is some distance back from the internal face of the wall, whilst in the upper range, or clerestory, it is within five or six inches of it. The lower windows being partially obscured by the open tracery in front are glazed with simple geometrical patterns whilst the clerestory being in full view has a row of figures and canopies in rich colour filling one half of the height, the rest being filled with simple diapers. The beauty of the whole arrangement is extreme, and supplies much matter for thoughtful study for architects, as it illustrates strikingly the extent to which mediæval architecture took into consideration the whole decoration of their works. I have no doubt whatever that with other arrangements of glazing it would be easy entirely to destroy the beautiful effect of the building, whereas now it is really wonderfully enhanced.

60

'STAINED GLASS AS AN ACCESSORY TO DOMESTIC ARCHITECTURE'

Chamber's Journal (1884, June 7), pp. 359–361

IN a former paper (September 1879) we briefly reviewed the growth and progress of the art of glass-staining and painting, and described the various processes necessary to its prosecution, and practised at the present day; and, after tracing its career in its application to the purposes of ecclesiastical decoration, hinted at its capability of adaptation to ornamental requirements beyond those pertaining to the embellishment of the sacred edifice. We propose in the present paper to deal more exhaustively with this branch of an art, and to endeavour to point out, as succinctly as possible, the more prominent and obvious cases where its introduction would be desirable in secular ornamentation.

Public buildings of course demand the first attention; and in a country like our own, owing its prosperity to its commercial enterprise, its political organisation, and its unequalled system of municipal government, we have witnessed in the course of the last few years the commencement, progress, and completion of costly and magnificently adorned buildings. Upon these noble buildings have been lavished the utmost resources of decorative art; and latterly, stained glass has formed an important element in the general scheme of decoration, and it is to its adaptation to this class of domestic architecture that we would first draw attention.

One of the first, as it is one of the most natural, motives prompting the enrichment of the ornamental accessories of a building, is discovered in a desire to see perpetuated the memory of its founder or founders. The most natural expression of this feeling is, of course, the desire to permanently retain a record of their features and personal characteristics in the shape of a pictorial representation. This desire at first sight seems to be susceptible of immediate gratification by a portrait, either on canvas or in marble; but further consideration will tend towards the conviction that the use of these media is not altogether free from objection. Little, perhaps, can be said against the statue in itself; but the elaborate and gorgeous decoration of our more sumptuous buildings is likely to be unpleasantly marred by the marble pallor of sculpture; and after all, dignified and stately as are many of our statuesque memorials, they convey little more than an idealised impression of the features of the person commemorated.

DOI: 10.4324/9781315400266-73

The employment of oil portraiture is also open to certain objections. It must be remembered that modern decoration means a great deal more than a mere picking out in gold and colour of the salient lines of a cornice, or the stencilled powdering of a conventional pattern over the area of a wall or a ceiling; it has advanced far beyond the province of the builder and house-painter, and demands no inconsiderable proportion of the genius of the artist. If the decoration of a room or hall is designed to constitute in itself a complete work of art, its effect may be grievously injured by the injudicious introduction of a heavy gold frame, and colours, which while admirably accomplishing the purpose of the artist, may in a great measure interfere with the surrounding harmony of colour. We have, then, no other place left but the window, and the problem seems to be in a fair way towards solution. The perfection to which the painting of glass has attained leaves no room for doubt as to the fidelity of the likeness; but apart from this fact, a far more extensive recognition of the virtues or services of the subject of the memorial is to be obtained by various devices and emblems, appropriate to the character and life of the person honoured, which could hardly with propriety be introduced into an oil picture. One example, recently erected, may serve to more clearly demonstrate our meaning. The lately erected town-hall of Lerwick has been enriched by two windows illustrative of persons and scenes connected with some of the primitive traditions of Orkney. In one window, divided by a central mullion into twin-lights, is represented the figure of Archbishop Eystein, one of the earliest of Orcadian prelates, clad in his archiepiscopal vestments; while a panel beneath the figure illustrates his consecration of King Magnus. Side by side with the figure of the archbishop stands Bishop William, the founder of the venerable cathedral of Kirkwall, the formal ceremony itself being depicted in the panel below. The corresponding window displays the gigantic form of the Norse warrior Harald Haarfager, with his landing in Zetland shown in the lower panel; and Jarl Rognvald, whose investiture as Earl of Orkney, 870 A.D., is represented in the panel beneath. In the 'tracery' above the two windows are shown respectively the Orcadian and Norwegian coats-of-arms. Now, a combination of such historical and traditional interest could hardly be otherwise so successfully treated, while the glowing colours and fine design materially add to the effect of the neighbouring beauties of the structure.

There is another consideration not without importance in connection with the establishment of a complete scheme of internal decoration. Light is one of the most important essentials in a building where exact and extensive business is transacted, and the presence of large and frequent windows is a necessity. But how painfully is the harmony and continuity of the ornament interrupted by the constant recurrence of these patches of white light. The eye, in following the progress of the decorative design, grows weary of the constant loss and recapture of its thread; and that which would otherwise have pleased and charmed by its beauty as a whole, only perplexes and tires by its division into parts. Here, then, is called into requisition the art of the glass-stainer; without any vital diminution of light, the scheme of colour is no longer disturbed, a perfect chromatic harmony is established, and the window serves a double purpose, by admitting the necessary illumination from without, and enhancing the beauty of the building within.

The foregoing remarks naturally have reference to all public buildings of more or less importance, though we have instanced the town-hall as a representative building, associated with the more imposing class of secular edifices.

There is an institution and building, without the existence of which the writing on subjects of beauty and art would be a serious waste of time – namely, the school; and here the introduction of stained glass may be found of beneficial effect. It is not to be denied that when the watchful eye of the master relaxes its vigilance, the youthful eye will wander too, and the direction of nearly every eye will be towards the window; and principals of schools and their subordinates are fully aware of the fact. They are also aware of the attractions or distractions presented by the tempting spectacle of green trees and spreading meadows in summer; or falling snow and ice-bound stream in winter, or even at all times the freedom of the open street; so, to remove the cause of temptation, the glass is made opaque by painting it over with a dull white mixture which effectually conceals the dangerous landscape. But by the introduction of cathedral glass, of the simplest patterns and pleasing tints, the unsightly whitewashed panes would be replaced by panels of unblemished glass more or less ornamental, perfectly effectual in their primary purpose, and at the same time affording some relief to the eyes from the monotony of the barren school walls. Tinted glass leaded in various geometric or flowing patterns might be made most useful as an excellent substitute for drawing copies of the elementary stage; the rudiments of freehand drawing could all be acquired from the glazed patterns; while, under competent hands, it could afford most valuable assistance in the teaching of the laws of the harmony and artistic contrasting of colours. The trifling initial expense would be speedily saved, as there would be no wear and tear of copies; there could be no *measuring,* most disastrous to the student; the copy would be always clean; the colour would be refreshing to the eye; and much labour would be saved to the teacher, as he could demonstrate his teaching to the whole class at once.

Passing from the consideration of public requirements to those of the private home, the increasing cultivation and appreciation of the fine arts, and their application to domestic necessities, are sufficient encouragement for the advancing of the claims of stained glass to hold a place in the general scheme of internal decoration. Of course, with such diversity as necessarily exists in the comparative size and extent of family abodes, from the lordliest mansion, standing in the midst of its own far-stretching grounds, to the more humble dwelling, forming a unit among the many that go to constitute a street, or terrace, or 'gardens,' it would be impossible to lay down any precise suggestions for their ornamentation; but it may be possible to offer a few general and broadly elastic ideas, capable of being expanded or contracted according to the means and wants of all.

The more pretentious of the mansions of the nobility and gentry are pretty sure to boast of at least one fine, large, and imposing window, affording ample scope for artistic design, and, whether in the family tracing its pedigree for centuries, or the *nouveau riche* who began life with a struggle, heraldry and its concomitants seem to be held, more or less, in equal reverence. It needs little apology, therefore, for suggesting the blazonry of shield, helmet, crest, mantling, motto, supporters, and other resources of the gentle science, as affording a most appropriate exercise of the glass-stainer's skill. Making use, as heraldry does almost exclusively, of the five most prominent colours, as well as white and gold, it is admirably adapted for its reproduction in stained glass, whose exquisite and transparent tints are seen to fine effect in heraldic compositions. The matter of expense is of course an important consideration; but the treatment of heraldic design can be almost endlessly modified or elaborated; so that, while within easy reach of the only moderately affluent, it may, on the other hand, be raised to such a height of gorgeous enrichment as to form no unworthy element in the decoration of a palace.

Nor is a large and finely proportioned window an absolute necessity. At Rydal Hall, Westmoreland, the seat of the family of Le Fleming, a window, the heraldic blazoning of which was designed by the present writer, consisted merely of nine upright oblong square panels, each about two feet high by eighteen inches wide, arranged three, three, and three; and separated by mullions and transoms. But this unpromising rigidity of construction was not only overcome, but made subservient to the general design, in the following manner: the arms of the Le Fleming family, in a shield of nine quarterings, occupied the centre panel; the quarterings (all divisions of a shield above two, no matter how many in number, are called quarters) being those respectively of Le Fleming, of course in the place of honour, the dexter chief; and of eight ancestral and collateral branches of the family; and each of these quarterings, thus brought together in one shield to form the perfect 'achievement of arms' of the present representative, was displayed separately on single shields occupying the eight surrounding panels.

One of the principal documents in the muniment rooms of the great is the genealogical tree, duly set forth on musty parchment, in itself a guarantee of its own antiquity. How admirably could this be executed in glass! The tree, very conventionally designed, trained over the whole surface of the window; the quaintly hung shields depending from its branches at intervals; the whole forming an interesting study for antiquary and genealogist.

But in less ambitious dwellings, stained glass under various forms may be introduced with picturesque advantage. It will be acknowledged that very often, while the front of a house may look on a well-kept garden, or form part of the side of a spacious and beautiful square or public garden, the back may very likely look out on equally spacious but not equally beautiful or savoury mews. We know it may be contended that most back-rooms are bedrooms, and only used at night. This is true enough. But in nine cases out of ten, in houses of this class, there is a staircase window on the first landing, which, as a rule, looks out on the back, and is continually calling the attention of those passing up or down the stairs to the interesting spectacle of an equine toilet, or some similarly delectable operation. In this case, a window, though consisting of only two or three tints of rolled cathedral glass, and leaded in geometric or ornamentally flowing lines, would completely shut out the offensive prospect, while in no way interfering with the necessary lighting of the stair, nor the opening or shutting of the window-frame; and the expense would be scarcely if any more than glazing the sashes with plate-glass, which, moreover, to look commonly decent, requires infinitely more frequent cleaning than the other. This, of course, is almost the simplest form of treatment; but, according to the length of purse of the householder, the window may be more or less ornate in its design. The owner's arms, or monogram; floral painted devices, heads, or figures representing the four seasons, field-sports, fables, nursery rhymes, and numberless kindred subjects, are all most appropriate for delineation, and can be obtained at far less cost than a doubtful 'old master,' or piece of Brummagem bric-à-brac. A very pretty effect is obtained at night by filling the sides of a hall-lamp, or any large conspicuous lamp, with painted glass of design according to the owner's fancy; the old-fashioned clumsy window-blinds are now frequently superseded by leaded glass screens, more or less ornamental in their details; and a great objection to the use of stationary firescreens hitherto – that while they screen, they also hide the fire, is removed by the use of screens of glass, leaded and painted according to the taste and purse of the buyer.

A great and most important consideration in the adoption of stained glass is the great variety of design of which it is susceptible, its range of artistic production being so extensive and pecuniarily elastic as to bring it, in one form or another, within the reach of almost any one occupying a house; while for cleanliness, durability, and pleasing effect, whether in the comfortable dwelling of the thriving tradesman, or adorning the noblest monuments of private munificence or national philanthropy, it cannot fail to charm the eye by its intrinsic beauty; while from the artist's practised hand, the jewels of design shed their lustre on the illuminated walls.

61

J. W. MACKAIL, *LIFE OF WILLIAM MORRIS*

(London, New York and Bombay: Longmans, Green & Co., 1899), Vol. 2, pp. 37–40

In the earlier years of the business Morris had accepted commissions for windows in old as well as new buildings: the most conspicuous instances being the well-known windows in the Latin Chapel at Christ Church, Oxford, and the southern choir-aisle of Salisbury Cathedral. When the Society for Protection of Ancient Buildings was founded, he was forced to reconsider the whole question of dealing with old churches more deeply than before; and the conclusions he drew with regard to the practice of restoration obliged him to take up a very stringent attitude when there was any question of alterations to an ancient building. As regards windows in particular, the casuistry of the matter is exceptionally delicate. "We are prepared as heretofore," Morris wrote in this circular, "to give estimates for windows in churches and other buildings, *except in the case of such as can be considered monuments of Ancient Art,* the glazing of which we cannot conscientiously undertake, as our doing so would seem to sanction the disastrous practice of so-called Restoration." The double ambiguity of the words in which the exception is couched is easily apparent. Even rules laid down with the utmost stringency must in some cases leave room for ambiguities and evasions, and the final decision will fall on the instinct of the artist. But Morris's principles prescribed that in all cases where there was any doubt, an existing building, or any part of an existing building, whether in strict terms a monument of ancient art or not, should be let alone. In most cases there was none. When Dean Stanley asked him to execute a window for Westminster Abbey, and upon his refusal, cited the Vyner window in Christ Church as a precedent, Morris replied that even that window, the excellence of which as a piece of modern work he did not affect to deny, was an intruder where it stood, and alien in character and sentiment from the building in which it was placed.

On the announcement now made and on Morris's own practice under it, Mr. Wardle makes some interesting remarks. "Its object was ill understood," he says, "and moreover so little liked, that we found it necessary to repeat orally and with asseverations our firm intention to abide by it, and at the back of this, to get it believed that we had not given up glass-painting altogether. For a year or two

 DOI: 10.4324/9781315400266-74

certainly our business suffered from the rumour, not wanting in echoes, that Mr. Morris had given up glass-painting; and we had to make many advertisements to the contrary."

"In the minds of most people," Mr. Wardle goes on, and here he touches the real truth of the matter, "who took any interest at all in Mr. Morris's work, the *raison d'être* of 'Morris glass' was its so-called mediævalism, and it was supposed nothing could be more suitable for an ancient building. The profound misconception which this opinion implied, and the other hopeless mistake which assumed that Mr. Morris's work was purposely 'mediæval,' made it impossible that the circular could be understood.

"The grounds of Mr. Morris's protest were two. The first was the obvious material damage ancient buildings suffer by the process of removing existing glass from the windows and the insertion of new. We had ourselves several frightful experiences, though we used every precaution in our power: how much damage has been done where no such care was taken, and where it was not even suspected that the original tracery and framing of a window was of any peculiar value! It was not uncommon, when a painted window was offered to an old church, that as part of the improvement new tracery and mullions were also decided on. Even when it was intended to preserve the old stonework, it was almost inevitable that some part of it would fall when the support of the ancient glass with its saddle-bars and stanchions was removed: and new stonework would then have to be prepared hastily. Even if all went well, which would be a large concession – for there was always the cutting of the old stonework for the new saddle-bars, the hammering, and the vibration, most dangerous to old masonry – there was the final blotting out of the entire window by the wire guards. These guards are almost equivalent to the abolition of the windows as part of the external architecture, since they hide much of the thickness of the masonry and all the refinements of the mouldings and tracery."

The other ground was that laid down with a firm hand by Morris himself in the original statement of the objects of the Society for Protection of Ancient Buildings, and continually impressed and re-impressed by him with tongue and pen whenever he dealt with the subject of ancient art: the essential dishonesty of any process which professed to be "restoration" of the old building; and the essential futility of anything which undertook to replace an original by a copy even when there was not the dishonest purpose of making the copy indistinguishable from the original.

"Never," Mr. Wardle justly adds – and the remark, of course, applies with equal force to the share which Burne-Jones, first as principal and afterwards as sole figure-designer, had in Morris windows – "let people say what they will about the suitability of Mr. Morris's glass to mediæval buildings, do the old and the new rightly harmonize. This last opinion very few were able to adopt, for so few recognized the real originality and modernness of his art. It was supposed to be mediæval. In popular estimation design necessarily takes one of several recognized forms which are called styles, and as his design had many of the characters of mediæval work, he was supposed to be intentionally imitating that style. On the contrary, Mr. Morris was too unaffected, and in the broadest sense natural, in his art to allow himself to imitate, and as he did not intentionally make his work mediæval, he did not pretend that it could be suitable for a mediæval building."

This, then, was Morris's theory, expressed in its rigour. In accordance with it he laid down a self-denying ordinance with regard to supplying painted windows for ancient buildings – self-denying doubly, because not only did this resolution, as has been noted above, injure, and for a time partly cripple, this branch of the business, but because the result in three cases out of four was simply that the owners, or guardians, of the mediæval building went somewhere else; and the window was filled with glass as much inferior to his in colour and design as it was more alien from the spirit of the Middle Ages, not least so when it was inspired by an insincere and pretentious mediævalism.

By abstaining himself, however, he hoped to set an example that others might gradually follow; and perhaps his action has not been wholly without effect. In a few instances he allowed exceptions: among these may be mentioned the five beautiful windows executed by him for the chancel of St. Margaret's, Rottingdean, at the special request of Burne-Jones. In that case the windows were plain lancets filled with modern glass, some of it unpainted, the rest admittedly and unrelievedly hideous. There was no tracery to injure, and no existing ancient glass to suffer from the juxtaposition of the new.

3.3

Style and taste

DOI: 10.4324/9781315400266-75

3.3 Style and taste

The building, rebuilding and restoration of churches were prolific activities in the Victorian period, and the desire to reintroduce decorative art and furnishings into these churches triggered an enormous demand for ecclesiastical stained glass. As we have seen, medieval precedents were held up as appropriate models for a revived era, and much stained glass in this period revived the 'mosaic' Gothic style as well as medieval imagery and symbolism. Figurative stained-glass windows were well populated with familiar religious images of saints, prophets, apostles and evangelists under Gothic canopies, biblical scenes with decorative borders, and tracery lights filled with Christian symbols, angels and archangels.

Medieval design was the main influence on Victorian stained glass, which persisted throughout the nineteenth century but was especially pertinent in the early years of its revival. 'A Card' published in the satirical *Punch* magazine in 1845 takes the form of a fake business card advertising a long list of objects available for purchase in the 'antiquated', Gothic or medieval style: some are 'designed to look old', others so convincing that they 'defy detection'.[1] Amongst the list is a 'Head from a piece of broken window found under a brick-kiln by the Archaeological Institute at Winchester', intended to ridicule the reverence which proponents of the Gothic revival bestowed upon archaeological fragments of medieval glass. To continue to poke fun at the fashion for medievalism, the Gothic revival architect and Catholic convert Augustus Welby Northmore Pugin (1812–1852) is caricatured as 'Pugsby', a figure wearing jester's boots beside a heraldic lion holding a banner bearing Pugin's own adopted motto 'En avant' and the initials 'AWP'. Pugin was a particular target for expressions of anti-Catholic sentiments, which here are veiled as comic satire. After Pugin converted to the Catholic faith in 1834, his promotion of the Gothic style and the reintroduction of church decoration fed into a widespread anxiety over the revival and popularity of material styles and art forms from Britain's Catholic past and their adaptation and use in the established Anglican church.

The satirical business card also includes a cartoon of a stained-glass window depicting a bearded saint with a decorated halo and gospel in one hand, standing under a Gothic arch and once again bearing the initials 'AWP'. The inclusion of this standard medievalising image serves to further the author's point that stock religious stained-glass windows in the Gothic style are predictable, repetitive and boring.[2] By the end of the century the 'Gothic' stained-glass window was the stock-in-trade of an increasingly saturated commercialised market. The ennui invoked by such figures is perhaps best exemplified in 'The Young Glass-Stainer', a poem written in 1893 by Thomas Hardy (1840–1928) and published in his 1917 collection of poems *Moments of Vision*. In this short poem, included here, the young glass painter is weary of painting stiff religious figures under Gothic niches and dreams instead of painting naturalistic and idealised figures from the classical mythologies of Ancient Greece and Rome.

By the 1850s, stained glass was a fast-growing Victorian industry. Following the publications of antiquarians such as Winston, along with treatises on stained glass by artists such as Scottish glass-painter James Ballantine (1806–1877) and London-based William Warrington (1796–1869), stained glass also became the subject of much discussion in the popular press. An anonymous article, which appeared in the *London Journal* in 1858, reveals how readers might encounter writings on stained glass in one of the best-selling weekly magazines of the period.[3] The article derides the popular practice of copying picture paintings by artists of the Nazarene movement, a group of German Romantic painters who formed a group originally known as the Brotherhood of St Luke in 1809. The Nazarenes, as they were later called, aimed to revive spirituality in art, and this group was one of the major influences on the British Pre-Raphaelite Brotherhood founded in 1848. The author alludes to the controversial decision to award the commission for glazing Glasgow Cathedral to the Königliche Glasmalereianstalt (Royal Bavarian Stained Glass Establishment) of Munich rather than British artists. The Munich artists were renowned for their naturalistic pictorial style and were directly influenced by the Nazarene movement.[4] The reglazing of Glasgow Cathedral was one of the largest public art commissions of the Victorian age, and the decision to award the commission to Munich artists injured national pride and stirred the debate on style, taste and technique.

Notes

The stained glass headnotes in this volume are written by Jasmine Allen.

1 'A Card', *Punch*, 8 (1845), p. 238.

2 Architect George Gilbert Scott acknowledged in his *Personal and Professional Recollections* (1879) that 'As it is, one constantly sees in painted glass, things which in Punch would pass for very good jokes, and caricatures in Punch, which, in glass, would be viewed as true Christian art.' G.G. Scott, *Personal and Professional Recollections, by the Late George Gilbert Scott* (London: Sampson, Low, Marston, Searle and Rivington, 1879), p. 218.

3 Anon., 'Stained Glass Windows', *London Journal* (20 March 1858), p. 40.

4 A group of German artists dating from the early nineteenth century, who were influenced by the early Renaissance.

62

'A CARD'

Punch, 8 (1845), p. 238

238 PUNCH, OR THE LO

A CARD.

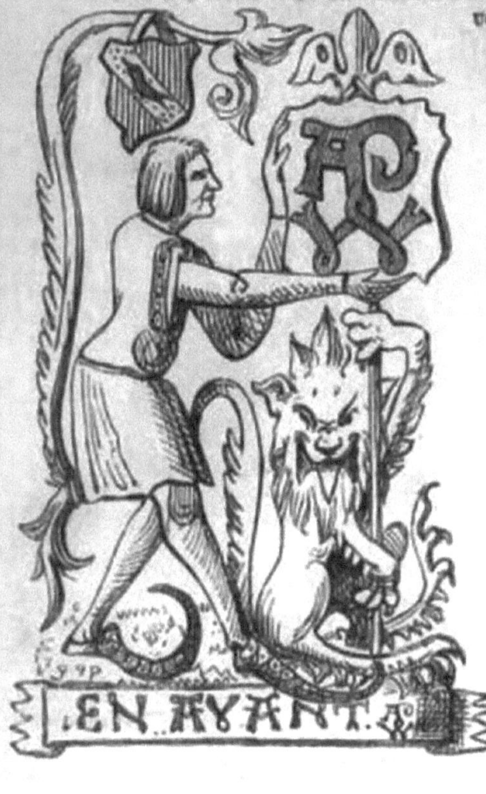

UGSBY begs to acquaint Bishops, Priests, Commissioners of Fine Arts, patrons of "Pure Art," and dealers in Ancient Windows, that he has opened a manufactory for every article in the Mediæval line at very reduced prices. All kinds of Metal Work, with imitation-rust of the best quality, done so as to defy detection from the remains of the middle-ages. New door-handles, pump-handles, water-vats, candlesticks, and weather vanes, warranted to look five hundred years old.

Modern Portraits, antiquated as per specimen annexed, at fixed prices, with lions or griffins extra, according to the length of their tails. Worthies made up from any number of authorities, as per other specimen annexed, namely :—

DOI: 10.4324/9781315400266-76

An unknown Saint, which has been faithfully copied from various originals, viz., Head from a piece of broken window found under a brick-kiln by the Archæological Institute at Winchester; Missal from a tomb-stone in Dublin Cathedral; Right Hand from half a Bishop picked up after the fire at York Minster; Left ditto from the nineteenth figure (counting from the right) in the oriel window of St. Peter's at Rome; Feet from part of a broken window (which has never been mended) in St. Stephen's, Walbrook; Drapery from the deal boards in Westminster Abbey.

N.B. Designs for Cathedrals made in five-and-forty minutes; superior ditto in one hour; ditto ditto for Churches in twenty-six minutes. Episcopal chapels in fifteen minutes—and, to save trouble, no Dissenters need apply. Elegant Designs of Tombstones done in five minutes, and ladies' and gentlemen's own Epitaphs worked in.

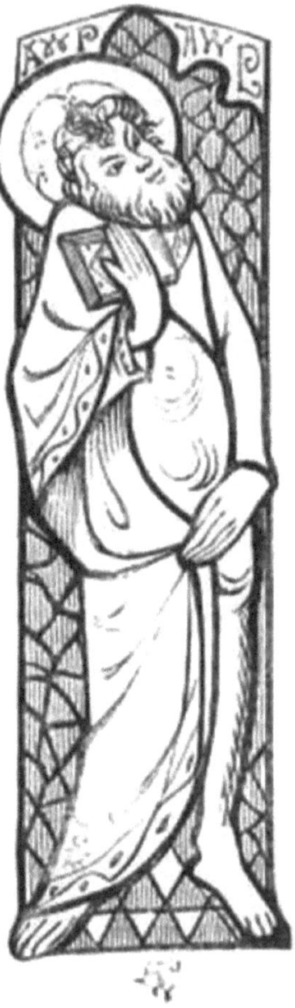

63

'STAINED GLASS WINDOWS'

London Journal (20 March 1858), p. 40

THE subject of stained glass windows in architecture is now occupying a considerable share of public attention. We can scarcely open a number of the publications devoted to the progress of building and decoration, without meeting with an article on this subject, or an account of some church or cathedral in which the practice of this art has been exemplified. The different styles, too, in which these mediæval decorations have been executed, have occasioned no small discussion among artists and amateurs. Among the zealous inquiries which have been made into the archæology of stained glass windows, the want of true principles in the art has become greatly apparent.

It has been asserted that our artists on glass have hitherto exhibited works which form an unfavourable contrast with those of the old masters, those artists to whom we are indebted for the painted glories of Chartres, Canterbury, and Fairford; and that they stand but poor comparison with those of the German artists of the present day. It appears that, notwithstanding the scenic trickery of the German artists, and their efforts to neutralise the finest, that is, the most natural elements of stained glass in its material and its individuality as an art, the new windows for the cathedral at Glasgow are to be, or have been, commissioned not by English artists, but by those of the school of Munich, by whom were lately erected the academic but vapid transparencies of Peterhouse College, Cambridge.

The following observations on this subject may serve to give our readers an idea of the state of the art of constructing stained glass windows as it at present exists among us. There is a wide-spreading error in looking upon this art more as a matter of manufacture than as a subject for the highest genius of pictorial artists. There is no aptitude which an artist can possess, either as a gift of nature or as the result of self-education, for colour, poetry, or composition – no power of expression, ingenuity of invention, or skill in drawing – which may not in glass be legitimately wedded to its materials, and made the true principles of its requirements in design.

With few exceptions, our modern windows, laying claim to high character in workmanship and design, emanate from establishments where art-skill is not even professed, and where the assumed authorship of that degree of art produced by them is not real, but borrowed. In matters of trade, no doubt the position of the vendor of stained glass-work, as a producer, may be paralleled in other departments of

DOI: 10.4324/9781315400266-77

art-skill: but the most powerful element of commerce may prove, as it has often done, the deadliest poison of true art. Were the great works bequeathed to us by former ages created under this cold shade of Mammon? Will an artist whose works are valuable in an artistic point of view, throw his full flow of invention and genius into a certain quantity of work at so much per day? Can such an individual keenly pursue his art under the cold calculation of pounds shillings and pence, estimated by time? Can anonymous art be considered art at all, or only commercial enterprise?

The following observations from a contemporary are so just, that we cannot refrain from giving them a place here: –

"We do not criticise a poem in favour or disfavour of the publisher, nor are poetic conceptions in architecture or sculpture attributed to the authorship of the mason or of the quarry masters of Carrara. In whose name, then, may most of our modern windows, good or bad, be fairly reviewed?

"As matters of detail, there are other pernicious influences acting with deadening effect upon glass-painting, to which allusion may be made – namely, those which have resulted from the importation of German prints after Overbeck, Schnorr, Fürich, and others of the school. These engravings and lithographs, together with those after Rubens and even West, have formed the stock-in-trade of many of those practitioners who enjoy, under the present state of things, a positive reputation as 'artists on glass.' Sometimes, by a not unusual effrontery, a whole composition derived from such sources, and cruelly mangled in the ignorant rendering, may be seen as intact as the circumstances of the case would permit; at others, an attempt to cloak the clumsy theft by a torturing of figures by, say Fürich, into part compositions of Overbeck, &c., may be easily detected; and then, worse than all, will come a few 'make up' figures, and accessories by the artist(?) himself. Thus has modern glass, in one of its most abject forms, been bolstered up, and encouraged.

"This is no exaggerated statement of the present condition of stained glass work, but the evil, deep though it be, is not past cure. Let those to whom art is something, and who at once regret and deride its position in relation to glass, who by their purse and influence would encourage it to better things, not despair of its easy emancipation. Let them probe the matter deeper than they have yet done, and seek the artist on glass as they would his brethren of painting, architecture, or sculpture. Let them, in simple justice to those who devote to the art their best years and warmest studies, open the doors of truth to true authorship. Let all evidence of the miserable print plagiarism and trade system be sought out, as a wholesome preliminary in determining the choice of him who shall commit to future centuries a thing of beauty.

"Pursuing such means, glass-painting will not long remain a reproach to English art. Those few true men who are steadfastly devoted to it, will, under fairer encouragement, be joined in art-brotherhood by others who are now scared from the pursuit; and the present *trade* of glass-painting will give due place to the banished *art,* which has so long yearned for the day upon which the veil shall fall from the eyes of those who, with good intent, have sought it in darkness and in error."

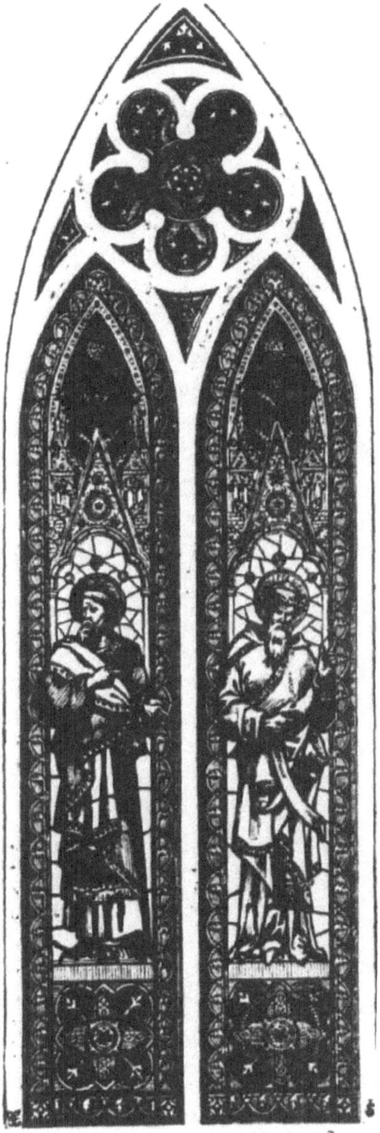

[STAINED WINDOWS—WESTMINSTER ABBEY.]

With reference to our engraving, which is a representation of one of the five stained glass windows which have been recently fixed in the south side of the clear story of Westminster Abbey. They were executed by Messrs. Clayton and Bell, and form the first instalment towards the completion of Mr. Scott's scheme for illustrating in the entire series of clear story windows around the building, the "Te Deum laudamus." The five windows to which we now allude contain representations of the "Prophets" David, Solomon, Isaiah, Jeremiah, Ezekiel, Daniel, Hosea, Joel, Amos, and Obadiah. The figures are each nearly ten feet in height, and are pointed to by the artists as the most colossal work in stained glass that has been done in England in modern times.

Objection has been taken to this colossal size as a mistake in architecture, and as serving materially to lessen the apparent height of the building. In this respect, however, every one can form a judgment for himself, when he views the *tout ensemble*. It is considered that the drawing is good, and the colours for the most part are sparkling. Green, however, is thought to be too predominant, and the arrangement by which some parts of the figure are made to break into the border, so as to give it the effect of standing out, is open to criticism.

As to the decorations of our abbeys, cathedrals, and churches, we are of opinion that a new style is wanting to give a fresh impulse to religion, and we agree with the poet when he says –

Artist attend – your brushes and your paint –
Produce them – take a chair – now draw a saint.
Oh sorrowful and sad! the streaming tears
Channel her cheeks – a Niobe appears!
Is this a saint? Throw tints and all away –
True piety is cheerful as the day.

64

THOMAS HARDY, 'THE YOUNG GLASS STAINER' (1893)

"THESE Gothic windows, how they wear me out
With cusp and foil, and nothing straight or square,
Crude colours, leaden borders roundabout,
And fitting in Peter here, and Matthew there!

"What a vocation! Here do I draw now
The abnormal, loving the Hellenic norm;
Martha I paint, and dream of Hera's brow,
Mary, and think of Aphrodite's form."

Nov. 1893.

DOI: 10.4324/9781315400266-78

3.4

Tools and artistic labour

DOI: 10.4324/9781315400266-79

3.4 Tools and artistic labour

In the second half of the nineteenth century, a younger generation reacted against the large-scale, increasingly commercialised and industrialised production of stained glass by large studios. The Arts and Crafts Movement's ideals centred on the role of artistic labour and the environment and conditions under which the artist worked. William Morris (1834–1896) and the firm of Morris, Marshall, Faulkner & Co. are often credited with transforming these approaches. However, although the design of stained glass by trained artists such as Edward Burne-Jones (1833–1898) invigorated the medium, these artists were far removed from the production of the stained-glass windows that they designed. As Morris' biographer Mackail demonstrates in this extract, the production of stained-glass windows at the Morris & Co. Merton Abbey workshop involved a division of labour at each stage.[1] Burne-Jones, who was the main designer for the firm, supplied full-scale cartoons, typically drawn in pencil and charcoal, to the Morris & Co. studio. Morris' own role was predominantly the careful selection of coloured glass and overall direction of its arrangement. Other trained craftsmen at Morris & Co.'s studio, located first in Bloomsbury and later at Merton Abbey, were responsible for cutting the glass, painting the pieces, firing and leading the panels.

Burne-Jones' designs were integral to the success of the Morris studio, but, as Hugh Arthur Kennedy (1854–1905) noted in his 1889 essay 'An Art Not Generally Understood', published in the *Contemporary Review* and included here, 'It is to be regretted that Mr. Jones has never executed a window of his own designing, by painting the absolute glass himself'.[2] Burne-Jones was a freelance designer for the firm. He kept detailed account books recording his payments from Morris & Co. for stained-glass designs and cartoons, which survive in the collection of The Fitzwilliam Museum, Cambridge. These have been transcribed and published along with a checklist of all Burne-Jones' designs for Morris & Co. in a special issue of *The Journal of Stained Glass* XXXV (2012). In contrast, Kennedy was a trained artist who worked in an Arts and Crafts manner, designing and making his own stained-glass windows in the workshops of Belham & Co. in London and with John Aldham Heaton (1830–1897). 'An Art Not Generally Understood' discusses the role of stained glass as a decorative art and the involvement of the artist. The making of stained glass is described poetically, conjuring up a medieval workman making a stained-glass window by hand within his humble studio. Kennedy's idealisation of the medieval workman approach to materials and the design and making of stained glass is held in direct opposition to the factory-like production of stained glass in large studios. In particular, Kennedy takes umbrage with the division of artistic labour in modern stained-glass work, stating that the artist should be with the work at every stage of its production and that a designer should be able to conceive his design 'in certain pieces of glass that he can put his fingers on'.[3]

Published in 1905, *Stained Glass Work* by leading exponent of the Arts and Crafts Movement Christopher Whall (1849–1924) had an enormous impact on the teaching and practise of stained glass as a craft. This manual was both poetic and instructive, striking a balance between the ideal and the practical. Whall elevates the art of stained glass by discussing the formal elements of the art and the artist's approach in a manner more typical of discussions of the fine arts of painting and sculpture. In an excerpt 'On Colour', he describes how the picture painter works to create a colour harmony by mixing pigments, and the glass-painter approaches the same task by arranging and rearranging many hundreds of specimens of glass, in varying colour tints, to reach a harmonious balance.

In addition to understanding the effect of the colour of the raw glass material, artists must also understand how pigments and stains applied to the glass surface, and made permanent by firing in the kiln, create a decorative pattern or bring an image to life. In another popular manual on stained glass, *A Treatise on the Art of Glass Painting* (1902), the application and compositions of the brown and black pigments used for tracing lines, outlines and shading, along with silver stain, flesh tint and vitreous enamels, are listed with hints on their use and effects. The author, stained-glass artist Ernest Richard Suffling (1855–1911), also provides an introduction to the many different brushes used by glass painters to paint onto the glass, along with other tools of the trade. The popularity of such manuals, which explained in layman's terms but also in ample technical detail, the materials, tools and processes of making stained-glass windows, encouraged independent artists and craftsmen to engage with every stage in the production of a stained-glass window.

Notes

1 See also Jim Cheshire, 'William Morris and Stained Glass' in Florence S. Boos (ed.) *The Routledge Companion to William Morris* (London: Routledge, 2020), pp. 188–206.

2 Kennedy, H. A. 'An Art Not Generally Understood', *Contemporary Review* 55 (1889, March), 442.

3 Kennedy, H. A. 'An Art Not Generally Understood', *Contemporary Review* 55 (1889, March), 438.

65

H. A. KENNEDY, 'AN ART NOT GENERALLY UNDERSTOOD' [SELECTED EXTRACTS]

Contemporary Review, 55 (1889, March), pp. 427–442

IN matters that may be discussed from several points of view a definition is useful, not so much for its conciseness or happiness of expression, as for its indisputability. Not that it makes a division exactly where one would like to have one, but that it divides things that, so separated, are for ever distinguishable. The division of poetry from prose, by its employment of certain recognized forms, is a handy one; none the less useful that we know well enough there is a limited amount of prose in the world vastly more poetical than an illimitable quantity of verse.

To find such a definition, one must look about for a point of departure in the nature of the things under discussion themselves: some point inherent in that nature that a mere difference in method of thinking will not disturb. Fahrenheit's zero, as a limit of conceivable coldness at thirty-two degrees below freezing point, was well enough until science began to recognize possibilities of cold far lower still; then it became an arbitrary and purposeless definition. Later on the scientific zero was fixed at the freezing point, and science henceforward could consistently measure from it up and down to any extent.

Discussion of the relative values of decorative and pictorial art is complicated by the fact that no two people are agreed as to where the one ends and the other begins. Nay, further, I believe that no man who has thought about the matter is at one with himself on the subject. For the two things do far worse than melt imperceptibly into each other; they interlace and overlap like interlocked fingers, and no distinction between them could approach accuracy without being too complicated for use. So that if our two supposed disputants were for the sake of argument to agree by mutual concessions on an arbitrary definition, it would be upset by the advent of a third.

But, well within the territory of decorative art, there is a natural landmark, trenchant as a river or mountain range; dividing an art, on the one hand, whose materials impose on it no limits but those common to all art whatsoever, from an art, on the other, that employs materials beautiful in themselves, whose beauty has

DOI: 10.4324/9781315400266-80

to be thought of and enhanced whilst other artistic necessities are being equally attended to. The art that deals with glass, silk, jewels, and metals, precious and brilliant, for distinctness' sake we may call "essentially decorative." Its first duty is towards the space it fills. You understand, when at too great a distance to decipher its representative qualities, not all its beauties, but distinctly that it is beautiful. For decorative art speaks at once to two audiences, as a good play appeals to the stalls by subtlety of finish, and to the gallery spectators by showing them at their less critical distance a natural, brilliant, and interesting sequence of events. But to the gallery first: give your play-wright (as distinguished from your play-writer) but half the time he really needs to write his drama in, and he will produce a work interesting and original in plot. For the rest he will probably employ old situations a little modified, and the stock *dramatis personæ,* or characters, of his own invention that he has used before. So give your decorator, as distinguished from your painter, half time to do his work in, and you shall yet have a design that adorns its place. Bring a close and critical eye to bear, and you will find perhaps that in its details he has employed old studies, or no studies at all. The term "applied art" sometimes bestowed on this essentially decorative work is misleading. It suggests either something artistic added to compensate for constitutional unsightliness, as a bronze statue to a hideous bridge, or decoration applied with questionable success to a thing already beautiful, as tattooing to the human body.

Real decorative art, however elaborate, springs from processes that adorn its material, and is not plastered on to it. Given a strip of sheet gold as material for bracelet or crown, the first effort in decoration is to hammer bosses on it to give increased play of light and reflection, and consequently more beauty. The bosses may come in time to be grouped and shaped until they represent warriors and chariots, or gods and goddesses, but the principle of enriching the metal is as obvious in the last as in the first development.

Art that is essentially decorative has a natural analogy with essentially lyrical poetry. A form of versification once chosen, the necessary conditions of metre and rhyme become to the poet, as the qualities of his material to the artist, opportunities, not restrictions; not only opportunities for beauty of metre and rhyme, but for an emphasis on the utterance of his thought not attainable outside that form of verse. He is no poet who finds rhyme and metre hamper his imagination, nor is he who is not inspired by the conditions of his material a decorator. From the exalted position assumed to-day by realistic painting, decorative art seems to run some risk of being shouldered into an altogether secondary and insignificant place. It can only be saved by its material, as poetry by its lyrical qualities from the assumptions of realistic prose. We must sing, and must have fresh words to sing; and as a song may touch our hearts as nearly as a novel, we shall not care to think of it as on a lower artistic level than the stories we get from the circulating library. Less elaborately imitative of the details of reality it will certainly be, but there is room in it for as much of Art, and, perhaps, in a more highly distilled form, for as much of Nature too. And so with the adornment of our rooms and the windows that we fill with colour in our churches; we should not, if we can help it, wish that, though different from, they should be intellectually beneath the pictures that we pay shillings to look at now and then.

Art, then, can express itself not only in the completely flexible media that admit the so-called realism of representation, but in materials that impose their own limits. In art, as in life, there is nobility in, and compensation for, self-restraint as well as for the wise acknowledgement of external restraining necessities. The actor, for instance, who reveals too soon the whole compass of his emotional resources, has lost his hold over us: the really impressive man showing us that only at the culminating instant, perhaps not the whole of it even then.

A happy incompleteness has qualities of its own; a rough sketch may denote character and expression so perfectly that no realism could do other than dilute it. To seek the reason of this would carry us too far away from our present subject, but the fact is on the surface.

Many human interests cling close to the productions of the decorative arts of the home and fireside, which enshrine memories of happiness or sorrow, gratify innocent vanities, recall pleasant hospitalities, and teem with homely everyday associations. It is to their advantage, as well as to their possessors', if, beyond this, the art in them is of a vital and clear-speaking nature that is intelligible, not only after their death, as it were, to the connoisseur who entombs them in a collection, but during their lifetime to the people who possess and live with them. In this direction we have made great all-round progress in the last twenty-five years, having struggled pretty clear of the worst period of decoration that ever existed. A comparison of the furniture, curtains, carpets, and the like, in general use now, with those of a quarter of a century ago, has been too often made to need repetition here, but one vital point in the change is well worth noting. People not only use better colours than they did, and more graceful furniture, but they appreciate them; taking real pleasure in the soft colours of their curtains and dress materials. The artistic revival has run its course, gained its nickname, been taken up by society, satirized, and dropped; but the preference for delicate colour over crude survives it and remains a permanent possession. Not now, in the most out-of-the-way country-place, do the least sophisticated natives walk to church clad in those ghastly aniline colours that once shocked the landscape, abashing the sober tints of Nature.

The art of stained glass is not yet fully fortunate in speaking a language understanded of the people. Indeed, "I don't understand stained glass," is the remark one most frequently hears made about it, and this even from people of considerable appreciation for other forms of art. This comes home to one when one sees what pitiful stuff people of taste are content to have in the doors and windows of their own houses. The purplish birds on the yellow leaves within a circle of harsh red, the whole backed up by alternate oblongs of bad pink and green; how frequently one notices that work of art, standing where it ought not! The builder inserts this, and the like of it in the first instance, but the occupants suffer them to remain, not perhaps confident that they could find anything else so much more agreeable to their feelings as to warrant the expense of a change. It means, perhaps, that about even the highest development of the art as usually practised, there still cling conventionalities of the parasitic or stifling sort; traditions that have arisen, that could only arise, in a period of bad art, and that have survived into a time of better things.

Wholesome conventionality, the acknowledgment of limits, and the determination to pull up well within them, is of the nature of a backbone to decorative art. Excellent, too, is healthy tradition. A man, or a school of men, who have practised a craft right well, bequeath to their successors, not a series of cast-iron rules and regulations, but a common-sense recommendation. "On such and such lines our art can be successfully carried out; adhere to them, we advise you, and see your way very clearly before you try to disturb them. If new possibilities arise, they must be dealt with; but do not change the old order for less than sufficient cause." Without some such tradition a craft may become experimental and amateurish, and its productions perplexing.

Let us, before going further, try and understand stained glass.

The germ of it lies, not in the wooden-framed sash-windows with which we are most familiar, but in lead-lattice, or, as it is perhaps most often called, casement. The simplest form of lattice consists of square or diamond-shaped panes of white glass of the same size, connected by "leads" – that is, by strips of that metal, with a groove on each side, into which the glass fits, the leads being joined by soldering at the corners, and the interstices filled in with cement, corresponding to the putty in our sash-windows. From this simplest form of a lead-latticed window, the next step is the introduction of coloured glass. By this we get square or diamond-shaped panes alternately of white and colour, or of several tints in succession – a series of arrangements being possible whilst we still cut our glass in panes of straight-lined shapes all of one size. More variety comes with the half-step from this to panes still rectilinear, but of different sizes and shapes; and we have made a stride when we have found out how to cut our glass into pieces with curved outlines. Our framing line of ductile lead is as ready to go round a circle as along a straight line, and now with curve contoured forms of varied colour arranged in groups we have already a handsome stained glass window of pattern.

The next move is a momentous one, and may have a word of preface. The best ornamentist of the present time[1] has acutely noticed that some simple pattern shapes that have been assumed to imitate natural forms are in reality dictated by the tool or material employed. When their resemblance to Nature struck the primitive artist, he did what he could to make it closer, but they arose at first independently. A single stroke of a full brush on paper beginning with a point spreading from that, and then ending with a sudden and more rounded diminution as the brush quits the paper, resembles the form of a leaf; the simplest combination of such touches suggests a leaf-cluster. Surround a large circle with a series of little ones, and you get a broad hint of a frequent flower type. So our window-maker, having advanced thus far, could not fail to be struck with hints of natural form in his pattern, and suddenly his brain took fire with the longing to complete the resemblance. This led to an application to transparent glass of the long-practised process of enamelling; lines and shadows were drawn on it with a material that, when fired at a sufficient heat, unites with the glass and becomes permanently fixed. The imitation of form seldom goes far in any art before the designer tries to imitate the most interesting of all forms: to take on him the God-like function of making man in his own image.

Glance with me, for a moment, at such a daring mediæval workman.

His studio is bare and rude, one of a little city of timber-built huts nestling at the feet of a stately cathedral, that is as yet but partly built. Hammering, chiselling, and sawing are going on all about him with a rhythmic noisiness. In other sheds like his are being hewn out the solemn figures presently to stand beside the doorways or in the niches of the west frontage. High overhead, clinging to scanty scaffolding, the carvers are shaping crocket and finial, are chipping the gargoyle into grotesque life, or enriching with ornament the niche to receive the statue. The dust from their chisels silts in through his unglazed window space. All about him is manufacture in the literal sense of the word – hand-work. There is no Art Department, for there is no department down to the laying of the courses of the masonry, where art is not. Interested monks come on the scene from time to time, pause for a few moments to watch, then disappear. They cluster at stated hours in the completed choir, and the chanting of psalms in sonorous Latin may be heard among the other sounds, telling how the day wears. Sometimes the great of the earth come to see, and the chisels pause whilst their wielders gaze downwards at the grand seignor, who appears richer clad even than he is against the white background of dusty road and fresh-cut stone, and at a grey-haired scarlet-robed church dignitary, followed by black-clad obsequious figures, and clinking men-at-arms.

Our glass painter's appliances are as simple and few as those of an Oriental weaver; he has no diamond to cut with, no pencils, no paper or tracing cloth for his cartoons and working drawings. A heavy wooden working-bench does, among other duties, that of drawing-paper. On it he sketches his designs with a piece of charred stick, and when they are to be used many times he goes over the lines with the red-hot iron he uses to crack his glass with, and makes them ineffaceable. His bench is dotted over with holes left by the nails that hold glass and lead in their places as they are being soldered together. When he wants an unencumbered surface to draw upon, he borrows a carpenter's plane and makes one.

He is working now on a tall lancet window, the ground of which is designed to be filled with a mosaic of interlaced forms, whilst the broad border and a series of super-imposed circles are to be of rich colour in foliated pattern. The pieces of glass for the ground are already cut and painted and lie piled in a rough box. In another are those for the border and several of the circles. The central round, which is to be of more emphasis than the others, remains to be done, and our workman is considering it. Why not, it flashes into his mind, a figure – a saint? The figure drawing of that time is simple, and he has learned its practice; why should not a saint be represented in glass as on a wall? Hurriedly he effaces from the board the half-sketched pattern within the branded circle, and recommending his new venture to God and Saint Luke, he begins to design his figure, planning it out by outlining the shapes of the pieces of glass of which it will be composed. The head shall be painted on a piece of tawny-pink glass, and as the background is to be of ruby-red, the drapery shall be of blue, cut in a good many pieces, for the sheets of glass at our artist's disposal are but little ones. Then the hand that holds the emblem, and the other on the bosom of the drapery, they again must be tawny, so must the feet be. The lining of the drapery where it shows itself may be a golden-yellow. With tremulous and eager care he sketches the lines of face, finger, and foot, of fold and twist of drapery, and then, roughly outlined within the scorched circle on his dinted bench, lies before him the first figure cartoon for glass. He sees no reason why the saint should not be as successful as the foregoing foliated patterns; but this that he has begun upon is a new thing, and he is in anxious haste to test its success through the slow processes of the material. Bit by bit he shapes the glass; each piece being laid in its place on the scored bench, roughly cracked with a hot iron in the direction of the desired form, and finished by laboriously biting the edges away with pincers. This completed, with a dark pigment he traces on the glass, piece by piece, the lines and shadows of drapery and face, and then the glass is passed through a kiln and the painting fused with it, pieces that require retouching and strengthening having to undergo a second firing. Finally he cuts the bits of ruby glass that, unpainted, are to form a background to his saint, lays all the pieces, painted and plain, in their places within the circle, and the little picture is ready to be put together: to be *glazed,* to use the technical word. Not until this process is over can he see the effect of his design, and as we must wait for him we may as well watch him at work, for it is an ingenious process, interesting to observe. He first selects and cuts to its approximate length the wide lead that is to surround the circle, and by hammering a series of nails just outside its circumference as drawn on the bench prevents it from exceeding its limits. Into the groove in this bounding lead are fitted the outermost pieces of the background; between each two is placed another slip of lead, rather narrower, to hold them together. As each piece of glass is put into its place a smart tap or two with the handle of the glazing-knife drives it well home into the grooves of the lead on each side of it, and a nail driven into the bench in front of it holds it in place until more lead and glass are added. So the work grows, each morsel of the glass is surrounded with strips of lead into whose grooves it is securely fitted; where the picture is as yet unfinished, there is a frontier of restraining nails, which are taken out to be replaced further on until the completed work gradually fills the circle. That done, the external lead is brought tightly round, its ends are trimmed and exactly adjusted, and the whole secured by nails. Then every one of the numerous points of junction of lead with lead in the whole work is greased to make the fixing solder adhere, and the solder is melted on to it with a red-hot iron, linking the whole together. The nails that confine it are hurriedly drawn from the board, the work is turned over, and the soldering process repeated on the other side; then – moment of moments – our patient workman holds up the circle to the window of his little hovel, and feasts a critical yet approving eye on the first figure ever painted on glass. The window is fixed in its place, the interested monks gather and applaud; brother workers in other arts cluster and discuss; the great of the earth arrive, and the new attempt is explained to the seignor by dignified ecclesiastics, all finally smiling on the new discovery. So we bid our adventurous workman good-bye, having lingered so long with him because the processes he employed have been, with slight modifications, in use from that time to this. Later, the possibility was realized of applying other enamel colours to glass besides the brownish black line and shadow pigment. Owing to their brilliancy being inferior to that of colour made in the glass, only two of these have played an important part in the history of the material; a yellow stain made from silver, and a reddish enamel applied to white glass to represent the flesh colour, no tint in the glass itself being quite satisfactory for this purpose, and the artist not being always content to make his heads and hands of white. There is one really perplexing element in stained glass that I will try and elucidate – that is the use of what are called *accidental leads*. An artist friend said to me the other day, "I understand the lead lines going all round the outlines perfectly, but I am puzzled as to why they sometimes go across the design when there seems no need for them." Suppose – to take an extreme instance – we had to cut out the shape of an hour-glass. It might, perhaps, be done with great care, but the danger of its cracking at the waist in cutting would be enormous, and if that were got over, it would have new perils to go through as it cooled after being fired. Even when finished and fixed in its place it would still be in danger. There is a certain elasticity in the leaden framework of a window, none worth speaking of in the glass itself; if the wind blew hard against the window that contained our hour-glass, the lead about it would yield a little, and it, being unyielding and brittle, would snap at its weakest point. Forseeing this, the artist arranges his leads so that instead of such weak places in his window there shall be flexible joints.

This then is what we have to grapple with in trying to understand stained glass. All the important colour is in the material itself; this is cut out and fitted together much like a dissected map, where the counties are of different tints. The modifications in the direction of shading are made with a grey or brownish tint, those of colour are merely the adding of a tone to represent flesh, and of a stain that shows yellow on white glass and produces a green when applied to blue. If we find anything unintelligible to us in modern stained glass that does not obviously spring from these necessities, we are justified in objecting to it.

I am convinced that the comparative indifference of the public to-day to glass-work indirectly results from the improper division of labour in its execution. The ordinary practice is that, having been designed by an artist who makes a small sketch in colour and full-sized cartoons, the most important work of all – that is, the choosing and painting the glass – is put into the hands of men who, though sometimes skilful workmen, are seldom artists. The scale of remuneration almost forbids that they should be, and in nine cases out of ten the glass-painter is an unambitious drudge, or a smart youth who only means to paint glass until he can persuade some one to give him cartoons to draw. This system puts the artist at the wrong end of the work – that is, if there could be a right one – when he really should be with it all through.

Take a literary parallel. Which would you prefer, a story of Mr. R. L. Stevenson's told by the anecdotist of the dinner-table, or a tale of the said anecdotist's related by the creator of Dr. Jekyll and Mr. Hyde? If, in the former case, the narrator could appreciate the Stevensonian charm, he could not transmit it; in the latter, the rendering would enrich the baldness of the original, leaving only a softened regret that the deftly told tale was not Stevenson's from first to last.

To be quite satisfactory, stained glass should have its colours selected and its painting executed by its designer; in this way it will have a unity of effect and a harmony of execution with invention not otherwise attainable.

Of this I am convinced by the opinions of many well qualified to pronounce on the subject, some indeed thinking as I do, in spite of their practice being opposite; by considerable personal experience; and perhaps chiefly by a study of the ins and outs of work done the other way. I have known artists designing for glass who not only did not care to see their work when executed, but who positively objected, knowing by experience that it would be a caricature of their intentions. Truly, with this method of dividing labour, the satisfactory work is that where the design is least artistic. Given a dry and unfeeling cartoon, the trade glass-painter executes it with very fair accuracy. The strongest evidence producible against the usual system is to be gathered from the more artistic of its attempts; from works where the designing is good, and the glass-painting has a measure of artistic skill, and between the two is produced a transparent picture, well designed and schemed in colour. In the qualities, however, that are essential to the material – the jewel-like brilliancy, the crispness and translucency, and all those sparkling beauties that we admire in early and in all good glass – it is completely deficient; the fact being that a design for glass ought never to crystallize and become unchangeable until it reaches its material. The fit use of that material is all-important, and the design should be kept, as it were, in solution until the requirements of the glass are satisfied. This of course is not possible where the artist who designs personally conducts his design no further than on to paper. He must leave it there, a thing fixed to be copied on glass without reference to the requirements of glass. Were the copier an artist, it is not easy for one such to modify the design of another; it is against the nature of things that a subordinate should ever be allowed to adapt the completed work of his superior.

An obvious instance of this is to be found in the continual mis-use of white glass. The artist designs his white drapery as for any other material, with very little absolute light, and a half-tone covering at least seven-eighths of it; the glass painter cannot do other than follow this pattern, seven-eighths of the material are obscured with shading, and the bulk of that drapery is without any of the beauties peculiar to glass. Look at the white draperies in any much-admired modern window – it is ten to one that you will find no more sparkle in them than in a wet newspaper, which they will much resemble in general tone. Sparkle and silveriness are the qualities appropriate to white glass; without them it is absolutely uninteresting. It is not shade on the glass, or even dark shade, that is objectionable; without some decided darks the white would not attain its brilliancy; it is the monotonous universal toning-down of white glass to get it into harmony with other colour not designed in the right key for it. You must not "perdooce tone" in glass by the use of paint, you must get it in your material or else go without it. If you design as well as paint, you will learn so to design it as to avoid the latter humiliation.

It is not that the men who do these things do not know, have not studied; it is that the art of inventing in glass must be built on the foundation of handling and painting it, and can no further be otherwise learned than swimming on dry land.

An instructive lesson of how the essential merits of glass may be lost in work whose other merits rank high, is to be found in the comparison of two windows placed side by side in the north wall of the nave of Westminster Abbey, commemorating two engineers. That to Trevithick, who devised a locomotive before Stephenson, is exceedingly satisfactory in execution and full of the silvery brilliancy appropriate to glass. For the design of it, it is simply an imitation of the glass of some centuries ago; it has nothing in common with modern feeling in art, or with modern thought. Except the drawings, displayed by angels in the lower part of it, of Trevithick's mechanical triumphs, there is nothing to connect it with the nineteenth century, or to attract nineteenth-century interest to it. It has a certain delight in neatness as opposed to impulsiveness, not characteristic of ancient work, or one might take it for an old window, and indeed by no means a bad one. The style of the angels as compared with the very modern machines they hold drawings of, suggests the fancy that Macaulay's New Zealander might carry such a figure home with him amid other English antiquities, and write learnedly in the "New Zealand Antiquary" of fourteenth-century steam-engines.

The window to Brunel is a very different thing. If we look first at the tracery, which is so high up that its execution does not go for much, we discern great beauty of design and a quite exquisite sense of colour. And the colour scheme is in accordance with the feeling of to-day, and is not in any sense imitative of earlier work in glass. Glancing down the window we still find the beautiful colour scheme and graceful modern drawing, instead of resuscitated archaism; but, compared with the other window, something seems amiss in the execution. If we include in our comparison the window beyond this one again, which is simply filled with white glass, we shall find that the Trevithick window is not only far more brilliant than its neighbour, but, though it contains a good deal of rich colour, it seems more luminous than the window of white glass. The Brunel window is throughout too monotonously covered with painting, and, in consequence, deficient in transparency. In parts this drawback amounts to absolute muddiness of effect; also, in places, the glass has not been sufficiently fired to completely fix this excess of paint, which has partly peeled off, giving a rotten and streaky effect that is highly unpleasant.

Not to leave the Abbey with our minds in a critical attitude towards what is in the main excellent, and that we may realize, whilst hoping for yet better things, from what we have recently risen, let us glance at the glass in the south transept. It is a production of that execrable period of art from which we have but lately emerged. The miserable design of these windows is a trifling fault as compared with their atrocious colour; they are a disgrace to the beautiful building they disfigure.

For colour is the key-note of stained glass, the all-important thing: no glass is worthy of the name that is not lovely in colour. The scheme may vary from silvery lightness to the richest intensity, but every bit of it must be beautiful, or the whole thing is a mistake. No other art can even approach the power of its colour; the sheeny loveliness of textile fabrics and the infinite modulations of tint of painting are alike paled by its fulness. Painting has an infinity of resources that the material in hand cannot command; like the human voice in singing, it may induce a variety of emotions. But the emotional effects that stained glass is particularly fitted to produce, it compels, like a blare of trumpets, by its volume and intensity. A great window of stained glass well placed in a cathedral, with the light of the sun on it, produces an effect on one more like in its vividness that of some beautiful aspect of Nature, than what can be given by a work of man's making.

Colour, then, is the first vital consideration in glass. Is there any other comparable to it? To answer this, we must go back for a moment to that primitive studio, and note the new element that was being introduced – the likeness of a man. For this new element brings rights of its own with it. The human figure may not be slighted in any material, but as far as the material allows must be as well represented as the art of the time can do it. If not, it is better away; it is not essential to stained glass, for perfect glass may exist without it. It is an invited guest, and courtesy must make its feelings deferred to. It is an important guest, who, where he comes, must be given the best place, and, like every guest, must show courtesy as full as he receives, lest he be not re-invited. Is there, then, a point where either host or guest must concede – where, to speak without metaphor, the figure painted on glass, to gain its perfect expression, must destroy some of the qualities of the material? It is very usual to insist that this is so; and it is easy to point out instances, in every school of glass-painting since the fourteenth century, where brilliancy of material has been sacrificed to pictorial considerations. Sir Joshua Reynolds' figures in New College Chapel, Oxford, are a typical instance; in them we have beautiful figure-work, and none of the beauties of glass itself at all. But there is a reason for all these lapses that is clear enough; it is that the artist, or the school of artists, has been summoned to paint glass too late. A man who has formed his habits in a material that admits of his making his shadows as interesting as his lights will overshade your glass for you to the end of his days.

To do good glass, an artist should not only design and paint it, he should steep his imagination in it, and get to know it with its possibilities so thoroughly that, when he conceives a design, he conceives it in certain pieces of glass that he can put his fingers on. These will be in his mind through all the processes of his work. He will not arrange a piece of drapery whilst making his studies without thinking of the precise amount of shadow necessary to bring out all the excellences of the material he will execute it on, and of the quality of shading, whether rich and trenchant or crisp and filmy. He will select the raw material for his work with anxious care, choosing from each sheet of glass he uses just such parts as are most beautiful and most fit. The drawings being his own work, and of the nature of studies rather than rigidly finished designs, he can as he paints his glass adapt them to the necessities of the material. The whole process being at his fingers' ends, he can in some places leave the work on the glass to the inspiration of the material itself.

Stained glass, as an art that by such means is trying to attain a fresher mode of thinking, and a nearer relation to Nature and the feelings of its own time, looks rather for sympathy to the public than to workers in other arts. Neither the architectural side of art, nor the realistic, looks with enthusiasm at possible departures in this way. As a rule, the architect has been fairly satisfied with the kind of trade glass that can be turned out to order, in the style of any century required. To him its shortcomings are atoned for by its respectfully subordinate position; accustomed to this, he naturally is not particularly anxious for work of less tractability, which may have a will of its own to be considered and even consulted.

The realistic artist has no interest in stained glass except as a background, when he usually paints it incorrectly. Satisfied that the school of to-day has attained the one complete method of representing Nature, he troubles his head not at all about the representation of her in any way to him less complete. And yet the very term realistic is a folly, if one compares the ocean of complicated fact, and the teaspoon in which it has to be contained, to produce realism. The most accurate historian tells not a tithe of the whole truth: the most inveterate romancer is not without a leaven of veracity.

Realist and decorator, though their attitudes differ, alike buy their stock-in-trade at the shop of that great universal provider, Nature.

The painter, in whose works design plays a subordinate part, presents himself at Nature's counter, puts his money down, and says, "I want you to give me the best value in goods for that, I am not particular as to what they are." Nature treats such a customer liberally, and because he is so accommodating as to take what is given him, he gets very good measure, and the transaction is a rapid and simple one, satisfactory to both parties.

But when the designer presents himself, Nature knits her brows at the sight of him – she has had so much trouble already with him. For he does not come to buy anything she wants to sell, but is provided with a list of troublesome requirements, and will have those and those only – a head with such an expression on it, such a cast of drapery of such a tint and no other, or such an effect of rock or storm-cloud, or tempest-tossed sea. Nature rummages her shelves, and article after article is rejected, while the exasperating customer declares that he has seen just the thing he wants in that very shop before. There has never been such a piece of goods in the trade Nature at last declares; it could not be turned out at any price; the gentleman must have dreamt it. The gentleman admits that he may have dreamt it, but is none the less anxious that it should be procured for him. In fine, when bargaining is over, the parties separate grumbling, and the designer goes home with his purchases, thinking he has spent a lot of money on them, and that, after all, his brain-children will have to accommodate themselves to circumstances, and put up with some rather tight fits in respect of the raiment he has been buying to clothe them with.

Selection of the fittest subjects for decorative art is never a very easy matter; in stained glass it particularly requires careful consideration. There are two ways of making the choice: one that the subject should be settled upon by the artist, the patron naturally retaining a right of veto; the other that it should be fixed by the patron, the artist being privileged to object to a subject not suitable to the work in hand. From some points of view the first way has advantages, but hardly to be set against the great additional interest to the possessor of the work if he is attached to it by associations connected with the subject, or even with such details as floral ornamentation or choice of predominating colour. It is a frequent misfortune that the all-pervading middle-man imposes a subject that is neither of special interest to the future possessor nor artistically fit.

In choosing subjects for a church window it is well to remember that, whilst many of the most sacred have been so often treated in art that their representation can be little else than a modification of what has gone before, there yet remains in the Bible a mine of almost unused themes for this art.

The stirring history of Gideon is full of subject-matter, from his first call by the angel as he threshed wheat by the wine-press to hide it from the Midianites, to his crowning victory over the high-souled and courtly spoken princes, Zebah and Zalmunna, who had ornaments like the moon upon their camels' necks. The other pair of princes in the same story, Oreb and Zeeb – the raven and the wolf – are picturesque figues; but the incident that presents itself to me most vividly is Gideon's interview with the inhospitable men of Penuel. They refused with a bitter jest to give bread to his wearied three hundred, and Gideon answered them, "When I come again in peace, I will break down this tower." One sees the fortress and the gesture against it of the man faint with pursuing, but God-befriended and certain of final victory. Fascinating too, from this point of view, is that chivalrous foray of Jonathan and his squire, when they clambered up the toothed crags and fought the Philistine garrison during the earthquake, surveyed from the distance by the watchmen of King Saul in Gibeah. And a grand subject, of which I have seen no representation, is to be found in a verse of the second Book of Kings: – "And Elisha prayed, and said, LORD, I pray thee, open his eyes, that he may see. And the LORD opened the eyes of the young man; and he saw: and, behold, the mountain was full of horses and chariots of fire round about Elisha" (2 Kings vi. 17).

Indeed, for the representation of visionary subjects, of which we find so many splendid examples in the prophets and the Apocalypse, stained glass, with its strength and mystery of colour, is particularly fitted.

In subjects for domestic glass, though the individual spaces to fill are usually smaller, the range is quite infinite, for lighter and even humorous themes may be appropriate here. What a pretty window, for example, one might make with playing cards as a theme. The borders might be decorated with hearts, diamonds, and the like, with royal and knavish personages in the central groups. It would be a pleasant conceit to fill a little window with painted glass to commemorate a marriage. It should contain medallion portraits of Edwin and Angelina; and other details might be introduced into a framing of appropriately fancied imagery. Where a consecutive series is required, the well-known fairy stories and the "Arabian Nights" are almost inexhaustible to draw upon. Some of the "Idylls of the King" are full of subjects, "Gareth and Lynette" being particularly rich in the symbolism and colour suggestion so treatable in our material. Indeed, besides his other gifts, the Laureate has a splendid feeling for essentially decorative art, a description in one of the "Idylls" being the best design by a poet that I have met with. It was treated in four bands of sculpture, and the subjects seem to suggest the style of the Pisani –

> "And four great zones of sculpture, set betwixt
> With many a mystic symbol, gird the hall:
> And in the lowest beasts are slaying men,
> And in the second men are slaying beasts,
> And on the third are warriors, perfect men,
> And on the fourth are men with growing wings."

The symbolism is perfect, and the succession of subject very decorative, the wings of the uppermost figures forming a natural decoration to the top of the work.

Against the great field of modern stained glass, so frequently pedantic or common-place, shine out the works of our really god-inspired designer. From the pencil of Mr. Edward Burne-Jones have come some of the best and fittest designs for glass that have been made at any time. Beyond his artistic genius, Burne-Jones has a special happiness with regard to art of this nature. Although his front door abuts on the rumble of the nineteenth century, his back garden is a fairy pleasaunce, through which he wanders, unobstructed by intervening centuries, into the studios of Orcagna and Donatello, and other workshops of earlier and later date, exchanging greetings with the sympathetic spirits within. He has watched the Byzantine-bred ivory-workers carving those lacey masterpieces wherein the sedate lover and lady sit to exchange caresses under large-leaved trees. The head of that wonderful mermaid of his was, one may fancy, sketched in the studio of Da Vinci from Leonardo's favourite, slow smiling model. In his own studio, Burne-Jones speaks the thoughts of his day in the language of the fifteenth century, unaffected on his gifted lips; and this natural archaism solves for him difficulties the cause of deep heart-searchings to the mere modern. His designs exhibited in the Grosvenor Gallery some years ago, for a Last Judgment window, were perhaps the highest flight in modern art in the direction of imaginative design. It is to be regretted that Mr. Jones has never executed a window of his own designing, by painting the absolute glass himself; one would look for a jewel-precious masterpiece had that ever been the case. The nearest approach is to be found in one of the windows in the cathedral church at Oxford, signed E. B. J. *inv.,* C. F. M. *pinx,* and painted on glass by Mr. C. Fairfax Murray, a pupil of Burne-Jones's, who has executed the master's design with great skill and sympathy, and has taken special pains that the record of it should be a lasting one. This, it is melancholy to find, is a degree of attention that has not always been given; all the other windows of Burne-Jones's design in the Oxford Cathedral showing symptoms of decay, and some of those in Jesus College Chapel, Cambridge, and one in the Chapel Royal, Savoy, being seriously dilapidated.

Besides the magnificent work of this great imaginative designer, a large amount of sincere artistic work has been bestowed on stained glass in the last quarter of a century, which no one appreciates more than I. But I strongly feel the shortcomings as regards results, and how, through an unfit system, artistic impulse has evaporated before the permanent record has been reached, and I grieve over the waste, being convinced of the only remedy.

The interest of that part of the world at large that is concerned with any art is its real support, and interest being a spontaneously given thing, it is clearly not the part of a specialist to lay down the law for the public. What he can do is to clear away any difficulties that may have accumulated between the appreciative outsider and his, the specialist's, own branch of art. He points out that this difficulty is a necessity of the material, explaining why; he shows that those other difficulties have arisen from unnecessary habits of pedantry into which the art has drifted. He sketches what results there might be if those habits were put aside, and retires to his workshop. For, to an artist, doing is a perpetual necessity, saying, fortunately, a very occasional one. If the necessity to speak has arisen, it is his apology for speaking; but for preaching no apology would suffice.

H. Arthur Kennedy.

Note

1 "Every-day Art." By Lewis F. Day.

66

J. W. MACKAIL, *LIFE OF WILLIAM MORRIS*

(London, New York and Bombay: Longmans, Green & Co., 1899), Vol. 2, pp. 41–42

As regards the personal part which Morris took in this branch of the firm's work, it was the invariable practice in early years, and remained the rule after the Merton Abbey works were started, that the interpretation of the design and the choice of the glass came under his own eye. He seldom at any time, and never in more recent years, made complete designs for windows himself. From the first, the figure-subjects were mainly supplied by those of his colleagues who were professional painters. As time went on, they came almost exclusively from the studio of Burne-Jones, who supplied no cartoons for glass except to the firm. But backgrounds and foliage were, as a rule, of Morris's designing, the animals and certain kinds of ornament being often drawn by Webb.

Morris never made his own glass. He often regretted that he did not; but for organizing this manufacture, time and money alike were required beyond what he could spare. There is little doubt that in the colouring of glass, as in that of yarns, his personal touch would have produced greater splendours of tone than could be got by other workers. As it was, his faultless eye for colour had to content itself with doing its best out of the glass supplied by the ordinary manufacturers. If the colour of a Morris window is to the present day unmistakable among all rivals or imitations, this is not from any difference in material, but from the skill in selection and variation which was an instinct in Morris himself, and which to some considerable degree he transmitted to his workmen.

When the cartoons for a window had been drawn, Mr. Wardle notes in speaking of the practice of this period, Morris personally "coloured" the window; that is to say, he dictated in detail to Campfield, the foreman of the painters, what glass was to be used for each part. The various parts were then distributed to the painters, whose work he watched as it went on, though he usually reserved any comments till the painter had done all that he could. Retouches were then made by his direction, and the glass was burned and leaded up. When this was done, there came the final review of the window, a work of great difficulty in any case, and to any ordinary eye impossible in the cramped premises

DOI: 10.4324/9781315400266-81

in Queen Square, where some of his largest windows were made. But here his amazing eye and memory for colour enabled him to achieve the impossible: he could pass all the parts of a large window one by one before the light, and never lose sight of the general tone of the colour or of the relation of one part to another. If any part did not satisfy him, new glass was cut and that piece of the window done again.

67

C. WHALL, 'OF COLOUR', *THE ARTISTIC CRAFTS SERIES OF TECHNICAL HANDBOOKS: STAINED GLASS WORK*

(London: John Hogg, 1905), pp. 205–207, 209–211

For the painter of pictures (we said) has his colour-box of a few pigments, from which all his harmonies must come by mixing them and diluting them in various proportions, dealing with infinity out of a very limited range of materials, and required to supply all the rest by his own skill and memory.

Coming each day to his work with his palette clean and his colours in their tubes;

Beginning, as it were, all over again each time; and perhaps with his heart cold and his memory dull.

But the glass-painter has his specimens of glass round him; some hundreds, perhaps, of all possible tints.

He has, with these, to compose a subject in colour;

There is no getting out of it or shirking it;

He places the bits side by side, with no possibility (which the palette gives) of slurring or diluting or dulling them; he must choose from the clear hard tints;

And he has the whole problem before him;

He removes one and substitutes another;

"This looks better;" "That is a pleasant harmony;" "Ah! but this makes it sing!"

He gets them into groups, and combines them into harmonies, tint with tint, group with group:

If he is wise he has them always by him;

Always ready to arrange in a movable frame against the window;

He cuts little bits of each; he waxes them, or gums them, into groups on sheets of glass;

He tries all his effects in the glass itself; he sketches in glass.

If he is wise he does this side by side with his water-colour sketch, making each help the other, and thinking in glass; even perhaps making his water-colour sketch afterwards from the glass.

DOI: 10.4324/9781315400266-82

Is it not reasonable?

Is it not far more easy, less dangerous?

He has not to rake in his cold and meagre memory to fish out some poor handful of all the possible harmonies;

To repeat himself over and over again.

He has all the colours burning round him; singing to him to use them; sounding all their chords.

Is it not the way? Is it not common sense?

Tints! pure tints! What great things they are.

[. . .]

At any rate, I throw out this hint for pupils and students, that if they will get a set of glass samples and try combinations of colour in them, they will have a bracing and guiding influence, the strength of which they little dream of, regarding one of the hardest problems of their art.

This for the student of painting in general: but for the glass-painter it is absolutely essential – the central point, the breath-of-life of his art.

To live in it daily and all day.

To be ever dealing with it thus.

To handle with the hands constantly.

To try this piece, and that piece, the little more and the little less.

This is the be-all and end-all, the beginning and the end of the whole matter, and here therefore follow a few hints with regard to it.

And there is one rule of such dominating importance that all other hints group themselves round it; and yet, strangely enough, I cannot remember seeing it anywhere written down.

Take three tints of glass – a purple, let us say, a crimson, and a green.

Let it be supposed that, for some reason, you desire that this should form a scheme of colour for a window, or part of a window, with, of course, in addition, pure white, and probably some tints more neutral, greenish-whites and olives or greys, for background.

You choose your purple (and, by-the-bye, almost the only way to get a satisfactory one, except by a happy accident now and then, is to double gold-pink with blue; this is the only way to get a purple that will vibrate, palpitating against the eye like the petal of a pansy in the sun). Well, you get your purple, and you get your green – not a sage-green, or an "art-green," but a cold, sharp green, like a leaf of parsley, an aquamarine, the tree in the "Eve" window at Fairford, grass in an orchard about sunset, or a railway-signal lamp at night.

Your crimson like a peony, your white like white silk; and now you are started.

You put slabs of these – equal-sized samples, we will suppose – side by side, and see "if they will do."

And they don't "do" at all.

Take away the red.

The green and the purple do well enough, and the white.

But you *want* the red, you say.

Well, *put back a tenth part of it*.

And how now?

Add a still smaller bit of pale pink.

And how now?

Do you see what it all means? It means the rule we spoke of, and which we may as well, therefore, now announce:

"HARMONY IN COLOUR DEPENDS NOT ONLY UPON THE ARRANGING OF RIGHT COLOURS TOGETHER, BUT THE ARRANGING OF THE RIGHT QUANTITIES AND THE RIGHT DEGREES OF THEM TOGETHER."

68

E. F. SUFFLING, 'THE COLOURS AND BRUSHES USED IN GLASS PAINTING'

A Treatise on the Art of Glass Painting (London: Scott, Greenwood & Co., 1902), pp. 81–93

THE colours used in mosaic glass painting are very few, being principally shading tints – a little enamel colour and silver-stain; but upon their quality and firing powers the permanence of a modern window entirely depends.

We do not propose entering into the composition and manufacture of the colours, as they may be bought ready to hand, and are not made by even the largest firms of glass painters. It is quite unnecessary to go into the actual composition of the colours, as our concern is more as to what they will do than as to what they are made from. We may note that they are made of certain metallic oxides ground with a certain proportion of borax flux, which is literally a kind of soft glass, possessing the property of causing the metallic oxide to adhere and incorporate itself with the glass upon which it is painted. Without flux the colour would not adhere to the glass at all after firing, but must be incorporated with the oxide as a medium between the metal and the glass.

When the correct amount of flux has been ground with the colour, the latter appears smooth and glossy when fired, but if insufficient has been used the colour comes from the kiln harsh and dull, and not being thoroughly incorporated with the glass can be scratched off with a knife or sharp piece of glass. Such colour will inevitably peel and chip in the course of a few years, leaving the window in a deplorable state. Buy your colour of a reliable maker, and you will have very little difficulty with it.

It used to be necessary to have a small box or bottle handy containing borax flux, a little of which was ground with the colour upon the palette, when it was found that the colour did not "go down" (or become glossy) in the firing; but such is now seldom requisite unless some very poor colour indeed is used.

The chief colour used by the glass painter is known as tracing brown, and is more largely used than any colour in the list. It is used for outlining the various patterns upon the glass before it comes to the painting or shading stage. It is of a rich red brown, and has a glaring appearance if used pure; it is therefore usually mixed with one-fourth of tracing black, which gives it a vandyke brown tone.

DOI: 10.4324/9781315400266-83

If the pure tracing brown is used in outlining it will be seen, by reason of its vividness, upon the surface of the glass, and in looking at a stained glass window we want to look *through* not *upon* the glass, as we should if it were an oil painting. Some knowing the glaring quality of the brown tracing colour go to the other extreme and use only black tracing colour, but this is going to the opposite error; and when we know that by reason of its softer nature black is apt to "fire away" and become transparent, thereby giving a poor outline, we are constrained to come to the commonsense view that a mixture of brown and black produce a happy medium – solid, dull and permanent.

Solidity of outline is a desideratum, for if the outline is transparent and washy, the object depicted on the glass will not be clearly defined, but will present a blurred, undefined and unsatisfactory appearance.

The writer personally uses a uniform mixture of one part black to two parts brown, but the amateur may vary the proportions to suit his individual taste.

Umber is a warm brown, somewhat fugitive, and not adapted to solid lines. It is used for painting in oil, and to imitate the shade of ancient colour in shading. By saying "painting in oil" it must always be understood that the oil used by glass painters is "tar-oil," the medium for painting in after the preliminary operations of outlining, matting, etc., have been finished.

Umber loses much of its depth in firing, so that one must paint the work very much deeper than it is wished to appear after firing. To prevent this "firing away," a little brown and black tracing colour may be added to it, but they must be well ground first, and afterwards again well ground when the colours are mixed.

Copper Black is an intense black of a soft nature, and is apt to fire away or become very transparent in the kiln.

If tracing brown is found to be a little harsh and rough on the surface when fired, a little copper black will greatly improve it, and may be added instead of the tracing black.

Shading Brown and **Shading Black** are used for the purpose denoted by their name, and are really the same as tracing brown and black, but of a slightly softer nature, having more flux used in their composition.

In many firms both outlining and shading are done entirely with the tracing colours.

China or **Flesh Red** is principally used as a "backing" or toning tint for flesh painting. For this purpose – if used at all – it must be applied very sparingly or the figures will look sunburnt – like a jolly farmer – an appearance not desirable in a saint, especially if of the female sex.

This pigment was not known to glass painters before about 1510–20, consequently it is never seen in fifteenth century work at all, and for this reason is seldom used by modern glass painters, who work in the style of the late fifteenth century or early sixteenth century era. Its use, according to some critics, was one of the first causes of decline in the art – it was a help to obtaining the picture or canvas style into which glass painting afterwards degenerated.

If therefore flesh red is used for toning flesh, it should be the merest film – just enough to "waken the dead" in the greenish corpse-like tone of the glass used for modern flesh. The flesh red is usually applied to the back of the glass.

Stain. – The golden glory of a window is one of the simplest and yet one of the most difficult to use. It is easy to apply to the glass, but requires great experience to know how thin or how heavily to apply to individual pieces of glass.

To make this more clear, let us take four strips of any kind of pale glass, and with the stain let us coat each of the four pieces, keeping the same strength of stain on each, and send them to the kiln to be fired.

When we receive them again we find one piece has a beautiful golden stain, the next a pale lemon, the third a deep, opaque film, and the last a deep orange stain.

From this we learn that by altering the strength of the stain on the first piece as we apply it, we can obtain any tint of stain we require, either pale or rich. The second piece, if we want rich stain, we must coat much more heavily. This glass will probably be found of a flesh tone, which is a hard glass, and wants more stain applied than the first piece, which was of a normal greenish-yellow tone, the painter's ideal tint for staining.

The third piece of glass was of a deep greenish-blue white, and is unsuitable for staining; the component parts of the glass are antagonistic to the stain, and we therefore reject that glass altogether, or else greatly reduce the strength of our stain by adding well-ground yellow lake.

The fourth proves itself to be good staining glass – too good, in fact – as it takes the stain too kindly. We therefore either apply the stain very much more thinned out with turpentine, or, what is better, add an equal bulk of ground yellow lake to the stain, which will then come from the kiln a beautiful golden tint instead of the fiery orange.

As so much has been said and written upon it from its invention at the beginning of the fourteenth century, our readers may like to make some for themselves. If so, here is the recipe – one which thirty years' practice has found to be equal to or better than any other: –

Obtain one ounce of virgin silver, in as small pieces as possible for quickness of melting, and place in a gallipot or glass jar. Warm the jar thoroughly, and in it, upon the silver, pour an ounce of nitric acid, to which add two ounces of boiling water.

Place it in the open air on a sill, or on the stove hob, as it gives forth a yellow vapour of a pungent and unpleasant kind.

If in a glass pickle jar, you will see the acid furiously attacking the silver, melting or decomposing it, and boiling and bubbling round it in a terrible rage.

By-and-bye the bubbling anger ceases and naught apparently remains in the jar but a beautiful, clear, emerald coloured liquid. But our silver is there, nevertheless, held in solution. Fill the jar nearly full of hot water, and pour in common table-salt till it will hold no more. Next pour the whole into a larger vessel and fill with cold water, stir well and allow to settle. When settled, a thick white pulp will remain at the bottom – this is the nitrate of silver. Carefully pour off the water, so as not to lose a particle of the sediment, and fill the vessel again with water and stir it well up. Repeat this a dozen times during the day to eliminate the salt and acid. In the meantime grind – in water – three ounces of yellow lake; grind it to an impalpable pulp – the finer the grinding the more successful the stain will be. Next day add the silver nitrate – which should have been allowed to drain as dry as possible – and grind them well and intimately together. When ground spread out on a glass slab and dry before a fire or in the sun. The stain is then ready for use.

Being in the form of a yellow powder, it is best kept in a wide-necked bottle.

For enamel painting on white glass a different set of colours is required. Enamel painting consists of firing several colours on one section of glass, quite different to mosaic stained glass, in which the glass employed is self-coloured or "pot metal".

Now and again the modern glass painter is called upon to use a little enamel for some little jewel, or enrichment of a border, a ring, or a crown. He has, therefore, by him tiny phials of blue, pink and, perhaps, green, though the latter can be made by applying the blue enamel to the front of the glass and staining the back; only he is not in this case so certain of the effect after firing as if he used the enamel green.

The mediums used in glass painting are sugar and gum for water-colour painting, and turpentine and tar-oil for oil painting.

If it is desired to simply outline a pattern on glass – such as in quarry work, and to stain the back – it is usual to mix sugar with the tracing colour so as to make it work smoothly, but if the outlining has to be painted over in water colour then the medium used is gum.

"Oil" colour is ordinary tracing or shading colour ground in turpentine and mixed with tar-oil to make it flow properly.

"Fat oil" is used as a medium for ordinary painting or shading colour, and for the stain.

"Fat oil" is simply turpentine placed in an open vessel and exposed for some days in the sun, or in a warm place by a stove, until it becomes thick and viscid.

The Brushes, etc., used in Glass Painting.

A glass painter's kit of brushes and tools is not at all an expensive one; the brushes are not very numerous in kind, but are of various sizes and substances. First come the brushes for outlining the various patterns on the glass, called "tracers". They are termed camel-hair, Siberian, and sable in quills, and are much like ordinary water-colour brushes, except that the hair is much longer, varying from an inch to an inch and a half. The quill should not be too full of hair, nor the hair too fine, neither should the quill be too lissom, as the colour used in glass painting is much heavier and denser than ordinary water colours used on paper. The quills should be mounted on long straight handles of hard wood—lancewood or yew being preferred, as they are of a tough, fine grain and do not warp.

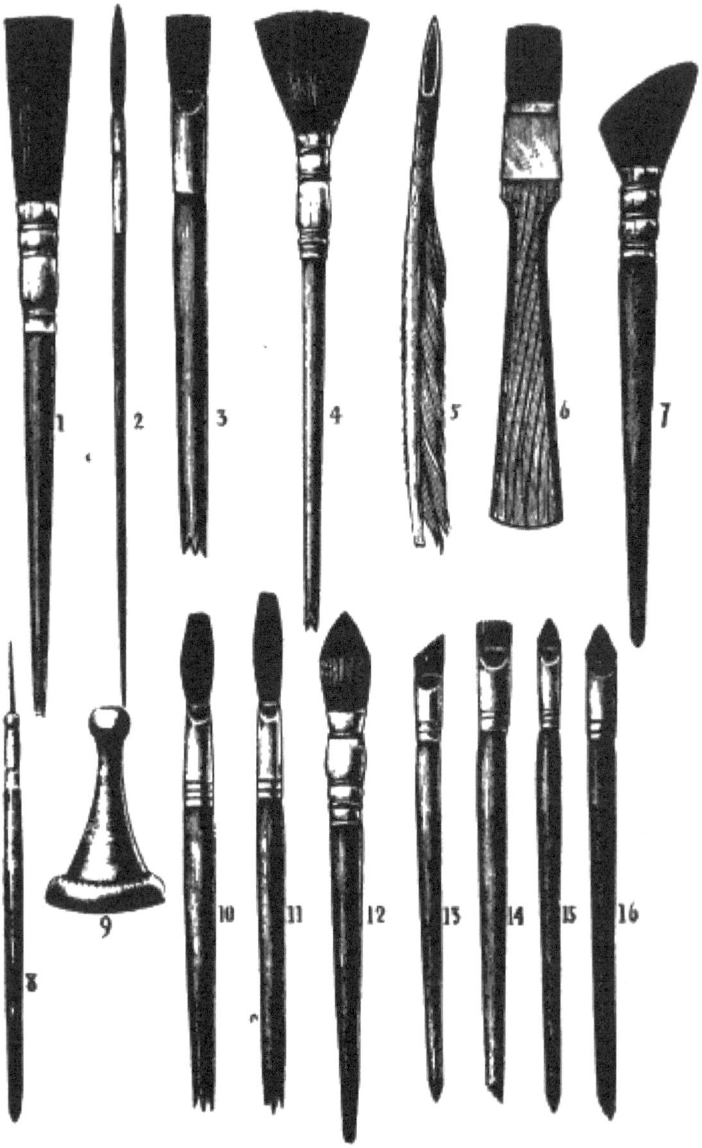

Figure 68.1 Glass Painting Brushes, etc.

1. Hog-hair Stippler.
2. Tracer.
3. Hog-hair Fitch.
4. Badger-hair Shader.
5. Quill Etcher.
6. Camel-hair Flat.
7. Skew Stippler.
8. Needle-point Etcher.
9. Glass Muller.
10. Camel-hair Painter.
11. Sable-hair „
12. Round Scrub.
13. Skew „
14. Square „
15. Pointed Round Scrub.
16. Pointed Flat „

For shading and painting, flat camel-hair brushes like those used for water colours will be best—say half a dozen camel-hair brushes in albata, of three different sizes.

Some artists prefer soft sable, as they are not so readily spoiled if accidentally left in colour, but a little care and experience in this respect will save the painter many shillings.

Where large surfaces have to be covered with colour, camel-hair "flats" in tin may be used. It will be well to have three half an inch wide, two an inch wide, and one an inch and a half wide. Keep one of the half-inch size for oil colour and the others for water.

Important among the brushes are really good "stipplers," or round hog-hair brushes, flat at the end for stippling in shadows, coating glass with stippled surfaces, etc. They look almost like ordinary house painting brushes, but are longer and straighter in the hair, of a better quality bristle, and of a flat surface at the end. They are rather expensive.

The French or skew stippler is of fine camel hair, and is used principally for flesh, as it gives a much finer grain than the ordinary stippler, which is more used for drapery.

Hog-hair fitches are converted into what glass painters call "scrubs"—that is, brushes for scrubbing away or removing paint from the surface of the glass—to produce half tones or high lights. To make these scrubs, first cut them down as near as possible to the required shape with a pair of scissors or a sharp pocket-knife, then very carefully singe the ends of the hair in a turned-down gas-jet, or at a lighted candle. The process must be done slowly and by degrees, so as to get fairly smooth ends to all the hairs, and a general rounding off of the whole scrub end.

During and after the singeing operation the scrub must be well rubbed on fine sand-paper or a piece of emery cloth. Scrubs are made in a variety of shapes—skew, round, flat, square, pointed, etc.

There is one kind of scrub which needs a little further comment, and that is the round scrub made from hog-hair brushes bound in quill. Two or three of these will be required for stippling out the lights from both flesh and drapery, principally the former. They are most useful brushes, and should be made in three sizes—one as large as the top of one's little finger, another not quite so large as the index finger, and the third for large work of about the size of one's thumb. These brushes must be cut down, singed, and rubbed smooth as above described.

Much of the success attending the painting of a window depends upon having well-made scrubs, so that great pains should be taken in making them, or the result will be a series of ugly scratches instead of gradated lights in the painted work. A badger-hair softener (or perhaps two of different sizes) will be required, and care should be taken, in selecting them, that no coarse hairs have been accidentally mixed in the making with the soft ones. These are about all the painter requires in the way of brushes, but there are several other accessories to mention. Three glass mullers of various sizes will be wanted, *viz.,* an inch and a half, a two-inch, and a two and a half-inch one.

A needle point mounted on the end of a piece of hard wood is an admirable etching tool for flesh, heradic charges, and wherever very fine hatched lines on a dark ground are required.

One of the simplest and most effective tools is a common goose-quill, cut like a pen, but without the slit for writing, for etching out the high lights in the hair or beard of a figure, for small diapered patterns, and a great variety of uses. The goose has aptly been called the glass painter's friend, not because birds of a feather flock together, but because in an able painter's hand the grey goose-quill can be made to do wonderful things, and to obtain peculiar effects upon matted grounds. Formerly the grey goose was the patron of archers, then of schoolmasters, and now of glass painters.

To make the quill-etcher, sharpen the quill as for a pen, but do not make the slit in it. Have some quills broad-nosed, others more pomted.

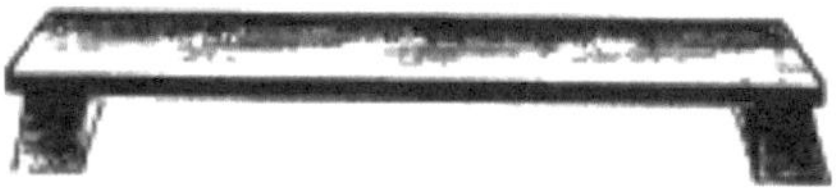

Figure 68.2 Hand Rest.

The hand rest is another useful tool, giving freedom to the tracer's hand when outlining, raising the hand from the work, and so keeping the sleeve and wrist from spoiling the wet work beneath. It is simply a piece of oak or mahogany, from twelve to twenty-four inches long, two inches wide, and three-eights of an inch thick, mounted on two little wooden legs or ends about an inch and a half high. Beginners find this somewhat difficult to use at first, but in time it becomes indispensable, and no work should be attempted without it.

For taking out sharp lights some pointed pieces of lancewood will be found useful, as they will not break at their points, because of their toughness.

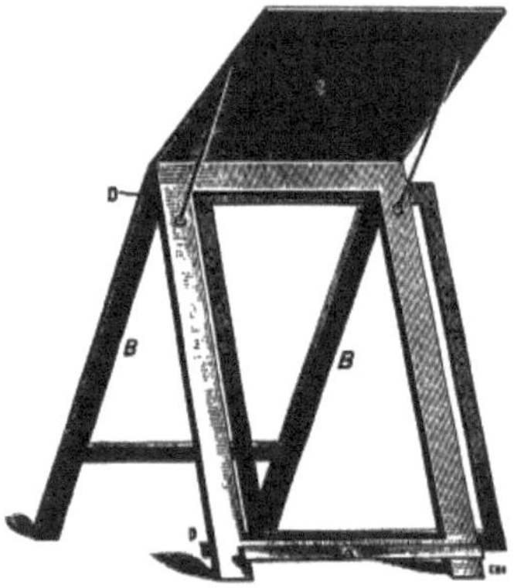

Figure 68.3 Improved Glass Painting Easel.

The last and most expensive requirement is an easel. This is of somewhat peculiar construction, but not at all difficult to make.

The front of the easel is a rectangle about three feet high by two feet broad, the side pieces being prolonged about three inches to form short legs. The wood of the front is three inches by an inch; upon the back at D. D are screwed two L-shaped runners to hold a thin sliding frame, called the "paper-frame," being covered, when in use, with white tissue paper to subdue and diffuse the light. This frame is made so as to slip easily in and out between the runners, D, D. Long back legs, B, with a strut near the bottom, and a top piece above, are hinged to the front of the easel by a couple of ordinary butt hinges. An L-shaped ledge, A, is next screwed along the front of the easel, and the whole is complete.

The use of the ledge, A, is to support a thick sheet of glass, three feet by two feet, called the easel glass, upon which is fastened, with a preparation of beeswax and resin, all the little pieces of glass which go to make up a figure or canopy, and to hold them in their correct places while they are being painted.

Sometimes the easel has an additional wooden frame, C, about two feet square, hinged to the upper part of the front, and covered with brown paper. This being held in position by two side rods, keeps the glare of light which streams over the top of the easel from the painter's eyes. It is, however, hardly necessary, though it is used by a few fastidious painters.

By the way, a few ground glass palettes, a quarter of an inch thick and seven to ten inches square, will be required for grinding the colour upon, and that is all.

Now having our tools, brushes and easel, we will proceed to consider the art of the painter.

PART 4

Art of the book

4.1

Book illustration: opinion pieces and debates

DOI: 10.4324/9781315400266-85

4.1 Book illustration: opinion pieces and debates

The sources included in this section explore nineteenth-century debates about book illustration. They discuss the dynamic between written text and accompanying image as well as the relationship between book illustration and the other arts (especially the developing art of photography).[1] As Ian Haywood et al. discuss, the modern meaning of illustration was crystallised in the romantic period. Words such as 'embellishment' and 'engraving' were more commonly used, with the term 'illustration' appearing for the first time in 1817.[2] The 1774 copyright act led to an exponential growth in the number of printed images appearing in books;[3] publishers such as John Bell and Charles Cooke, for example, began to produce cheap, multivolume illustrated editions of British poets and novelists.[4] These cheaper illustrated editions of books enjoyed huge popularity, but caused consternation among some writers. On this theme, our first source is Charles Lamb's poem addressed to the poet Samuel Rogers, which appeared in *The Times* in 1833. Lamb's poem discusses a new illustrated edition of Rogers' *The Pleasures of Memory,* which reproduced work by painters J. M. W. Turner and Thomas Stothard. Lamb attributes a form of moral degeneracy to Rogers' lavishly illustrated book; its showy extravagance might appeal to 'The eye of pampered aristocracy', but it provides nothing 'Of healthful action to the soul-conceiving/Of the true reader'. A more conciliatory letter to Rogers from Lamb, written as an acknowledgement of an early copy of Rogers' *Illustrated Poems*, uses the example of illustrated editions of Shakespeare's works to articulate an argument about the 'combination of the sister arts', which should, in Lamb's opinion, be left to 'sparkle apart'.[5] The *Quarterly Review*'s 1844 review of four illustrated books discusses 'the rage for ornamented, or as they are now termed "Illustrated" or "Pictorial" editions of books'. In this posthumously published piece, the author, John Murray (second head of the John Murray publishing house), acknowledges the impact of modern advances in engraving, such as stereotyping or electrotyping.[6] Bemoaning the quality of present day book illustration, the author describes its increasing popularity as a 'return to baby literature – to a second childhood of learning'. He quotes the Roman poet Horace's statement that things presented to the eye rouse the feelings more quickly than those presented to the ear, arguing that the impetus behind the explosion in print illustration is market driven: 'a low utilitarian wish to give and receive the greatest possible amount of knowledge at the least possible expense of time, trouble, money, and [. . .] intellect'. Looking back to previous, more meretricious (in Murray's view) examples of book illustration as well as forward to the impact of photography, the full article sketches a history of illustration and considers its role across different genres: travel writing, poetry, natural history writing and novels. William Wordsworth's 1846 sonnet 'Illustrated Books and Newspapers' responds to the rapid developments in print that had taken place over the preceding 50 years.[7] Wordsworth appears to take a negative view of illustration, describing it as a return to a 'lower stage' of man's development, though recent critics have suggested that Wordsworth's conservative stance towards the development of book illustration can be complicated by the fact that his previous published work contained engravings and that he spoke in favour of illustration to his publisher in 1846.[8]

Moving forward in the century, some commentators are more positive about the possibilities of book illustration, though concerns about the quality of illustration are often aired. The 1860s is often referred to as a golden age of book illustration, based on the huge outpouring of illustrations in both books and periodicals during that period.[9] However, the term 'golden age' was also used to describe illustration in the 1880s and 1890s, as well as the early twentieth century, and many of the sources included here (like the piece in the *Quarterly Review*) look back to prior golden ages of book illustration, both in the Victorian period and in previous centuries. The article from the journal edited by Charles Dickens, *All the Year Round*, looks back from 1867 to a golden age of 1840s illustrators dominated by George Cruikshank and Hablot Knight Browne, who illustrated many of Dickens' own novels when they appeared in serial form, including *Oliver Twist* (1837–1839) and *David Copperfield* (1849–1850). The extract reproduced here considers how modern illustrators tend not to help the author 'make himself understood', preferring to produce work that might enhance their own reputations. This inclination leads them to reproduce scenes from novels 'wholly devoid of action or stir', and the author laments the inability of modern illustrators to combine action with beauty. The full article goes on to explore this dynamic in the work of French illustrator Gustave Doré.

Henry Blackburn discusses the modern state of book illustration in the first of a series of lectures on book and newspaper illustration delivered at the Royal Society of Arts (RSA) in 1893. Discussing developments in this area since his 1875 lecture, also to the RSA, he draws attention to 'the deterioration in the character of book illustration in England', attributing this to a lack of detailed knowledge on the part of artists, publishers and authors, the low estimation of book illustration as a profession, and the difficult relationship between book illustration and photography. Illustrator and artist Walter Crane's 1889 lecture on the decoration and illustration of books was also part of the annual Cantor Lecture series. In the short excerpt reproduced here, Crane is largely concerned with the challenge posed to the book illustrator by photography. The radical designer, artist and craftsman, William Morris, discusses the idea of the beautiful book in relation to modern utilitarian manufacturing models and lost golden ages of woodcuts in a paper read to the RSA in 1892. Morris emphasises the importance of viewing the whole book as a work of art and criticises the practice of illustrating the publication of novels in serial form, describing periodicals as 'a mass of utilitarian matter [. . .] absolutely helpless and dead'. Morris goes on to discuss techniques and approaches for the production of beautiful books.

George Du Maurier's essay 'The Illustrating of books from the serious artist's point of view' appeared in the *Magazine of Art* in 1890. Du Maurier was himself an established illustrator – perhaps best known for his work on the satirical magazine *Punch* from the 1860s to 1890s. In the extract included here, Du Maurier describes two different types of reader: one who 'visualises what he reads' and one who does not possess this capacity. It is for the 'greater happiness' of those in the latter category that the illustrator 'plies his trade'. The full article gives an account of Du Maurier's favourite illustrators from across the century. The final piece in this section discusses the art of book and print collecting. In his 1897 book on illustration, Gleeson White proposes the 1860s as the period to which the keen collector should turn. White discusses the material challenges of collecting and arranging wood engravings from periodicals:

> must the collector retain intact a whole set of an illustrated periodical for the sake of a few dozen pictures within it [. . .] Must he mutilate a Tennyson's *Poems* [. . .] for the sake of arranging his specimens in an orderly fashion?

White describes the process of 'print-splitting' in which printed backs are removed from wood engravings. He suggests this as a possible occupation for 'young lady artists' instead of the low-paid activity of producing 'head-pieces', otherwise known as head-banding, where women workers hand sewed the edges, head and tail of a book.

Notes

1 There is a vast literature on Victorian book illustration. Important edited collections include Catherine J. Golden (ed.), *Book Illustrated: Text, Image and Culture 1770–1930* (New Castle, DE: Oak Knoll Press, 2000); Paul Goldman and Simon Cooke (eds.), *Reading Victorian Illustration 1855–75: Spoils of the lumber room* (London: Routledge 2016), first published 2012 by Ashgate Publishing. See also Catherine J. Golden's recent study *Serials to Graphic Novels: The evolution of the Victorian illustrated book* (Gainesville: University Press of Florida, 2017). On caricature-style illustration see John Harvey, *Victorian Novelists and their illustrator*s (New York: New York University Press, 1971). On Dickens see Robert L Patten, *Charles Dickens and his Publishers* (Oxford: Clarendon Press, 1978; second edition Oxford University Press, 2017). On the relationship between illustration and narrative painting see Julia Thomas, *Pictorial Victorians: The Inscription of Values in Word and Image* (Athens: Ohio University Press, 2004).

2 Ian Haywood, Susan Matthews and Mary L. Shannon, 'Editors' Introduction', *Romanticism and Illustration* (Cambridge: Cambridge University Press, 2019), p. 2.

3 See William Sinclair, *The Reading Nation in the Romantic Period* (Cambridge: Cambridge University Press, 2004), p. 134.

4 See Thomas F. Bonnell, *The Most Disreputable Trade: Publishing the Classics of English Poetry 1765–1810* (Oxford: Oxford University Press, 2008).

5 The exact date of the letter is unknown, though E.V. Lucas estimates December 21st 1833.

6 Both of these were facsimile processes that used moulds to produce copies of the original woodblock. For helpful technical definitions see Michael F. Suarez, S.J. and H. R. Woudhuysen (eds.), *The Oxford Companion to the Book* (Oxford: Oxford University Press, 2020); Susan Doyle, Jaleen Grove and Whitney Sherman (eds.) *History of Illustration* (Fairchild Books, New York, 2018), p. 202.

7 For a discussion of this poem in context see Sophie Thomas 'Poetry and Illustration: Amicable Strife' in Charles Mahoney (ed.) *A Companion to Romantic Poetry* (Wiley-Blackwell, 2011), pp. 354–373.
8 Peter Manning, 'Wordsworth's 'Illustrated Books and Newspapers' and Media of the City', in Larry H Peer (ed.), *Romanticism and the City*, (Basingstoke: Palgrave, 2011), pp. 223–240 (p. 224).
9 On the mid-century golden age see Goldman and Cooke (eds.), *Reading Victorian Illustration*, (Farnham: Ashgate, 2012).

69

CHARLES LAMB, 'TO SAMUEL ROGERS, ESQ.'

The Times, 13th December 1833

To Samuel Rogers, Esq., on the new edition of his "Pleasures of Memory"

When thy gay book hath paid its proud devoirs,
Poetic friend, and fed with luxury
The eye of pampered aristocracy
In glittering drawing-rooms and gilt boudoirs,
O'erlaid with comments of pictorial art,
However rich and rare, yet nothing leaving
Of healthful action to the soul-conceiving
Of the true reader – yet a nobler part
Awaits thy work, already classic styled.
Cheap-clad, accessible, in homeliest show
The modest beauty through the land shall go
From year to year, and render life more mild;
Refinement to the poor man's hearth shall give,
And in the moral heart of England live.

C. Lamb.

DOI: 10.4324/9781315400266-86

70

LETTER FROM CHARLES LAMB TO SAMUEL ROGERS

Sir Thomas Noun Talford (ed.) *The Complete Works of Charles Lamb containing his letters, essays, poems, etc. with a sketch of his life* (Philadelphia: William T. Amies, 1879), pp. 291–292

"Dec. 1833.

"My dear Sir, – Your book, by the unremitting punctuality of your publisher, has reached me thus early. I have not opened it, nor will till to-morrow, when I promise myself a thorough reading of it. The 'Pleasures of Memory' was the first school-present I made to Mrs. Moxon; it has those nice wood-cuts, and I believe she keeps it still. Believe me, that all the kindness you have shown to the husband of that excellent person seems done unto myself. I have tried my hand at a sonnet in the 'Times.' But the turn I gave it, though I hoped it would not displease you, I thought might not be equally agreeable to your artist. I met that dear old man at poor Henry's, with you, and again at Cary's, and it was sublime to see him sit, deaf, and enjoy all that was going on in mirth with the company. He reposed upon the many graceful, many fantastic images he had created; with them he dined, and took wine. I have ventured at an antagonist copy of verses, in the 'Athenæum,' to *him,* in which he is as everything, and you as nothing. He is no lawyer who cannot take two sides. But I am jealous of the combination of the sister arts. Let them sparkle apart. What injury (short of the theatres) did not Boydell's Shakspeare Gallery do me with Shakspeare? to have Opie's Shakspeare, Northcote's Shakspeare, light-headed Fuseli's Shakspeare, heavy-headed Romney's Shakspeare, wooden-headed West's Shakspeare (though he did the best in Lear), deaf-headed Reynolds's Shakspeare, instead of my, and everybody's Shakspeare; to be tied down to an authentic face of Juliet! to have Imogen's portrait! to confine the illimitable! I like you and Stothard (you best), but 'out upon this half-faced fellowship!' Sir, when I have read the book, I may trouble you, through Moxon, with some faint criticisms. It is not the flatteringest compliment in a letter to an author to say, you have not read his book yet. But the devil of a reader he must be, who

DOI: 10.4324/9781315400266-87

prances through it in five minutes; and no longer have I received the parcel. It was a little tantalising to me to receive a letter from Landor, *Gebir* Landor, from Florence, to say he was just sitting down to read my 'Elia,' just received; but the letter was to go out before the reading. There are calamities in authorship which only authors know. I am going to call on Moxon on Monday, if the throng of carriages in Dover-street, on the morn of publication, do not barricade me out.

"With many thanks, and most respectful remembrances to your sister,

"Yours, C. LAMB.

"Have you seen Coleridge's happy exemplification in English of the Ovidian Elegiac metre?

In the Hexameter rises the fountain's silvery current,
In the Pentameter aye falling in melody down.

"My sister is papering up the book – careful soul!"

71

JOHN MURRAY, 'ILLUSTRATED BOOKS'

Quarterly Review, June 1844, pp. 168–172 [selections]

AMONGST the characteristics of the literature of the present age there is one which, if neither the most striking from its novelty nor the most important in its tendency, is certainly the most familiar to us all, and silently exercises no little influence upon society; we allude to the rage for ornamented, or as they are now termed, 'Illustrated' or 'Pictorial' editions of books. Be the books what they may, sacred or profane, old or new; good, bad, or indifferent – destined to remain as monuments to their authors, more durable than brass, or to pass away and be forgotten like the last year's Annuals – still all must be adorned with whatever the arts of engraving and fine printing can supply, to form what our Gallic neighbours call 'Editions de luxe' – or else, for the most part, be condemned to small type, and, perhaps, double columns, as 'Editions for the people.' Nearly forty years since, when 'Illustrated' books were of comparatively rare occurrence, Professor Christian[1] querulously remarked, 'we do not grow wiser than our forefathers; the fury for prints proves the frivolity of the times, and our books, I fear, will shrink from a comparison with those of the age of Queen Anne, which were not adorned with such superfluous and meretricious decorations.' How would the professor lament over the 'Illustrations' of the present day!

The skill of the engraver has indeed been singularly assisted by modern discoveries in science and in art: the Formschneiders and the Intagliatori of the fifteenth and sixteenth centuries would start with surprise at the stereotyped woodcuts and the electrotyped engravings of the present day. Maso Finiguerra and Albert Durer, Melchior Pfintzing, and Raimondi (Marc Antonio) would, perhaps, be less astonished at the steam-engine and its wonders, than at the reproduction *ad infinitum* of their most laboured and most finished efforts; their own handiwork remaining the while unsoiled by ink, uninjured by the press, and serving only to produce metallic copies for the printers' use.

Five lustres since and a few hundreds only of impressions could be taken from a copper-plate engraving without its delicacy being materially injured; a 'retouching' – almost amounting to a re-engraving – was necessary to produce some few copies of inferior beauty and debased value. Now the 'Art Union' can supply its

 DOI: 10.4324/9781315400266-88

twelve thousand subscribers with impressions from an engraving, of which the last shall be scarcely, if at all, inferior to the first, and could do the same were its numbers tenfold what they are. Five lustres since, and a few small woodcuts, mostly of very questionable design and execution – the works of Bewick and two or three others being the alone exceptions – were with difficulty 'inked' with 'balls' and 'worked' by hand: the price of any book being materially enhanced by the pains and labour necessarily incurred in the printing of its woodcut 'embellishments' – for such was then the term. In Johnson's '*Typographia,*' published in 1824, is a detailed account of the difficulties experienced in finding either a printing-press of sufficient power, or proper ink, or the requisite skill to print a few copies of 'the very elaborate and most extraordinary engraving on wood, executed by Mr. William Harvey, of the Assassination of L. S. Dentatus, from a celebrated painting by Mr. B. R. Haydon.' This engraving was composed of eleven pieces of wood, 'through which passed four strong iron bolts with nuts at each end,' and measured fifteen inches by eleven and a half inches. We may now smile at this difficulty, but the worthy typographer might then boast of his success in achieving such a task with the means at his command. A few months ago the 'Illustrated London News' circulated to its twenty or thirty or forty thousand subscribers a well-executed and well-printed view of London measuring four feet by two feet, having a superficies about six and a half times that of the Haydonian Dentatus; and, more lately, the 'Pictorial Times' put forth a wood-cut of Wilkie's 'Blind Fiddler,' of the same size with Burnet's line-engraving!

[. . .]

Five lustres since, and, with the exception of Bewick's works, scarcely twenty books of modern date could be named having woodcut embellishments with any pretensions to merit. Amongst the few were a small Shakspeare in seven volumes, with designs by Thurston; an edition of Fairfax's translation of Tasso; and especially Rogers's Pleasures of Memory, with designs of exquisite beauty by Stothard.[2] The number of works with cuts steadily increased; but without doubt the greatest impulse was given by the publication of the 'Penny Magazine' of the Society for the Diffusion of *Useful* Knowledge – followed, '*haud passibus æquis,*' it must be confessed, by the 'Saturday Magazine' of the Society for Promoting *Christian* Knowledge. The first still continues, we believe, in its original course; the second has been long since cast off by the Society which originated it, although it still bears a stamp resembling, in outward appearance, that Society's distinctive mark. There is no doubt that these two publications, each with many woodcuts weekly, have been the pioneers in the present march of woodcut illustration

The improvements in the art of wood-cutting, or of embellishment in relief, have been followed by their natural consequence – a great increase in the demand, greater means of supply, a lower price for 'the article,' and a corresponding increase in the 'factories,' some masters employing from twenty to thirty, or even more hands. If the present taste continues to exist, and shall spread, as is not by any means improbable, we may well anticipate that mechanical means will be found necessary, and something like a Brunel's block-machinery in miniature be adapted to the xylographic process, to aid the engraver in his suburban garret, as the larger machinery does the rigger in Portsmouth-yard.

A natural effect of all this is, that those means, which at first were called in to aid, now bid fair to supersede much of descriptive writing: certainly they render the text of many books subsidiary to their so-called illustrations. In this partial return to baby literature – to a second childhood of learning – the eye is often appealed to instead of the understanding, not so much on the ground that

> 'Segnius irritant animos demissa per aurem,
> Quam quæ sunt oculis subjecta fidelibus, et quæ
> Ipse sibi tradit spectator,'

nor from an acute and accurate perception of beauty of design, as from a low utilitarian wish to give and receive the greatest possible amount of knowledge at the least possible expense of time, trouble, money, and, we may add, of intellect. Verily it is a superficial knowledge which now pervades the country from Berwick to the Land's-End – from Maidenkirk to John O'Groats – wherever the English language is known, and where it is not known: we have seen the 'Penny Magazine' in Polish.

One publisher has put forth a 'Pictorial Bible,' a 'Pictorial Shakspere,' and a 'Pictorial' History of England. The Napoleon Museum is advertised as an 'Illustrated' History of Europe. The hoards in the streets are placarded with puffs of some refuse of American literature (?) called Peter Parley's 'Illustrated' Histories, written, we suppose, by 'drab-coloured' Philadelphians, and savouring of democracy and repudiation of honest debts. We have a Weekly 'Illustrated News,' and a 'Pictorial Times;' besides scores and scores of baser newspapers 'illustrated' but unstamped. In all these cases it will be seen that the adjective is more prominent than the substantive. We do not know that it would be fair to say the same of 'Punch.' Mr. Punch has pens of no common mark at his orders, as well as pencils – very clever writers (we are sorry to see not so good-humoured as they were at the start); yet George Cruikshank and his fellows are real artists, and to their grotesque fertility this most diverting paper owes at all events half of its attraction.

[. . .]

Notes

1 'Vindication of the Right of the Universities of Great Britain to a Copy of every New Publication.'

2 Mr. Rogers, as it might be expected, has preserved some of these in the recent more elaborately ornamented editions of his Poems. We, however, prefer the wood to the copper.

72

WILLIAM WORDSWORTH, 'ILLUSTRATED BOOKS AND NEWSPAPERS'

The Poetical Works of William Wordsworth D.C.L., Volume VI (London: Edward Moxon, 1846), p. 212

DISCOURSE was deemed Man's noblest attribute,
And written words the glory of his hand;
Then followed Printing with enlarged command
For thought – dominion vast and absolute
For spreading truth, and making love expand.
Now prose and verse sunk into disrepute
Must lacquey a dumb Art that best can suit
The taste of this once-intellectual Land.
A backward movement surely have we here,
For manhood – back to childhood; for the age –
Back towards caverned life's first rude career.
Avaunt this vile abuse of pictured page!
Must eyes be all in all, the tongue and ear
Nothing? Heaven keep us from a lower stage!

1846.

DOI: 10.4324/9781315400266-89

73

'BOOK ILLUSTRATIONS'

All the Year Round, Aug 10th 1867, pp. 151–152

THE Art of book-illustration is, just now, passing through a curious phase. When George Cruikshank, or Hablot Brown, two artists whose names are here associated solely for chronological reasons, had to make the illustrations to a work of fiction, it would seem to have been their practice to select as subjects all the most dramatic situations, whether of a comic or tragic sort, which were treated of in the narrative. On the one hand, violent encounters, terrible accidents, exciting adventures, crises through which the characters described in the book were compelled to pass; on the other, situations characterised by their extreme absurdity, in which the persons represented were shown in a ridiculous light, or exhibited under laughable circumstances – these were almost invariably the themes chosen for illustration. Their ambition appears to have been to put the more remarkable scenes described by the author, before the reader's eyes, rather than to display their own artistic powers.

But this principle has got to be now regarded as antiquated and obsolete. Our modern men appear to occupy themselves less with the thing to be done than with the manner of doing it. Their ambition seems to be confined to the desire of producing a beautiful work of art. The modern illustrator, when a book is put into his hands, proposes to himself – judging by results – rather to produce a set of drawings which shall redound to his own credit, than to help the author whose work he illustrates, to make himself understood. The consequence is, that he ordinarily chooses those situations which are the tamest and least dramatic, because they fetter him less, and lend themselves more readily to his purpose of producing a complete and agreeable picture, than those more stirring situations which both the author and the public would have liked to see illustrated.

A large proportion of the drawings with which such works are embellished represent scenes wholly devoid of action or stir. Two or three people seated round a table, partaking of a meal; a couple of young fellows chatting over their wine; a lady showing a picture-book to her little girl; lovers in pairs, without end; single figures, also without end; young ladies reading love-letters, or overwhelmed with some piece of ill news just received.

It must be acknowledged, at starting, that the execution of such drawings as are here spoken of is, in many cases, well-nigh faultless. The figures are evidently

 DOI: 10.4324/9781315400266-90

drawn elaborately from nature. They are well placed, both as to attitude and as to their relative positions with regard to each other. Nor are the accessories neglected. If the scene represented take place in a room the objects about the room are well copied; if a landscape be introduced, this also is well studied, and is often a pretty picture in itself. Yet, admitting all this, at times one gets weary of these well-executed nothings; these well-written tales without story; these harmonious symphonies destitute of tune.

[. . .]

74

GEORGE DU MAURIER, 'THE ILLUSTRATING OF BOOKS'

Magazine of Art, January 1890, pp. 349–350

FROM THE SERIOUS ARTIST'S POINT OF VIEW. – I.

BY GEORGE DU MAURIER.

WHEN the Editor of this Magazine first expressed to me his flattering wish that I should write down, for him to print, my ideas on the subject of book illustration, I was much embarrassed. I felt that of all subjects in the world, this was perhaps the one on which I had the least and fewest ideas; that such ideas as I had consisted principally in my admiration for so many illustrations by others, in my dissatisfaction with so many illustrations of my own, in the wonder that there should be so many illustrated books, good, bad, and indifferent; and that the taste for them should rather seem to be on the increase than otherwise.

Evidently the illustrated book is a "felt want." The majority of civilised human nature likes to read, and a majority of that majority likes to have its book (even its newspaper!) full of little pictures. Evidently, also, there are two classes of readers.

There is the reader who visualises what he reads (at the moment of reading) with the mind's eye, unconsciously, perhaps, and without effort, but in a manner so satisfactory to himself that he wants the help of no picture; indeed, to him a picture would be a hindrance. Another man's conception of the scene or character would interfere with his own, and probably seem to him inferior; just as many people would sooner read their Shakespeare for themselves than see him acted on the stage or hear him declaimed by an elocutionist. To such a man two is company, three is none.

The greater number, I fancy, do not possess this gift, and it is for their greater happiness that the illustrator exists and plies his trade. To have the author's conceptions adequately embodied for them in a concrete form is a boon, an enhancement of their pleasure. Their greatest pleasure of all, of course, is to see it all acted on the stage. In this way the story unfolds itself to them without any effort on their part; nothing is left to the imagination, which they may not possess, or, possessing, may not care to exert.

DOI: 10.4324/9781315400266-91

But the stage is not always at one's command, and failing this, the little figures in the picture are a mild substitute for the actors at the footlights. They are voiceless and cannot move, it is true. But the arrested gesture, the expression of face, the character and costume, may be as true to nature and life as the best actor can make them. Within the limits assigned, these little dumb motionless puppets may be as graceful, or grotesque, or humorous, or terrible as people in real life – indeed, more so; they may continue to haunt the memory when the letterpress they illustrate is forgotten. When they produce this effect, it may be said, I think, that they are the work of a good illustrator; and if, in addition to this, there is the charm of fine handicraft and the cunning of a well-trained faculty, the result is a delightful and valuable work of art – although its scale be a small one, and the means of its production very simple and slight – a very precious possession.

[. . .]

75

WILLIAM MORRIS, 'THE WOODCUTS OF GOTHIC BOOKS', ADDRESS TO THE APPLIED ART SECTION OF THE SOCIETY OF ARTS IN LONDON

Journal of the Society of Arts (40), 12th February 1892, pp. 254–257 [selection]

[. . .]

Now you have seen my examples, I want once more to impress upon you the fact that these designs, one and all, while they perform their especial function – the office of telling a tale – never forget their other function of decorating the book of which they form a part; this is the essential difference between them and modern book illustrations, which I suppose make no pretence at decorating the pages of the book, but must be looked upon as black and white pictures which it is convenient to print and bind up along with the printed matter. The question, in fact, which I want to put to you is this, Whether we are to have books which are beautiful as books; books in which type, paper, woodcuts, and the due arrangement of all these are to be considered, and which are so treated as to produce a harmonious whole, something which will give a person with a sense of beauty real pleasure whenever and wherever the book is opened, even before he begins to look closely into the illustrations; or whether the beautiful and inventive illustrations are to be looked on as separate pictures embedded in a piece of utilitarianism, which they cannot decorate because it cannot help them to do so. Take as an example of the latter, Mr. Fred. Walker's illustrations to "Philip" in the "Cornhill Magazine," of the days when some of us were young, since I am inclined to think that they are about the best of such illustrations. Now they are part of Thackeray's story, and I don't want them to be in any way less a part of it, but they are in no respect a part of the tangible printed book, and I do want them to be that. As it is, the mass of utilitarian matter in which they are embedded is absolutely helpless and dead. Why it is not even ugly, at least not vitally ugly.

Now the reverse is the case with the books from which I have taken the examples which you have been seeing. As things to be looked at they are beautiful taken as a whole; they are alive all over, and not merely in a corner here and there.

DOI: 10.4324/9781315400266-92

The illustrator has to share the success and the failure, not only of the wood cutter, who has translated his drawing, but also of the printer and the mere ornamentalist, and the result is that you have a book which is a visible work of art.

You may say that you don't care for this result, that you wish to read literature and to look at pictures; and that so long as the modern book gives you these pleasures you ask no more of it; well, I can understand that, but you must pardon me if I say that your interest in books in that case is literary only, and not artistic, and that implies, I think, a partial crippling of the faculties; a misfortune which no one should be proud of.

However, it seems certain that there is growing up a taste for books which are visible works of art, and that especially in this country, where the printers, at their best, do now use letters much superior in form to those in use elsewhere, and where a great deal of work intending to ornament books reasonably is turned out; most of which, however, is deficient in some respect; which, in fact, is seldom satisfactory unless the whole page, picture, ornament, and type is reproduced literally from the handiwork of the artist, as in some of the beautiful works of Mr. Walter Crane.

But this is a thing that can rarely be done, and what we want, it seems to me, is, not that books should sometimes be beautiful, but that they should generally be beautiful; indeed, if they are not, it increases the difficulties of those who would make them sometimes beautiful immensely. At any rate, I claim that illustrated books should always be beautiful, unless, perhaps, where the illustrations are present rather for the purpose of giving information than for that of giving pleasure to the intellect through the eye; but surely, even in this latter case, they should be reasonably and decently good-looking.

Well, how is this beauty to be obtained? It must be by the harmonious co-operation of the craftsmen and artists who produce the book. First, the paper should be good, which is a more important point than might be thought, and one in which there is a most complete contrast between the old and the modern books; for no bad paper was made till about the middle of the 16th century, and the worst that was made even then was far better than what is now considered good. Next, the type must be good, a matter in which there is more room for excellence than those may think who have not studied the forms of letters closely. There are other matters, however, besides the mere form of the type which are of much importance in the producing of a beautiful book, which, however, I cannot go into to-night, as it is a little beside my present subject. Then, the mere ornament must be good, and even very good. I do not know anything more dispiriting than the mere platitudes of printers' ornaments – trade ornaments. It is not uncommon now-a-days to see handsome books quite spoiled by them – books in which plain, unadorned letters would have been far more ornamental.

Then we come to the picture woodcuts. And here I feel I shall find many of you differing from me strongly; for I am sure that such illustrations as those excellent black and white pictures of Fred. Walker could never make book ornaments. The artist, to produce these satisfactorily, must exercise severe self restraint, and must never lose sight of the page of the book he is ornamenting. That ought to be obvious to you, but I am afraid it will not be. I do not think any artist will ever make a good book illustrator, unless he is keenly alive to the value of a well-drawn line, crisp and clean, suggesting a simple and beautiful *silhouette*. Anything which obscures this, and just to the extent to which it does obscure it, takes away from the fitness of a design as a book ornament. In this art vagueness is quite inadmissible. It is better to be wrong than vague in making designs which are meant to be book ornaments.

Again, as the artists' designs must necessarily be reproduced for this purpose, he should never lose sight of the material he is designing for. Lack of precision is fatal (to take up again what I have just advanced) in an art produced by the point of the graver on a material which offers just the amount of resistance which helps precision. And here I come to a very important part of my subject, to wit, the relation between the designer and the wood-engraver; and it is clear that if these two artists do not understand one another, the result must be failure; and this understanding can never exist if the wood-engraver has but to cut servilely what the artist draws carelessly. If any real school of wood-engraving is to exist again, the wood-cutter must be an artist translating the designer's drawing. It is quite pitiable to see the patience and ingenuity of such clever workmen, as some modern wood-cutters are, thrown away on the literal reproduction of mere meaningless scrawl. The want of logic in artists who will insist on such work is really appalling. It is the actual touches of the hand that give the speciality, the final finish to a work of art, which carries out in one material what is designed in another; and for the designer to ignore the instrument and material by which the touches are to be done, shows complete want of understanding of the scope of reproducible design.

I cannot help thinking that it would be a good thing for artists who consider designing part of their province (I admit there are very few such artists) to learn the art of wood-engraving, which, up to a certain point, is a far from difficult art; at any rate for those who have the kind of eyes suitable for the work. I do not mean that they should necessarily always cut their own designs, but that they should be able to cut them. They would thus learn what the real capacities of the art are, and would, I should hope, give the executant artists genuine designs to execute, rather than problems to solve. I do not know if it is necessary to remind you that the difficulties in cutting a simple design on wood (and I repeat that all designs for book illustrations should be simple) are very much decreased since the 15th century, whereas instead of using the knife on the plank section of the wood, we now use the graver on the end section. Perhaps, indeed, some of you may think this simple wood cutting contemptible, because of its ease; but delicacy and refinement of execution are always necessary in producing a line, and this is not easy, nay it is not possible to those who have not got the due instinct for it; mere mechanical deftness is no substitute for this instinct.

Again, as it is necessary for the designer to have a feeling for the quality of the final execution, to sympathise with the engraver's difficulties, and know why one block looks artistic and another mechanical; so it is necessary for the engraver to have some capacity for design, so that he may know what the designer wants of him, and that he may be able to translate the designer, and give him a genuine and obvious *cut* line in place of his *pencilled* or *penned* line without injuring in any way the due expression of the original design.

Lastly, what I want the artist – the great man who designs for the humble executant – to think of is, not his drawn design, which he should look upon as a thing to be thrown away when it has served its purpose, but the finished and duly printed ornament which is offered to the public. I find that the executants of my humble designs always speak of them as "sketches," however painstaking they may be in execution. This is the recognised trade term, and I quite approve of it as keeping the "great man" in his place, and showing him what his duty is, to wit, to take infinite trouble in getting the finished work turned out of hand. I lay it down as a general principle in all the arts, where one artist's design is carried out by another in a different material, that doing the work twice over is by all means to be avoided as the source of dead mechanical work. The "sketch" should be as slight as possible, *i.e.,* as much as possible should be left to the executant.

A word or two of recapitulation as to the practical side of my subject, and I have done. An illustrated book, where the illustrations are more than mere illustrations of the printed text, should be a harmonious work of art. The type, the spacing of the type, the position of the pages of print on the paper, should be considered from the artistic point of view. The illustrations should not have a mere accidental connection with the other ornament and the type, but an essential and artistic connection. They should be designed as a part of the whole, so that they would seem obviously imperfect without their surroundings. The designs must be suitable to the material and method of reproduction, and not offer to the executant artist a mere thicket of unnatural difficulties, producing no result when finished, save the exhibition of a *tour de force*. The executant, on his side, whether he be the original designer or someone else, must understand that his business is sympathetic translation, and not mechanical reproduction of the original drawing. This means, in other words, the designer of the picture-blocks, the designer of the ornamental blocks, the wood-engraver, and the printer, all of them thoughtful, painstaking artists, and all working in harmonious co-operation for the production of a work of art. This is the only possible way in which you can get beautiful books.

76

WALTER CRANE, 'THE DECORATION AND ILLUSTRATION OF BOOKS'

The Journal of the Society of Arts (Vol. 37), November 1, 1889, pp. 887–898, p. 895

[. . .]

I have some pages here from several of my own books. My own poem of the "Sirens Three," which is being in some measure influenced by the series of Omar Khayyam, may not inappropriately be shown here perhaps. Then the others which follow serve at least to show the direction in which I have myself aimed in the decoration and illustration of books, and in the treatment of the page as a whole, if I have not always succeeded to my own satisfaction.

The facile methods of photographic-automatic reproduction certainly give an opportunity to the designer to write out his own text in the character that pleases him, and that accords with his design, and so make his page a consistent whole from a decorative point of view, and I venture to think when this is done a unity of effect is gained for the page not possible in any other way.

Indeed, the photograph, with all its allied discoveries and its application to the service of the printing press, may be said to be as important a discovery in its effects on art and books as was the discovery of printing itself. It has already largely transformed the system of the production of illustrations and designs for books, magazines, and newspapers, and has certainly been the means of securing to the artist the advantage of possession of his original, while its fidelity, in the best processes, is, of course, very valuable.

Its influence, however, on artistic style and treatment has been, to my mind, of more doubtful advantage. The effect on painting is palpable enough, but so far as painting becomes photographic, the advantage is on the side of the photograph. It has led in illustrative work to the method of painting in black and white, which has taken the place very much of the use of line, and through this, and by reason of its having fostered and encouraged a different way of regarding nature – from the point of view of accidental aspect, light and shade, and tone – it has confused and deteriorated, I think, the faculty of inventive design, and the sense of ornament; having concentrated artistic interest on the literal realisation of certain aspects of superficial facts, and instantaneous impressions instead of ideas.

[. . .]

 DOI: 10.4324/9781315400266-93

77

HENRY BLACKBURN, 'THE ART OF BOOK AND NEWSPAPER ILLUSTRATION: THE ILLUSTRATOR OF TODAY'

The Journal of the Society of Arts (Vol. 42), December 29, 1893, pp. 93–99 [selections]

By Henry Blackburn.

Lecture I. – Delivered November 27th, **1893**

The Illustrator of To-day

Education of the Artist – Drawing for Reproduction – Modern Methods and Requirements – Examples of Drawings for Reproduction, Good and Bad.

Eighteen years ago, in this room, the general question was discussed "whether, in the matter of book and newspaper illustration, we are really 'keeping pace with the times'; whether those who provide the illustrations, which are tossed from steam printing presses at the rate of several thousand an hour, are doing the best work they can." The meeting was largely attended by experts, and the general conclusion arrived at was, that much remained to be done.

Thus in 1875 it was admitted, almost without dissent, that the system of illustrating books of travel and scientific research by means of wood engravings was "too elaborate and costly"; that, in consequence, there was much valuable material that never saw the light, and that in the case of news the public was continually deprived of what it would most care to see.

In the illustration of newspapers, it was further argued that there, should be a clearer distinction between fact and fiction, between illustrated news and pictures. The exact words may be thought worth repeating: –

"In the production of illustrations we have arrived at great proficiency, and from London are issued the best illustrated newspapers in the world. But our artistic skill has led us into temptation, and by degrees engendered a habit of making pictures when we ought to be recording facts. We have thus, through our

DOI: 10.4324/9781315400266-94

cleverness, created a fashion and a demand from the public, for something which is often elaborately untrue.

"Would it then be too much to ask those who cater for (and really create) the public taste, that they should give us one of two things, or rather *two things* in our illustrated papers, the real and the ideal.

"1st. Pictorial records of events in the simplest and truest manner possible.

"2nd. Pictures of the highest class that can be printed in a newspaper.

"Here are two methods of illustration which only require to be kept distinct, each in its proper place, and our interest in them would be doubled. We ask first for a record of news and then for a picture gallery; and to know, to use a common phrase, *which is which*."

At the time referred to, drawing on the woodblock and engraving was almost universal – instantaneous photography was in its infancy, "process blocks," that is to say, mechanical engraving, was very seldom employed, and (for popular purposes) American engraving and printing was making great strides.

Let us now glance at some of the changes which have taken place in illustration (bridging over a distance of nearly twenty years), and consider the work of the illustrator, the photographer, and the maker of blocks, as presented in books and newspapers at the end of 1893; speaking principally of topical illustrations, on which so many thousand people are now engaged.

It may seem strange at first sight to include "newspapers" in the title of these lectures; but the fact is that the weekly newspapers, with their new appliances for printing, and in consequence of the cheapness of good paper, are now competing with books and magazines in the production of illustrations which a few years ago were only to be found in books. The illustrated newspaper is one of the great employers of labour in this field, and distributors of the work of the artist in black and white, and in this connection must by no means be ignored. The Post-office carries a volume of 164 pages (each 16 by 22 inches), weighing from two to three pounds, for a half-penny. It is called a "weekly newspaper," but it contains, sometimes, 100 illustrations, and competes seriously with the production of illustrated books.

In the next lecture we shall see how the illustrations of one number of an illustrated newspaper are produced; what part the original artist has in it, what part the photographer, what part the wood engraver.

It was time, perhaps, that the "Society for the Encouragement of Arts, Manufactures, and Commerce" should take into consideration the state of book illustration in the present day. The words which head the proceedings of this Society are singularly applicable; the "Art, Manufacture, and Commerce" of a book is well worth examining.

The modern publisher, it may be said without offence, understands the manufacture and the commerce of a book, better than the art in it. And how should it be otherwise? The best books that were ever produced, from an artistic point of view, were inspired and designed by students of art and letters, men removed from the commercial scramble of life, and to whom an advertisement was a thing unknown!

The ordinary education of a publisher, and the multitude of affairs requiring his attention, unfit him for the task of deciding whether an illustration is good or bad; or how far – when he cheapens the production of his book by using photographic illustrations ("snap shots" from Nature) – he is justified in calling it "art."

It would be difficult, I think, to point to a period when so much bad work was produced as at present. The causes are not far to seek. As matters stand at present, the beautiful processes for the reproduction of drawings for the type press are scarcely understood by the majority of artists, publishers, authors, or critics. It is the misuse of these processes which is dragging our national reputation in the mire. Our best artists have neither the time nor the inclination to make themselves acquainted with the methods, and it is hardly to be expected that a reviewer who has a pile of illustrated books to pronounce upon should know the reason of the failures that he sees before him. Thus the public is grievously misled by those who should be its guides as to the value and importance of the new systems of illustration.[1]

The deterioration in the character of book illustration in England is a serious matter, and public attention may well be drawn to it. The first and most serious difficulty to contend against is the comparatively low estimate of this class of work, and the competition of photographs. The second is the want of good technical education in this direction. Students leave art schools by hundreds not properly equipped for the business of life. The business of many will be to contribute, in some form, to the making of pictures and designs to be multiplied in the press; and, in order to learn the technique and obtain employment, some of the most promising pupils have to fall into the ways of the producers of cheap illustrations, Christmas cards, and the like. On the other hand, a knowledge of the mechanical processes for reproducing drawings (as it is being pressed forward in technical schools) is leading to disastrous consequences, as may be seen on every railway bookstall in the kingdom.

It is the special purpose of these lectures to inquire into the conditions under which process illustrations (to use the common phrase) are now produced, and to see how far, and in what way, we may obtain the best results.

[. . .]

Note

1 There seems but one rule of criticism in this connection. If a book illustration comes out coarsely and (as is often the case) a mere smudge, the process is blamed, when the drawing or photograph may have been quite unsuitable for the process employed.

78

GLEESON WHITE, *ENGLISH ILLUSTRATION, 'THE SIXTIES, 1855–70'*

(London: Archibald Constable and Co. Ltd., 1897), pp. 1–4 [selections]

Another point of conscience arises which each must decide for himself. Supposing that the collection of wood-engravings of the sixties assumes the proportion of a craze, must the collector retain intact a whole set of an illustrated periodical for the sake of a few dozen pictures within it, or if he decides to tear them out, will he not be imitating the execrable John Bagford, who destroyed twenty-five thousand volumes for the sake of their title-pages? Must he mutilate a Tennyson's *Poems* (Moxon, 1857) or *The Music-master*, or many of Dalziels' gift-books, for the sake of arranging his specimens in orderly fashion? The dilemma is a very real one. Even if one decides to keep volumes entire, the sets of magazines are so bulky, and in some cases contain such a small proportion of valuable work, that a collector cannot find space for more than a few of them. Possibly a fairly representative collection might be derived entirely from the back-numbers of periodicals, if any huge stores have yet survived the journey to the paper-mill or the flames; the one or the other being the ultimate fate of every magazine or periodical that is not duly bound before it has lost its high estate, as 'a complete set,' and become mere odd numbers or waste-paper.

[. . .]

Having decided to collect, and bought or obtained in other ways, so that you may entitle your treasures (as South Kensington Museum labels its novelties) 'recent acquisitions,' without scrupulous explanation of the means employed to get them, you are next puzzled how to arrange them. It seems to me that a fine book should be preserved intact. There are but comparatively few of its first edition, and of these few a certain number are doomed to accidental destruction in the ordinary course of events, so that one should hesitate before cutting up a fine book, and be not hasty in mutilating a volume of *Once a Week*or the *Shilling Magazine*. But if you have picked up odd numbers, and want to preserve the prints, a useful plan is to prepare a certain number of cardboard or cloth-covered boxes filled with single sheets of thick brown paper. In these an oblique slit is

DOI: 10.4324/9781315400266-95

made to hold each corner of the print. By this method subjects can be mounted quickly, and, as the collection grows, new sub-divisions can be arranged and the subjects distributed among a larger number of boxes. This plan allows each print to be examined easily, the brown paper stands wear and tear and shows no finger-marks, and affords a pleasant frame to the engraving. Pasting-down in albums should be viewed with suspicion – either the blank leaves for specimens still to be acquired are constantly in evidence to show how little you possess, compared with your expectations; or else you will find it impossible to place future purchases in their proper order.

There is a process, known as print-splitting, which removes the objectionable printed back that ruins the effect of many good wood-engravings. It is a delicate, but not a very difficult operation, and should the hobby spread, young lady artists might do worse than forsake the poorly-paid production of nasty little head-pieces for fashion-papers and the like, and turn deft fingers to a more worthy pursuit. It needs an artistic temperament to split the print successfully, and a market would be quickly opened up if moderate prices were charged for the new industry.

4.2

Author-illustrator-engraver relations

DOI: 10.4324/9781315400266-96

4.2 Author-illustrator-engraver relations

Victorian discussions of book illustration were often shaped by the idea of primacy: which was the most important element – the writing or the illustration? New techniques of reproduction added a further dimension to this debate, and the role of the engraver, often unsung, is one that garners a good deal of attention in Victorian art periodicals and journals.

The relationship between author, illustrator and engraver did not always run smoothly. Writers feared that their literary efforts would not be imagined accurately by illustrators, while painters and illustrators balked at the idea of being confined by an author's particular vision. George Eliot's correspondence with painter Frederick Leighton over the illustrations for her 1863 novel *Romola* was generally cordial; nonetheless, her letters reveal some of the tensions that could arise between author and illustrator. In the selection reproduced here, Eliot writes of the 'impossibility of producing perfect correspondence between my intentions and the illustrations'. In an early letter, she praises Leighton's illustration of 'the blind scholar and his daughter', while at the same time expressing regret at one or two details that were not rendered as she had hoped. In a subsequent letter, however, she counters this sentiment by expressing a new understanding of the role of the illustrator: that it was not the objective of book illustration to produce a 'perfect correspondence between the text and the illustration'.

Pre-Raphaelite painter and poet Dante Gabriel Rosetti collaborated with the London wood engraving firm the Dalziel Brothers over a number of projects, including the illustrations for the Moxon Tennyson, an edition of Tennyson's *Poems* edited by Edward Moxon and published in 1857.[1] In a letter to his friend, the Irish poet William Allingham, Rossetti expresses frustration at the services of the engravers working on the woodcuts for one of his designs: 'Dalziel; has made such an incredible mull of it in the cutting that it cannot possibly appear'. In a later letter he describes the Dalziels as 'minsters of wrath' who wreak havoc with artists' drawings.[2] Dalziel's response was to argue that Rossetti had little idea of how to produce a drawing suitable for the engraver's purposes.[3]

Philip Gilbert Hamerton tried his hand at poetry, art criticism and painting during his career. In the first of two dialogues on the subject of literature versus illustration, Hamerton imagines an exchange between a poet, who represents a 'purely literary culture', an artist 'opposed to scientific views', a scientist opposed to the 'picturesque order' of the artist, and a critic, who takes on the role of moderator. The dialogue explores how illustrations will provide the poet with posthumous fame, the concept of 'literary asceticism' in which illustration is rejected as it appeals to 'the luxury of the eyes', and the merits of an author producing her own illustrations. The dialogue between painter and illustrator Edward F. Brewtnall and decorative artist and designer Lewis Foreman Day, reproduced in the *Art*

Journal of 1902, begins with a direct question about the merits of book illustration – 'why presume to illustrate the story that an author has put into words?'[4] In a rather provocative retort, Brewtnall describes the author as a 'lame dog', who needs to be helped to achieve his purpose. He draws attention to the popular demand for book illustration, while Day argues for its superfluity, adding a moral dimension to the debate: 'I do not admit that whatever pays is right'. The dialogue addresses the issue of the reader's imagination (or lack thereof) and the question of whether popularity is a marker of artistic merit. Examples discussed include John Tenniel's illustrations for Lewis Carroll's *Alice in Wonderland* and John Gilbert's illustrations for an edition of Shakespeare's plays.

In lecture three of his 1893 Cantor Lectures, Henry Blackburn recounts an experiment in which a scene from a book was read out to a group of artists. All produced completely different drawings, none of which was 'correct'. In the extract reproduced here, Blackburn opines, 'how useless and absurd many illustrations are in books, as *illustrations*', preferring instead to see them as works of art that have a different function than merely illuminating the text. The lecture goes on to bemoan the Victorian penchant for copying the techniques and approaches of past ages: 'nearly everything ornate or beautiful has been stolen or copied from another country of period'. Blackburn criticises the fraudulent approach of modern book production that seeks to imitate past golden ages, singling out the typefounder, the engraver on steel, and the paper manufacturer for particular criticism. Writing two years later, the art critic Joseph Pennell draws attention to the difficulties of researching the work of illustrators and engravers. None but the most well-known illustrators are catalogued in the collections of the South Kensington and British Museums. Periodicals, too, ignore artists and engravers in their indexes. Pennell asserts that illustrations are constantly reused and links this with a drive to expediency on part of the author and publisher, who 'desire to palm off old blocks as new'.

Notes

1 For a fine analysis of the Dalziel brothers and their work see Bethan Stevens, 'Wood engraving as ghostwriting: the Dalziel Brothers, losing one's name, and other hazards of the trade', *Textual Practice* 33(4), 645–677.

2 George Birkbeck Hill (ed.) *Letters of Dante Gabriel Rossetti to Willingham Allingham* (London: Fisher and Unwin, 1897), December 18th 1856 p. 191.

3 Quoted in Susan Doyle, Jaleen Grove and Whitney Sherman (eds.) *History of Illustration* (Fairchild Books: New York, 2018), p. 234.

4 Lewis Foreman Day was a decorative artist and designer with strong links to the Arts and Crafts Movement.

79

CORRESPONDENCE BETWEEN GEORGE ELIOT AND FREDERICK LEIGHTON

Mrs Russell Barrington, *The Life, Letters and Work of Frederic Baron Leighton*, Vol. 2, pp. 96–99

16 Blandford Square, N.W.,
Friday.

Dear Mr. Leighton, – Thanks for the sight of the Vignettes. They are satisfactory.

Your delicious drawing was with me all day yesterday and made the opera more delightful to me in the evening. I never saw anything comparable to the scene in Nello's shop as an illustration. There could not be a better beginning.

I should very much like to have a little conversation with you, and will arrange to see you at any hour that will best suit you, in the evening if you like, any time after the morning working hours, which last till two o'clock. I know your time is very precious to you just now, but I think we shall both benefit by a little talk together after you have read the second proof. – Yours very truly, M. E. Lewes.

F. Leighton, Esq.

16 Blandford Square, N.W.,
Wednesday.

Dear Mr. Leighton, – I feel for you as well as myself in this inevitable difficulty – nay, impossibility of producing perfect correspondence between my intention and the illustrations.

I think your sketch is charming, considered in itself, and I feel now with regret that if we had seen each other and talked a little together after you had read the proof, the only important discrepancy might have been prevented. It is too late for alterations now. If it had not been, I should have wished Bardo's head to be raised with the chin thrust forward a little – the usual attitude of the blind head, I think – and turned a little towards Romola, "as if he were looking at her."

DOI: 10.4324/9781315400266-97

Romola's attitude is perfect, and the composition is altogether such as gives me a very cheering prospect for the future, when we have more time for preparation. Her face and hair, though deliciously beautiful, are not just the thing – how could they be? Do not make yourself uneasy if alteration is impossible, but I meant the hair to fall forward from behind the ears over the neck, and the dress to be without ornament.

I shall inevitably be detestable to you, but believe that I am

(Unfinished)

16 BLANDFORD SQUARE, N.W.,
Thursday.

DEAR MR. LEIGHTON, – Unmitigated delight! Nello is better than my Nello. I see the love and care with which the drawings are done.

After I had sent away my yesterday's note, written in such haste that I was afterwards uncomfortable lest I had misrepresented my feelings, the very considerations you suggest had occurred to me and I had talked them over with Mr. Lewes – namely, that the exigencies of your art must forbid perfect correspondence between the text and the illustration; and I came to the conclusion that it was these exigencies which had determined you as to the position of Bardo's head and the fall of Romola's hair. You have given her attitude transcendently well, and the attitude is more important than the mere head-dress. I am glad you chose Nello's shop; it makes so good a variety with Bardo and Romola. In a day or two you will have the second part, and I think you will find there a scene for Tessa "under the Plane Tree." But perhaps we shall see each other before you begin the next drawings. – Ever yours truly, M. E. LEWES.

16 BLANDFORD SQUARE, N.W.,
Monday.

DEAR MR. LEIGHTON, – Your letter comforts me particularly. I am so glad to think you find subjects to your mind. I have no especial desire for the view from S. Miniato, and indeed a plan we started in conversation with Mr. Smith this morning, namely, to have moderately sized initial letters – the opening one being an old Florentine in his *Lucco* and generally the subjects being bits of landscape or Florentine building – seems to do away with any reason for having the landscape to begin with. The idea of having Tessa and the mules, or Nello's sanctum, smiles upon me, so pray feel free to choose the impression that urges itself most strongly. Your observation about the "che, che" is just the aid I besought from you. With that exception, I have confined myself, I believe, to such interjections as I find in the writers of the fourteenth and fifteenth centuries, and in them, curiously enough, this exclamation now said to be so constant and "to mean everything" (according to our authority) does not seem to occur.

Thank you. Pray let me have as many criticisms of that kind as you can. I am more gratified, I think, by your liking these opening chapters than I have yet been by anything in these nervous anxious weeks of decision about publication. – Very truly yours, M. E. LEWES.

F. LEIGHTON, Esq.

16 BLANDFORD SQUARE, N.W.,
Tuesday Evening.

DEAR MR. LEIGHTON, – I am enchanted! purely delighted! which shall I begin with, to tell you that I delight in Baby's toes or that exquisite poetry in the scene where Romola is standing? Is it not a pleasant change to have that opening made through the walls of the city, so as to see the sky and the mountains? In the scene with Baldassarre and Tessa, also, the distant view is charming. Tessa and her Babkin are perfect – Baldassarre's is, as you say, an impossible face to draw, but you have seized the framework of the face well, both in this illustration and the previous one.

I want to tell you that a man of some eminence in art was speaking of your drawings to a third person the other day as "remarkable" in a tone of genuine admiration. I don't know whether you care about that, but it is good to know that there is any genuine admiration in one's neighbours.

I am glad to have the drawings left. I shall go now and have a long look at them. The February number will soon be out of my hands, but you will have it when it pleases the pigs – or printers. – Ever yours truly, M. E. LEWES.

PARK HOTEL, LITTLE HAMPTON,
Sussex, *September* 10, '62.

DEAR MR. LEIGHTON, – Thanks for your letter, which I have received this morning.

My copy of Vasari has a profile of Piero di Cosimo, but it is of no value, a man with a short beard and eyes nearly closed. The old felt hat on his head has more character in it than the features, but the hat you can't use.

Of Niccolo Caparra it is not likely that any portrait exists, so that you may feel easy in letting your imagination interpret my suggestions in the First and the Fifth Parts of Romola. There is probably a portrait of Piero di Cosimo in the portrait room of Uffizi, but in the absence of any decent catalogue of that collection it was a bewildering and headachy business to assure oneself of the presence or absence of any particular personage.

If you feel any doubt about the *new* Romola, I think it will be better for you to keep to the original representation, the type given in the first illustration, which some accomplished people told me they thought very charming. It will be much better to continue what is intrinsically pretty than to fail in an effort after something indistinctly seen. If you prefer the action of *taking out* the crucifix, instead of the merely contemplative attitude, you can choose that with safety. In the scene with Piero di Cosimo, I thought you might make the figures subordinate to those other details which you render so charmingly, and I chose it for that reason.

But I am quite convinced that illustrations can only form a sort of overture to the text. The artist who uses the pencil must otherwise be tormented to misery by the deficiencies or requirements of the one who uses the pen, and the writer, on the other hand, must die of impossible expectations. *Apropos* of all that, I want to assure you again of what I had said in that letter, which your naughty servant sent down the wind, that I appreciate very highly the advantage of having your hand and mind to work with me rather than those of any other artist of whom I know. Please do not take that as an impertinent expression of opinion, but rather as an honest expression of feeling by which you must interpret any apparent criticism.

[. . .]

80

GEORGE BIRKBECK HILL (ED.), *LETTERS OF DANTE GABRIEL ROSSETTI TO WILLINGHAM ALLINGHAM* (London: Fisher and Unwin, 1897), Saturday March 18th 1855, pp. 108–109

Saturday, March 18, 1855.

DEAR ALLINGHAM,

I am going to write a most vexatious letter – however, the news cannot be more so to you than to me, and its extreme disagreeableness has prevented my writing it before. That woodblock! Dalziel has made such an incredible mull of it in the cutting that it cannot possibly appear. The fault, however, is no doubt in great measure mine – not of deficient care, for I took the very greatest, but of over-elaboration of parts, perplexing them for the engraver. However, some of the fault is his too, as he has not always followed my lines, but a rather stupid preconceived notion of his about intended "severity" in the design, which has resulted in an engraving as hard as a nail, and yet flabby and vapid to the last degree. In short, it is such a production as could give no idea of anything like care or skill on the part of the designer – of anything but the most conceited attempt of a beginner to be grand and "severe." Before I sent in my drawing, however, to the engraver, I consulted a friend – Clayton, who has drawn much on wood – as to whether it were done in the right way for cutting, and he assured me it was not only adaptable but remarkably so: certainly I kept every line as distinct as I could; and on this account Clayton was of opinion that it was very much more the thing for the purpose than the drawings made by Hughes, which, however, turns out a complete mistake, as Hughes's drawings, also cut by Dalziel, have come, with one exception, quite remarkably well. Three or four of them are most beautiful designs, and will be worthy of your book. Before sending in the block I took the precaution to write to Routledge that, if not approved by me when cut, it must not appear, and Dalziel himself called on me before cutting it, and understood this, so that I must trust they will act accordingly, as I have written to Dalziel since also. If you like, I will send you the proof of it which I have, though at cost of considerable

DOI: 10.4324/9781315400266-98

humiliation to myself, as you cannot possibly imagine by looking at it, even after this letter, *how far* different it is from my drawing – Hughes, Boyce, Woolner, and Clayton, who saw it before the cutting would tell you this. I would enclose the proof now, but really don't like to, before you've been prepared for the horror of it.

[. . .]

81

'BOOK ILLUSTRATION'

Art Journal, October 1902, pp. 315–316

A FRIENDLY DISPUTE BETWEEN EDWARD F. BREWTNALL, R.W.S., AND LEWIS F. DAY.

L. F. D. – WHY presume to illustrate the story which an author has put into words?

E. F. B. – Why not help a lame dog over the stile if you can?

L. F. D. – If there is a lame dog in the case it is possibly not the author. But it is no question of lame dogs but of competent writers quite capable of running alone.

E. F. B. – The competent writer is, of course, quite capable of running alone, as you say; but it has been discovered that, as a rule, he runs in double harness just as well – sometimes even better.

L. F. D. – In double harness they would run together. In illustration the artist comes after the author. Fair collaboration is another story.

E. F. B. – Then I will say tandem – in which case the artist is in the shafts. How do you like that?

L. F. D. – You are playing with the question. An author says his say. If he says it adequately, the artist's commentary on it is superfluous.

E. F. B. – I should say, on the contrary, that most fiction and much poetry distinctly gain by being adequately illustrated.

L. F. D. – Alas, poor Fiction! Do you really mean to say you would rather read your favourite novel in an illustrated edition?

E. F. B. – Yes, if I might choose the illustrator.

L. F. D. – But we do not choose the illustrators of our books, and so your answer is tantamount to *no*.

E. F. B. – To "No"? Oh, no, no! I pray you, do not take me too literally. It is but my way of saying that I want the chooser of the illustrator to choose properly. "Your *favourite* novel" implies choice on my part. My favourite novel is, in my opinion, one of the best. I desire that the illustrations shall be of the best also, or I would none of them.

L. F. D. – I take it we are discussing current book illustration, not the best illustration of the best book – which is a rare exception.

DOI: 10.4324/9781315400266-99

E. F. B. – I seem to remember that we began by discussing the presumption of the illustrator – but no matter! I should say the person who really ought to settle this question is the Reader (with a capital R, to whom prefaces are generally addressed). And the Reader, in his thousands, seems to say that he is distinctly anxious for illustrations. If he were not, if he were even indifferent about them, the publishers would no longer supply them on every hand in the way they do now.

L. F. D. – Quite right: it is the presumption of the illustrator we are discussing. I will not deny that a great artist may, by exception, justify the illustration of a perfect story, nor yet pretend that in the case of a bad one the presumption is very great. All I say is that from my point of view illustrations are commonly superfluous if not a positive annoyance. But then my standpoint is not that of the publisher; and I do not admit that whatever pays is right.

E. F. B. – But whatever pays is not necessarily wrong. It is all a question of the honesty and wholesomeness of the demand. It is no more commercially immoral to supply illustrations than to supply stories, or Academy pictures, or tin-tacks, or wall-paper, or sausages, or glue. If you will pardon my being serious for a moment, I think the almost universal demand for illustration (I am, of course, one of the demanders) is perfectly sane and wholesome, and an adequate reason for its existence. It sounds a commonplace one, but if examined, will, I think, be found quite satisfactory.

L. F. D. – Why wander into the ethics of trade? The demand is commercially cause enough for production. Artistically it has nothing to do with it.

E. F. B. – I am wondering whether, after all, it would not save trouble to condense this discussion in what I may call the "Soap Advertisement" manner, as thus – "Good morning! Do you dislike illustrations?" "No, I don't. Good evening!"

L. F. D. – First you try and hide behind trade, and now you escape under a lather of soap!

E. F. B. – The reason why I, and most of the rest of the world, like our stories illustrated, is that we have little or no imagination; and that "things seen are mightier than things heard" – or read. The small minority that likes its stories "plain," does so either because it finds all pictorial work rather a bore, or, more often, because it is *highly* imaginative and requires no pictorial assistance. It would be manifestly unfair that the more gifted should have things arranged entirely for them; and this is the reason why the true umpire in this matter is The Reader.

L. F. D. – To purchase an illustrated book does not prove any preference for illustrations. I have had to buy books with pictures in them which I promptly tore out. I doubt the longing of the cultivated reader for cuts, a large part of which do not really illustrate, but are mere artistic trimmings to the book, of no real assistance to the reader.

E. F. B. – Would "Alice in Wonderland" have had so robust a life, think you, without Tenniel's White Rabbit and Mock Turtle? Do not Walker's illustrations accentuate the charm of Miss Thackeray's stories? Do not Houghton's magnificent drawings realise for every one of us the very atmosphere of the Arabian Nights? Can the most imaginative conjure up a better Sir Galahad than the one that Rossetti has given us, or decline to accept as absolutely satisfactory Holman Hunt's Lady of Shalott? Could anything be more touchingly in harmony with the text than Millais' Edward Grey? I know a boy that found Gilbert's illustrations to Shakespeare a revelation. He hung over the drawings – he devoured them – he loved them – he copied them. And they led him to read Shakespeare.

L. F. D. – I grant you the possibility of picturing some one scene in a book (that is not what is understood by book illustration), and, by exception, of really throwing light upon the author's words. I cannot in a breath discuss all your instances of illustration; but you mention Shakespeare – what have his illustrators done for him? I admire John Gilbert's work as much as any one; but he translated Shakespeare into Gilbert. I prefer my poet untranslated.

E. F. B. – I am not careful to maintain that Shakespeare should be illustrated. Probably he should not, any more than he should be acted (see Charles Lamb). Of course he is not fiction at all in the ordinary sense – nor even ordinary drama. With regard to Gilbert's illustrations to his plays, I spoke, with deliberate intent, of their effect upon a *boy*. Before Alice reached Wonderland she peeped into her sister's book, but it had no pictures or conversations in it. "What is the use of a book," thought Alice, "without pictures or conversations?" A wise young person Alice.

L. F. D. – Now you are sheltering yourself behind the child. I believe you don't want your stories illustrated any more than I do; but, having been guilty of illustration, you can't quite say so.

E. F. B. – I will put my name to any form of words that will make you realise that I *prefer* an illustrated edition; and that (competent) illustrations greatly enhance my pleasure in a book. You do not like illustrations. You are hopelessly in the minority. The great majority of people, cultivated or uncultivated (and I don't know which section is the better judge) do like them. To my mind that settles the matter. You say the demand for them is commercial. You have just as much right to say that Tennyson's and Browning's poetry owed its existence to a commercial demand.

L. F. D. – I only said that you justify illustrations on the ground of the demand for them – which no more argues their artistic nature than does the liking of the great majority. I grant great work must appeal to the many; but their liking does not prove great work, which only the few ever appreciate at its worth. On the main question we must agree to differ; but I will take up your qualifying parenthesis, and say that "competent" illustration is so rare that it hardly counts.

E. F. B. – I should say that competent anything is pretty rare. But I do not think you disposed of the instances I gave you. I will add to them Phiz's illustrations to Dickens, which I think are about as good as they could be.

L. F. D. – I give you Phiz, and some of your other instances, especially Tenniel's illustrations to Alice. I will even go so far as to say that children's books are perhaps better illustrated. In any case, I do not mean to say that a book cannot be helped by illustration, if the artist is wholly in sympathy with the author, or may not be bettered by it, if he is the greater artist of the two; but I maintain that illustration, as it is done by professional illustrators, is, with rare exceptions, superfluous or worse.

E. F. B. – I think we are a good deal in agreement; but I would point out that Phiz, Tenniel, and the rest, were "professional illustrators." Probably there are many superfluous drawings; but are there not also many superfluous stories? I fancy that, as a rule, these are as well illustrated as they deserve to be. A dull and lifeless story has a very paralyzing effect upon the illustrator.

L. F. D. – Tenniel is more an illustrator of events than of books – more a symbolist than an illustrator. However, it is not a question of drawings good enough for the book, or of books good enough for the drawings, but of the need of illustration generally, or the help of it, which I do not think you have shown.

E. F. B. – In the case of stories of bygone times, the illustrator realises for the reader the costume and the surroundings, which most readers would be incapable of realising for themselves. In a modern story the sympathetic illustrator (and I will have none other) realises the characters and the action. The reader has the pleasure of having his conceptions corroborated and defined more clearly for him, and of saying, "Ah! of course it was like that." This in addition to the pleasure the drawing gives as drawing.

L. F. D. – It comes then to the sympathetic illustrator, who occurs only by exception – the rule being that the draughtsman selects two or three characters in a story and does the best he can with them in the time and for the money given. Mind, I don't blame him; the conditions are not in favour of sympathetic co-operation; but the story gains nothing by his mere drawings, however good they may be.

E. F. B. – What little fiction I read is of the best, and is well illustrated. If there are such cases as you speak of, doubtless the writers of the stories have also to "do the best they can in the time and for the money." I do not wonder that you occasionally tire of the inferior mixture.

L. F. D. – What little fiction I read is of various degrees of excellence; but the illustrations to it are seldom of the best, or so much as adequate. Sometimes they don't merely "tire" me, as you say, but exasperate me so that I have to tear them out of the book before I can read it – and this even in the case of writers admittedly the best.

E. F. B. – You really seem very unfortunate. We clearly see the matter with different eyes, but I think I am the person to be congratulated, as what is a source of irritation to you usually brings an added pleasure to me.

L. F. D. – Unfortunate? Yes, and the pest is spreading to my newspaper – of which also I wish you joy!

82

JOSEPH PENNELL, *MODERN ILLUSTRATION*

(London: George Bell & Sons, 1895), pp. xvii–xxi [selections]

[. . .]

There is another most serious, really insurmountable difficulty, for me or anyone else who attempts to write of modern illustration: no illustrations are catalogued to any extent; only the most important illustrators find a place in either the catalogues of South Kensington Art Library or the British Museum; therefore a few years, even a few weeks, after an illustrated book is published, if it has already passed through several editions, it may require hours to find the edition one wants. And as for a special illustration, that necessitates almost always turning over thousands of pages – unless one knows exactly where to find it. I know of but one magazine – "Once a Week" – in the bound volumes of which the artist's work is properly indexed, and even here the engraver's name is omitted.[1] In Harper's most excellently conducted magazine, for some unknown reason artists and engravers are ignored in the index. Even "The Century" leaves much to be desired in this way. Again, it is almost impossible to obtain the date or the name of the work in which many an important illustration first appeared. Illustrations are used over and over again, this has always been done; even a publisher at times cannot help one: for this reason it is very difficult to tell when one is consulting a first edition of an illustrated book. Sometimes I fancy this carelessness is not altogether unassociated with the author's or publisher's desire to palm off old blocks as new. It is by no means uncommon to omit the name of the artist altogether from the work he has illustrated; rarely indeed is it that the engraver's name is given; sometimes no mention that the work is illustrated is even made on the title page, or only that it contains so many illustrations; usually if an attempt is made to describe the method by which the designs have been reproduced, it is wrong; in rare cases, I am glad to say, this is intentional – photogravures being called etchings, for example – but it is mainly the result of sheer ignorance on the part of publisher, author, or at times, the illustrator.

Hence there are two matters to which I should like to call attention; that all library catalogues give the name of artist and engraver whenever these are printed in the book being catalogued; naturally in a work like this or a magazine, such

DOI: 10.4324/9781315400266-100

a course would be impossible, but at least the number of illustrations might be given. The name of the illustrator should always appear on the title page when possible; if his work is worth printing he should have a decent amount of attention drawn to it. This matter is not so difficult, nor would it entail in new catalogues so much work as librarians might think, for I may say in the British Museum and South Kensington I find that Menzel's work is so catalogued already.

Secondly, that bibliographers everywhere should turn their attention more to modern illustrated works, even if from the bibliographer of the future it removed much of that pleasant uncertainty which enhances, for some, the work of to-day. There is scarce an illustrated book of the fifteenth or sixteenth century, in which we are absolutely sure of the artist and engraver; but the bibliographers of the future will have a far bigger puzzle to solve, unless we pay some attention to the work of to-day, when they come to catalogue and describe the books of this century.

Most illustrators, it is true, now sign their drawings, but I should not care to attempt a catalogue of my own work.

I have no doubt that I have omitted to mention some really important books, but they have been omitted because I have never seen them; with no good catalogue, no guide, many of the artists dead, and the books dead too, how is one to find them? I have done what I could to make a start; I only hope some one will carry it on; certainly I am sure some of my sincere flatterers will imitate me, as they always do.

But to-day the output of illustration is overwhelming; to study the subject properly one must see all the books, magazines, and papers published all over the world. No one man has a chance to do this, and, if he had, the mere looking at such a mass of material would take up all his time. Yet one must get some idea of what is being done, for in the most unexpected places the best work often appears; originality is barred in many, so-called, high-class journals, and has to struggle, in the cheapest publications, with the printing-press, ink, and paper.

Note

1 The "Pall Mall Magazine" has just commenced to index artists and engravers completely.

83

HENRY BLACKBURN, 'THE ART OF BOOK AND NEWSPAPER ILLUSTRATION', LECTURE 3 (DEC 11 1893)

Journal of the Society of Arts, Vol. 11, January 12 1894, pp. 121–123

By Henry Blackburn

Lecture III. – Delivered December **11, 1893**

The Author

His part in the illustration of books – His handwriting – – The decorative page – Examples of illustration: archaic, decorative, topical – The Book of the Past – The Book of the Future.

We come now to the consideration of a class of illustrations in which the artist of the future will have to come more into personal contact with the author than he has been in the habit of doing, and wheret he distinction I referred to in the first lecture between illustrations which are to be (1) records of facts and (2) works of art should be more clearly drawn.

Here we ask for the active co-operation of the author. The far-reaching spread of education – especially technical art education – is tending to bring together, as they were never brought before in this century, the author and the illustrator. The author of a book will give more attention to the appearance of his pages, to the decorative character of type and ornament; whilst the average artist will be better educated from a literary point of view, and, to use a French word for which there is no equivalent, more *en rapport* with the author. By means of the cheap processes for reproducing any lines to print with the letterpress in the pages of a book, the author will have the opportunity of explaining himself, by his own notes, diagrams, &c., on the page which he never had before. This is illustration in the true sense of the word.

How false and imaginative many of the pretty illustrations in books, especially books of travel were, before the days of photography, every one knows. How easy

DOI: 10.4324/9781315400266-101

it is to go astray in an illustration, without direct communication with the author of a book, is also well known.

To show how easily the cleverest artists may go astray without the aid of the author, I exemplified the other day, where the verbal description of a scene was read out carefully several times before a company of artists, whilst three were selected to draw upon blackboards (simultaneously and without seeing each other's work) the principal lines of composition as presented to their minds. Each was, in a sense, a work of art; each differed widely from the other, and all were wrong! The exhibition was highly stimulating and interesting, but the immediate object was to show how useless and absurd many illustrations are in books, *as illustrations*. If they are works of art they may be accepted as worthy decorations of a book; but, in the face of what photography is doing now, there is less and less demand for the imaginative landscape compositions which graced so many books of travel twenty years ago. As to purely imaginative illustrations, in which the mind in them plays the most important part, there is happily plenty of scope for the educated illustrator of to-day. But first as to –

The Author

Considering the small amount of interest which the author – whether historian, poet, essayist, man of science, or discoverer – seems to take in the production of his book, and the personal interest with which he might endow it, let me draw a picture of the average author of to-day – or yesterday; the "man of letters," the student, who lives apart from the whirl of journalism and hand-to-mouth literature. The picture may be a little fanciful, but it is intended to be suggestive, not only to the author, but to all who are engaged in the production of books, whether "olde style," or otherwise.

If there be one characteristic which should enhance the interest attaching to the expression of a writer's thoughts, it should be that his individuality, or personality so to speak, should be in some way expressed on the printed page. Chaucer, Shakespeare, Milton, Scott, Byron, Dr. Johnson, and the men of letters of the past, are, each of them, deeply interesting to us in their personality, in their costume, in their handwriting, and in whatever they have left behind them as the work of their own hands. As matters stand at present, the the high pressure of work imposed upon anyone who has something to say, is turning the picturesque figure of the "author" (as we read of him in past times) into a more or less highly-strung, preoccupied, steam-driven "literary machine."

Looking backward to the Victorian age (say from the end of the twentieth century), what pictures will be formed in the minds of those who come after us, of the *entourage* of the man of letters of to-day? Clothed in a degrading, characterless costume, which takes all appearance of manliness and suppleness from his figure, living in houses and in cities in which nearly everything ornate or beautiful has been stolen, borrowed, or copied from another country or period, he is found engaged in the production of books in which, as far as the mechanical parts are concerned, nearly everything is a sham.

The nineteenth century author's love for the literature of his past has led him to imitate not only the style, but the outward aspect of old books; and, by a series of frauds (to which his publisher seems to have lent himself only too readily), to produce something which appears to be what it is not.

The genuine outcome of mediæval thought and style – of patience and leisure – is treated at the end of the nineteenth century as a fashion to be imitated in books, such as are to be seen under glass cases in the British Museum. The twentieth century reader, looking back, will see few traces worth preserving, either of originality or of individuality.

The typefounder of to-day takes down a Venetian writing master's copy-book of the sixteenth century [which I will show presently on the screen] and, imitating exactly the thick downward strokes of the reed pen, forms a set of moveable type, called in printer's language "old face," a style of letter much in vogue in 1893; but the style and character of which belongs altogether to the past. Thus, with such aids, the man of letters of to-day – living in a whirl of movement and discovery – clothes himself in the handwriting of the Venetian scholar as deliberately as the Norwegian disguises himself in a bear skin.

The next step is to present in his book a series of so-called "engravings," which are not engravings. The advance of science in producing blocks, from photographs of steel and other intaglio plates, for the type printing press, at a small cost per square inch, is not only taking from the artistic value of the modern *édition de luxe,* but also from its personal interest and genuineness.

The next step is to manufacture rough edged, coarse-textured paper, purporting to be carefully "hand-made." The rough edge, which was a necessity when every sheet of paper was finished by hand labour, is now imitated successfully by machinery, and is handled lovingly by the book-worm of to-day, regardless of the fact that these roughened sheets can be bought by the pound in Drurylane. The worst, and last fraud (I can call it no less) that can be referred to now is, that the clothing – the "skin of vellum" – that appropriately encloses our modern *édition de luxe* is made from pulp, rags, and other *débris*. That the gold illuminations on the cover are no longer real gold, and that the handsomely bound book, with its fair margins, cracks in half with a "bang," when first opened, are other matters connected with the discoveries of science, and the substitution of machinery for hand labour, which we owe to modern enterprise and invention.

[. . .]

84

P. G. HAMERTON, 'BOOK ILLUSTRATION'

The Portfolio: an artistic periodical, Jan 1888, pp. 17–21

THE following study has been cast into the form of dialogue for the reader's convenience. The subject is one that has to be considered from different points of view, and it is tiresome to be continually told that from another point of view it has another aspect. In dialogue this transition is effected frequently and instantaneously by simply changing the speaker. In the present instance the too frequent practice of introducing a speaker who utters opinions only that they may be controverted is avoided by limiting the argument to the strong points on every side. In order that there may be no ambiguity about my own opinions, and that I may not seem to avoid responsibility by getting behind different *dramatis personæ,* I may say that the art-critic is the writer purely and simply, whereas the other personages express opinions which the writer puts forward, not necessarily as his own, but as well deserving to be taken into consideration. The scientist (I dislike the word, but it is convenient and not less legitimate than 'artist'[1]) expresses what I have heard said by scientific men in real life; the artist is of the picturesque order and opposed to scientific views. The poet represents imaginative literature generally, and has that want of sympathy with the graphic arts which so often accompanies a purely literary culture, whilst he is positively hostile to science, – a natural antipathy that Professor Bain will admit to be consistent. The critic is in some degree a reconciler, not by desiring the others to abandon any position that they have a right to hold, but by inducing them to consider the interests of others.

Conversation I

The Rivalry between Art and Literature

POET (*opening a volume on the table, and shutting it at once contemptuously*). Another illustrated edition of a popular poet! I wonder he tolerates these things.

ARTIST. Perhaps he feels rather flattered. At any rate, an illustrated edition is a confirmation of his fame. Publishers do not select unknown men for illustration.

POET. That is one of the numerous advantages of obscurity.

DOI: 10.4324/9781315400266-102

CRITIC. When you are dead you will probably be illustrated also, and appear amongst the Christmas books with some astonishingly showy binding. Add to this the gilt edges, the toned paper, the faultless typography, and the 'exquisite illustrations by the first artists of the day,' as the advertisements have it.

POET (*with a look of anguish*). Say no more, I pray you, those dreadful words have already added a new bitterness to death! And to think that a dead poet is powerless to prevent this, and that if his works live it is almost certain to happen!

CRITIC. Almost? Why not say *perfectly* certain? It is as certain as anything can be in this world, that when your copyrights have expired there will be illustrated editions of your poems. Then will the arts of the draughtsman and the photographic reproducer be married to immortal verse!

POET. There ought to be a law to preclude the possibility of that.

ARTIST. May it not occasionally happen that the illustrator perpetuates a poetical reputation that would perish without his help? There is the well-known case of Rogers, who purchased immortality with a definite sum of money, by going to Turner and the wonderful vignette engravers of that day; just as you may buy a kind of temporary fame by paying for advertisements in the papers.

POET. A most undesirable and unnatural kind of existence after death. It is like paying for being embalmed. Rogers' poems are really dead, yet instead of being permitted to pass into oblivion quietly, according to the kindly natural law, there they are, existing still like mummies! A poet needs no help from illustration. If his works have not vitality enough to do without it, they gain no advantage from the kind of factitious immortality that illustration may confer.

CRITIC. I may, perhaps, be able to suggest a case in which illustration would do a real service to a poet's memory. Suppose the case of a poet who had genius deserving durable fame, yet who might be overlooked and forgotten by a mere change of fashion. He has, however, the good luck to be illustrated by an artist who remains in fashion during a generation indifferent to the poet. This would carry the poet through a time that would otherwise be fatal to him, and afterwards he might be really appreciated for himself.

POET. The illustrator, in that case, would be a sort of camel carrying the poet across a stretch of desert, a sort of *nefood* that would be death to him if he were alone. The worst of it would be the difficulty of getting rid of the camel afterwards. It is an inversion of the fabled 'Old Man of the Sea.' In that story the difficulty was to get rid of the rider.

ARTIST. Nothing can exceed your ingratitude to the Fine Arts. You seem to look upon them not merely with indifference, but with antipathy.

POET. I can attain to indifference when the Fine Arts keep to their proper place, and illustrate subjects of their own; I mean subjects that the artist finds for himself in nature, and especially on condition that the illustrations be kept out of the books and exhibited separately as pictures are at the Royal Academy, or like etchings that are published by themselves. What I dislike is to see the text of a poet encumbered by illustrations.

ARTIST. We have here, as it seems to me, a case of jealousy. The Poet is jealous of the illustrator, and of the attention that the illustrator attracts to himself.

CRITIC. There may be a reasonable jealousy. In this case I think the poet may reasonably be jealous, as the illustrator, under pretext of doing honour to the poet, really gets upon his shoulders and attracts most of the public attention to himself.

POET. We can do without illustrators as ships can do without barnacles. The old poets did without them for ages.

SCIENTIST. The best way to elucidate this question would be to take some particular instance. May I suggest Doré's illustrations to Dante as a case in point?

CRITIC. Certainly, one of the best instances you could have selected. We have only to examine that single case to get to the bottom of the whole subject.

POET. As for me, the mere juxtaposition of the two names leaves me no patience for argument. Doré and Dante! The names by themselves are enough. The preposterous Frenchman stands for grotesquely impudent pretension; the illustrious Italian represents all that is most august in the grandeur of the human mind.

CRITIC. I have nothing to say against your high estimate of Dante, but you are harder on Doré than you would have been if he had only illustrated authors you cared for less. Your objection to Doré as an illustrator of Dante would, in fact, apply to all illustrators that are inferior to so great a poet; and what illustrator is not?

POET. Well, I could be content to regard Doré with simple indifference if he had not used Dante as a convenience to attract attention to himself. It is a terrible example of the rivalry between the illustrator and the poet. Nobody ever thinks of *reading* Dante in the huge, unwieldy edition with Doré's illustrations. The mere size of the page and weight of the paper are insuperable obstacles to quiet reading. All that people do with these editions is to turn over the leaves and examine the cuts. My contention is that the artist, under the utterly false pretext of glorifying the poet, does, in reality, 'exploit' him in the sense of the French verb *exploiter*. He makes use of him for his own perfectly selfish purposes. My view is that an artist like Doré, with his coarse interpretations of the poets, is an active evil in literature. He makes use of the poets simply as a matter of business to sell his illustrations better. It is a nefarious pact between artist and publishers. They plot together to get up a trade: they trade on illustrious names.

SCIENTIST. Is it not possible that the artist may help to keep alive the reputation of the poet?

POET. I hope you do not mean to imply that Dante stands in need of Monsieur Gustave Doré's good offices.

SCIENTIST. The readers of Dante are not very numerous, except in Italy. There every educated man has read the 'Divina Commedia,' and many women, too, like the Countess Guiccioli, are Dantean scholars; but in France and England, the countries Doré worked for, how many know the Italian poet at first hand?'

CRITIC. I have known about half-a-dozen Dante scholars in England.

SCIENTIST. And how many in France?

CRITIC. One.

SCIENTIST. My experience has been much the same. Now, I venture to remark that Doré has made the principal scenes in the 'Inferno' known to thousands in both countries, and this may have induced many to read at least a translation, or enough of it to understand the pictures. Doré has acted in a manner analogous to that of a professor or commentator who draws attention to a great poet; but he has been a hundred times more efficacious because a hundred times more attractive than a prose commentator could ever be. I confess, for my part, that many of the scenes in the 'Inferno' have been fixed in my memory more permanently by the illustrations. The tortures in the drawings are at any rate horrible enough. I don't profess to be a judge of art, but when I see several men with their heads fixed in a frozen lake, and still living, I feel cold and uncomfortable.

POET. Well, for my part I would rather my writings were totally forgotten than kept before the public by the speculations of an illustrator. The mere material aspect of illustrated books is too much for me. I hate their superfine paper, their excessive margins, their obtrusively big and fine typography, their showy bindings. My notion of suitable publishing is that which consults the convenience of the reader without attracting any attention to itself; consequently, the volume should be easily held in the hand, the print legible, the paper thick enough to hide what is on the other side of the leaf, but not thick enough to be heavy, and the binding simple, smooth, and light. I like Morris's 'Earthly Paradise' as a material book. It has all these qualities, and the great negative one of being without illustrations.

ARTIST. We might, perhaps, find a ground to agree upon. Illustration is sometimes quite subordinate, and when it is so even you might possibly tolerate it. For instance, in Hood's 'Whims and Oddities,' the little pen-sketch woodcuts are of quite secondary importance, and do not interfere with the literature in the least. On the other hand, when illustrations become big and important, why not publish them separately from the text in albums? When this is done, the reader may enjoy his poet in a handy edition, and refer to the illustrations when he chooses.

CRITIC. The publishers do not take to the last system you propose. In fact, it would embrace two different branches of trade, – book-selling proper for the readable volume, and print-selling for the album. There cannot be a doubt that the question of rivalry between literature and art really exists, though few of us feel so acutely on the subject as our friend the Poet. I remember the case of a young writer of verse who had a certain modest degree of accomplishment as an artist, so he published a book of poems with his own illustrations. The consequence was that without at all intending it, he set up a conflict between the two. He told me that the reviewers invariably compared the poet with the artist, and generally sacrificed one to the other. One reviewer would sacrifice the poet, another the illustrator. His own intention had been to make the illustrator auxiliary but subordinate.

SCIENTIST. The conflict you speak of cannot be avoided. It is in the nature of things. But what strikes me as remarkable is that when literature and art are put together it is generally literature that suffers. People do not read splendidly illustrated editions, and the fewer and more insignificant the illustrations the better is an author's chance of being read. Why should pictorial art have this advantage over literature?

CRITIC. The reason is simply because an engraving can be understood at a glance, whereas to read a page requires a little effort, and also a little time. In some cases a sustained intellectual effort would be necessary. We have talked about Dante and Doré. Nobody, however intelligent, can read Dante without close mental application, but any one can glance at the woodcuts. Therefore the woodcuts receive at once the slight degree of attention that they claim, and the poet, as we see, is neglected.

SCIENTIST. This accounts for the great prevalence and great success of illustrated books in the present day. People take a certain faint interest in a number of subjects, and engravings supply their demand for knowledge.

ARTIST. You might add that there is really a much stronger appreciation of the fine arts than there used to be, so that engravings or reproduced drawings have an interest for the present generation which they could not have for a generation ignorant of art.

POET. Then there is the stronger reason for jealousy on the side of literature, for if illustrations are appreciated for high artistic reasons they are the more dangerous as rivals, and we who write have the stronger reasons for keeping them out. I say nothing against pictorial art in its own domains, that is, on the walls of an exhibition or in a portfolio of prints, but I want to keep it out of ours.

ARTIST. No one knows better than an artist the great importance of avoiding conflict in any appeal to attention. No real artist would tolerate an ornamental engraved border round a print of any artistic merit. Even the ordinary engraved letters under a print are an injury to it, and are avoided in the early proofs as much from artistic reasons as any other. When lettering is given it is always purposely made as light and thin as possible so as not to catch the eye. Only imagine the effect of heavy lettering under a delicate print!

SCIENTIST. We have said nothing yet about colour. We have talked about the attractiveness of engravings, but even these lose their power of catching attention when works in colour are to be seen. In exhibitions the rooms set apart for black and white art are invariably empty when galleries of coloured pictures are close by; and these, notwithstanding their vastly greater extent, are often crowded. We may therefore suppose that the recent introduction of coloured illustrations, printed with sufficient delicacy and taste to make them admissible in works of a high character, must be an additional blow to literature.

POET. There can be no doubt that the work of the old illuminators was anti-literary. Can you imagine any one really praying from an illuminated missal with elaborate borders and miniatures? Such things could only distract attention, unless the ornaments had become so familiar that they were entirely forgotten, as we forget the designs in the coloured glass of a church that we go to every Sunday.

SCIENTIST. Your feeling on this subject might be described as a kind of literary asceticism, the rejection of the luxury of the eyes for the higher needs of the intellect.

POET. 'Asceticism' is, perhaps, hardly the proper term, as I am grateful for every luxury that is a help to reading. I like good print, good paper, a volume that can be held pleasantly, an easy chair, and a well-shaded lamp. These are delightful luxuries. But I don't want superfluities that seem to me inimical to reading any more than, on going out for a walk, I should care to be encumbered with the Lord Mayor's state robes. In placing the *perfect* convenience of the reader above every other consideration, I speak not only as an author but as a reader too. The bibliophile may think differently. My reasons fall to the ground when books are purchased merely to be looked at and very carefully handled.

SCIENTIST. You are wonderfully rational, for a poet. The voice of Reason herself seems to issue from your lips.

ARTIST. All artists are rational when the interests of their own art are concerned, because they understand them. Our friend is like a painter, who wants a good frame and a good light, but would rather not have the attention of his visitors distracted by anything remarkable in surrounding colour or architecture.

SCIENTIST. Or you might say that he resembles a musician, who likes a room with good acoustic properties and hates conversation, however intelligent, that goes on during a musical performance. This kind of jealousy is most reasonable. Let us have talk or music, one or the other; we cannot attend to both at the same time.

POET. Nor to poetry and illustrations.

ARTIST. You mentioned a case in which a poet was his own illustrator. When that is so there can be no occasion for jealousy, as the attention of the public could only be diverted from himself to himself. We admit that you might be reasonably jealous of me if I illustrated your books, but if *you* were to illustrate them would you be jealous of yourself?

POET. I should do as Rossetti did. I should keep the two talents separate. Have you not noticed how careful Rossetti was to publish his poems without illustrations? All he did in the way of graphic art was to decorate the back of his volumes and design the paper lining with a sort of unmeaning pattern.

SCIENTIST. But might it not be very advantageous in various ways that an author should illustrate his own works if he could draw well enough?

CRITIC. That is one of those suggestions which always seem excellent at first. I remember hearing a very distinguished author say that it was most desirable, but there is a fallacious idea underlying every fancy of this kind. The fallacy lies in the supposition that the artist's talent would answer in every respect to the author's, because the two were united in the same man. It would do nothing of the kind. All examples show the extreme narrowness of gift and accomplishment in the graphic arts. I presume, to begin with, that you would not desire the illustrations to be bad, as art. Very well, if you admit that, you must accept the narrow range of all successful work, and a probable want of connection between the graphic and the literary performance.

ARTIST. In most cases the author who illustrated his own works would not be, as Rossetti was, an artist. He would only be an amateur like Thackeray, and therefore unable to draw. Amateurs are *never* able to draw in our sense of the word.

CRITIC. Thackeray's illustrations have a great interest, but it is only psychological. His books, with all their satire, are kindlier in their views of human nature than his drawings. The people in the drawings are generally disagreeable, besides being defectively drawn. They have a habit of looking mean, or else of wearing a peculiarly vapid expression. No one would infer from Thackeray's drawings that he possessed a powerful intellect, still less that his nature was really and deeply sympathetic. A critic who judged Thackeray from his drawings only might possibly not under-estimate the works of art, but he would be sure to under-estimate the artist.

POET. In another way the same may be said of Thomas Hood and his rude little pen-sketches. They are always comic, whereas his genius as a poet was serious and sometimes profound. Hood's sketches are the playful exercise of a small part of his mind. For one thing they have no delicacy, yet there was much delicacy, as well as tenderness, in his work as a writer.

ARTIST. That is true, and still I like Hood's sketches far better than those of most amateurs; they are unpretending, and quite sound and straightforward in method. He used a simple kind of art, which is better than attempting something beyond his power.

CRITIC. There are two other instances of authors whose drawings may be compared with their literary work – Mr. Ruskin and Victor Hugo.

ARTIST. Ruskin is not an artist; he draws like an amateur.

CRITIC. I knew you would say that; but you are rather unjust. Mr. Ruskin does not draw as an artist could because he has not the same purposes. An artist's object is simply to produce a good work of art – not to teach people anything about nature. Mr. Ruskin's drawings are observant and didactic; sometimes strictly scientific. At the same time it is not fair to speak of him as an amateur, because that word may be taken to mean a feeble imitator of the style of artists without their knowledge, and that Mr. Ruskin is not. He has no *style* as a draughtsman; yet his knowledge has always been sufficient for the clear statements of fact which are all that he has attempted to make. It would be just to call him a student – a student of nature.

POET. Still, the difference between Ruskin as a writer and as a draughtsman is very striking. He is a powerful writer, fond of strong effects and able to produce them; in short, he seems to be gifted with poetical power, but so far as I can see anything in drawings I should not say that his drawings display poetical power.

CRITIC. As Mr. Ruskin has himself said, the literary and artistic faculties cannot be both cultivated to the same extent. He is an artist when he writes, a student when he draws. In writing he unhesitatingly sacrifices accuracy to effect, and that is quite characteristic of an artist. In drawing he seems always anxious, above all things, to be accurate, and that is characteristic of the painstaking and conscientious student.

SCIENTIST. It must follow from what you say that the draughtsman, in Ruskin, only accompanies the writer half-way.

CRITIC. Exactly, or even less than that. The drawings express little of the artist's idiosyncrasy, which is the more remarkable that they are evidently sincere.

ARTIST. Anyhow they are not impudent like Victor Hugo's.

CRITIC. 'Impudent' is a strong word. Victor Hugo's drawings are violent; they express at the same time an energetic and a vain disposition, but there is in them no false pretension to artistic refinement. They are a savage utterance, partly made in fun, like the thumping on the piano of some vigorous but uncultivated amateur who has a rude notion of music, and who turns round and laughs at his own performance. There is a sort of grim humour and a real turn for the grotesque in Victor Hugo's drawings. They show one side of his mind.

SCIENTIST. We seem in each case to arrive at the same conclusion, namely, that when an author illustrates himself he will do it very partially.

CRITIC. Quite as partially and imperfectly as any other artist. There is no practical advantage in illustrating one's own works, beyond a certain convenience. A critic likes to see drawings by an author just as he likes to read writings by an artist, because they may gratify his curiosity by revealing another side of a mind that interests him, but that is all.

SCIENTIST. If a novelist illustrated his own novels we should at least get an idea of the outward appearance of the people that he imagined. We might see his creations as he saw them in his mind's eye. No other illustrator could give us that kind of authenticity.

CRITIC. The seeker for this kind of revelation in Thackeray's drawings would generally come away disappointed. He would feel that the character in the drawing was poorer and more vapid than the character in the text. Frederick Walker's illustrations to 'Philip' are more satisfactory, because more living than those which Thackeray began to make. It is difficult to believe that he would have given us a better Colonel Newcome than Doyle's. Yet Doyle, as a draughtsman, was not to be compared for one moment with such a consummate artist as Charles Keene, for example. Had Thackeray possessed the technical and artistic knowledge of Keene, he would have held in his hand an instrument as good as his pen, and we should have seen his characters as he conceived them. I cannot believe that Thackeray was able to realise his own conceptions in drawing, indeed, there is distinct evidence in one of his letters that he knew his own weakness as a draughtsman – at least in some degree. He thought that he had not the knack of giving lively touches. In reality the drawings were weak throughout, and no mere touches could have strengthened them.

POET. Then your conclusion is that authors do better not to illustrate their own works.

CRITIC. I think the rivalry we have been speaking of as existing between literature and art displays itself in a peculiar way when the author is his own illustrator, and it is more prudent to follow Rossetti's example than Thackeray's. This refers, however, chiefly to imaginative literature. When matters of fact are in question an author may give useful illustrations. Utility is worth considering, but it lies outside of the subject of our present conversation. We may talk about it another time.

P. G. HAMERTON.

Note

1 How inconvenient it would be to say 'man of art' every time we say 'artist!'

4.3

Engraving

DOI: 10.4324/9781315400266-103

4.3 Engraving

While copperplate etchings and engravings were commonly used to illustrate publications in the eighteenth century, the nineteenth century saw massive growth in the range of materials and techniques used to reproduce images.[1] Intaglio techniques, in which images are formed by the ink retained in grooves that have been carved into the printing surface, continued to be used and developed, while new relief techniques using wood, where the raised portion of the surface is inked and the rest cut away, grew in popularity. Thomas Bewick's *The History of British Birds* (1797) is the volume of choice for Charlotte Brontë's Jane Eyre, before she is interrupted by the infuriating and cruel John Reed, and it contains images produced using a new technique.[2] Bewick developed a relief process that increased the capacity for reproducing detailed drawings by using end-grain sections of hard boxwood and jewellers' tools. This removed the time-consuming business of hand inking the plates, which is necessary in intaglio methods, and allowed engraved woodblock and letterpress text to be printed together. As wood was cheaper than metal, Bewick's method, and its subsequent modifications, were a key driver of the expansion in image reproduction in the nineteenth century.[3] The first source in this section is from Bewick's memoir (written in 1829 but not published until 1862), in which he describes his own contribution to wood engraving.[4] Bewick discusses the deficiencies of pelt balls made of sheepskin used to cover the surface of the engraving with ink and reveals the thinking behind his abandonment of cross-hatching in favour of a more direct and unfussy style.

Henry Cole's 1838 essay discusses the relative merits of wood and copper engraving. He emphasises the advantage of wood engraving as a cost-effective method of reproduction, as the woodblock can be used for much longer than the metal plate. An advantage of this cheaper method is that it allows a wider audience access to prints. According to Cole, 'bringing copies of beautiful pictures to the cottages of poor men' will foster joy and increase the moral fortitude of the working man. He singles out the work of Charles Knight, editor of *The Penny Magazine*, an illustrated weekly aimed at the working class that contained numerous engravings.[5]

John Ruskin's *Ariadne Florentina* (1872) contains six lectures given by Ruskin on different engraving techniques. In the extract reproduced here, Ruskin muses on definitions of engraving and the relationship between different forms of engraving, and he looks forward to a time when wood engraving might be superseded by photography. For Ruskin, the evolution of wood engraving as an assembly line process was problematic; no longer was the line of the artwork directly under the control of an individual artist or engraver. Instead, it lay in the hands of the 'woodpeckers', workers employed to remove the wood from among the drawn lines.[6] The mezzotint, an intaglio process discussed by Ruskin in his piece, is the subject of a ghost story titled 'The Mezzotint' (1904), written by medieval scholar and antiquarian Montague Rhodes James. In the extract reproduced here, the protagonist, Mr Williams, is presented with 'an indifferent mezzotint, and an indifferent mezzotint is, perhaps, the worst form of engraving known'. This mediocre image, however, has peculiar powers that are revealed to the reader as the story unfolds.

Our next source is an image of a wood engraver at work engraved by the firm Dalziel Brothers.[7] Their engraving firm was hugely successful in the mid-nineteenth century, supplying a number of newspapers and periodicals (including *Punch*), as well as a wide range of artists. The source reproduced here is from *The Boy's Book of Industrial Information* by Elisha Noyce. Published in 1863, it contains 370 engravings produced by the Dalziels. The extract from the official catalogue of the fine art section of the 1862 International Exhibition (the next source) discusses the differences between engraving on wood, stone (lithography) and metal, while the full piece focuses on engraving metal, which it describes as the superior technique. Engraving was the fifth of five classes included in the British section of the exhibition (the others being architecture, painting, art designs for manufacture and sculpture).

The challenges of keeping up with new techniques is reflected in Charles Dickens' article 'Engraved on Steel', which satirises the process of steel engraving. Appearing in *All the Year Round* in October 1866, it charts the experience of Pickpeck, a 'stipple engraver' (a technique used in intaglio) who is flummoxed by the instruction to produce an engraving of a photographic portrait of Bunglebutt, author of a 22nd edition of 'Our empty coal sellers and What's to fill them'. Pickpeck is tasked with producing a portrait 'beautifully engraved upon steel in the highest style of art', 'as quick as "a flash of lightening"'. The article goes on to discuss the travails of the put-upon Pickpeck, providing a commentary on the labour involved in steel engraving, as well as summarising its processes in great detail.[8] The final source is from Charles Booth's monumental *Life and Labour of the People in London* (1889–1903), which surveyed the living and working conditions of the working class. In a section titled 'Art and Amusement', Booth discusses both wood and copperplate engraving and opines that, 'No other occupation has suffered more than engraving from the competition of new inventions and the change from ancient to modern methods'. He also examines the hours of work and earnings of engravers.

Notes

1 The term 'intaglio' refers to a number of techniques including etching (in which acid is used to make incisions into a, usually metal, plate), engraving (in which tools are used to mark the image on the plate), drypoint (similar to engraving, but the pieces of metal that are left when the line is cut are retained, forming a 'burr') and mezzotint (a 'dark to light' method in which the metal plate is roughened, and the image created by a process of burnishing the plate with metal tools. This creates smoother sections, which print lighter tones). For detailed descriptions of these techniques See Doyle, Grove and Sherman (eds.) *History of Illustration.*

2 Charlotte Bronte, *Jane Eyre* (London: Smith & Elder, 1847), p. 3.
3 For details of this process see Susan Doyle, Jaleen Grove and Whitney Sherman (eds.) *History of Illustration* (Fairchild Books, New York, 2018), p. 219.
4 There are various theories as to the reasons for this delay. See Frank Graham's introduction to the 1862 edition for more details, *A memoir of Thomas Bewick: written by himself*, (Newcastle, Frank Graham, 1974).
5 With this sentiment, Cole echoes Thomas Bewick whose 1828 memoir looks back to a time when cheap woodcuts were affordable to the rural poor. See Bewick, *Memoir*, p. 247.
6 See Ruskin, 'Appendix. Article 1. Notes on the Present State of Engraving in England', *Ariadne Florentina*, pp. 256–78.
7 See Bethan Stevens, 'Wood engraving as ghostwriting: the Dalziel Brothers, losing one's name, and other hazards of the trade', *Textual Practice* 33(4), 645–677.
8 For discussions of this article see Katherine Haskins, *The Art-Journal and Fine Art Publishing in Victorian England, 1850–1880* (London and New York, Routledge, 2017), p. 48. (First published Ashgate, 2012); Gordon Fyfe, *Art, Power and Modernity: English Art Institutions, 1750–1950* (London and New York: Leicester University Press, 2000), p. 113.

85

THOMAS BEWICK, *A MEMOIR OF THOMAS BEWICK, WRITTEN BY HIMSELF*

(London: Longman, Green, Longman and Roberts, 1862), pp. 237–341

HAVING already noticed my beginnings, or first efforts, in engraving on wood; and as at that time this department of the arts was at the very lowest ebb in this country, and, I believe, also in every other country in Europe, it may perhaps be of some use, or at least may excite some curiosity, to know the part I took in renewing, or bringing into use, this to me new art, as far as I was able, with the slender means in my hands, and the many difficulties I had to contend with and surmount, before anything like an approach towards perfection could be arrived at. I ought first distinctly to state that, at that time, it never entered into my head that it was a branch of art that would stand pre-eminent for utility, or that it could ever in the least compete with engraving on copper. I ought also to observe that no vain notions of my arriving at any eminence ever passed through my mind, and that the sole stimulant with me was the pleasure I derived from imitating natural objects (and I had no other patterns to go by), and the opportunity it afforded me of making and drawing my designs on the wood, as the only way I had in my power of giving vent to a strong propensity to gratify my feelings in this way. In process of time, however, as I began to improve, and seeing the practical use printers were making of wood cuts, the utility and importance of them began to be unfolded to my view; and the more I have since thought upon the subject, the more I am confirmed in the opinions I have entertained, that the use of wood cuts will know no end, or, so long as the importance of printing is duly appreciated and the liberty of the press held sacred.

The first difficulty I felt, as I proceeded, was in getting the cuts I had executed printed so as to look anything like my drawings on the blocks of wood, nor corresponding to the labour I had bestowed upon the cutting of the designs. At that time pressmen were utterly ignorant as to any proper effect that was to be produced; or even, if one of them possessed any notions of excellence beyond the common run of workmen, his materials for working were so defective that he could not execute even what he himself wished to accomplish. The common pelt balls then in use, so

DOI: 10.4324/9781315400266-104

daubed the cut, and blurred and overlapped its edges, that the impression looked disgusting. To remedy this defect, I was obliged carefully to shave down the edges round about; and this answered the end I had in view. The next difficulty was worse to surmount, and required a long time to get over it; and that was, to lower down the surface on all the parts I wished to appear pale, so as to give the appearance of the required distance; and this process will always continue to call forth and to exercise the judgment of every wood engraver, even after he knows what effect his *careful pressman* maybe enabled to produce, from this his manner of cutting. On this all artists must form their own ideas. I think no exact description can be laid down as a rule for others to go by: they will by practice have to find out this themselves. While I was patiently labouring and contending with difficulties which I could not overcome, I was shown some impressions from wood cuts done long ago, with cross-hatching, such as I thought I should never be able to execute. These were from wood cuts by Albert Durer, and perhaps some others of his day, in the collection of the Rev. John Brand, the Newcastle Historian; and from these I concluded that Albert Durer must have had some very easy way of loading his blocks with such an useless profusion of cross-hatching, or he would not have done them so, unless, indeed, he had found out some easy means of etching the wood (or perhaps metal plates), quite unknown to me; but, if otherwise, I then, in changing my opinion, could think of no other way than that he must have cut his blocks on the plank or side way of the wood, on which it would be more easy to pick out the interstices between the squares, or the lozenge-shaped lines, than as I (at that time) thought it possible to do on the end way of the wood. One of these plank blocks, said to have been drawn by Albert Durer, was shown to me by my kind friend George Allan, Esq., of the Grange, Darlington. The drawing, which was done with great accuracy, seemed to me to have been done by a crow-quill, with a kind of varnish ink, the strokes of which, from their regularity, looked as if they had been printed from a well-executed copper plate, and transferred to the block. After labouring for some time, endeavouring to produce the like effect on my blocks, on the end way of the wood, not indeed to my satisfaction, I felt mortified in not succeeding to my wish; and I then began to think the impressions must have been printed from two blocks. This, indeed, I soon found to be quite easy to do, as well as being beautifully correct; and any artist may see this in a few minutes, by cutting parallel lines on a piece of wood, and from it taking, by his hand, an impression on a piece of paper, and then again inking the same cut, and printing it in the same way, either directly in a cross or in an oblique direction, upon the first impression. This can also easily be done, from two cuts, at a printing press, and is much easier to do, and better than the labour necessarily bestowed upon one cross-hatched block. When I had accomplished this, and satisfied myself that the process was both simple and perfect, as to obtaining the object I so much wanted, my curiosity on this score ceased, and I then concluded that in this way the cross-hatching might be set aside as a thing of no use at all. The artists indeed of the present day have brought it to such a pitch of perfection that I do not know that it can be carried any further; and in this they have also been so marvellously aided by the improved methods now used in printing their cuts, that one would be led to conclude that this department has also attained to perfection; and, had this not been the case, the masterly execution of wood cuts, either by crossed lines, or otherwise, would have continued to be beheld with disgust or contempt. I have long been of opinion that the cross-hatching of wood cuts, for book work, is a waste of time; as every desired effect can be much easier obtained by plain parallel lines.

86

HENRY COLE, 'MODERN WOOD ENGRAVING'

London and Westminster Review, 31:2, August 1838, pp. 265–278 (pp. 268–269)

[. . .]

The great end of the whole art of engraving is to render the spirit and genius of a great artist accessible to the thousands, or the millions, by embodying them in cheap and portable forms. Wood engraving, professedly the cheapest and most portable of all the representations of great pictures, excels equally in fulfilling the highest mission of its art, by the superior accuracy and fidelity with which it represents the spirit and genius of the picture. In wood engraving the draughtsman makes black lines with a pen or pencil, which the engraver leaves untouched; thus the black lines are the original designs themselves put into a shape for printing.

Cheapness is the advantage of engravings over paintings, and one of the advantages of wood-cuts over copper-plates. A plate of metal is useless after a few thousand impressions have been taken from it, while a wood-block will yield sometimes two or three hundred thousand impressions: and thus the expenses – and it costs much less to produce a first rate wood-cut than it does to produce a first rate copper-plate – are divided among nearly a hundred times as many purchasers.

This circumstance, by bringing copies of beautiful pictures to the cottages of poor men, will help to lessen the rudeness which is not necessarily, but is too usually associated with poverty. There is a deep morality in the love of the beautiful. The Spartan blessing, "the Beautiful to the Good," had its fulfilment in itself, for beauty is only one of the qualities of goodness. The character or action which is right, is of necessity also beautiful, or noble, and he must be prepared to overlook everything great in the civilization of the ancient Greeks who does not see that great things may come of creating a love of art among all ranks, since all the inner life of that wonderful people was derived from their reverence of beauty, – their religion was the religion of the beautiful. Serene and harmonious objects, by the very emotions which those words express, make the soul into which they sink, like themselves by doing so; the beauty which the eye drinks re-appears in the affection which the heart feels; the moral qualities which the beautiful has in itself are brought out variously and sweetly in the lives of the lovers of it: the white

 DOI: 10.4324/9781315400266-105

light falls on the flowers and re-appears in iris hues. The mind which has fresh upon it the disgust excited by the affectations of those whose talk is of tone, of chiar'oscuro, of Claudes and of Guidos, may be disposed to think any approach to such talk a degradation of a bold peasantry, – and we sympathise in the thought, – but a single conception of what our peasants really are, a reminiscence of red-faced, bare-necked men in smock frocks, sitting at the ale-house door with their pipes and porter pots, will more than suffice to exhibit the improvement which would be evinced by them even in conceited criticisms on cross-hatchings and deep tones, stipplings and good taste. It ought, therefore, to be admitted that his fellow men owe no slight obligations to Mr Charles Knight for the great impulse he has given to wood engraving, for the adaptations he has made of it, and the moral good he has done by it to the poor of the whole civilized world; – thanks and praise be to the man who has multiplied and extended the pleasures of the beautiful where they were scarcely known before![1]

Note

1 So completely did the 'Penny Magazine' bring the art of engraving on wood into general notice, that a certain young lord is reported to have said, wood engraving was invented with the 'Penny Magazine.' The 'Pictorial Bible,' and the 'Pictorial History of England,' 'the Pictorial Prayer Book,' the new edition of the 'Arabian Nights,' with a close and excellent new translation, and illustrations so accurate, that the appropriate turbans for every hour of the day are given; and lastly, the new 'Pictorial Shakspeare,' just announced, continue the good work which the 'Penny Magazine' began, while casts of the engravings in the latter are now sent to every part of the civilized world.

87

JOHN RUSKIN, 'DEFINITION OF THE ART OF ENGRAVING'

Ariadne Florentina: six lectures on wood and metal engraving: given before the University of Oxford in Michaelmas term, 1872 (Orpington: George Allen, 1873), pp. 7–11 [selections]

Lecture I

Definition of the art of engraving

[. . . .]

9. First then, to-day, of the Differentia, or essential quality of Engraving, as distinguished from other arts.

What answer would you make to me, if I asked casually what engraving was? Perhaps the readiest which would occur to you would be, "The translation of pictures into black and white by means admitting reduplication of impressions." But if that be done by lithography, we do not call it engraving, – whereas we speak contentedly and continually of seal engraving, in which there is no question of black and white. And, as scholars, you know that this customary mode of speaking is quite accurate; and that engraving means, primarily, making a permanent cut or furrow in something. The central syllable of the word has become a sorrowful one, meaning the most permanent of furrows.

10. But are you prepared absolutely to accept this limitation with respect to engraving as a pictorial art? Will you call nothing an engraving, except a group of furrows or cavities cut in a hard substance? What shall we say of mezzotint engraving, for instance, in which, though indeed furrows and cavities are produced mechanically as a ground, the artist's work is in effacing them? And when we consider the power of engraving in representing pictures and multiplying them, are we to recognize and admire no effects of light and shade except those which are visibly produced by dots or furrows? I mean, will the virtue of an engraving be in exhibiting these imperfect means of its effect, or in concealing them?

11. Here, for instance, is the head of a soldier by Dürer, – a mere gridiron of black lines. Would this be better or worse engraving if it were more like a photograph or lithograph, and no lines seen? – suppose, more like the head of Mr.

DOI: 10.4324/9781315400266-106

Santley, now in all the music-shops, and really quite deceptive in light and shade, when seen from over the way? Do you think Dürer's work would be better if it were more like that? And would you have me, therefore, leaving the question of technical method of production altogether to the craftsman, consider pictorial engraving simply as the production of a light-and-shade drawing, by some method permitting its multiplication for the public?

12. This, you observe, is a very practical question indeed. For instance, the illustrations of my own lectures on sculpture are equivalent to permanent photographs. There can be little doubt that means will be discovered of thus producing perfect facsimiles of artists' drawings; so that, if no more than facsimile be required, the old art of cutting furrows in metal may be considered as, at this day, virtually ended. And, indeed, it is said that line engravers cannot any more get apprentices, and that a pure steel or copper plate is not likely to be again produced, when once the old living masters of the bright field shall have been all laid in their earth-furrows.

13. Suppose, then, that this come to pass; and more than this, suppose that wood engraving also be superseded, and that instead of imperfect transcripts of drawings, on wood-blocks or metal-plates, photography enabled us to give, quite cheaply, and without limit to number, facsimiles of the finished light-and-shade drawings of artists themselves. Another group of questions instantly offers itself, on these new conditions; namely, What are the best means for a light-and-shade drawing – the pen, or the pencil, the charcoal, or the flat wash? That is to say, the pen, producing shade by black lines, as old engraving did; the pencil, producing shade by gray lines, variable in force; the charcoal, producing a smoky shadow with no lines in it, or the washed tint, producing a transparent shadow with no lines in it. Which of these methods is the best? – or have they, each and all, virtues to be separately studied, and distinctively applied?

14. See how curiously the questions multiply on us. 1st, Is engraving to be only considered as cut work? 2d, For present designs multipliable without cutting, by the sunshine, what methods or instruments of drawing will be best? And now, 3dly, before we can discuss these questions at all, is there not another lying at the root of both, – namely, what a light-and-shade drawing itself properly *is*, and how it differs, or should differ, from a painting, whether by mere deficiency, or by some entirely distinct merit?

[. . .]

88

M. R. JAMES, 'THE MEZZOTINT'

The Ghost Stories of an Antiquary (London: Edward Arnold, 1905), Second impression, pp. 57–65 [selections]

Now, in February of last year there appeared upon Mr. Williams' desk at the museum a catalogue from Mr. Britnell's emporium, and accompanying it was a typewritten communication from the dealer himself. This latter ran as follows:

'Dear Sir,

'We beg to call your attention to No. 978 in our accompanying catalogue, which we shall be glad to send on approval.

'Yours faithfully,
'J. W. Britnell.'

To turn to No. 978 in the accompanying catalogue was with Mr. Williams (as he observed to himself) the work of a moment, and in the place indicated he found the following entry:

'978. – *Unknown.* Interesting mezzotint: View of a manor-house, early part of the century. 15 by 10 inches; black frame. £2 2s.'

It was not specially exciting, and the price seemed high. However, as Mr. Britnell, who knew his business and his customer, seemed to set store by it, Mr. Williams wrote a postcard asking for the article to be sent on approval, along with some other engravings and sketches which appeared in the same catalogue. And so he passed without much excitement of anticipation to the ordinary labours of the day.

A parcel of any kind always arrives a day later than you expect it, and that of Mr. Britnell proved, as I believe the right phrase goes, no exception to the rule. It was delivered at the museum by the afternoon post of Saturday, after Mr. Williams had left his work, and it was accordingly brought round to his rooms in college by the attendant, in order that he might not have to wait over Sunday before looking through it and returning such of the contents as he did not propose to keep. And here he found it when he came in to tea, with a friend.

The only item with which I am concerned was the rather large, black-framed mezzotint of which I have already quoted the short description given in Mr. Britnell's

DOI: 10.4324/9781315400266-107

catalogue. Some more details of it will have to be given, though I cannot hope to put before you the look of the picture as clearly as it is present to my own eye. Very nearly the exact duplicate of it may be seen in a good many old inn parlours, or in the passages of undisturbed country mansions at the present moment. It was a rather indifferent mezzotint, and an indifferent mezzotint is, perhaps, the worst form of engraving known. It presented a full-face view of a not very large manor-house of the last century, with three rows of plain sashed windows with rusticated masonry about them, a parapet with balls or vases at the angles, and a small portico in the centre. On either side were trees, and in front a considerable expanse of lawn. The legend 'A. W. F. sculpsit' was engraved on the narrow margin; and there was no further inscription. The whole thing gave the impression that it was the work of an amateur. What in the world Mr. Britnell could mean by affixing the price of £2 2s. to such an object was more than Mr. Williams could imagine. He turned it over with a good deal of contempt; upon the back was a paper label, the left-hand half of which had been torn off. All that remained were the ends of two lines of writing: the first had the letters – *ngley Hall;* the second, – *ssex.*

[. . .]

'It's from that man Britnell, I suppose, isn't it?' said Binks. 'Is it for the museum?

'Well, I think I should buy it if the price was five shillings,' said Williams; 'but for some unearthly reason he wants two guineas for it. I can't conceive why. It's a wretched engraving, and there aren't even any figures to give it life.'

'It's not worth two guineas, I should think,' said Binks; 'but I don't think it's so badly done. The moonlight seems rather good to me; and I should have thought there *were* figures, or at least a figure, just on the edge in front.'

'Let's look,' said Williams. 'Well, it's true the light is rather cleverly given. Where's your figure? Oh yes! Just the head, in the very front of the picture.'

And indeed there was – hardly more than a black blot on the extreme edge of the engraving – the head of a man or woman, a good deal muffled up, the back turned to the spectator, and looking towards the house.

Williams had not noticed it before.

'Still,' he said, 'though it's a cleverer thing than I thought, I can't spend two guineas of museum money on a picture of a place I don't know.'

[. . .]

It was by this time rather late in the evening, and the visitors were on the move. After they went Williams was obliged to write a letter or two and clear up some odd bits of work. At last, some time past midnight, he was disposed to turn in, and he put out his lamp after lighting his bedroom candle. The picture lay face upwards on the table where the last man who looked at it had put it, and it caught his eye as he turned the lamp down. What he saw made him very nearly drop the candle on the floor, and he declares now that if he had been left in the dark at that moment he would have had a fit. But, as that did not happen, he was able to put down the light on the table and take a good look at the picture. It was indubitable – rankly impossible, no doubt, but absolutely certain. In the middle of the lawn in front of the unknown house there was a figure where no figure had been at five o'clock that afternoon. It was crawling on all-fours towards the house, and it was muffled in a strange black garment with a white cross on the back.

[. . .]

89

'WOOD ENGRAVING'

Elisha Noyce, *The Boys Book Of Industrial Information* (London: Ward and Lock, 1863), p. 134

Arts and processes

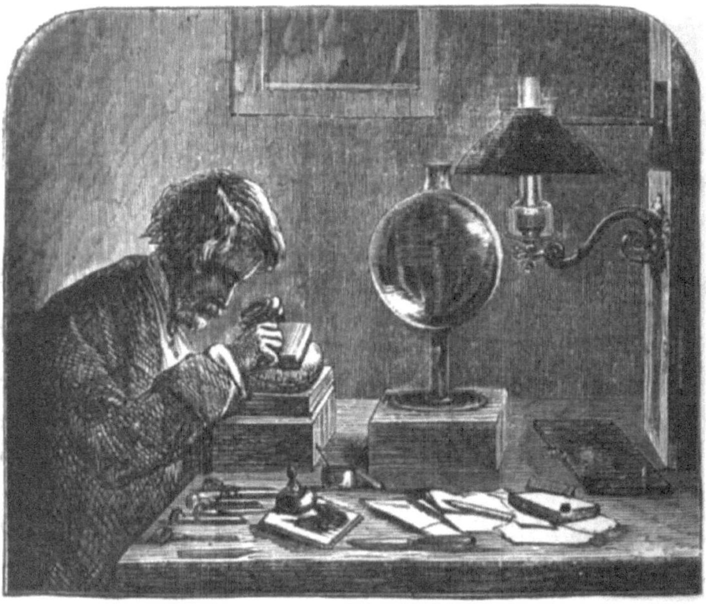

Wood engraving.

DOI: 10.4324/9781315400266-108

90

INTERNATIONAL EXHIBITION 1862: *OFFICIAL CATALOGUE OF THE FINE ART DEPARTMENT*

(London: Truscott, Son, & Simmons, 1862), p. 103

Engraving

I This, of all the Fine Arts of design the most popular and the most generally diffused, appears to be at the same time that of which the technical processes are least familiar. It is, therefore, thought that a few words mainly on this point will be the most useful introduction to the masterpieces of modern work here collected.

The three forms of Engraving which include almost the whole art employ respectively the surfaces of Wood, Stone, and Metal to give the impression. In the first, the ink is laid *on* projecting portions: in the second, on portions of *plane* surface chemically prepared to receive it: in the third, within hollows sunk *below* the surface, whence it is removed by wiping. In Wood Engraving what the artist cuts away, forms the light; what he leaves, the lines. In Lithography, – whether plain or in colours, – what he lays on with ink or chalk is repeated on the paper. It is on metal only that the lines he cuts in are reproduced by the printing-ink. This latter art is therefore *Engraving* in the strict sense, and the one which bears the name by custom. It is also by its nature capable of the greatest variety in style, and of the most powerful or the most delicate effects in execution. The texture of wood does not carry cuttings of the freedom and complexity possible in metal, and strokes cannot be laid over strokes to strengthen and gradate the effect. Nor can the surface lines of lithography in its different forms, drawn with ink or chalk, approach the united force and tenderness of the lines which may be sunk into the steel or the copper. Engraving on Metal thus holds the first rank, and may claim precedence in our brief notice.

[. . .]

 DOI: 10.4324/9781315400266-109

91

CHARLES DICKENS, 'ENGRAVED ON STEEL'

All the Year Round, October 27 1866, pp. 372–376

BUNGLEBUTT, the great Bunglebutt, member of parliament for the flourishing town of Lower Pighurst, has come out decidedly strong this time! Bunglebutt, at any time, is an awfully knowing blade; a regular Adam Smith over the nation's wealth collectively, and over his own wealth individually.

Bunglebutt – who has been returned by a majority of nine hundred and ninety-nine of the most enlightened of Lower Pighurst, to serve in the imperial parliament – is admitted, on all hands, to be up to a thing or two; his grasp over the mysteries of political economy is so tremendous, and his appetite for statistics is so alarming, that ever since he came out with his exhaustive pamphlet, "What will Britannia do when her last shovel of coals has been put on the fire?" not only the Lower Pighurstians to a man, woman, and child, but the political economists and the most cunning staticians in all parts of the kingdom have combined to consider the great Bunglebutt as a match for any two chancellors of the exchequer, one down and the other come on. Yet, all this is nothing to what the great Bunglebutt has since done on the momentous coal question. Bunglebutt is, himself, a great manufacturer, and consumes no end of tons of coals every week. Our daily increasing consumption of coals so rankles in his heart that he sees the day when it will be all up with England and her coals, together. To avert this stupendous calamity, the mighty mind of the far-seeing Bunglebutt has been hard at work, both in and out of parliament, until the interesting result has been the production of his truly stunning work, "Our empty Coal-cellars, and What's to fill them?"

Only think! A book on the great coal question consisting of one thousand and one closely printed pages, filled from beginning to end with a never-ending variety of statistical tables, from which even the most hungry statician can appease his appetite to his heart's content!

Only think! Twenty-one editions – one thousand each – of "Our empty Coal-cellars, and What's to fill them?" devoured in the short space of twenty-one days, by twenty-one thousand admiring political economists and stunned staticians, each and every one of whom talked himself clean out of breath to twenty-one more almost driven-mad political economists and stunned staticians who had

DOI: 10.4324/9781315400266-110

not been fortunate enough to make a purchase of "Our empty Coal-cellars, and What's to fill them?"

Nevertheless, twenty-one editions, of one thousand copies each, demolished in twenty-one days, is not half enough to satisfy the craving of the public upon this home-touching topic. All heads (especially the thickest and hardest) are filled with Bunglebutt. The fame of Bunglebutt resounds everywhere – morning, noon, and night. Every twenty-four hours the name of Bunglebutt turns up in every column of every morning and evening newspaper, no matter what may be its price or its political colour. Then who can wonder that the twenty-second and much-augmented edition of "Our empty Coal-cellars, and What's to fill them?" has gone to press?

But at the last moment, when the panting public are almost at the point of frenzy for this twenty-second and much-augmented edition, the splendid idea strikes somebody that it should be adorned with a portrait of the great Bunglebutt, "beautifully engraved upon steel, in the highest style of art."

Jolterhead, the eminent photographic artist of Lower Pighurst, who has accomplished no end of cartes de visite of the mighty Bunglebutt in every possible pose – sometimes with his left foot thrown over his right foot, with his hat in his right hand, and sometimes with his left hand upon his left hip, and his hat upon the table, against which he rests gracefully – has just accomplished a great triumph, in the shape of a large portrait of Bunglebutt. Hence the splendid idea of somebody – perhaps the immortal Bunglebutt himself – that "Our empty Coal-cellars, and What's to fill them?" should hereafter be delivered to the panting public embellished with this photographic portrait of the great Bunglebutt, "beautifully engraved upon steel, in the highest style of art."

The dreadful consequence of this "at the last moment" determination is, that Pickpeck, the engraver, is sent for, and is commandingly requested to engrave upon steel the portrait of Bunglebutt in the "highest style of art," from a muzzy and black-as-your-hat photograph, as quick as "a flash of lightning." There is no help for it; the public are panting for the twenty-second and much-augmented edition of "Our empty Coal-cellars, and What's to fill them?" The book is ready to go to the binder. It is, therefore, Pickpeck, the stipple engraver, the dawdling Pickpeck, who alone keeps, as it were, the cellar-door of publication shut up, and simply because he cannot engrave, "in the highest style of art," the portrait of Bunglebutt as quick as "a flash of lightning."

However, whether the great Bunglebutt is "beautifully engraved in the highest style of art" or not, the art and mystery of engraving a portrait upon steel is not to be accelerated beyond "putting on the screw," in the shape of working night and day; this poor Pickpeck does, but engraving even a book-portrait upon steel is a work of time for all that; besides which, Bunglebutt is the proud possessor of a peculiar obliquity of vision in one eye, and that simple, if not beautifying, circumstance will bring much wailing and woe upon Pickpeck, the engraver, before Bunglebutt is done with.

It happens to be half-past one P. M. on Monday, when Pickpeck has undertaken the "flash of lightning" impossibility. The muzzy and black-as-your-hat photograph has been delivered to him; the size of the steel plate has been settled upon; and so, to save time, although it is two miles out of his way yet on his way home, Pickpeck posts along to the steel-plate maker, to order his plate; but somebody has ordered half a dozen "flash of lightning" plates five minutes before the arrival of Pickpeck, so Pickpeck is content to accept the promise that he shall have his "flash of lightning" plate last thing on Wednesday night, or first thing on Thursday morning. Here's delay – what is to become of "Our empty Coal-cellars, and What's to fill them?" What is to become of the panting public? Down with Pickpeck!

Pickpeck returns to his home to prepare for action. The first serious thing to be accomplished is, to carefully trace the outline of the portrait. Pickpeck selects a fine clear piece of gelatine, or glass paper, fastening it down over the portrait, which, being a photograph, does not show as perfectly through the glass paper as Pickpeck could desire; nevertheless, with the aid of a magnifying-glass and his properly sharpened etching-needle, Pickpeck manages to trace, that is to say, slightly to scratch or cut, on the upper surface of the glass paper, the outline of Bunglebutt's majestic countenance, as it shows itself through the transparent sheet of glass paper.

At length the steel plate arrives; whereupon Pickpeck well washes with turpentine the polished side thereof, besides further polishing that same side by friction with whiting; then he prepares to lay an etching-ground. Having firmly fastened a hand vice to one end of the steel plate, by which it may be held out at arm's length, then, with sundry pieces of paper crumpled up, and placed all alight in a fire-shovel, Pickpeck proceeds to warm the steel plate through, from the underneath side, against which he is slowly moving the flame arising from the ignited print paper; the heat being adjusted to that degree which, in his long experience, Pickpeck conceives to be sufficient to cause the etching-ground to melt and flow freely.

The mysterious compound called etching-ground – carefully tied up in a piece of silk – is a small globe, not unlike, in size and colour, a rather corpulent brandy-ball: a sweetstuff known to most of us in our childhood.

The steel plate being sufficiently heated, Pickpeck passes his silk-covered ball of etching ground up and down the polished side of the steel plate: the warmth contained in it causing the etching-ground to flow out freely through the pores of the silk covering; thus leaving across the front of the steel plate what look like so many streaks of treacle. Pickpeck then takes up his dabber, also made of silk, stuffed with wadding, and to which a holder is attached; the entire dabber resembling most completely a two and a half-inch inverted mushroom. With this inverted mushroom-looking dabber, Pickpeck dabs up and down, and backwards and forwards, over the treacle-like streaks of etching-ground, until the latter have become beautifully manipulated into one harmonious and level tint, very much, in appearance as to colour, like the top of a hot-cross-bun. One more operation, and the etching-ground will be complete. Lighting a wax taper – which, to yield a good body of flame, has been doubled up into lengths so as to make a cable of eight wicks, the whole gently twisted together, and presenting the appearance of a peppermint-stick, only not quite so white to look at – Pickpeck makes of the steel plate, by holding it at arm's length aloft, a temporary ceiling above his head, but with the etching-ground-covered side of the steel plate turned downwards. Beneath this extemporised ceiling, Pickpeck flickers the lighted wax taper of eight wicks to and fro, so that the smoke arising from the wax-taper flame ascending to the steel-plate ceiling, that smoke sinks into and amalgamates itself with the etching-ground, which is still meltingly hot; the consequence of this last performance is, when the steel plate becomes cold, that the mixture of wax-taper smoke and melted etching-ground has produced a polished lacquer-like coating on the steel plate, causing it to resemble a well-japanned piece of black tea-tray.

The steel plate being quite cold, and the etching-ground perfect enough to satisfy Pickpeck – who is very fastidious in all these operations – he prepares to "turn off the tracing." Putting the glass paper, upon which the countenance of the wise Bunglebutt has been cut, or scratched, or traced, over a piece of white paper, but with the tracing uppermost, Pickpeck proceeds to sprinkle a little lead-pencil dust on it, and then, with a small piece of cotton rag, sweeps, or brushes, as much of the lead-pencil dust into the traced lines as they will hold. He soon ascertains when each line is well filled, by their suddenly appearing black, owing to the white paper underneath the transparent sheet of gelatine, or glass paper.

And now to effect the transfer of the tracing on to the etching-ground. The glass paper, on which is the "counterfeit presentment" of the tremendous Bunglebutt, is laid with the traced side downwards upon the etching-ground itself, and, when it is fastened in position, Pickpeck, with one of his choicest burnishers, proceeds to burnish over the upper or non-traced-upon side of the glass paper. The pleasing result of this operation is, that, as the burnisher passes along, it presses the lead-pencil dust out of the lines of the tracing on to the etching-ground, and all so perfectly, that, upon the removal of the glass paper, the eye of Pickpeck beholds every line of the tracing shining like threads of silver upon the black japanned-looking etching-ground.

Now the valorous Pickpeck can commence his etching; that is to say, he, with his etching-graver, begins to perforate the etching-ground with divers and innumerable dots, dug down into the steel, along the transferred lines of silvery pencil-dust, representing in outline the figure-head of the profound Bunglebutt. Pickpeck arranges his dots accordingly along the lines aforesaid, just as his judgment conceives they will best carry out, in an artistic manner, this much-desired representation. The etching completed, the bright dots dug into the steel – bright because surrounded and relieved by the black etching-ground – now blaze away until the etching seems to represent a kind of starry firmament turned upside down, and composed of countless illumination-lamps on a small scale.

The etching completed, Pickpeck has nothing to do but to prepare himself, and the steel plate, for the "biting-in;" a process whereby a certain acid, called nitric, antagonistic to steel in all its notions, will do, in a few minutes, what even an engraver could not accomplish so well, were he to labour no end of days. But, before biting-in, the steel plate must be "walled," and then "stopped out."

For the purpose of walling the plate Pickpeck gets a small pan of lukewarm water, into which he puts the wall-wax, or bordering-wax, as it is variously called; the same being a compound of common pitch and beeswax, in equal proportions. When this wall-wax is sufficiently softened by the warmth of the water, Pickpeck, upon his table, rolls it out, until it looks like an extra-long piece of stick-liquorice, but not quite so big in its circumference; then with the thumb and the first finger of both hands he presses the round stick of wall-wax to a flat, about the eighth of an inch in thickness by one inch in breadth. The next thing to be done is to place this flat strip of wall-wax on its side edge, round the entire etching; where it somewhat resembles a little great wall of China, made of hardbake, but without the almonds. The edge of the wall-wax resting on the steel plate, being securely pressed down, so as to cause it to adhere firmly to the plate, and not allow the acid to escape beneath the wall, the remainder of the plate – between the wall and the etching – although it is already covered with the etching-ground, is nevertheless now covered over with a coating of Brunswick black, fresh from the bottle, and laid on with a camel-hair brush; the Brunswick black being carried round the base of this little great wall of China, with every possible care, the more effectually by such attentive stopping-out, to keep the acid within bounds, and thereby prevent "foul biting" – a kind of accident most repugnant to the soul of Pickpeck. On the left side of the steel plate, while erecting the wall, and while the wax is still warm and pliable, Pickpeck, by a dexterous action of his fingers, presses out a spout to allow of the acid being poured off the plate with increased facility.

At length the stopping-out being perfectly dry, with a small-spouted jug half full of malignant-smelling acid grasped in his left hand, Pickpeck looks one moment down upon the bright shining dots of his etching; the next moment the deed is done; the acid is poured on to the etching – confined within the limits of the little great wall of China. The etching-ground and the Brunswick black being both impervious to all acidical attacks, the acid has nothing to do but to tumble headforemost into the dots, dug through the etching-ground into the steel below. The acid no sooner tumbles into the dots, than they almost immediately lose their brightness: just as though the acid, being so pugnaciously inclined towards steel, had suddenly given every individual bright dot a black eye. Anyhow, the acid is fighting for its life in these dug-out dot holes; the acid is tearing off minute particles of steel, and throwing them up out of the dot holes in such multitudes as to cause a brownish cloud to be seen floating about the little lake, the pungent odour from which has already begun to tickle the nose of Pickpeck. But the time has now come for Pickpeck to interfere. Swiftly he pours off the acid from within the little great wall of China, rapidly supplying the place of the acid with pure water; which operation he repeats again and again, so as to wash thoroughly the dots that have been so much belaboured by the violent conduct of the acid. Upon pouring off the water and drying up the few bubbles that have remained fondly hanging about the etching, Pickpeck comes to the conclusion, on a close examination, that the biting is sufficient. Removing, therefore, the wall, and washing off the etching-ground and the Brunswick black with turpentine, the steel plate once again appears silvery white: while the dots, owing to the vigorous performance of the acid, appear jet black; whereby the mighty Bunglebutt looks up at Pickpeck in brilliant outline.

All things, such as acid, Brunswick black, wall-wax, and other "biting traps" being carefully put away, Pickpeck sits down to begin engraving in earnest. First, then, he proceeds – by digging the point of his stipple-graver down into the steel plate, and thence chipping out a minute particle of that metal – to lay a tint of tiny dots all over the expressive face of Bunglebutt; sometimes placing the dots close together, thereby to render the finer markings of the features; sometimes placing the dots wider apart, as various muscles swell out and give the varied rotundities of Bunglebutt's countenance. When one tint of dots has been laid down all over the great man's face, Pickpeck, by means of a powerful magnifying-glass, is enabled to place a second dot close to the side of the first dot – Siamese-twins fashion; thus he proceeds upon his way, putting a dot here, and a dot there, and a dot wherever his artistic judgment tells him a dot should be placed. Such is the art and mystery of stipple-engraving upon steel; and so Pickpeck goes on dotting from day to day, until he has wrought out, by means of these multitudinous dots, a fair representation of the "form and pressure" of a Bunglebutt "in his habit as he lives."

But, say what you will, engraving upon steel *is* a very slow process; therefore Pickpeck has no help for it but to go on dot, dot, dotting, with his greatest vigour; first oppressed by the heat of the sun during the day; then, baked almost beyond endurance by the heat from his oil lamp at night. And thus, although the head of Bunglebutt, as it is being engraved, is no bigger than a bronze penny-piece, Pickpeck has to dot, dot, dot, his countless dots day after day, besides suffering from all the ills which an engraver's flesh is heir to. These are ills that come in the shape of indifferent gravers; one graver is too hard, and away flies its point as soon as it touches the steel plate, making, instead of a dot beautiful in shape and clearness, an ill-formed dent, probably twice as big as was required for the purpose. Sometimes the result of this sudden snapping of the point of the graver is a slip, which brings with it loss of time – first to erase the slip, and then to make good the surface of the steel plate. The next graver, and the next after that, will be, in all probability, too soft, and here is more trouble for Pickpeck; nearly half his time is lost in re-sharpening his gravers, for, the moment some of them touch the steel plate, their points get doubled up. Thus, Pickpeck frets and fumes, and fumes and frets, and carries on his work "through difficulties of which it is useless to complain," as Johnson observed concerning the labour of his Dictionary. Yes; all this Pickpeck has to do, to an extent which makes him feel with bitter force the further words of the great lexicographer; for the engraver dots away, day after day, "without one act of assistance, one word of encouragement, or one smile of favour" from anybody.

But after all this work and labour, after all this dot, dot, dotting, to get out the true light and shade of Bunglebutt's sage countenance – upon taking a proof at this middle stage of the engraving, the proof looks rather white and ghostly; consequently, increase of power must be had quickly, and can be had quickly by what is called re-biting; therefore, Pickpeck prepares for the more than usually delicate operation of "a re-bite."

For laying his re-biting ground, Pickpeck does not use the ground he employed for etching upon, although that would serve the purpose very well; but Pickpeck is a particular fellow in these matters, and has, therefore, his special corpulent-looking brandy-ball-coloured ground for re-biting; yet the materials composing these grounds are the same in both cases – that is to say, virgin wax, Burgundy pitch, and asphaltum; but it is by the most subtle cunning that the proportions have been varied, so as to make each ground the more efficacious for its particular department.

In this operation of re-biting, the first thing that Pickpeck has to do, is, beautifully to clean the engraved surface of the steel plate with turpentine; then, placing a lady's silver thimble full of whiting upon the well-cleaned surface, with a little fresh turpentine added, wherewith to make the whiting into a kind of paste, the same is then laid completely over the plate, and, when quite dry, the superfluous whiting being brushed off with a clean piece of cotton rag, the surface of the steel plate will suddenly appear as bright as polished silver, while every-individual engraved dot and line looks somewhat pretty, being perfectly filled with dry and hard whiting. But this must be removed before the ground can be laid; so, with a piece of carefully selected stale bread, quite free from the least speck of grease, Pickpeck gently rubs the stale bread over the engraved parts: when forthwith the whiting leaves the dots and lines, which are then observed to sparkle like diamonds of the purest water.

The steel plate being thus prepared for a re-biting ground, and at the back or under side of the plate the proper amount of warmth having been applied, the first important thing for Pickpeck to do is to pass down the margin of the plate the silk-covered ball of re-biting ground, which, as if by magic, leaves in the wake of its passage what looks like a stroke of treacle. This is then gently manipulated about the margin of the plate by means of a series of delicate pats or dabs with the re-biting dabber, until the ground is diffused about and thinned down into a homogeneous tint, like a layer of leaf-gold. Now comes the trial of skill; from this leaf-gold looking tint of re-biting ground, lying on the margin of the plate, Pickpeck begins to pass with his dabber over the engraved surface with the gentlest of all gentle pats, and, as his manipulation is this time perfect, the satisfactory result is, that over Bunglebutt's expressive head and shoulders there presently appears a golden film of re-biting ground, the same resting upon the blank bits of steel situated between and around each line and dot that has been engraved upon the steel plate; moreover, every dot is shining away through the golden film of re-biting ground, like so many homœopathic spangles; for if the smallest particle of the re-biting ground had flowed over the sides of any line or dot, and so down into these graver-made cavities, the acid would very politely decline to act therein.

The next thing to be done is for Pickpeck to carefully cover over with his Brunswick black all such parts of the engraving as he does not desire to re-bite. Then, once again, Pickpeck surrounds the steel plate with a second little great wall of China, composed of the same kind of wax that the first was made with. The Brunswick black being carried home to the base of this little great wall of China, the process of stopping-out the plate for re-biting is complete, while the Brunswick black will in a comparatively short time be dry enough and hard enough to decline letting the acid make way through its coat, so as to do damage to the surface of the steel beneath.

Pickpeck prepares to pour his re-biting acid on the plate and within the mystic circle of wall-wax. As before observed, the engraved portion of the plate, not stopped out with Brunswick black, is only covered with a delicate gold-leaf-looking film of re-biting ground, which, thin and delicate as it is, being nevertheless perfectly laid, scorns the most desperate attack of the acid; consequently the acid aforesaid is no sooner poured upon the plate than it pops down into the dots, taking their shine off in no time. As in the case of the etching, so with the engraving, minute particles of metal are torn away, whence every dot is being enlarged by this violent mode of proceeding on the part of the acid. And very sharp and attentive work is this re-biting, for all that Pickpeck wishes to accomplish, though of such great importance, is nevertheless – on steel – almost of a momentary nature in its working. An instant too long – nay, the winking of Pickpeck's eyelids – and the work of days may be undone in half a second. But fate is this time kind to Pickpeck; his re-biting is a success. Nay, more, though Pickpeck, in his anxiety to see a proof, starts off himself to the steel and copper-plate printer at full speed in the broiling sun, as though he were walking for a heavy wager, his proofs are beautiful, for all the nice operations of the skilful "prover" are successful. Pickpeck would, notwithstanding his toils, begin to feel a little happy, were it not for that obliquity of vision on the part of Bunglebutt; which circumstance fills the heart of the engraver with misgivings. But still he works on manfully, toning here, burnishing a little there, and attending to all the refinements of drawing in every part of Bunglebutt's face, until he is enabled to submit what is, as he flatters himself, a very satisfactory finished proof. This, however, does not end the woes of Pickpeck. The sons and daughters of Bunglebutt – to say nothing of the wife of Bunglebutt's bosom – all make their remarks upon the engraving. These remarks are highly complimentary to Bunglebutt, and, as a natural consequence, very uncomplimentary to the engraver. The prodigious Bunglebutt himself writes a letter of remarks. This letter fills four pages of the largest cream-laid note-paper. The writing is very small and very close, and the remarks are directed at the inartistic manner in which Pickpeck has rendered the expression of "the left-hand eye."

To speak in plain and honest English, Pickpeck believes that the obliquity of Bunglebutt's left eye is a positive squint – an uncompromising squint; and that he has rendered its expression perfectly, even to its most subtle refinements of drawing. However, the Bunglebutt family perceive in "the left-hand eye" of their great papa – the real live eye – only "a stern expression of deep meditation, combined with a profundity of philosophical thought." Upon that, Bunglebutt criticises, in three pages of closely written note-paper of the largest size, the refinement of expression to be observed in what he calls "the left-hand eye;" all of which intellectual expression, in the united opinion of the Bunglebutt family, he, Pickpeck, has entirely missed. After this, nothing is left for Pickpeck but to throw, as well as he can, his whole soul into the soul of Bunglebutt, and to do his best to coax and coquet with that same left-hand eye, engraving divers dots, first a little on this side, then a little on that side, then a trifle above, then a trifle below: with a few very refined dots placed in the very apple of "the left-hand eye" itself. After doing all this, there are more journeys to the steel and copper-plate printer, and more finished proofs to be submitted, to be followed by more criticism; for the Bunglebutt family think a great deal of the "profundity of philosophical thought" which they perceive in that parental "left-hand eye," a most evil eye to Pickpeck. But all this monstrous long time the panting public are clamouring with frenzy for the twenty-second and much-augmented edition of "Our empty Coal-cellars, and What's to fill them?" embellished with the portrait of the author, which was to have been engraved "like a flash of lightning," but is not done yet.

Consequently a finished proof has to be submitted for a third time, and has to be a third time criticised; this necessitates a fourth finished proof, which, although the Bunglebutt family still think the engraver has not quite entered into all the depths of expression to be observed in "the left-hand eye," is happily accepted by them: while, taken altogether, they admit the engraving to be a very nice engraving, which will doubtless be received by the panting public as a decided adornment to "Our empty Coal-cellars, and What's to fill them?"

92

CHARLES BOOTH, *LIFE AND LABOUR OF THE PEOPLE IN LONDON*

(Second series: Industry) (London: Macmillan and Co., 1903), pp. 109–113

Wood engraving

This work may be pictorial or mechanical, and the men employed usually confine themselves to one or other branch. Anatomical work, which may also be considered apart, lies about midway between the other two.

Pictorial engraving includes the production or reproduction of many kinds of drawings, and demands often a high degree of skill. The business of illustration is as a whole very active, but hand labour and the use of wooden blocks are being superseded by the new photographic processes to which we shall refer later. Mechanical engraving includes technical drawings and plans, and most of the illustrations for trade circulars and advertisements. This business too is active, and, although it is now attacked, has so far held its own better than pictorial work, since the saving to be made by using the newer methods is not so great as with pictorial work.

The improvement and cheapening of various methods of reproducing drawings has resulted in a reduction in the number of men employed in wood engraving. Some firms formerly employing twenty engravers have not more than half a dozen now, and the majority of those employed only work about half time. Competition has been consequently very keen, and although the cost of work on wooden blocks has decreased nearly 50 per cent. within the past ten years, the advantage of price still remains with "process," as the new method is termed, and the wood engraver can only depend upon work that requires special treatment.

Engraving readily adapts itself to a system of home work, and while many take work in this way, others combine, two or three together, to hire a work-room, each man having his own clients and retaining his own earnings. As work has become more difficult to obtain, increased numbers have adopted these methods, and have set up a competition amongst themselves as well as with the large firms which has furthered the fall in prices and brought about a general demoralization of the trade. Employers, finding they can have their work done as well and more cheaply outside, give out their orders, and decrease the number of those regularly employed on their own premises.

DOI: 10.4324/9781315400266-111

Several engraving machines are in use for cutting straight lines or parts of circles. The cost of these machines, however, precludes their use by engravers with a small business, and moreover they are only suited for technical drawings in which straight lines and circles play a considerable part.

Copper-plate engraving

The men who engrave on copper are sharply specialized among themselves. There are heraldic engravers, ornamental engravers, map engravers, and writing or script engravers.

Heraldic Engravers are a small body of men who, besides the ability to cut the lines correctly, should have a fair knowledge of the subtleties of heraldry, in order to do their work intelligently. A few of them work on their employers' premises; others at home or in a hired workshop. Of the latter, several are to be found on the upper floors of the old houses in Soho, where good light can be combined with a comparatively cheap rent, and the engraver is not far from the fashionable shops, whence he receives his orders.

Ornamental Engravers cut scrolls and patterns. They are a very small but highly skilled body of men, skin to the heraldic engravers.

Map Engraving is almost entirely a London industry – the only important exception being the work for the Ordnance Surrey carried on at Southampton. Much of this work used to be done on steel, but copper has superseded steel for this purpose. The maps are not printed directly from the plates, but a transfer is made from the plate to a lithographic stone, and from this the maps are more easily printed. The men engaged are either "outline" or "hill" engravers. The outline engraver does his part, including the lettering, and the plate then passes to the hall engraver, who inserts the mountains and other elevations in the conventional shading to which our eyes are accustomed, and which most of us find more suggestive than "contour lines." The number of men employed in this way in London would not exceed fifty all told. Good hill engravers, we are told, can be counted on the fingers.

Map engravers, like the root, have suffered in recent years by the competition of other "processes," and the best men are apt to monopolize the reduced volume of work, making the earnings of the others more and more precarious.

Script or Writing Engravers form the largest section of those working on copper. They do a great deal of commercial work, such as invoice and bill heads, cheques, share certificates, &c., as well as note-paper headings and visiting cards for all the world. The last is one of the most important branches. A large proportion of these men work on their employers' premises and have fairly regular work. Men describing themselves as copper-plate engravers will generally belong to this group; those in the other sections would describe themselves by their special marce.

Banknote Engraving is another specialized branch finding employment for a small but highly skilled and well-paid body of men. The work is in the hands of two or three firms. In addition to those required for the Bank of England, notes are sometimes made here for foreign governments, but most of this work is said to go to America if not done by the country issuing the note. In some of this work, as with maps, lithography is combined with engraving.

No other occupation has suffered more than engraving from the competition of new inventions and the change from ancient to modern methods. Every branch of the business has been affected in this way.

Hours of Work vary widely. In the employers' workrooms 9 A.M. to 6 or 7 P.M., with intervals for dinner and tea, is the usual time, or from forty-two to forty-eight hours a week. With the men working in their own homes the hours are at least as irregular as the work. Every man is a law unto himself. Too frequently he stands idle through lack of employment, and must work early and late to make up for lost time; but even without such enforced irregularity it is rarely found that men who are their own masters keep very regular hours.

Earnings. – The system of employment and the uncertainty of the trade make it difficult to obtain reliable information as to actual earnings. Employers only know the amount they pay weekly, but men may work for more than one master. On the other side the men may perhaps state what they can earn in a full week, but are unable or do not care to state what the average amount is. Piece-work is the usual method of remuneration. For wood engraving a price is fixed per square inch or for the block – varying according to the character of the work. When a time-rate is adopted it will vary from 10*d* to 2*s* an hour, but this generally resolves itself into a piece-rate, as a certain time is allowed for a block. Pictorial engravers can earn from £3 to £5 a week if in regular work; mechanical engravers about £3. Very few, however, actually earn these amounts. Ordinary piece-workers range from 30*s* to 40*s*, home-workers often making loss. Some men employed by time earn only 35*s* a week. The men engaged on heraldic and ornamental work are paid the highest rates. Piece-work is usual, and the men earn anything up to £4 or £5 a week; but the work is very uncertain and earnings sometimes fall to 20*s*. Script or writing engravers can seldom exceed 60*s*, but their work is more regular and may yield a larger average amount of wages. Map engravers in full work earn £4 to £5 a week, but to do this is exceptional. A few men are regularly employed on weekly wages of 70*s* to 80*s*, and those rates secure the best men. "Hill" engravers are paid a higher rate than the outline men, but the work is more precarious so that the average incomes of the two classes differ little. The lettering on the maps is paid so much a word of five letters.

Apprenticeship is the recognized mode of learning the trade. The period varies from five to seven years. A premium of £30 to £80 is usually paid; but few lads are entering the business. As a rule employers do not care to take apprentices. It is easy for a lad to spoil work, while he seldom becomes really useful within two years. It is only the men who work on their own account who will take boys to learn the trade.

4.4

Bookbinding

DOI: 10.4324/9781315400266-112

4.4 Bookbinding

The component parts of a book include paper, covers made from different materials, stitching, lettering and embossing, as well as paratextual elements such as illustrations in various forms, endpapers and title pages.[1] The art of bookbinding brings together all of these elements; the sources in this section examine the materials, equipment and labour involved in bookbinding and consider its aesthetic role.

The first is from an 1842 article in *The Penny Magazine,* which charts 'a day at a bookbinders'. Drawing attention to the recent increase in print publications 'at a small weekly price', which has transformed publishing, the article provides a highly detailed account of the daily activities of Messrs Westleys and Clark, a large bookbinding establishment in London. The article takes the reader through a series of spaces within the factory. In the basement we find the warehouses containing heavy machinery, while on the ground floor is the 'boarding-shop', where cloth binding takes place. The next floor contains the 'roan-shop' where books to be bound in sheep leather are produced, as well as a whole room devoted to the sewing and covering of 'the little ninepenny books called "Pinnock's Catechisms"'. The top two floors contain a 'blocking-shop' for lettering and ornamenting book covers and a room in which different kinds of leather are cut to the required shape. The full article goes on to discuss the processes of bookbinding and the different kinds of labour it involves.

We move from the 1840s to the 1880s and to Oscar Wilde's anonymised piece in the *Pall Mall Gazette,* which meditates on the art of bookbinding. In this review of a recent lecture given by Thomas James Cobden-Sanderson (an artist and bookbinder with links to the Arts and Crafts Movement), Wilde criticises Cobden-Sanderson's rushed exposition of the history of bookbinding, but praises the practical demonstration in which 'Mr Sanderson described and illustrated the various processes of smoothing, pressing, cutting, paring and the like'. Wilde takes issue with Cobden-Sanderson's view that bookbinding is an expressive art that 'come[s] from the man himself'. Instead, Wilde argues, bookbinding is an 'impressive art' with an 'abstract decorative beauty' and not 'a mode of expression for a man's soul'.

The Bookbinder was a periodical which ran from 1888 to 1894, becoming *The British Bookmaker* from July 1890 onwards. Billed initially as 'An illustrated Journal for Binders, Librarians, and all Lovers of books', it published an eclectic range of pieces from bibliophilic poetry to articles on 'disinfecting books' and 'finishing on pigskin'.[2] Its aim, as stated in the Preface to Volume 1 was to

> raise the Binders' craft of the present day to a higher level than before, both by showing examples of the best work of the Old Masters in the art, and by inculcating what all good critics admit to be the first principles of book ornamentation.[3]

But its remit was, in fact, far broader than this; as well as questions of design, taste and the aesthetics, a number of articles are concerned with the working lives of those engaged at different levels of the profession.

The first source from this periodical picks up on Wilde's theme and considers whether bookbinding deserves the status of a fine art. It examines this idea from the perspective of 'three classes': 'the artistic bookbinder, the bibliophile and the custodians of libraries'; 'country town bookbinders, botchers of jobs, dabblers in the art'; and 'the public at large'. These three groups have very different attitudes towards the idea of bookbinding as an art form. While the public at large (class three) 'fails to regard bookbinding as one of the fine arts', the author makes a case for the art of bookbinding, arguing that it was a 'branch of art work long before the invention of printing'.

The advert included in this section is for bookbinders' rollers made from India rubber from supplier M. Lindner. Benignly referenced here as an exciting new material, the story of rubber production in the Victorian period is one of exploitation and violence, as detailed in the *Raw Materials* volume of this series.[4] The handwritten note reproduced in the advert testifies to the way in which the rollers 'save a great deal of time and trouble'. The penultimate source from *The Bookbinder* meditates on a new material, xylonite, a form of early plastic formed by combining nitrocellulose, camphor, and castor oil that was used for covering the front, sides and backs of books. Xylonite was developed by Daniel Spill, who founded the British Xylonite Company and established a large factory on Homerton High Street, Hackney, in 1877.

Nearly 50 years after the *Penny Magazine* article, *The British Bookmaker* ran a piece on a new bindery established by the bookbinding firm Zaehnsdorf. It charts new developments, which include a lavatory on every floor for the use of workers, and a darkroom in which photographs were taken of 'high-class' bindings and used for advertising. Of particular note is the fact that Zaehnsdorf uses no heavy machinery – 'ours is all hand work' – indicating a buoyant market for the hand-produced book. The piece excerpted here also includes images of workers involved in the bookbinding process: the collator, sewer, cutter out and coverer. Joseph W. Zahensndorf's detailed account, *The Art of Bookbinding*, was published in 1880 and contains engravings of some of the tools and machinery used in the book industry at the time. His 'glossary of the technical terms and implements used in bookbinding' is a particularly useful reference source.[5]

Notes

1 On the anatomy of the book see Denis Duncan and Adam Smyth, *Book Parts* (Oxford: Oxford University Press, 2019).

2 By 1890 the periodical's target audience was 'The Book Printer – the Book Illustrator – The Book Cover Designer – the Book Binder – Librarians, and Lovers of Books generally'.
3 *The Bookbinder: an illustrated journal for binders, librarians and all lovers of books* (vol. 1), 1888, p. iv.
4 Adelene Buckland, *Raw Materials* (this series).
5 Joseph W. Zahensndorf, *The Art of Bookbinding* (London: George Bell and Sons, 1880).

93

'A DAY AT A BOOKBINDERS'

The Penny Magazine for the diffusion of useful knowledge, September supplement, 1842, pp. 377–384 (377–378)

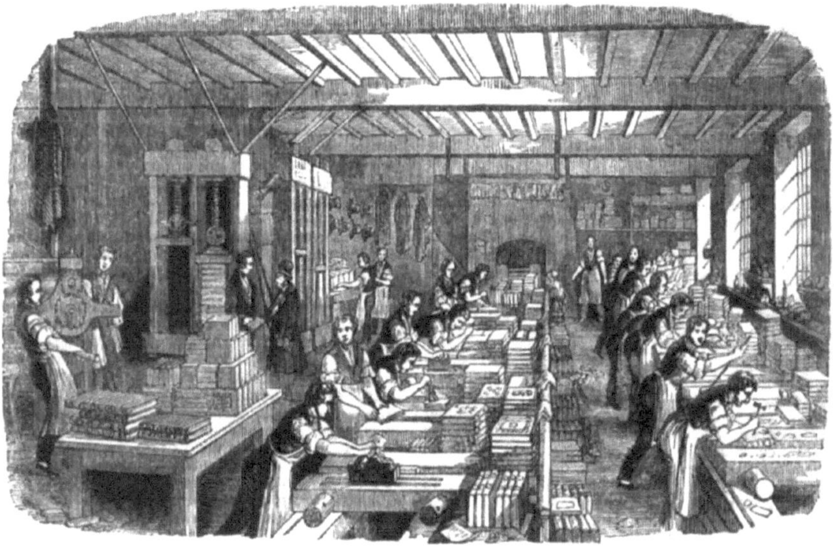

[Roan-binding Shop. – Messrs. Westleys and Clark's Factory.]

IT is a necessary consequence of the connexion existing between different branches of manufacture, that no one of them can receive any notable increase or advancement without benefiting many of the others. Thus, the spur which was given ten or a dozen years ago to popular reading by the establishment of works issued at a small weekly price, and many of them illustrated by wood-engravings, has been the means of inducing changes and eliciting improvements in nearly all the arts connected with publishing: – wood-engraving, paper-making, printing, bookbinding – all have been affected by a moving-power which at first sight might appear a trivial one. Some of the works now published at a penny or three-halfpence weekly can vie with the costly works of bygone years in illustrations, paper, and printing; and those persons who were schoolboys in the days when

DOI: 10.4324/9781315400266-113

schoolboys were whipped through 'Vyse's New London Spelling-book,' will not fail to see how rapidly such books are assuming the neat gilt-lettered cloth covers of modern times in place of the nankeen 'roan' of past years.

In one of our early volumes a sketch, under the title of 'The Commercial History of a Penny Magazine,' was given of wood-engraving, paper-making, type-founding, stereotyping, and printing, sufficient to convey a popular notion of those departments of 'book-making;' but the subject of *Bookbinding* was touched upon so slightly as to leave ample room for the present article. The mechanical and social economy of a large bookbinding establishment at the present day are of much interest; and we have been favoured by Messrs. Westleys and Clark with the requisite facilities for presenting the details which will now occupy our attention.

Any one who knows London intimately is aware that many of our large factories are so hemmed in on all sides by houses as to be scarcely visible externally. Such is the case with the building now under our notice. It is a large pile, built expressly for its present purpose, and presenting much the appearance of a cotton-factory; yet we can scarcely catch a glimpse of it till nearly close to its walls. To say that it is situated in 'Shoemaker Row' will not perhaps convey a very precise idea of its locality to the mass of readers; and we must therefore be content with saying that it has Ludgate Hill a little on the north, Doctors' Commons a little on the east, and Apothecaries' Hall a little on the west. The building is six stories or floors in height, and has an extensive range of windows from north to south, with an entrance in the middle. Into this entrance we will suppose the reader to accompany us.

Each floor of the building is in general appropriated to one class of operations, under the superintendence of a foreman, who is responsible for that department. A winding quadrangular staircase extends up the centre of the building from bottom to top, with landing-places, at which are several doors leading to the workshops. The basement story consists of many rooms occupied as warehouses, or for processes wherein heavy machines are employed. Thus, one room is the 'board warehouse,' where the mill-board, purchased from the stationer in sheets of various sizes and thickness, is deposited in classified recesses till wanted. Another is the 'cloth-warehouse,' where the cotton-cloth, now so extensively used for covering books, is kept and cut to sizes. Near this is the 'embossing warehouse,' filled with pieces of leather or cloth which have received some of those ornamental devices to be described hereafter. One room, which we will call the 'cloth-cylinder room,' contains two machines for imparting to cloth the diamond or granulated or speckled appearance usually presented by books in cloth boards; an appearance which nearly hides the rectangular interlacings of the warp and weft threads. The 'embossing shops,' on the same range, contain three powerful machines for giving to the flat covers of books those beautiful devices which now so often distinguish them: if the book be a Bible, we have an emblematical device of a religious character; if it be a 'Shakspere,' we have something pertaining to the great dramatist; if it be a lady's album or portfolio, or letter-case or blotting-book, we have a device of a graceful and ornamental character. This is an approach towards what may perhaps be termed a 'principle' in bookbinding, viz. that the subject of a book may be known from its cover; a principle which seems to have much to recommend it.

On ascending to the ground-floor, or that which is nearly on a level with the street, the hum of voices tells us that a numerous body of workpeople of both sexes are here employed. In the counting-house of the principals is one of those simple but valuable expedients for saving time, now so much employed in large factories; we mean a series of 'speaking-tubes.' Tubes pass from this room to the counting-houses or offices of all the foremen above and below stairs, and with these are associated a range of bell-wires; a bell is first rung, which draws the attention of the foreman to his end of the tube; and a message being then whispered or spoken through the tube, he hears it readily, and gives the necessary reply. All the tubes are inscribed with the names of the department to which they belong.

The main portion of this floor is occupied by the 'boarding-shop,' a technical name for the shop wherein all the operations are conducted for binding books in cloth boards, the most prevalent style at the present day. In one part of this room females are engaged in folding the sheets, gathering them into groups, sewing them into the form of a book, &c.; while in other parts are men pursuing the subsequent operations of glueing, pasting, cutting, hammering, pressing, &c., by which the book is brought to a finished state. This is a very busy scene, and one presenting much variety, from the distinct nature of the processes carried on. In many branches of manufacture it is found convenient to locate the workmen according to the kind of labour required; but in bookbinding on a large scale it is found desirable to classify with respect rather to the style in which the book is to be bound, than to the nature of each individual process. Hence nearly all the workpeople required for binding an extensive order of books in boards are here congregated on one floor. The folding-tables for the folders, the sewing-frames for the sewers, and the various benches and presses for the workmen, are the scenes of many remarkable and ingenious processes, of which we shall speak more hereafter.

The next range (which, if we reckon the basement as the commencement, must be called the third) exhibits another example of the classification just alluded to. This is called the 'roan-shop,' or the 'sheep-shop,' in allusion to the preparation of those books which are covered with roan, or sheep-leather. Most readers are perhaps aware that books bound in 'sheep' are less expensive than those bound in 'calf;' the leather itself is less costly, and the general style of workmanship less elegant. Hence workmen who are accustomed to one sort of binding are generally employed upon that kind; and hence the preparation of roan-bound books in a workshop different both from that above described and from that devoted to more elegant work. This range is, however, not strictly confined to roan-bound books, since 'school-books,' whether bound in cloth or in leather, are prepared here. The large room exhibits nearly similar features to that below stairs; females, in one department, are forwarding the earlier operations; and men, in another department, are finishing the volumes. Our frontispiece represents the appearance of this room.

Another room on the same range, known in the factory as the 'Pinnock' room, affords us a curious insight into the amount of sale which popular works sometimes command. This room is appropriated mainly to the sewing and covering of the little ninepenny books called 'Pinnock's Catechisms.' Of these small productions the sale is so large and so uninterrupted, that the processes of sewing and covering them proceed continuously. The numbers sold must be enormous; and indeed a glance through the operations of this range of the factory shows that such school-books as are so fortunate as to obtain a "name" command an extent of sale scarcely equalled by any other kind of literary productions, with the exception of Bibles and Prayers. 'Goldsmith's England,' 'Mangnall's Questions,' 'Carpenter's Spelling,' and other schoolbooks, were piled in such heaps and groups in various stages of preparation as to indicate pretty clearly to us the extent of the demand. What improvements these books may have received from time to time as literary productions, or may be susceptible of receiving hereafter, is no part of the present subject; but exteriorly they have marched with the march of the times, and have yielded to the bookbinding reforms of 'embossed-roan' and 'cloth-lettered.'

The fourth range of the factory is occupied by the 'extra' workmen; that is, those who are employed on the finer kinds of binding, such as Bibles and Prayers, gilt-edged books generally, and books exhibiting all the costly and elaborate varieties of 'Russia,' 'Morocco,' and 'Calf binding. One shop, called the 'extra-forwarding shop,' is occupied by the folders, pressers, sewers, &c., while the 'extra-finishing shop' sufficiently explains itself.

In the two upper floors of the factory are numerous rooms more or less subsidiary to those below stairs. One or two are 'blocking-shops,' for lettering and ornamenting the covers of books; another is occupied by the men who make cloth-cases for books; in another, the edges of books are gilt. One is the 'leather-warehouse,' where all the various kinds of leather are kept, as procured from the leather-dresser, and cut to the required sizes. Another is the 'Annual' shop, in which the Annuals are bound at the particular period of the year when they are wanted. One of the rooms is termed the 'Caoutchouc-shop,' as being devoted principally to those workmen who produce the caoutchouc or Indian-rubber binding; and there are a few others, which are used, or not, according as the amount of business fluctuates at different seasons.

Among several indications of a well-arranged factory, we noticed one which is always pleasing wherever observed. Many of the superintendents and workpeople appear to have been old standards, to have grown old with the growth of the factory, and to have shared with the proprietors the progress and fluctuation to which all manufactures are subject. This is a feature which we have more than once had occasion to notice in reference to large factories, and is one of considerable importance to the well-being of both the employers and the employed.

[. . .]

94

OSCAR WILDE, 'BEAUTIES OF BOOKBINDING'

Pall Mall Gazette, November 23, 1888, p. 3

The Beauties of Bookbinding

Mr. Cobden-Sanderson at the Arts and Crafts

"The beginning of art," said Mr. Cobden-Sanderson last night in his charming lecture on Bookbinding, "is man thinking about the universe." He desires to give expression to the joy and wonder that he feels at the marvels that surround him, and invents a form of beauty through which he utters the thought or feeling that is in him. And bookbinding ranks amongst the arts: "through it a man expresses himself."

This eloquent and pleasantly exaggerated exordium preceded some very practical demonstrations. "The apron is the banner of the future!" exclaimed the lecturer, and he took his coat off and put his apron on. He spoke a little about old bindings for the papyrus roll, about the ivory or cedar cylinders round which old MSS. were wound, about the stained covers and the elaborate strings, till binding in the modern sense began with literature in a folded form, with literature in pages. A binding, he pointed out, consists of two boards originally of wood, now of millboard, and covered with leather, silk, or velvet. The use of these boards is to protect the "world's written wealth." The best material is leather, decorated with gold. The old binders used to be given forests that they might always have a supply of the skins of wild animals; the modern binder has to content himself with importing morocco, which is far the best leather there is, and which is very much to be preferred to calf. Mr. Sanderson mentioned by name a few of the great binders, such as Le Gascon, and some of the patrons of bookbinding like the Medicis, Grolier, and the wonderful women who so loved books that they lent them some of the perfume and grace of their own strange lives. However the historical part of the lecture was very inadequate, possibly necessarily so, through the limitations of time. The really elaborate part of the lecture was the practical exposition. Mr. Sanderson described and illustrated the various processes of smoothing, pressing, cutting, paring, and the like. He divides bindings into two classes, the useful and the beautiful. Among the former he reckoned paper covers such as the French use, paper boards and cloth boards, and half leather or calf bindings. Cloth he disliked as a poor material, the gold on which soon fades away. As for beautiful bindings,

DOI: 10.4324/9781315400266-114

in them "decoration rises into enthusiasm." A beautiful binding is "a homage to genius." It has its ethical value, its spiritual effect. "By doing good work we raise life to a higher plane," said the lecturer, and he dwelt with loving sympathy on the fact that a book is "sensitive by nature," that it is made by a human being for a human being, that the design must "come from the man himself" and express the moods of his imagination, the joy of his soul. There must, consequently, be no division of labour. "I make my own paste, and enjoy doing it," said Mr. Sanderson as he spoke of the necessity for the artist doing the whole work with his own hands. But before we have really good bookbinding we must have a social revolution. As things are now, the worker diminished to a machine is the slave of the employer, and the employer bloated into a millionaire is the slave of the public, and the public is the slave of its pet god, cheapness. The bookbinder of the future is to be an educated man, who appreciates literature, and who has freedom for his fancy and leisure for his thought.

All this is very good and sound. But in treating bookbinding as an imaginative expressive human art we must confess that we think that Mr. Sanderson made something of an error. Bookbinding is essentially decorative, and good decoration is far more often suggested by material and mode of work than by any desire on the part of the designer to tell us of his joy in the world. Hence it comes that good decoration is always traditional. Where it is the expression of the individual, it is usually either false or capricious. These handicrafts are not primarily expressive arts, they are impressive arts. If a man has any message for the world he will not deliver it in a material that always suggests and always conditions its own decoration. The beauty of bookbinding is abstract decorative beauty. It is not, in the first instance, a mode of expression for a man's soul. Indeed, the danger of all these lofty claims for handicraft is simply that they show a desire to give crafts the province and motive of arts such as poetry, painting, and sculpture. Such province and such motive they have not got. Their aim is different. Between the arts that aim at annihilating their material, and the arts that aim at glorifying it, there is a wide gulf.

However, it was quite right of Mr. Cobden-Sanderson to extol his own art, and though he often seemed to confuse expressive and impressive modes of beauty, he always spoke with great sincerity. Next week Mr. Crane delivers the final lecture of these admirable "Arts and Crafts Series," and no doubt he will have much to say on a subject to which he has devoted the whole of his fine artistic life. For ourselves we cannot help feeling that in bookbinding art primarily expresses, not the feeling of the worker, but simply itself, its own beauty, its own wonder.

95

'BOOKBINDING AS A DECORATIVE ART'

The British Bookmaker,
January 1892 (Vol. 5), pp. 158–9

Whether bookbinding is to be regarded as one of the fine arts is a subject upon which opinions are very divided. There are three classes especially in the community who hold widely different ideas on this subject. The first embraces the artistic bookbinder, the bibliophile and the custodian of libraries containing books and art collections. This class entertains no doubt that bookbinding is a fine art. The second class includes country town bookbinders, botchers of jobs, dabblers in the art, those who scamp their work, and those in the trade who never realise to what a degree bookbinding can be developed because they hardly give a though to the subject, seldom use cutting machines, are still in the habit of beating books in the old fashioned way, and hire incompetent help in the bindery. This class is larger than is generally realized, and its members never read a journal devoted to the interests of the craft, never see an exhibition of objects connected with the trade, nor visit an art museum; but in ignorance of all suggestions of improvement in taste, style, and methods continue to work in the old grooves, to which they have become accustomed in the past half century. They simply regard bookbinding as their means of livelihood, and have never asked themselves whether it could be anything more.

The third class is the public at large. This class admires the ornamental gold binding, but cares little for stamped leather or leather mosaic work, and it recognizes no difference between hand and machine gilding. It possesses more taste, however, than the dabblers in the art above mentioned, but it is not sufficiently enlightened as to the difficulties involved in hand work to correctly estimate its importance, and it accordingly gives other trades a higher position in the arts than bookbinding. So the great public fails to regard bookbinding as one of the fine arts.

We have, therefore, the three classes. The first does consider bookbinding as one of the fine arts, but its number is still composed of only a few individuals. The second gives no thought for the morrow and pays little attention to the question under discussion. This class, too, is small in number and will after a while die out. The third class considers the matter as of no importance. The second

DOI: 10.4324/9781315400266-115

class is incapable of improvement, and every effort to arouse its members from their lethargy would be in vain; but the third class may be influenced to undergo a change for the better if this task is undertaken in the right way; for the public mind is formed by an exhibition and comparison of artistic and everyday objects and by lectures and explanatory talks. Hence the future of the bookbinding art and the economical as well as the artistic development of bookbinding depends upon a proper recognition of these facts; for eh greater number capable of appreciating the art in our trade, the easier it will be to obtain artistic employment. The more deeply the art is felt, the more remunerative will the market become and the higher the material return will be.

A person who has laboured for years for the recognition of art in the bookbinder's trade cannot entertain a doubt that bookbinding belongs to the fine arts. Indeed, bookbinding was a branch of art work long before the invention of printing, with which the development of the trade has ever since marched hand in hand. We need not go back to remote antiquity, but can refer to artistic bookbinding which dates from the eleventh century, when the material was not such as is used in or bindings of to-day, but consisted of wood, ivory etc. Even when the shape of the book differed from that in use at present, and the written leaves were glued together under instead of back of one another, and rolled upon a piece of wood – even then these covers or rolls were artistically ornamented [. . .]

96

ADVERTISEMENT FOR LINDNER'S ROLLERS

The Bookbinder, 1889 (Vol. 2), p. iv

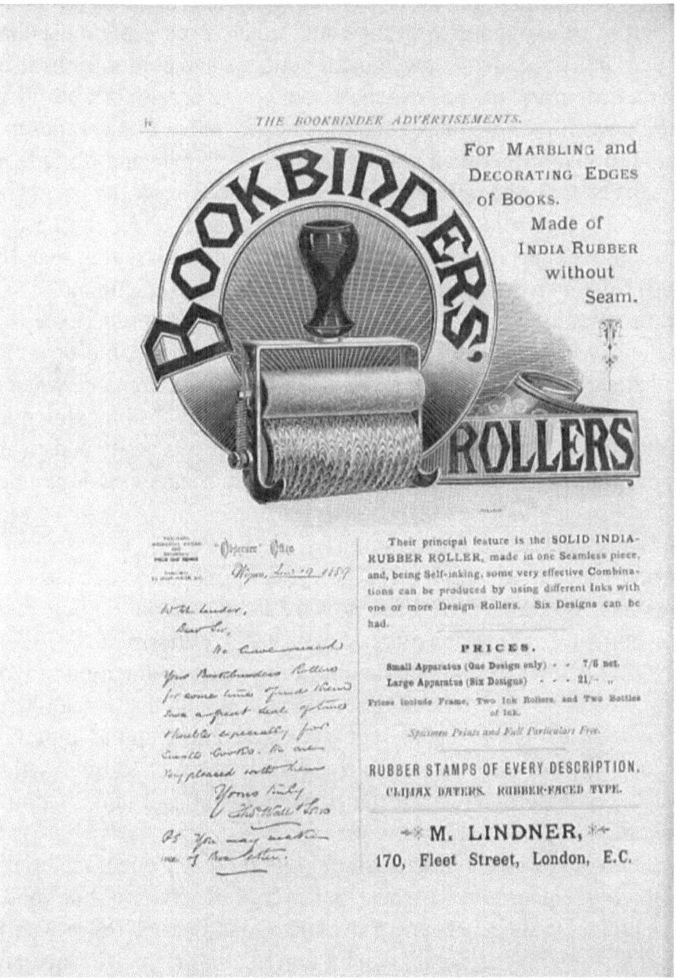

Source: Reproduced by kind permission of the Syndics of Cambridge University Library.

DOI: 10.4324/9781315400266-116

97

'XYLONITE FOR BOOK BINDING'

The British Bookmaker, March 1891 (Vol. 4), p. 19

XYLONITE is a material but little known in the bookbinding trade, yet it has points that need but to be explained to bring it into much more general use than it has hitherto been. It is not exactly new, though binders have used it for little else than tablets, but a firm in Ireland has executed some large orders for Catholic work in this material, much of which has gone to America. What it is composed of I am not prepared to say, further than that it has a base of paper, and is made in sheets of any thickness, from the $^{1}/100$th of an inch up to one inch, the usual size being 35-inches by 20. It is sold by weight at 4/- per pound, or for the best "grained ivory" 5/-, and its cheapness may be easily calculated by saying that 18-inches (superficial) by 1-inch thick weighs as nearly as possible one pound.

In texture xylonite is close and compact, without any grain, except the best variety which is veined rather than grained. It may be flexible or stiff, with a highly polished surface, or rough, and though highly inflammable when brought into direct contact with fire, will stand a moderate heat in the blocking press without shrivelling. It is hard enough to retain form, yet it cuts easily and cleanly with no tendency to tear, either in the board machine or shears, and it can be carved with ordinary carving tools.

The forms best suited for bookbinding are the following: –

A thin unpolished kind mainly used for tablets, can also be used as end papers for many books in which it is desirable to have some material for note taking, and is very convenient, as the pencil marks can be easily obliterated.

Another kind, known as one-line flexible xylonite, is in imitation of ivory, with a beautifully polished surface, and is so thin and pliable that it may be used for covering, and turned in like leather, yet without cracking up the joint. Of course the joint goes in time, but it wears fairly well. It is better to bind with a white leather back, using the xylonite for the sides only, but as it may be turned in no rim is necessary.

The "grained ivory" is the most beautiful imitation of the real material, both in the creamy white colour and the veins, and would deceive any but good judges. This can be bought in sheets of similar thickness to ordinary ivory as used on sides of books, and should be especially useful now that ivory has reached an almost prohibitive price.

 DOI: 10.4324/9781315400266-117

Besides these forms xylonite is worked up into book sides and backs already for binders. The bevelled sides however differ in this respect: being moulded rather than bevelled, to secure lightness, the under side is hollowed out in proportion to the bevel. We have some very fine samples before us with sunk oval centres, having a raised one line or dotted line inside the oval, and in the centre a latin cross, with a delicate spray of ivy leaves in the closest imitation of carving ivory work. Others have a cross and lilies, or a cross with the sacred heart, and other catholic emblems, but the cross with the ivy leaves is the prettiest, and the design is repeated in several sizes, from diamond 48mos upward. The front side in this style, back plainly bevelled, and a rounded back for the smaller size, cost but 8/- per dozen sets, while a real carved ivory would probably cost about 10/- for the one set.

The difficulty of moulding the xylonite is too great for binders to attempt that work for themselves as the material has to be softened by steam, and special machinery used into which steam is forced during the moulding, the dies being very costly, but the manufacturers would no doubt have special designs worked up if the orders were large enough to repay the cost. With the plain material no difficulty exists, while the quality and general appearance is so good that it may benefit some of our readers to know of this substitute for the dearer animal product.

The tortoise-shell, either of the red or dark shell, almost defies detection, and there are imitations of many other substances, but it is with these two that the trade is particularly interested, and on both we have seen some excellent gold blocking for pocket calendars and note tablets, so we hope these hints may be useful.

98

'ZAEHNSDORF'S NEW BINDERY'

The British Bookmaker, November 1890 (Vol. 4), pp. 12–16 (14–15)

[. . .]

The basement has been used to great advantage. It is perfectly lighted all round and is exceedingly cool and lofty. The folding, sewing, collating, and washing are all carried on here. There is a special apparatus for washing, but we were quite unable to grasp its mysteries. As most of our readers are aware, this department is one necessitating special experience and in which very few binders excel. A number of neatly attired young ladies were quietly engaged at their sewing presses, performing that portion of the work which Mr. Zaehnsdorf contends is the foundation of good bookbinding. He says that for sewing purposes: "The thread should be of the best quality; the cords upon which the book is sewn, and which secures sheet to sheet and sheets to boards, should be of good hemp and of long fibre. Without a doubt the strength of a book is in the sewing and a badly sewn book has but a short life to run." In a corner of this basement was erected a photographic dark room. Photography is Mr Zaehensdorf's pet pastime, and he is, perhaps, one of the cleverest amateurs in London. Photographs are taken of all the high-class bindings executed, and, we believe, customers residing at a distance can obtain, upon application, photographic reproductions of the covers of any book mentioned in the catalogue issued by the firm. It will thus be seen that the proprietor is enabled to render his favourite amusement very practically useful.

Passing upstairs we noted a lavatory and other conveniences on every floor. Finishing, covering and pasting down are the departments allotted to the second floor. Everything here is most conveniently arranged, and the men proceed noiselessly and calmly with their several tasks, the most noticeable feature being the entire absence of "rush". A large stock of leather was stowed away in a special apartment on this floor, and rows of tools in circular boxes lined the walls close by. A long rack, placed down the centre of the floor, was also laden with tools – many thousand in all. In passing through the workshops the visitor cannot but be impressed with the absence of machinery, especially when it is remembered what a large part machinery plays in a binder's work. "We use no machinery" remarked Mr. Zaehnsdorf, "Ours is all hand work. The screw presses are almost our only assistance, and you see I use a black japanned board for placing between the

DOI: 10.4324/9781315400266-118

books when in the press to enable us to get that high polish which is so desired in morocco bindings." We watched for a few moments the finisher at work, for we felt that after all here was the artist of the establishment.

[. . .]

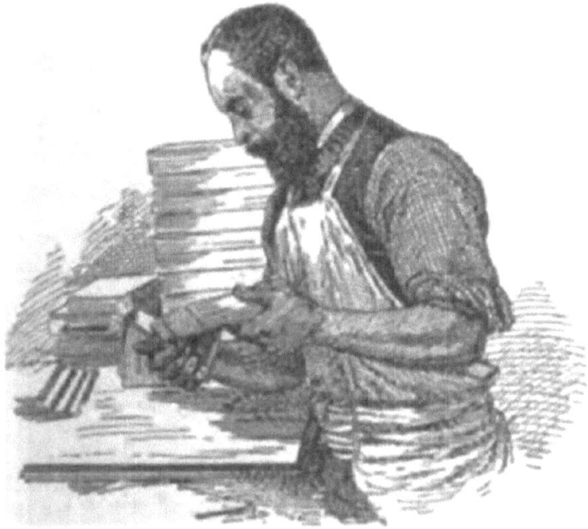

COLLATING.

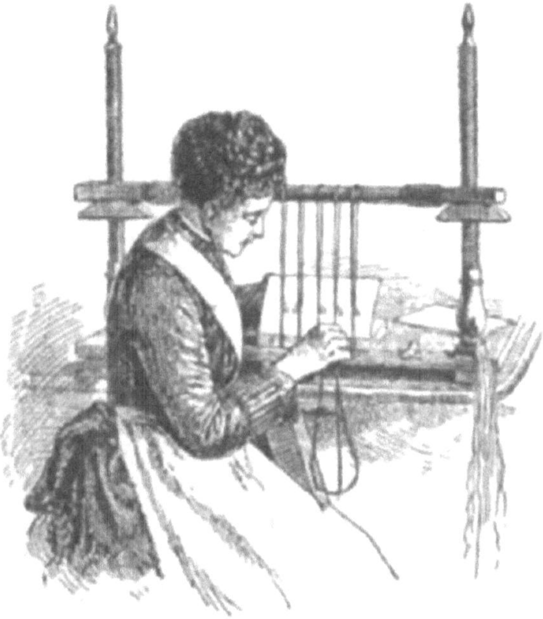

SEWING.

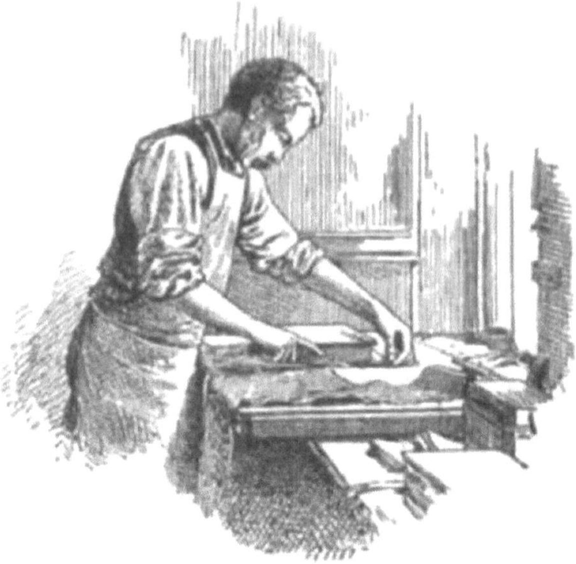

THE CUTTER OUT.

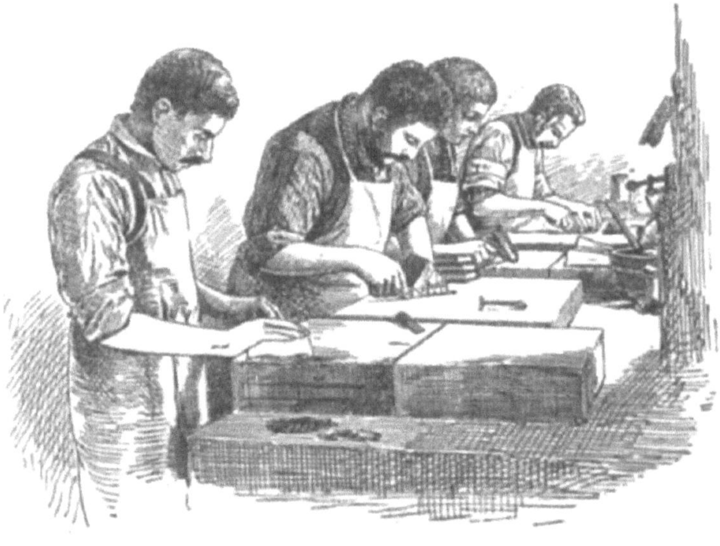

COVERERS.

4.5

Book art as a profession for women

DOI: 10.4324/9781315400266-119

4.5 Book art as a profession for women

There were growing opportunities for women to earn money from wood engraving, printing and bookbinding in the second half of the nineteenth century.[1] The first source in this section is an article from the *Englishwoman's Review* of 1881, which looks to America as a model for the employment of female engravers. The article contains detailed advice for those seeking to enter the profession; it advocates the importance of having a 'special workroom' away from the home, and it encourages girls and women to protect their time:

> a girl's time is generally considered of little value and is frittered away in little interruptions and social 'duties'; everyone thinks they may make demands upon it. You must shake yourself clear of all this if you are ever to become a professional engraver.

The article refers to two fictional representations of the relationship between women and wood engraving, both of which give the false impression that wood engraving is quick to learn and quick to remunerate. On the contrary, according to Burton, girls looking to enter the profession must expect a lengthy apprenticeship.

The two fictional depictions of women and their engagement with wood engraving discussed in the *Englishwoman's Review* are Charlotte Yonge's *The Clever Woman of the Family* (1865) and Jean Ingelow's *Off the Skelligs* (1872). The conservative, Yonge's, work intervenes in mid-century debates about unmarried, 'surplus' women.[2] The novel charts the disastrous attempts of Rachel Curtis to set up her own asylum for girls to save them from the privations of the local lacemaking industry. This new venture will enable young women to 'learn handicrafts that might secure their livelihood, in especial, perhaps, wood engraving and printing'. The asylum produced an illustrated monthly magazine, the 'Journal of Female Industry', printed and illustrated by the female workers and dubbed by Curtis the F.U.E.E. (Female Union for Englishwomen's Employment). The plot's denouement (an extract from which is reproduced here) revolves around an investigation of the material properties and provenance of a proof engraving, which is passed off by the corrupt head of the F.U.E.E. (Mr. Mauleverer) as the work of the Union when in fact it had been cut out from the *Illustrated London News* and pasted onto a card.[3]

Yonge's novel satirises the Victoria Press set up by the Society for Promoting the Employment of Women under the leadership of Emily Faithful, which trained girls to be printers.[4] Among other publications, it printed *The Englishwoman's Journal*, one of the founders of which was Bessie Rayner Parkes, a prominent member of the Langham Place Circle.[5] Our source comes from the *Illustrated London News* and describes the activities of the press and depicts female compositors arranging the type on composing machines.

Off the Skelligs charts the fortunes of Dorothea Graham, who learns wood engraving in order to support herself, and teaches the art to other young women. Wood engraving is interwoven with a romance plot; Dorothea has some success with her venture, but she is aware that she will never excel in the trade, and she eventually marries. The first extract focuses on Dorothea's training and her calculations about how much money she might expect to earn from wood engraving, while the second is a short depiction of the wood-engraving process in which a white ground is applied to the woodblock as part of the etching process.

The Englishwoman's Review of October 1879 carries a notice of a new opportunity for women to learn wood engraving at the Council of the City and Guild of London Technical Institute, which had been founded the year before. The notice emphasises a commitment of 'at least three years' for 'the acquirement of the art', while also highlighting how it is especially fitted for women, requiring 'great delicacy of execution, and nicety of perception, but little physical strength'. Richard Taylor's 'Wood engraving as an employment for girls' ran as a series in *The Girls Own Paper* in 1886. The September article discusses possible routes into the profession and the benefits for a woman of working 'with competent engravers of her own sex'. It also contains an image of a female wood engraver at work. The last piece on engraving is from the weekly *Hearth and Home*. Titled 'What to do with our daughters', it again speaks to the pressing question of finding a profession for young women for whom marriage was not an immediate prospect. Like other sources, it posits a relationship between a woman's 'natural' capabilities and the skills required for wood engraving, drawing attention to a female 'lightness of touch'.

Two sources from *The Bookbinder* discuss the role and status of women involved in bookbinding as a profession. The first is an extract from a report by the chief inspector of factories and workshops. It discusses the way in which the development of new machinery has reduced the work involved in hand stitching, and it comments on decreasing wages. The second item documents the opening of a small bookbinding factory by the Salvation Army in Hackney, East London. Staffed by women, it was linked to the Salvation Army's rescue home movement, which sought to save women from domestic violence and prostitution.

Emily Hill challenges the idea that women can deal only with work that is 'delicate and dainty', describing the female bookbinder as both 'artist' and 'artizan'.[6] In an article on bookbinding for *The Woman's Signal*, she makes a distinction between binding as a remunerative employment for gentlewomen (so-called artistic bookbinding) and the less appealing and more poorly paid aspects of the trade, such as 'folding, collating pages, stitching, pasting'. The article refers to a trade union formed for women engaged in these more laborious activities, most likely the Book-folders union established in 1892. The first union for female bookbinders,

The Society for Women Employed in Bookbinding, was formed by Emma Patterson in 1874. An early example of a women's trade union, short notices detailing the activities of the Society often share space with debates about women's suffrage in the periodicals.[7] A 1904 study of women in the print trades draws attention to the considerable distance in class terms between the Book-folders union and the Society:

> It is a significant fact, and one which throws a great deal of light upon the very little which one section of workers knows even of those working at their elbow, that the organisers of the new Union were quite unaware of the existence of the Women Bookbinders' Society.[8]

Note the reference at the end of Hill's article to Queen Victoria's purchase of two volumes from the women's bookbinding exhibition at Frank Karslake's establishment on the Charing Cross Road in London. The Queen buys two volumes 'bound in the new rich red leather produced in the Congo Free State'. Easy to miss, but a reminder, once again, of the colonial trading links underpinning the market for bookbinding materials.[9]

The Guild of Women Bookbinders was established in 1897 by Karslake, an antiquarian and secondhand book seller. Karslake had viewed book bindings produced by female binders at the Victorian era exhibition held at Earl's Court, West London, in 1897. This exhibition had an entire section devoted to 'Woman's work', including exhibits showcasing the advances of women in both fine and applied arts and handicrafts. The final source in this section is excerpted from the lengthy introduction to a record of the Guild's work produced in 1902. It describes how the Guild's approach to bookbinding is a riposte to dominant utilitarian approaches to book production and discusses how the artistic aspects of women's bindings are likely to 'surpass that of men-binders as a whole'. The book contains reproductions of work by female binders, including Constance Karslake, Florence de Rheims and Dorothy Holmes.[10]

Notes

1 In 1887, the highly skilled engraver Clemence Housmann published *Occupations for Women Other Than Teaching*, a pamphlet promoting wood engraving as a profession for women, one of many publications dealing with this subject. On Housmann's work see Lorraine Kooistra, ' Victorian Women Wood Engravers: The Case of Clemence Housman' in Alexis Easley, Clare Gill, Beth Rodgers (eds.), *Women, Periodicals and Print Culture in Britain, 1830s-1900s: The Victorian Period* (Edinburgh: Edinburgh University Press, 2019).

2 See the photography section in this volume for a discussion of these debates.

3 For a discussion of the novel in its broader historical context see Charlotte Younge, *The Clever Woman of the Family* ed. By Clare A. Simmons (Ormskirk: Broadview Press Ltd., 2001).

4 See William E, Freedman, 'Emily Faithfull and the Victoria Press: An Experiment in Sociological Bibliography', *The Library* 29:2 (1974), 138–64; Sheila Herstein, 'The

Langham Place Circle and Feminist Periodicals of the 1860s', *Victorian Periodicals Review* 26:1, 1993, 24–27.

5 A group of middle-class women who campaigned for the improvement of women's lives and situations in the mid nineteenth century.

6 Hill also wrote a piece on women and printing for the *Woman's Signal* as part of a series 'What can our daughters do for a living' (23rd September 1897).

7 For example, *The Woman's Signal*, December 8th 1898.

8 J. Ramsay Macdonald (ed.), *Women in the Printing Trades: A Sociological Study* (London: P.S. King & Son, 1904), p. 38.

9 On Britain's relationship to the Congo in the late Nineteenth Century see David M. Gordon, 'Precursors To Red Rubber: Violence In The Congo Free State, 1885–1895', *Past and Present* 236:1 (2017), 133–68.

10 For a discussion of the work of the guild's bookbinders see Marianne Tidcombe, *Women Bookbinders 1880–1920*. (Newcastle, Delaware: Oak Knoll Press, 1996).

99

E. P. BURTON, 'A FEW HINTS TO WOMEN ADOPTING WOOD ENGRAVING AS A PROFESSION'

Englishwoman's Review: A Journal of Woman's Work, October 15th 1881, pp. 440–449 (440–444)

WOOD ENGRAVING, or the cutting of pictures on blocks of wood, though of almost older date than printing, may be said to be only now advancing towards the development of which it is capable in the way of book illustration. Within this century especially it has made rapid progress, and a great deal has been done for the improvement of the art. We would like any of our readers to compare the coarse woodcuts of the 18th century with the soft tints and delicate texture of the illustrations in *Scribner's* popular and well-known magazine. But much remains yet to be done for the advancement of wood engraving, especially on this side of the Atlantic, for in the production of woodcuts we have let the Americans get before us. There are various reasons for this; for one thing engravers are better paid there, but another reason may be that in the United States women are admitted into the profession on the same equal terms as men, and thus there is twice the amount of material to draw upon for good engravers; whereas in this country engraving has hitherto been a monopoly in the hands of one sex only. But now that it is possible for women to obtain proper professional training as engravers, we hope that many ladies who possess taste and steady perseverance will turn their thoughts in this direction. We say designedly "steady perseverence," for it is not an employment that can be learnt in a few months, it requires hard work and some years training to make a good engraver. We have known ladies bring their daughters to learn wood engraving, expecting that they would begin to earn a competency at the end of a few months, and on finding that it would be years before they could attain that object, take their departure again. We suspect Miss Yonge's "Clever Woman of the Family," and Jean Ingelow's "Off the Skelligs," have done something to foster this delusion, and the sooner it is exposed the better.

Educated women seem to be specially adapted from their early training to form good engravers; as they have been accustomed from childhood to use hand and

DOI: 10.4324/9781315400266-120

eye in fancy work, drawing and other things that require neat-handedness. Let them show therefore what can be done by their sex for the development of the art; and show what work the graver is capable of producing when used with freedom and delicacy. We would have them make it their endeavour to introduce a higher style of art and break through the monotony, the commonplaceness, that characterises the engravings in our illustrated books and magazines. Engravers are apt to get into a groove, and cut their blocks always in the same style, skies in one way, water in another, without reference to the character of the original designs, and pencil and charcoal sketches are often turned out identical. Apprentices follow their masters, and the result is a sameness in all our illustrations; the drawings of different artists, each of which had a character of its own, being reduced to the same dead level, as if they had all been drawn by the same hand. Engravers ought to bring out the "individuality" of the sketch, picture, or drawing they are cutting, to seize the colour, texture, spirit, and in fact all the peculiarities of the original and reproduce them in their own work. Now women must make it their aim to do this, and, breaking through the monotony that characterises our English woodcuts, improve, develop, raise the art, till engraving on wood takes its place among the fine arts alongside of painting and sculpture. It is this faithfulness to the original that has in a great measure led to the superiority of American engravers, whose work will be seen at its best in the pages of *Scribner's Magazine*. In a letter from one of the editors of the magazine the writer says, referring to this point, "we endeavour to give every phase of art which is good a hearing, through the medium of the best wood engraving procurable – by the best I mean that which adheres the closest to the original in form, colour, and sentiment." Certainly American woodcuts have not yet been equalled by any we have been able to produce in this country, not, we believe because we have not the native talent, but because the attempt has never been made to break through the commonplaceness of our style, and both artists and engravers hold themselves too much aloof from each other. The artist complains that the engraver spoils his design in the cutting, the engraver thinks the artist very hard to please, they do not work together in the best way to ensure success.

I trust soon to see a large number of educated women enter the profession, and that they will soon rival their American sisters in the excellence and beauty of their work. To them I would say, Do not be discouraged if you should hear it said, as perhaps you may, "women have not the talent to produce such work;" for a good part of the staff of engravers employed on *Scribner's Magazine* are women, and the woodcuts in that magazine are universally admired, and are, we believe, considered the best that the United States produces. The art editor of *Scribner* in the letter above quoted, speaking of the employment of women as wood engravers continues: "A fact which you might use in your advocacy of the right of women to earn their living by means of wood engraving – is, that we have some eight or nine ladies constantly working for our magazine, and that one of these we entrust with the most subtle of our work." I hope this "fact" will encourage women to persevere, and endeavour to become first-class engravers. But in order to become this I must remind you that it is necessary to work steadily and constantly, remembering that you are in training for a profession, and not learning an easy employment to fill up vacant time. Do not, however, make the mistake of working too hard the first few months, begin with a few hours a day and gradually increase, in six or nine months you may be working your fifty-two hours a week (an engraver's week), but if you plunge *at once* into nine hours a day (Saturday six hours) you will probably find it too much for you. Never take a long holiday while you are learning, (of course I am not speaking of cases of illness); if you were to leave off work for two or three months together it would throw you back, and you would find on beginning work again that you had lost ground; therefore, if you have to leave home for any length of time provide yourself with plenty of work, and do not let more than two or three weeks elapse without taking it up again. A couple of hours a day even would keep your hand in. Let nothing interfere with your regular hours of work, you have so many hours a day to do, take care that you do them. A girl's time is generally considered of little value, and is frittered away in little useless interruptions and social "duties"; every one thinks they may make demands upon it. You must shake yourself clear of all this if you are ever to become a professional engraver, you would need to have as much command over your own time, and be as free from interruption, as any of your brothers are.

Do not be in too great a hurry to obtain remunerative employment, if you begin by turning out bad work it will go far towards preventing your getting the best kind of work when you are really fit to undertake it. If you take paying work too soon, it will be only the inferior and cheap kind that you will get, and by spending your time over that you will make no progress, and will end by being only a second-rate engraver. Women ought to aim at being first-rate engravers, and try to stand in the front ranks of the profession. Wait, therefore, till you can do excellent work, and have some good proofs to show, before you try to get employment.

A great deal has been said about the suitability of wood engraving as an occupation for ladies to carry on in their own homes, as it is neither laborious nor untidy, and can be carried on in a small space and without disturbing the other members of the family. This is true, it is a very good home employment, but all the same, we believe that the greatest success will be achieved by those women who, like male engravers, have a special workroom, unless they happen to live near the centres of business. In the latter they will easily obtain plenty of work, but if their home is a long distance from the city (I speak specially of London), their best chance is to hire chambers in the city where employers can easily find them, and go there to their work every day. They cannot expect anyone to send work several miles when it can be done as well and as cheaply in the next street. The only remedy for those who live out of town is to make arrangements for sending for, and returning, their work without giving trouble to their employers. The post will help them a great deal in this; but still, the nearer the engraver is to the centre of the publishing trade the greater will be her chance of obtaining full employment. Could not two or three ladies, good engravers, join together, hire one or two rooms in the city, and set up in business as a firm? They would live in their own homes and go to their work daily, but all orders and business letters would be received at their chambers. Such an arrangement would put them more on an equality with other professional engravers, and they would also be enabled to take girls as apprentices.

[. . .]

100

CHARLOTTE YONGE, *THE CLEVER WOMAN OF THE FAMILY*

(London and Cambridge: MacMillan and Co., 1865), pp. 45–48

[At this point in the novel, Rachel Curtis is beginning to suspect Mr Mauleverer (head of the F.U.E.E) of malpractice, though she defends him to the last]

[. . .] In good time, Rachel made her appearance in Miss Williams's little sitting-room. "I am ready to submit to any test that Captain Keith may require to confute himself," she said to Ermine; "and I do so the more readily that with all his mocking language, there is a genuine candour and honesty beneath that would be quite worth convincing. I believe that if once persuaded of the injustice of his suspicions he would in the reaction become a fervent supporter of Mr. Mauleverer and of the institution; and though I should prefer carrying on our work entirely through women, yet this interest would be so good a thing for him, that I should by no means reject his assistance."

Rachel had, however, long to wait. As she said, Captain Keith was one of those inborn loiterers who, made punctual by military duty, revenge themselves by double tardiness in the common affairs of life. Impatience had nearly made her revoke her good opinion of him, and augur that, knowing himself vanquished, he had left the field to her, when at last a sound of wheels was heard, a dog-cart stopped at the door, and Captain Keith entered with an enormous blue and gold volume under his arm.

"I am sorry to be so late," he said, "but I have only now succeeded in procuring my ally."

"An ally?"

"Yes, in this book. I had to make interest at the Avoncester Library, before I could take it away with me." As he spoke he placed the book desk-fashion on a chair, and turned it so that Ermine might see it; and she perceived that it was a bound-up volume of the "Illustrated London News." Two marks were in it, and he silently parted the leaves at the first.

It revealed the lace-making beauty in all her rural charms.

"I see," said Rachel; "it is the same figure, but not the same shaped picture."

DOI: 10.4324/9781315400266-121

Without another word, Alick Keith opened the pages at the lace-school; and here again the figures were identical, though the margin had been differently finished off.

"I perceive a great resemblance," again said Rachel, "but none that is not fully explained by Mr. Mauleverer's accurate resemblance and desire to satirize foolish sentiment."

Alick Keith took up the woodcut. "I should say," he observed, holding it up to the light, "that it was unusual to mount a proof engraving so elaborately on a card."

"Oh, I see what your distrust is driving at; you suspect the designs of being pasted on."

"There is such a test as water," suggested Alick.

"I should be ashamed to return the proof to its master, bearing traces of unjust suspicion."

"If the suspicion you impute to me be unjust, the water will produce no effect at all."

"And you engage to retract all your distrust and contempt, if you are convinced that this engraving is genuine?"

"I do," he answered steadily.

With irritated magnanimity Rachel dipped her finger into the vase of flowers on the table, and let a heavy drop of water fall upon the cottage scene. The centre remained unaltered, and she looked round in exultation, saying, "There, now I suppose I may wipe it off."

Neither spoke, and she applied her pocket handkerchief. What came peeling away under her pressure? It was the soft paper, and as she was passing the edge of the figure of the girl, she found a large smear following her finger. The peculiar brown of Indian ink was seen upon her handkerchief, and when she took it up a narrow hem of white had become apparent between the girl's head and its surroundings. Neither spectator spoke, they scarcely looked at her, when she took another drop from the vase, and using it more boldly found the pasted figure curling up and rending under her hand, lines of newspaper type becoming apparent, and the dark cloud spreading around.

"What does it mean?" was her first exclamation; then suddenly turning on Ermine, "Well, do you triumph?"

"I am very, very sorry," said Ermine.

"I do not know that it is come to that yet," said Rachel, trying to collect herself. "I may have been pressing too hard for results." Then looking at the mangled picture again as they wisely left her to herself, "But it is a deception! A deception! Oh! he need not have done it! Or," with a lightened look and tone of relief, "suppose he did it to see whether I should find it out?"

"He is hardly on terms with you for that," said Ermine; while Alick could not refrain from saying, "Then he would be a more insolent scoundrel than he has shown himself yet."

"I know he is not quite a gentleman," said Rachel, "and nothing else gives the instinct of the becoming. You have conquered, Captain Keith, if it be any pleasure to you to have given my trust and hope a cruel shock."

"With little satisfaction to myself," he began to say; but she continued, "A shock, a shock I say, no more; I do not know what conclusion I ought to draw. I do not expect you to believe in this person till he has cleared up the deceit. If it be only a joke in bad taste, he deserves the distrust that is the penalty for it. If you have been opening my eyes to a deception, perhaps I shall thank you for it some day. I must think it over."

She rose, gathered her papers together, and took her leave gravely [. . .]

101

'THE VICTORIA PRESS'

Illustrated London News, June 15 1861, p. 555

THE introduction of women into the printing trade can now claim the consideration due to a successful experiment. The Victoria Press was opened in March, 1860, and has therefore stood the test of one year's work, and has triumphed over all the preliminary difficulties with which such an undertaking could not fail to be attended. The originators of this enterprise believed that former failures were to be traced to causes altogether apart from the nature of the work. They believed that these failures arose from the small scale of the experiments, which from the nature of the work, and the considerable outlay of capital required before economical success can be secured, carried in this alone an element of loss. They resolved, therefore, to incur the risk of a larger experiment than any hitherto tried, feeling that the time was ripe for it. The public mind, long either strongly opposed or utterly indifferent to such innovations, was in enlightened quarters beginning to feel the necessity for extending the industrial employment of women. A certain amount of support was to be expected, an expectation which has been amply realised. The footing of the concern is that of a private business in which a considerable capital has been embarked. Miss Emily Faithfull, as one of the proprietors, undertook the sole management, and a year ago the office opened with a few girls, five of whom were apprenticed by the Society for Promoting the Employment of Women. In time these were joined by a few who had been trained by male relatives, but who could find no other outlet for their industry.

The site of the office of Great Coram-street is somewhat out of the bustle of business, but it was chosen as a quiet and respectable neighbourhood for the experiment. Several large volumes have issued from the Victoria Press, showing efficient workmanship. Among others we may mention "The Transactions of the Social Science Association," a volume of nine hundred pages; also "The Report of the Committee on Trade Societies," published by John W. Parker. "The Englishwoman's Journal," a monthly publication devoted to the interests of women, is also issued from the office. If the Victoria Press continues to obtain the public support which has hitherto been extended to it there is no doubt of its ultimate entire success, even as a commercial undertaking, and this is earnestly to be desired as the only ground on which the extension of the experiment can be justly urged.

DOI: 10.4324/9781315400266-122

Visitors are allowed to inspect the establishment between three and five o'clock daily, and we recommend any one interested in the employment of women to take advantage of the permission thus extended to them.

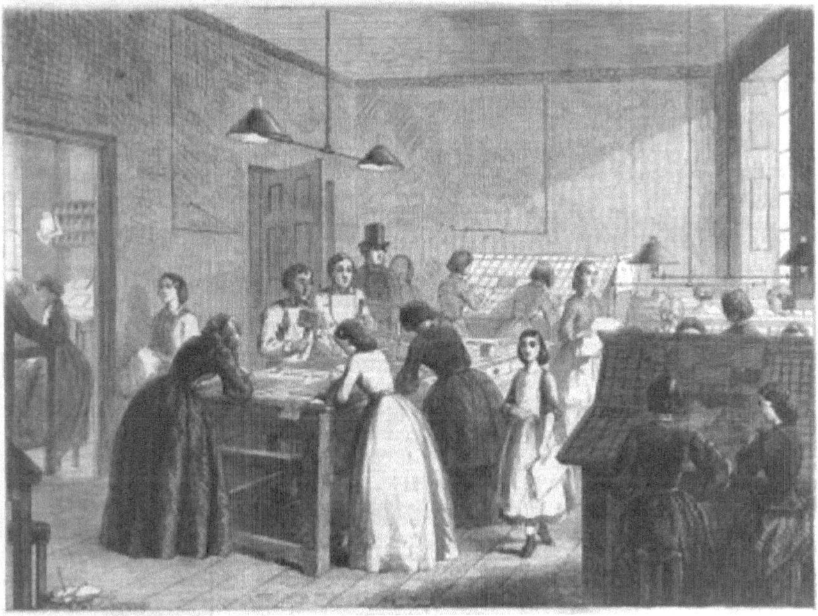

Printing-office (the Victoria press) in Great Coram-Street, for the employment of women as compositors.

102

JEAN INGELOW, *OFF THE SKELLIGS*

(Boston: Roberts Brothers, 1872), pp. 469–476 [selections]

[. . .]

I think it was when I had learned wood-cutting about four months, that one day my usually silent master expressed himself greatly pleased with one of my performances, and asked whether I knew that I was learning the art much faster than most people did.

As he had never volunteered any praise before, but generally looked at my drawings and my cuts with a silent elevation of the eyebrows, I had become accustomed to think that I surprised him by the slowness of my progress, and had risen early to work before breakfast, and had always spent two hours in the evening over my performances, in the vain hope that some day he would smile, instead of so provokingly indicating his amazement, and as I thought his discomfort. This remark astonished me, and I said that it was most unexpected.

'A friend of mine,' he continued, 'that I often show your proofs to, was saying, ma'am' – here he paused in his work to blow away some minute shavings which the tool was turning up, and went on with a deliberation which tired my patience greatly, – 'he was saying that he'd give you five shillings apiece for cuts like these, if you wanted to sell 'em.'

'Indeed,' I exclaimed; 'then wouldn't it be better to let this friend of yours have them?'

'I wouldn't,' he answered, 'if I was you.'

'Why not, Mr. Curtis?'

'Why, miss, because they're worth more.' He continued to examine my work with his glass; then laid it down and slowly plodded through the rest of his speech. 'You see, miss, you can draw, that's where your talent lies. You've had good instruction too – consequently you've learnt no more of me than how to engrave your own drawings. There's hardly a wood-engraver that I know who does that. If they get a book to illustrate, they employ artists to make the drawings, and then they engrave 'em, and so you see two people have to live – the artist and the engraver. Now you don't draw first-rate by any means, but there's a vast lot of drawings engraved that are worse than yours.'

'What do you advise me to do, then?'

DOI: 10.4324/9781315400266-123

'Why, ma'am, you want some first-rate drawing lessons. You want lessons for the next six months.'

'I cannot afford them, Mr. Curtis.'

Mr. Curtis elevated his eyebrows and said no more; but the next lesson he gave me he had a long fit of silence, and when he had set my work in order he grew red in the face and breathed heavily, as he often did when some mistake of mine, or some information to be given, compelled him to open his mouth. At last he said –

'My friend, miss, that I spoke to you about – '

'Yes, Mr. Curtis.'

'He is an artist.'

'Is he?'

'Yes, miss; he has a good many books to illustrate. He illustrated that book of arctic travels that I showed you, and that new work on natural history.'

I wondered what was coming, but to have spoken would only have put my master out.

'He and I have been thinking of a plan,' pursued Mr. Curtis.

'About me?' I exclaimed.

'Yes, miss; you see you want drawing lessons. Now he says, does my friend, that he would instruct you in drawing twice a week for six months, and let you see him draw on the block occasionally, if you'll pay him with all the engravings you do in the six months.'

'Would you advise me to accept his offer?'

'Decidedly, miss, if you mean to go on taking lessons of me at the same time. He will lose by you the first three months; but unless we're both very far out, you'll make it up to him the second, for you'll know more of drawing by what he'll teach you, and more of engraving by what I shall.'

'Then by that plan I make my drawings under his superintendence, and engrave them under yours? I still pay you half-a-crown a lesson, and I pay him nothing but the result of my work?'

'That is all, miss.'

'But if I agree to this, what do you think I shall be able to earn at the end of the six months if I spend about four hours a day on the engraving?'

'About two pounds a week, perhaps, ma'am.'

[. . .]

He too seemed curious about the wood-engraving; and when Valentine had pushed him into a chair, and placed a block of wood before him, he recovered himself so far as to ask some questions about it; not of me, however, but of his brother.

'What's this stuff for? It looks like whitening.'

'Why, you put your finger into it, and smooth it carefully over the surface of the block to make it white.'

'Well, I have stuck my finger in.'

'Smooth away then, old fellow.'

'There – what next? But, Miss Graham, you see this: I suppose you don't disapprove?'

'No – I'll answer for her – you don't D. dear. Now, Giles, draw something on the white surface, and I'll show you how to cut it out.'

'You will, will you? I should hope I have sense enough to do that myself. Here's a little digger that looks just suitable.'

He began to draw, and Valentine and I, seated on the sofa close at hand, went on talking at our ease till he suddenly announced that he had made a drawing.

'Well, dig it out then,' said Valentine, 'since you will have it that you know how. I say, D. my dear, what's this thing? it looks like an empty oil-flask corked and turned upside down, and I declare it's full of water.'

'It's only to throw a light upon my engraving when I work by lamp-light. Look, here is a wide-necked bottle full of sand. I insert the narrow neck into the wide neck to make it steady, and set a candle behind: the result is that a beautifully clear and soft spot of light falls through upon the bit of the wood I am engraving.'

'I wish you'd throw a light, then, on this fellow's work. Look what he's doing! – he's cutting away all the strokes and leaving the ground.'

'Just what you were going to do yourself!'

'D., I shall learn to engrave – will you teach me?'

'I am not far enough advanced for a teacher.'

'Well, but sit down and let us see you do a little piece.'

103

'WOOD ENGRAVING FOR WOMEN'

Englishwoman's Review, October 15th 1879, pp. 451–453

AN excellent opportunity for learning wood engraving is now offered to women, which we hope may be eagerly seized on. The Council of the City and Guild of London Technical Institute is about to form a class for them under the charge of Mr. Charles Roberts, an engraver of very high standing. The class will be held in the south of London, and there will be eight hours of study daily, from 10 a.m. to 4 p. m., and again in the evenings. The candidates must possess a fair knowledge of elementary drawing, and they must be prepared to devote at least three years to the acquirement of the art. The fees will be £5 for the year. On three evenings of the week two hours will be devoted to drawing, and two months holiday in the year will be given.

The art of wood engraving is one that is specially fitted for women. It requires great delicacy of execution, and nicety of perception, and but little physical strength. It can be carried on at home, although in this case there are sometimes difficulties in procuring or finishing work, and ladies practising the art would find great advantage in combining together to have an office where orders for work could be received. An engraving is frequently made from several blocks of wood, each the work of a separate artist, which are afterwards screwed together to form the entire picture; and though it is not absolutely necessary to the successful rendering of the picture that an engraver should see the blocks which lie contiguous to her own, it certainly would help in the finish of the picture. An *atelier,* therefore, where several ladies could work together, would be of no small use.

The art of wood engraving is one that it takes at least three years to acquire properly; but once learned it is well paid, and is a certain provision, inasmuch as it is not dependent upon the caprice of fashion, like embroidery or carved wood or brass work. So long as there are books, there will be pictures to those books, and the engraver's art will be brought into play. Moreover, there is a real vacancy for women in this profession, which is so far from being overstocked, that much of our best engraving has to be done by foreign workmen. There is, therefore, likely to be immediate employment for those ladies who thoroughly learn the trade. But it must be thoroughly learnt, and not taken up as an amateur employment. It is

DOI: 10.4324/9781315400266-124

stated that at least three years will be necessary for its acquirement, and it need hardly be added that the students should be young women, as in later life neither hand nor eye can be trained to sufficient accuracy.

All further particulars respecting the classes can be learnt at the Office of the Society for Promoting the Employment of Women, 22, Berners Street, W.

104

RICHARD TAYLOR, 'WOOD-ENGRAVING AS AN EMPLOYMENT FOR GIRLS'

The Girl's Own Paper, Saturday, September 25, 1886, pp. 822–827 (823)

SUPPOSING that a girl be willing to make the indispensable sacrifices as to time that have been named, and determined to become an engraver, it is still most difficult to say how she had best proceed. To work in company with competent engravers of her own sex would be most favourable to success, and would place her on an equal footing with youths against whom she will have one day to compete for employment; and the nearer she can place herself in such circumstances the better it will be. But as far as I know there is no office conducted by ladies at present open to her. Perhaps she may be able to find some male engraver who would take her as an apprentice. Much of the work in London is done by engravers working by themselves in their own homes, and there would be fewer objections to her working with one of these in the house with his family than to her doing so with him in an office in the City.

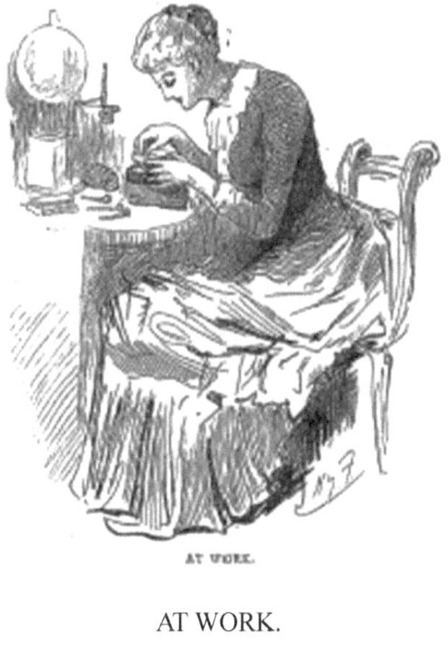

AT WORK.

DOI: 10.4324/9781315400266-125

Personal instruction and constant supervision would be ensured in such a case, but there would still be the drawback before alluded to as to materials for practice, the engraver under these circumstances, as a rule, having only such work entrusted to him as he cannot delegate to another.

In an office an apprentice usually pays a fee of £30, for a term of not less than five years; and this sum, with an additional £50 or £60, is returned to him during the term in the form of weekly wages, none being paid during the first year.

Probably if an office were open to girls it would be on similar conditions, as their general usefulness would not be greater than that of boys. An engraver working in the way named might accept a lower fee, but in any case it behoves the would-be pupil to be very careful indeed as to the integrity and trustworthiness of the person with whom she might be engaging, as unfortunately there are some – indeed many – who advertise and take apprentices with no other object in view than to get possession of the apprenticeship fee, and practically there is no remedy at law for this species of dishonesty.

I have said I doubt very much the utility of class practice, still it may be that a girl, having formed the resolution spoken of, and having other means open to her, might like to know that there is a class for instruction in wood engraving, established by the City and Guilds of London Institute, at 124, Kennington Park-road. It is in charge of a thoroughly competent engraver, and if it be possible to learn this art by such means, the object should be attained there; and there is also a class at the Lambeth School of Art, Miller's-lane, Kennington-lane.

[. . .]

105

'WHAT TO DO WITH OUR DAUGHTERS'

Hearth and Home (London, England), Thursday, June 18, 1891, p. 146

Wood engraving

IN these days people want a great deal for their money, and insist upon having it good; therefore those whose business it is to supply the public demand are compelled to substitute, as far as possible, mechanical processes for manual skill and labour, which are comparatively costly. If this fact is for some reasons to be deplored, it has its advantages. The workers find that they are competing not only against one another, but also against machinery, and unless they exert themselves to the uttermost, they do not receive adequate remuneration for their time and trouble. In consequence those who have drifted into occupations for which they are unsuited, are driven elsewhere. The fittest alone survive. The result is seen in the improved quality of the work turned out, and the tendency is towards further improvement. There is no such thing as standing still.

Fortunately at the top there is room – plenty of room – and always will be. For those who get there are few in number, and in no industry can any mechanical process compete successfully with human effort backed by human skill. Wilkie, the artist, in reply to a question, said that he mixed his colours "with brains." Thank goodness, machinery cannot do that. Therefore it can never become a dangerous rival to men and women who bring to their tasks special training and special aptitude.

These remarks particularly apply to wood engraving. There are so many cheap processes now a-days that it has almost gone out of fashion, and as the work executed by these means is in most cases fairly good, it is only when real excellence is required that the art of the wood-engraver is called into requisition. Of course, there are exceptions. Out of the many cheap books and journals which are daily being produced, a certain proportion are illustrated by woodcuts which have very little in their favour. These give employment to a number of persons who can never expect to rise above mediocrity, but the payment is correspondingly small. No girl should think of depending upon such a means of livelihood. The higher she aims, provided that she has not mistaken her vocation, the further she is likely to go. Unless she strives incessantly to get to the top of the tree, she is bound to remain at the bottom, and down there lies something very like starvation.

On the other hand, if she has a bent for wood-engraving to commence with, and if she sets herself diligently to acquire the necessary skill, she may be quite sure of plenty to do, and her earnings will be large, for first-class engravers are handsomely paid. The work will then be profitable as well as pleasant. Moreover, it is peculiarly adapted to women, for it needs the lightness of touch in which men are usually deficient. It has, however, one drawback – it is as trying to the eyes as watch-making. Only those with strong sight should attempt it. But to all who possess this qualification, together with the others which have been mentioned, we have no hesitation in recommending it as a profession. It is not necessary that they should have any marked originality; all that is required of them is the power to reproduce in wood the drawings entrusted to them, but this they must be able to do faithfully and well.

Next comes the question as to how the necessary training is to be obtained. Not at home certainly – at least without the aid of a competent instructor; the work is far too technical. Those who wish to learn it should put themselves under the guidance of some well-known engraver. In Edinburgh there are two ladies who have already started in business on their own account, and they would doubtless be glad to receive pupils. But in London probably the best, and certainly the cheapest instruction, is to be obtained at the City Guilds Institute, in the Kennington Park Road. Girls of the age of sixteen are admitted, and, for a nominal fee of three guineas a year, receive daily lessons. They have, it is true, to serve a five years' apprenticeship, but during the latter part of that time they can earn something, some of them as much as a pound a week. When fully trained they should not have much difficulty in making a fair income, the average being about a hundred and fifty a year, while the work possesses this great advantage – that it can be done at home. Of course, if they show exceptional ability, they may confidently expect to go far beyond the sum named, for there are some fortunate engravers whose yearly receipts run into four figures. But in any case their earnings will compare favourably with those of any other occupation open to women.

The start presents the greatest difficulty. It always does. But the young engraver has one advantage over her sisters in other professions, for even during her term of apprenticeship she can be gathering together a little body of clients, and these will be ready for her as soon as she commences business in downright earnest. If she has always done her best, and has under no circumstances palmed off work which she considered merely "good enough," perhaps because the remuneration happened to be rather small, she may be quite sure that those who have employed her once will employ her again. They will stand by her when she endeavours to stand alone, and others will soon join them. Each client who is thoroughly satisfied with her work is the best advertisement she could possibly have. For he not only comes again himself but also brings his friends. But one thing she must bear in mind: she must produce better work than her rivals, or equally good work at a cheaper rate. If, then, her charges at the commencement are rather lower than she thinks she has a right to expect, she will not be a loser in the long run.

But suppose, it may be said, a girl who has learned the art of wood-engraving knows nobody likely to help her, what is she to do? Is she not then quite helpless? Not at all. She is no more helpless than an author who can use his pen. He can send his manuscripts to publishers and editors; she can do the same. If her work is good, she is bound sooner or latter to find employment.

But in order to shorten this probationary period we would suggest a partnership. If every girl who is skilled in wood-engraving would combine with some other who is equally skilled in drawing, they would both double their chances of success. For they would then be in a position to offer to publishing firms not merely sketches which might or might not reproduce badly, but the actual blocks at a stated price, and these would always command a readier sale than the unfinished article. Moreover, the difficulty of introducing themselves to the notice of employers would be greatly diminished. Instead of the slow process of submitting sketches to one firm after another, they could send reproductions to a score or more at once. If they selected for illustration some particular book, they would of course first send their specimens to the firm that published it, for in that case they might even dispose of their first blocks. But from others they would simply invite offers for similar work to be done to order, their terms being distinctly stated.

Such partnerships, if conducted on business principles and equipped with the necessary skill, should do really well, especially as the co-operation of artist and engraver must produce better results as regards workmanship than where each is acting independently of the other. Nor should they have any difficulty in coming together. An advertisement or two should do that.

Here, perhaps, we may be of some assistance. We will register the names of any ladies who would like to enter into a partnership of the sort, and when we find two who reside in the same district, the one skilled in drawing and the other in wood engraving, we will place them in communication. All we ask in return is that, if a partnership should result from the negotiations, they will let us hear from them from time to time, for we should be glad to learn that they were doing well.

106

'BOOKBINDING BY WOMEN'

The Bookbinder, Volume 1 (1887–88), p. 171

BOOKBINDING BY WOMEN. – A small bookbinding factory for women has lately been started at 14, Ashgrove, Mare-street, Hackney, under the supervision of the Salvation Army, in connection with their rescue homes for women. The providing of a suitable means of livelihood for these women is one of the great problems of the work, and bookbinding seems to solve the question in a satisfactory manner for those girls who are unfitted for domestic service. The elements of the trade are taught in the Mare-street home itself, and in due time the learners are dratted into the workshop, which at present gives employment to about a dozen girls. In a large, well-lighted workroom they may be seen at work, folding and stitching, under the direction of a capable foreman. After a few weeks' application they are able to earn from seven to nine shillings a week. The girls board in carefully-selected homes, often with members of the Salvation Army, and attend services at the Home. Unfortunately, in spite of a certain amount of work provided by the army, it is difficult to obtain sufficient orders to keep the hands in full employment, and any one who wishes to help a most needful work would afford material assistance by sending any books which require simple binding addressed to the manager, who will pay every attention to orders.

DOI: 10.4324/9781315400266-127

107

'ON FEMALE LABOUR IN THE CENTRAL DISTRICTS'

The Bookbinder, Volume 1 (1887–88), p. 167

THE Report of the Chief Inspector of Factories and Workshops has been recently issued. Mr. Lakeman, one of the Inspectors, contributes an interesting paper upon the "Social Condition of Female Operatives in the Central Districts." Referring to Bookbinding, he says: –

"This industry employed an army of workers now greatly reduced by the introduction of motive power to stitching machines; the value of hand-sewing has fallen in consequence, producing a redundancy of labour and causing much misery during slack times. The work being light and clean attracted young girls, who were bound for two years, and received 3*s*. and 4*s*. a week each year. Young persons could earn 8*s*. to 10*s*. on fair work, and experienced hands 12*s*. to 15*s*., though when on cheap work this sum is not reached; forewomen earn 21*s*. as a maximum. As in other trades, greater advantages can be found in some binding factories than in others, and workers are classed accordingly.

"The commercial book-sewer finds regular employment, and can earn 15*s*. a week at machine work; the publishers' sewers are subject to the uncertainties of trade. Generally, girls work in threes, two of them at machines, one to prepare work, changing places by rotation; they earn 12*s*. to 15*s*. each, but hand-sewing has fallen to 8*s*. to 10*s*. Religious publications are very poorly paid for; and masters accept orders upon barest margin of profit. In the houses of the best publishers' binders, the hands are not sent away in ordinary slack times, that is from March to end of July; the little work to be done then is divided equally, affording less than half wages; but in extra slack periods large numbers are dispensed with, but as the slack time of one class of binders may be the busy season of another, girls can go to and fro. The price of labour is governed by the trade, which is said to be unable to bear a higher strain in advancing wages. I believe that publishers' binding work is now amongst the poorest paid of city industries. It is undisputed that great and sore trials are undergone by many young hands out of season."

It is a well-known fact that publishers' binding is done at the very lowest margin of profit. The fierce competition that prevails, and the rivalry of little masters, have brought about the present unsatisfactory state of things. It is to be hoped that before long a remedy will be found that will benefit both employers of labour and their workpeople.

DOI: 10.4324/9781315400266-128

108

EMILY HILL, 'ARTISTIC BOOK BINDING'

The Woman's Signal, March 17 1898, pp. 166–167

What can our daughters do for a living?

Artistic bookbinding

By Emily Hill.

IN speaking of bookbinding as a remunerative employment for gentlewomen there are two points to be always borne in mind. The first is that we have in view only the highest branch of the craft – artistic bookbinding; the second is that the would-be worker is possessed of artistic faculty and feeling, and has been through, or is prepared to go through, some training of eye and hand. For many years past girls and women have been employed in what goes under the general term, bookbinding, but is, in fact, only the worst paid and most mechanical part of the trade – folding, collating pages, stitching, pasting, and so on. The women so engaged number several hundreds, and have formed themselves into a Trade Union; but the work they do and the social stratum from which they are drawn differ *toto cœlo* from the occupation and the workers now being touched upon.

This does not by any means imply that the lady who takes up artistic bookbinding is to do nothing but what is delicate and dainty. On the contrary she must be both an artist and an artizan. She has to paste and stitch, and manipulate a whole battery of implements – some of them formidable enough weapons to look at – and she must not be afraid of putting on her apron. But the aim in view is the creation of something original and unique, something that is to stand alone, as every work of art must – single and individual.

Within quite the last few years several ladies possessed of artistic talent, and a painstaking capacity for deft manipulation, have turned their attention to the binding of books in a manner which recalls the beautiful individual work of many, many years ago. Calf or morocco embossed with original designs, or with a scene illustrative of the letterpress within, white kid painted on with delicate touch and tint, vellum illuminated in Mediæval manner with colour and gold, are some of

 DOI: 10.4324/9781315400266-129

the media employed. Schools of Art find endless possibilities in silk, gold and silver thread and pearl embroideries on velvet and satin, for books, book covers, and book boxes. One lady, a young art student, Miss Gloria Carden, has struck out quite a new line for the illustration of books by her delicate colouring of pen and ink sketches. While producing an effect of rare daintiness, so firm and accurate are her lines that they could hardly be more so were they printed in colour. Miss Carden has in this way illustrated "The Midsummer Night's Dream," and Keats's poems, notably "Hyperion." The result is quite as delightful as it is novel.

One primary condition of success in this highest kind of bookbinding is that it should be studied and followed up with the seriousness of a profession. It is not necessary merely to be accurate and precise; one has to be mathematically so. Training is a *sine quâ non.* Some students turn out good work at the end of a year; others cannot do as much in twice or thrice that period. Individual capacity and taste, and individual industry and painstaking are determining factors in the result.

Training can be obtained at the Chiswick Art Workers' Guild, Bedford Park, at the Royal School of Art Needlework in the Exhibition-road, and at some of the County Council technical classes. The Chiswick Art Workers' Guild have turned out remarkably good work during the short two years that the bookbinding department has been in existence. The charges for tuition are very moderate. The bookbinding members of the Gentlewomen's Guild of Handicrafts have exhibited some beautiful Russia leather bindings. The members' subscription is 4s. a year, and a commission is, of course, charged on work sold. The Working Ladies' Guild has also a bookbinding department.

[. . .]

At the permanent Exhibition of Artistic Bookbinding by Women, opened by Messrs. Karslake at 61, Charing Cross-road, the work of about twenty ladies who have made a name in bookbinding is represented, while a large number of beautiful examples are sent unnamed from the various centres above referred to. Miss Birkenruth, Miss Sorley, Miss E. M. MacColl and Miss Sophia Smith exhibited at the same place, but as independent exhibitors. Miss Lynch makes a speciality of illuminated bindings.

Artistic bookbinding by women may, therefore, be said to have passed beyond the experimental stage. At present orders for work are more likely to come from private persons than from the ordinary publishing houses, but the opportunity that is now offered for the exhibition and sale on commission of bound books brings the occupation into the region of practicability as a remunerative employment.

A small room in one's dwelling would need to be set aside for the work, a sum, which ought to be a moderate one, spent on obtaining instruction, and a few pounds laid out on the purchase of tools and materials. For any girl who is strong enough to cycle, or garden, or even to play tennis, the physical effort involved in the process of bookbinding is anything but arduous. The interest is, one may say, inexhaustible, as there is constant scope for fresh design and the whole range of colour is at the artist's service.

Two or three ladies are regularly employed at the Chiswick Art Workers' Guild; but those who take up bookbinding as a profession must not do so with the idea that they will drop into paid posts. On the contrary, they must be ever on the alert for opportunities, always ready to push forward, and never cease seeking to bring their work to such perfection that it shall command success.

A box of books from the Women's Bookbinding Exhibition in Charing Cross-road was submitted for inspection to the Queen. Her Majesty purchased two volumes – "Italian Book Illustrations" – bound in the new rich red leather produced in the Congo Free State.

109

GEORGE ELLIOT ANSTRUTHER, *THE BINDINGS OF TOMORROW: A RECORD OF THE WORK OF THE GUILD OF WOMEN BINDERS AND THE HAMPSTEAD BINDERY*

(London: Printed for the Guild of Women Binders, 1902), pp. vii–viii, x

IN an age largely given over to utilitarianism it is gratifying to find purposes and persons at variance with the conditions around them, and in no field is the discovery more productive of satisfaction than in that of industry. Terms which have their significance in the business world, such as Competition, Output, and the like stand in the aggregate for a condition of things which has practically killed the nobler qualities that belonged to the industries of bygone centuries, creating in their stead a system of work and wages which has usually no outlook beyond the prospect of individual gain. The introduction of machinery has nearly lost to us the self-reliant, consciously-proud figure of the English craftsman; the old Trade Guilds, with their dignified constitutions and worthy aims, had little in common with their corporate successors of to-day, and the stress of competition has driven thousands of women and girls into the already overcrowded ranks of suppliant labour. While it is impossible, save in almost imperceptible degrees, to alter the present day aspect of affairs, it has been found practicable to exercise thought and skill in certain channels of restoration, and it is one such channel which forms the subject of these remarks. I am going to speak of a work which has greatly dared and has lived to rejoice in its daring; of a work which sought the attainment of a twofold object: the organization of bookbinding as a remunerative employment for women, and the elevation of the handicraft itself to a proud association with art and beauty. Begun inauspiciously, in the face of discouraging criticism that was at times hardly to be distinguished from hostility, the work went steadily on, realizing its purpose by a consistent loyalty to its own ideal. In the result, criticism has become praise, and even the scoffers of a few years back are constrained to devotion. A new force has established itself in an important branch of industry, and the Guild of Women-Binders is doing for the craft of bookbinding what the

DOI: 10.4324/9781315400266-130

Kelmscott Press accomplished for modern printing. So few are the years dividing us from William Morris and his work that we recall his prospectuses, his productions and his triumphs, among the memories of yesterday; yet even now the Kelmscott books find an honoured place in the showcases of the British Museum. Is it too fond a thought which opens up a similar prospect for some of these bookbindings, supposing the Guild were to end its existence to-morrow?

[. . .]

The Guild has shown that the craft of bookbinding offers a remunerative field for women's labour; that women can, and do, bind books extremely well; and that, under proper instruction, the artistic side of their work is likely to surpass that of men-binders as a whole. The Guild would hardly claim to have initiated the practice of bookbinding as an industry with individual women; on the contrary, its existence grew out of the contemplation of such examples of women's work. What it has done, however, has been to crystallize and focus existent talents and ability, to face the question of bookbinding as a profession for women vigorously and practically, and to set a standard of merit which must constitute the minimum of attainment by its members.

[. . .]

PART 5

Photography

5.1

Inventions and techniques

DOI: 10.4324/9781315400266-132

5.1 Inventions and techniques

Photography was born in the nineteenth century, though experimentation with the projection of images (for example, the camera obscura) and with chemically fixing the image has a much longer history. The advent of photography spawned a vast range of new objects and materials. From the 1830s to the end of Queen Victoria's reign, this new medium developed in many different directions; apparatus evolved, techniques changed and more and more applications of photography were conceived and introduced. While by no means comprehensive, the sources in this section give a flavour of different photographic methods and the associated apparatus, as well as the ways in which these were marketed to new audiences.[1]

It is difficult to establish who produced the first image by photochemical reaction. According to Geoffrey Batchen, '[. . .] at least twenty people from seven European countries entertained the idea of photography between about 1790 and 1839'.[2] In the 1830s, the development of different photographic techniques took place simultaneously in England and France.[3] Louis-Jacques-Mandé Daguerre produced the first 'daguerreotypes' by coating a copper plate with silver, which is then sensitised using iodine fumes, exposed to light and chemically treated with mercury vapour to produce a single, positive photographic image, a unique image with no negatives.[4]

Henry Fox Talbot invented two different processes. The first, 'photogenic drawing', was presented and patented by Talbot in 1839. This involved exposing sensitised paper (paper dipped in sodium chloride with one side coated with silver nitrate) to sunlight while it was in contact with opaque objects. The first source in this section is a report summarising Fox Talbot's lecture to the Royal Society in 1839 in which he discussed the 'photogenic' process. The second, the calotype/Talbotype process, was a negative-positive process that vastly reduced exposure times. This process produced stable paper negatives from which it was possible to generate multiple, positive salted-paper prints. This was an improved version of the earlier photogenic method and was used to produce the images in Talbot's *The Pencil of Nature*. This book was published in fascicles (instalments) between 1844 and 1846, charting different applications for photography. *The Pencil of Nature* was the first major commercially published volume to contain original photographs, and, while it was not a commercial success, it is an important landmark in both photography and the history of the printed book. Included here are Fox Talbot's introductory remarks to the volume along with his discussion of photographing sculpture based on an image of a bust of Patroclus, now in the British Museum.

Elizabeth Sheridan Carey's 'Lines written on seeing a daguerreotype portrait of a lady' is an early example of a form of photographic ekphrasis.[5] Extolling the indexical virtues of the photograph over the painted portrait, Carey writes, 'why prate of Art,/Where nature only plays the part?/No gifted touch could this excel;/ No pencil breathe so sweet a spell'. The reference to 'La Creevy's dark despair' alludes to Miss La Creevy, the miniature painter in Charles Dickens' *Nicholas Nickelby* (1838–1839) who worked from an apartment on the Strand. Note Carey's careful explications of her poem and its arguments in the extensive endnotes. While the daguerreotype in the poem's title is not reproduced in the *Illustrated London News* (*ILN*) piece, an engraving depicts the 'photographic process at Mr. Beard's establishment, Parliament-street, Westminster' and shows the ophthalmic surgeon Jabez Hogg taking a photograph for a client. Hogg published a manual of photography in 1843 and worked for the *ILN* for many years.

Photographic entrepreneur Richard Beard took an early interest in the commercial potential of photography and secured patents on some early camera models and photographic processes. He opened the first public photographic studio in the United Kingdom at the Royal Polytechnic Institute in Regent Street in London. His Parliament Street studio opened in 1842 and was previewed by Prince Albert, who sat for six daguerreotype portraits in March of that year.[6] George Cruikshank's 'Photographic phenomena, or the new school of portrait painting' was included in his 1842 *Omnibus*.[7] The illustration shows a sitter in Beard's studio on a 'posing chair' placed on a raised rotatable platform. Studios were often placed at the top of a building to take advantage of the light. To ensure complete stillness, the subject's head is held in a clamp. The cameras visible on the high shelf are those designed by Alexander Wolcott, an American who opened the first US photographic studio in 1840 and then sold exclusive rights to Beard. The photographer stands on a stepladder and uses a pocket watch to time the exposure. Wolcott's plates were tiny, necessitating the use of magnifying glasses by the customers on the left of the image. The accompanying poem pokes fun at the process of sitting for a portrait and is divided into three sections: 'Invitation to sit', 'The process of the portraiture' and 'The criticisms of the sitters – the moral'.

In 1851, Frederick Scott Archer invented the wet collodion process. Frustrated with the limits of both the daguerreotype (which required a long exposure time) and the calotype (which could produce lots of prints from one negative, but the paper base meant they were less clear), Archer began to experiment with using glass as a negative support. The wet collodion process involved mixing a number of potentially dangerous chemicals. Collodion was made from highly explosive gun cotton (cellulose nitrate), produced by soaking ordinary cotton in sulphuric and nitric acids. This was then mixed with ether, alcohol and potassium iodide to form the collodion substance used to coat glass plates, which replaced the albumen (egg white) used previously. This new technique offered a much faster process for developing photographs.[8] Reproduced here is Archer's short article from the March 1851 issue of the journal *The Chemist,* in which he describes the new process. Though it appears as a rather innocuous ingredient in the wet collodion process, cotton was, of course, a commodity linked to the transatlantic slave trade as well as to poor working conditions in Lancashire cotton mills in the UK. Sources discussing both of these contexts can be found in the *Raw Materials* volume in this series.

The news item from the *Pall Mall Gazette* of 1892 reports a terrible accident involving the spillage of '15 quarts' of collodion in a Paris manufacturer of dry plates, the fumes of which caught fire. As well as highlighting the dangers inherent in using photographic chemicals, it also reflects a move from the wet collodion process to the dry plate process, which gave more flexibility for outdoor photography as it no longer required the use of a portable darkroom tent, chemicals and water. Such a tent, complete with travelling case, can be seen in the advert for W. W. Rouch and Co., a company that supplied optical instruments for chemists and photographers. The advert refers to the recent International Exhibition of 1862 in which the company had exhibited.

The next two sources are also adverts, this time for the Imperial Dry Plate Company established in 1892 by Joseph John Acworth. This company was one of a number of dry plate companies operating towards the end of the nineteenth century.[9] Dating from June 1901, the first advert depicts Lord Roseberry, a liberal politician and prime minister from 1894 to 1895. The tag line 'we are all imperialists nowadays' misquotes one of Roseberry's speeches from 1899 in which he asserts, 'now that we are all Imperialists – and I think we are all Imperialists'.[10] The advert depicts Roseberry in Parliament and makes a connection between the quality of Imperial dry plates and the politics of late-Victorian imperialism. The second advert from June 1909 plays on the same theme: this time depicting a Britannia-type figure in a boat heading overseas, it suggests that Imperial dry plates will conquer a global market, mirroring the contemporary appetite for British colonial expansion. The final source from the Imperial Dry Plate Company is a short article from its 1916 handbook. Musing on the meaning of the term 'imperial', it draws attention to its 'literal translation' as 'commanding'. Note the boxed advert for dry plates at the bottom of the page that speaks to this idea: 'The TESTED Best MUST Lead the Rest'.

As photography advanced, so did its market potential on the basis of the development of new apparatus and devices. The next source is an advert for stereoscopes and stereographs produced by the London Stereographic Company. A stereoscope is an optical device for viewing stereographs; two photographs taken with a stereoscopic camera mounted next to each other which, when viewed through the apparatus, are combined by the brain to give the appearance of a 3D image.[11] Using a tag line from Shakespeare's *Hamlet*, 'It seems nay madam it is', the advert plays on the relationship between reality and illusion effected by the stereoscope.

Two sources in this section are aimed at potential investors in the Birmingham Mutoscope Company. One of a number of 'scopes and 'tropes that developed across the period, the mutoscope was an early device capable of producing animated pictures invented in 1894 by W. K. L. Dickson and Herman Casler.[12] Here, the company advertises for potential shareholders in a business proposition for coin-operated mutoscopes within 15 miles of Birmingham town hall. According to the advert, the device 'presents to the eye objects of such startling appearance of reality as to border on the marvellous' and has the potential to be 'a most seductive and untiring money earner'. The cartoon from an 1899 issue of *Punch* imagines the usefulness of the mutoscope to the gallery visitor who is pressed for time. Our final source is from Cuthbert Bede's *Photographic Pleasures*. Bede's series of satirical sketches mocks the overwhelming array of new photographic processes under development in the 1850s. These include Archer's wet collodion process, William Crooke's waxed-paper process and Farnham Maxwell-Lyte's work on 'instantaneous' photography.[13]

Notes

1 We have not included any sources relating to the theme of photography and colour as this is covered comprehensively in Lindsay Smith (ed.) *Color and Victorian Photography* (London: Routledge, 2020).

2 Geoffrey Batchen, *Burning with Desire: the Conception of Photography* (MIT: 1999), p. ix. See, for example, Thomas Wedgwood and Humphry Davy's 'An Account of a Method of Copying Paintings upon Glass' (1802) reproduced in Smith, *Colour and Photography*, pp. 101–5.

3 For full technical details of these processes see John Hannavay (ed.) *Encyclopaedia of Nineteenth Century Photography* (London: Routledge, 2018), p. 367; pp. 1376–1379.

4 On Daguerre's collaboration with Joseph Nicéphore Niépce see Batchen, pp. 24–35.

5 Elizabeth Carey was the daughter of William Sheridan, an Irish art critic and engraver. Elizabeth was a writer and privately printed a book of poems, *Ivy Leaves,* in 1837.

6 *The Times*, 22nd March, 1842, p. 5.

7 It illustrates a poem by Sidney Laman Blanchard.

8 For more details on the life and work of Archer see *The Encyclopedia of Nineteenth Century Photography* entry on Archer by Martin Barnes from which this description is taken. (pp. 55–57).

9 Others included Ilford Limited, founded by Alfred Hugh Harman. Harman set up the 'Britannia Works' in the late 1870s to manufacture dry plates. These became known as 'Britannia plates', but following an argument with his agent (Marion's and Co. In London), he lost the right to prevent Marion's from using the Britannia name and thenceforth marketed his plates as 'Ilford' plates. The business continued to grow and in 1918, Ilford acquired control of the Imperial Dry Plate Company that had been established in 1892. For a detailed narrative on the history of Ilford Limited see https://collection.sciencemuseumgroup.org.uk/people/ap8818/ilford-limited [accessed 1st May 2021].

10 *Lord Roseberry his life and speeches* (London: Hutchinson and Co., 1900), p. 963. The line 'We are all imperialists nowadays' can be attributed to the editor of the *Oxford Magazine* who wrote 'we are all "imperialists" nowadays' in an editorial on 6th February 1895, p. 196. Quoted in MG Brock MC Curthoys (eds.) *The History of the University of Oxford: Volume VII: Nineteenth-Century Oxford*, Part 2: 7, p. 690.

11 As Lindsay Smith records, in 1832 'Charles Wheatstone invented the first instrument by which stereoscopic effect could be observed' (this was the reflecting stereoscope that combined two drawings). However, 'it was David Brewster's refracting instrument described to the Royal Society of Edinburgh in 1849, that established public interest in the medium'. Lindsay Smith, *Victorian Photography, Painting and Poetry* (Cambridge: CUP, 1995), p. 8. For more sources on the stereoscope see the *Inventions and Technology* volume in this series.

12 Others include the stereoscope, luxoscope, kinetoscope, zoetrope and praxinoscope.

13 A photograph was considered to be instantaneous when the exposure time was short enough to freeze action. For full details of the development of this process across the century see *The Encyclopaedia of Photography*, p. 746.

110

REPORT OF HENRY FOX TALBOT'S LECTURE 'SOME ACCOUNT OF THE ART OF PHOTOGENIC DRAWING OR THE PROCESS BY WHICH NATURAL OBJECTS MAY BE MADE TO DELINEATE THEMSELVES WITHOUT THE AID OF THE ARTIST'S PENCIL'

Read January 31st 1839 and report printed in *Abstracts of the Papers Printed in the Philosophical Transactions of the Royal Society of London,* pp. 120–121

January 31, 1839.

JOHN W. LUBBOCK, Esq., Vice-President and Treas., in the Chair.

John Wesley Williams, and James Yates, Esqrs., were severally elected Fellows of the Society.

A paper was read, entitled, "Some account of the Art of Photogenic Drawing, or the Process by which Natural Objects may be made to delineate themselves without the aid of the Artist's Pencil." By H. F. Talbot, Esq., F.R.S.

In this communication the author states, that during the last four or five years he has invented and brought to a considerable degree of perfection, a process for copying the forms of natural objects by means of solar light, which is received upon paper previously prepared in a particular manner. He observes, that a prior attempt of this kind is recorded in the Journal of the Royal Institution for 1802; by which it appears that the idea was originally suggested by Mr. Wedgwood, and afterwards experimented on by Sir Humphry Davy. These philosophers found, that their principle, though theoretically true, yet failed in practice, on account of certain difficulties; the two principal of which were: *first,* that the paper could not be rendered sufficiently sensible to receive any impression whatever from

DOI: 10.4324/9781315400266-133

the feeble light of a camera obscura; and *secondly,* that the pictures which were formed by the solar rays could not be preserved, owing to their still continuing to be acted upon by the light.

The author states that his experiments were begun without his being aware of this prior attempt; and that in the course of them he discovered methods of overcoming the two difficulties above related. With respect to the latter, he says, that he has found it possible by a subsequent process, so to fix the images or shadows formed by the solar rays, that they become insensible to light, and consequently admit of being preserved during any length of time: as an example of which, he mentions, that he has exposed some of his pictures to the sunshine for the space of an hour, without injury.

With respect to the other point, he states that he has succeeded in discovering a method of preparing the paper which renders it much more sensitive to light than any which had been used previously; and by means of which he finds, that there is no difficulty in fixing the pictures given by the camera obscura and by the solar microscope.

He states that in the summer of 1835 he made a great number of portraits of a house in the country of ancient architecture, several of which were this evening exhibited to the Society.

After some speculations on the possibility of discovering a yet more sensitive paper, the author mentions, that the kind employed by him may be rendered so much so, as to become visibly affected by the full light of the sun, in the space of half a second.

The rest of this paper contains an account of various other ways in which this method may be employed in practice, according to the kind of object which it is required to copy: also, a brief mention of the great variety of effects resulting from comparatively small differences in the mode of preparation of the paper: and, of certain anomalies which occur in the process, the cause of which has not hitherto been rendered distinctly manifest.

In conclusion, the author designates this as "a new process, which he offers to the lovers of science and nature."

111

HENRY FOX TALBOT, 'INTRODUCTORY REMARKS'

The Pencil of Nature (London: Longman, Brown, Green and Longmans, 1844), pp. 1–2

Introductory remarks

The little work now presented to the Public is the first attempt to publish a series of plates or pictures wholly executed by the new art of Photogenic Drawing, without any aid whatever from the artist's pencil.

The term "Photography" is now so well known, that an explanation of it is perhaps superfluous; yet, as some persons may still be unacquainted with the art, even by name, its discovery being still of very recent date, a few words may be looked for of general explanation.

It may suffice, then, to say, that the plates of this work have been obtained by the mere action of Light upon sensitive paper. They have been formed or depicted by optical and chemical means alone, and without the aid of any one acquainted with the art of drawing. It is needless, therefore, to say that they differ in all respects, and as widely us possible, in their origin, from plates of the ordinary kind, which owe their existence to the united skill of the Artist and the Engraver.

They are impressed by Nature's hand; and what they want as yet of delicacy and finish of execution arises chiefly from our want of sufficient knowledge of her laws. When we have learnt more, by experience, respecting the formation of such pictures, they will doubtless be brought much nearer to perfection; and though we may not be able to conjecture with any certainty what rank they may hereafter attain to as pictorial productions, they will surely find their own sphere of utility, both for completeness of detail and correctness of perspective.

The Author of the present work having been so fortunate as to discover, about ten years ago, the principles and practice of Photogenic Drawing, is desirous that the first specimen of an Art, likely in all probability to be much employed in future, should be published in the country where it was first discovered. And he makes no doubt that his countrymen will deem such an intention sufficiently laudable to induce them to excuse the imperfections necessarily incident to a first attempt to exhibit an Art of so great singularity, which employs processes entirely new, and having no analogy to any thing in use before. That such imperfections will occur in a first essay, must

DOI: 10.4324/9781315400266-134

indeed be expected. At present the Art can hardly be said to have advanced beyond its infancy – at any rate, it is yet in a very early stage – and its practice is often impeded by doubts and difficulties, which, with increasing knowledge, will diminish and disappear. Its progress will be more rapid when more minds are devoted to its improvement, and when more of skilful manual assistance is employed in the manipulation of its delicate processes; the paucity of which skilled assistance at the present moment the Author finds one of the chief difficulties in his way.

112

HENRY FOX TALBOT, BUST OF PATROCULUS (PLATE 17)

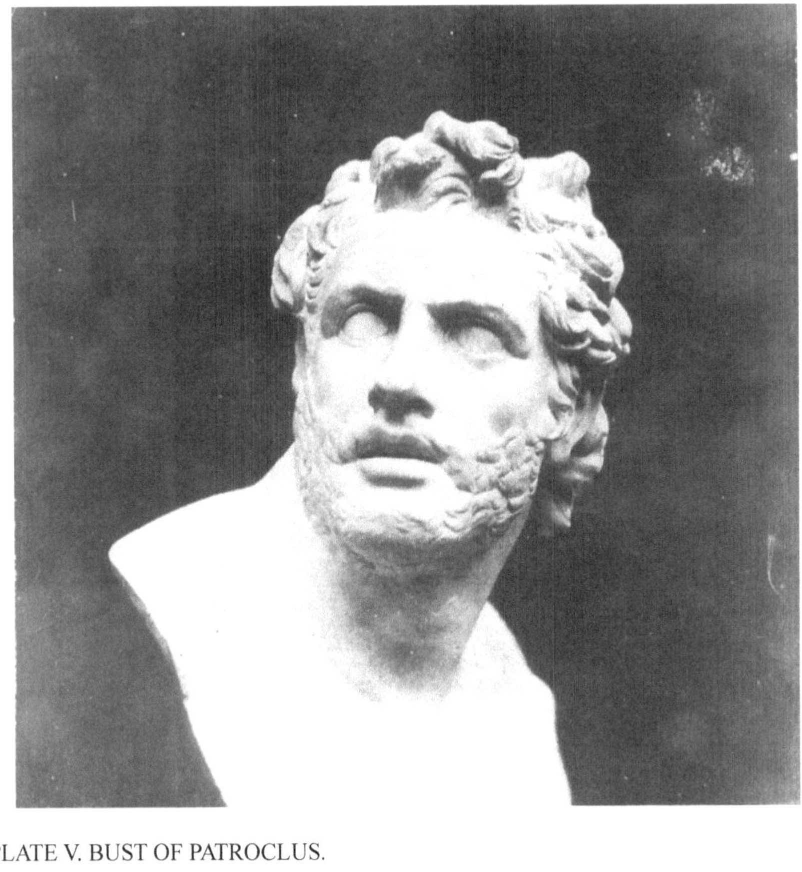

PLATE V. BUST OF PATROCLUS.

Plate V. Bust of Patroclus

Statues, busts, and other specimens of sculpture, are generally well represented by the Photographic Art; and also very rapidly, in consequence of their whiteness.

DOI: 10.4324/9781315400266-135

These delineations are susceptible of an almost unlimited variety: since in the first place, a statue may be placed in any position with regard to the sun, either directly opposite to it, or at any angle: the directness or obliquity of the illumination causing of course an immense difference in the effect. And when a choice has been made of the direction in which the sun's rays shall fall, the statue may be then turned round on its pedestal, which produces a second set of variations no less considerable than the first. And when to this is added the change of size which is produced in the image by bringing the Camera Obscura nearer to the statue or removing it further off, it becomes evident how very great a number of different effects may be obtained from a single specimen of sculpture.

With regard to many statues, however, a better effect is obtained by delineating them in cloudy weather than in sunshine. For, the sunshine causes such strong shadows as sometimes to confuse the subject. To prevent this, it is a good plan to hold a white cloth on one side of the statue at a little distance to reflect back the sun's rays and cause a faint illumination of the parts which would otherwise be lost in shadow.

113

ELIZABETH SHERIDAN CAREY, 'LINES WRITTEN ON SEEING A DAGUERREOTYPE PORTRAIT OF A LADY'

Illustrated London News, August 19 1843, p. 125

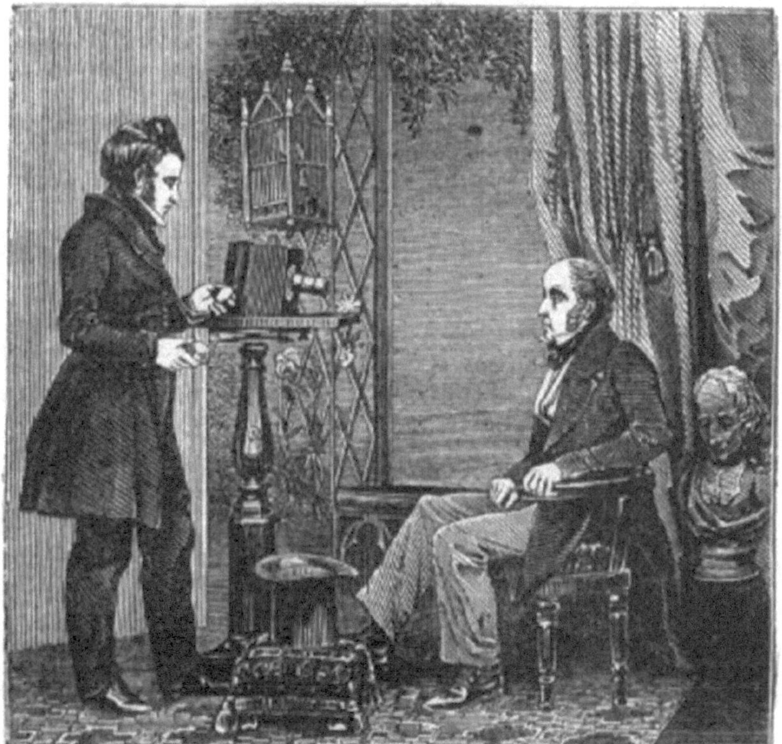

LINES WRITTEN ON SEEING A DAGUERREOTYPE PORTRAIT OF A LADY.

BY MISS ELIZABETH SHERIDAN CAREY.

DOI: 10.4324/9781315400266-136

"To the artist and true connoisseur, the mere vehicle employed will be a matter of little importance, and he will be delighted with whatever is excellent of its kind." – D. C. Read. *Preface to the Catalogue of his Etchings.*

Wondrous it is! form, face, and air,
Dress, attitude, are pictured there!
Nay, pictured not – why prate of Art
Where Nature, only, plays the part?
No gifted touch could this excel;
No pencil breathe so sweet a spell!
Not *Reynolds,* in his "noon of fame,"
Could put this magic head to shame,
Nor with the splendour of his hues,
O'er canvas, worthier traits diffuse;
Not *Lawrence,* with his suasive line,
His pearly shades, and soft carmine;
Not *Hayter,* who, with wizard hand,
Limns forth the "Layde of the Land,"
And shows how fair, how all serene,
In sov'reign beauty shines a Queen;
Not one with chalk, and ductile oil,
And varied tints, and patient toil,
Back'd by the love of ancient schools,
Their hints, their practice, sleight, and rules, –
Could *in veracity* surpass[1]
A portrait truer than the glass.

Here is no feature half awry,
Too large a nose, too small an eye,
No forehead just an inch too low,
No faulty stroke, no faithless glow;[2]
And, best of all eulogia! here
No false deceiving charms appear;
But the fair face as Nature made it,
So hath the regal sun portray'd it!
The cordial, frank, old English air
Sits nobly on the features there;
And shrewd and bland, with cheerful wile
She seems to seek an answ'ring smile.
That is her turn – you may compare it, –
And that her very glance – I'll swear it!
There is her brow, *sans* cap or wimple,
And there her mirth-enjoying dimple –
That comely cheek, and rounded chin –

To mar them were a mortal sin!
There clusters each bright waving tress,
And there's, I vow, her last new dress –
A shaded silk, each stripe and fold;
And, as I live! the chain of gold
Whose glitt'ring circles lightly deck
the alabaster of that neck;
And, see, the brooch – that petted snake,
More happy than in flow'ry brake.

Most marvellous! so soft, so true!
A priceless pearl – a rare bijou!
So much herself – keep it beside you,
Nor time nor tide can e'er divide you;
Or place it, in the sun, before you,
And strangest fancies will creep o'er you;
Those sportive eyes will seem to glisten –
That little ear, well pleased, to listen –
That arch and coaxing smile to play,
And snare your very heart away –
Those lips to breathe, to move, to talk,
And, with a gentle aspiration,
To share their owner's morning walk,
Give you right courteous invitation.

Oh! hence-immortaliz'd *Daguerre* –
The fair *La Creevy's*[3] dark despair!
Whoe'er shall wisely wish to be
Portray'd in pure reality,
And in the likeness of his friend,
Would have no borrow'd beauties blend;
Nor yet, by clumsy art defaced,
Find charms and much lov'd traits erased,
And view, disgusted, crude outline –
Vile colour, attitude, design –
With bold pretence assume the place
Of beauty, intellect, and grace:[4]
Whoe'er, in short, seeks life and truth,
In health or sickness, age or youth,
And need not beg "some pow'r to gie 'em
To see themselves as others see 'em" –
Will to the sunny roof repair,
And start to find their shadow there;
But wither'd beau, and wrinkled belle,

Whose mirrors fatal tidings tell;
Who fret and fume, and peak and pine
O'er youth and beauty's long decline,
And ban the glass that e'er declares
Their shrunken mien and silver hairs –
Those tott'ring knights and ancient dames
Who still aspire to kindle flames,
And dream of love and Cupid's darts,
And Hymen's bonds, and bleeding hearts,
And think it very hard to show 'em
As all the world has chanced to knew'em;
And they, though young, of homely air,
Who die to be esteem'd most fair,
Who, closely wrapt in self-conceit,
Believe themselves perfection sweet,
And loathe the pictures that disclose
Not tints of lily and of rose,
Nor in the false, obsequious line
Make Venus or Adonis shine –
Of fop, and fool, and sere old maid,
Of truth's unflatt'ring forms afraid,
Hope not the patronage, Daguerre.
With them thy art is foul, not fair,
"*Mere trick!*" and "*stuff!*" and "*imposition!*"
"*Unfit for any exhibition!*"
"*Black, dirty daubs!*" "Faugh! *coarse and vile!*"
"*Old, ugly things that never smile!*"
And "*why* the Good Queen Dowager
Should mount to CLAUDET's studi – *o,*
And Louis Philippe come to err
So much as to the Baron go.
They cannot for their lives declare!"
So hate ye, Beard, Claudet, Daguerre.[5]

Take back the picture now, Lucrece
(Reluctantly we must resign it!);
And, doating on its ev'ry trace,
Ere in its casket you enshrine it,
Whene'er you gaze, and gaze and feel
Its mystic influence o'er you steal,
And seem to commune, though apart,
With the sweet sister of your heart,
Bethink you she would prize, like you,
A sister's faithful semblance too.

We wot a certain hazel eye,
Bright as the star in yonder sky –
A pencill'd brow, a forehead fair –
And glossy braids of raven hair –
A merry glance – a sunny smile,
Whose playful sweetness doth beguile –
A winning, heart-illumin'd face,
Where goodness hath impress her trace,
Proclaiming o'er each flexile trait
Her own supreme eternal sway.
But why these items here recall?
Peep in your glass, you'll see them all;
And, if you would "dear Sarah" please,
Send her the portraiture of these –
A sparkling, speaking, fond reflection,
For ever priz'd by pure affection.

E. S. C.

Our engraving represents the photographic process at Mr. Beard's establishment, Parliament-street, Westminster.

Notes

1 Nothing can be further from my intention than to decry the brilliant productions of these masters, or to snatch from painting the highest honours awarded to it by its most ardent admirers – among whom I desire to be ranked: I refer only to that *unerring accuracy of resemblance* which, unattainable by the pencil, renders the Daguerreotype invaluable in portraiture.

2 Defects "plenty as blackberries" in the productions of the *La Creevy* school.

3 Who can have forgotten the warm-hearted little miniature-paintress, Miss La Creevy, afterwards Mrs. Tim Linkin water, in "Nicholas Nickleby?"

4 The dazzling, but often fugitive, lights of expression, which not infrequently elude the practised and accomplished pencil, are rarely, if ever, caught by an inferior hand. To copy the features is a task of little difficulty; but to inform them with the character, and animate them with the expression of the sitter, require gifts and attainments not possessed by the ordinary face-painter. Here the Daguerreotype is *unrivalled,* and preserves, for ever, the fleeting sunbeam of a smile.

5 It is impossible to purge poor human nature of conceit. "*Amour-propre aime les portraits;*" but, as the Daguerreotype tells "the truth – the whole truth – and nothing but the truth," they who, innocent of the attributes, pretend to youth, beauty, grace, and intellectual character, and to whom many years' close consultation of the glass has failed to dispel the "dear delusion," are ludicrously dismayed when they espy their honest resemblances, and as they can be in no wise persuaded of the unpalatable fact that the Daguerreotype is infallible, they fall foul on it, and denounce it with a heat and vindictiveness unspeakably amusing. It is needless to say that such aspirants only can be disappointed by a discovery that cannot be too highly estimated by the social affections. What treasure can we possess more coveted than the *perfect* likeness of the friend or relative most dear to our heart, and when did the pencil thoroughly satisfy the expectations of the eye familiar with the form, air, and bearing of the portrayed?

114

GEORGE CRUIKSHANK, 'PHOTOGRAPHIC PHENOMENA, OR THE NEW SCHOOL OF PORTRAIT PAINTING'

George Cruikshank's *Omnibus*
(London: Tilt and Bogue, 1842, pp. 29–32)

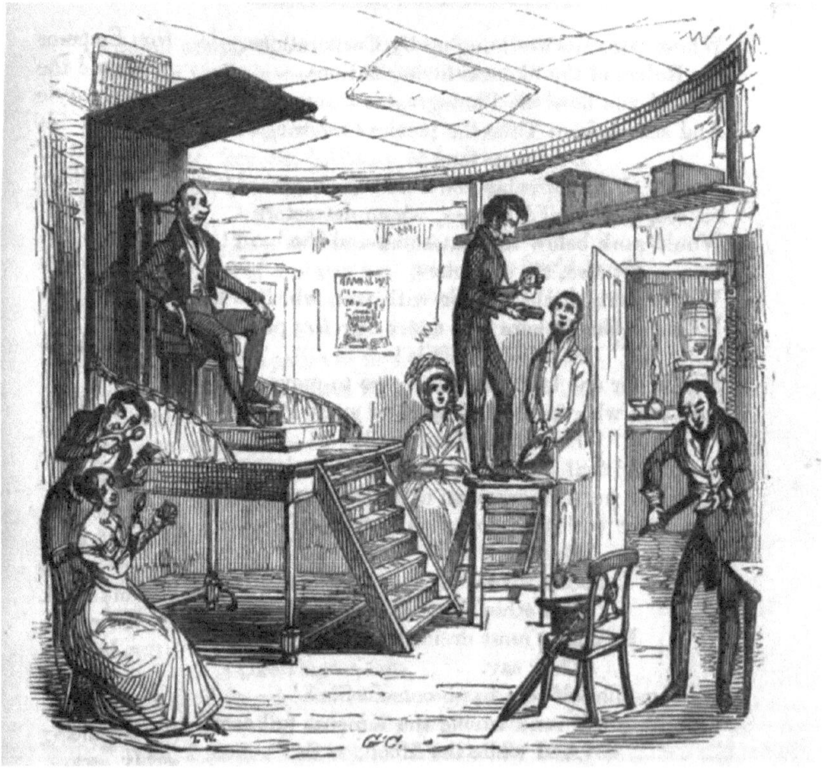

DOI: 10.4324/9781315400266-137

"Sit, cousin Percy; sit, good cousin Hotspur!"—HENRY IV.
"My lords, be seated."—*Speech from the Throne.*

I. – INVITATION TO SIT.

Now sit, if ye have courage, cousins all!
Sit, all ye grandmamas, wives, aunts, and mothers;
Daughters and sisters, widows, brides, and nieces;
In bonnets, braids, caps, tippets, or pelisses,
The muff, mantilla, boa, scarf, or shawl!
Sit all ye uncles, godpapas, and brothers,
Fathers and nephews, sons, and next of kin,
Husbands, half-brother's cousin's sires, and others;
Be you as Science young, or old as Sin:
Turn, Persian-like, your faces to the sun!
And have each one
His portrait done,
Finish'd, one may say, before it's begun.

Nor you alone,
Oh! slight acquaintances! or blood relations!
But sit, oh! public Benefactors,
Whose portraits are hung up by Corporations.
Ye Rulers of the likeness-loving nations,
Ascend you now the Photographic throne,
And snatch from Time the precious mornings claim'd
By artists famed
(In the Court Circular you'll find them named).
Sit too, ye laurell'd Heroes, whom detractors
Would rank below the statesman and the bard!
Sit also, all ye Actors,
Whose fame would else die with you, which is hard:
Whose *Falstaffs* here will never *Slenders* prove,
So true the art is!
M.P.'s, for one brief moment cease to move;
And you who stand as Leaders of great Parties,
Be sitting Members!
Ye intellectual Marchers, sit resign'd!
And oh! ye Authors, men of dazzling mind,
Perchance with faces foggy as November's,
Pray sit!
Apollo turned R.A.
The other day,
Making a most decided hit.

They say.
Phœbus himself – he has become a Shee!
(Morning will rank among the Knights full soon)
And while the Moon,
Who only draws the tides, is clean outdone,
The Stars are all astonishment to see
Earth – sitting for her portrait – to the Sun!

II. – THE PROCESS OF THE PORTRAITURE.

It's all very fine, is it not, oh! ye Nine?
To tell us this planet is going too fast,
On a comet-like track through the wilderness vast:
Instead of collision, and chances of splitting
In contact with stars rushing down the wrong line,
The world at this moment can't get on – for sitting:
And Earth, like the Lady enchanted in *Comus,*
Fix'd fast to her chair
With a dignified air,
Is expecting to sit for a century there;
Much wondering, possibly, half in despair,
How the deuce she's to find her way back to her domus.

"Keep moving," we know, was the cry long ago;
But now, never hare was "found sitting," I swear,
Like the crowds who repair
To old Cavendish Square,
And mount up a mile and a quarter of stair,
In procession that beggars the Lord Mayor's show!
And all are on tiptoe, the high and the low,
To sit in that glass-cover'd blue studio;
In front of those boxes, wherein when you look
Your image reversed will minutely appear,
So delicate, forcible, brilliant, and clear,
So small, full, and round, with a life so profound,
As none ever wore
In a mirror before;
Or the depths of a glassy and branch-shelter'd brook,
That glides amidst moss o'er a smooth-pebbled ground.
Apollo, whom Drummond of Hawthornden styled
"Apelles of flowers,"
Now mixes his showers
Of sunshine, with colours by clouds undefiled;

Apelles indeed to man, woman, and child.
His agent on earth, when your attitude's right,
Your collar adjusted, your locks in their place,
Just seizes one moment of favouring light,
And utters three sentences – "Now it's begun," –
"It's going on now, sir," – and "Now it is done;"
And lo! as I live, there's the cut of your face
On a silvery plate,
Unerring as fate,
Worked off in celestial and strange mezzotint,
A little resembling an elderly print.
"Well, I *never!*" all cry; "it is cruelly like you!"
But Truth is unpleasant
To prince and to peasant.
You recollect Lawrence, and think of the graces
That Chalon and Company give to their faces;
The face you have worn fifty years doesn't strike you!

III. – THE CRITICISMS OF THE SITTERS – THE MORAL.

"Can this be *me!* do look, mama!"
Poor Jane begins to whimper;
"I *have* a smile, 'tis true; – but, pa!
This gives me quite a simper."
Says Tibb, whose plays are worse than bad,
"It makes my forehead flat;"
And being classical, he'll add,
"I'm blow'd if I'm like *that.*"

Courtly, all candour, owns his portrait true;
"Oh, yes, it's like; yes, very; it will do.
Extremely like me – every feature – *but*
That plain pug-nose; now mine's the Grecian cut!
Her Grace surveys her face with drooping lid;
Prefers the portrait which Sir Thomas did;
Owns that o'er this *some* traits of truth are sprinkled;
But views the brow with anger – "Why, it's wrinkled!"
"Like *me!*" cries Sir Turtle; "I'll lay two to one
It would only be guess'd by my foes;
No, no, it is plain there are spots in the sun,
Which accounts for these spots on my nose."

"A likeness!" cries Crosslook, the lawyer, and sneers;
"Yes, the wig, throat and forehead I spy,

And the mouth, chin, and cheeks, and the nose and the ears,
  But it gives me a cast in the eye!"
Thus needs it the courage of old Cousin Hotspur,
  To sit to an artist who flatters no sitter;
Yet Self-love will urge us to seek him, for what spur
  So potent as that, though it make the truth bitter!
And thus are all flocking, to see Phœbus mocking,
  Or making queer faces, a visage per minute;
And truly 'tis shocking, if winds should be rocking
  The building, or clouds darken all that's within it,
        To witness the frights
        Which shadows and lights
Manufacture, as like as an owl to a linnet.
        For there, while you sit up,
        Your countenance lit up,
The mists fly across, a magnificent rack;
And your portrait's a patch, with its bright and its black,
Out-Rembrandting Rembrandt, in ludicrous woe,
Like a chimney-sweep caught in a shower of snow.
    Yet nothing can keep the crowd below,
    And still they mount up, stair by stair;
    And every morn, by the hurry and hum,
    Each seeking a prize in the lottery there,
    You fancy the "last day of drawing" has come.

L. B.

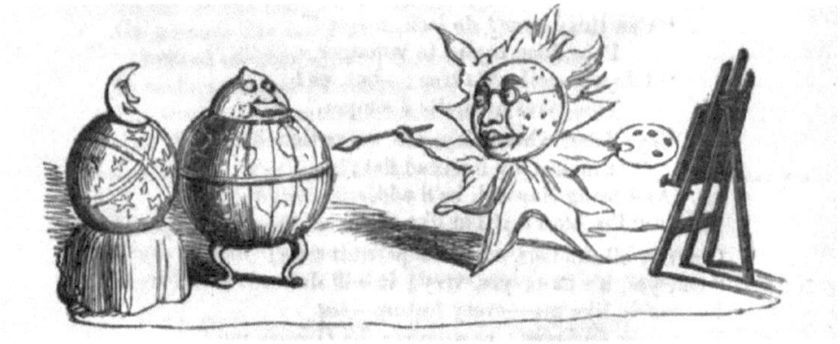

[All the World and his Wife must recollect that they are not figuring before a mere mortal artist with whom they may all the while laugh and chat. Here you must sit mute and motionless. You *may* wink; you may perhaps just put on a smile; but you *must not* laugh; for if you do, one half of your head will go off!]

115

FREDERICK SCOTT ARCHER, 'ON THE USE OF COLLODION IN PHOTOGRAPHY'

The Chemist, March 1851, pp. 257–258

by frederick scott archer, esq.

THE imperfections in paper photography, arising from the uneven texture of the material, however much care may be taken in the manufacture of it, and which from its nature, being a fibrous substance, cannot, I believe, be overcome, has induced me to lay it aside and endeavor to find some other substance more applicable, and meeting the necessary conditions required of it, such as fineness of surface, transparency, and case of manipulation.

A layer of albumen on glass answers many of these conditions, producing a fine transparent film, but it is difficult to obtain an even coating on the glass plate; it requires careful drying, and is so extremely delicate when damp that it will not bear the slightest handling; besides these objections, the necessity of having a large stock of glass when a number of pictures are to be taken, is much against its general use. My endeavor, therefore, has been to overcome these difficulties, and I find from numerous trials that *Collodion,* when well prepared, is admirably adapted for photographic purposes as a substitute for paper. It presents a perfectly transparent and even surface when poured on glass, and being in some measure tough and elastic, will, when damp, bear handling in several stages of the process.

I will now give a short outline of my mode of using it. The first step in the process is to prepare the solution of collodion. There are several ways of doing this, but I will briefly allude to two.

Pour a quantity (say 1 oz.) of collodion into a bottle containing dry iodide of silver. Shake them well together, and then allow the excess of iodide of silver to settle. The collodion will in this way take up a certain quantity of the silver salt, and become opaque; it should then be transferred to another bottle containing iodide of potassium, to be again well shaken up until the iodide of silver is entirely dissolved, and the solution becomes perfectly transparent.

Or this: – To a solution of iodide of potassium in spirits of wine add a small quantity of iodide of silver sufficient to saturate the iodide of potassium; let,

DOI: 10.4324/9781315400266-138

however, the latter salt be in excess. Add a small quantity of this solution to the collodion, between 5 and 10 grs. by measure to 1 oz. of collodion will be sufficient, and if any of the iodide of silver should precipitate, a small quantity of iodide of potassium must be added to dissolve it. In this way, or by the former mode, the collodion may be prepared.

The next step is to spread this solution evenly on a plate of glass. This can be done by pouring a sufficient quantity on the glass to run in a body freely. When it has entirely covered the glass plate, let the superabundance be drained off at one corner into the bottle again; this operation cannot be done too quickly, for the other rapidly evaporating would prevent the collodion running evenly over the surface of the plate, from becoming too thick.

The plate is now plunged into a bath of nitrate of silver, allowed to remain there for a few seconds, and then washed in water. (This washing is intended to remove all the ether from the surface of the collodion, which, if allowed to remain, would cause an unevenness in the sensitiveness of the surface, producing streaks or spots.) Immediately after washing, it may be exposed to the action of light for the time necessary to obtain a picture. This picture can be developed either by gallic or pyrogallic acid. If the latter acid be used, a few precautions are necessary, to which I will allude presently. The former acid may be used as a bath, in the ordinary way. After the picture is developed, the film of collodion should be loosened from the edges of the glass plate with a flat glass rod. By doing this, it will easily separate from the plate and can be allowed to float freely in the water bath, previous to being placed in the bath of hyposulphite of soda, and then again thoroughly washed.

The drawing can now be mounted on a plate of glass, and when dry can be varnished, to protect it from injury.

If thought more convenient (and, in fact, this mode is the best when pyrogallic acid is used), the film of collodion, after being exposed to light and the image developed, can be removed from the glass plate (leaving the fixing and final washing to be done at leisure) by rolling it up on a glass rod, thus: – Take a sheet of ordinary white wrapping or thick blotting paper (if glazed it will be better), about the same breadth and about one-third longer than the drawing to be removed, soak it in water, and place it with the glazed side in contact with the surface of collodion. Turn the end of the collodion picture over the edge of the paper lying upon it, then place the glass rod just within the edge, and commence rolling it upon the rod; with a little dexterity, this can be accomplished without injuring the drawing. The cylinder thus formed, is easily removed from the glass rod, and can be preserved for any length of time in this state by being kept damp and away from the light, to be finally fixed at some more convenient time. Thus one plate of glass will be sufficient to make any number of drawings upon, the above operations being repeated for each picture.

The plate of glass should be rather larger than the drawings intended to be made upon it, to allow for rough edges, &c. The back of the glass may be ground to get the focus upon, and one side should be formed into a kind of handle to prevent the hand of the operator being near the solution when the glass is in use.

30 grs. of nitrate of silver to 1 oz. of water will be sufficient for the nitrate of silver bath.

3 grs. of pyrogallic acid to 1 oz. of water, to which must be added about 1 drachm of acetic acid.

Between 5 and 10 grs. of nitrate of silver to 1 oz. of water.

The two latter solutions are to be mixed in equal proportions when a picture is to be developed. A wide-mouthed glass measure will be necessary to hold this mixture.

I have found it convenient to have a trough made of gutta percha, the two sides and bottom of which are about ¼ inch high and just large enough to hold the glass plate. With this trough the mixed solution can be poured rapidly over the plate, without fear of any being thrown over the edges.

18th February, 1851.

116

'DREADFUL COLLODION EXPLOSION IN PARIS'

Pall Mall Gazette, September 12 1892, p. 5

Four persons burnt to death

An explosion which occurred on Saturday in Paris in the Rue Buffon, opposite the Jardin des Plantes, and which, during the first excitement, was attributed to dynamite, has been discovered to have been caused by collodion. The upper floor of the house, No. 25, is occupied by M. Chapron, a manufacturer of special dry-plates for photographers. M. Chapron was in his workshop, together with Madame Chapron, their two daughters, the servant, and two workgirls, when Madame Chapron let fall a jar containing about fifteen quarts of collodion, which broke and covered the floor with its contents. Everybody present commenced to mop up the precious liquid with sponges (telegraphs the Paris correspondent of the *Chronicle*), but in their anxiety to save the collodion they neglected to open the windows, and the fumes of the collodion reached a stove in an adjacent drying-room, and produced a most formidable explosion. One by one all the other vessels containing collodion and other chemicals exploded, setting fire to the place; the floor of the apartment fell through, and communicated the flames to that beneath. M. and Mdme. Staude and the other tenants had fortunately fled at the first explosion. The neighbours were soon on the spot; they heard the groans of the victims in the burning house, and soon saw the two workgirls, terribly burnt, jump from the window, followed by a son of M. Chapron, who was saved by catching hold of a window bar until a neighbour brought him down a ladder. His sister had escaped by the staircase with all her clothes in flames. Mdme. Chapron also escaped the same way, but would not leave the spot until she was informed that her husband had been conveyed to the hospital. This, said to calm the unfortunate woman, was, however, untrue, for when the firemen had extinguished the flames they found his body hanging between two rafters of the fallen floor, and burnt out of semblance to a human being. The charred corpse of the servant, Marie Peyrout, was found among the burning débris on the ground floor. The two children, Réné and Suzanne Chapron, died at the hospital during the night. Mdme. Chapron and the two workgirls are not expected to recover from their injuries.

DOI: 10.4324/9781315400266-139

117

ADVERTISEMENT FOR W.W. ROUCH AND CO.

From *the Photographic News Almanac or the Yearbook of Photography for 1863*, p. x

W. W. ROUCH AND CO.

(Formerly **BURFIELD & ROUCH**),

MANUFACTURING CHEMISTS,

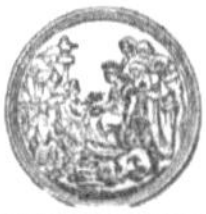

Opticians & Photographic Instrument Makers,

180, STRAND, W.C., LONDON.

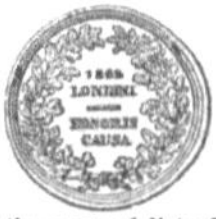

CLASS 14, INTERNATIONAL EXHIBITION.

W. W. ROUCH and Co. respectfully direct the attention of Photographers to the annexed list of specialities, which may be seen, with every requisite of the Art, at their Show Rooms, 180, Strand, W.C.

Rouch's (Edwards') Improved Model Photographic Tent,

(REGISTERED.)

"Moderate in price, and far superior to any other substitute for a dark room."—*Official Illustrated Catalogue.*

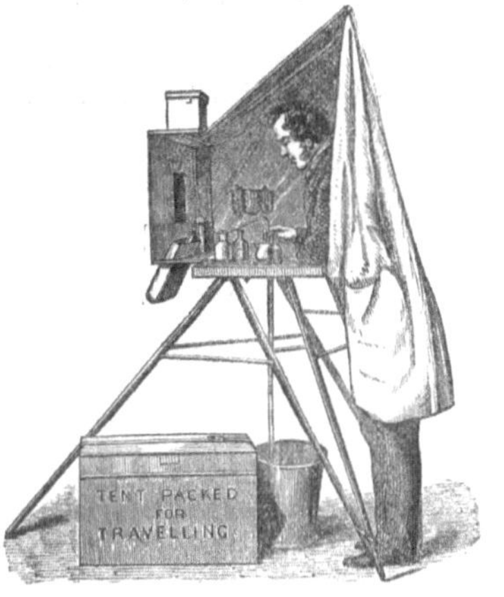

"The best of the kind yet invented."—*Popular Guide to the International Exhibition.*

Section, showing the method of working the Model Photographic Tent.

"One of the most complete and conveniently arranged tents which we have yet seen."—*Photographic News*, Nov. 7th, 1862.

"A very perfect arrangement for the photographer, whether in the field or *en route.*"—*British Journal of Photography*, Dec. 1st, 1862.

Mr. F. BEDFORD (Photographer to H.R H. the Prince of Wales in the East), writes :—"I shall be able quite conscientiously to recommend your new tent to any of my friends."

The above arrangement is intended to supersede, and is an improvement suggested by Mr. ERNEST EDWARDS, on ROUCH'S Operating Chamber; it has since been further improved by Mr. ROUCH, and is now unhesitatingly pronounced to be perfect by all who have seen and used it. Further particulars and price on application.

ROUCH'S MODEL OPERATING-ROOM STAND,

The most elegant, efficient, and firm Stand in the Market,
Possessing all the movements of the best French Table Stands, at one-third less cost.

DOI: 10.4324/9781315400266-140

118

THE IMPERIAL DRY PLATE CO., 'WE ARE ALL IMPERIALISTS NOW-A-DAYS', JUNE 1901

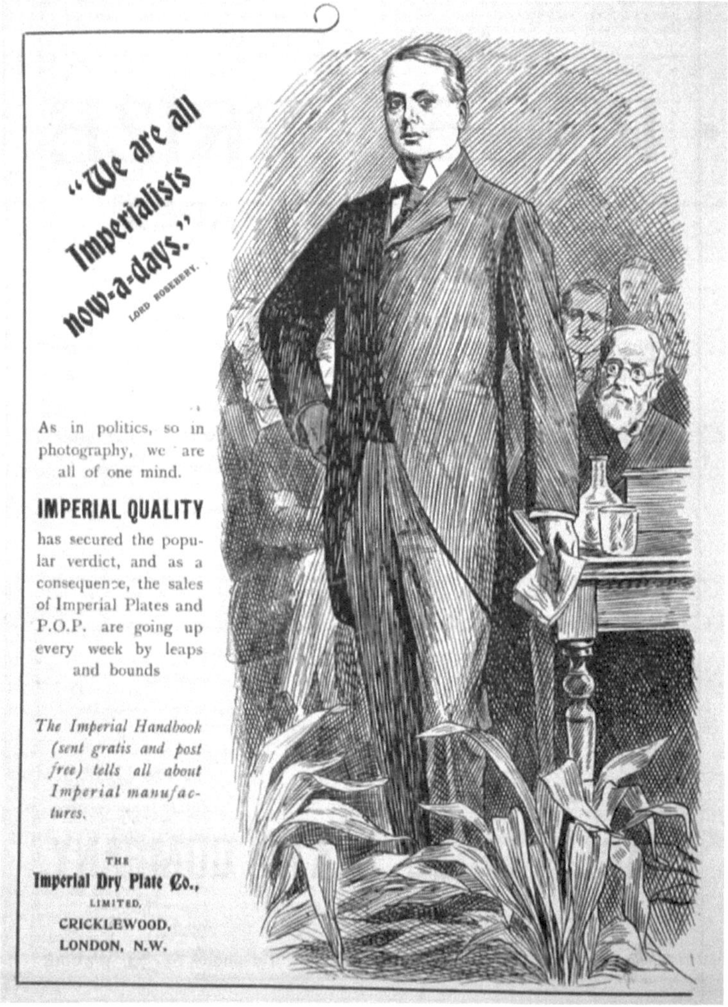

 DOI: 10.4324/9781315400266-141

119

THE IMPERIAL DRY PLATE CO., 'IMPERIAL PLATES PILOT THE WAY'

Photography, June 5th 1909, p. 19

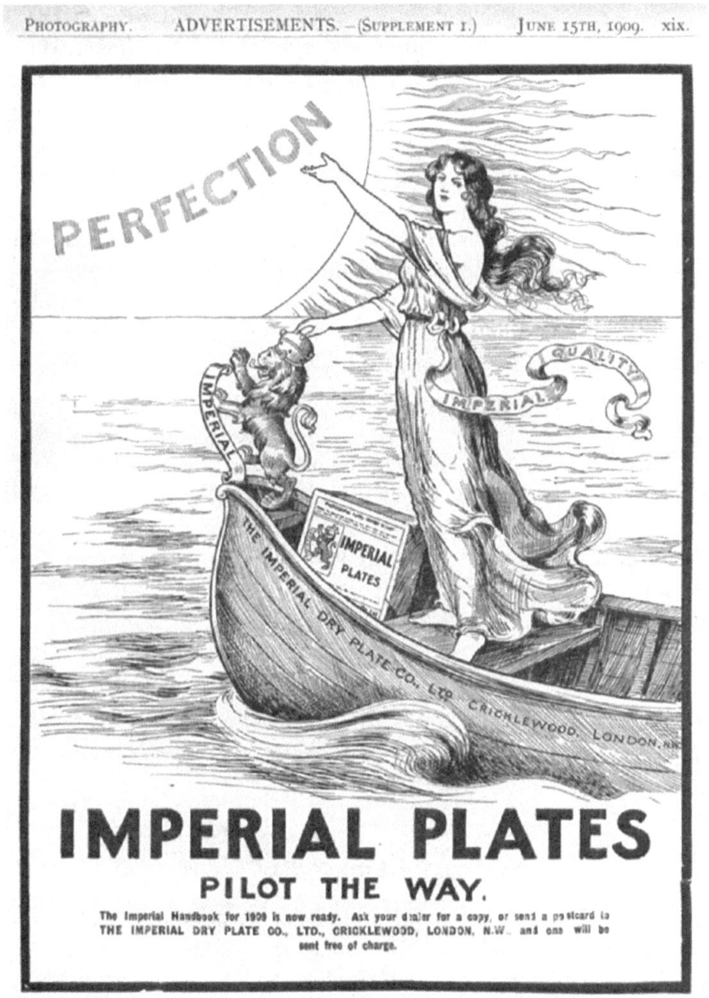

DOI: 10.4324/9781315400266-142

120

'THE GENESIS OF THE WORD IMPERIAL'

The Imperial Handbook, (London: The Imperial dry Plate Company, 1916), p. 21

WE are often felicitated upon the appropriateness of the name under which Imperial plates are marketed, and a note on the word itself may be of interest.

Although the word IMPERIAL, in its modern acceptation, has become one with a meaning of world-wide influence, it must not be forgotten that its literal translation is "commanding." A thing is "Imperial" because it attracts imperiously by reason of its special and superior qualities.

The strength and power of the first emperors of Rome were based upon their ability to command; they became the natural governors of their nations from just that fact. Napoleon stepped from the position of a Corsican officer to the Imperial pinnacle by virtue of the same abilities. These men commanded because they were proved, reliable, of the higher calibre.

Note from Ogilvie's Imperial Dictionary: –

> IMPERIAL (Latin, imperialis, from imperium, empire, command). 1. Meaning of, or pertaining to an Empire. *ITEM: Imperial Plates are used throughout the greatest empire in the world.* 2. Of or pertaining to supreme authority; supreme. *ITEM: All photographers know of the supremity of Imperial Plates.* (3) For, or suitable for, an emperor; hence meaning of superior quality or excellence. *ITEM: Is not this the very note of Imperial Plates*?

Our readers may be interested to remember that in Handbooks of former years we have reproduced photographs, from Imperial negatives, of every living emperor and monarch of modern times.

The tested best must lead the rest

"**That which is Best Must Lead.**" After the most exhaustive tests of the various brands of dry plates we are in a position to say that Imperial Plates now represent the most perfect plate-quality obtainable, and our world-wide

DOI: 10.4324/9781315400266-143

sales at the present time prove, in the most emphatic manner, that photographers everywhere realize this truth also. For years Imperial Plates have led the way; to-day they are still paramount. Any one article that continues from year to year to dominate other similar articles must be the acknowledged leader. This is an established fact in commercial circles. That which is best must lead.

121

'OPTICAL WONDER OF THE AGE'

Peter Parley's Annual: a Christmas and New Year's present for young people, n.d., p. 12

OPTICAL WONDER OF THE AGE.

"Seems, madam ; nay, it IS!"—HAMLET.

STEREOSCOPES IN MAHOGANY.—LENSES WARRANTED.

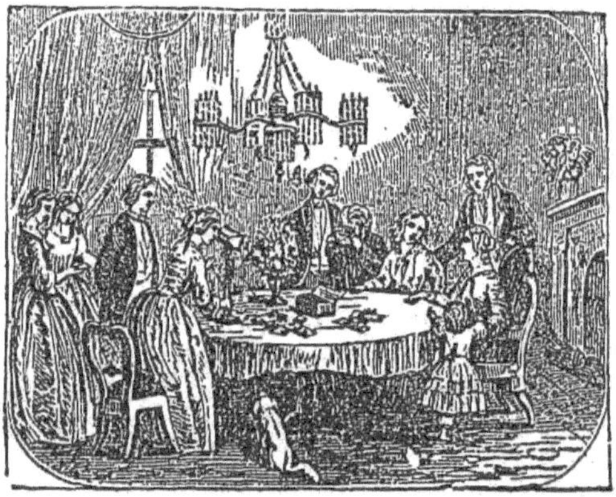

Price 3s. 6d. to 21s., Groups and Views, 1s. and 3s., Ditto in choice Woods to 30s. 100,000 GROUPS ranging from the most solemn subjects to the most amusing, and VIEWS from all parts of the World, from the renowned empire of Antiquity, with their selectest treasure, of Ancient Arts and Nature, from its loveliest nook and dell, to its grandest Alpine Glacier. SIXTY VIEWS from SWITZERLAND.

LONDON STEREOSCOPIC COMPANY, 54, Cheapside, and 313, Oxford-street.

A selection made, if desired, and carefully packed and sent into the country on a remittance. A beautiful selection sent for £3 3s., with Stereoscope.—"Marvels of beauty."—DAILY NEWS. "A most remarkable collection."—ATHENÆUM. "Of unsurpassed beauty."—PATRIOT. "The finest we ever saw."—ART-JOURNAL.

Just Out.—Scenes from the Winter's Tale.— As put on the Stage by Mr. and Mrs. Kean. Price 3s. each, exquisitely coloured, or 42s. the set of 15. Sent free by post, on remittance.—Now ready—Some exquisite Scenes from Dovedale.

DOI: 10.4324/9781315400266-144

122

'THE BIRMINGHAM MUTOSCOPE COMPANY, LTD.'

The Birmingham Pictorial and Dart, March 11, 1898, p. 5

The List of Applications will close on Monday, the 14th day of March, 1898, at 4-0 p.m.

(Incorporated under the Companies' Acts, 1860 to 1890.)
CAPITAL · · · £21,000

Divided into Shares of £1 each. Payable 2/6 on Application, 2/6 on Allotment, and the balance in Calls of 5/- each, as and when required.

DIRECTORS:

Walter Harley, J.P., Capethorn, Smethwick (Chairman.)
James Adie, Rolandseck, Hagley Road, Edgbaston, City Councillor.
Lewis John Murray, Vesta House, Lodge Road, Birmingham, City Councillor.

The Licensors have the right to appoint two additional Directors to represent their interest.

BANKERS: The City of Birmingham Bank (Limited,) Birmingham.
SOLICITORS: Pinsent & Co., Bennett's Hill, Birmingham.
AUDITORS: Leigh Elkington, Neal & Co., 39, Newhall Street, Birmingham.
SECRETARY AND REGISTERED OFFICE: Hugh C. Aston, 7a, Newhall Street, Birmingham.

PROSPECTUS,

This Company is formed for the purpose of acquiring an exclusive license under the Letters Patent held by the Mutoscope and Biograph Syndicate, (Limited,) for working coin-operated Mutoscopes within a radius of fifteen miles from the Town Hall, Birmingham.

The Mutoscope is a little instrument not unlike a stereoscope in appearance, and is the latest and most perfect invention in the art of producing animated photographic Pictures. It presents to the eye objects in motion with such startling appearance of reality as to border on the marvellous. Attempts in this direction have hitherto been made by means of cumbersome and complicated mechanisms, with very unsatisfactory results. The Mutoscope is simplicity itself, and yet presents views with a steadiness and distinctness that, although the eye may behold

DOI: 10.4324/9781315400266-145

thousands of successive pictures, they are presented with such evenness as to give the effect of one continuous scene.

Equipped with a "penny-in-the-slot" attachment the Mutoscope becomes a most seductive and untiring money earner. A penny is inserted; the spectator from that moment achieves entire control of the apparatus by means of a handle which regulates the speed of the pictures according to the rapidity with which it is turned, until the entire scene contained has passed before the eye. The fascination of the view can only be realised by actual experience.

The first public exhibition in England was at the Cycle Exhibition, Bingley Hall, Birmingham, when between the 20th and 29th January, 1898, in nine days, eight Mutoscopes earned an average of 17s. 10½d. per machine per day. Ten Mutoscopes exhibited at the Birmingham Photographic Society's Exhibition, from the 28th of February to 5th of March, 1898, took an average of 17s. per machine per day. In both these cases the attendance was small, except during the evenings.

Whilst Birmingham and the immediate district could, it is believed, profitably employ a larger number, it is proposed, in the first instance, and at as early a date as practicable, to place 500 Mutoscopes on exhibition, and assuming these to earn on an average a total revenue of 2s. each per day for 300 days in the year, a gross revenue of £15,000 would be realised.

The expenses of management and operation are small, but if an allowance of £4,500 be made for this, a surplus of £10,500 remains, which is equal to 50 per cent. upon the capital of the Company.

The Company acquires its rights and hires the Mutoscopes from the Mutoscope and Biograph Syndicate, Limited (who hold the patents for Great Britain) upon the following terms: The Company allots to the licensors as fully paid one-third of the present issue of capital, namely, £7,000, and pays to the licensors for the use of each Mutoscope, with subject complete, a license fee of £10, and an annual rental of £1.

It is now proposed to allot the remaining 14,000 shares, producing £14,000, available for the business, which will be thus applied:

License Fee on 500 Mutoscopes at £20 each	£10,000
Working Capital	4,000
	£14,000

Arrangements have also been made by which, from time to time fresh views (or subjects) shall be supplied to this Company by the licensors, at a charge the maximum of which has been agreed upon, thus enabling the public interest to be maintained from year to year.

The well-established success of "penny-in-the-slot" automatic machines is a guarantee that the public do not grudge a penny for anything that yields an adequate return, and the high premiums at which shares in well-managed companies of this class now stand prove their commercial value. The Directors believe that as a money earner, the Mutoscope possesses qualities superior to any of these machines.

It is not a vending machine, and does not need to be refilled or replenished.

It works at all hours and at any time.

It can be placed at isolated points requiring no attendant—in hotels, theatre lobbies, popular shops, restaurants, bazaars, fairs, exhibitions, and all places where the public resort.

Appreciating the great advantage of local administration and local interest, local companies are now in course of formation in the principal cities of the United Kingdom.

The Directors believe that there is every prospect of the Company being able to pay substantial dividends on its capital.

The only agreement entered into by this Company is dated 8th March, 1898, and is made between the Mutoscope and Biograph Syndicate (Limited,) of the one part, and this Company of the other part.

This agreement, together with the Memorandum and Articles of Association, can be inspected at the offices of the Solicitor.

March 9th, 1898.

123

'SUGGESTION FOR THE R.A.'

Punch or the London Charivari,
May 10th 1899, p. 225

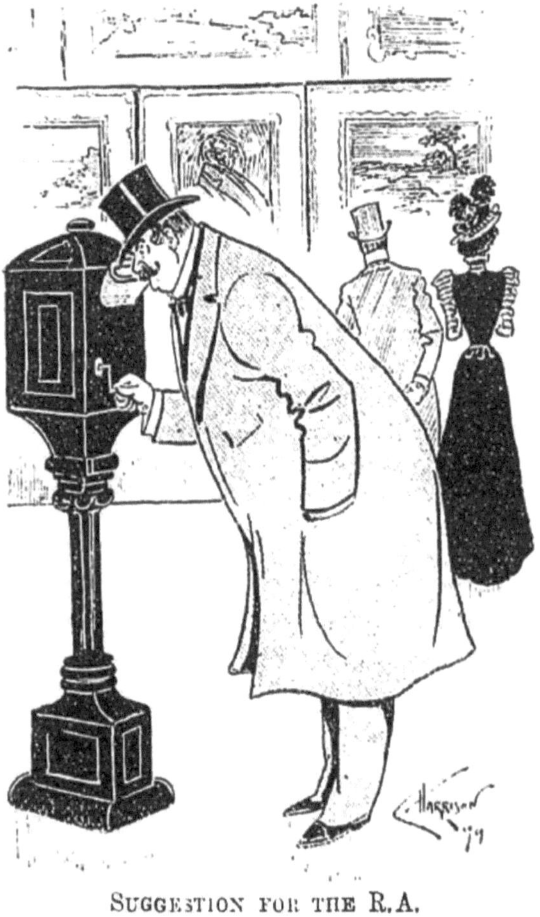

SUGGESTION FOR THE R.A.

A Mutoscope of the Pictures, for the use of visitors in a hurry. The Royal Academy "done" in five minutes.

 DOI: 10.4324/9781315400266-146

124

CUTHBERT BEDE, 'PHOTOGRAPHY PROCESSES'

Photographic Pleasures: popularly portrayed with pen and pencil
(London: Thomas McLean, 1855), p. 29

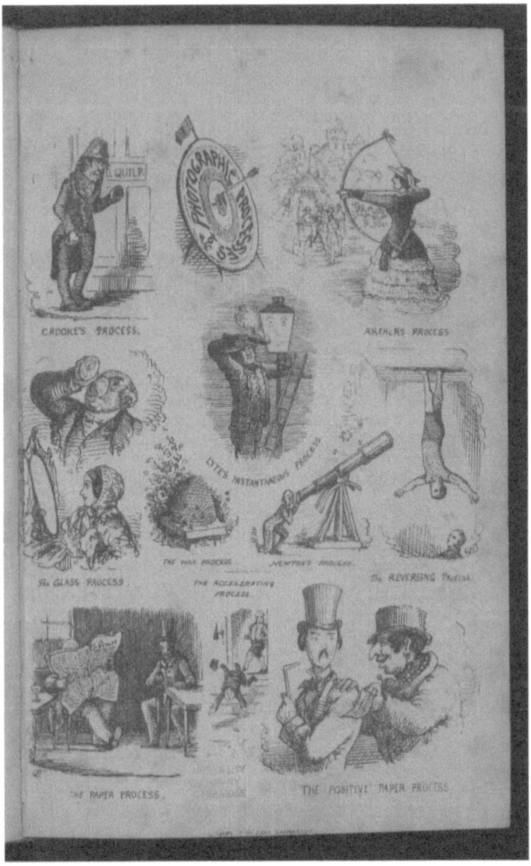

Source: Reproduced by kind permission of the Syndics of Cambridge University Library.

DOI: 10.4324/9781315400266-147

5.2

Materials and equipment

DOI: 10.4324/9781315400266-148

5.2 Materials and equipment

Following on from inventions and techniques, this section focuses on the new materials and equipment available to photographers in the second half of the nineteenth century and demonstrates the uses of photography in a number of different contexts. Many of the sources included here are taken from a regular column in *The Photographic News* titled 'Photography – in and out of the studio', which appeared in the 1870s and 1880s. These articles highlight the relationship between photography and chemistry (photographic materials were often for sale in chemists' shops), as well as indicate the dizzying array of apparatus that evolved in association with the new medium.

Our first source, however, returns us to Cuthbert Bede's *Photographic Pleasures* (1855). One of the sketches produced by Bede as part of a page of 'photographic fancies' shows an image of a black man applying black varnish to his face. Early collodion images on glass required a backing material to make them visible. This might be a type of black paint, cloth or varnish, as shown here. Bede's caricature speaks to a nineteenth-century history of blackface, 'the application of any prosthetic – makeup, soot, burnt cork, minerals, mask etc. – to imitate the complexion of another race'.[1] In fact, what is being applied here is not a form of varnish but a jar of 'Day and Martin' boot blacking, and this is part of the intended joke. In his satire of the craze for new photographic processes and materials, Bede combines a form of racial stereotyping (note the exaggerated depiction of facial features) with a sense that skin colour is a form of make-up that can be applied at will.

While India rubber was used largely in the bicycle, automotive and military industries, it was also one of the material components of photography. Colonial enterprise led to the greater availability of rubber in the second half of the nineteenth century, but as Adelene Buckland attests, 'the real story of rubber production is of some of the worst violence of the imperial period' – a story in which Britain was implicated.[2] Our source discusses the solubility of India rubber. A solution of India rubber was used as a substratum for developing photographs using glass plates and for storing photographic paper by keeping it dry and excluding air.[3] The article discusses the relative merits of different kinds of India rubber for making a coating solution, and it gives a very good sense of the reach of the rubber trade, which flourished in Britain in the second half of the nineteenth century through companies such as the North British Rubber Company, the Leyland and Birmingham Rubber Company and the Avon India Rubber Company. Some photographers had vested interests in these companies; John Dudley Johnston, for example, who was an expert in gum platinum prints, worked for Helibut, Symons and Co., who were rubber merchants in Liverpool in the late nineteenth century. The source discusses guajaquil rubber coming from Ecuador, Para rubber from across South America and rubber from Africa and Madagascar.[4]

'Travellers and dry-plate photography' discusses the merits of the dry-plate process for use in foreign travel. As discussed in Part 5.1, the invention of dry plates meant that photographers could dispense with a portable dark room, but as the piece in the *Photographic News* suggests, the disadvantage here was that development of photographs no longer took place at the scene so the photographer must 'run the risk of failure with his dry-plates'. As a result, it became common practice for the travelling photographer to take dry plates *and* materials for the wet collodion process. The article goes on to discuss the 'vicissitudes of travel in an Eastern country', including the perils of traveling in high temperatures with photographic chemicals. Later in 1879, the regular section 'Photography – in and out of the studio' ran a piece on the development of photographic equipment for use in warfare. It references a newly published government pamphlet on wartime equipment, including a section on 'Photographic Implements and Materials forming the Equipment of a Photographic Waggon'. The article describes the equipment and materials contained in a typical horse-drawn photographic wagon (including various cameras, albumenised paper, chemicals, dipping baths and dark room facilities) all for the costly sum of £209. The last section of the piece discusses the relationship between photography and war, focusing on the Crimean War and the Franco-German war of 1870. The photographer, Roger Fenton, used a photographic van to carry his equipment during the Crimean War. A photograph of the van from 1855 shows its size and cumbersome nature.[5]

'The Poisonous Properties of Bichromate of Potash' is one of hundreds of articles and opinion pieces that were published on the subject of photographic chemicals. This source responds to a paper by a Mr Duchochois in which he discusses his experience as a victim of poisoning. Duchochois reports that,

> the skin of the hands, on which at first appeared small itching vesicles, split and fell out in scales, leaving the flesh bare and tumulated.[6] The disease extended to the interior of the nose, under the eyes, the feet; in fact, to all parts of the body.[7]

Bichromate of potash was used in 'gum printing', otherwise known as the pigment process, a photographic process in which potassium bichromate (the sensitiser) was mixed with an appropriate 'colloid' or liquid (for example, gum arabic, gelatin, fish glue or egg white) to produce a photographic emulsion.[8] The article concludes that frequent exposure to these chemicals would result in harm. It discusses the case of an assistant in a photographic studio in Paris, who was

> cooped up near the roof, whose duty from morning till afternoon had to be carried on in a hot cupboard full of ether and alcohol fumes, the only relief being when he momentarily opened the door to hand out or receive the slides.

The article assumes that because the assistant in question is 'half-caste', he will be 'in a better condition to bear the hot close air around him'. Despite the evident sympathy of the author, the article indicates the existence of a form of slave labour in the photographic studio, and it makes racialised assumptions about the nature of the human body.

The final two sources are adverts for photographic materials and apparatus. The first contains a half-page advertisement for Thomas' Collodion. Richard Wheeler Thomas was a key supplier of photographic chemicals through his establishment at 10 Pall Mall, London. Note the advert's insistence on the efficacy of Thomas' collodion 'for use around the world' – in particular, 'it is **the** collodion for India', the implication being that it is able to withstand high temperatures. The other adverts included here (for studio accessories, a bookkeeping system especially for photographers, and a substitute for photographic plates made of glass) give a sense of the range of photographic accoutrements marketed in the second half of the nineteenth century. The second advert, from London-based firm Marion and Co., reveals the variety of photographic products available from just one supplier – from a 7-foot-high tree for use as a studio accessory to a new type of camera shutter. It also indicates the wide range of chemicals available for purchase by both amateur and professional photographers.

Notes

1 Ayanna Thompson, *blackface,* (London: Bloomsbury Academic, 2021), p. 19.
2 See the *Raw Materials* volume in this series.
3 See Peter Duchochois, *Photographic Reproduction Processes* (New York: The Scovill and Adams Company, 1891), pp. 51, 66.
4 For a detailed description of the India rubber trade in the nineteenth century see *The Journal of the Society of Arts*, Vol. 28, July 30, 1880), pp. 753–762.
5 Roger Fenton, 'The artist's van' (1855). https://www.loc.gov/pictures/item/2001697111/ [accessed 20th June 2021].
6 Possibly the author of *Photographic Reproduction Processes* (see note 3).
7 *Photographic News*, January 3rd 1879 pp. 2–3.
8 For further information on the 'gum print' see *Encyclopaedia of Nineteenth-Century Photography*, p. 624.

125

CUTHBERT BEDE, 'PHOTOGRAPHIC FANCIES', 'APPLYING THE BLACK VARNISH'

Photographic Pleasures: popularly portrayed with pen and pencil
(London: Thomas McLean, 1855), p. 37

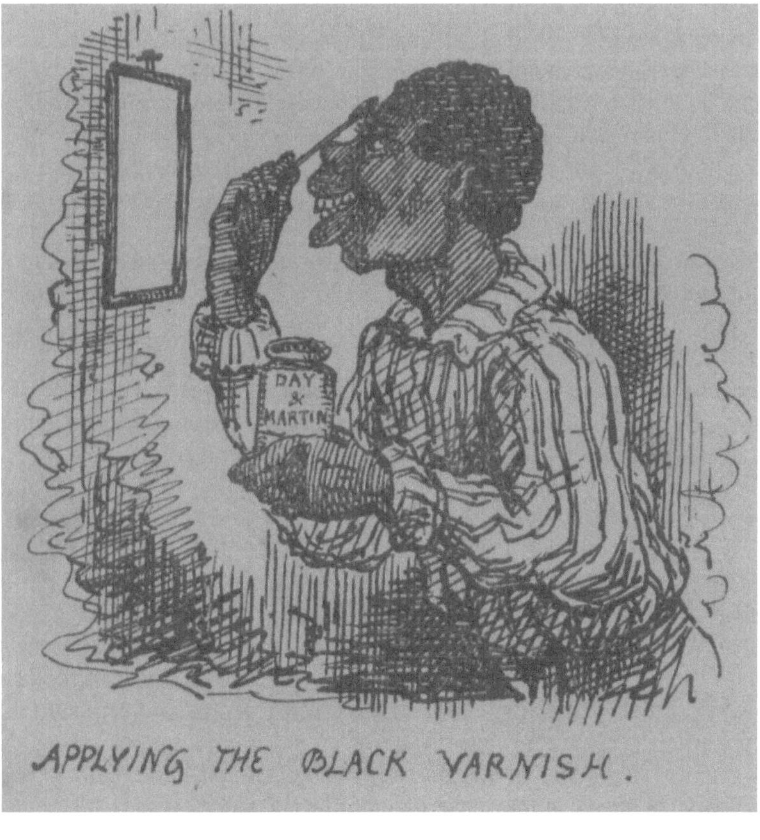

DOI: 10.4324/9781315400266-149

126

'INDIA-RUBBER AND ITS DEGREE OF SOLUBILITY', IN 'PHOTOGRAPHY – IN AND OUT OF THE STUDIO'

Photographic News, April 6 1877, p. 167

India-rubber, and its Degree of Solubility. – Photographers are well aware of the difficulty with which some samples of india-rubber dissolve in benzole, even when the former has been masticated with great care – and, indeed, this circumstance has stood in the way of its application in photographic processes frequently. Sometimes it has been affirmed in these columns that rubber will easily dissolve, while at other times complaints of the impossibility of getting anything but a thin solution on the application of benzole have been rife. The reason for this appears to be that rubber from various countries differs very greatly in its solubility, and a German chemist, Heeren, has shown that benzole will take up in solution four times as much of one rubber than of another. This chemist has made a careful examination into the solubility of a dozen different species of rubber, and having first worked the samples between hot rollers to masticate them, he cut them into thin strips, and added benzole. After frequent shaking, and securing solutions of as thick a consistence as possible, it was ascertained how much in a certain volume of liquid there was of india-rubber. Guajaquil rubber was found to be the most soluble, one hundred parts of benzole taking up as much as twenty-five parts of this description of caoutchouc. Next came Para, of which one hundred parts of benzole took up twenty of rubber, and this was followed in solubility by Carthagena and Borneo samples. The worst examples, so far as solubility is concerned, were so-called Africa – Knökels, Africa – Niggara, and Madagascar. This last was very difficult indeed of solution, one hundred parts of benzole only taking up six parts of the rubber – a fact that may afford some consolation to photographers who have been trying their hardest to get a sample of caoutchouc to dissolve. We do not know much about Guajaquil rubber, which stands at the head of all the samples examined by M. Heeren, but Para rubber, which stands second, is always to be had in the market, and in this country enjoys a reputation for being the best article. Very little rubber is, however, soluble before being masticated, photographers should remember, and those who employ it, either in the form of a preliminary coating or in the preparation of films, should bear in mind that a vast amount of trouble and labour may be avoided by purchasing the material already

DOI: 10.4324/9781315400266-150

masticated. It is to be bought in the form of thin sheets, something resembling tripe in appearance, and in this worked condition it will be found very soluble in benzole. Some photographers, we know, purchase india-rubber cement, which is but rubber dissolved in benzole, and this they dilute with more liquid till of the required consistence; but this cement, unless very pure and of exceptionally good quality, is not adapted to photographic manipulation. It contains a large amount of foreign matter from dirty rubber or from impure benzole spirit, and this, so soon as the cement is diluted, appears most unmistakably upon the film in the form of black particles and coarse fibre. The best plan, therefore, unless the solution is simply required as a cementing material, is to purchase the finest rubber in a masticated form, and, after washing it in hot water and drying, to dissolve the same in the best sample of benzole that can be obtained. Some advise the previous softening of the material in chloroform, but this we have never found to be necessary if good soluble rubber is at hand.

127

'TRAVELLERS AND DRY PLATE PHOTOGRAPHY', IN 'PHOTOGRAPHY – IN AND OUT OF THE STUDIO'

Photographic News, March 15 1879, p. 121

Photography in and out of the studio

Travellers and dry-plate photography

Travellers and Dry Plate Photography. – It would be well, indeed, if travellers could derive more benefit from the improvements that are taking place in dry plate photography. It is no longer a novelty to employ dry plates in the studio in preference to wet ones. Several of our correspondents have now been employing gelatine emulsion plates in the studio for months past, and the silver bath, if not put on one side altogether, has not been called into requisition. But in the studio there is a dark room always at hand, a haven of safety and refuge to the photographer, which the traveller, unfortunately, lacks. If things do not go quite as they should do, the stay-at-home photographer has always his dark room to go into, wherein to investigate the circumstances of his failure. He can always see how far he has succeeded or failed on the instant, and may at once investigate the cause of failure. His sitter is still in the next room, and another plate can be taken without loss of time. The traveller, unfortunately, is in a far worse position. If he does not burden himself with a dark tent, then he must run the risk of failure with his dry plates; if he carries a dark tent with him, the advantages of dry plate work cease to have their full importance with him. There is no doubt, too, that a photographer who is not well versed in dry plate development gets nervous over the manipulations when he knows that the object he has photographed is, perhaps, left far behind in his journey, and there are no means of retaking it should his plate turn out a failure. He is not working under favourable circumstances, and he gets more failures than would otherwise be the case. Under the circumstances a traveller never seems to feel confidence unless he carries materials for the wet process, and, when he has these with him, he naturally employs them. The experiences recently detailed by Dr. Stolze before the Berlin Photographic Society are not likely to give travellers

DOI: 10.4324/9781315400266-151

any further confidence in dry plate work. Dr. Stolze has made a journey through Persia, and his results, obtained not with a few, but a large series of dry plates, must have been very discouraging. He tried during his wanderings, he tells us, no less than three hundred emulsion plates, with which he obtained very poor results, owing, he explains, to the yellow glass of his transfer box not being proof against a Persian sun. If the emulsion plates had been prepared with gelatine, we can well believe the traveller's explanation, and it certainly behoves travellers to bear in mind that protection which may be sufficient in a European climate, fails to preserve plates from immunity in the East; but Dr. Stolze's other dry plates were not more satisfactory. Films, whether prepared with coffee, tea, or beer, were not to be relied upon, and, in the end, Dr. Stolze had to do what many before him have done, namely, get along as well as he could with the wet process. This resolution did not at once remove all thorns from his path. The want of water and a dark tent, together with the insupportable heat, compelled him in the end to cut short his photographic tour in Persian territory. He did not wash and fix his plates, but contented himself with developing them and coating them with a solution of sugar. Dr. Stolze's woes as a travelling photographer appeared to be never-ending. He had believed so sincerely in his dry plates that he had come almost unprepared to work by the wet method. He complains that at Bombay no collodion of any worth was to be obtained, and he hints that dealers appear to be in the habit of sending out such photographic material to India as they cannot get rid of elsewhere. Ether it was impossible to procure, since the bottles arrived always nine-tenths empty. We suspect the circumstance goes a good way to explain the dearth and inferiority of other articles – such as collodion, alcohol, &c. Ninety degrees in the shade must play a good deal of havoc with photographic chemicals, although we have many correspondents in India who have never complained against difficulties from this source. Dr. Stolze would have us believe that at last he was so reduced in the matter of supplies that only lunar caustic and raw collodion remained to him, with which he prepared some emulsion that secured very good views of the ruins of Persepolis. No doubt climatic influence must work an impression upon dry films, and an emulsion or coffee plate prepared in England or Germany no doubt would hardly give such successful results after the vicissitudes of travel in an Eastern country; at the same time, we remember, Captain Abney had little difficulty at Thebes with films prepared in England prior to his departure. The plates in the latter case, it is true, were prepared by himself, and, as Captain Abney is *facile princeps* in all that pertains to dry work, no doubt the films were handled with unusual skill; but still there is the fact that they were not found wanting. Captain Waterhouse, the Assistant Surveyor-General at Calcutta, has also worked repeatedly with dry plates, and has secured eminently satisfactory results. In the case of both these officers, of course, they are well acquainted with the Tropics, and it would be well if they could be prevailed upon to place on record their experiences on the preparation of dry plates to be employed in hot climates.

128

'PHOTOGRAPHY AND WARFARE', IN 'PHOTOGRAPHY – IN AND OUT OF THE STUDIO'

Photographic News, September 12 1879, p. 433

Photography and photographic equipments in warfare

No better evidence of the importance with which the British Government regards photography as an aid to military science is afforded than that displayed in a recent publication giving a complete detail of warlike stores which has just been issued by the Secretary of State for war. It is entitled "Priced Vocabulary of Stores used in Her Majesty's Service," and to those interested in the matter we may mention that it is to be obtained of any bookseller for the sum of three shillings. For the most part, no doubt, it furnishes but sorry reading, but still there are many who like to know how much a big gun costs, or what is the price of the orthodox "gaiter-button." But photographers will certainly be interested in the portion appertaining to "Photographic Implements and Materials forming the Equipment of a Photographic Waggon." It must be borne in mind that modern armies are furnished with necessaries and apparatus that were quite unknown to our forefathers, and a well-equipped force now-a-days carries with it the means for erecting telegraphs, surveying and making roads, printing and lithographing documents, mining and diving, laying down railroads and blowing them up, and last, if not least, the wherewithal to make photographs. Every army corps, which consists in the British army of some 36,000 of all ranks, is not complete unless it numbers among its *personnel* a serjeant-photographer and assistants, and among the *materiel* a photographic waggon and a very complete list of stores. To judge by the *Vocabulary,* this military photographic outfit is very sound and substantial, and calculated, therefore, to excite the envy of many a brother in the craft. That it is costly goes without saying, for only good apparatus and sound workmanship could be trusted to endure the vicissitudes of a campaign. To begin with, the photographic waggon itself, drawn by a pair of stout army horses, is an object to admire. It is entered by a door from behind, and, under ordinary circumstances, presents the appearance of a small and compact travelling office, provided with seats and well lighted. In these circumstances it fulfils all the conditions of an ordinary workroom, where prints can be toned and fixed, and trimmed and

DOI: 10.4324/9781315400266-152

mounted without difficulty. To convert it into a dark room, it is only necessary to adjust the coloured glass windows and make use of a screen if necessary. There are shelves and cupboards, trays and stands proper to manipulation, to the stowage of baths and chemicals, all made in the most substantial and durable manner. In fact, when we state that the price of the waggon complete is no less than £209, our readers will readily understand that a very perfect carriage must be at hand. We shall not go through the various items that are contained in this waggon, for, as we have said, anyone who desires the information can obtain it, and much more besides, for a few shillings. Still our readers will probably like to know what sort of apparatus and to what extent photography is employed in the army. In the way of cameras, for instance, we find the soldier-photographer is provided with three, two of which are capable of securing any size plate up to 12 by 10, while the third is a small hand camera provided for taking 7½ by 5 pictures. The camera-stands chosen by the War authorities are marked "Paget's Pattern," and these also are three in number. So that in case of accident the photographer has more than one string to his bow. Of collodion, the supply provided is ten pints of plain and ten of prepared, while of pyroxyline and alcohol and ether there are also certain quantities, to permit of further supplies of collodion being made. The lenses provided for service in the field are six in number, viz., a pair of stereoscopic lenses for small rapid pictures, two rapid rectilinears of Dallmeyer for 12 by 10 and one for 7½ by 5 plates, and one wide-angle rectilinear, also of Dallmeyer, for 12 by 10 and 7½ by 5 pictures. A cone for copying is not forgotten, and of 12 by 10 plates "crown glass, thick, polished, the supply taken is a gross, and 7½ by 5, half as many. Besides the waggon itself, which can be employed as a dark-room, there is provided a box tent, "Abney's pattern," together with a supply of tammy and fitments for the improvising of dark chambers. Of course provision is made for the employment of dry plates, and double backs for dry plate box are not forgotten. Three dipping baths, one of ebonite and two of glass, form part of the equipment, and eight large and eight small printing frames. A ream of albumenized paper is supposed to furnish sufficient material for printing, and the amount of nitrate of silver deemed sufficient is ten pounds. A copper still with condenser allows the soldier-photographer to make his own distilled water if he happens to fall short of that commodity, and altogether, as we have said, the equipment is of a most perfect character. Several such equipments are kept in the military stores ready for use at any moment, so that when war is declared no delay shall occur in providing photographic necessaries. As to the uses to which photography may be put in the field, these have by no means been exhausted, albeit many Continental nations have availed themselves of the art. The first application of the camera in warfare dates from the Crimean war, when two young officers, Ensigns Brandon and Dawson, were sent out from England by Lord Panmure, after they had in the first instance received proper instruction from Mr. Mayall. Some of the work of these officers is still in existence, Mr. Mayall having presented several of the pictures which came into his hands to Mr. Baden Pritchard, of the General Photographic Establishment of the War Department. In the Franco-German war of 1870, both the Germans and French made use of photography in the field. The Prussians organised a corps of photographers under the command of a captain and lieutenant, and sent them to Strasburg, to help in the reduction of that fortress. Many valuable measurements and reconnoitring pictures were taken before Strasburg by the camera, and when that fortress fell the military photographers were transferred to the Paris lines of investment, there to perform further service. On the side of the French, apart from the invaluable aid photography rendered in producing microscopic despatches for transmission by pigeon to the besieged capital, photography in the hands of the French engineers did much good service. Plans and maps were prepared and copied by its agency, and indeed in the military topographical department of France the camera has for years past held a prominent position. The Cammandant Laussedat was one of the earliest to foresee the valuable aid of photography in war, and it was under his auspices that M. Auguste Chavalier developed his invention, the *planchette photographique*. The photographic plane-table is still employed by the French War Department as a rapid means of surveying, and had it not been for M. Chevalier's premature death, there is no doubt that further applications of photography to warfare would have been forthcoming. The Emperor himself ordered that every facility should be given to M. Chevalier to carry out his experiments on a large scale at Vincennes, that gentlemen having pledged to obtain with the plane-table the following results: 1. By employing two proofs obtained with the instrument, to regulate in the most certain manner, during the night-time, the direction of tire against an enemy's works, as likewise the angle of reflection of the electric light to be used for illuminating the same; 2. In like manner to regulate the convergent fire of one or more batteries as well during the night as during the day. Our readers will thus see that photography and war are likely in the future to see a good deal of one another.

129

'THE POISONOUS PROPERTIES OF BICHROMATE OF POTASH', IN 'PHOTOGRAPHY – IN AND OUT OF THE STUDIO'

Photographic News, January 10 1879, p. 13

– A complaint comes across the sea from America, that sufficient warning has not been given those who practise carbon printing of the deleterious nature of the bichromate of potash solution with which we have to work. M. Duchochois read a paper at the American Institute, in which he put himself forward as a victim and sufferer of the effects of bichromate, and we can readily believe that the poisonous nature of the salt is in some cases of a most virulent character. M. Duchochois is wrong, however, in supposing that attention has not been drawn to the gravity of the subject, for not only in this country, but in America, has it been referred to, a volume by the Editor of this journal published by Messrs. Anthony & Co. having specially directed readers to the fact. Bichromate of potash solution works upon some systems more strongly than others, but in any case it cannot be without injury to those who are constantly employing the salt. Thus, although to wet one's fingure [sic] with a solution daily for a few minutes may not harm, it is another matter altogether when a photographer or his assistant does nothing all day long but sensitize carbon tissue in a bichromate bath. To do this, with a stout constitution or a weak one, cannot be beneficial, to say the least of it. It is like collodionising plates. To breathe the ether fumes now and then, when you enter a dark room to coat a plate, may not be injurious; but to be an assistant confined all the morning, doing nothing else, may lead to serious consequences. We have seen this in one of the finest Paris studios – an assistant cooped up near the roof, whose duty from morning till afternoon had

DOI: 10.4324/9781315400266-153

to be carried on in a hot cupboard full of ether and alcohol fumes, the only relief being when he momentarily opened the door to hand out or receive the slides. Even supposing the cupboard to have been as well ventilated as possible, the tainted atmosphere must necessarily have been bad to breathe day after day, and we took some consolation, we remember, in the fact that the assistant in question was a man of half caste, and we hoped, therefore, in a better condition to bear the hot close air around him. We cannot help thinking that bichromate solution, however harmless it may appear in some cases, can hardly be employed with immunity day after day without having some deleterious results. It may be argued that as bichromate of potash has been used for coating articles of food – to wit, the pea-sausage to which wo adverted last week iu these columns – it cannot be strictly considered poison. But the cases are widely different, as will be seen at a glance. In the first place, there is no need of the bichromate to penetrate the gelatine skin at all; the sausage, if first of all covered with a thick layer of gelatine, and then dried, before the application of the bichromate, might not come in contact with the latter at all; but even if it did, the food would be of a greasy repellent character, while at the same time it would lack that absorbent power which a living system represents. There would be no absorbing action constantly going on and carrying the poison into the system, which constitutes the main injury when we dip our fingers into a solution. So that, although bichromate liquids may not act as poison in trivial cases, there can be little doubt about the risk photographers run who systematically wet their fingers with the solution; and we owe our thanks to M. Duchochois for so vividly pourtraying [sic]the effects which may arise from disregarding ordinary means of precaution. No doubt when carbon tissue comes more generally into use we shall be able to purchase our material already sensitised, and thus obviate the danger altogether.

130

ADVERTISEMENT FOR THOMAS'S COLLODION

Photographic News, January 3rd 1879, p. v

vi THE PHOTOGRAPHIC NEWS. [JANUARY 24, 1879.

THOMAS'S COLLODION — 10, PALL MALL, LONDON. — **THOMAS'S COLLODION**

USED BY EMINENT PHOTOGRAPHERS FOR NEARLY A QUARTER OF A CENTURY.

THE LEADING COLLODION.	KNOWN AS THE BEST.
IT IS USED BY THE BEST MEN,	IT HAS THE LARGEST SALE.
AND AT THE GOVERNMENT OFFICES,	IT IS THE COLLODION FOR INDIA.
THE ADMIRALTY, ROYAL ENGINEERS,	IT IS THE MOST SENSITIVE.
FOR THE ORDNANCE SURVEYS OF	THE IMAGE IS ROUND AND BRILLIANT
INDIA, NEW ZEALAND, ETC.	IT IS NOT SURPASSED IN QUALITY.

THOMAS'S COLLODION is pronounced by many of the most accomplished Photographers to be, WITHOUT EXCEPTION, **the Best Collodion for Iron Development** ever yet manufactured. With a view, also, to **subsequent enlargement**, there is no collodion that surpasses it in the delicate qualities of the negative. **THOMAS'S COLLODION**, the first introduced commercially, has been from time to time modified to suit the requirements of the day. The Manufacturer announces with some pride that at the present moment the sale for his collodion is more than ten times greater than when for years he stood alone as a manufacturer of collodion, almost without a rival; and notwithstanding the introduction of preparations sold at a lower price, the demand for **THOMAS'S COLLODION** is yearly increasing.

IT IS USED, AND MAY BE OBTAINED THROUGHOUT THE WORLD.

CAUTION.—Observe the TRADE MARK—

FORREST'S PATENT PLATE SUBSTITUTE.

PRICES per Gross—4¼ × 3¼, 10/- 5 × 4, 14/9; 6½ × 4¾, 24/-; 7¼ × 4½, 25/9; 8½ × 6½, 48/-; 10 × 8, 9½d. ft.; 12 × 9, 10½d.

Not above 1 foot per square, 11d. per ft.; 1½ foot, 1/- per ft. Usual terms to the Trade. It is superior to Patent Plate, because it is non-absorbent, and consequently is not able to stain with Chemicals or Damp, and has also the advantage of being scarcely HALF THE PRICE OF PATENT PLATE. Crown Glass is rapidly growing out of use, and Messrs. F. & Co. have anticipated this difficulty at great expense to themselves, and are happy to find Photographers appreciate their efforts.

N.B.—One side of our Glass is especially prepared for the Collodion, and is distinguished by a diamond mark on one corner of each square.

J. A. FORREST & SON, 58 & 60, LIME STREET, LIVERPOOL.

NON-ACTINIC PHOTO. GLASS, for Operating Rooms, tested by Spectrum Analysis. **OPAL GLASS**, smoothed and flashed to order.

THE NEW

REGISTERED FLOWER STAND ACCESSORY,

A light elegant Accessory made of Iron, finished in different colours and gold to suit the lighting of any Studio. The Price of these Stands is so low that a very large Sale is anticipated. Orders should be sent at once.

No. 1 Grey or Bronze, 15s.; No. 2 Black and Gold, 17s. 6d.; No. 3 White and Gold, 21s.

Carte and Cabinet Mounts EQUAL to the FRENCH in STYLE and FINISH, printed on the **PREMISES**, and delivered in **TEN DAYS** or LESS if required.

Every description of Mounts, tinted, plain, or printed.

SOLE MAKER OF THE IMPROVED 'EAGLE ALBUMENIZED PAPER.'

MANUFACTURER AND DEALER IN EVERY REQUISITE FOR THE PHOTOGRAPHIC ART.

C. E. ELLIOTT,

THE CITY OF LONDON PHOTOGRAPHIC WAREHOUSE,

36, JEWIN STREET, CITY, LONDON.

BALANCE EVERY MONTH, AND SEE HOW YOU STAND.

TRY

"Hooper's System of Book-keeping for Photographers."

(REGISTERED AT STATIONERS' HALL.)

The Books are handsomely and strongly Bound, and are gaining favour in all well-regulated Establishments. The system is sel checking, and made so simple that a knowledge of Book-keeping is not even essential.

Set of Three Books, with Instructions ... £3 3s 0d. Address and Day Book (separate) ... **£1 10 0**

SAMPLE SHEETS, with Instructions showing the system, will be sent anywhere on receipt of Thirty Stamps, which will be returned on Set being ordered.

ACCOUNTANCY WORK PROMPTLY EXECUTED, AND VALUATIONS MADE.

GEORGE HOOPER, 3, CHEAPSIDE LONDON, E.C

DOI: 10.4324/9781315400266-154

131

ADVERTISEMENT FOR MARION AND CO.

The Photographic News, November 14th 1879, p. ix

MARION & Co.

ARTISTICALLY MODELLED ACCESSORIES—No. 104, Haddon Hall Steps, an original and striking accessory; 103, Balustrade, Pillar, and on the reverse side a Rough Wall; 105, a Tree, about seven feet high; No. 100, Gate and Stile; No. 106, Swiss Cottage Front, with changeable window and door No. 101, a Column on square base, about eight feet high, one side in Ionic the other in Gothic style. **FURNITURE**—No. 145, a Settee in the fashionable style of furniture, upholstered in figured velvet; No. 144, a Velve Table to match; No. 146, Velvet Chair with two rising backs. Photographs and Lists of the above sent free **THE SOHO COLLODION**, for Portrait Work or for copying purposes; we strongly recommend a trial. **NEW MOUNTS** for Cartes or Cabinets; ask for samples of the Granite Mounts. **PROMENADE PORTRAIT**—A new size, bound to be popular; if not already seen, write for samples and list of articles to start it; it can be started at a mere trifling expense. NOW READY, **CADETT'S PATENT PNEUMATIC SHUTTER**, A NEW FORM ADAPTED FOR THE INSIDE OF THE CAMERA, price **42s.** each. By using the inside shutter and the dry plates, taking a portrait now becomes an invisible and nstantaneous operation, much to the pleasure and surprise of the sitter. **DRY PLATES**—All the best makes **MARION'S MOUNTS**—Better and more highly finished than any other makes, the board manufactured expressly by Marion and Co., and the printing executed in the best French Lithography; Manufactory, Courbevoie near Paris. **ALBUMENIZED PAPERS**—Marion's Helio Rive, best picked, best superfine, white, or in all tints. **MR. CADETT'S MATTLINE**—A new Retouching Medium; one drop sufficient or a negative. **ENLARGEMENTS IN ALL STYLES**—A new style called Semi-tint, very popular. **PHOTO. REQUISITES AT CASH PRICES.**

All Orders for Goods as listed below must be accompanied by Cash.

Packing Cases extra. Delivered Free in London.

COLLODIONS—Mawson's Pints, Iodizer separate, bottles included, 6s. 1d.; in 5-lb. Winchesters, Iodizer eparate, bottles included, £1 2s. 11d.; Thomas's Pints, Iodizer separate, bottles included, 6s. 4d.; Winchester 4 Pints, Iodizer separate, £1 3s.; Huggon's Pints, bottles included, 5s. 10d.; Winchester, 4 Pints, Iodizer separate bottles included, £1 2s. 6d.; The "Soho" Pints, Iodizer separate, 7s.; Copying Pints, 7s. **ACIDS**—Glacial Acetic, in bottles of 1½ lbs., price, inclusive of bottles, 2s.; Winchester, 6 lbs., bottles included, 6s. 8s.; Pyrogallic in bottles of 1 oz., bottles included, 1s. 7½d. **SPIRIT**—Methylated, jar included, per gallon, 4s. 5d. **AMMONIA LIOUID**—Pints, bottles included, 1s. 1d.; Winchester, 4½ lbs., bottle included, 3s. 4d. **AMMONIUM BROMIDE**—Per lb., bottle included, 3s. 8d.; per oz., 5d. **IRON PROTOSULPHITE**—Per lb., 1½d. **IRON AMMONIA SULPHATE**—Per lb., bottle included, 7d. **POTASSIUM CYANIDE**—Cake, per lb., bottle included, 1s. 5d.; stick, per lb., bottle included, 1s. 7½d. **POTASH OXALATE**—Per lb., bottle included, 2s. 6d.; per oz., bottle included, 3d. **POTASSIUM BROMIDE**—Per lb., bottle included, 3s. 1d.; per oz., bottle included, 4d. **SODA ACETATE**—Per lb., bottle included, 9d. **HYPOSULPHITE SODA**—English, per cwt., cask included, 10s. 9d. **MARION'S ALBUMENIZED HELIO. RIVE**—Per Ream, £3 15s.; per Quire, including post, 4s. 6d. **CHANCE'S CHEAP GLASS**—Direct from Chance's Works, per gross—4¼ by 3¼, 3s.; 5 by 4, 4s. 6d.; 6½ by 4½, 6s.; 6½ by 4¾, 6s. 9d.; 7¼ by 4½, 7s. 2d.; 8½ by 6½, 12s.; 9 by 7 15s. 9d.; 10 by 8, 22s. 6d.; 12 by 10, 38s. 6d.; 15 by 12, 67s. 6d. **GOLD, CHLORIDE OF**—15-grain tubes, per doz., 19s.; **SILVER, NITRATE OF**—Per oz., 3s. 2d.

PLEASE NOTE—CASH WITH ORDER.

---

22 & 23, SOHO SQUARE, LONDON, W.

DOI: 10.4324/9781315400266-155

5.3

Photography in relation to the other arts

DOI: 10.4324/9781315400266-156

5.3 Photography in relation to the other arts

The impact of photography on other art forms was debated throughout the second half of the nineteenth century.[1] This section includes a range of sources on this topic, including the heated discussions about the classification of photography in the International Exhibition of 1862. We begin, however, with John Ruskin's early views on the new medium of photography. Writing to his father from Padua in October 1845, Ruskin enthused about the invention of the daguerreotype, indeed he possessed some of the earliest daguerreotypes in Britain: 'Among all the mechanical poison that this terrible 19th century has poured upon men, it has given us at any rate one antidote – the Daguerreo-type. It's a most blessed invention; that's what it is'.[2] The first source in this section is another letter from Ruskin to his father, sent a week earlier, in which he marvels over the indexical nature of photography. Daguerreotypes of Venetian palaces are described as 'glorious things. It is very nearly the same thing as carrying off the palace itself'. In a further letter to William Henry Harrison, Ruskin expands on his positive view of the daguerreotype, describing it as a recording device with which it is possible to preserve 'evidence'. He includes a note of caution, though, about its relationship to art: 'As regards art, I wish it had never been discovered, it will make the eye too fastidious to accept mere handling'.[3]

The inaugural issue of the *Photographic Art Journal* (January 1851) devotes its first editorial to the subject of 'The Art of Photography'.[4] The author complains that photography 'is viewed too much, in the light of a mere mechanical occupation [. . .] without the least appreciation of its merits as an art of exquisite refinement' and advocates a closer relationship between photography and its sister arts of drawing, painting and sculpture. During the 1850s and 1860s, the relationship between other arts and the new medium of photography continued to provoke debate. Was photography an art, a science or some kind of hybrid of both? Edward Bradley, a clergyman and minor novelist who wrote under the pseudonym Cuthbert Bede invokes both art and science in his satirical *Photographic Pleasures* (1855).[5] In the 1850s, he writes, photography was still in its infancy, 'the most beautiful baby yet born to Science'. Bede's chapter 'Photography in an artistic light' begins by emphasising the differences between photography and art, using the names of the seventeenth-century French painter Claude Lorrain and the nineteenth-century French photographer Antoine Claudet for comic effect. 'The pictures of Claudet are the results of scientific invention: those of Claude; of inspired observation. There was poetry in Claude: there is no poetry in a Claudet'. Bede is of the firm opinion that 'Photography is not (strictly) "Art:" neither is a Photographer an artist. Photography is but the handmaid of art'. Photography, though, can be of use to the artist because 'it enables him to secure truthfulness of detail'. Bede's book also pokes fun at various photographic processes as discussed in Parts 5.1 and 5.2.

The Illustrated Magazine of Art makes a similar point in a short piece on the relationship between photography and fine art: photography is good for 'accustoming the eye to accuracy of outline and fidelity of light and shade'. Though it exists in an antagonistic relationship with art, photography should become a 'friend and ally' with a view to improving the draughtsmanship of artists. The article discusses photographs that had formed part of an exhibition that toured Britain in 1853–1854 following the 'Recent Specimens of Photography' exhibition at the Society of Arts in 1853.[6] Included in the exhibition and singled out for merit by virtue of its handling of architecture is Philip Henry's Delamotte's 'Boy in the Arch', a salted-paper print, an engraving of which is included in the article. A short piece in *The Crayon*, a weekly, and later monthly, periodical devoted to the graphic arts, sees photography not as a rival but as a 'most important auxiliary to the resources of the artist'. Fears of the new medium are assuaged by the sense that photography 'only aspires to *copy*, it cannot invent'. The article goes on to discuss the production of photographic facsimiles of engravings and the new commercial opportunities this provides.

The controversial omission of photography from the fine arts section of the 1862 International Exhibition provoked arguments about the relationship between photography and art and raised questions about the connection between photographic apparatus and the finished photograph, as well as the nature of different kinds of labour. The page from the official catalogue to the 1862 International Exhibition included here reveals that, instead of being classified as one of the fine arts (architecture, painting, sculpture, art designs for manufacture and engraving), photography was placed in the Industrial Department, sitting alongside mining, quarrying and mineral products, naval architecture and animal and vegetable substances used in manufacture. *The Photographic Journal* documents the opposition of the Council of the Photographic Society to this decision. The author of this piece registers dismay at photography's relegation from '"Arts and Sciences" where it has hitherto figured in similar entertainments, to the humbler class of "mechanical contrivances"'. The piece discusses the 'arbitrary' nature of this classification, asking why photography should not take its place among the 'modern fine arts'. The second piece from *The Photographic Journal* comes from its next issue (May 1861). Here the author calls for 'an immediate alteration of the obnoxious classification', and the piece reproduces the correspondence between Francis Richard Sandford, the Secretary of Her Majesty's Commissioners of the International Exhibition, and Frederick Pollock, Lord Chief Baron of the Exchequer and President of the Photographic Society. Pollock argues that photography is far more than 'the mere mechanical application or use of certain apparatus', making a distinction between the photograph as the finished product and photographic equipment. A photograph involves '*thought, selection, taste,* and *sometimes design*' yet is placed 'among carpenters' tools and agricultural implements! The incongruity is not so glaring, but it is of the same kind as if architecture were placed along with trowels and scaffolding'.

The final source in this section is from Peter Henry Emerson's *Naturalistic Photography*, a book which champions the ability of photography to accurately reproduce the natural world. 'Photography, Not Art' is a short essay dating from 1899 that replaced a section titled 'Photography – a Pictorial Art' from the original 1889 edition. Emerson caused controversy when he wrote a pamphlet titled 'The Death of Naturalistic Photography' in 1891 in which he changed his mind about the idea of art being linked to the faithful depiction of nature. In the extract included here, Emerson expands on the ideas expressed in his earlier pamphlet, insisting on the fact that, whereas 'Art is personal; photographs are machine-made goods', '*The photographer does not make his* picture – A MACHINE DOES IT ALL FOR HIM'.

Notes

1 For a detailed discussion of the relationship between photography and painting in the nineteenth century see Jan von Brevern, 'Two or three things photography did to painting' in Nicoletta Leonardi and Simone Natale (eds.) *Photography and Other Media in the Nineteenth Century*, (University Park, Pennsylvania: Pennsylvania State University Press, 2018), pp. 103–115. On Ruskin and photography see Lindsay Smith, *Victorian Photography, Painting and Poetry* (Cambridge: CUP, 1995, 2008), pp. 10, 88–91.

2 John Ruskin letter to his father from Padua (October 1845) quoted in *Modern Painters* in E.T Cook and Alexander Wedderburn (eds.) *The Works of John Ruskin* (London: George Allen, 1903), p. 210. See Ken and Jenny Jacobson's *Carrying Off the Palaces: Ruskin's Lost Daguerreotypes* (London: Bernard Quaritch Ltd., 2015). This was written following the Jacobsons' discovery of a mahogany box of daguerreotypes once belonging to Ruskin in a small auction in 2006.

3 Ruskin's views on photography fluctuate throughout his work. See Cook and Wedderburn (ibid.) for a list of references to photography in Ruskin's other work.

4 In the United States, *The Photographic Art Journal* was established in 1851 devoted in part to such debates. Its first issue contains articles with titles such as 'The Art of Photography' and 'Photography, the handmaid of art'. This journal ran for four years and was then published as *The Photographic and Fine Art Journal* until 1860.

5 For a discussion of Bede's work in context see B.A Henisch and H.K Henisch 'Cuthbert Bede and the Photographic Scene in the 1850s', *History of Photography* 28:4 (2004), pp. 348–356.

6 For further discussion of the exhibition see Roger Taylor, *Impressed by Light: British Photographs from Paper Negatives* (Yale University Press: New Haven and London, 2007), pp. 53–6.

132

JOHN RUSKIN, LETTERS TO HIS FATHER FROM VENICE (7TH OCTOBER 1845) AND TO WILLIAM HENRY HARRISON FROM VEVAY (AUGUST 12TH 1846)

Modern Painters, in *The Works of John Ruskin*, eds. E. T. Cook and Alexander Wedderburn (London: George Allen, 1903), p. 210

Letter from Ruskin to his Father (7th October 1845)

'I have been lucky enough to get from a poor Frenchman here, said to be in distress, some most beautiful, though very small, Daguerreotypes of the palaces I have been trying to draw; and certainly Daguerreotypes taken by this vivid sunlight are glorious things. It is very nearly the same thing as carrying off the palace itself; every chip of stone and stain is there, and of course there is no mistake about proportions. I am very much delighted with these, and am going to have some more made of pet bits. It is a noble invention say what they will of it and any one who has worked and blundered and stammered as I have done for four days, and then sees the thing he has been trying to do so long in vain, done perfectly and faultlessly in half a minute, won't abuse it afterwards.

Letter from Ruskin to W. H Harrison (August 12th 1845)

My drawings are truth to the very letter too literal, perhaps; so says my father, so says not the Daguerreotype, for it beats me grievously. I have allied myself with it [. . .] and have brought away some precious records from Florence. It is certainly the most marvellous invention of the century; given us, I think, just in time to save some evidence from the great public of wreckers. As regards art, I wish it had never been discovered, it will make the eye too fastidious to accept mere handling.

DOI: 10.4324/9781315400266-157

133

'THE ART OF PHOTOGRAPHY'

Photographic Art Journal (Vol. 1), January 1851, pp. 1–3

The art of photography

EXPERIENCE has taught the world that secresy is the great bar to all earthly well-being, and if it has not grown wiser by a knowledge of the fact in its domestic relations, it certainly has in business matters; and for this reason it is we see over the whole inhabitable globe, where man has been enlightened by the power of the press, each commercial, mechanical, agricultural, or political class, supporting its own printed organ of intercommunion, for their own special benefit. That each derives great advantages – far, very far beyond the amount invested – from these publications, is a fact now totally beyond dispute. Ask the merchant who first caviled at the publication of Hunt's Merchants' Magazine, and he will tell you, no consideration would induce him to part with it. Ask the mechanic who once thought and declared that for his business, a paper was worse than useless, to relinquish the Scientific American, or any other periodical devoted to his trade, and he would laugh at you – and last but not least, look at that stubborn old farmer, who once scorned to introduce what he ironically was pleased to call book learning, in his practice of Agriculture, poring over the columns of the Cultivator – do you think he will deny its usefulness? Ask him, and he will point to his fields and say to you, there where I once got only twenty bushels of wheat to the acre by my old method, this paper has taught me to get forty – there is land that five years ago yielded me naught but stalks and stones, now produces me two hundred bushels of potatoes. And such you will find to be the experience of all – in every branch of business – who have devoted their leisure hours to the perusal of congenial prints.

And why should not the Daguerreotypist be equally benefitted by a periodical devoted to his interests, particularly when his art is so susceptible of improvement? We can see no reason to doubt it; and it is in consideration of this – admiring and loving the art as we do – that we are induced to undertake the pleasing task of communing monthly with the Daguerrian world, and it shall not be our fault if they fail to derive pleasure and profit from the intercourse.

Our intentions are before the public in our prospectus, and we shall content ourselves by looking a little ahead and predict what we conceive and trust may be

 DOI: 10.4324/9781315400266-158

the fruits of our labor. We do it not egotistically, for we rely more upon the good sense and ardent desire of Daguerreotypists for their accomplishment than we do on our efforts, whatever they may be.

Even as the art of engraving and sculpture has improved under the criticisms of the press, so must that of Photography. – At the present day it is viewed, too much, in the light of a mere mechanical occupation to arrive at any high degree of excellence. In too many instances men enter into it because they can get nothing else to do; without the least appreciation of its merits as an art of exquisite refinement, without the taste to guide them, and without the love and ambition to study more than its practical application, neglecting the sciences intimately connected with it, and leaving entirely out of the question those of drawing, painting, and sculpture, sister arts, a knowledge of which must tend to elevate the taste and direct the operator into the more classical and elegant walks of his profession.

Daguerreotyping is comparatively rude to what it will be a few years hence. The pictures now produced stand in relation to those that will be executed within a quarter of a century, very little better than the ancient Egyptian paintings compared with the beautiful works of the present day, or the early copper engravings of Germany with the exquisite steel productions of our own times. We look forward to a period not far distant, when our best Daguerreotypists will wonder how they could, for so long a time, be content with the specimens of their art they now put forth, as much as they do at this day at the shadows of six and eight years ago.

But a far different feeling must exist among them than that entertained to be productive of the result we predict. In all our intercourse with Daguerreotypists we have found but two who are enthusiastic lovers of the art; and the greatest ambition we detect is a desire to produce a *good* picture so far as the present process will permit – very few, if any, experiments are made to improve the whole system. We have never yet seen a perfect picture, and the fault lies with all the various manipulations in a more or less degree. These are to be corrected only by the most careful and intense study, more than the art has ever yet received from an American operator. We think one fact will illustrate the correctness of our assertion. We know of one of our *best* artists who frequently gets into difficulty from the imperfect working of his material and is quite incapable of discovering the cause, and yet he professes to despise what he calls – and what is partially – the theory of the art; quite ignorant, probably, of the fact that it is to *theoretical* analysis and deduction he is indebted for his art. Had Daguerre and Niepce been ignorant of the sciences of Chemistry and Philosophy, they never would have discovered photography; and as yet none can assert that the latter is perfect, it must be conceded that a more intimate investigation of chemistry and philosophy in connection with photography will lead to new discoveries of the most surprising results.

The philosophers of Europe are daily toiling in search of the still hidden principles of the art, and every year brings forth from their laboratories some new application. But why should we wait for new developments to be wafted to us across the Atlantic, when we have from our extensive practical knowledge of the business so many advantages for noticing its various phases, developing and applying them, and successfully experimenting.

Since the time of Professors Morse and Draper's experiments, what new discoveries – apart from various "Quick stuffs" – have been made by our ten thousand Daguerreotypists? None; at least none have come to light. If any have been made, we must deprecate the selfishness which induces the miserly hoarding of such discoveries. It is a great mistake to suppose that individual benefit can result from such a course; it is only by free communication and interchange that permanent advantage can be derived from them. Many may be drawn to an operator's room by the announcement of a new discovery, but many more will think and judge for themselves, and consider it a mere catch-penny affair, unless they are assured of its adoption by others. Thus we have heard numbers reason, and in this age of so much deception it is quite plausible.

Photography must assume a higher sphere and maintain it. It is a noble science, and as such it must be regarded and preserved. If personal considerations do not now make men sensible of this, they soon will exist, for we feel assured, from the eagerness with which our "History and practice of the art of Photography" has been sought after within the last few months, that the minds of Daguerreotypists are awakening to the importance of knowing something more than the mere mechanical portion of their art.

Occasionally I have found men opposed to the publication of works on the art; giving as their reason, that everybody would know as much about it as themselves. The narrow-mindedness and selfishness of this reason is too apparent to merit any thing but contempt. Such men must fall by their own ignorance, and the sooner the profession is relieved of them the better.

That we are not singular in the views above expressed, may be seen from the following extract from a letter received from one of our best artists.

"Dear Sir – Your note, together with circular of the Photograpic Art-Journal, is duly received; and I hasten to reply that I am truly gratified that you have taken so important a step in the diffusion of knowledge in practical Photography. I hope and really believe that the best of success will attend your noble effort. Long has the art of Photography grovelled in darkness – long has it been enshrouded in mystery, and long has it been practised with very ill success – not because it is of trifling importance, or should rank beneath any one of the fine arts, for the world has christened it king over all; but because its devotees, especially those who have led the craft, have been so self-conceited that they have refused a reunion of thought and action; consequently but little, comparatively, has been done for the perfection of the art. One man may possess great selfishness, but he has not all the knowledge of Photographic manipulation and cannot attain that high state of perfection in thus relying wholly on his own ability, that might be attained by the united efforts of twenty, each, perhaps, as well informed as himself, and I deprecate all those whose constant efforts have been to enshroud the art in mystery. In regard to your requesting me to correspond with the Journal I have only to say that perhaps there are others better qualified than myself; however, I am at the service of the cause – I have dedicated my life to the art and will use my exertions whenever I can be in any way useful. Yours, &c."

Such is the language of an artist. He speaks feelingly and truthfully, although severely, and we cherish the hope that among the chaff we shall find in the course of our editorial career many more kernels like him.

134

CUTHBERT BEDE, 'PHOTOGRAPHY IN AN ARTISTIC LIGHT'

Photographic Pleasures: popularly portrayed with pen and pencil (London: Thomas McLean, 1855), pp. 32–34

"BY the aid of Photography," says Mr Hogg, "any one may now become an artist." A dictum which – at the risk of making Mr Hogg bristle up at my temerity – I deny, even in this artist-dubbing age, when people, from modists and mountebanks to ballet-dancers and barbers, dignify their trades, and call themselves "*artistes*."

But before a man can be an "artist," in the commonly received meaning of the word, not only is there required of him a very different kind of manipulation to that demanded in Photography, but also brains to guide his handiwork. There is a vast difference between a Claudet and a Claude; just as there is a vast difference between a steam engine and a "Hamlet." Each one is a triumph of inventive genius; but, how different are their natures!

The pictures of Claudet are the results of scientific invention: those of Claude; of inspired observation. There was poetry in a Claude: there is no poetry in a Claudet. The former can throw beauty and grace over the rugged and harsh; but the latter is the Gradgrind of Art, and represents nothing but stern facts. The Claudets can show but little judgment or discretion in the selection or rejection of component parts for their pictures: the Claudes chiefly depend upon this, and are able to omit at pleasure anything that interferes with the harmony of the composition. There may be a thousand Claudets, but only one Claude.

Photography is not (strictly) "Art;" neither is a Photographer an artist. Photography is but the handmaid of art. We hear and read a good deal of "Photography in its relation to Art;" but, if we inquire into that relationship, and search the registers of art for information on the subject, we shall find that the connexion is little nearer than that of a Scotch cousin. "It must always be borne in mind," says Sir William Newton, "that, essentially speaking, the Camera is by no means calculated to teach the principles of art; but, to those who are already well-informed in this respect, and have had practical experience, it may be made the means of considerable advancement."

The greatest use that an artist derives from the Camera is, that it enables him to secure truthfulness of detail, when he might otherwise be unable to give it. He

 DOI: 10.4324/9781315400266-159

can paint, on the spot, the broad effects – giving all the play of light and shade, the local colour, and the atmospheric tints, and then – having secured what the Camera could not give him – he can make his Calotype, and afterwards, by its aid, complete his picture at his leisure. This method would be especially useful to the artist, in views wherein he would have to paint intricate masses of architecture; and it would enable him to compete in accuracy of detail, with the painstaking fidelity of a Canaletti, or an Edwin Cooke.

And yet, after all, Photography can but help the artist up to a certain point. It cannot supply him with "the gift divine;" and so, when the pre-Raphaelites were accused of painting from Photographs, they replied, "Let our accusers do the same, and produce pictures of equal merit and truth:" and the accusers tried in vain.

The Camera will only help that painter who has deeply studied the principles of his art, and has worked faithfully and laboriously in the minute representation of Nature. We may rest satisfied that there is no "Royal road" to anything; and that genius only becomes great by careful study and perseverance. Power of hand, and freedom of execution in Art, can only be acquired by the diligent perusal – not of the works of the Camera, but of the works of Creation; and a scientific invention, like Photography, can never be made to usurp the place of true Art in the eyes of the true artist.

135

'PHOTOGRAPHY AS A FINE ART'

The Illustrated Magazine of Art,
Vol. 3, No. 13 (1854), p. 1

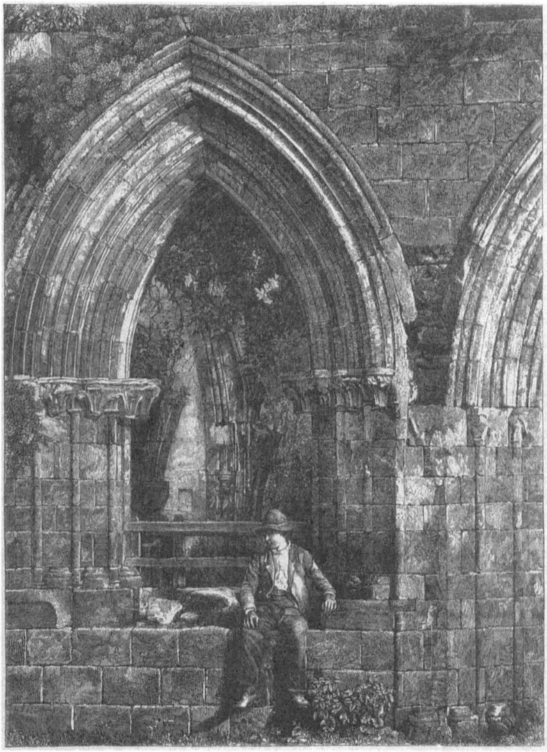

THE BOY IN THE ARCH, FROM A PHOTOGRAPH BY DELAMOTTE.

Photography as a fine art

LIMITED as the powers of photography are, at present, to the representation of form by the agency of light and shade only, photographic pictures possess a *severity of truth* which renders them invaluable as a means of accustoming the eye to

DOI: 10.4324/9781315400266-160

accuracy of outline, and fidelity of light and shade. Colour cheats the eye to a great degree in its perception of form; therefore we hope that the so-much coveted discovery of the means of producing images in their natural colours, may be delayed until the more important result of training the eye to the appreciation of correct form has been accomplished.

The necessity for this education of the eye, both on the part of the artist and the public, must be evident to every one who can skilfully criticise the artistic productions which cover the walls of our exhibitions; it will be seen that amid the crowd of *painters* the good draughtsman is the exception rather than the rule. And this deficiency arises from the ordinary practice of young artists, who, in their eagerness to make pictures, rush to colour before they can produce a really finished drawing; hence it is that neither this country nor England show more than three or four eminent lithographers who can compete with the crowds of the same class of artists to be found in France and Germany. And thus the public, seldom having an opportunity of seeing accurate drawing, accepts the bad with so much favour, because its falsehood is glossed over by meretricious colour: and further, it is incapable of detecting the gross distortions presented to view even in the pictures of many artists of note. A correct eye for the appreciation of form, as well as colour, is seldom found combined in the same individual; the former is capable of great improvement, while the latter, like an ear for music, cannot be acquired, although, when latent, it may be more or less correctly developed.

It will at once be evident that this art must come into antagonism with the pencil of the artist, and great has been the fear and consternation that the draughtsman's and painter's occupation was gone. It is said that photography is hated by artists, but if so, it can only be by those who are unworthy of their calling: an inferior mechanical artist may be jealous of such a rival, since it must compel him to be more faithful in his representations; but the artist with a true genius for his calling welcomes photography as a friend and ally; he will find scope enough beyond the limits of mechanical reproduction for the full play of his genius. Photography takes no liberties with nature, it never sacrifices truth to tricky effect. The light and shade in a photograph are not the less effective for being nature's own, and in nothing is this fact more evident or striking than in architectural views, when compared with an ordinary artist's sketch of the same structure. In the latter it is frequently difficult or impossible to make out the details of the ornamentation, in consequence of the conventional manner in which the artist delineates them; while, in the former, every variation of surface, the most delicate chiselling, and even the qualities of texture, are given with wonderful truth, which an examination by the microscope even confirms.

We are led to these remarks by an examination of the interesting collections of photographs now exhibiting both in this country and in England. Here we have collected into a focus the choicest productions of this wonderful art, contributed by practitioners of various countries, and fully representing the great state of perfection at which photography has arrived. Every department of art and nature is laid under contribution, and each adequately represented. Nature, animate and inanimate (the animals "taken unawares"); the leafless tree with its perplexing anatomy of branches and twigs, or crowned with its luxuriant foliage; the corn-field, the rural lane, the copse and dell, the lofty battlemented castle or lowly cottage, the bridge, the stream, are mirrored before us with picturesque effect and microscopic fidelity. But the happiest sphere of its operations appears to us to be architecture. How striking the countless details of the Gothic cathedral, or the crumbling ruin, or distant city with its spires, turrets, and domes, or the nearer view with the portraiture of public buildings. Some of these views present charming *pictures,* the effect of which it would be impossible for art to improve. One of these views, simple in its subject ("The Boy in the Arch," photographed by Mr. Delamotte, an English artist), but most brilliant in effect, from its pleasing variety of light and shade, has so much merit that, by permission of the photographer, we have had it engraved for this Magazine, for which purpose it is extremely well suited; for while lacking those minute details which give so much value to certain representations, yet are so difficult to render by the artist's pencil, it has a sufficient breadth of *chiar'oscuro* to form a good picture. The boy, too, with his natural easy attitude, immediately attracts the eye, and imparts life to a scene which, without him, would lose much of its interest.

Among other architectural photographic views which we have seen, there are two, at least, which we cannot pass by without special mention: a view of "The Cathedral of Notre Dame," at Paris, and "The Hotel de Ville," in the same city. There are, doubtless, others of equal merit, but in them we recognise *all* the conditions we require to be fulfilled in admitting photographic pictures to the rank of works of art; for, be it observed, that there are two classes of photographers, the *mechanical* and the *artistic:* and the same object taken by two individuals will be insipid or interesting according to the amount of artistic feeling employed in taking the view. It is needless to observe that during almost every hour in the day the pictorial aspect of a building varies, owing to the state of the atmosphere, and to the play of the sun's rays upon its principal or lateral façades. The artistic photographer will select the hour for taking his view when the building is most picturesque; the mechanical photographer will take his view at any hour indifferently; but the resulting photograph will loudly proclaim by which of the two it was taken. It is just the same in the art of painting; the majority of pictures exhibit merely mechanical or technical skill: all the higher qualities demanded in a truly artistic production are to be found only in the works of the few; hence the majority of pictures pass through three periods or stages of existence – production, exhibition, oblivion; or, as has been quaintly remarked, through hell, purgatory, and paradise.

But to return to photography; beside its suitableness for representing objects of the kind already named, there are also its applications to the delineation of sculptured works and portraits from life, and a wide field of usefulness in its power of reproducing *fac simile* copies of rare etchings and engravings, drawings, manuscripts, &c. In portraiture it has many advantages over the daguerreotype, and has nearly superseded it. In the multiplication of *fac simile* copies of etchings, we have some very choice specimens, in a portfolio of examples obtained from Rembrandt's works: indeed, almost every day yields its surprise in new applications of this magical art.

Although photography dates its existence but fourteen years back, its progress has been wonderfully rapid, considering upon how delicate and refined a series of observations its development is based. Continental photographers were far outstripping those of the land of its birth: within a few months its progress has been incredibly rapid; and this progress dates from the abandonment of Mr. Talbot's patent rights.

136

'PHOTOGRAPHY'

The Crayon, Vol. 1, No. 11 (Mar. 14, 1855), p. 170

THE marvellous productions of Photography continue to engross the attention of the lovers of Art in a high degree. The apprehensions once entertained that this art would, to a certain extent, thrust the artist and his vocation aside, are now no longer indulged; but, on the contrary, it is seen that Photography, so far from being a rival, is in truth a most important auxiliary to the resources of the artist. If it encroaches on any department of Art, it is that of the engraver; for books illustrated by photography, in place of the productions of the graver, are finding their way into the book market. But even this application is limited to the mere reduction and copying of works previously engraved or drawn; for, however ingenious the processes or surprising the results of photography, it must be remembered that this art only aspires to *copy,* it cannot invent. The camera, it is true, is a most accurate copyist, but it is no substitute for original thought or invention. Nor can it supply that refined feeling and sentiment which animate the productions of a man of genius, and so long as invention and feeling constitute essential qualities in a work of Art, Photography can never assume a higher rank than engraving.

As an auxiliary to Art, Photography comes opportunely to the aid of the artist in those preparatory studies always necessary in the production of a work of Art. It obtains for the painter or sculptor, in a few moments, a number of studies of all kinds – landscapes, posés, draperies, &c.; for the architect, models and detail, without which they would, perhaps, have remained but imperfectly known; to the engraver, it furnishes reductions of pictures, &c., of all sizes. These results are attained with the utmost accuracy of form and correctness of effect, such as the most accomplished artist could have attained only by an enormous expenditure of time and labor.

It is in France that the applications of Photography have taken their widest and most practical extension. Not the least interesting and important of these is the production of *fac similes* of rare engravings, such as the productions of Rembrandt, Albert Durer, Callot. Among those now in course of reproduction are the works of Marc Antonio Raimondi. It is well known that a single impression of one of this artist's plates can only be obtained by much persevering assiduity, and at great expense; but a photographic *fac simile* can be procured for as many shillings as the engraving costs pounds.

 DOI: 10.4324/9781315400266-161

Anything like a complete collection of the works of the artists we have named, is only possible to the wealthy amateur. But the taste and appreciation for these things is not confined to that class; and photography comes to the aid of the pictorial art as printing did to literature, and the enjoyment of such works, hitherto the exclusive privilege of the few, is now, by the aid of the new art, extended to a large circle of admirers.

The production of these *fac similes* of engravings is exceedingly easy, and opens up a delightful source of amusement to the fair sex, much more rational and artistic than the uncouth vagaries of crotchet and Berlin wool. An engraving is copied by mere superposition on prepared paper; no camera is required, or other apparatus, except a porcelain dish or two, and a pressure-frame. Moreover, the integrity of the original engravings is in nowise impaired; their value to the possessor is not depreciated; they remain as highly prized as ever, while the delight and instruction they are capable of imparting are widely extended, and with an increased knowledge of, and taste for, works of Art.

To obtain a *fac simile* of an engraving we proceed as follows: – The engraving is placed face downwards upon the glass of the pressure-frame, and a piece of prepared sensitive paper laid upon it. Pressure being applied, the glass is exposed for a sufficient time to a strong light. This soon produces a *negative;* for, as the engraving only admits of the light passing through those portions of the paper left uncovered by the ink, it follows that what is black in the original is left white in the copy, and *vice versâ;* but from this negative any number of *positives* – that is, *fac similes* of the engraving – can be obtained; and by this means the portfolio of the collector may become enriched with productions which, but for the aid afforded by Photography, could never have found a place in it. – *The Artist.*

137

INTERNATIONAL EXHIBITION 1862, OFFICIAL CATALOGUE OF THE INDUSTRIAL DEPARTMENT

(Third ed.) (London: Truscott, Son and Simmons, 1862), p. viii

CONTENTS.

UNITED KINGDOM.

COLONIAL POSSESSIONS.

DOI: 10.4324/9781315400266-162

138

THE PHOTOGRAPHIC JOURNAL, APRIL 15 1861

(Journal of the Photographic Society of London), April 15 1861, pp. 149–150

THE programme of the Commissioners for the International Exhibition of 1862 has been issued in the *Gazette*. In it is detailed, rather elaborately, the objects which are admissible in one or other of the four grand sections into which the intended Exhibition is to be divided. On looking it over, of course we were anxious to see how photography would fare; and we must confess our great astonishment at the arbitrary arrangements of the Commissioners. We find that photography is to be placed in Section 2, and is thus designated, "No. 14, Photographic Apparatus and Photography." We are at a loss to conceive why photography should be thus unceremoniously ousted out of its proper section, which we consider to be No. 4. Why should photography be placed among "Railway plant, locomotive engines and carriages, agricultural and horticultural machines and implements," and things of this class? Why should not photography, the youngest sister of art, be represented in Section 4, which is to contain paintings in oil and water colours, drawings, sculpture, models, die-sinking and intagli, etchings and engravings? To show how unjust and arbitrary this system of classification is, we need only point out the fact that if a photographer were to send untouched photographs, they would go among the ploughs, harrows, and watering-cans! and if he were to send coloured photographs, they would go into Section 4, with the objects of art above enumerated. Is not the photographic branch of the Department of *Science and Art* considered so important that the Government, to promote *art-education,* has entered into a fierce competition with traders in order the more fully to carry out their scheme? If photography is not a branch of art, why did not the managers of the *Art Treasures* Exhibition, held in Manchester in 1857, exclude it? What, on the contrary, is the fact? They had a special gallery for the purpose of exhibiting the various productions of photographers. There is neither reason nor sense in this arrangement; and we trust that photographers will not quietly submit to see themselves thus pushed aside. True that, by being placed in Section 2, they will be entitled to prizes and medals as rewards for merit. But do photographers desire to be brought to the level of mere mechanicians? We think and hope not. The wonderful progress made in photography during the last ten years will be

DOI: 10.4324/9781315400266-163

one of the greatest and most marked features in the Exhibition of 1862. In 1851 it had not then attained importance enough to be classed particularly; but during the past ten years every day has shown more clearly than ever, that it is destined to be the great means of reforming many of the conventionalities of art, and at the same time the only means of rendering intact the reproduction, in a cheap form, of great works of art.

139

THE PHOTOGRAPHIC JOURNAL, MAY 15 1861

(Journal of the Photographic Society of London), May 15 1861, pp. 171–174

In our last Number we took occasion, in a hurried manner, to call the attention of our readers to the extraordinary classification decided upon by Her Majesty's Commissioners for the Exhibition of 1862. Since, then, an official communication from Mr. F. R. Sandford, the Secretary to the Commissioners, has been addressed to our President, requesting the Council of the Photographic Society to appoint a Committee to organize Class 14, "Photographic Apparatus and Photography." Under these circumstances the Lord Chief Baron assembled the Council to consider the proposition. The Council express themselves unanimously as feeling aggrieved at the manner in which the Art of Photography is classed. In a reply, which will be found below, the Lord Chief Baron puts the grievance in a manful and logical manner. It is needless to recapitulate the various points in this powerful and effective reply. From the manner in which the case is put, we cannot anticipate anything other than an immediate alteration of the obnoxious classification. Last month we quoted instances which we think sufficiently prove that Photography by common consent is acknowledged to be a branch of the *Fine Arts*. Since then, in the discussion of the new Copyright Bill, the Attorney-General, and the various Members of the House of Commons who spoke on the subject, placed Photography on the same footing as Engraving; that being the case, the Lord Chief Baron is undoubtedly right when he says "that the Council of the Photographic Society claim for it a position (however humble) among the *Fine Arts* (if etching and engraving may be so placed, as no doubt they may)." He then goes on to say that "Photography, quite as much as engraving, gives room for the exercise of individual genius, so as to stamp a special character on the works of photographers, and give to the result of their labours the *impress of the mind of each artist*." The truth of this succinct statement is annually to be found on the walls of our Exhibitions, where any one who has the least knowledge of the productions of our leading photographers can instantly, without the assistance of a catalogue, single out the productions of Messrs. Fenton, Bedford, Llewellyn, Lake Price, Robinson, Vernon Heath, G. Washington Wilson, Maxwell Lyte, and others too numerous

DOI: 10.4324/9781315400266-164

to mention. It is this "impress of the mind of each artist" that enables us to do so without any trouble.

Sir Charles Eastlake, in his speech at the Royal Academy dinner recently, alluded to the satisfaction felt by the artistic profession at the decision that no prizes would be given in the *Fine Art* Department of the forthcoming Exhibition. Knowing, as we do, the strong feeling on that subject in the same direction, felt and expressed by photographers, we can easily account for the strong expressions which have reached us in letters on this subject.

To any one who knows the arduous labours of those who direct the organization of such a gigantic undertaking as the Exhibition, it will be easily understood how impossible it is, in the overwhelming mass of details which have to be considered by the Commissioners, to watch with care every little matter; and the simple mis-classification, though of great importance to photographers, is one of the many little correctible mistakes inseparable from the undertaking.

As we have already said, we have no hesitation in stating that, when the Commissioners read the conclusive and able statement of the matter as put by the Lord Chief Baron, they will immediately rectify it. In one of the concluding paragraphs of the Lord Chief Baron's letter he says, "The incongruity is not so glaring, but it is of the same kind as if architecture were placed along with trowels and scaffolding." Now, strangely enough, something of this sort does happen; and the *Saturday Review,* which is a great organ on everything architectural, makes a somewhat similar complaint to ourselves, and, while doing so, glances at our grievance as an illustration of its own peculiar little trouble. We will quote the paragraph: –

"When we come to the classification itself of the sections, *the confusion of ideas* as to the meaning and value of architecture, which reveals itself, is a proof that the danger to be apprehended is not imaginary. To be sure, 'Architecture' stands as No. 1 of Section 4, that of 'Fine Arts,' followed by paintings and drawings; but we have to turn back to the second section, in which railway plant forms the first item, and surgical instruments and appliances the last, for a class (the 10th) of 'Civil Engineering, Architectural and Building Contrivances;' while the 14th Class *bears the very suspicious title of 'Photographic Apparatus and Photography'*– A DESIGNATION WHICH, IF IT REALLY MEANS ANYTHING, IMPLIES THAT PHOTOGRAPHIC REPRESENTATIONS OF BUILDINGS (THE MOST TRUTHFUL CONCEIVABLE METHOD OF ARCHITECTURAL EXHIBITION) ARE TO BE JUMBLED UP WITH TENDERS AND BANDAGES IN THE COMMISSIONERS' MINDS. *We cannot conceive that this crude classification will be persisted in by the Commissioners*."

The italics in the above are our own. But that we have reason and common sense on our side, the foregoing quotation amply proves. We leave the matter now, with a firm conviction that the right thing will be done.

International Exhibition, 1862.
454 West Strand, London, W.C.
April 26, 1861.

Sir, – I am directed by Her Majesty's Commissioners to forward for your information the enclosed copy of the Decisions which they have published up to this date, on points relating to the management of the Exhibition of 1862.

Her Majesty's Commissioners having had under consideration the arrangements that will be required for securing an adequate representation of the various branches of industry of the United Kingdom, and having had the benefit of the advice of a large and influential Committee whom they specially consulted on the subject, have determined to organize those Classes of the Exhibition which appear to admit of such an arrangement, by means of Central Committees, and to invite the cooperation of such Societies, or other public bodies, as are generally recognized as the representatives of these Classes, in the selection of the members of the several committees that will be appointed.

One of these Committees will be formed in connexion with the Class of "Photographic Apparatus and Photography" (Number 14); and Her Majesty's Commissioners have directed me to inquire whether the Council of the Photographic Society would be willing to submit the names of six or eight gentlemen whom they would recommend for appointment as members of such Committee.

The duties of the Committee will consist generally in advising Her Majesty's Commissioners on the measures to be taken for obtaining an adequate representation of the class with which it is connected, – in examining the demands for space sent in by intending exhibitors, which will be classified and submitted to the Committees in a condensed form by the officers of Her Majesty's Commissioners, – in encouraging the production of suitable objects for exhibition, – and in settling the final distribution of space among the exhibitors in the class.

Her Majesty's Commissioners trust that they may not only have the assistance of your Council in the selection of this Committee, but that the officers and members of your Society in general will give them the benefit of their cooperation, by communicating such information, or such results of their experience, as may seem likely to assist the Commissioners in those departments of the Exhibition with which the Photographic Society is mainly concerned.

I have the honour to be,
Your obedient servant,
F. R. Sandford,
Secretary.

To the President of the
Photographic Society.

Baron's Room, Court of Exchequer,
Westminster, 6th May, 1861.

Sir, – I have to acknowledge your communication of the 26th inst., *inquiring* whether the Council of the Photographic Society would be willing to assist in appointing a Committee to advise Her Majesty's Commissioners on the measures to be taken to procure an adequate representation of Photographic Apparatus and

Photography, Class No. 14, and *expressing* "that Her Majesty's Commissioners trust that the Officers and Members of the Society will give the benefit of their cooperation, and assist the Commissioners in those departments of the Exhibition with which the Photographic Society is mainly concerned."

I lost no time in assembling the Council, and laying before them your letter and its enclosure (containing the decision as to Sections and Classes), and I have been desired by the Council to communicate to you the result of their deliberations, in which I entirely concur. It appears to them that some mistake has occurred with reference to the objects of the Photographic Society, indeed to photography itself, which it is desirable to point out and have corrected before they appoint a committee. The Class to which their attention is directed is Section 2, No. 14, "Photographic Apparatus and Photography" (as if photography were nothing more than the mere mechanical application or use of certain apparatus, and to be considered of less account than the apparatus itself).

The Section in which No. 14 is placed includes every species of machinery, implement, or tool which is used for the purposes of social life; and photography is the only *result* or *product* which is placed among the machinery or apparatus necessary to produce it; it furnishes the solitary exception to what is otherwise a universal rule; even the paper on which a photograph is printed is put into a section above the machine that is used to make it.

In the investigation of the properties of light, upon which the visible phenomena depend, photography is as much a science as astronomy or chemistry; it has led to discoveries of the greatest interest and importance as to the composition of the rays of the sun, and the properties of the different portions of the solar spectrum, as was lately expressed in a part of Prof. Faraday's lecture at the Royal Institution. It has also enlarged the bounds of chemical science, by ascertaining the qualities of a great variety of substances with which it had to deal, and it is in these respects chiefly that I personally have any connexion with it.

In the observations of natural scenery, and in the selection of what shall be represented with reference to the effect of light and shade, and from what point of view, – in the grouping and arranging of the principal or accessory objects for the purpose of forming a picture, photography is no doubt an art, *an imitative* art; but the Council of the Photographic Society claim for it a position (however humble) among the *fine arts* (if etching and engraving may be so placed, as no doubt *justly* they may). Photography, quite as much as engraving, gives room for the exercise of individual genius, so as to stamp a special character on the works of photographers, and give to the result of their labours the impress of the mind of each artist.

The Photographic Society has been founded chiefly with a view to promote photography in connexion with *science* and *the fine arts*; and the Members interest themselves about photographic apparatus in the same manner only as a Raphael or a Reynolds might select and use the most convenient easel, the best brushes, or the most appropriate and enduring colours – the instrument is comparatively nothing. Photography consists in the artistic use of any apparatus upon a subject properly selected, and occasionally arranged or prepared. They are quite willing to contribute as much as lies in their power to illustrate what photography has done, and is daily doing, in producing the most accurate copies of the finest works of art, ancient or modern, in multiplying representations of the fairest or the wildest scenes of nature, and whatever art has done to adorn or improve nature in building cities and constructing magnificent works and buildings of all sorts, from the cathedral or palace to the humblest cottage – from the bridge that spans a mighty river to the plank that crosses a brook, or in giving enduring pictures of private and domestic life. They do not complain that the apparatus they use is put among all the other apparatus, but they do complain that results such as have been exhibited for many years by the Society, and have been honoured by the presence and encouragement of Her Majesty and His Royal Highness The Prince Consort, are deemed worthy of no better place than among tools and mechanical devices of whatever merit; and they would appeal to the Royal and illustrious patrons of their body to be rescued from the comparative degradation of being mixed up with the last improvement in ploughs or cart-wheels, or ships' tackle.

The very clear and luminous arrangement of the articles to be exhibited gives the greater force to the objection of the Council.

Section 1 contains all natural substances, whether mineral, vegetable, or animal, which minister to the wants and comfort of man.

Section 2 contains all the machinery and apparatus (including instruments and tools of every description) that conduce to a mechanical end; and, with one exception, it contains *nothing else.*

Section 3 contains the result produced by Section 2 acting upon Section 1.

There is something so remarkably distinct and simple in the arrangement, that it is to be regretted that its beautiful simplicity should be marred by any exception. But Photography as a *result* is put in Section 2; it is the only thing that is out of place in the whole arrangement. A result that involves *thought, selection, taste,* and *sometimes design,* is put among carpenters' tools and agricultural implements! The incongruity is not so glaring, but it is of the same kind as if architecture were placed along with trowels and scaffolding, or Humboldt were put among commercial travellers.

Section 4 comprehends all that genius and labour have done in the departments by common consent called the Fine Arts, in which Engraving has been *tardily* admitted.

But at last it *has* been admitted (now one of the latest discoveries in photography is) that an actual engraving (without the use of any graving tool) can be produced by chemical agency and the light of the sun. Is the impression from the result of such a process to be received as an engraving (which most undoubtedly it is)? and the other results of photography to be excluded? I am sorry to have troubled you at such length; but these are the views of the Council, which I have to submit to you in answer to your letter, and remain

Your obedient Servant,
Frederick Pollock.

To F. R. Sandford, Esq.,
Secretary of Her Majesty's Commissioners,
International Exhibition, 1862.

Decisions of Her Majesty's Commissioners on points relating to the Exhibition. April 1861.

The articles exhibited will be divided into the following Classes: –

SECTION I.

Class 1. Mining, Quarrying, Metallurgy, and Mineral Products.
Class 2. Chemical Substances and Products, and Pharmaceutical Processes.
" 3. Substances used for Food, including Wines.
" 4. Animal and Vegetable Substances used in Manufactures.

SECTION II.

Class 5. Railway Plant, including Locomotive Engines and Carriages.
" 6. Carriages not connected with Rail or Tram Roads.
" 7. Manufacturing Machines and Tools.
" 8. Machinery in general.
" 9. Agricultural and Horticultural Machines and Implements.
" 10. Civil Engineering, Architectural and Building Contrivances.
" 11. Military Engineering, Armour and Accoutrements, Ordnance, and Small Arms.
" 12. Naval Architecture, Ships' Tackle.
" 13. Philosophical Instruments, and Processes depending upon their use.
" 14. Photographic Apparatus and Photography.
" 15. Horological Instruments.
" 16. Musical Instruments.
" 17. Surgical Instruments and Appliances.

SECTION III.

Class 18. Cotton.
" 19. Flax and Hemp.
" 20. Silk and Velvet.
" 21. Woollen and Worsted, including Mixed Fabrics generally.
" 22. Carpets.
" 23. Woven, Spun, Felted, and Laid Fabrics, when shown as specimens of Printing or Dyeing.
" 24. Tapestry, Lace, and Embroidery.
" 25. Skins, Fur, Feathers, and Hair.
" 26. Leather, including Saddlery and Harness.
" 27. Articles of Clothing.
" 28. Paper, Stationery, Printing, and Bookbinding.
" 29. Educational Works and Appliances.
" 30. Furniture and Upholstery, including Paper-hangings and Papier-mâché.
" 31. Iron and General Hardware.

" 32. Steel and Cutlery.
" 33. Works in Precious Metals, and their imitations, and Jewellery.
" 34. Glass.
" 35. Pottery.
" 36. Manufactures not included in previous Classes.

SECTION IV. – Modern Fine Arts.
(*See Decisions* 111–123.)

Class 37. Architecture.
" 38. Paintings in Oil and Water Colours, and Drawings.
" 39. Sculpture, Models, Die-sinking, and Intaglios.
" 40. Etchings and Engravings.

140

PETER HENRY EMERSON, 'PHOTOGRAPHY, NOT ART'

Naturalistic Photography for Students of the Art (London: Dawbarn & Ward, 1899), pp. 53–63

Let us, lest we be misunderstood, preface our article by acknowledging without stint the great and invaluable uses of *scientific* photography – that is, photography taken with the best corrected optical instruments that give mathematical reproductions of objects before them – reproductions scientifically true in *some* respects, but not in all; *e.g.*, false in color translation. No doubt science will remedy these defects, and then we shall have an invaluable *machine* by which *impersonal* drawings can be made. The uses of such drawings it were superfluous to consider; they are already widely known to many, and their increased usefulness can be trusted to gain ground without any advocacy. But it must never be forgotten that such mathematical plottings of persons and things are not true in the sense that they reproduce objects as we see them. I first called attention to the fact as regards form and perspective drawing, and subsequently, in conjunction with Mr. T. F. Goodall, published a paper on the subject. Our observations have, in many cases, been corroborated by one of the greatest living psychologists; and one or two of the results, we have since found, were previously discovered by another psychologist. In addition, a well-known teacher, the author of a work on simplified "perspective," has accepted our pamphlet, and intends withdrawing his work. Our investigations easily explain why photographs so often do not resemble the people they are meant to represent, why landscapes are nearly always so disappointing and petty, and why architectural photographs are useless to the seeing draughtsman, as Mr. J. Pennell so ably pointed out.

I may briefly say that perspective drawings (and such are correct photographs) are useful purely as "measurements" – as surveys, in fact for topography; when photography is invaluable. In the matter of textures photography sometimes serves – sometimes other methods are truer. But in most transient landscape effects photographs are disappointing. Look at the full moon just rising, and take a photograph of it, then compare the proportion of the moon to the rest of the landscape; the photograph will give an absurdly "small" impression of the scene.

This brings us to the subject of photography and art. It has often been asked, "Is photography an art?" We answer: "*No,*" and with Mr. Pennell agree that "it can never be an art."

 DOI: 10.4324/9781315400266-165

It is amusing to watch the wrigglings of various vain persons who would be known as "artists," and yet are living on from day to day practising some other trade or profession, persons who – provided photography were an art, and all that some say of it – could never be classed as anything but "amateurs." They belong chiefly to a body of well-meaning persons well known to neural pathologists – a class that fills our galleries and libraries with rubbish done at their own expense. But there are some who really are puzzled to know why photography is not an art.

We will endeavor to enlighten them. Let us assume we are going to prove to the world photography is an art; that the most fastidious and critical judges of the period (artists of all schools), have assembled for us to demonstrate to them that photography is an art.

We begin then the "proof" (?).

First, we must select a subject, a real objective picture in the world before us. We select a landscape, say, that experience has taught us would make an artistic painting. We may in that act of selection prove we have artistic judgment. We will assume we have proved this fact. Next we arrange it on the screen, focus it as we like, place our diaphragm in the appropriate slit, and put on the cap – all ready to expose. No special photographic knowledge is required for all this – any artist amongst our judges could do the same thing – his purely *artistic knowledge* would tell him when the focus was right for his desired effect. *Up to the taking off the cap, then, nothing is required but artistic knowledge* (saving a trifle of mechanical knowledge learnt in a *few minutes* by any intelligent person). The person who really wishes to arrive at an impartial judgment must hold *this fact closely*. All done so far has nothing to do with photography, but with art; as for example, any great painter might come and do all this, and then any operator could take the picture. Whatever artistic value it had, would of course belong to the artist who selected, arranged, and focused the view. For "taking" the picture is a pure science, as for ever proved by Messrs. Hurter & Driffield.

Taking negative

Having selected a good view, artists next have *to paint or etch, etc., it. The photographer does not make his picture* – A MACHINE DOES IT ALL FOR HIM. Whatever subtlety of tones, of drawing, there are in the photograph, these are the work of a machine. The operator has no part in it, and he cannot control the result at all, as the classical researches referred to have proved beyond a doubt. The fact that the photographer does not do the work is nearly always overlooked; he gets to talk of *his works* so much that he forgets that after all he has *only set the machine to work,* and he has no more done the work than the engineer who starts the locomotive pulls the train. This must be realized to justly estimate the credit attached to the producer. Now since the machine does the work, and since any intelligent person can easily learn to manipulate the machine, nearly all the credit of all so-called "artistic" photographs is in choice of view, arrangement on screen and choice of focus. In these matters the photographer is absurdly limited in power as compared with hand-work, by the mechanical conditions of the camera. It is therefore very easy to imitate an original worker in photography – a practice, I regret to say, far too common; mediocrity is ever imitative. In addition, the limited powers of the machine tend to level all workers, and prevent genius from fully expressing itself as it can in all individual arts. Very little credit really attaches to *any photographer,* and such work can never reach any but a mediocre plane; it will never fully satisfy any genius, nor any first-rate intellect. But to proceed. We have now got the negative – *and by pure photography nothing more can be done.*

An *artist* now *might* improve the negative by retouching, local intensification, and reduction, etc.; but it must be remembered that everything done by these methods *is not photography at all,* but hand-work, and only art when done by an accomplished and trained artist; and I know of no artist capable of doing such work who would waste time upon negatives. Such work must be judged, and the credit put down to art, not photography. This work is done to-day for commercial ends, and fulfils a commercial need, but all that has nothing to do with art or photography.

Next comes the "printing" from the negative. An *artist* has the power of choosing the process, and paper that will best suit his subject. *That is purely a matter of art-knowledge* if the object be artistic; but, if scientific, the paper will be chosen for scientific considerations. The choice here is very limited. After the paper is chosen, again comes the mechanical photographer and starts the engine, and *light does the printing,* he merely stopping the engine when the printing is done. In this respect the merest journeyman copper-plate printer is a greater artist than the photographer. If the photographer dodge in printing by masking, that is merely a crude form of art, and not photography.

Et voila! He presents his print to the judges whom we imagined assembled. They discuss it, and the spokesman sums up as follows: "You selected the view: that was art (we allow you have an eye for the picturesque). You arranged it well; focused it well (we think): that was art. But you were so limited by the machine that your individuality could but barely assert itself in this respect. Then you started a machine, and *that machine drew* the picture for you; you merely fixed its work by chemicals, which is photography, not art. You selected some ready-prepared paper, and the *sun printed your picture,* and you fixed it again. That is photography, with an iota of art in the selection of the paper. We find you have not proved to us you are an artist, for *you* can execute nothing. You cannot even draw a cube fairly; and, moreover, we find your machine does not give us any idea of the magnificent scene you selected. One of us – an accomplished landscape painter – has been drawing the scene in black and white (we omit to refer to your color impotency), and his *proportions* and tonality are altogether different from those of your photograph. His picture is altogether grander and bigger, yours being merely a *mechanical perspective drawing, false in many respects*. We find that, if you think photography to be art, you must decide who is the artist in the case of an automatic machine – the penny, the person who drops the penny in the slot, or the automatic machine."

Perhaps, convinced by this inexorable logic, you would say: "Yes, I yield to reason, for only fools live in a fool's paradise; but would I not be an artist if I were to reproduce my negatives on copper, photo-etch them, and hand-print them myself?" They, knowing the process, would answer, "No! The laying of the ground is a mechanical process. The biting, if scientifically conducted – and all other ways are mere bungling – is mechanical; and finally but chiefly you are doing a set task, viz., to REPRODUCE your photograph. You are not like the etcher *creating a new work,* but merely mechanically reproducing the work of a machine, Any hand-work put on the plate will, of course, not be photography, though it *may* be art."

Finally the spokesman says to you: "You have demonstrated to us most clearly that photography *is not art,* and never can be. If, however, you like the results (we do not include the invaluable scientific results), do them; you can by them show in a VERY LIMITED way whether you have anything of the artistic temperament (we refer always to the unphotographic part of the work, as we have explained), but do not hold yourself up to ridicule by calling yourself an artist, unless you have been trained as an artist and follow art as a *profession*; for remember that many of us here could pay persons to do the merely photographic work, and soon take the wind out of the sails of all but the three or four of you whom we allow are masters in the selection of pictures in nature, and could these three or four paint what they select as well as they photograph it we allow they would be master-artists. To be an artist you must have the power of SELECTION AND EXECUTION. No matter what the medium chosen, the lack of either is *fatal,* just as there are many real poetic natures who cannot write a stanza."

I may finish this little paper by a suggestion as to why I think artists invariably consider, and will continue to think, hand-work superior to machine-work. Photographs often interest them for a time, yet the interest is *never lasting;* people soon tire of them. I believe the reason of this to be that mankind will always value the personal element in a work; they constantly recur to the etching or painting because it has been done by a man.

Photography then, when not scientific or topographical, is a *pastime,* dangerous in many respects, as apt to foster morbid vanity in the degenerate, but useful often as leading its practitioners to think about art and to visit picture galleries, thus helping them to cultivate an æsthetic sense. But the snares of vanity are too strong to be resisted by the weak, and the cheap press hurries them to their doom. It has been well said that the chief use of the multiplication of cheap journals and increased facilities given to every one to "have his say," has been the increased facility they offer for the *discovery of* fools – since in their columns alone fools are allowed to "have their say." Certain it is that photographic papers have helped photographers to discover many fools who would otherwise have lain *perdus* – amateur writers upon optical matters, upon art, upon science, and what not. We would suggest that the common fool in future hesitate before discovering himself.

Let photographers take the modest and legitimate ground that photography is not an art but a science, and further, that in one invaluable branch – topography – the *machine pictures* selected by an artist must always be superior to others, for a topographer may sacrifice detail for breadth, or accuracy for general topographical sentiment. Let there be no misunderstanding about the use of the word artist. An artist is a man thoroughly trained in the practice of an art (photography is a science), who devotes his life to his art to the exclusion of everything else; his sole end and aim being the production of æsthetic works, whose object is to give emotional pleasure. Art is personal, and machine work can never be art. One must understand something of music to get the best work from a hand-organ, yet an organ-grinder with musical tastes is no artist. If any photographer aspires to become an artist he must cultivate some artistic method of expression, such as painting, sculpture, literature, acting, music, singing, – and practice it as his profession. Then, and not till then, will he be recognized as an artist; and then he may be aggrieved to find that the masters of his profession allow but few even of such trained practitioners the name of artist.

There is much good scientific work to be done by photographers, and if I am permitted to reopen the subject in another paper, I would suggest some systematic work to be undertaken by enthusiastic amateurs – work that would lead them to a far higher level than any taking of "pictures" during a short period of the year will ever do; and they will be relieved of keeping up the pretentious title of artists, bickerings will cease, and photography be more universally respected and advanced.

There was excuse until quite recently for men who contended that photography was art. For men are justified in fighting for a cause, provided they base their fight on knowledge *up to date;* and until quite recently it was justifiable to contend that photography might be a fine art in the hands of an artist. That position, in the light of recent investigations, is untenable and foolish; but, like all old "truths," it will be for a time perpetuated as a superstition amongst the vain and uncultured. Photography is an easily acquired *science,* and never can be anything else.

Finally, there are some who may say – "But Carmine a second-rate painter, or Stylus a third-rate etcher, says – photography is art, and that is sufficient answer." It is no more an answer than when third-rate scientists or first-rate theologians deny the theory of Natural Selection. What one or two men say on this side or that matters not a rap; but the general consensus of opinion of a body of first-rate specialists upon their own subject matters much; and the best artists are unanimous that photography is not art, and never can be, though till recently many able artists were doubtful. Art is personal; photographs are machine-made goods, useful, as is machine-made furniture, machine-made fabrics, and perhaps – for the slums – machine-made music.

5.4

Women and photography

DOI: 10.4324/9781315400266-166

5.4 Women and photography

Periodicals aimed at a female audience carried a number of articles on photography in the second half of the nineteenth century. Focusing on photography as employment, these publications took part in the debate over women and work, addressing the issue of how women might support themselves in ways that made them less dependent on marriage as the only economically viable outcome.[1] Beyond this, though, there is a real sense in these pieces that women have something to offer photography, not merely that a career in this area was a means by which to save them from a form of penury associated with the status of 'old maid'. The sources also discuss women's interaction with the materials, processes and equipment involved in photography.

The anonymous author of the article in *The Englishwoman's Review* of 1867 begins by suggesting the ways in which photography is suited to women. The list of 'requisites' for a female photographer speaks to a stereotypical model of ideal womanhood and includes 'delicacy', 'patience' and 'carefulness'. Only minimal skill is needed; no 'deep researches into chemistry and optics' are required. However, the broader claim of the article is that photography offers an opportunity for women. Citing acclaimed photographers Julia Margaret Cameron ('Mrs Cameron') and Lady Clementina Hawarden as examples, it suggests photography as an occupation in which women might rival men, though it also argues that cheaper female labour would make photographic products more accessible to the working classes. The long extract included in the article on the uses of photography is from *The English Mechanic and Mirror of Science and Art*, a weekly publication which discussed new scientific inventions and discoveries.

Julia Margaret Cameron is also celebrated in a piece from the *Women's Herald* of 1891. Described as the 'founder of photography as a fine art' and a 'wonderful woman who has surpassed all men', the article charts her early life and the first steps she took in learning the art of photography. The article makes reference to Cameron's autobiographical fragment *The Annals of my Glass House* (1890). In this, Cameron discusses the material challenges of attempting photography in the home; she reveals that she 'turned my coal-house into a dark room and a glazed fowl house I had given to my children became my glass house!' and she recounts how her habit of 'running into the dining room with my wet pictures has stained an immense quantity of table linen with nitrate of silver'.[2]

Adeline Anning's article in *The Woman's Signal* of 1895 refers to a recent book by Edith Barnett, *The Training of Girls for Work* (1894). Barnett recommends that women should be taught to do 'one sort of work well', and Anning suggests that photography is one such area in which women can 'specialise'.[3] The article refers to the success of London portrait photographer Alice Hughes, who studied at the School of Photography on Regent Street in London and opened her own studio in 1891. Anning gives her female readers details of various photographic processes that include the taking of the photograph, developing, 'spotting' or retouching, toning, boxing and mounting. Anning suggests that the opening of a studio at the seaside would be an excellent venture for a family of sisters, which echoes the theme of Amy Levy's *The Romance of a Shop* (1888), discussed later in this introduction. Ruth Young, a regular contributor to the monthly magazine *Atalanta* discusses the training on offer for women at the Polytechnic School of Photography in an article from 1898. As well as advice on the purchasing of equipment, the Regent Street School gives private tuition in a wide range of photographic techniques, including 'Retouching, [. . .] Printing in Permanent Carbon, Printing Transparencies for the magic lantern [. . .] Enlarging [. . .] and Photogravure', an intaglio process of photographic reproduction described by Young as 'the highest development of photography'.

Funny Folks was a comic paper published between the mid-1870s and mid-1890s. With its subheading, 'a comic camera,' it is fitting, perhaps, that this publication occasionally focused its comic lens on developments in photography. In 1885, it ran a four-part series titled 'Photography at home', which satirises the efforts of the 'lady' amateur photographer. Following the exploits of sisters Blanche and Ethel, the series takes a disparaging look at the efforts of female amateurs, poking fun at their lack of understanding about specialist equipment and materials. The last source from *Funny Folks* categorises the lady photographer as a 'social fad of the day'. The cartoon depicts a female photographer in a glass house studio surrounded by fashionable onlookers, about to take a photograph of a male sitter against a mocked-up backdrop.

Finally, Amy Levy's *The Romance of a Shop* charts the fortunes of four sisters who, left to fend for themselves after the death of their parents, resolve to open a photographic studio and shop in order to support themselves. Included here is an extract in which the sisters discuss the issues involved in setting up their new venture. The novel discusses photography in a range of contexts: the classes on offer at the British Museum, the sisters' first commission for a post-mortem photograph, and the common perception that 'the sex of the photographers [is] a ground for greater cheapness in the photographs'.

Notes

1 For example, France Power Cobbe's 'What Shall We Do With Our Old Maids', appeared in *Fraser's Magazine*, in 1862, and championed the idea that women should have unfettered access to the employment market. The article was a response to William Rathbone Gregg's 'Why are women redundant?', published in the *National Review* earlier in 1862 in which he expresses concern about an 'excess' of unmarried women.

2 Julia Margaret Cameron 'Annals of my glass house' (1890) reprinted in Beaumont Newhall (ed.) *Photography essays and images: illustrated readings in the history of photography* (New York: Museum of Modern Art; Boston: New York Graphic Society, 1980), pp. 135–139 (pp. 135, 136).

3 Edith Barnett, *The Training of Girls for Work* (London: Macmillan and Co., 1894), p. 111.

141

'PHOTOGRAPHY AS AN EMPLOYMENT FOR WOMEN'

The Englishwoman's Review, July 01, 1867, pp. 219–223

Any employment which has its main requisites in delicacy of manipulation, patience and carefulness, with a greater or less degree of refined or artistic taste, is pre-eminently suited for women – and this is precisely the character of photography. It requires no manual strength, only skill, not difficult to attain. Taste and dexterity of finger in delicate work are woman's natural gifts, patience and perseverance are also peculiarly her attributes. It is the possession of such qualities, rather than any deep researches into chemistry and optics, which makes the successful practical photographer. It is therefore not surprising that women have been very successful in the practice of this fascinating and useful art. Ladies of the highest rank have practised it as an amusement. It is said that Her Majesty has displayed considerable photographic skill. The late respected Lady Hawarden carried off the London Society's gold medal, the first prize in the art. Few professional photographers have gained as much fame, or more honours, than Mrs. Cameron. It is therefore not a little surprising that there are few female names in the long list of London photographers, although numbers of women are employed in almost every London photographic studio. One well-known artist and photographer, who stands high in his profession, and exercises unusual care in the printing of his pictures, has never employed any but female labourers in this department of his art, and has given his reason for so doing, that he could only meet with the necessary care, attention, delicate manipulation and patience, in female printers. Similar statements were made some time since in one of the public journals by another photographer of note. The same qualities that would enable women to print would also enable them to do the whole process as well, at least, if not better, than any of their male rivals; but in very many studios they are not permitted to learn or to practise the higher branches of the art. In photography, as in almost every other trade or profession, men will thankfully employ women as their subordinates, while they are jealously careful and anxious to exclude them from the knowledge which might permit them to practise the art independently. Women are graciously permitted to labour at the drudgery, while men reserve to themselves the easy task of directing the work and of taking the profit.

DOI: 10.4324/9781315400266-167

I lately met with a lady, recently left a widow with two children, who was anxious to engage in some employment for their support. Before her marriage she had been employed for five years in a photographer's studio, long enough to learn the profession in all its branches. If she had been properly taught she might have established a business for herself, and so have supported her children, but during that long time she had learned only to "touch" and mount, for which but little remuneration is given. Unless the glass plate on which the photograph is taken is very equally and completely covered with collodion, little white spots and stripes appear in the photograph, and these must be carefully painted in by the hand. This is called "touching." If the clumsy fingers of an operator leave many of these spots to be filled up, the girls who do it require to possess such a degree of taste and neatness as would enable them to learn all the other processes of photography, if they were properly taught. I know one young lady, who was lately employed in a studio of no mean note, in painting defective photographs, and who could with much less labour have taken much better originals, had she been permitted. It seems, therefore, most desirable that a photographic school should be established, in which women might be thoroughly taught every branch of the profession.

When we recommend photography as an employment for women, it is often alleged, that the art has had its day, that its profitableness and usefulness are nearly over, and that even if it were taught to women, they would not easily find sufficient employment. Those who make this objection think of photography as mere portrait taking, and do not sufficiently consider the numerous purposes to which it is at present applied, or the still more extensive usefulness that may be expected of it in future. In order to meet such objections, we quote a brief extract from an account of what photography is doing, which appeared in the *Mirror of Science:* –

> There are few discoveries to which we owe more valuable results than are attributable to photography. In the course of its brief career it has achieved, both as an art and as a science, a degree of usefulness quite unsurpassed. Wherever we look for its influence, whether it be in the sciences, in the arts, or in matters of social importance, we find it occupying an important position. By virtue of its numerous processes, and the modifications thereof, it serves a great and ever increasing variety of valuable and comprehensive purposes, the bare enumeration of which would more than suffice to fill the present number of our magazine. Its power of registering microscopical minutiæ in natural objects, and the perfection with which its productions can be enlarged, the chemical nature of its operations, the optical principles it embodies, and the rigid accuracy of its productions, have each created for it new and important uses, by means of which existing theories have either been exploded or established, fresh facts have been demonstrated within the sphere of the applied and physical sciences, and new or more accurate means of investigation have been placed within the philosopher's reach. It would be

> difficult to exaggerate the importance of the revolutions, improvements, applications, and discoveries for which we have to thank photography.
>
> If you attend the meetings of our learned, scientific, or artistic societies – to say nothing of those devoted specially to this art-science – the wide scope and increasing utility of practical photography will speedily be realised. You will find in each that photography and its productions are employed to originate, demonstrate, or illustrate the facts discussed. The students of geology, astronomy, botany, chemistry, geography, meteorology, ethnology, optics, microscopical science, natural history, archæology, mechanics, war, and jurisprudence, each owe much to this new power. There is scarcely a profession in which it is not more or less useful, and in the trades and more ordinary business of life, it has its daily applications.
>
> In the Fine Arts it is no less active. The painter, the sculptor, the architect, the engraver, the scene painter, the book illustrator, and the decorator, have all found it subservient to their labours; and we have little doubt but that it will ultimately, by decreasing the mechanical technical drudgery of the studio, enable the artist to devote that time to those higher and nobler aspirations of true art which is the main want detected in most modern works.

In connection with book illustration, photography has as yet made comparatively slow progress; but there are various improvements now in the course of being perfected which, it is expected, will enable it to rival wood engraving. Besides, it is probable that photography will be much more extensively used for book illustration, if really good photographs could be produced sufficiently cheap for this purpose; and this cheapness might be in a great measure secured by the exclusive employment of female artists who usually charge less for their work.

Our space forbids us to mention numerous other objects for which it is likely that photography will be used; we shall name only one more, namely – its application to Ceramic Ware. Various processes have been invented by which photographic pictures may be applied to, and burnt in, upon articles of porcelain or glass.

Photography has likewise a literature of its own, represented by several flourishing journals, to which we refer the reader for a further account of the numerous discoveries recently made in this interesting art.

Photography is peculiarly the friend of the poor. Many can remember when the possession of family pictures and miniatures was a luxury enjoyed only by the rich; and this is now within the reach of all. What words can express the inestimable value of this art to the friends of the numerous emigrants who every year leave our shores. Next to the great blessing of cheap postage, it has perhaps done more than anything else to lessen the pain of separation between families whose members are divided often by the distance of the globe. The numerous pictures that may be mutually exchanged between them keep up the remembrance, on the one hand, of dear home faces and home scenes; and, on the other, picture to friends in this country the emigrant's home, and the scenes by which he is surrounded. From the small carte de visite that can be sent in a letter, an enlarged photograph can now be taken to adorn even the cottage wall. These enlarged pictures are still rather expensive, but it is to be hoped, by the introduction of more female labour, the price may be considerably reduced, till even the cottager who wishes for it may be able to possess his gallery of family pictures, hitherto the boast of the rich.

To the toiling artisan, compelled to spend the greater part of his life in towns, to the invalid, confined to a bed of sickness, to all deprived of the pleasure of country life, it must be a great enjoyment to possess pictures of those beautiful scenes which they once have enjoyed in reality. Photography can now offer, at a comparatively cheap rate, copies of the most beautiful pictures, representing everything on which the eye loves to look, thus bringing the enjoyment of art within the reach of the poor.

The indefatigable Society, which has already done so much to promote the employment of women, have had their attention called to the suitable field for female labour afforded by photography. By the generosity of some of the members of this Society, a sum of money has been subscribed in aid of the establishment of a Ladies' School of Photography. Premises have been taken in Belgravia, which are now open under the superintendence of Miss Gauntlett, and under the patronage of the Society for the Promotion of the Employment of Women.

All that are favourable to the cause of female employment, are earnestly requested to pay a visit to the Studio, 10, Lower Belgrave Place, nearly opposite the Grosvenor Hotel, Victoria Station. If this establishment be successful, it is proposed that branch establishments shall be formed on the co-operative principle in various other districts of the Metropolis, so as to allow the female workers to participate in the profits of their work.

142

'PHOTOGRAPHY AT HOME', 'THE EXPERIENCES OF A LADY AMATEUR – NO. 1'

Funny Folks: A Weekly Budget of Funny Notes, Funny Pictures and Funny Stories,
March 28, 1885, p. 99

PHOTOGRAPHY AT HOME.

THE EXPERIENCES OF A LADY AMATEUR.—NO. 1.

DEAR MR. EDITOR,—Blanche and I are going to exhibit at the Amateur Photographic Exhibition in Bond-street next month. Isn't it fun? We have both bought apparat—should it be in the plural, apparati or apparatuses?—and as soon as they were sent home we got to work. But really I had no idea it was so difficult. Though we kept on all day, and went without our dinners, the nasty thing somehow would not come right. Which way should the thing like a brass cannon with a bull's-eye lantern in it go? Blanche thinks it should look towards the sitter, but that's absurd, isn't it? Poor dear Pa was so good, and sat to us for hours; but of course he got a little tired at the last. We haven't got a portrait of him yet; but Blanche declares that *on one of* her negatives (they're called negatives, I suppose, because you can see nothing on them) there is something which looks like his nose. We find the focussing cloth tumbles our hair dreadfully, and with the next experiments we think of wearing our indiarubber bathing caps. Isn't it a capital idea? Hope to let you know next week how we get on.—Yours, ETHEL.

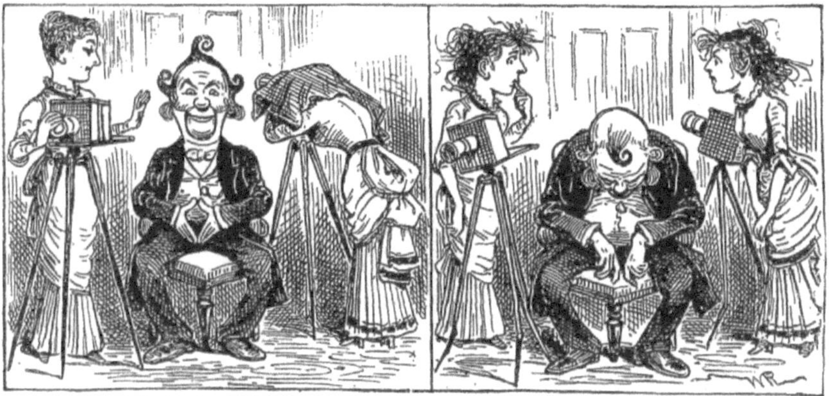

POOR PA SITTING FOR HIS FIRST PORTRAIT. POOR PA AFTER SIX HOURS' SITTING.

DOI: 10.4324/9781315400266-168

143

'PHOTOGRAPHY AT HOME', 'THE EXPERIENCES OF A LADY AMATEUR – NO. 2'

Funny Folks: A Weekly Budget of Funny Notes, Funny Pictures and Funny Stories, April 4 1885, p. 107

PHOTOGRAPHY AT HOME.

THE EXPERIENCES OF A LADY AMATEUR.—NO. 2.

DEAR MR. EDITOR,—At present we haven't got on very well. The developing (Algy spells the first syllable of this word quite differently, but then he is so (silly) is *dread/ul*. You see, you must have a dark room, and a sink, and plenty of water; and when Blanche and I went down into the kitchen and told the cook we should want it for an hour or two, the nasty cross thing flew into quite a passion, and said she'd go and give warning to mamma at once. Well, she went off, and after she'd gone we put a table-cover over the window, fastening it up with a couple of forks, and began our developing. But what the stupid people at the shop meant by "dry plates" I don't know, for they got quite wet when we put them in a dear little dish, and poured some stuff out of a bottle over them, and I was just saying to Blanche it couldn't be right, when the door opened and in marched Ma and Pa! The language Pa used was dreadful. *He* wasn't going to wait two hours for his dinner. *He* wasn't going to give the cook warning just because of our messy photography. *He*—but there, Mr. Editor, I daren't tell you all he said. I believe the photographs would have been splendid if the door hadn't been opened and let in all the light. Of course they were spoilt.—Yours,

ETHEL.

P.S.—Next week we mean to try a little outdoor photography.

P.P.S.—Our bathing caps answer splendidly. Never have our hair ruffled now by focussing cloth.

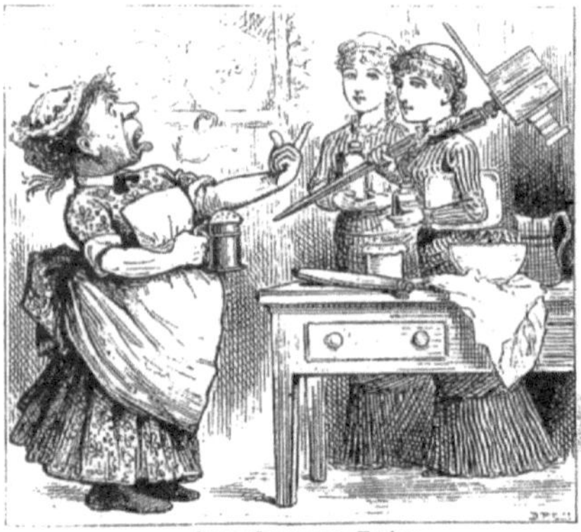

SCIENCE INVADING THE KITCHEN.

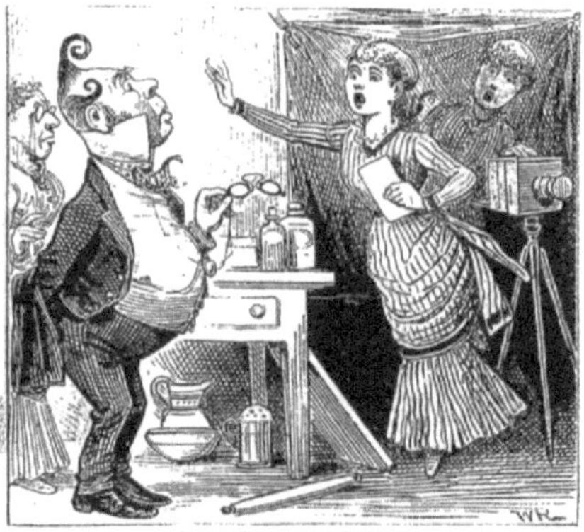

SCIENCE DEFEATED BY HUNGER!

DOI: 10.4324/9781315400266-169

144

'PHOTOGRAPHY AT HOME', 'THE EXPERIENCES OF A LADY AMATEUR – NO. 3'

Funny Folks: A Weekly Budget of Funny Notes, Funny Pictures and Funny Stories, April 18, 1885, p. 123

PHOTOGRAPHY AT HOME.

THE EXPERIENCES OF A LADY AMATEUR.—NO. 3.

Dear Mr. Editor,—Thinking everybody was away for a holiday, we tried a little outdoor photography in the back garden on Easter Monday. I never shall forget the dreadful time we had. You see poor dear Pa thought he would like Fido taken; and so he was taken—with a violent desire to drive the next-door cat out of our garden. Well, directly Fido flew at the cat, the cat flew on to the camera; the boys next door attacked poor dear Pa with a horrible pea-shooter; the vulgar servants made most rude remarks; and worst of all, we saw that low young Fitzkins, whom we always cut, laughing. Blanche and I have determined that outdoor photography is quite a mistake, and we are going to do all our experiments indoors for the future. I'm told that it's possible to take likenesses by burning some wire made out of citrate of magnesia. I forget the exact name of the process, but I think it is Luxurygraph—I suppose, because it's such a little trouble. I shall try it, of course, because I want to learn *everything*.—Yours,

ETHEL.

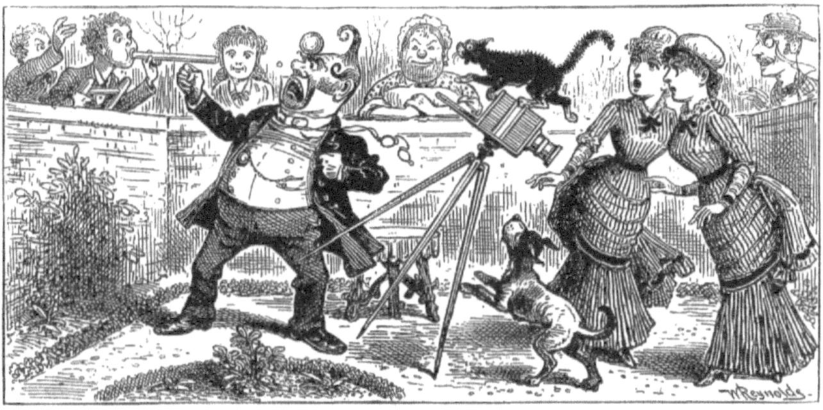

DOI: 10.4324/9781315400266-170

145

'PHOTOGRAPHY AT HOME', 'THE EXPERIENCES OF A LADY AMATEUR – NO. 4'

Funny Folks: A Weekly Budget of Funny Notes, Funny Pictures and Funny Stories, April 25, 1885, p. 131

PHOTOGRAPHY AT HOME.

THE EXPERIENCES OF A LADY AMATEUR.—No. 4.

DEAR MR. EDITOR,—We have been very hard at work all the week, because the *very* latest day for the Amateurs' Exhibition in Bond-street is the 21st, and there is no varnishing day, like at the darling Royal Academy. Well, as I told you, we determined to try some artificial light, and it was so fortunate Harold (he is our cousin, you know) was in town, because we got him to bring the lovely Troubadour's Dress he wore at the last Fancy Ball to be taken in. He laughed when we said we were going to burn some wire made of citrate of magnesia, and said we meant magnesium ribbon, though it isn't a bit like ribbon. Of course I arranged everything, and it was so fortunate, because a gas bracket on the wall was just the height, and so we stuck him against it, and it made a splendid head-rest, only he kept complaining that it hurt his cheek. Blanche held the burning wire, and I took the cap off the lens and counted ten. . . . .

But how *do* you account for this? Actually I got Blanche's portrait as well as *Harold's*, and—and they look as if they were *kissing!* I shall never dare to send it to the Exhibition. Not but what Blanche's portrait flatters her, though it is so large. She was always plain. Had it been *my* face with Harold's I shouldn't have minded so much. What *am* I to do?—Yours, ETHEL.

P.S.—I have just discovered that Harold has taken away the picture, and he declares he will send it. I am almost distracted.

P.P.S.—I have consulted eleven instruction books, and I find that Blanche must have got between Harold and the camera, and so was photographed. Of course she was nearer to the lens, and came out larger. Disagreeable thing; I believe she did it on purpose.

P.P.P.S—Do you know anybody who wants to buy photographic apparatus cheap?

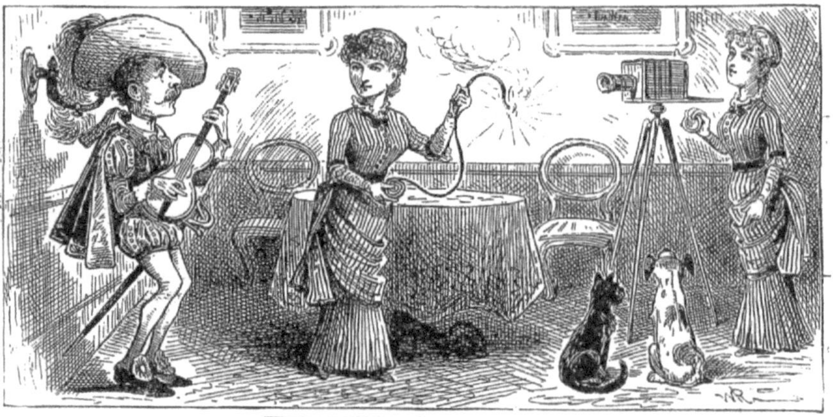

DOI: 10.4324/9781315400266-171

146

'SOCIAL FADS OF THE DAY', 'THE LADY AMATEUR'

Funny Folks: A Weekly Budget of Funny Notes, Funny Pictures and Funny Stories, 6th Feb 1892, p. 41

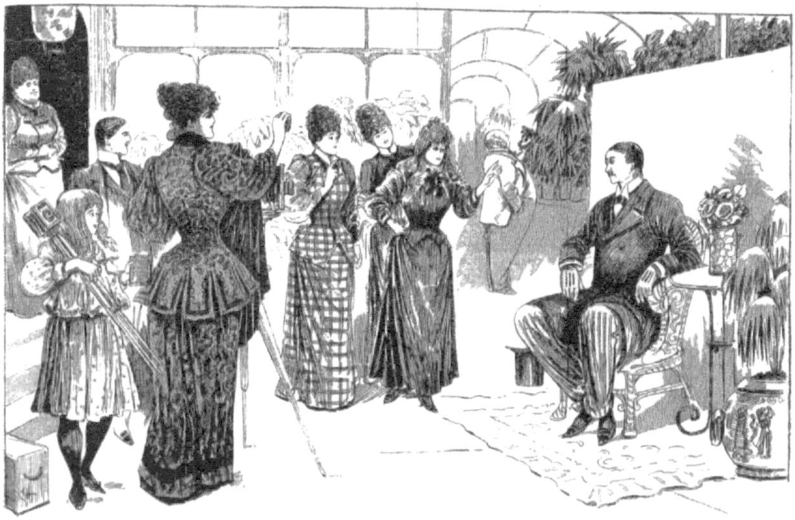

SOCIAL FADS OF THE DAY.—No. 5: The Lady Amateur Photographer.

DOI: 10.4324/9781315400266-172

147

ADELINE ANNING, 'A PROFESSION FOR WOMEN: PHOTOGRAPHY'

The Woman's Signal, March 07, 1895, p. 149

By Adeline Anning

A MONTH or two ago a very interesting and amusing account was published in an Irish paper of a meeting of the College Historical Society in Dublin, when "The Position of Women, Social and Political" was the subject under discussion, and at which most of those who gave their views were apparently possessed by the idea that a woman had to choose between becoming a telegraph clerk, a typewriter! – not a typist – or a nurse.

We are sorry that civilisation has advanced no further than this in Dublin. On this side of the water we are learning that there are very few professions or employments – call them what you will – into which women cannot enter if they choose. Adequate equipment is the most important qualification now-a-days when every profession is opening its door to women. It is not always the clever and talented people who are the most successful; rather those who are best and most thoroughly equipped.

SPECIALISE! SPECIALISE! SPECIALISE!

What is the trend of the times calling us to do? Specialise! specialise! specialise! As Miss Barnett says in her book on "The Training of Girls for Work," "Every girl ought to be taught to do *one* sort of work so well that the world will readily pay her money for doing it should she need the money."

In the choice of a profession one great aim should be to keep away from the crowd. Work with a *future* rather than with a *past* should be sought for, and this essential surely is to be found in photography.

In Pope's oft quoted line we are told that character, which is man, is the proper study of mankind. Then in photography there is an opportunity to prosecute that study in a more or less scientific manner, for there undoubtedly are, in this profession, quite special opportunities for seeing character at its best and worst.

DOI: 10.4324/9781315400266-173

There are but few professional women photographers in London. Miss Alice Hughes, has been pre-eminently successful. But although London is by no means over-stocked, there are excellent openings where women might do well in the country, or, possibly better still, at the seaside.

Then and now

In the old days the photographer tramped the fields with his tent and laboratory strapped upon his back, and when anything presented itself as being "takeable," the apparatus was unloosened, the mysterious shrouded figure on three legs fixed its one eye, and, hey, presto! he had his view. Many a pretty scene must rise up before us as we think of those times. The cottage far away in Devonshire covered with roses and honeysuckle; the bright flowers in the little garden, holly-hocks, stocks, and sweet peas; two or three sturdy youngsters standing shyly against the gate as they say – probably with their mouths full – "Take me too, mister, – take me too"; the busy mother at the door with arms bare to the elbow, fresh from her wash-tub – all go to make a quaint and homely picture – realistic we should call it to-day – a triumph of amateur art.

But we are more technical now, and not so easily satisfied, although one cannot but think tenderly of the old times, when we fostered our artistic sense at the sacrifice of art. The artistic sense is not, as we used to think it, the first requisite in photography. It is necessary, of course, in arranging the details of the picture.

The absolute essentials

For instance, in the matter of costume, it is frequently advisable to alter or re-arrange the dress of the sitter, and here taste and judgment are needed; light colouring and soft draperies play by no means an unimportant part in the making of a pretty and graceful picture, but a trained eye is wanted to choose and refuse these accessories, and to adjust them against an appropriate background. In every part of the profession, technical excellence is required, a knowledge of drawing, and the capacity for taking pains.

These are the absolute essentials, and without them any woman would be making a disastrous mistake in taking up photography as a profession. For the amateur who is content with resemblance, and disregards the charm of artistic detail, and one who has no desire to gain appreciation beyond the circle of his immediate family, training does not matter. But the professional must understand that it is necessary to begin at the *beginning* and serve the preliminary apprenticeship.

How to begin

There is no better way of starting than by attending the classes at the Polytechnic. Miss Hughes, whose name has already been mentioned, secured her elementary training at this school, where the teacher is an able man happily possessed of that "infinite capacity for taking pains" which is the genius of photography, as of every other branch of work.

Much ignorance prevails even now about the methods of photography. There are still many people, more or less enlightened – rather less than more, one is inclined to think – who imagine you have simply to take a camera, turn on the tap, as it were, and, lo and behold! you have your photograph. They do not realise how many processes have to be gone through before the photograph is finished. There is, first the actual taking, then the developing, or bringing out of the latent image that which has been impressed on the negative plate. This is usually done by the use of pyrogallic acid, other chemicals being used to assist the development when necessary. Spotting is simply touching out pinholes or other small defects in the negatives or prints, while the toning is preparing the paper with certain chemicals which replaces the silver image with a gold one; the boxing and mounting, as everyone knows, is simply fixing the photographs on to the cards. As may be readily understood, all these processes require care, skill, and judgment.

Not a mistaken idea

And yet, after all, it is not an altogether mistaken idea that "anyone can take a photograph." Anyone can, but the result would not be a picture. To those who aspire to make artistic pictures, photography means a study of art principles, a constant outlook for subjects and combinations, perseverance and hard work, with a proper appreciation of disappointments and failures. These last are particularly beneficial. As a lady said not very long ago, speaking of photography, "All I have learned was by experience, and some of my failures have proved the most interesting and amusing part of my work."

A suggestion

In a family where there are several daughters it would be an excellent thing for two, or even three, to go through the necessary training, and then to open a studio at the seaside. One sister might take the photographs, another could do the retouching, while the third might undertake the printing. This would be a fair division of labour and a very pleasant one, and would, in the course of time, prove a remunerative way of earning a living. For the start a certain capital would be required, as the accessories are many and the plant is expensive. But no well-equipped enthusiast in the profession need fear failure. As in other professions, although photography is crowded below stairs, there is plenty of room in the upper storey.

148

RUTH YOUNG, 'PHOTOGRAPHY AS A PROFESSION FOR WOMEN'

Atalanta, April 1, 1898, p. 407

I THINK very few of the professions open to women are so pre-eminently fitted to the feminine mind as is Photography, which is an art which appeals to the love of the beautiful inherent in every woman, and to the love of perpetuating what is graceful and beloved, which most women possess. Men, with their minds set on money-gaining, or pre-occupied with scientific research, have no time to devote to small things. Photography appeals to a degree to the affections, and to that sentimentality which is womanly. The charm of a photograph is that it carries to one, it may be from afar, the features of a friend; perhaps it re-awakens in the heart of the beholder the love which, maybe, has grown a little cold; for "out of sight" is sometimes "out of mind."

Years have passed since a "photograph" was a synonym for a portrait of a crinoline and an elegant lace shawl, or a top hat and a new suit of clothes, together with a representation of the obviously artificial background of the photographer's studio, generally an Italian garden, with here and there a rustic armchair.

To glance round Mrs. Flora Fraser's receiving-room, at 9 Regent Street, is to forget the photographic oddities of the past in a contemplation of specimens of the art in its most modern development, specimens which must surely be classed amongst "the joys for ever."

Mrs. Fraser informed me that she has only been at work professionally for eighteen months. She received her training in Photography under Mr. Howard Farmer, at the Polytechnic School of Photography, in Regent Street. The length of time usually allotted for a training in Photography is two years, though an apt pupil would perfect her work in a shorter period.

I asked Mrs. Fraser if it is necessary for a photographer who aims at very high results to study chemistry, and become thoroughly acquainted with the qualities of the different acids; but she told me she had been advised not to dabble too deeply in such matters, as a knowledge thereof was needless from a practical point of view, and conducive to the wasting of time and materials.

Of course, to start a Studio requires some capital, and anyone before deciding definitely to open business on her own account would do well to consider whether she had the wherewithal to keep herself and her Studio going for at least a year,

DOI: 10.4324/9781315400266-174

counting on no profit from her business, as it is not well to expect great things at first. A good private connection is by no means to be despised; in fact, it is greatly to be prized.

To make a financial success of a photographic business many qualities are needed. No woman should take up the work, if she intends actually to take the photographs herself, unless she has an innate notion of "posing" her subject; to a certain extent, photographers, like poets, are born, not made. With an artistic mind, and that conversational power with which some women are blest, of setting strangers at their ease, a woman should have a good chance of success. It is surprising how painfully nervous some models, or should they be termed "subjects" (or even "patients"), are. Probably they remember former occasions when they have endured the affliction of being photographed by some small county practitioner! In Mrs. Fraser's pleasant studio, the nervous depression would be heavy that could not be shaken off.

A branch of photography which requires rather manipulative skill than artistic perception is re-touching. There is a good opening for women's work in this branch of photography. The work is well paid, but to be paid well it must be well done. To make a good worker, over a year's practice is required. A clever re-toucher is sure of plenty of work.

At the Polytechnic School of Photography, 307 Regent Street, anyone can receive instruction, either for professional purposes, or merely for recreation, and the fees are moderate.

From this School assistance is given to pupils in choosing and testing photographic apparatus; beginners would do wisely who did not trust to their own judgment in purchasing instruments and materials.

Evening classes are held at the Polytechnic, but pupils can take a private course of lessons, either at the School or by correspondence, until they are "proficient in producing with certainty good negatives and silver or platinum prints" within a period of twelve months from commencement of the course. It is guaranteed on the prospectus that beginners who take this course will produce work in two months equal to that produced unaided in five or six years. "The glorious privilege of being independent" is all very well in theory, but in photographic practice it is evidently far from satisfactory! The charm of this course of lessons is that it can be broken at intervals and continued at the convenience of the learner.

In this course pupils receive instruction with regard to lighting, the conditions to be guided by in lighting, the best light and disposition of light for distant views, landscapes, portraits out of doors and in, architectural subjects, interiors, etc.; also with regard to focussing, how to choose the point of view and set up the camera, together with the rules for obtaining a correct and sharp image; and the rules and conditions of exposing; the relative exposures required by different subjects; the effects produced by varying the exposure; and the exposures required by different lenses and stops.

Pupils are also carefully instructed in the development of negatives; and in fixing the developed image, and washing and drying the finished negative. They are also taught intensifying and reducing, and the causes which produce, or tend to produce, defects in sensitive plates and negatives, and how to remedy them. The mysteries of printing, toning, and mounting are also fully explained. At the Polytechnic private tuition is given in Retouching, Printing with Platinum Paper, Silk, and other textile fabrics, Printing in Permanent Carbon, Printing Transparencies for the magic lantern or window decorations, and Enlarging; and lessons can be received in Photogravure, which is the highest development of Photography.

Surely the wisest course for a woman to pursue who has set her heart on Photography as a profession, is to take a course of lessons at the Polytechnic, and then to choose her studio with careful regard to its situation. If she is so happy as to find a sphere of labour where London fogs are unknown, she is to be congratulated.

RUTH YOUNG.

149

AMY LEVY, *THE ROMANCE OF A SHOP* (LONDON 1888)

First American edition (Boston: Cupples and Herd), 1889, pp. 2–13

Amy Levy, *The Romance of a Shop* (1888) – this extract taken from chapter 1 of the first American edition – (Boston: Cupples and Herd), 1889), pp. 2–13.

[pg 2]

Gertrude Lorimer was not a beautiful woman, and such good looks as she possessed varied from day to day, almost from hour to hour; but a certain air of character and distinction clung to her through all her varying moods, and redeemed her from a possible charge of plainness.

[Pg 3]

She had an arching, unfashionable forehead, like those of Lionardo [sic] da Vinci's women, short-sighted eyes, and an expressive month and chin. As she stood in the full light of the spring sunshine, her face pale and worn with recent sorrow, she looked, perhaps, older than her twenty-three years.

Pushing back from her forehead the hair, which, though not cut into a "fringe," had a tendency to stray about her face, and passing her hand across her eyes, with a movement expressive of mingled anxiety and resolve, she walked quickly to the door of the conservatory, opened it, and went inside.

The interior of the great glass structure would have presented a surprise to the stranger expectant of palms and orchids. It was fitted up as a photographer's studio.

Several cameras, each of a different size, stood about the room. In one corner was a great screen of white-painted canvas; there were blinds to the roof adapted for admitting or excluding the light; and paste-pots, bottles, printing-frames, photographs in various stages of finish – a nondescript

[Pg 4]

heap of professional litter – were scattered about the place from end to end.

 DOI: 10.4324/9781315400266-175

Standing among these properties was a young girl of about twenty years of age; fair, slight, upright as a dart, with a glance at once alert and serene.

The two young creatures in their black dresses advanced to each other, then stood a moment, clinging to one another in silence.

It was the first time that either had been in the studio since the day when their unforeseen calamity had overtaken them; a calamity which seemed to them so mysterious, so unnatural, so past all belief, and yet which was common-place enough – a sudden loss of fortune, immediately followed by the sudden death of the father, crushed by the cruel blow which had fallen on him.

"Lucy," said the elder girl at last, "is it only a fortnight ago?"

"I don't know," answered Lucy, looking round the room, whose familiar details stared at her with a hideous unfamiliarity; "I don't know if it is a hundred years or yesterday since I put that portrait of Phyllis in the printing-frame! Have you told Phyllis?"

[Pg 5]

"No, but I wish to do so at once; and Fanny. But here they come."

Two other black-gowned figures entered by the door which led from the house, and helped to form a sad little group in the middle of the room.

Frances Lorimer, the eldest of them all, and half-sister to the other three, was a stout, fair woman of thirty, presenting somewhat the appearance of a large and superannuated baby. She had a big face, with small, meaningless features, and faint, surprised-looking eyebrows. Her complexion had once been charmingly pink and white, but the tints had hardened, and a coarse red colour clung to the wide cheeks. At the present moment, her little, light eyes red with weeping, her eyebrows arched higher than ever, she looked the picture of impotent distress. She had come in, hand in hand with Phyllis, the youngest, tallest, and prettiest of the sisters; a slender, delicate-looking creature of seventeen, who had outgrown her strength; the spoiled child of the family by virtue of her youth, her weakness, and her personal charms.

Gertrude was the first to speak.

"Now that we are all together," she said,

[Pg 6]

"it is a good opportunity for talking over our plans. There are a great many things to be considered, as you know. Phyllis, you had better not stand."

Phyllis cast her long, supple frame into the lounge which was regarded as her special property, and Fanny sat down on a chair, wiping her eyes with her black-bordered pocket-handkerchief. Gertrude put her hands behind her and leaned her head against the wall.

Phyllis's wide, grey eyes, with their half-wistful, half-humorous expression, glanced slowly from one to the other.

"Now that we are all grouped," she said, "there is nothing left but for Lucy to focus us."

It was a very small joke indeed, but they all laughed, even Fanny. No one had laughed for a fortnight, and at this reassertion of youth and health their spirits rose with unexpected rapidity.

"Now, Gertrude, unfold your plans," said Lucy, in her clear tones and with her air of calm resolve.

Gertrude played nervously with a copy of the *British Journal of Photography* which she held, and began to speak with hesita-

[Pg 7]

tion, almost with apology, as one who deprecates any undue assumption of authority.

"You know that Mr. Grimshaw, our father's lawyer, was here last night," she said; "and that he and I had a long talk together about business. (He was sorry you were too ill to come down, Fanny.) He told me all about our affairs. We are quite, quite poor. When everything is settled, when the furniture is sold, he thinks there will be about £500 among us, perhaps more, perhaps less."

Fanny's thin, feminine tones broke in on her sister's words –

"There is my £50 a-year that my mama left me; I am sure you are all welcome to that."

"Yes, dear, yes," said Lucy, patting her shoulder; while Gertrude bit her lip and went on –

"We cannot live for long on £500, as you must know. We must work. People have been very kind. Uncle Sebastian has telegraphed for two of us to go out to India; Mrs. Devonshire offers another two of us a home for as long as we like. But I think we would all rather not accept these kind offers?"

[Pg 8]

"Of course not!" cried Lucy and Phyllis in chorus, while Fanny maintained a meek, consenting silence.

"The question remains," continued the speaker; "what can we do? There is teaching, of course. We might find places as governesses; but we should be at a great disadvantage without certificates or training of any sort. And we should be separated."

"Oh, Gertrude," cried Fanny, "you might write! You write so beautifully! I am sure you could make your fortune at it."

Gertrude's face flushed, but she controlled all other signs of the irritation which poor hapless Fan was so wont to excite in her.

"I have thought about that, Fanny," she said; "but I cannot afford to wait and hammer away at the publishers' doors with a crowd of people more experienced and better trained than myself. No, I have another plan to propose to you all. There is one thing, at least, that we can all do."

"We can all make photographs, except Fan," said Phyllis, in a doubtful voice.

"Exactly!" cried Gertrude, growing excited, and walking across to the middle of the room; "we can make photographs!

[Pg 9]

We have had this studio, with every proper arrangement for light and other things, so that we are not mere amateurs. Why not turn to account the only thing we can do, and start as professional photographers? We should all keep together. It would be a risk, but if we failed we should be very little worse off than before. I know what Lucy thinks of it, already. What have you others to say to it?"

"Oh, Gertrude, need it come to that – to open a shop?" cried Fanny, aghast.

"Fanny, you are behind the age," said Lucy, hastily. "Don't you know that it is quite distinguished to keep a shop? That poets sell wall-papers, and first-class honour men sell lamps? That Girton students make bonnets, and are thought none the worse of for doing so?"

"*I* think it a perfectly splendid idea," cried Phyllis, sitting up; "we shall be like that good young man in *Le Nabab*."

"Indeed, I hope we shall not be like André," said Gertrude, sitting down by Phyllis on the couch and putting her arm round her, "especially as none of us are likely to write successful tragedies by way of compensation."

[pg 10]

"You two people are getting frivolous," remarked Lucy, severely, "and there are so many things to consider."

"First of all," answered Gertrude, "I want to convince Fanny. Think of all the dull little ways by which women, ladies, are generally reduced to earning their living! But a business – that is so different. It is progressive; a creature capable of growth; the very qualities in which women's work is dreadfully lacking."

"We have thought out a good many of the details," went on Lucy, who was possessed of less imagination than her sister, but had a clearer perception of what arguments would best appeal to Fanny's understanding. "It would not absorb all our capital, we have so many properties already. We thought of buying some nice little business, such as are advertised every week in *The British Journal*. But of course we should do nothing rashly, nor without consulting Mr. Grimshaw."

"Not for his advice," put in Gertrude, "but to arrange any transaction for us."

"Gertrude and I," went on Lucy, "would do the work, and you, Fanny, if you would, should be our housekeeper."

[pg. 11]

"And I," cried Phyllis, her great eyes shining, "I would walk up and down outside, like that man in the High Street, who tells me every day what a beautiful picture I should make!"

"Our photographs would be so good and our manners so charming that our fame would travel from one end of the earth to the other!" added Lucy, with a sudden abandonment of her grave and didactic manner.

"We would have afternoon tea in the studio on Sunday, to which everybody should flock; duchesses, cabinet ministers, and Mr. Irving. We should become the fashion, make colossal fortunes, and ultimately marry dukes!" finished off Gertrude.

Fanny looked up, helpless but unconvinced. The enthusiasm of these young creatures had failed to communicate itself to her. Their outburst of spirits at such a time seemed to her simply shocking.

As Lucy had said, Frances Lorimer was behind the age. She was an anachronism, belonging by rights to the period when young ladies played the harp, wore ringlets, and went into hysterics.

[pg. 12]

Living, moving, and having her being well within the vision of three pairs of searching and intensely modern young eyes, poor Fan could permit herself neither these nor any kindred indulgences; but went her way with a vague, inarticulate sense of injury – a round, sentimental peg in the square, scientific hole of the latter half of the nineteenth century.

Now, when the little tumult had in some degree subsided, she ventured once more to address the meeting.

That was the worst of Fan; there was no standing up in fair fight and having it out with her; you might as soon fight a feather-bed. Convinced, to all appearances, one moment; the next, she would go back to the very point from which she had started, with that mild but terrible obstinacy of the weak.

"I suppose you know," she said, having once more recourse to the black-bordered pocket-handkerchief, "what every one will think?"

"Every one will be dead against it. We know that, of course," said Lucy, with the calm confidence of untried strength.

Fortunately the discussion was inter

[pg. 13]

rupted at this juncture, by the loud voice of the gong announcing luncheon.

150

'MRS JULIA MARGARET CAMERON'

Womans Herald, April 4 1891, pp. 369–370

We now enter upon the period which becomes of greatest interest to women. Mrs. Cameron, at Freshwater, commenced her photographic career, and from this moment her progress was a long record of success. The chemicals and apparatus were of the simplest description, the barest necessities for the wet collodion process and silver printing. She writes: "I turned my coal-house into my dark-room, and a glazed fowl-house I had given to my children became my glass-house. The hens were liberated – I hope, and I believe, not eaten – and all hands and hearts sympathised in my new labour, and the society of hens and chickens was soon changed for that of poets, prophets, painters, and lovely maidens, who have immortalised the hen-house. The glass-house was fitted with simple white roller blind, no head rests, or other abominations finding place there!" Her first sitter was Farmer Rice, who was paid half-a-crown an hour. "After many half-crowns and many hours spent in experiment, I got my first picture, and *effaced* while holding up triumphantly to dry. I longed to arrest all beauty that came before me, and at length the longing has been satisfied. I began with no knowledge of the art. I did not know how to place the dark-box, how to focus my sitter. I spoilt my first plate by rubbing my hand over the filmy side of the glass to my utter consternation." These are Mrs. Cameron's own words from a sketch written in Ceylon, giving an account of how she came to take up photography and called *The Annals of My Glass-house*.

Her sitters were the men, women, maidens, and children in the island; her friends often sat to her, and her son tells the following good story, illustrative of her enthusiasm in her search for the beautiful. She was at Oxford, and walking in the "High" she passed a very beautiful girl. Going up to her she asked excitedly, "Oh, who are you?"

"I am Mrs. Donkin's cook," replied the blushing girl.

Mrs. Cameron got her address, called on Mrs. Donkin, and obtained permission to take the girl to Freshwater for a time as a model. The girl is "Œnone." While at Putney she had picked up a starving Irish girl whom she converted into a neat sewing-maid. She was, like many Irish, singularly beautiful, and often served Mrs. Cameron as a model. She was the original of "Maud," and when Mrs.

DOI: 10.4324/9781315400266-176

Cameron had an exhibition in London, "Maud" went up to explain the pictures to the public. A gentleman who saw her here, and afterwards passed into the Indian Civil Service, finally returned and came to Freshwater to claim "Maud" as his wife. He had fallen in love with the beautiful model, whom he married, and lived happily with ever after, as the stories say.

Mrs. Cameron believes her first success, *i.e.,* her out-of-focus pictures, were, as her son Henry Herschel told her, "a fluke."

"That is to say, when focussing and coming to something which to my eye was very beautiful, I stopped then instead of screwing on the lens to the more definite focus, which all other photographers insist upon."

It may easily be imagined Mrs. Cameron was subjected to much criticism from jealous craftsmen. Unable to produce, with all their appliances, work in anyway approaching hers, the photographers sought to belittle her pictures by every possible pretext, though they failed signally, her work being beyond compare, and possessed of undying merit. But while trade jealousy and commercial instincts were thus striving to lower her, Mr. Watts was calling some of her works "divine," and the greatest English artists were praising her masterly productions. Mrs. Cameron treated these small traducers with the contempt they deserved, and answered none of them. Her pictures set men thinking, and the result was an immense improvement in photography.

Mrs. Cameron, after many failures, photographed a little child, which she entitled "My First Success," and thus writes of it: – "I was in a transport of delight. I ran all over the house to search for gifts for the child. I felt as if she entirely had made the picture. I printed, toned, fixed, and framed it, and presented it to her father that same day; size, 11in. by 9in. I exhibited as early as May, 1865. I sent some photographs to Scotland – a head of Henry Taylor and a Raphaelesque Madonna. They did not receive the prize; the picture that did, called 'Brenda,' clearly proved to me that detail of table cover, chair, and crinoline skirt were essential to the judges of the art, which was then in its infancy." Mrs. Cameron next sent her photographs to Germany. "Berlin, the very home of photographic art, gave me the first year a bronze medal, the succeeding year a gold medal, and one English institution a silver medal. Personal sympathy has helped me much. My husband from first to last watched every picture with delight, and it is my daily habit to run to him with every glass upon which a fresh glory is stamped. This habit of running into the dining-room with my wet pictures has stained such an immense quantity of table linen with nitrate of silver – indelible stains – that I should have been banished from any less indulgent household."

Sir Henry Taylor lent himself greatly to her early efforts. "Regardless of the possible dread that sitting to my fancy might be making a fool of himself, he, with greatness which belongs to unselfish affection, consented to be in turn Friar Lawrence with Juliet, Prospero with Miranda, Ahasuerus with Queen Esther, to hold my poker as his sceptre, and do whatever I desired him."

Sir John Herschel watched every step of her career with the keenest appreciation, and wrote often to warn her of the deadly powers of "cyanide." Mr. Watts also encouraged her greatly, so that she wrote: –

"I felt as if I had wings to fly with."

The following ten years record nothing but success, and the production of the pictures which have made her name famous. In 1875 the Camerons left England and went to Ceylon, where Mrs. Cameron commenced, but never finished, alas! *The Annals of her Glass-house*. She died in 1878, the period of her photographic work reaching over ten years – from 1865 to 1875.

Her finest works are, perhaps, "The Day Dream," "Kiss of Peace," Mrs. Jackson, Maud, Œnone, Christabel, Sir John Herschel, and Tennyson. The Poet Laureate has said of his picture "that he likes it better than any photograph that has been taken of him," and Henry Taylor, "that the picture was as fine as Alfred Tennyson's finest poem."

In photographic portraiture Mrs. Cameron still remains unapproached. She was a grand woman, and our sex may well feel proud of her and regret she is not still in our midst to lead us on with her loving, helpful sympathy and splendid work. We have still, however, her best portraits, which will survive all time, and can be seen at the Cameron studio in Mortimer-street, where her son, Henry Herschel Hay Cameron, himself a remarkable photographer, now conducts a studio. The fine portrait which we have the pleasure to reproduce, is taken from one of Mr. Cameron's photographs of his mother.

5.5

Photography as a hobby

DOI: 10.4324/9781315400266-177

5.5 Photography as a hobby

The sources in this section demonstrate the ways in which photography developed as a popular hobby in the late nineteenth century. Periodicals such as *The Photographic News* (later *The Amateur Photographer*) and the *Yearbook of Photography and Photographic News Almanac* published by Piper and Carter met the demand for information and tips from an increasing number of photographic hobbyists. However, many other general interest journals also carried regular pieces on photography, together with (as we have seen in other sections) large numbers of adverts for photographic equipment and materials.

Alfred Harmsworth's 'How to take a photograph' extols the virtues of photography as a hobby for the young amateur.[1] Published as a series in *Young Folks Paper*, a late-Victorian weekly children's magazine, it discusses how photographic equipment has become much cheaper over the past 15 years and is more widely available to those with limited means. Harmsworth references the demise of the wet collodion process and its mixing of dangerous chemicals, reassuring his readers that photography is now unlikely to cause 'damage to clothes or carpet'. In a section on female hobbyists, the reference to the way in which the 'black art' of photography in earlier times 'lent an Ethiopian tint to the fair figures of the [female] operator', while meant as an amusing play on words, is a reminder of the widespread 'othering' of people of colour that pervades nineteenth-century discourse.[2]

In his article, Harmsworth recommends the 'Meritoire' and 'Merveilleux' cameras. Despite the French resonances of these names, both of these cameras were produced by Birmingham-based firm J. Lancaster and Son. In an advert published in the Birmingham monthly, *The Dart*, the cameras are listed as part of a new patented range, with the Meritoire illustrated along with a camera called the 'International'. The Meritoire was made from polished mahogany with cloth bellows, which allowed the user to arrange the plate in different positions in relation to the lens.[3] Note also the fact that women were appealed to as a distinct customer base, with the firm offering a 'ladies complete set'. In a contemporary advert featured in *The County Gentleman: A Sporting Gazette and Agricultural Journal*, the London firm Marion and Co. targets a range of different consumer groups, including 'young people' and 'students'. The alliterative advertising rhetoric used for its 'U series of photo sets' is particularly rangy. Depending on one's budget, the customer could purchase the 'united', 'unique', 'useful', 'utilitarian', 'universal' or 'unequalled'. Marion and Co. was based in Soho Square in London from the early 1860s onwards. Founded by Augustin Marion in the 1830s, the firm was based first in Paris and sold stationary before diversifying into photographic equipment in 1854. Marion and Co. was one of the first firms to introduce *cartes-de-visite* to Britain. These small photographs (54 mm × 89 mm mounted on a 110 mm × 170 mm card) were often used as visiting cards and became extremely popular and highly collectable in the second half of the nineteenth century. Another advert in the same journal gives a sense of the various accoutrements associated with photography that were seen as a marketing opportunity. Here, the London Stereoscopic Company advertises a 'photographic bag' to its potential customers. Branded with a Latin name, the 'Semper Paratus' (the 'always ready'), the bag enables the amateur photographer to carry all of their photographic apparatus and chemicals in one handy piece of portable luggage. Replacing the more cumbersome photographic tent, the bag contains a compartment for dry plates, and prospective purchasers were also offered 'free lessons in photography'.

The fusion of two nineteenth-century technological innovations can be seen in the late-Victorian craze for cyclo-photography.[4] The bicycle and the camera come together in the penultimate source in this section, which is from *Cycling* magazine, an illustrated weekly published in the 1890s. It describes the new phenomenon of cyclo-photography, a leisure activity in which photographs could be taken while cycling. Photography is described as a sister pastime to cycling, and the piece included here is the first in a series on the topic. Specially adapted cycles and cameras were produced for this market. Note the reference to the Elswick machines (types of bicycles) on display in the windows of the London Stereoscopic Company, 'each one fitted with specially made camera carriers'.[5] The accompanying image shows a would-be cyclo-photographer wrestling with his photographic equipment.

The final source in this section is an article by Horace Eckert from *Pick-me-up*, a comic periodical launched in 1888. Eckert's piece is part of a series that takes a wry look at different kinds of hobbies. Photography is described as an 'expensive, and quite useless' hobby and a very effective 'breaker-up of friendships and [. . .] severer of family ties'. This idea is explored in the article, in which a series of misadventures befalls the amateur photographer, who tussles haplessly with a range of photographic equipment and materials.

Notes

1 Harmsworth was later to develop a newspaper empire, purchasing and running the *Evening News*, *Daily Mail* and the *Daily Mirror*.

2 An excellent study on the relationship between gender, race and class in the contexts of British imperialism is Anne McClintock's *Imperial Leather: Race, Gender and Sexuality in the Colonial context* (London: Routledge, 1995).

3 For a literary take the imperial contexts of mahogany production and consumption see chapter one of Elaine Freedgood, *The Ideas in Things: Fugitive Meaning in the Victorian Novel* (London: University of Chicago Press, 2006).

4 For an analysis of this phenomenon see Sara Dominici, 'Cyclo-Photographers', Visual Modernity, and the Development of Camera Technologies, 1880s–1890s', *History of Photography*, 42:1 (2018), pp. 46–60.

5 Originally founded in Newcastle in 1880, the Elswick Cycle Co. merged with F. Hopper and Co. in 1910.

151

ALFRED C. HARMSWORTH, 'HOW TO TAKE A PHOTOGRAPH'

Young Folks Paper, May 01, 1886, p. 278

By Alfred C. Harmsworth,
Author of "Practical Photography for Amateurs," &c.

Chapter I

COST OF APPARATUS – THE DELIGHTS OF PHOTOGRAPHY – A POPULAR DELUSION – THE CAMERA – FOCUSSING – DRY PLATES.

THE improvements which have taken place in photography during the past few years have rendered it a pastime which can be enjoyed by those of the most limited means and acquirements. Ten or fifteen years ago photographic amateurs were few and far between, for apparatus and materials were expensive, and the taking of a photograph an operation requiring much care and practice. Fortunately, however, most of the recent discoveries in this delightful art have tended towards economy and simplicity, with the result that numberless young people are able to indulge in what is rapidly becoming a popular pursuit.

A complete set of photographic apparatus with all necessary chemicals and accessories can be purchased for very little. A cheap outfit would not of course enable an aspirant to produce pictures of great artistic merit; but I have seen many excellent photographs which have been taken by young amateurs whose "stock-in-trade" had not cost a sovereign.

The chemicals, of which fond mothers have such a dread, are not particularly poisonous and expensive. Since the abolition of the old process, in which many deadly solutions were used, photographers can, with ordinary care, get through their work without damage to clothes or carpets.

With an experience extending over several years, I can truly say that photography is one of the most charming amusements in existence. I know of no more pleasant way of spending a holiday than in rambling into the country with a camera and a good stock of "dry plates." When you reach a favourite nook, a bend in a river, a quaint old building, or any piece of the handiwork of man or Nature which

DOI: 10.4324/9781315400266-178

pleases your fancy, you can adjust your apparatus and in the fraction of a second obtain a pleasing reminiscence of a happy day. The painter must sit sketching away for hours before he can produce a perfect picture, and in the time that he is delineating one scene the photographer could, if he wished, accurately portray a dozen. The artist must learn much, and study deeply. The photographer can in the space of a few months attain very considerable proficiency in his work. Once the simple rules are mastered, there is nothing to prevent any reader of *Young Folks Paper* from becoming fairly skilful in the course of a week or two of practice. It would be absurd to expect that a young beginner should be able to produce photographs of express trains, of birds in the act of flying, or of graceful swans mirrored in smooth pools. Such subjects can be dealt with by skilful operators only. Yet even these difficult themes may be undertaken after a few months of careful work. Lest, however, my readers are disappointed in their first experiments, I may say that unless the greatest care and precision are exercised, disappointment and failure are likely to ensue. The careless handling and mixing of the various chemicals has often led to disgust.

In these papers I shall endeavour to reduce the whole art to its simplest elements.

Before proceeding to my first lesson, I should like to remark that those who take up photography provide themselves with a hobby that can be ridden at all seasons and in the evening as well as in the daytime. A photographic camera and tripod stand can be carried easily, the former in the pocket, the latter as a walking-stick. With these, one can wander about at one's sweet will. In the evening the "plates" may be "developed," and printing proceeded with.

A large number of ladies have recently "gone in for" photography, and among those who exhibited their work in London last season were many of the fair sex. In the good old days of photography no one who cared for white hands could venture to become a knight of the camera. "The black art," as it was facetiously called gave employment to many noxious acids, and these in their turn lent an Ethiopian tint to the fair fingers of the operator. Gloves could be worn, but those who cared for accurate work found free fingers a *sine qua non*. With the introduction of what is known as the dry plate process, numerous poisonous and disagreeable chemicals were banished for ever from the dark room; and recently the dark room has itself been partially superseded by a lamp which any person can make out of a cigar-box and a small piece of ruby-coloured glass. Before the gelatine dry plates came in, the photographer who wished to take a view had to carry with him a portable dark room in which to conduct his very complicated manœuvres. The enthusiast who essayed to photograph the summit of a mountain was obliged to stagger up with a tank of water, a folding dark room, a camera (and cameras were heavy in those days), and many other things which the rapid strides of advancement have rendered unnecessary. Moreover, the whole operation of exposing and developing the plate had to be proceeded with then and there. The photographer of these days has a much more agreeable time of it.

There is a popular delusion respecting photography which it may be well to dispel from the minds of those who read these articles. Photographers are given to advertise what they are pleased to call "the instantaneous process." There is no process of the kind. On a bright, sunny day, a photograph can be taken in, it is said, the two-hundredth part of a second; but if the weather is dull, three or four, or even more, seconds will not suffice. The speed with which a portrait or view can be taken depends, therefore, upon the state of the light; and when our young beginner has conquered the first difficulties, he will find that the study of the atmosphere will occupy no small portion of his time.

I would advise any one intending to take up photography to look about him a little before purchasing his materials. There are numerous ingenious advertisers who offer complete sets for amateurs, and many of these sets are utterly valueless. Were I about to commence, I should advertise in a suitable paper for "A five by four camera, with rapid rectilinear lens, folding tripod stand, and two double dark backs, in good condition." Such an advertisement would be certain to produce replies, as most beginners speedily discard the apparatus with which they learnt in order to obtain implements for the execution of more ambitious work. A five by four camera, with lens, dark backs, and tripod stand, is often to be purchased for fifteen shillings. Should, however, the beginner have a pound to spare, he may, after judicious examination of the maker's advertisements, obtain an "amateur's set." The best of these are the "Meritoire" and the "Merveilleux." The size I mention is that known as the "quarter plate," and with it a photograph five inches by four may be taken. Larger sizes, six inches by four and three-quarters, or seven inches by five, and so on, are to be had; but the expense attending the development and printing of these is in proportion. With no more expensive apparatus than this, I have taken capital instantaneous sea views and portraits, which are at least as good as those sold by photographers in small provincial towns.

The first endeavour of the young photographer should be to become an accurate and expert focusser. At the end of the camera, opposite to that at which the lens is fixed, is a ground glass focussing screen. When the cap is removed from the lens, and the camera is directed towards any object, the object is found reflected upside down upon the screen. By screwing the lens in and out, the object will grow blurred or distinct as the case may be, and no photograph should be taken unless every detail on the screen is sharply and clearly outlined. With practice, one can adjust the lens in an instant. The cap (I write for those who know nothing whatever of the subject) is used for giving the exposure. As the beginner becomes more proficient, he will discard the cap for an instantaneous shutter, concerning which I shall speak in my last paper.

The dark backs contain the plates on which the photograph is taken, and which, after development, are known as the negatives. It is essential that these backs should be absolutely impervious to light, and for this reason the greatest care must be taken in handling them. They are usually in the form of flat cases of some strong wood; vulcanite and metal backs are also used. With the cheap sets, single backs are often sold. These hold only one plate. The plates on which the photographs are taken are sold in boxes by makers. The best plates are the "Kingston," "Lancaster," and the "Britannia." These are all very cheap and good.

152

ADVERTISEMENT FOR THE MERITOIRE CAMERA

The Dart, July 22nd 1887, p. 5

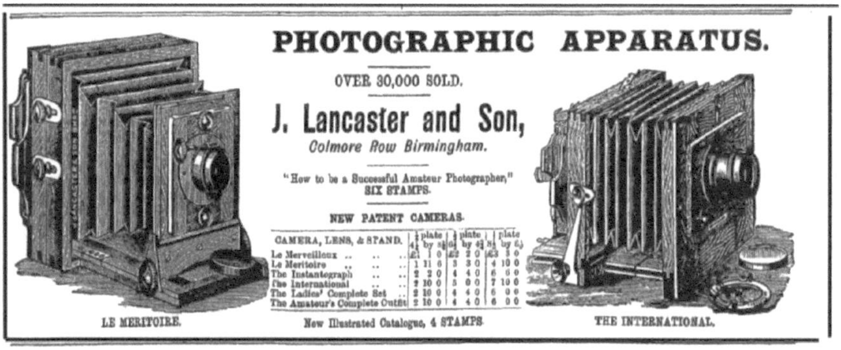

DOI: 10.4324/9781315400266-179

153

ADVERTISEMENT FOR MARION'S AMATEUR PHOTOGRAPHY

The County Gentleman: A Sporting Gazette and Agricultural Journal, January 29, 1887, p. 154

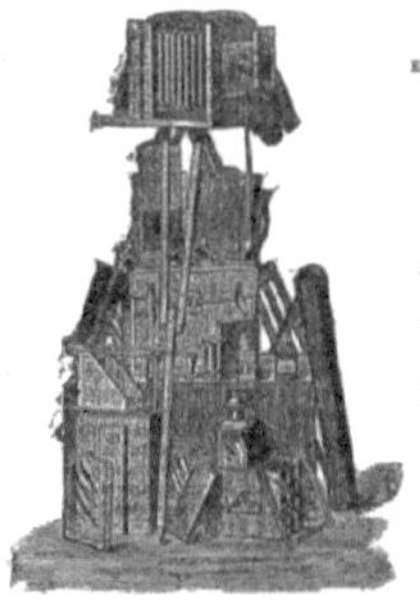

MARION'S AMATEUR PHOTOGRAPHY.

Complete Sets for Taking Negatives.

Containing.

EVERYTHING REQUISITE, WITH CLEAR INSTRUCTIONS HOW TO WORK.

The NONPAREIL SET for Young People	£1 10 0
The STUDENT'S SET, size of Plate, 5 by 4	3 10 0
The OXFORD SET, size of Plate, 4¼ by 3¼	5 0 0
The UNIVERSITY SET, size of Plate, 6½ by 4¾	10 0 0
The COMPACT SET, for Ladies, size of Plate, 4¼ by 3¼	7 15 0

The SUPERIOR SETS	£17	£20	£28	£34
for Plates	6½ by 4¾	8½ by 6½	10 by 8	12 by 10

LESSONS FREE TO PURCHASERS.

ENLARGING APPARATUS, complete with Lenses, for ¼-plate, £4 4s.; ½-plate, £9 10s.

"MARION'S PRACTICAL GUIDE TO PHOTOGRAPHY," 2s. 6d. post free.

"THE ART OF RETOUCHING NEGATIVES AND COLOURING PHOTOGRAPHS," 2s. 3d. post free.

Middlemiss Patent Camera, with Three Double Backs.

The most Improved form of Camera for Plates.

6½ by 4¾	8½ by 6½	10 by 8	12 by 10
£8	£9 10s.	£11 5s.	£14 10s.

Britannia Dry Plates.

BEST AND CHEAPEST PLATE MADE.

¼-plate	½-plate	6 by 4	7½ by 5	8½ by 6½	10 by 8	12 by 10
1s.	2s. 3d.	1s. 7d.	2s. 6d.	[illegible]	[illegible]	[illegible]

EXTRA RAPID Ditto.

1s. 3d.	2s. 0d.	2s. 0d.	4s. 6d.	5s. 6d.	[illegible]	[illegible]

Per Dozen.

Marion's Ferro-Prussiate (Blue Printing) Paper.

For Copying Drawings, Plans, &c., &c.

Suitable for Engineers, Architects, Builders, &c.

Marion's "U" Series of Photo Sets.

Each comprising a Camera, with one Double Back, a Lens, and a Strong Tripod Stand. The first three have, in addition, a Drop Shutter. These Sets are of excellent value.

THE UNITED.—No loose parts; folds into small compass; well made, with all the most improvements; good Rectilinear Lens, Drop Shutter, for Plates 6½ by 4¾, £7 [illegible]

THE UNIQUE.—Substantial Camera, Screw Adjustment, Double Swing, Double Rising Front, good Rectilinear Lens, Drop Shutter, for Plates 6½ by 4¾, £6 [illegible]

THE USEFUL.—Strong Camera, with Rack and Pinion Adjustment, View Lens and Shutter, for Plates 6½ by 4¾, £4 4s.

THE UTILITARIAN.—Leather Bellows Camera, Single Lens, &c., &c., for Plates 6½ by 4¾, £3 10s.

THE UNIVERSAL.—Strong Camera, &c., &c., for Plates 5 by 4, £2 [illegible]

THE UNEQUALLED.—Well-made cheap Camera, &c., &c., for Plates, 4¼ by 3¼, £1 [illegible]

Collections of Photographs and Prints put into Order, Mounted, Fitted, and Bound into Albums, Portfolioed or Framed.

MARION'S PHOTO. SUPPLY WAREHOUSE, 22 & 23, SOHO SQUARE, LONDON.

DOI: 10.4324/9781315400266-180

154

ADVERTISEMENT, 'FREE LESSONS IN PHOTOGRAPHY'

The County Gentleman: A Sporting Gazette and Agricultural Journal, December 19, 1885, p. 1626

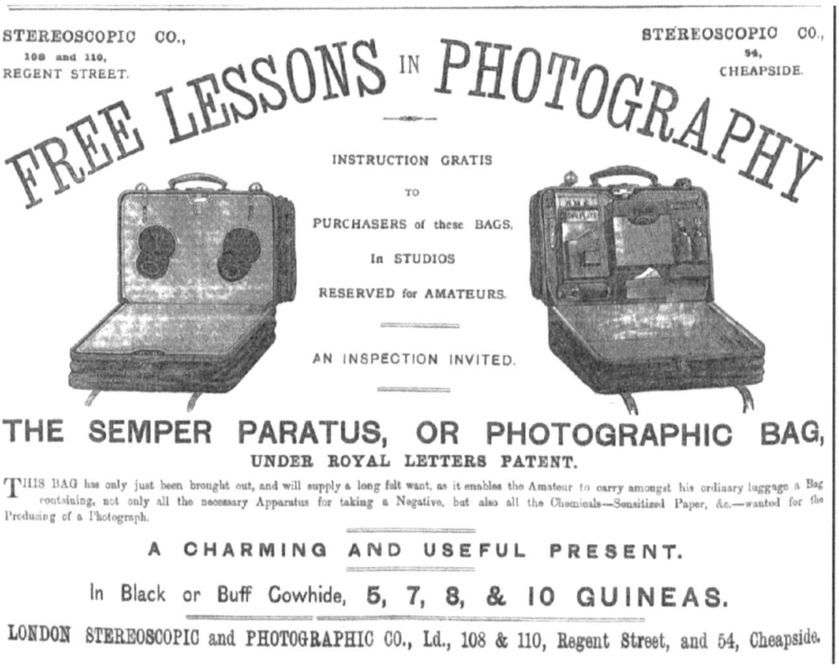

 DOI: 10.4324/9781315400266-181

155

'CYCLO-PHOTOGRAPHY'

Cycling, May 13, 1899, p. 370

If ever there were two pursuits supremely fitted to go hand in-hand, those two are photography and cycling, and now that both photographers and cyclists are beginning to so generally recognise this fact, there is surely no incongruity in what has hitherto been an essentially Cycling paper starting a column devoted to the sister pastime. Many a cyclist who has taken up photography, after his first burst of enthusiasm is over, relegates his text-books, &c. to his book-shelves and proceeding in the same very elementary way as when he first adopted this pursuit, never studies a periodical devoted entirely to it, and consequently many a little interesting and useful hint which experienced workers give forth to the world pass him by, and too often his work, instead of improving in quality, remains constantly distinctly mediocre, and sometimes even worse. And to this type of photographer, very often an enthusiastic and diligent reader of Cycling – these notes will especially appeal, for we shall endeavour, as far as possible, to assist him by many a little hint, in the pursuit of a pastime at once interesting and elevating.

As an instance of how photographic depots are beginning to cater for cyclists, we noticed the other day that the London Stereoscopic Co's West End Depot had a large number of Elswick machines in one of their windows, and, it is needless to say, that each one of these machines was fitted with some form of a carrier specially adapted for carrying the various cameras made by this firm.

[. . .]

Working large plates is, of course, quite out of the question for the Cyclo-Photographer, who has to have everything as light and portable as possible, and is therefore restricted, generally speaking, to quarter-plate or 5 by 4, but with a good lens and enlarging apparatus, there need be no reasonable limit to the ultimate size of his prints, and in the writer's opinion, enlarging is one of the most profitable and interesting branches of photography. If a lantern be used, thus rendering oneself independent of the light of day, this becomes an essentially Winter pursuit. Nothing can be more pleasing or satisfactory in the long Winter evenings than to make enlarged pictures, suitable for framing and hanging on the walls of our

DOI: 10.4324/9781315400266-182

homes, of the many beautiful places and scenes visited on the cycle during the Summer months.

THE writer believes that he has tried almost every form of cycle luggage-carrier on the market, and all with more or less unsatisfactory results, until, a short time ago, he purchased from Messrs. R. & J. Beck, 68, Cornhill, one of their carriers, specially adapted for the Frena camera. These carriers can be purchased for 5s., are splendidly made, can be used for almost any camera case, and weigh only a few ounces. They also have the merit of saving the camera from absolutely all vibration; and we can unhesitatingly pronounce them as being the best things of their kind we have yet struck.

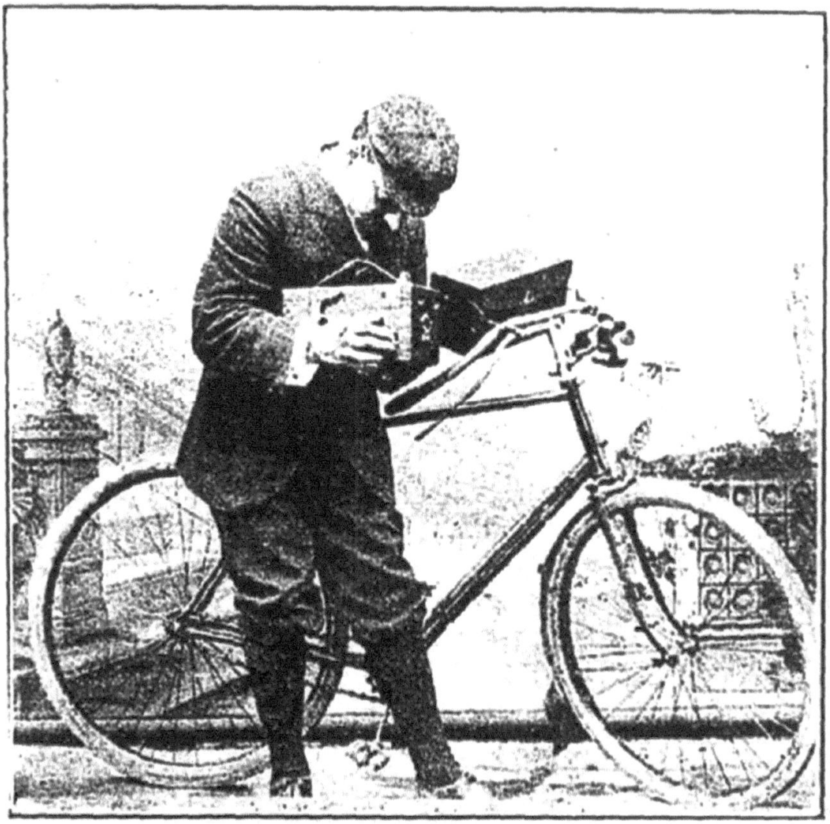

THE AMATEUR CYCLO-PHOTOGRAPHER.

156

HORACE ECKERT, 'SOME HOBBIES'

Pick-Me-Up, October 20, 1900, p. 36

Some hobbies. No. 1. – photography

PHOTOGRAPHY possesses a fascination that is simply miraculous. Why it should do so is still more miraculous. As a hobby it is expensive, and quite useless; but as a breaker-up of friendships and a severer of family ties it may be equalled but never surpassed. You take a photo of your best friend, and show it to him. He thinks you have done it on purpose, and looks a little grieved; and if you try to pacify him by saying, "It is not so bad," he thinks you are getting at him and the trouble begins. Looking at it from a moral point of view, too, I don't think the camera is in the front rank of influences for good, because if anything is more provocative of lurid language than getting a splash of mud on your collar when you are going to meet your best girl, it is photography.

I suppose it is only a natural tendency for getting into trouble that prompts you to begin by taking portraits instead of confining your early efforts to landscapes – you can't offend a landscape very well. Of course, when your maiden aunt, the only person in the family who has any money to speak of, pays you a visit, you make it the occasion of honouring her by taking her photo. You start badly. You can't get her to sit properly. Not that it will matter much in the resulting photo how she sits, but it sounds professional to make a fuss about it, and that's good enough. When you have succeeded in placing your victim to your artistic satisfaction, she is beginning to look disagreeable, and you put your foot in it when you ask her not to look as if she had backed a twenty to one winner, and been done for the money. At last you are ready; covering your head with the cloth, you take the cap off the nozzle, and look through the camera. To your great horror, you see the good lady upside down; and, being of a modest disposition, you hurriedly replace the cap, and blush a dark-room red. You put it as delicately as you possibly can to her that you hardly think she would like to appear upside down in the photo, and as it is an optical peculiarity that reverses the image, you suggest that if she stands on her head she will come out all right. She probably would.

But your victim doesn't seem to think so. She gets out of temper, and says something about never seeking the shelter of your roof again, and that if you are mentioned in her will it will be in a clause saying that all her money is to go to charity before you have any of it, so there!

DOI: 10.4324/9781315400266-183

Little set-backs like this damp the ardour of the photographer for a short period. But the fever soon breaks out again, and you are getting on fairly well, when you are seized by a mad desire to show the family how it is done from start to finish. Of course, being only an amateur, you haven't a proper dark room, and you have to make shift with the scullery, which is hardly large enough for six people to see what you are doing all at the same time. You say "Now then!" with the air of a man who is going to show something marvellous, and you turn out the gas, leaving the congregation blinking in a faint red light. Then you get your first plate out. Tommy, in his anxiety not to miss anything, rushes forward and knocks over a pail of water which was to be used for washing the plates. Somebody at the back, who has evidently had a cheap but unwelcome paddle, says D., and lights the gas. This spoils the plate, and you start a few irrelevant remarks of your own. You are not the only one. Directly Tommy is located in the suddenly flashed-up light he receives a thump which starts him crying. The governor is cussing freely, with a perfect disregard for the presence of the ladies, who are wringing out the bottoms of their skirts. Tommy is sent off to bed, the scullery is mopped out, and when peace is eventually restored, you get out your second plate.

In pouring the developer over the plate somebody pushes your arm accidentally, and sends all the liquid that doesn't go up your sleeve, over Annie's summer skirt. Then the governor bends over the plate to watch the image appear and drops his pipe on it. In your hurry to get the plate under the tap to wash it, you give Matilda a dig in the whalebone and send her with startling suddenness on to somebody's pet corn. A shriek rends the air and the gas is again lit.

Plate Number Two done for.

The family have had enough of it by this time, and they all file out to dry their feet, leaving you in a crockery-breaking state of nervousness.

With some misgivings you start another plate, after issuing a manifesto to the effect that nobody is to open the door and let the light in to spoil any more plates. You have nearly finished developing it, and you reach up on the shelf for a bottle of the next mixture. You feel about for it, and find it by knocking it over on the dim red lamp, plunging the room into a darkness that can be felt. You don't feel the darkness though nearly as much as your shin feels the water-pail after being forcibly brought into contact with the edge of it. In mortal agony you reach for the matches but only succeed in putting your hand on the hot – very hot – remains of the lamp. Removing your hand rather quickly you knock over a bottle, which after gurgling its valuable contents down your trousers, falls on the floor with a crash, which proves the saying that empty vessels make the most noise. In sheer desperation you burst open the door, and rush in upon the family who are cheerfully playing cards, and ask them if they want you to perish miserably without putting a hand out to save you. They reply that you particularly told them not to open the door. They admit that they heard an unusual noise, but thought it was part of the developing business.

5.6

The new photography

DOI: 10.4324/9781315400266-184

5.6 The new photography

Though included in this volume primarily as an example of an art form, Victorian photography, as we have seen, was discussed in both arts and science contexts. The sources in this section discuss the scientific applications of what became known as the 'New Photography', and consider some of its unintended consequences. The end of the nineteenth century saw a proliferation of phenomena to which the term 'new' was appended. The New Woman, New Imperialism, New Journalism, New Realism and New Drama, as well as the emergence of new sciences, such as psychology. The New Photography takes its place in what Sally Ledger and Roger Luckhurst have called a 'constellation of new formations'.[1] The term refers to the work of Wilhelm Conrad Röntgen, who discovered a means of photographing through solid substances, an invention that transformed investigative approaches to material culture. This discovery was widely reported in scientific journals such as *Nature* and the *British Medical Journal,* in which its medical applications were widely debated.[2] The first source in this section comes from *Nature* and discusses the application of this new technique in army surgery. It includes a photograph of a hand taken by German chemist Walter Nernst, which shows a gold ring on one of the fingers, as well as the anode wire and Crooke's tube used in the process of taking the images.[3]

So-called 'Röntgen rays' also received wide coverage in the popular press. The second source is from the periodical *Hearth and Home*, a publication aimed at a female audience, which began its run in 1891. The extract included here carries a report of experiments undertaken by Allan Campbell Swinton, an electrical engineer. While appreciative of the wonders of the new photography, the author expresses concerns about some of its implications, especially the ability of Röntgen rays (or X-rays as they later came to be known) to penetrate flesh, bone and clothes: 'our clothes and flesh are no longer to hide our interior economy from the gaze of the curious'. *The Woman's Signal* also discusses the applications of this new discovery. The author muses on the possibility that it will put an end to vivisection, 'that awful method of prying into physiology that preys on the hearts and consciences of so many of us'. The article contains another photograph taken by Swinton using Röntgen's method, this time showing the contents of a calico pocket.

X-rays also provided a subject for satire. *Judy*'s cartoon of the 'New Photography' from February 1896 shows 'Burglar Bill' with his coats stuffed full of stolen (we assume silver) cutlery. In the same year, *Punch* carried a cartoon which shows the capacity of X-rays to thwart a nosey landlady, or possibly a servant, caught eavesdropping at the door of a lodger's sitting room. The comic magazine *Illustrated Chips* published a number of cartoons on the New Photography. Three are included here, all drawing on the idea of the newly transparent solid object. The first imagines the way in which X-rays might affect domestic relations between husband and wife by giving the latter the means by which to see into her husband's jacket pockets. The second considers a range of situations in which Röntgen rays might be usefully enlightening, for example, in revealing the contents of a dubious pie or a hand in a game of cards. The last source from *Chips* speaks to the way in which the stereotype of the 'savage cannibal' was normalised in the Victorian period. Playing on the idea of 'civilising the natives', the cartoon shows a cannibal chief using the apparatus of the New Photography to locate the whereabouts of a Victorian businessman. This hapless individual is discovered through the use of X-rays, which show him to be inside the stomach of a fellow cannibal.[4] The final source in this section returns us to *Nature*. It is an advert for Crooke's tubes (electrical discharge tubes used by Röntgen in his discovery of X-rays) and a special 'cabinet' for lecturers containing equipment for demonstrations. It is interesting to note that the advert for 'Röntgen photography' from Brady and Bartin, surgical and scientific instrument makers based in Newcastle-upon-Tyne, appears next to one for De Vere's conjuring apparatus, a juxtaposition which suggests an affinity between the almost magical capabilities of the New Photography and the types of 'tricks and illusions' advertised by Charles De Vere's touring magic company based in London and Paris.

Notes

1 Sally Ledger and Roger Luckhurst (eds.). *The Fin de Siècle: A reader in Cultural History c. 1880–1900* (Oxford: Oxford University Press, 2000), p. xiii. The New Photography does not appear in Ledger and Luckhurst's list of new formations.
2 For more on Röntgen rays see the *Inventions and Technology* volume in this series.
3 An early electrical discharge tube.
4 For more on the nineteenth-century discourse of 'civilizing the natives' see Patrick Brantlinger, *Taming Cannibals: Race and the Victorians* (Ithaca N.Y, Cornell University Press, 2011).

157

'THE NEW PHOTOGRAPHY: WILL IT STOP VIVISECTION?'

The Woman's Signal, February 13, 1896, pp. 97–98

TRULY we live in an age of unceasing wonder! The newest thing in photography is interesting to us women, not only because we are intelligently concerned with all that is new and wonderful, but because it is not impossible that this may prove to be the means of putting an end to that awful method of prying into physiology that preys on the hearts and consciences of so many of us, vivisection; and also because it will probably serve to lighten for our children the mysterious burden of deep-seated pain and disease.

All this, indeed, is going rather in advance of the immediate facts. These are wonderful, but they are so very newly discovered that the practical applications of them are still in the future.

The new discovery is that it *is possible to photograph through a solid substance* and so to see what is inside it.

Thus, it is possible to photograph the bones inside the flesh; and it will be perfectly easy for the surgeon to see the position of a bullet, or for the physician to perceive the first symptoms of the "deposit" that is going to be visible presently in the shape of pain and constitutional disturbance as gout or rheumatism. Hip disease, again, so often neglected and called only "growing pains," even when surgical aid has been sought in the first stage, will be earlier recognised. All this *is* already in practical reach, for it is an actual fact that the new photography can and does photograph the bones through the solid flesh – the flesh appearing only like a shadow around the clearly defined bones. Whether it will prove possible to see the working of the organs, and so cut the ground from under the feet of the vivisector, is not yet certain.

The illustration that we give is of something as wonderful as, but a little less gruesome than, the bones of a living person's hand. It is the contents of a calico pocket, taken by the photographic camera through the calico, which of course hides from the eye what it contains, but thus plainly gives up its secrets to the photographic operator. The coin, the latchkey, and the corkscrew are easily identified. The third long object is yet more interesting; it is a lead pencil, that pulls up and down in a metal sheath; the darkest part of the object is the metal case, and below that the lead is seen distinctly inside the shadow of the wood of the pencil. Thus we perceive

DOI: 10.4324/9781315400266-185

that not only is the calico pocket in which the whole lot were enclosed pervious by this means, but also that wood, like flesh, can be seen through, looking only like a sort of shadow around what is inside it. Such is indeed the fact. In a special issue of the *Photogram,* that is dedicated to this new discovery, there is a translation from the German of the paper in which the original discoverer of the new photography, Professor Röntgen, of Wurzberg, gives his own account of it. He says: –

"Paper is so transparent that a book of a thousand pages offers practically no resistance, and printer's ink makes no difference. Similarly the fluorescence shows behind two packs of cards; a single card does not visibly diminish the brilliancy of the light! So, again, a single thickness of tin-foil hardly casts a shadow on the screen; several have to be superposed to produce a marked effect. Thick blocks of wood are still transparent. Boards of pine two or three centimetres thick absorb only very little. A piece of sheet aluminium, 15 mm. thick, still allowed the X-rays (as I will call the rays, for the sake of brevity) to pass, but greatly reduced the fluorescence. Glass plates of similar thickness behave similarly; lead glass is, however, much more opaque than glass free from lead. Ebonite several centimetres thick is transparent. If the hand be held before the fluorescent screen, the shadow shows the bones darkly, with only faint outlines of the surrounding tissues. Water and several other fluids are very transparent. Hydrogen is not markedly more permeable than air. Plates of copper, silver, lead, gold, and platinum also allow the rays to pass, but only when the metal is thin. Platinum thick allows some rays to pass; silver and copper are more transparent. Lead is practically opaque."

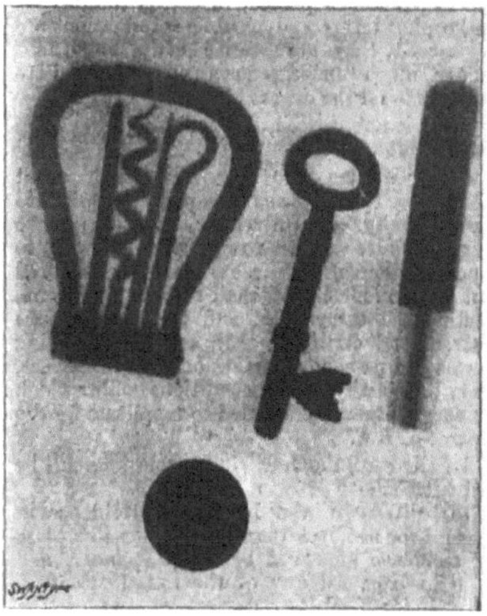

SHADOW PHOTOGRAPH OF CALICO POCKET
(showing contents, corkscrew, pocket-pencil with metal guard and lead in black, key, etc.)

Taken according to PROFESSOR RÖNTGEN's method on an ordinary photographic dry plate enclosed in a slide, and exposed for about five minutes to the rays of a Crookes vacuum tube, by MR. A. A. C. SWINTON AND MR. J. C. M. STANTON.

If a sheet of vulcanite, aluminium, or fibrous material is laid over the calico, it does not affect the resut.

It is not, of course, possible for anyone who has no knowledge of physics to properly understand exactly how this extraordinary result is brought about by the photographic process. But it is not too obscure for anybody to get a brief idea. That which we call "white light," the ordinary light of the sun, is proved by the prism (a simple apparatus for breaking it up into rays) to really consist of a number of different coloured rays. This anybody who has a prism can see; and certain comparatively simple experiments have shown, too, that beyond what we can see with our poor eyes, there are finer gradations of colour. Photography is a main factor in teaching science to-day that there *are* rays in light that we cannot take cognisance of by our eyes, just as the microscope teaches us that we cannot see with our unaided eyes an infinite variety of minute facts that are around us, or as the telescope shows us distant wonders that men had gazed towards unseeing for ages before this help to our vision was made. Well, it is known by photography that there are many rays that exist, and are not recognised by the eye, and some of these have been rendered visible by electricity, which is a main factor in the production of the new photographs.

The light employed in taking these pictures of objects inside others is produced in a vacuum tube, *i.e.,* a tube from which air has been withdrawn as far as possible, and then electricity is passed through, so as to get a brilliant light. It is some one or more of these pure rays that can pass through the solid objects.

The discoverer, it will be observed, calls them "X-rays" (X being used in mathematics to denote unknown quantities) by way of stating that he has not yet ascertained what rays they are to which the solid bodies named are transparent. Mr. Wall, in the *Photogram,* observes: –

"The discovery of these X-rays by Professor Röntgen was due, as is so often the case, entirely to an accident. He was experimenting with a Crookes' tube wrapped in an opaque material, and on his bench lay a piece of sensitive paper on which he found, after a powerful current had passed through the tube, that a black line had been formed on the paper. Keenly alive to all extraordinary phenomena, the learned professor proceeded to investigate, with the result of the discovery of what is practically something absolutely new, and the value of which we cannot at present appreciate. The subsequent developments may be of such a nature as to totally change our ideas of things in general.

"Whilst the experiments hitherto made are from the utilitarian point of view of but little value, there is not the slightest doubt that in the near future they will be of considerable value, as has already been shown by Professor Mosetig, of Vienna, who obtained by this means shadowgrams of a man's hand, in which was embedded a bullet from a revolver, and also in the case of a girl who had a malformation of the foot. In both cases the exact location of the injury was obtained, and considerable assistance rendered to the surgeon. It will be possible, as here sketched out, to obtain not only the location of a foreign substance in the body, but possibly also valuable aid as to the displacement or injury to internal organs of the human body.

"As it has been proved that metals possess a different transparency to these rays, it does not seem chimerical to assume that we have in these new rays a power to determine the perfect nature of an alloy, for instance, or the presence or absence of flaws in castings, in forgings, such as our heavy ordnance, etc."

The matter cannot be made more clear without undue attention. Enough is shown and said to enable our readers to see the great possibilities of the future in this way of discovering that which has been hidden, and its possible application to that decrease of suffering both to man and brute that interests the tender heart of woman.

158

'THE NEW PHOTOGRAPHY', *HEARTH AND HOME*

Hearth and Home, February 20 1896, p. 552

BUT a few weeks since the world was startled by the announcement that Professor Röntgen had discovered a means of photographing through wood, paper, leather, and human flesh, and that it would be possible, for instance, to photograph the structure of a person's body through his or her clothes. The news was at first received with considerable incredulity, but subsequent information proved the practicability of the weird discovery, and since then the leading savants in every country have been at work on similar experiments.

No one has been more active in this respect, or more successful, than Mr. A. Campbell Swinton, the well-known electrical engineer, who has by the new process produced some shadow photographs, four of which I am enabled to reproduce here by his kind permission and that of the proprietors of *The Photogram*.

In the full account of his experiments which appeared lately in *Nature,* Mr. Swinton says that with the assistance of Mr. J. C. Stanton, he repeated Professor Röntgen's experiments with entire success. In one of their early experiments an ordinary photographic plate was placed in the ordinary camera back, the sliding shutter made of wood kept closed, and on this such articles as coins, pieces of wood, carbon, ebonite, vulcanised fibre, aluminium were placed, and above them a Crookes' tube, through which a current was allowed to pass for some minutes. On development, shadows of all objects were obtained, some proving more opaque than others. Perhaps the most interesting of Mr. Swinton's shadowgrams, to coin a new word, given here are those of the living frog, and of his own hand showing the bones. One very curious shadowgram which, however, space prevents me from reproducing, is that of the blade of a closed razor, taken through not only its own handle, but through the cardboard case as well.

Wonderful, indeed, is the march of science, of which these strange X rays have given the latest proof, but where is it to stop? Apparently our clothes and flesh are no longer to hide our interior economy from the gaze of the curious, and the scientific are not satisfied with what they have done, but are aiming at nothing less than penetrating solid bone and laying bare our brains, or at least whatever occupies the space where our brains should be. Science doubtless has its claims, and we should put up with a good deal of inconvenience and discomfort in its cause; but against the

DOI: 10.4324/9781315400266-186

possibility of such an outrage as photographing the inside of our skulls a firm stand must be made.

The case is bad enough as it is, for, if the savants are to be believed, our present clothes will be no protection against the inquisitiveness of the new photography, while glass, the only substance that does seem to be an efficient screen, unfortunately is transparent to everything else. Besides, glass garments hardly strike one as likely to be cosy or comfortable.

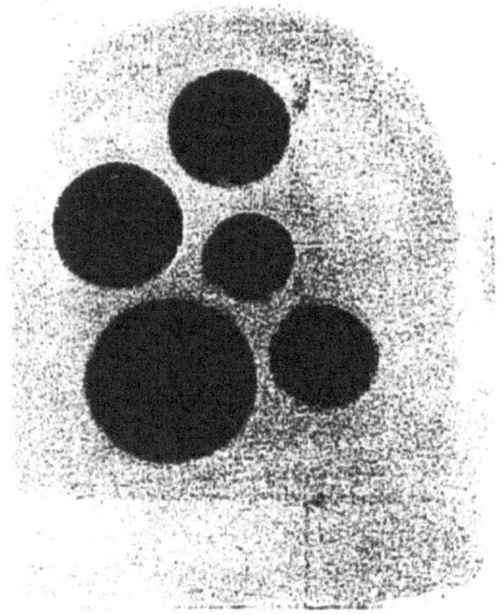

Coins inside leather purse. Exposure four minutes.

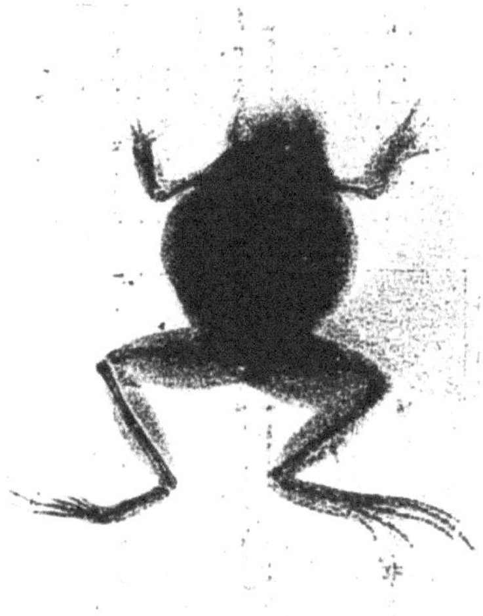

Living frog through sheet of aluminium. Exposure twenty minutes.

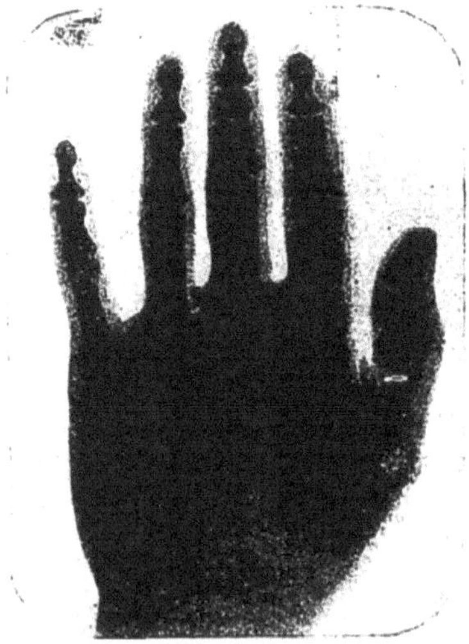

Living hand through black vulcanise 1 fibre. Exposure four minutes.

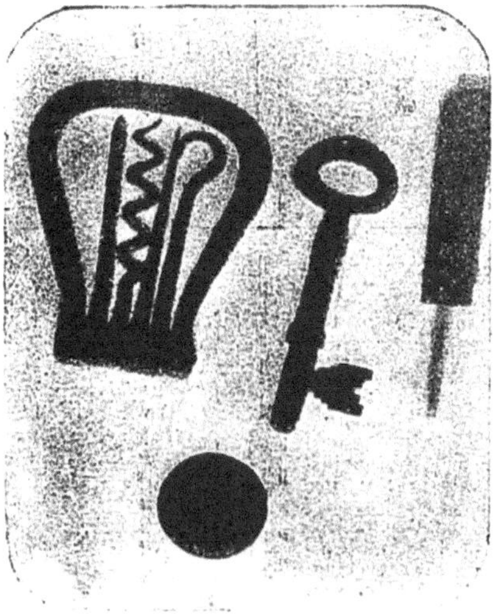

Metal objects through calico pocket and sheet of aluminium. Exposure four minutes.

159

'THE NEW PHOTOGRAPHY', *JUDY, OR THE LONDON SERIO-COMIC JOURNAL*

Judy, or the London Serio-Comic Journal, 26 Feb. 1896, p. 410

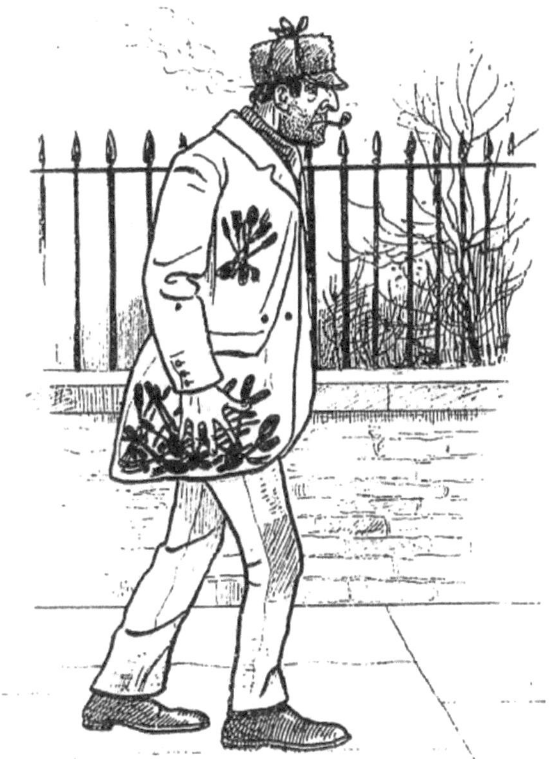

THE NEW PHOTOGRAPHY.

Snapshot of Burglar Bill, showing silver spoons and forks in his pockets.

DOI: 10.4324/9781315400266-187

160

'THE NEW PHOTOGRAPHY AND THE LOST MISSIONARY WHO WENT ON A VISIT INTO THE INTERIOR'

Judy, or the London Serio-Comic Journal, March 25 1896, p. 462

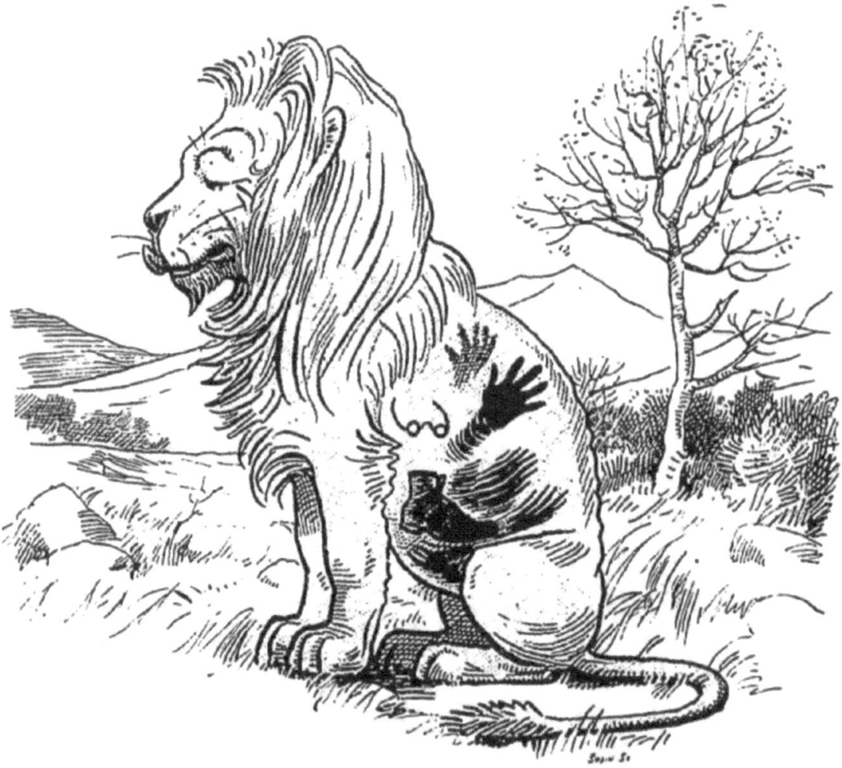

The New Photography and the lost Missionary who went on a visit into the Interior.

DOI: 10.4324/9781315400266-188

161

'THE MARCH OF SCIENCE'

Punch, or the London Charivari, March 7 1896, p. 117

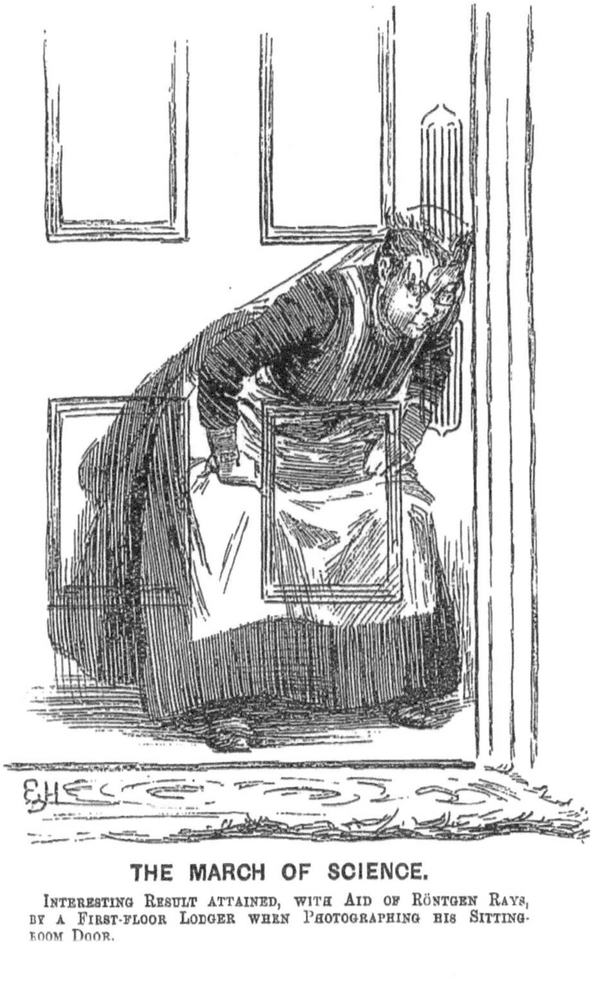

THE MARCH OF SCIENCE.

INTERESTING RESULT ATTAINED, WITH AID OF RÖNTGEN RAYS, BY A FIRST-FLOOR LODGER WHEN PHOTOGRAPHING HIS SITTING-ROOM DOOR.

DOI: 10.4324/9781315400266-189

162

'AWFUL POSSIBILITIES OF THE NEW PHOTOGRAPHY'

Illustrated Chips, 25 Apr. 1896, p. 4

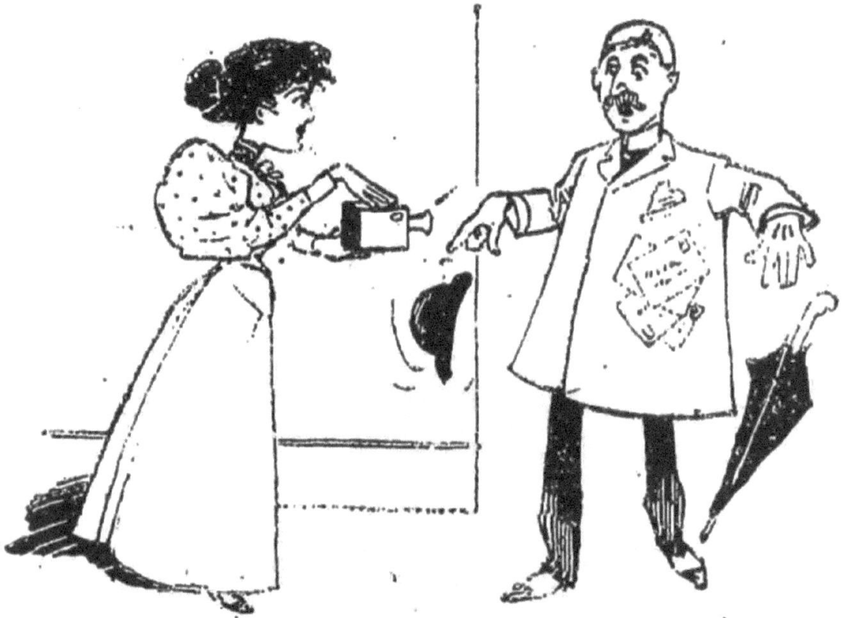

MR. CITTEY, MAN: "For the love of heaven, Kate! what is that machine you've got there?" MRS. C. M.: "This is the housewife's patent camera, John; built especially to enable a woman to see if the letters entrusted to her hubby's care have been posted. You have four there!"

DOI: 10.4324/9781315400266-190

163

'THE NEW PHOTOGRAPHY', *ILLUSTRATED CHIPS*, 25 JULY 1896, P. 1

Illustrated Chips, 25 July 1896, p. 1

THE NEW PHOTOGRAPHY

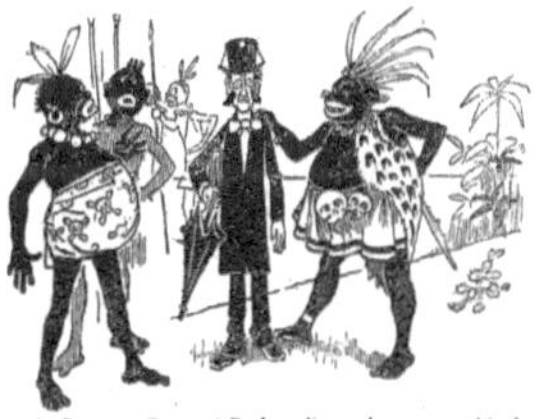

1. CANNIBAL CHIEF: "Bredren, dis genelman am ma friend. He not to be eaten. I tole you!"

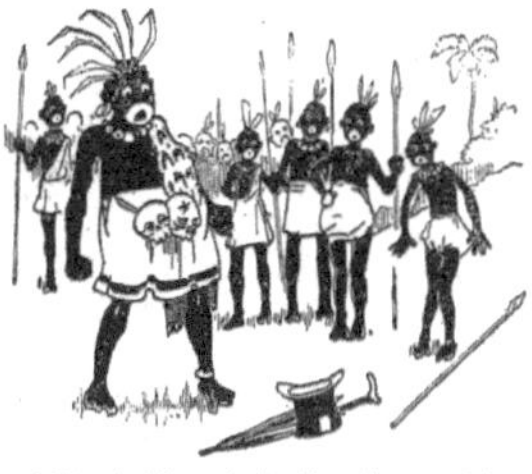

2. But on the following day the white gentleman was missing, and his umbrella and hat alone remained.

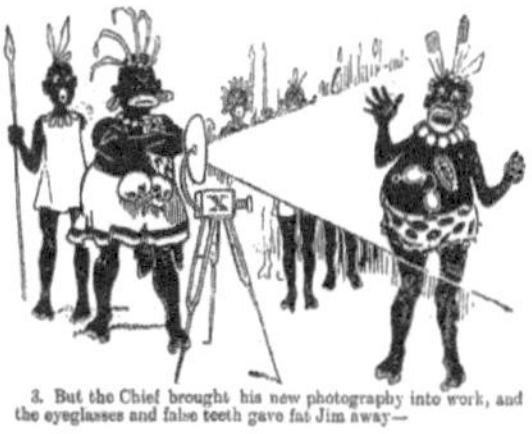

3. But the Chief brought his new photography into work, and the eyeglasses and false teeth gave fat Jim away—

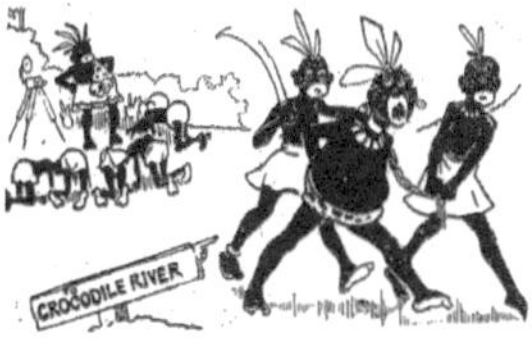

4. And he was led off as a dainty meal for the crocodiles. 25/7/96

DOI: 10.4324/9781315400266-191

164

'THE NEW PHOTOGRAPHY', *ILLUSTRATED CHIPS*, 4 APR. 1896, P. 1

Illustrated Chips, 4 Apr. 1896, p. 1

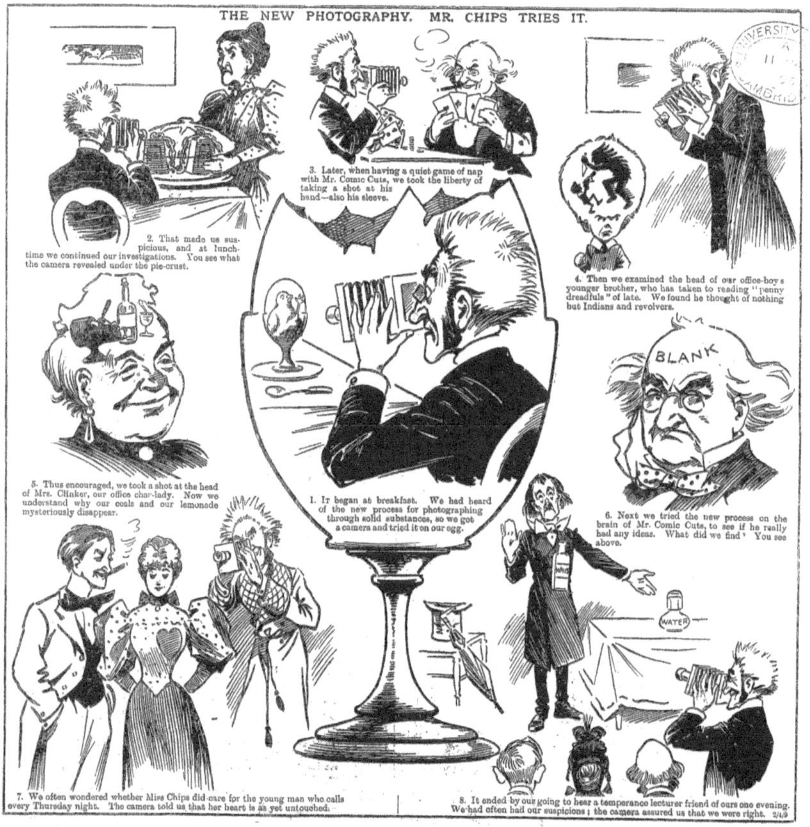

DOI: 10.4324/9781315400266-192

165

'THE NEW PHOTOGRAPHY', *ILLUSTRATED CHIPS*, 19 DEC. 1896, P. 7

Illustrated Chips, 19 Dec. 1896, p. 7

Never before has a purely scientific-discovery created such world-wide interest among all classes as has Professor Roentgen's discovery of the X rays.

The rays are not rays of light, such as the rays that emanate from a lamp or the electric light, neither are they heat rays. In point of fact, neither Professor Roentgen, nor any other scientist, has been able to positively declare what rays they are. They are sometimes called the Roentgen rays, but their discoverer prefers to call them the X rays – X, as every schoolboy knows, signifying an unknown quantity.

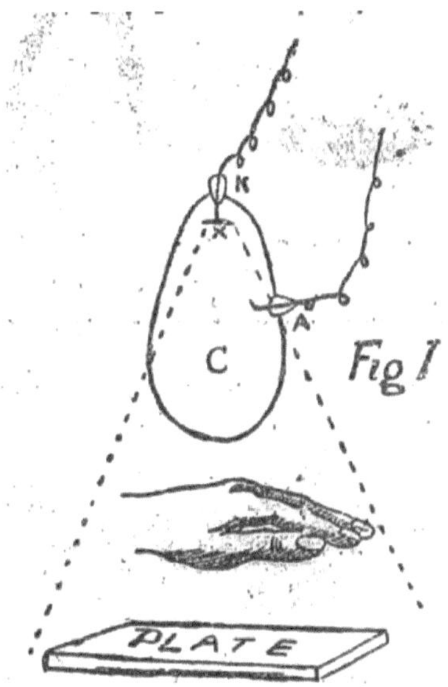

The apparatus necessary for the production of these searching rays can be procured from £7 upward. It consists, in the first place, of four cells – Grove's or Bunsen's. These give the necessary excitation, or, to use a more easily understood phrase, they charge the wires, of which, of course, there are two, with the electric power.

DOI: 10.4324/9781315400266-193

The wires pas [sic] from the cells to a Rhumkorff coil, and are then connected to a glass pear-shaped bulb, called a Crookes tube.

When electricity can be obtained direct from a dynamo, or an electric-lighting station, the jar, the battery, and the Rhumkorff coil can be dispensed with, and the wires connected directly to the Crookes tube.

This tube, as it is called, though its form is more suggestive of a bulb, is a complete vacuum; that is to say, all air has been exhausted from it before it is hermetically sealed, so that the pressure of air within the glass is about one-millionth part of the atmosphere without. Into this perfect vacuum the terminals, or ends, of the two wires – the positive and the negative – are conducted.

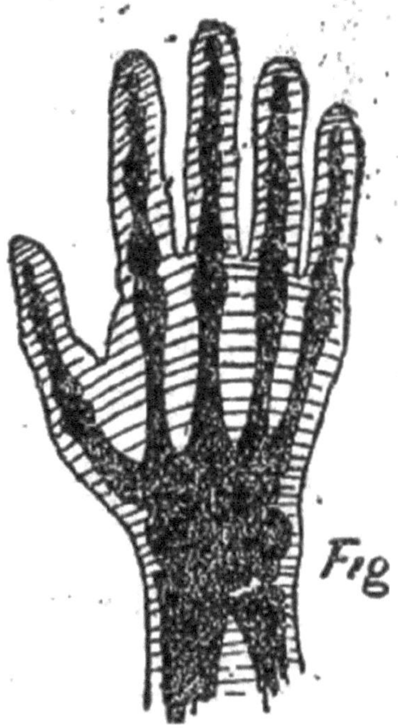

Fig 2

The negative wire is termed the kathodic wire (see K, Figure 1), and terminates in the form of a small disc or plate inside the Crookes tube. (See X, Figure 1.) The other wire, the positive one, is called the anodic, and ends in a point which is directed towards the plate of the kathodic (see A, Figure 1, C being the Crookes tube). It will now be seen that these two wires, or poles, are not actually connected; and under ordinary circumstances there would be no result; but in the vacuity of the Crookes tube it is different. The positive current emanating from the anode pole passes through the intervening vacuum, and impinges upon the plate of the negative, or kathodic, pole. Thus the circuit is completed; and from the small plate forming the termination of the kathodic pole emanates that current or ray which we call the Roentgen, or X, ray.

We will now see in what manner, and for what purpose, the ray is put into actual use.

There are certain substances or bodies which are opaque to the rays; that is to say, through which the rays are powerless to pass. Metals are of this class, so are bones; and glass, curiously enough, which is transparent to ordinary light rays, is opaque to the X rays.

There is another class of subjects which are transparent to the rays, and through which the rays pass as easily as though they did not exist.

Wood, paper, leather, rubber, the human flesh, cloth, of cotton or of wool, and linen are some of the subjects which are wholly, or nearly so, transparent to the ray, for instance.

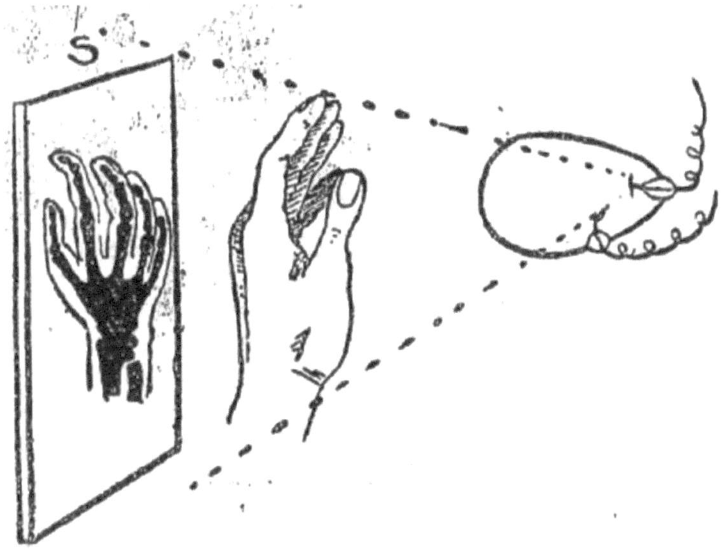

Professor Roentgen says that bodies of low specific gravity appear to be more transparent than those which are specifically heavier; that is to say, the weightier a body is the less transparent is it to the X rays. Taking, for example, metals. Aluminium and magnesium, which are the lightest of metals, have a higher degree of transparency than platinum or mercury, which are the heaviest. Flesh does not weigh so much as bone, hence the former is transparent to the rays, while the latter is opaque.

This brings us to that part of the subject which has most appealed to the public mind, and that which makes the X rays invaluable on account of the surgical uses to which they may be put – namely, the power the rays possess of passing through the fleshy covering of the human body, and producing a shadow of the living skeleton.

Turning again to Figure 1, we see that beneath the Crookes tube is placed a photographic plate – gelatino-bromide – which is wrapped in several thicknesses of ruby paper to protect it from the light of day. Between the tube and the bromide plate a human hand is interposed – the hand resting on the plate. The apparatus is then set into motion, and the rays from the kathodic plate x pass through the fleshy covering of the hand, through the paper in which the sensitised plate is wrapped, leaving upon the plate a shadowgraph – i.e., a photograph in shade – of the bones of the hand, the surrounding flesh being faintly reproduced, as in Figure 2.

The value of the shadowgraph for the purpose of detecting such defects as malformation, decay, necrosis, fractures, and faulty setting of fractures of the bones, or of ascertaining the precise locality of any foreign substance, such as a bullet or a needle, &c., may be readily appreciated.

It is said that one of the reasons for opacity to the X rays is the presence of lime salts in the bones.

Figure 3 shows another method of using the rays, this time without the aid of a photographic plate.

A screen (S. Figure 3) is coated with a chemical substance called barium-platino-cyanide. Between the screen and the rays is interposed the object to be operated upon, and when the rays are set into motion a shadowgraph of the subject is thrown on the screen. The shadowgraph will of course disappear when the power of the rays is removed, and the screen will be left clear for the next subject.

It will be noticed that I have said glass is one of the substances which the rays cannot pass through. There are two kinds of glass; lead-glass – so called because that metal is used in its manufacture – and white glass, the base of which is soda, potash, and lime. The lead glass offers resistance to the passage of the X rays, but the white glass is really permeable or transparent, therefore it is of the latter kind that the Crookes tube is made.

166

'THE NEW LIGHT AND THE NEW PHOTOGRAPHY'

Nature, August 20 1896, p. cxxviii

THE NEW LIGHT AND THE NEW PHOTOGRAPHY.

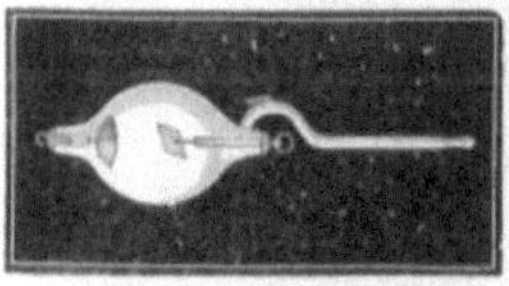

This form of Tube has become celebrated in connection with the name of Mr. Jackson, of King's College.

CROOKES' RADIANT MATTER TUBES, for Experiments, supplied at the shortest notice. Various patterns and sizes kept in stock. Any design made to order.

J. J. HICKS

(THE ORIGINAL MAKER OF CROOKES' RADIOMETERS),

8, 9, & 10 HATTON GARDEN, LONDON, E.C.

Telegraphic Address—"LENTICULAR, LONDON."

TO LECTURERS ON "X" RAYS, &c.

Attention to details in the construction and arrangement of a Lecturer's Apparatus makes *all* the difference sometimes.

Time occupied in adjustments or readjustments that would be tolerated in the Laboratory, might be fatal to success at a public Lecture. Every Lecturer knows this, and my only object in mentioning it is to let the reader know that I know it too.

My Cabinet for Induction Coil is not a simple box of no further use than to pack the Coil and to carry it by; it is what I say it is, a *Cabinet* opening at the side—and forms a useful piece of apparatus in itself. Packed for travelling the Coil is inside, of course; but when in use, the Coil may be left inside or placed outside on top of Cabinet; the Battery or Accumulator can then be placed inside. A Resistance Coil, "Cut out" or Fuse, with suitable terminals and connections, are all fitted inside the Cabinet—at one end—accessible for use whilst *in situ*; adjustable supports are provided—at the ends of the Cabinet—for carrying and elevating the wires from secondary terminal pillars (to be out of the way of the operator), and to these elevating supports may be attached one or more small incandescent lamps, with suitable switch—also fixed inside the Cabinet. Thus we may have the light on when the Coil is off, and as the Coil is switched on the light is switched off.

The whole is convenient, complete, and compact for either the Laboratory or the Lecture Table, and may be packed or set to work in half the time it takes to describe it.

Our Resistance Coil is adjusted by a lever switch to the greatest nicety—no screws to bother with, our "Cut out" is similarly arranged with six Fuses adjusted for, say, 10 amperes each; if one gets fused there is no loss of time, the next may be switched on instantly.

A series of seven Crookes' Tubes exhausted to show phenomena from Spark in air to fluoresence, fitted in special Cabinet with connections.

W. I. CHADWICK,

SCIENTIFIC INSTRUMENT MAKER, MANCHESTER.

RÖNTGEN PHOTOGRAPHY.

Full descriptive Price List of the best Apparatus for the above, containing every requisite, sent by Post on application.

BRADY & MARTIN,

SURGICAL AND SCIENTIFIC INSTRUMENT MAKERS,

NEWCASTLE-ON-TYNE,

Importers, Manufacturers, and Dealers in CHEMICAL, PHYSICAL, PHYSIOLOGICAL and METEOROLOGICAL APPARATUS.

Guaranteed Pure Chemicals for Analysis, and Standardized Solutions.

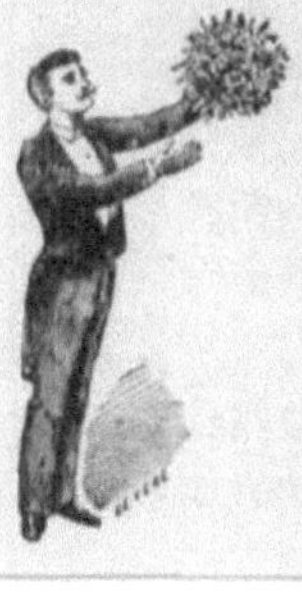

DE VERE,

Manufacturer of every description of

CONJURING APPARATUS AND MECHANICAL NOVELTIES.

Tricks and Illusions for Theatres, Marionettes, Guignols, Automatons, Juggling Apparatus, &c.

39 RUE DE TREVISE 39, PARIS.

Catalogue in English, Post Free, 2½d. Large Catalogue in French, 120 pp., Post Free, 1s.

DOI: 10.4324/9781315400266-194

INDEX

Note: Numbers in *italics* indicate a figure.